The Anglophone Question and Postcolonial Hegemony in Cameroon

The Anglophone Question and Postcolonial Hegemony in Cameroon

The Past that Did Not Pass

Volume II

Edited by
Lyombe Eko

SPEARS BOOKS
Denver, Colorado

Spears Books
An Imprint of Spears Media Press LLC
7830 W. Alameda Ave, Suite 103-247
Denver, CO 80226
United States of America

First Published in the United States of America in 2025 by Spears Books
www.spearsbooks.org
info@spearsmedia.com
Information on this title: www.spearsbooks.org/the-anglophone-question-vol2

ISBN: 9781957296517 (Paperback)
ISBN: 9781957296524 (eBook)

Designed and typeset by Spears Media Press LLC
Cover designed by Doh Kambem

Distributed globally by African Books Collective (ABC)
www.africanbookscollective.com

Dedicated to the following persons who fought for freedom of speech and expression in Cameroon and paid the penalty for it:

Mola Njoh Litumbe
Tataw Obenson (Ako Aya), pioneer West Cameroon journalist
Barrister Felix Agbor Nkongho (Balla), human rights lawyer,
Justice Ayah Paul Abine
Nyo' Wakai, judge and author
Pius Njawé, Founder of Le Messager
Nyemb Ntoogue Paul (Nyemb Popoli), Cartoonist
Mancho Bibixy Tse, radio announcer and activist
Christian Penda Ekoka, Humanist
Cardinal Christian Wiyghan Tumi, Catholic Cardinal
Samuel Ajiekah Abuwe (Wazizi), journalist
Martinez Zogo, Journalist
All journalists detained or imprisoned in Cameroon.

Contents

Preface

LYOMBE EKO

The Anglophone Question in Cameroon is, first and foremost, a consequence of authoritarian governance. It is a problem of a government of the rule of one man, the Chief of State, rather than the rule of law. The problem was ironically transformed into an active crisis that ultimately became a "frozen conflict" due to the preponderance and superiority of "law" over human rights and human dignity. Case in point. On October 9, 2024, Cameroon's Minister of Territorial Administration, Honorable Mr. Atanga Nji Paul, sent a "very urgent" directive entitled, "Injunction against certain discussions in the media." The directive was addressed to the Biya-appointed governors of the country's 10 regions, including the English-speaking Northwest and Southwest regions.

The directive was written in French because in Cameroon, power and language are interconnected, and the appointed governors of the English-speaking regions are Francophones. Honorable Minister Atanga Nji lamented that:

> For a period of time, unscrupulous persons have been flooding social media with fake news about the condition of the health of the President of the Republic. The ill-intentioned objective of these elucubrations is to perturb the quietude of Cameroon, sow confusion and doubt in the minds [of the public] in order to create uncertainty in the country....The Minister Director of the Civil Cabinet of the Presidency and the Minister of Communication, have each published a press release condemning these excesses and formally denied the whimsical rumors spread about the state of the President of the Republic. After these clarifications... no other commentary or discussion should be tolerated from anyone whatsoever, in the private media within the week or during weekends...The Chief of State is the First Institution of the Republic...discussions on the state of his health fall within the domain of national security. From today, I direct that each Governor create in his offices, surveillance teams, responsible for monitoring and recording all programs and discussions broadcast by

> the private media and identify the authors of tendentious commentaries, including those that act through the social media.
>
> All discussions in the media on the state of the President of the Republic are therefore formally forbidden. Violators will face the rigors of the law. (Translation by the author).

This thunderous, chilling, censorious directive from the High, Honorable Minister was triggered by a phenomenon that was discussed in volume I of this project, namely, the frequent disappearances of 92-year-old President Paul Biya from public view, and his notoriously lengthy stays in the lap of luxury at a reserved presidential suite of the Inter-Continental Hotel in Geneva, Switzerland. This round of rumors about the state of health of 92-year-old President Paul Biya started in September 2024. After attending the 2024 Forum on China-Africa Co-operation (FOCAC) in Beijing from September 4-6, 2024, President Biya was expected to travel to New York to attend the 79th session of the United Nations General Assembly that took place from September 10-28, 2024. The annual UN General Assembly meeting, whose detractors have described it as a mere "talking shop where no issue is too small to be debated endlessly," (Ki-moon, 2008) is the platform where pompous, self-righteous presidents, bloody dictators, potentates, kings, and autocrats from around the world strut across the stage and present their perspectives on world crises ranging from the Taliban's war against women in Afghanistan, to shopworn litanies of the alleged sins of Zionism, to Russia's ethno-nationalistic war in Zaporizhzhia, Ukraine. The fact that President Biya simply vanished from the political and diplomatic radar between Beijing and New York in September 2024 spawned a new tsunami of rumors about the state of health of the 92-year-old president in the national and international media in real space and cyberspace. It turned out that the president had gone to his favorite hideout, Switzerland, after the Forum on China-Africa Co-operation in Beijing.

The disappearance of President Biya from public view for weeks at a time, and the subsequent social media rumors about the state of his health were not new phenomena. What was different in the September/October 2024 incident was the Cameroon government's total ban on discussions of "the state" of the president as well as the state of his health on the media in real space, as well as on Internet social media platforms. The ban was the subject of international news given that the Constitution of Cameroon protects freedom of speech and expression, and Cameroon is a signatory to the African Charter on Human and People's Rights, and the Universal Declaration of Human Rights. Neither the Universal Declaration of Human Rights nor the African Charter of Human and People's Rights have exception for ailing chiefs of State. The Atanga Nji affair demonstrated two phenomena that were discussed in the first volume:

a). Politically, Cameroon is a neo-patrimonial, *chefferie républicaine* (republican chiefery), with a governmentality (logic of governance) in which the Chief of State incarnates the government and the country for life. On January 1, 2025, President Biya presented his 42nd New Year message to the nation (in French, as usual, followed by a translation read by a government journalist). In that message, he announced that he was still prepared "to serve" the nation. That was the clear message that he would stand for another 7-year term in the 2025 elections. No one in the country dared to present a contrary view. It was a crime to comment on the "state"–or fitness for office of the Chief of State. In the *chefferie réuplicaine*, a climate of fear ensures that there is silence–a tyrannical peace (Davenport, 2007), tyrannical unity, tyrannical "living together," tyrannical muting of minorities and of dissent, tyrannical erasure, tyrannical inertia, and tyrannical perpetual rule of the republican Chief of State. The argument of overwhelming force, which takes precedence over the force of argument, is the structured and structuring value of the *chefferie républicaine*. The argument of force, erasure and enforced forgetfulness, are designed to de-memorialize Anglophone culture, nay, Cameroon national culture, and consign the horrendous misdeeds and atrocities of the republican chieftain into what the Kpe/Mboko (Bakweri) people call *Inameh*, the ocean of oblivion, the sea of forgetfulness.

b). The Anglophone Question is a national problem with multiple international dimensions and connections. Indeed, like most crises in Africa, it has colonial antecedents and disconnections. Things have been that way from time immemorial. The great documents of Western Civilization in their multiple linguistic, ethnic, cultural and political manifestations–from Homer's *Iliad* & *Odyssey*, through the Bible to the American Constitution–demonstrate a certain "reticent fascination" with Africa, the so-called "Dark Continent" to borrow the expression of Jacques Portes (1987). This attraction/revulsion towards Africa, was best expressed by Roman naturalist and writer, Pliny the Elder (23-79 A.D.) who wrote: "Out of Africa, always something new." In Western literary and journalistic discourse, "Africa" is the archetypal "Other World" that has served as the foil of Europe, from antiquity to the present (Mudimbe, 1994; Mbembe, 2001; Eko, 2010). Africa is thus the original exotic "Other." Jacques Lacan (1986) asserted that the "Other" with a capital 'O,' is the mythical "prehistoric Other that is impossible to forget" (p. 71). A 19th-century European writer described the continent as follows: "Africa is a lovely charnel house" (Godbey, 1889). Nevertheless, as we saw in Volume I, at the Berlin Africa Conference of 1884-1885, European geo-political, balance of power realities transformed Africa into a series of European colonial possessions. The European colonizers declared that they were driven by a humanitarian, "civilizing colonial mission" (Gann, 1988; Betts, 1961, p. 28) that Kipling (1940) called the "white man's burden." The Anglophone Question in Cameroon emerged in part from late 19th century and early 20th century European historical and geo-strategic arrangements, and post-World War I rearrangements. It is, therefore, unfinished business of 19th-century European colonialism, World War I, and the Treaty of Versailles of 1919. It was compounded and transformed into a crisis by the anti-democratic postcolonial regime that emerged at the end of European colonialism in the 1960s.

The Anglophone Question, Collective and Corrective Memory

The order of the Honorable Minister of Territorial Administration banning all discussion of "the state," with a small "s," of President Paul Biya, was not only an authoritarian injunction against the human rights of freedom of expression set forth in the United Nations Universal Declaration of Human Rights, the African Charter on Human and Peoples' Rights and the Constitution of Cameroon, it was a counter-memorial act. Public phenomena, occurrences, happenings, and matters of public concern, like the health of the Chief of State, that are banned from discussion in the public sphere are also banned from collective memory. One of the organizing values of the *chefferie républicaine* is denial, denial of collective and cultural memory. This counter-memorialization posture extends to major events in the history of the Cameroonian State, notably the death and burial of Cameroon's first president, Ahmadou Ahidjo, and his wife, Germaine, in Dakar, Senegal, narratives of the bloody aftermath of the 1984 abortive *coup d'etat* against President Paul Biya, prohibitions against discussion of federalism, silence over the death in military custody of journalist, Samuel Wazizi, among other phenomena. Reality, ideas, events, and occurrences don't cease to exist just because the State plays the ostrich and bans them from the official state media, and from the public sphere in physical space and cyberspace.

The central premise of this volume is that the Anglophone Question is grounded in the collective and cultural memory of the people of the English and Pidgin-speaking former state of Southern Cameroons. It is thus a collective and corrective memory project. The membership of Southern Cameroons (the Northwest and Southwest regions) in the global Anglosphere was anchored in a number of sites of cultural memory. These include a heritage of the English language, which was introduced to the Cameroon coast in the early 19th Century by British missionaries, Rev & Mrs. Joseph Merrick, Rev. & Mrs. Alfred Saker and others, and maintained by Christian religious literature, specifically the King James version of the Bible, church hymnaries and prayer books. Beside the church, two major sites of memory connected Southern Cameroons to the global Anglosphere: its English-medium educational system that is roughly patterned after the British educational system, and its common law system that is generally patterned after the British common law system. As such, this book is all about "a past that did not pass," to borrow the expression of Ofer (2009). It is about a past that has not passed, a past that is sustained by the collective and cultural memory of Anglophones. Additionally, Southern Cameroonians are virtually connected to the post-World War II international English-language media that consisted of Radio Nigeria, the British Broadcasting Corporation (BBC), The Voice of America (VOA), and the English-language services of Radio Vatican, Radio Deutsche Welle (the Voice of Germany), Radio Moscow, and so on. Globalization and global communication spawned for the most part by American Information and Communication Technology innovations–the Internet and its networked social media platforms, mobile telephony, databases, and the like, made English the lingua franca of the global village.

The Socio-political and Cultural Meaning of Collective Memory

Given the fact that the history of Cameroon is replete with prohibitions, deliberate omissions, denials, distortions, misrepresentations, mischaracterizations, bans, erasures, and muting of the past, we conceptualize these volumes as a project of collective/corrective and cultural memory. The term collective memory is used in three ways: The socio-political and cultural sense of the term is collective societal or group remembrance of past events of historical, political, religious, and cultural significance. The seminal ideas on the socio-political and religious foundations of collective memory were advanced by Halbwachs (1925). He conceptualized collective memory as a socially constructed act of selectively remembering (and forgetting) that happens on at least two levels: the individual—which is shaped by one's personality and experiences—and the collective. The collective dimension involves a self-identified group with a collective sense of history, culture, identity, and religion (Halbwachs, 1925). For many organized groups, collective memory is grounded in a traumatic past that does not pass (Ofer, 2009). The basic premise of collective memory is that since human memory often functions within collective contexts, "memory groups," usually minorities that believe they have been the victims of historical wrongs and injustices, reconstruct pasts and instrumentalize these pasts to solve untenable socio-political realities of the present. As a result, collective memory "sees" (Bommas (2012, p. xxxi) in specific circumstances, images, actions and reactions, memory cues that rouse their emotions and indignations, and reinforce their memories. The outcome is that concerned memory groups "play memory games" to attempt to redress injustices of the present (Mink & Neumayer, 2013, p. 4; Eko & Mielczarek, 2015). A fundamental feature of collective memory is that it is an ideological tool that is often manipulated and instrumentalized by organized interest groups for political, social, economic, religious, and identitarian purposes (Ricoer, 2000). In order for it to be "useful" for the needs of the moment, collective memory has to be dynamic, evolving, malleable. It has to have the ability to take the "coloration" of the political or social cause that it is being deployed to promote. Halbwachs (1925) called collective memory "the cult of the past" in which individuals "transfigure the past to the point of yearning for it" (p. 51). It thus becomes a dynamic phenomenon in which groups use past collective memories to meet the politico-cultural needs of the present. For his part, Assmann (2011) advanced the concept of cultural memory). The basic premise of cultural memory is that cultural artifacts are imbued with or associated with memory to the point where they become sites of memory. In Southern Cameroons, colonial edifices like the Schloss, German Governor Jesko von Puttkamer's castle in Buea, which was transformed into the West Cameroon Prime Minister's Lodge, the educational and legal systems, historic churches like the Ebenezer Baptist Churches in Limbe and Rzoph'a Mokongo mo Kongami (The Big Soppo on the Sloping Hill, aka Great Soppo), are sites of collective and cultural memory. By the same token, agricultural institutions like the Cameroon Development Cooperation (CDC), PAMOL, as well as the multiple British-style senior service and junior service clubs in Buea, Limbe, Tiko, Ekona, Likomba, and other locations, are sites of Southern Cameroons' collective memory of British colonial social hierarchies.

The African Collective and Corrective Memory Perspective

On his 89th birthday, 18th July 2007, Nelson Mandela, former President of South Africa, announced the formation of "The Elders," a small group of elder statesmen and women from around the world–and they included former presidents Jimmy Carter of the United States, Mary Robinson of Ireland, Fernando Henrique Cardoso of Brazil, Gro Harlem Brundtland, former Prime Minister of Norway, Kofi Annan, former United Nations Secretary-General, and others who had agreed to work to help address global challenges. President Mandela said that the action of the Global Elders would be grounded in "the spirit of Ubuntu – that profound African sense that we are human only through the humanity of other human beings" (Mandela, 2007).

Nelson Mandela and the Global Elders in 2007

President Nelson Mandela's launching of the "Elders" was an actualization and globalization of an ancient informal, African collective/corrective memory institution, known in Swahili as *Wazee Hukumbuka* (The Elders Who Remember). This group is made up of village Elders of high repute who serve as the heirs, custodians, and repositories of collective memory. Elders are essentially *"lieux de mémoire" (sites of memory),* to borrow the expression of Nora (1997). The task of *Wazee Hukumbuka* is ritualistic memorialization or preservation of collective cultural and social memory through rites, rituals, performances, and ceremonies. The importance of elders in African collective and cultural memory was succinctly put by Malian sage, Amadou Hampâté Bâ who wrote that, "In Africa, when an old person dies, a library burns down…An old African teacher used to say: 'There is my truth and your truth, but the truth is in the middle. To get close to it, everyone must move slightly out of their truth to take a step towards the other" (Waberi, 2018). The search for truth is one of the collective/corrective memory roles of the Elders. In his novel, *Things Fall Apart,* Chinua Achebe expressed the idea of elders as an institution for persons who had attained a level of maturity and demonstrated responsibility: "As the elders said, if a child washed his hands, he could eat with kings. Okonkwo had clearly washed his hands and so he ate with kings and elders." (1996, p.6). In Africa, *Wazee Hukumbuka* or village elders are repositories of collective, cultural and social memory. These African perspectives on memory draw on notions of collective and cultural memory, which have strong undercurrents of concertation, peer input, consensus, and collective decision-making. The result is collective/corrective memory that stands the test of time. When they get together, elders share individual information, knowledge, and lived experiences, which, taken together, crystallize into collective memory, cultural memory and wisdom.

The Media and Collective/Corrective Memory

While these concepts of collective and cultural memory are widely studied in the social sciences, they are put into practice by the media. Indeed, newspapers, radio, television, the Internet, and social media platforms are sites of memory. The African satirical press has added a playful, yet critical dimension to African journalism and political communication (Eko, 2007; Eko, 2015). Pape Samba Kane of Senegal produced a two-volume collection of the cartoon portraits of one of Africa's most celebrated satirical newspapers, *Le Cafard Libéré* (The Liberated Cockroach). This collection, entitled *Mémoire Corrective* (Corrective Memory), is a safari into the past, into Senegalese collective memory. The title is a clever play on the expression "collective memory." The sub-text is that the media are watchdogs of the public interest. Kane (2023) revisits key events in Senegal's history through *Le Cafard Libéré's* cartoon portraits of some of the major actors of the Senegalese political scene (Kane, 2023). The ultimate aim is to keep the record "straight" through satirical re-presentations of historical events and characters. The context is that in democratic societies, the role of the media is to denounce governmental, corporate and individual predatory activities and excesses. In the field of communication, governmental unethical activities include propaganda, the technique of manipulating information to shift public opinion. Propagandists only highlight information that supports given viewpoints while downplaying or omitting those that do not (Cummings & Kong, 2019). Anything can be considered propaganda, from half-truths to lies, from facts to arguments to rumors (Jowett & O'Donnell, 2018). A major type of unethical communication that distorts the contemporary and historical record of crises around the world is disinformation. Disinformation is counter-information. It is the act of intentionally disseminating false, inaccurate, or sensational information to deceive and mislead national and international publics.

The Anglophone Revolt in Cameroon was spear-headed by three of the heirs, custodians, and bulwarks of the collective memory (the political, cultural and identitarian heritage) of the English-speaking regions of Cameroon–the legal profession, the educational sector, and the churches. The English-speaking common law lawyers, and the English-speaking teachers' unions kicked off the Anglophone Revolt in 2016, with the blessing of their cultural, identitarian and spiritual guides and partners, the Roman Catholic Church, the Presbyterian Church in Cameroon and the Cameroon Baptist Convention, to name the major denominations. This book is a collective/corrective memory project. It describes, explains and analyzes the multiple problematic situations and realities brought about by the tyrannical peace (Davenport, 2007), tyrannical unity, tyrannical harmonization, tyrannical assimilation, and tyrannical living together imposed on the multi-cultural, two-state federation of Cameroon by force of arms, the Ahidjo/Biya neo-patrimonial republican chiefdom of *la République du Cameroun*. It is also a work of "corrective memory" because it discusses and sets the record straight on banned groups and political ideologies like federalism, as well as human rights abuses, atrocities, and exactions carried out by the Israeli-trained and armed security forces.

The Information Technology/Artificial Intelligence Sense of "Memory"

The term "memory" has a special meaning in computer science and Artificial Intelligence. The term was advanced by Alan Turing in 1948. According to him, the term "memory" refers to "the number of states (configurations)" a machine can have. These configurations are essentially the memory or storage capacity of the machine (p. 110). This computer memory perspective is used because this book is very much a product of Internet social media platforms. It is the result of the use of the huge "memory capacity" of Internet social media platforms to host vast amounts of digitized and uploaded historical and current affairs information from government documents, archives, repositories, and databases, as well as the ease with which this information can be downloaded or retrieved for research on the collective and cultural memory of Cameroonians who happen to be in the Anglosphere. At the outset of the Anglophone Revolt in 2016, social media platforms, particularly Facebook and Twitter, which had been catalysts for the so-called Arab Spring in North Africa and the Middle East as early as 2010, became instrumental in furthering and publicizing Anglophone identitarian narratives and discourses, as well as organizing and enabling civil society actions. Social media platforms were used to promote strikes, ghost-towns, civil disobedience activities, and above all to publicize the repressive measures and unspeakable human rights violations of the Biya regime in the Northwest and Southwest regions. These social media platforms, particularly Facebook, soon became digital bulletin boards on which government documents of all types and classifications were posted for the world to see. These platforms also featured the images of the collective civil disobedience actions of Anglophone civil society activists and grouping of all political and ideological stripes, in all parts of the world. These platforms essentially became sites of Cameroonian collective memory in general and Anglophone visual, politico-cultural memory, in particular. As we saw in Chapter 10 (Volume I), the Internet and social media platforms were so effective in galvanizing and instrumentalizing Anglophone collective and cultural memory and channeling them into communitarian revolts that the government of Cameroon banned the Internet in Anglophone Northwest and Southwest Cameroon for a record-breaking nine long months. This was a clear demonstration that in Cameroon, the English and pidgin-speaking Southern Cameroonians are a muted, identitarian "memory group" whose collective memory-based political, and cultural grievances were banned in real space and virtual space in Cameroon (Ardener & Ardener, 1992; Mink & Neumayer, 2013). Nevertheless, images of Cameroon military atrocities and human rights violations continued to seep through the Biya regime's tropical Napoleonic firewall and find their way to the social media platforms, which had become megaphones of resistance. This book would not have been possible without the Internet and the social media platforms, which provided a daily stream of official and unofficial documents, media reports and videos of torture and atrocities shot by Cameroon soldiers eager to impress their relatives and friends or to keep video records of their macabre exploits and excesses.

Negative Collective Memory

Halbwachs (1925) claimed that the past is the "cement" that binds individual and collective memory. The past, which is the stuff of collective memory, is almost always composed of traumatic historical events. Indeed, Heller (2006) suggests that collective trauma is the "cement" that binds collective memory. In past traumatic situations involving memory groups, collective memory is negative collective memory, a past that is recalled with extreme bitterness and negativity. Some negative memories may be repressed by individuals. However, from a group or social psychology perspective, collective memory consists of concerted efforts made to remember the past in order not to forget it, lest it be repeated. Negative collective memory is, therefore, traumatic memory that individuals and memory groups remember not to forget. This often leads to the politics and journalism of nostalgia (Eko, 2003). In many African cultures, negative collective memories are immortalized in the names given to sites of memory, the names given to children born in times of tragedy, natural catastrophes, war, and so on. In the Anglophone crisis, there are multiple sites of negative collective memory. They include the infamous detention and torture center of the National Gendarmerie at the *Secretariat d'Etat à la Defense* (SED), the Yaoundé Military Tribunal, the Douala, Buea, Bafoussam and other military tribunals, the Kondengui Central Prison (Chapter 22), and other locations. Indeed, sites of clashes between Anglophone separatists and Cameroon security forces are places of manslaughter, negative sites of memory. The Muyuka, Mamfe and Kumba hospitals are now sites of negative collective memory. The settlements for internally displaced persons (IDPs) in Cameroon, and Anglophone refugee camps in Nigeria, are all sites of negative collective memory spawned by the Anglophone crisis. In the Kpe/Mbolo and Duala Bantu languages of the coast of Cameroon, negative collective memory is commemorated by "negative" names given to children in times of tragedy: Kpwedi (Death), Tonde (flood), Njuma (war), Manyaka (wonders), and so on. The Anglophone Question is a negative collective memory problem that has created a new generation of children with negative collective memories–and negative names. Anglophone negative collective memory is fueled by past injustices that have not passed, that will not be allowed to pass as long as the Anglophone Question is not resolved through democratic dialogue Anglophones remember and bristle at the intolerable historical wrongs visited on them by the British colonialists and the United Nations who denied them the right of self-determination. Above all, they toil under the yoke of the tyranny of the Ahidjo/Biya *chefferie républicaine,* which deceitfully destroyed their autonomous state, alienated their lands and natural resources, took away their rights and freedoms, and imposed an over-centralized, tyrannical, neo-patrimonial, Napoleonic regime on them. To add insult to injury, the republican chiefdom turned a deaf ear to their pleas, and proceeded to subjugate them militarily when they revolted against its brutal excesses.

Africa as Site of Negative Memory

If Cameroon is a site of negative collective memory for many Cameroonians, that is also the lived reality of millions of other Africans. Due to its multiple authoritarian regimes, human rights violations, wars, famines and massacres, Africa is, for most Africans, a giant site of negative collective memory: Biafra in Nigeria, Sharpeville and Soweto in South Africa, the Derge (Ethiopia military regime), Darfur, Mugabe's *Gukurahundi* massacres in Matabeleland, Zimbabwe, the Rwanda genocide, Idi Amin's mass murders, Sekou Toure's Camp Boiro detention, torture and murder center in Conakry, Guinea, Mobutu Sese Seko and Dennis Sassou Nguesso's murderous excesses in Congo Kinshasa and Brazzaville, together with the unspeakable atrocities in Somalia, Eritrea, and Sudan, explain why Africans rush to emigrate to other parts of the world. One of the most famous sites of negative historical memory on the African continent is the city of Bulawayo in Matabeleland, Zimbabwe. In Ndebele, the language of the region, the original name of that site of negative collective memory is "KoBulawayo" (The Place of Slaughter) in reference to the location as the site of bloody internecine conflicts and colonial wars of conquest. Ethiopia has Lalibela, a magnificent site of religious and cultural memory, but it is also a site of negative memories, from famines to war. In Senegal, the slave port of Gorée is a national site of negative memory, while Elmina Castle in Ghana and Zanzibar, are major sites of African negative collective memory. In Egypt, the pyramids are sites of memory par excellence.

In volume one of this project, my co-authors and I demonstrated that President Paul Biya was the quintessential archetype of the authoritarian republican chieftain. The Biya regime's relationships with its main international partners–Nigeria, France, Israel, the United Kingdom, Switzerland, Russia and China, represent diverse connections, partnerships, angles–geometries of national self-interest–and self-interest alone. While history will be the ultimate judge of the Ahidjo/Biya regime and its international partnerships, we can conclude without a doubt that in his combined 50 years as Prime Minister and President, His High Excellency, the Chief of State, President Paul Barthélémy Biya bi Mvondo was the quintessential, authoritarian, neo-patrimonial, African republican chieftain. He was known as the "absentee" Chief who spent a total of years at the expensive presidential suite of the Intercontinental Hotel in Geneva, Switzerland. It is, therefore, no accident that Switzerland, Anglo-Swiss conglomerates, Glencore, and Hotel InterContinental, were chief international beneficiaries of Biya's "spoils system," whose stock-in-trade was mostly the natural resources of Southern Cameroons (Soboth, 1993). This volume describes and explains how Nigeria, Israel, France, the United Kingdom and Switzerland were self-interested partners in the "slothmanship" rule-by-decree, bureaucratic inertia and human rights violations of the republican chiefery of Cameroon under President Paul Biya. This volume focuses on the human rights aspects of the Anglophone Question and the geometries of international self-interest that made violations of these rights possible. An interesting angle, a positive development in the geometries of human rights violations of the Anglophone Question is the emergence of a small, eclectic group of Cameroon Francophone voices whose actions echo Wole Soyinka's admonition: intellectuals who keep silent in the face of injustice, repression, and human rights violations, die! (See Chapter 25). It is also worth noting that when the Internet was shut down in the English-speaking regions, "Internet refugees" traveled to Douala, Mbouda, Bafoussam, Yaoundé and other towns in the French-speaking regions where cybercafés, private businesses, and even government offices granted them access to the Internet discreetly, often free of any charge. That is how the world received images of human rights violations by the Cameroon military and the Anglophone separatists.

References

Achebe, C. (1996). *Things Fall Apart*. London: Heineman.

Ardener, S. (2005). Ardener's "Muted Groups": The genesis of an idea and its praxis. *Women and Language*, Vol. 28, (2), Pp. 50-54.

Assmann, J. (2011). *Cultural memory and early civilization*. Cambridge, UK: Cambridge University Press.

Betts, *R. (1961). Assimilation and Association in French Colonial Theory, 1890-1914.* New York: Columbia University Press.

Bommas, M. (2012). Introduction: Sites of memory and the emergence of urban religion. In M. Bommas, J. Harrisson, & P. Roy (Eds.), *Memory and urban religion in the ancient world* (pp. xxvi–xxxviii). London, UK: Bloomsbury.

Cummings, C. L., & Kong, W. Y. (2019). Breaking down "fake news": Differences between misinformation, disinformation, rumors, and propaganda. In *Resilience and hybrid threats* (pp. 188–204). IOS Press.

Davenport, C. (2007). State Repression and the Tyrannical Peace. *Journal of Peace Research*, 44(4), 485-504. https://doi.org/10.1177/0022343307078940.

Eko, L & Mielczarek, N. (2015). When Memory Sees Signs and Plays Games: *Visual Communication Quarterly*, 22:3, 160-173, DOI: 10.1080/15551393.2015.106919

Eko, L. (2003) The English-Language Press and the Anglophone Problem in Cameroon: Group Identity, Culture and the Politics of Nostalgia, *Journal of Third World Studies* 20 (1) pp. 79-102.

Eko, L. (2015). The art of satirical deterritorialization: Shifting cartoons from real space to cyberspace in Sub-Saharan Africa. *International Communication Gazette*, 77(3), 248-266. https://doi.org/10.1177/1748048514568759

Eko, L. (2007). It's a Political Jungle Out There: How Four African Newspaper Cartoons Dehumanized and 'Deterritorialized' African Political Leaders in the Post-Cold War Era. *International Communication Gazette*, 69(3), 219-238. https://doi.org/10.1177/1748048507076577

Eko, L. (2003). The English-Language Press and the Anglophone Problem in Cameroon: Group Identity, Culture and the Politics of Nostalgia, *Journal of Third World Studies 20 (1)* pp. 79-102.

Gann, L. (1988). The Berlin Conference and the Humanitarian Conscience, in Stig Förster, Wolfgang Mommsen & Ronald Robinson (eds). *Bismark, Europe and Africa: The Berlin Africa Conference 1884-1885 and the Onset of Partition, pp.* 321-331. Oxford: Oxford University Press.

Halbwachs, M. (1925). *Les cadres sociaux de la mémoire (The Social Contexts of Memory).* Paris: Félix Alcan.

Heller, J. (2006). Alternative narratives and collective memories: Israel's new historians and the use of historical context. *Middle Eastern Studies*, 42(4), 571–586.

Jowett, G. S., & O'Donnell, V. (2018). *Propaganda & persuasion*. Sage publications.

Kane, P. (2023). *Mémoire corrective* (Tomes 1&II, 1987-1991). (Corrective Memory Vols. 1 &II) *Recueil de portraits satiriques publiés* dans le Cafard Libéré sous la Rubrique Profil (Collection of Satirical portraits published in *le Cafard Libéré* under the Profile Section). Dakar L'Harmattan Sénégal

Ki-Moon, B. (2008). More than Just Talk. United Nations Secretary General. https://www.un.org/sg/en/content/sg/articles/2008-06-17/more-just-talk

Kipling, R. (1940). *The White Man's Burden. Rudyard Kipling's Verse.* New York, Double Day,

Lacan, J. (1986). *The seminar of Jacques Lacan, Book 7 (1959–1960): The ethics of Psychoanalysis.* New York: Norton. (D. Porter, Trans.)

Mandela, N. (2007). Nelson Mandela introduces The Elders, Johannesburg, 18 July 2007. The Elders https://theelders.org/news/nelson-mandela-introduces-elders-johannesburg-18-july-20

Mbembe, A. (2001). *On the Postcolony.* Berkley: UCLA Press.

Mink, G., & Neumayer, L. (Eds.). (2013). *History, memory and politics in Central and Eastern Europe: Memory games.* Houndsmill, UK: Palgrave Macmillan.

Mitchell, WJ.T. (2005). *What do Pictures Want? The Lives and Loves of Images.* Chicago, University of Chicago Press.

Mudimbe, V.Y. (1994). *The idea of Africa.* Bloomington, Indiana: Indiana University Press

Pliny, G. (The Elder) (1952) *Natural History V* (H.Rackham, trans.). Cambridge, MA: Harvard University Press.

Portes, J. (1987). *Une Fascination Réticente: Les Etats-Unis Dans L'Opinion Français, 1870-1914.(A reticent fascination: The United States in French Public Opinion 1870-1914).* Paris: Université Paris I Panthéon-Sorbonne.

Nora, P. (1997). *Les lieux de mémoire* (Sites of Memory) Vol. 3. Paris: Gallimard.

Ofer, D. (2009). The past that did not pass. *Israeli Studies*, 14(1) 1--35.

Pacepa, I. M., & Rychlak, R. J. (2013). *Disinformation: former spy chief reveals secret strategies for undermining freedom, attacking religion, and promoting terrorism.* Wind Books Washington, DC.

Ricoeur, P. (2013). *Hermeneutics.* (D. Pellauer, trans). Cambridge, UK: Polity.

Soboth, J-M (1993). Le partage du butin pétrolier del'ex-Cameroun occidental: Cambriolage electoral en Mai 1972? (Sharing of the petroleum spoils of the former West Cameroon: Electorial Burglary on May 1972?) *Expression Nouvelle*, No. 21, April., p. 11.

Turing, A. (1992). Intelligent Machinery. In *Mechanical Intelligence Collected Works of A.M. Turing*, Volume 1, pp. 107-127, D.C. Ince, ed.). North Holland.

Waberi, A. (2018). A Missive for Youth. The UNESCO Courier. https://courier.unesco.org/en/articles/missive-youth

INTRODUCTION

The International Connections and Human Rights Dimensions of the Anglophone Question & Crisis in Cameroon

LYOMBE EKO

In January 2023, the world witnessed one of the most bizarre incidents in modern diplomatic history of conflicts. On January 20, the Canadian Ministry of Foreign Affairs issued a "Statement on Peace Process in Cameroon." The statement said inter alia:

> The Honourable Mélanie Joly, Minister of Foreign Affairs, today issued the following statement on the announcement of a peace process aimed at resolving the ongoing crisis in the North-West and South-West regions of Cameroon:
>
> "Civilians are bearing the brunt of the ongoing crisis in Cameroon, with more than 6,000 people having lost their lives since 2017. In addition, nearly 800,000 people have been displaced as a result of this crisis, and 600,000 children do not have full access to education.
>
> Canada welcomes the agreement by the parties to enter a process to reach a comprehensive, peaceful and political resolution of the conflict. The parties have also agreed to form technical committees to begin work on confidence-building measures.
>
> The agreement to enter a formal process is a critical first step toward peace and a safer, more inclusive and prosperous future for civilians affected by the conflict.
>
> We commend all parties for engaging in substantive dialogue. We encourage all stakeholders to support and work with the parties to advance and

> contribute to an inclusive process to reach a lasting and sustainable political settlement.
>
> Canada has accepted the mandate to facilitate this process, as part of our commitment to promote peace and security and advance support for democracy and human rights. Our role also reflects Canada's engagement to work with our African partners to build a better future for everyone.
>
> The parties to this agreement are the Republic of Cameroon, the Ambazonia Governing Council and the Ambazonia Defence Force, the African People's Liberation Movement and the Southern Cameroons Defence Force, the Interim Government, and the Ambazonia Coalition Team. The parties further express the hope that other groups will join the process (Government of Canada, 2023).

The United Nations, the European Union, the Vatican, the British and American governments, as well as the international community and the media hailed this breakthrough, which followed years of futile behind-the-scenes, cat-and-mouse diplomatic and humanitarian efforts to bring Cameroon's enigmatic, 92-year-old autocratic, Chief of State, President Paul Biya, who had ruled Cameroon for more than 40 years, to the negotiating table for peace talks with leaders of the fractious Anglophones to resolve the protracted Anglophone crisis. The 2016 Anglophone Revolt and the Cameroon government's extremely violent response to it had caused thousands of deaths, the displacement of hundreds of thousands of civilians as either internally displaced persons in Cameroon or refugees in Nigeria and other countries (York & Njie, 2023). The euphoria with which the Canadian announcement was received seemed to be well-placed because Canada was the ideal country to play the role of mediator in the Anglophone crisis. Not only is it a rich and thriving multicultural country, but it is also officially a bilingual English/French country like Cameroon. Canada's own history of peaceful, democratic resolution of issues of political co-existence between French-speaking Quebec and English-speaking Canada could serve as a model for resolution of the Anglophone Question in Cameroon. The Quebec sovereignty referendums of 1980 and 1995, in which the federalist side, led by Francophone Prime Ministers from Quebec, Pierre Trudeau and Jean Chrétien, succeeded in convincing French-speaking Quebecois to vote against the idea that "Québec should become sovereign." Canada had mastered the art of peaceful political and cultural co-existence or co-habitation between English-speaking and French-speaking Canadians. When the Anglophone crisis erupted in Cameroon in 2016, the Canadian High Commissioner (Ambassador) in Yaoundé made efforts to bring the Anglophones and Francophones together to dialogue but the republican chiefery in Yaoundé was not interested in the niceties of dialogue. Therefore, this announcement came as a breath of fresh air. It gave rise to a wave of euphoria in the Anglophone and international community. This intractable conflict was about to be tackled through peaceful negotiations and dialogue.

Snubbing Canada...and Switzerland

Exactly four days after the Canadian Foreign Minister Melanie Joly's office announced that "Canada has accepted the mandate to facilitate this process, as part of our commitment to promote peace and security and advance support for democracy and human rights," Cameroon's Minister of Information and Government Spokesman, Réné Sadi, dashed the hopes of all concerned by contradicting the Canadian Foreign Minister. Sadi released a lengthy statement which said in part:

> Following recent information disseminated by certain media, the Government of the Republic of Cameroon informs the national and international community that it has not entrusted any foreign country or external entity with any role of mediator or facilitator to settle the crisis in the Northwest and Southwest regions (Resolving Anglophone Crisis, 2023).

Minister Réné Sadi effectively slammed the door on any negotiations to resolve the Anglophone Question. There was shock and despair in the Anglophone Northwest and Southwest regions, where the Cameroon military, led by the Israeli-trained and armed, *Bataillon d'Intervention Rapide* (BIR) had unleashed a reign of terror on civilians alleged to be separatists, suspected of being relatives of separatists, or suspected of harboring separatists. The houses of those suspected of giving aid to, or sheltering separatists, were burned to ashes, and their owners killed. Many people fled to the bush. In response, Anglophone leaders in exile called for the intensification of the so-called Monday "ghost towns," symbolic acts of civil disobedience and resistance par excellence, which consisted of general boycotts of all outdoor activities in the Northwest and Southwest regions. These ghost towns continue to be observed every Monday, seven years after the Anglophone Revolt began in 2016.

Cameroon's denial that it had requested, and Canada had accepted to mediate the Anglophone problem, made a mockery of diplomacy. It was a terrible snub of Canada, which insisted that the talks about talks that had taken place prior to the announcement were at the initiative of the Cameroon government. The decision to go public with the information about Canada's mediation was apparently made with the knowledge and consent of the parties. If the Canadians were upset, they did not show it. Despite the humiliating disavowal by the Biya regime, Foreign Minister Melanie Joly's Press Secretary, Adrien Blanchard, put a positive spin on events: "We are in touch with the parties and our previous statement still stands...Representatives of Cameroon's government had attended all of the earlier meetings in Canada that led to the agreement" (Canadian Government, 2023). The Canadian initiative quickly fizzled into an embarrassing diplomatic non-incident that demonstrated the political bad faith, unpredictability, and unreliability of the republican chiefery in Yaoundé.

Solicitation and Rejection of Swiss Mediation

The diplomatic fiasco over Canada's mediation of the Anglophone crisis in Cameroon was just one of multiple international diplomatic games of smoke and mirrors in the

Anglophone crisis. Indeed, plausible deniability is the structuring modus operandi of the Biya regime. Cameroon's Chief of State, President Paul Biya, whose home away from home is an expensive presidential suite at the Geneva InterContinental Hotel, had already played an identical game of plausible deniability–denial of participation in Swiss-mediated pre-negotiation talks with Anglophone groups. After months of behind-the-scenes talks between representatives of Cameroon and a few of the main Anglophone separatist groups. On June 27, 2019, the Swiss Federal Government issued the following press statement:

> At the request of the parties, Switzerland is acting as a facilitator in the crisis in north-western and south-western Cameroon. To this end, a second preparatory meeting with various Cameroonian opposition groups took place in Switzerland between 25 and 27 June 2019. The Federal Department of Foreign Affairs (FDFA), working in close partnership with the Centre for Humanitarian Dialogue (HD Centre), is committed to finding a peaceful, lasting negotiated solution to the crisis in north-western and south-western Cameroon. Switzerland was tasked by a majority of the parties with facilitating an inclusive negotiation process. To this end, a second meeting with various Cameroonian opposition groups took place in Switzerland between 25 and 27 June 2019. The aim of the meeting was to prepare the future peace negotiations between the Cameroonian government and the political opposition. The FDFA is concerned about the continuing violence in the north-western and south western regions of Cameroon, which is taking a heavy toll on the civilian population.
>
> Switzerland has long been committed, both at bilateral and multilateral level, to finding a peaceful solution to the crisis and to promoting respect for human rights in Cameroon. Switzerland is also committed to providing humanitarian aid to the affected local population and has supported Cameroon in dealing with multilingualism.
> Facilitation is an instrument of Switzerland's traditional good offices. In this role, Switzerland can establish contacts and provide communication channels. Switzerland's good offices are open to all concerned parties who wish to participate in facilitation processes. Switzerland adheres to the principles of strict neutrality and discretion. In order not to jeopardise the process, the FDFA does not comment on the content of ongoing mediation efforts (Government of Switzerland, 2019).

This announcement was greeted with euphoria in the war-torn Anglophone Northwest and Southwest regions. After years of painstaking, on-again, off-again, behind-the-scenes, pre-negotiation talks between the Cameroon government and the main Anglophone separatist groups, it appeared that progress was finally being made to peacefully resolve the problematic situation of Anglophones in *la République du Cameroun*. International involvement would ensure that the Biya regime did not resort to the political subterfuge and deceptive ways for which it was notorious. Leaders of the main Anglophone groups attended a number of Swiss-mediated preparatory talks with representatives of the Cameroon government in Switzerland. The Biya regime soon started dragging its feet. On September 13, 2019, the Cameroonian government announced that it had rejected Swiss mediation aimed at resolving the Anglophone crisis and opted for continued military operations (Sahill & Latimer, 2022).

President Biya could afford to snub the Swiss and get away with it because he was the guarantor of Swiss "commodity" interests in Cameroon– oil, natural gas, and agricultural products like cocoa and coffee. Was Biya not a regular customer of the Geneva InterContinental Hotel? Biya had the upper hand in the Biya-Swiss relationship. Months later, Biya was back at his favorite location in the Swiss Alps, the InterContinental Hotel in Geneva. Swiss business interests (national self-interest) outweighed the vicissitudes of an enigmatic republican chieftain.

As the abortive Canadian and Swiss mediation efforts demonstrate, if the Anglophone crisis has persisted since 2016, it is not for want of international efforts to resolve it. The United Nations, the African Union, the European Union, the British Commonwealth, la *Francophonie*, the Vatican, the United States, and others made efforts to resolve the crisis peacefully. Alas, these efforts were all in vain, due to the duplicity, lack of forthrightness, obduracy, and bad faith of the enigmatic, authoritarian republican monarch, the Chief of State, President Paul Biya. His main political strategy is bureaucratic inertia, political "slothmanship" based on the belief that time and eternity are on his side, that he can afford to turn an authoritarian blind eye and a deaf ear to their plight of disgruntled citizens, that he can use military force and unspeakable atrocities and human rights violations to subjugate them, that he can ignore the entreaties of human rights groups and the appeals of the international community. *Slothmanship* is the art of playing for time, slowing things down, delaying, doing nothing, stringing things out, paying lip service to peace initiatives like those of Switzerland and Canada, only to repudiate them at critical moments. The aim was to buy time to militarily crush and subjugate the separatist Ambazonian groups. This was a clever strategy because it was based on the belief that Anglophones were a fractious lot that have a tendency to splinter into factions, engage in internecine fighting, and self-destruct. That strategy worked perfectly. The fractious, unsophisticated Anglophone groups soon splintered into rival factions that turned on each other. Every single one of their faction leaders and warlords wanted to be the authoritarian "President of Ambazonia." Everyone wanted to change Cameroon; no one wanted to change himself or herself. None of them wanted to compromise and speak with one voice. This gave the republican chieftain in Yaoundé the perfect excuse–he was not sure whom to negotiate with. The Canadian and Swiss mediation efforts ultimately failed because the absolutist republican chieftain does not negotiate with the Other; he only believes in negating and subjugating that Other, who contributed to the impasse by a lack of unity and foresight. The result is a tyrannical system of bureaucratic rule-by-decree governance that is sustained by military force and external self-interested allies. In the Republican chiefery, the law of jungle is supreme: might is right; the argument of force is always preferable to the force of argument. The republican chieftain wants to change humanity but is aggressively hostile to the idea of changing himself or his chiefdom.

Christian Cardinal Wiyghan Tumi's Abortive Anglophone General Conference

Not only did the Biya regime frustrate international efforts to organize peace talks aimed at resolving the Anglophone Conference, it also negated efforts by the Roman Catholic Church to organize a peace conference in Buea, Cameroon. A well-publicized, Catholic-church peace forum, the Anglophone General Conference, a framework for dialogue between all parties to the conflict initiated by the late Christian Cardinal Wiyghan Tumi, the Emeritus Archbishop of Douala, fizzled out because the Cameroon government did not give the Cardinal the authorization to hold the Anglophone General Conference, despite prior encouragement from the regime for the Cardinal to proceed with the conference (Mares, 2021).

These national and international happenings, or lack thereof, demonstrated that under the republican chiefery of Cameroon, *le Chef de L'État est l'État* (The Chief of State is the State). He reigns over his people not as citizens, but as colonial-style subjects over whose welfare he demonstrated a reckless disregard for decades. Cameroonian intellectuals, engineers, doctors, lawyers, politicians, and so on are masters of their area of expertise but at the end of the day, they are all servants and subjects of the Chief of State who has absolute away over their lives and can affect them negatively or positively with a stroke of his mighty pen. The rule of the Cameroonian Chief of State is geometric and pervasive. It is felt in all angles and directions by anyone who has any connection, no matter how remote to that country. The Chief of State has established a "*matrice elargi de predation*," (an enlarged matrix of predation) to use the expression of Mbembe (2025).

The Republican Chieftain's International Partners in Crimes (Against Humanity)

Volume I of this project presented the historical, political, and cultural background of the events that ultimately led to the Anglophone Revolt and abortive attempts by the United Nations, the African Union, Canada and Switzerland to mediate between the Cameroon government and Anglophone separatist groups to reach a peaceful solution to the conflict. The main reason the crisis has become a protracted, frozen conflict is that some countries have a stake/steak in maintaining the status quo in Cameroon. That is to say, they have vested economic interests in the longevity of President Biya and his regime. As we saw in volume I, the Anglophone crisis is being fueled by the dreaded "resource curse" that stalks resource-rich, corrupt, neo-patrimonial African countries. Despite their abundant natural resources, these countries are perpetually on the verge of failure, while their people are perpetually on the verge of starvation. This volume focuses on the major partners –in crimes against humanity–of the republican chiefery of Cameroon–Nigeria, Israel, France, the United Kingdom, and Switzerland. These countries have directly or indirectly supported the military subjugation of the people of English-speaking Southern Cameroons through their military partnerships, as well as their diplomatic and economic support. The quid pro quo has been lucrative arms contracts, and concessions to the natural resources–oil and natural gas, as well as agricultural, forestry and mineral resources that are mostly in the territory of the former Southern Cameroons.

American Engagement in the Fight Against Boko Haram Terrorism in Cameroon

The Boko Haram terrorist activities in North Cameroon, the Chad Basin and Nigeria increased American engagement in West Africa. In 2015, the Obama Administration said that the United States had declared Boko Haram a foreign terrorist organization and deployed approximately 90 troops to Cameroon to provide airborne intelligence, surveillance and other reconnaissance operations and training to the Cameroon military at the request and invitation of the Cameroonian government (Kindzeka, 2018). Israeli and American military officers worked side by side. In 2018, the United States US Africa Command provided two CESSNA 208B Grand Caravan EX aircraft to the *Armée de l'Air du Cameroun* (Cameroon Air Force) for a project called Building Partnership Capacity C-208B Intelligence, Surveillance and Reconnaissance Program. The aim of the program was to support counter-terrorism efforts against Boko Haram in North Cameroon and Chad. This program had been in the pipeline since 2015 (Key Aero, 2018). A provision of the program was that the United States would maintain the aircraft and train Cameroonians to fly and maintain them for a two-year period (Kindzeka, 2018). According to the Cameroon Ministry of Defense (2023), the two CESSNAs are based in Garoua. In the meantime, the Anglophone Revolt had begun in 2016, and the Cameroon military was given the task of crushing the Anglophone uprising, which gradually morphed into a separatist movement. Some of the American weapons were diverted from North Cameroon to the Anglophone Northwest and Southwest. When he transferred the two Cessna aircraft to the Cameroon Airforce, U.S. Ambassador to Cameroon Peter Henry Barlerin, said that the aircraft were intended to carry out surveillance and reconnaissance against Boko Haram in North Cameroon, not against Anglophone separatists in the Northwest and Southwest regions. In the meantime, the massive atrocities and human rights violations of the Biya regime in the Anglophone Northwest and Southwest regions rendered American military cooperation with Cameroon impossible. Between Congressional hearings attended by sizeable segments of the Anglophone Cameroon diaspora in the United States, and during which Cameroonian intellectuals, Felix Nkongho Agbor Balla, and Professor Patrice Nganang, testified, the American government concluded that the Biya regime was carrying out gross human rights violations against civilians. Under American law (the Leahy Law or Leahy Amendments), the U.S. State Department and U.S. Department of Defense (DOD) are ordered to ensure that: "No assistance shall be furnished...to any unit of the security forces of a foreign country if the Secretary of State has credible information that such unit has committed a gross violation of human rights." For its part, the DOD is barred from providing funds "for any training, equipment, or other assistance for a unit of a foreign security force if the Secretary of Defense has credible information that the unit has committed a gross violation of human rights" (Leahy Act, 2007).

The United States Congress soon found that the Cameroon military and Anglophone separatists were engaged in atrocities and human rights violations in the Northwest and Southwest regions of Cameroon, thereby making the country ineligible for further military aid.

Figure. 1.1. U.S. Ambassador to Cameroon Peter Henry Barlerin, transferring American CESSNAs to Cameroon Ministry of Defense

Removal of Cameroon from the US African Growth and Opportunity Act (AGOA)

In view of Congressional findings that the Cameroon security forces systematically carry out torture and other gross human rights violations. The first Trump administration revoked Cameroon's eligibility for the US African Growth and Opportunity Act (AGOA), which affects market access and investment and reduces or eliminates tariffs on US imports from Cameroon. The White House announced it had revoked Cameroon's eligibility, with effect from January 1, 2022 due to its human rights violations:

> Despite intensive engagement between the United States and the Government of Cameroon, Cameroon has failed to address concerns regarding persistent human rights violations being committed by Cameroonian security forces. "These violations include extrajudicial killings, arbitrary and unlawful detention, and torture (AGOA.Info, 2019).

In 2020, the Senate Foreign Relations Committee passed a resolution "calling on the Government of Cameroon and armed separatist groups to respect the human rights of all Cameroonian citizens, to end all violence, and to pursue an inclusive dialogue to resolve the conflict in the Northwest and Southwest regions" (Senate Foreign Relations Committee, 2020). These decisions were taken in part due to the pressures exerted on individual members of Congress by the Anglophone Diaspora in the United States as well as public demonstrations by members of the Anglophone Diaspora, notably the women's group known as Takumbeng. These declarations and actions caused Cameroon to move closer to Russia and reinforce bilateral military ties with the Kremlin, which paid no heed to the niceties of human rights like the Americans.

Figure 1.2. "Takumbeng" women demonstrating in Washington D.C. at the height of the Anglophone Revolt, 2018

The Russian Connection

On 12 April 2022, less than two months after Russia's invasion of Ukraine, Cameroonian Defense Minister, Joseph Beti Assomo flew to Moscow and signed a military cooperation agreement with his Russian counterpart, Sergei Choigou, despite the Western condemnation of Russia's invasion of Ukraine (Sahil & Lattimer, 2022). The agreement did not mention Boko Haram or the Northwest and Southwest regions. The timing of the 2022 agreement was interesting, given that in 2015, just months after Russia had invaded Ukraine and annexed its Crimean Peninsula in 2014, Cameroon had signed a first bilateral military cooperation agreement with Russia. During the UN General Assembly vote calling for the Russian withdrawal from Ukraine in February 2022, Cameroon was absent for one vote and abstained in the second (Cameroon signs agreement with Russia, 2022). This was a geo-strategic realignment towards Russia, which was making its presence felt in many parts of Africa, and had no patience with the niceties of democracy and human rights.

The International and Human Rights Dimensions of the Anglophone Question

In volume one of this project, we showed that the Anglophone Question in Cameroon can be summarized as *la présence Anglophone,* the problematic place of the English and Pidgin-speaking Anglophones in the republican Cameroon. The premise is that the Anglophone Question, in the philosophical and political senses of the term, is an unsolved left-over, nay, a hangover from 19th-century European colonialism, the First World War, and postcolonial, authoritarian governance. The latter took the form of neo-patrimonial republican chiefery that imposed a suffocating tyrannical unity, a tyrannical harmonization, a misapplied, tyrannical version of the French concept of "living together," a tyrannical policy of assimilation, and a "tyrannical peace," to borrow the formulation of Davenport (2007).

Volume two explores three major aspects of the Anglophone Question, namely:

1. The international connections and partners that have contributed to shoring up and sustaining the republican chiefery of Yaoundé, and furthering the Machiavellian goals and strategies of its enigmatic, implacable, unswerving, strong-headed and hard-hearted tyrannical chieftain, 92-year-old President Paul Biya, who had been in power first as Prime Minister, and then as President of *la République du Cameroun* for a record half a century. Those fifty years in the corridors of power is a record that makes President Paul Bya one of the longest-reigning chiefs of state in the world. The volume focuses on the following countries: Nigeria, France, Israel, the United Kingdom, and Switzerland, countries that are major participants in the entrenchment of the republican chiefery.
2. Absolutist, tyrannical, rule-by-decree has no place for dissent. This volume also focuses on the consequences of Anglophone resistance to the extreme political obduracy, reckless disregard for human rights and human life demonstrated by the atrocities of the autocratic Biya regime. This volume presents the voices of Anglophone political prisoners in the insalubrious and inhuman detention/torture centers, dungeons, and prisons of the republican chiefery. It also features the voices of refugees in UN refugee settlements for Anglophones in Nigeria. Internally displaced persons (IDPs) within Cameroon are also given opportunities to speak about their predicament. The volume also features the voices of select Francophone intellectuals whose acute sense of humanism and fairness moved them to speak up against the tyrannical ecosystem of silence and *oubli* (the sea of forgetfulness) to which the republican chiefery has sought to consign Anglophone history and collective memory. This volume also contains the voices of historic Anglophone opinion leaders who, over the years, tried in vain to persuade the republican chieftain to be visionary enough to enter into negotiations to avert the impending catastrophe that became the Anglophone crisis. The volume ends with international legal analyses of two important aspects of the Anglophone Question: the Bakweri land problem, refusal by the republican chiefery to correct the injustices of colonial and post-colonial appropriation of vast tracks of native land for plantation agriculture and oil refinery construction without input from, or compensation for the land owners. The second legal analysis is a trial observation report of the

trial, before the Yaoundé military tribunal, of Anglophone civil society leaders. The chapter ends with a visual case study of Anglophone newspaper front pages that recount the major milestones and occurrences of the Anglophone Revolt. In President Biya's republican chiefery, where the rule of man trumps the rule of law, and law takes precedence over right, journalists are perpetual victims.

3. The Anglophone press as a site of collective/corrective memory. In Cameroon, there is freedom of speech on paper (the made-to-measure constitution of the republican chieftain) but "freedom after speech" is not guaranteed to anyone, including contributors to this volume, to paraphrase sentiments attributed to late Ugandan dictator, General Idi Amin Dada. However, the Anglophone press has been a site of memory that has been the site of crystallization of Anglophone collective memory.

Structure and Content of Volume II

The Anglophone Question in Cameroon–French-speaking Cameroonians speak of *le problème anglophone*–is grounded in the history of 19th-century European colonialism and imperialism in Africa. It is one of the few items of unfinished business of the First World War and the Treaty of Versailles of 1919. The first part of this volume is concerned with the international, geo-strategic aspects of the Anglophone Question, specifically, the contemporary role of Nigerian, French, British, Israeli, and Swiss self-interest-driven engagements and interventions in aspects of the crisis. The premise is that since the 1970s when oil and natural gas were discovered in large quantities off the coast of the territory of the former British Southern Cameroons, the territory became the subject of French Cameroun annexation and subjugation. Indeed, the Anglophone Question has been compounded by one of the major paradoxes of modern African politics and economics, what economists call the "resource curse." The basic idea is that in specific politico-cultural contexts, countries endowed with abundant natural resources, particularly oil, natural gas, and minerals, tend to be neo-patrimonial governments. As Fukuyama (2014) put it, these are "governments staffed by the [tribal] family and friends of the ruler, and run for their benefit…a neo-patrimonial government has the outward form of a modern state, with a constitution, presidents and prime ministers, a legal system, and pretensions of impersonality, but the actual operations of the government remains at core a matter of sharing state resources with friends and family" (pp. 287-288). As a result, neo-patrimonial states are often kleptocratic (the ruler and his ethnic elite use proceeds from natural resources as their personal slush funds). These countries have less economic growth, more conflicts, and poorer economic outcomes than countries less endowed with natural resources (Smith & Waldner, 2021; Wright & Frantz, 2017; Wright et al., 2015; Ross, 2012). The reasons for this paradox are systemic, institutional, and postcolonial hegemonic relations. In 2008, the United States Senate Foreign Relations Committee issued a report entitled: "Petroleum and Poverty Paradox: Assessing U.S. and International Community Efforts to Fight the Resource Curse." The report concluded that:

> Paradoxically, history shows that rather than a blessing, oil or natural gas

> reserves can be a bane for many poor countries, leading to fraud, corruption, wasteful spending, military adventurism and instability. Too often, oil money that should go to a nation's poor ends up in the pockets of the rich, or it may be squandered on grand palaces and massive showcase projects instead of being invested productively" (United States Foreign Relations Committee, 2008, p. 2).

Several African countries are classified as having a resource curse. They include Nigeria, the Democratic Republic of Congo, Congo Brazzaville, Gabon, Sudan, South Sudan, Equatorial Guinea, the Central African Republic, and Cameroon (Berman et al., 2017). Studies have shown that "great power alliances," and postcolonial hegemonic relationships are key drivers of "petrostate aggression," which is one of the main characteristics of the African resource curse. This is the reflex to solve political and diplomatic problems through repression and violence rather than negotiations because autocrats can use natural resources to acquire the best repressive security apparatus money can buy (Kim & Woods, 2016).

Cameroon is an exemplar of a neo-patrimonial state with a resource curse. The enigmatic President Biya personally controls the country's natural resources. Ironically, when President Biya came to power on November 6th, 1982, his political slogan was "*riguer et moralization*" (rigor and moralization). This slogan was intended to signal a new beginning, a break with the rigid authoritarianism and corruption of the Ahidjo regime. The Biya regime, which celebrated its 42nd year, in power in 2024, turned out to be anything but moral and humane. It is a tyrannical regime of *rigeur sans moralité* (rigor without morality), a kleptocratic republican chiefery that has been propped up by an Israeli-trained and armed presidential praetorian guard, as well as a notoriously brutal *Bataillon d'Intervention Rapide* (Rapid Intervention Battalion, or BIR). This Israeli-trained and armed elite "army within the Cameroon army," reports directly to President Biya. It is infamous for its use of violence, torture, the murder of civilians, and extra-judicial killings of perceived opponents of the regime. It is also responsible for burning scores of villages accused of aiding and sheltering Anglophone separatists and killing thousands of people. The BIR, which has also had a partnership with, and funding from U.S. Special Forces (Turse & Speri, 2022; O'Grady, 2019), is funded directly by the state oil company, *la Société Nationale des Hydrocarbures* (the National Hydrocarbons Corporation). It is an open secret that the rent-seeking ruling elite of autocratic kleptocracies often collude with multi-national commodities extraction and trading companies in the domains of oil, natural gas, forestry, agriculture, and mining, to further the interests of these companies while amassing fortunes through bribery, kickbacks and other forms of corruption. This goes on while the African citizens of these countries are mired in poverty and misery. A good example is the international, multi-state prosecution and conviction of Swiss multinational commodities (oil, natural gas) and mining conglomerate, Glencore Plc, in the United States, the United Kingdom and Brazil for bribery and corruption in a number of African countries (see chapters 19 and 20). The premise of this section of the volume is that the over-centralized, tyrannical, kleptocratic republican chiefery of Cameroon is a unique exemplar of the resource curse. The chapters explore, describe, and explains how France, the United Kingdom, Israel, and

Switzerland have woven a web of lucrative, and often corrupt postcolonial relationships with the Ahidjo/Biya republican chiefery that have been highly lucrative for the extracting companies of the above countries, and for the Chief of State, President Paul Biya and his Beti-Bulu tribal ruling elite. Natural resources–oil, natural gas, minerals, agricultural and forestry resources–are exploited, controlled, and spent by the Chief of State (first Ahmadou Ahidjo, and after 1982 by his successor, Paul Biya and their respective tribal elite, with utmost opacity, in true neo-patrimonial fashion, while much of the country lacks clean drinking water, many schools do not have classrooms and desks (see Vol. I, Chapter 8), the public healthcare system is not worth the name (see Vol. I, Chapter 13), and the roads are deplorable death traps, to name just those indicators of underdevelopment. The Anglophone Problem is an international human rights problem that is being fueled by countries that claim to be democratic promoters of human rights but are, at best, direct beneficiaries of the frits of the African resource curse. These lucrative relations thrive despite the horrendous human rights violations of the Biya republican chiefery, and Biya's decision to order–from Swiss territory–his military to subjugate the Anglophone minority rather than engage in political dialogue with it.

Chapter fifteen explores the role and place of Nigeria in the Anglophone Question. Nigeria has, over time, become the main partner in crimes against humanity of the republican chiefery of Cameroon. Nigeria is also, ironically, the host of numerous refugee camps for Cameroon Anglophones. When the peaceful Anglophone Revolt got underway in 2016, under the leadership of common law lawyers, teachers, churches (Catholic, Presbyterian and Baptist), students, and other members of the civil society, the Biya regime set out to crush it by overwhelming force of arms. The Cameroon government unleashed the might of the Israeli-trained and armed BIR, and other branches of the military, the army, navy, air force, gendarmerie, and the police to crush the movement by all means necessary. Tens of unarmed Anglophone civilians were killed in the Northwest and Southwest regions. The massive repression and bloodshed led to a transformation of the Cameroon Anglophone movement from a civilian federalist movement advocating political change, to a nascent Anglophone separatist movement and armed resistance based near the border with Nigeria. It was no longer a matter of changing the highly centralized, tyrannical, republican chiefery that had been imposed by Presidents Ahidjo and Biya to assimilate the English and Pidgin-speaking Southern Cameroons into French Cameroon, *la République du Cameroun*. The demand for a return to federalism and autonomy for the former League of Nations Mandate turned United Nations Trust Territory had fallen on deaf ears. Anglophones likened President Biya to the proverbial African Chief, Ikol'a Mato (the chief with a thousand ears who refuses to hear). According to the folkloric tale, the gods gave the chief 1000 ears to listen to the cries, petitions, pleas, and prayers of his people. Mighty and arrogant Chief Ikol'a Mato got tired of hearing the daily cacophony of pleas, prayers, petitions, cries and groans of the people. He decided to plug 999 of the ears the gods had given him. He listened only to the one ear tuned to his courtesans and tribal elite who praised, worshipped and flattered him. The result was disaster for the village, the people and ultimately Chief Ikol'a Mato.

Having concluded that Cameroon's Chief of State was a reincarnation of the proverbial

African Chief, Ikol'a Mato, Anglophone separatist groups, calling themselves "Ambazonians" (after Ambas Bay, the stretch of coast between Victoria/Limbe and Bota) emerged to resist the murderous atrocities of the Cameroon military in the former Southern Cameroons.... One of these groups, the Ambazonia Defense Force (ADF), led by Lucas Cho Ayaba, attacked and killed several Cameroonian soldiers in Agbokem-German, Manyu, Southwest region, in retaliation for Cameroon government killings of unarmed civilian demonstrators in the Northwest and Southwest regions on October 1, 2017. In November 2017, President Biya declared war on the separatists. Biya's hand-picked Prefect, the chef de terre (lord of the land) in the area, Mr. Joseph Oum II, issued a prefectorial decree that ordered the residents of 11 villages in the area to vacate their homes to avoid being caught in impending military operations in the area. The expulsion order was read several times on the radio (see Vol. I, p. 397 for expulsion order). Cameroon Anglophone refugees started streaming across the border into Cross River State, Nigeria. These refugees were initially welcomed with open arms by Nigerians on the other side of the Cross River due to ethnic and linguistic proximities and affinities between Cameroonians and Nigerians on both sides of the river. The United Nations High Commission for Refugees (UNHCR), working with the Nigerian National Commission for Refugees, Migrants, and Internally Displaced Persons (NCFRMI), and the Cross River and other state authorities, set up several refugee camps for Cameroon Anglophone refugees in Nigeria. The population of refugees in these camps increased as more refugees crossed the border, and children are born in the camps. Ironically, during the Nigeria Civil War of 1967-1970, many Nigerians had crossed over to Southern Cameroons, then a federated state in the Francophone-dominated Federal Republic of Cameroon. The Anglophone crisis caused a reversal of population movements from Southern Cameroons to Nigeria. Chapter 15 focuses on the Nigerian connection in the Anglophone problem.

Nigeria's attitude towards the Anglophone problem in the Northwest and Southwest regions was driven by self-interest, maintaining its partnership with the Cameroon government in their joint fight against the Boko Islamist terrorists, an offshoot of the Islamic State of Iraq and Syria (ISIS) that had instituted a reign of terror in large swathes of territory in Northeastern Nigeria, Northern Cameroon and the Lake Chad Basin. Incidentally, troubled and impoverished Northeastern Nigeria used to be British Northern Cameroons. The Anglophone problem in Cameroon was a lucrative opportunity for the Nigerian "securicrats," the top bureaucrats of the national security apparatuses. A number of them received suitcases of cash to facilitate the arrest and rapid extra-judicial rendition of Cameroonian political refugees and asylum seekers to the Biya government. These deportations were taking place even as Nigerian human rights lawyers were challenging their legality in the slow, ponderous, and labyrinthine legal system of the country. By the time the Nigerian courts could begin to examine these deportation cases, judges were faced with a fait accompli. The civilian arrestees were quickly deported to French Cameroun where they were held in inhuman condition in detention centers, tortured, and tried before military tribunals (see Chapter 22). Nigeria soon became the partner of Cameroon in the illegal, extra-judicial rendition of Southern Cameroonians and in subjugating Southern Cameroons separatist ambitions. The outcome is that Southern Cameroonian refugees found themselves caught between the hammer of *La République du Cameroun* and the anvil of Nigerian contempt for international law. One demonstration of the relationship of convenience between Nigeria and Cameroon was the kidnapping of the Nera 10 affair, the case of the so-called interim government of the separatist Federal Republic of Ambazonia in exile, that was holding a meeting at the Nera Hotel in Abuja, the capital of Nigeria. The 11 Ambazonians, led by their Interim President, Sisiku Ayuk Tabe, were arrested, held incommunicado, and ultimately deported in secrecy to Cameroon, without benefit of an opportunity to contest their arrest and deportation in a Nigerian court. This deportation took place despite the legal challenges filed by the lawyers of the NERA 10, most of whom had legal residency or official political refugee status in Nigeria. The extra-legal deportations were carried out despite the appeals of the United Nations High Commission for Refugees (UNHCR) in Nigeria. This extraordinary rendition of the NERA 10 and dozens of other Anglophone political refugees was a clear violation of due process of law and of international human rights law. It was also the height of the Buhari administration's contempt for the Nigerian judiciary and the rule of law. The civilian and military deportees (Anglophone deserters from the BIR and other branches of the Cameroon military) were court-martialed at the French language only Yaoundé Military Tribunal and sentenced to life imprisonment. This chapter focuses on the Machiavellian relationship between Nigeria and Cameroon in suppressing the Anglophone separatist movement. In 2021, the separatist Ambazonia Defence Forces (ADF), announced that it had allied with the separatist Indigenous Peoples of Biafra (IPOB). This development added another complication to the Anglophone Question.

Chapter sixteen focuses on the contemporary French connection in the Anglophone crisis. It explores the tension between French traditional universalistic human rights rhetoric and its postcolonial policies and actions regarding the assimilation of the former Southern Cameroons into *la République du Cameroun* and the *Organisation Internationale de la Francophonie*. The main premise of the chapter is that after the reunification of *La Republique du Cameroun* and Southern Cameroons in 1961, France had a *mission assimilatrice* (a mission to assimilate the English-speaking Southern Cameroons into the French language sphere of influence, *la Francophonie*). When the Anglophone Revolt began in 2016, France became a hidden partners in crimes against humanity with the Biya regime, and French media outlets like *TV5 Monde* reported the crisis with a Francophone slant.

Chapter seventeen describes, explains, and analyzes the Israeli connection in the human rights tragedy that is the Anglophone crisis. For more than 40 years, Israel has been responsible for setting up, training, and arming President Biya's personal praetorian guard, the *Garde présidentiel*, and the BIR, the notorious, elite, army within the Cameroon army that is infamous for its brutality, torture, extra-judicial killings, burning of villages, and other gross human rights violations and crimes against humanity in the English and Pidgin-speaking regions of Cameroon. Since the onset of the crisis, members of the BIR recorded inhuman torture sessions in their detention facilities and posted them on Facebook, WhatsApp and other social media platforms. Former Israeli Defence Forces officials, whose official title has been "*conseiller technique*," (technical adviser) have served as presidential security advisers to President Biya since a failed army mutiny and *coup d'état* in 1984 made the president abandon France and turn to Israel for presidential security and communications. This chapter explores the opaque military relationship between Israel and the Biya regime. Israeli human rights advocates and activists have denounced and demonstrated against the unholy alliance between the Netanyahu government of Israel and the Biya republican chiefery. This chapter recounts some of the realities, brutalities, atrocities, and human rights violations spawned by the Israeli connection in the Anglophone crisis.

Chapter eighteen covers the British connection in the Anglophone Question in Cameroon. As the United Kingdom scrambled to forge new political and economic alliances around the world in the wake of Brexit, its exit from the European Union, it did so under an existential imperative– the very economic survival of the U.K. was at stake. Prime Ministers Theresa May and Boris Johnson reenforced ties with the Biya regime despite its human rights record that was denounced by the British Commonwealth Human Rights Initiative (see Vol. 1, Chapter 3). As the human rights violations against lawyers, teachers, students, and members of the civil society mounted in the English-speaking regions of Cameroon that were once the League of Nations Mandated Territory and UN Trust Territory of British Southern Cameroons, the former British trustees turned their backs on these people who had been under British colonial rule from the Treaty of Versailles of 1919 to the plebiscite of 1961. The older generation of citizens of the former British Southern Cameroons had grown up in the British Commonwealth. The Ahidjo/Biya regime, which had seized control of the natural resources of Southern Cameroons through legally dubious means, decided to eliminate the collective memory and cultural specificity of Southern Cameroons, and assimilate the now divided territory into the highly centralized, Napoleonic, neo-patrimonial, republican chiefery of French Cameroon. When Anglophones rejected that total assimilation by Revolting in 2016, the Biya regime set out to subjugate the territories militarily amid massive human rights violations: the imposition of a reign of terror that included shutting down the Internet, killing of unarmed civilian protesters, the arrest, detention, torture and murder of suspected Anglophone separatists, and burning down hundreds of villages suspected of separatist sympathies. This reign of terror triggered a massive refugee crisis. The British Commonwealth Human Rights Initiative, CHRI (2017), whose self-described mission is "working for the practical realisation of human rights in the countries of the Commonwealth," addressed a letter to the Commonwealth Ministerial Action Group on Cameroon, outlining the massive human rights violations in the English and Pidgin-speaking Northwest and Southwest regions. The Conservative British government, led by Lady Theresa May, Prime Minister from 2016 to 2019, a period that coincided with the apogee of the Anglophone revolt, ignored the spirited submissions and protestations of the CHRI, as well as Anglophone protest in the UK, and cast its lot with the oppressive republican Chief of State in Yaoundé. The British Commonwealth was reduced to a deafening silence, demonstrating once again that British short-term economic interests trump the human rights ideals of the Commonwealth. The irony is that Nigeria, Zimbabwe, Pakistan, and Fiji had been expelled from the Commonwealth for less serious human rights violations. As we saw in Chapter 15, a Commonwealth member, Nigeria, has been the active partner in crimes against humanity with the republican chiefery of Cameroon. This chapter explores British human rights amorality in the Anglophone Question in Cameroon. This was exemplified by the Machiavellianism of British High Commissioner,

Rowan James Laxton, whose effusive submissions on British economic partnership with the tyrannical, neo-patrimonial, republican Chief of State of Cameroon, bordered on obsequious sycophancy that "o'er flowed the measure," to use a Shakespearean expression.

The theme of chapter nineteen is the Swiss connection in the Anglophone crisis in Cameroon. Historically, Switzerland or to be more specific, Swiss Germans, came to Cameroon through the colonial acquisition of the Kamerun territories by the founder and first Chancellor of the German Empire, the "Iron Chancellor," Prince Otto von Bismarck, at the partition of Africa during the Berlin Africa Conference of 1884-1885. In effect, at the Berlin conference of Frederick William of Prussia, Bismarck, who had undergone a Christian conversion, which led him to believe "in a God who invariably agreed with him on all issues" (Barkin, 2023) paved the way for the Swiss German Basel Evangelical Missionary Society, later known as the Basel Mission to begin work in Kamerun. The Basel mission had been formed by Swiss Calvinists and German Lutherans from the Kingdom of Württemberg, Bismarck's home state. They began missionary work in German Kamerun in 1886, two years after Germany acquired the territory. The colonial relic, Bismarck's Fountain, constructed in the colonial capital, Buea, is a legacy of the connection between Swiss-German missionary work and late 19th-century pan-Germanism. However, the Basel Mission was forced to leave Kamerun when German armies in Africa were defeated during World War I (1916) in Kamerun by British and French forces. Germany's defeat in Europe in 1918, marked the end of German Kamerun. However, the work of the Basel mission continued in the mission stations it had founded in the territory. Today, the Presbyterian Church in Cameroon is the heir and custodian of the work of the Basel Mission in Cameroon.

Interestingly, the German presence in Cameroon continued through the missionary work of bilingual German American immigrants in the United States and Canada, who were working under the auspices of the German-speaking General Conference of German Baptist Churches in North America (Purpose and Priorities, 2024). The conference was renamed the North American Baptist Conference in 1944, in the middle of World War II, to remove its German ethnic identity and adopt English as its primary language. The North American Baptist Conference was instrumental in founding the Cameroon Baptist Mission, later renamed the Cameroon Baptist Convention (CBC), the heir and custodian of the work of German American missionaries like Rev. Drs. Karl Jacob Bender, Dr. Gebauer, Rentz, George Dunger, Bender, Lang, Meinerts, Schroeder, Michelson, Fluth, Schmidt, Westerman, Lemke, Zimbelmann, Haupt, Fluth, Lake, Kirschman, and so on.

Fast forward to 2015. The Swiss are back in Cameroon, this time not as Protestant missionaries but as entrenched multinational business conglomerates like Glencore International, in agricultural commodities and natural resource (oil and natural gas) extraction, as well as the main managers of the logistics and security of the port of Douala and other infrastructures. The federalist Swiss Confederation and the anti-federalist Biya republican chiefery had forged such close ties that Switzerland became President Biya's second home, a place where he spent weeks and sometimes months at a time, and like the proverbial Ikol'a Mato, he was oblivious to the dire and desperate realities of the people of Cameroon. On May 24, 2022, the United States Department of Justice accused Swiss commodities (natural resources) trading conglomerate, Glencore International AG of Baar, Switzerland, of bribing national oil company officials in Nigeria, Cameroon, Ivory Coast, Equatorial Guinea, Congo, and South Sudan to have profitable access to the oil and other natural resources (minerals) of these countries. Glencore International AG pled guilty to the charges. The British Serious Fraud Office also charged Glencore with high-level international corruption, saying it had paid officials of the Cameroon National Hydrocarbons Company (SNH), and the national refinery, SONARA bribes to have profitable access to oil and natural gas in Cameroon in furtherance of the interests of Glencore International AG (*United States v. Glencore International AG*, 2022, Tobin, 2022). Furthermore, in August 2024, the British Serious Fraud Office (SFO) charged the former head of Glencore Oil for bribery offenses in Nigeria and Cameroon (Glencore's ex-head of oil charged with bribery offences by UK fraud agency, 2024). For obvious reasons, the Swiss have not found President Biya's lucrative "Short private trips" to Geneva, Switzerland, problematic in any way, even when the president ordered human rights violations against the English-speaking minority of Southern Cameroons from his sponsored presidential suite at the InterContinental Hotel in Geneva, Switzerland (Crawford & Spoerndli, 2019). This chapter focuses on Switzerland's amoral, self-interested partnership in crimes against humanity with the Biya republican chiefery in Cameroon. Given Swiss secrecy, only history will reveal the full extent of the symbiotic relationship between Biya and the Swiss.

Chapter twenty examines another aspect of the relationship between the Swiss Confederation and its enigmatic, authoritarian, anti-federalist bedfellow, President Paul Biya. It delves deep into this twisted irony of the Anglophone crisis, namely, the close political, diplomatic, and especially economic relationship between the Swiss Confederation and the hardline, anti-federalist Paul Biya, whose regime arrested, imprisoned, tortured, and murdered Anglophone federalists, merely because they espouse or believe in the political ideology of federalism, which was once the system of government in Cameroon. Biya wallows in the joys and freedoms of federalism in Switzerland and violently suppresses it in his own country. This chapter describes and explains the deterritorialization of the Anglophone Question and other associated political problems from Cameroon to Switzerland, whose national policy is Machiavellian in the purest sense of the expression. It is Swiss national and corporate self-interest above all else. The result is that Anglophone and Francophone Cameroonians who were also feeling the consequences of Biya's authoritarian regime, held unprecedented demonstrations against President Paul Biya and his Swiss "accomplices" at his favorite Swiss hideout, the InterContinental Hotel in Geneva, Switzerland. This chapter narrates the long history of President Biya's fondness for his hideout in the Swiss Alps. Its premise is that the close relationship between President Biya and the Swiss is due to the fact that the Swiss are partners with the Biya in the "lawful plunder" of the natural resources of English and Pidgin-speaking Southern Cameroons, to borrow the expression of Bastiat (1998, p. 7). Bastiat pointed out that this type of plunder is "plunder [that] is organized by law for the profit of those who make the law," the Biya regime. This chapter surveys how Swiss engagement in Cameroon evolved from a 19th- century colonial, missionary (Christian humanitarian) engagement backed by German Chancellor Otto von Bismarck to a 21st-century capitalist, politico-corporate partnership with the Biya regime despite its authoritarianism and crimes against humanity.

The second part of this volume focuses on the impact of the political impasse and the republican chieftain's failure to solve the Anglophone crisis. It explores the impact of Biya's failure to find a lasting consensual, democratic solution to the crisis. Chapter twenty-one presents the two ideological mentalities that came to characterize the conflict: the force of argument advanced by the Anglophones and the argument of force deployed by the Biya regime to counter Anglophone demands for change. It presents Anglophone voices that raised the alarm that the status of the Anglophone minority in *La Republique du Cameroun* was neither tenable nor tolerable, and President Biya's violent response to these demands for change. This section includes the voices of Anglophone civil society, and Anglophone political prisoners at the Kondengui Central Prison in Yaoundé, Anglophone refugees in Nigerian refugee camps, and internally displaced Anglophone persons (IDPs) in Cameroon. It also presents the Ayah Foundation, a humanitarian group that works with Anglophone refugees and internally displaced persons. The section also includes the voices of a select group of Francophone intellectuals, humanitarians who opposed the human rights violations of the Biya republican chiefery in the Northwest and Southwest regions.

Chapter twenty-one is a catalog of the enigmatic Chief of State's political intransigence, tone-deafness, bad faith, and authoritarian abuse of power. It presents the voices not heeded on the road to Cameroons' national disaster. It brings to the fore the voices of the historic actors at the center of the Anglophone Problem. Starting with Hon. John Ngu Foncha, Premier of Southern Cameroons' naïve and unsophisticated panegyric to President Ahmadou Ahidjo on the occasion of *la République du Cameroun's* accession to independence from France on January 1, 1960, it goes full circle and returns to Hon. Jonh Ngu Foncha and Hon. Solomon Tandeng Muna's 1992 open letter to President Paul Biya entitled, "A call to the Head of State to save the nation before it is too late." The letter demonstrates the complete transformation of the relationship between French Cameroun and English-speaking Southern Cameroons. The relationship evolved from a status of equality between two equal states to an unequal, hegemonic relationship between a dominant French Cameroon State and two subservient, subaltern regions, the Northwest and Southwest. It presents the Buea Declaration of the All Anglophone Conference of 1993 (AAC I), which bemoaned the suppression of Anglophone cultural and identitarian specificity. It also contains discourses and counter-discourses on the make-believe, plagiarized, partially implemented Cameroon constitution of 1996, the demands of firebrand Bui MP, Joseph Mbiydzenyuy Wirba that the rubber-stamp Cameroon National Assembly discuss the Anglophone crisis, the 2018 open letter of John Fru Ndi, Chairman of the Social Democratic Front to President Biya, and the submissions e of the Anglophone Churches on the Anglophone Problem. These voices represent a historical snapshot of Anglophone political and civil society resistance against the decades-long measures undertaken by the autocratic, republican Chiefs of State, Presidents Ahmadou Ahidjo and Paul Biya, to harmonize, mute, and eventually erase the linguistic, cultural, educational, and legal specificities of the former Southern Cameroons, a state that had merged with the French-speaking *La Republique du Cameroun* to form the Federal Republic of Cameroon in 1961. The premise of the chapter is that the Anglophone Question is a question of the contested form of the Cameroonian State. This is the bone of contention between Francophones and Anglophones who inherited different colonial logics of governance and have different interpretations of the understandings–or lack thereof–of the balance of power between the three branches of government, the role of religion in the life of the state, local governance, and the rights of the citizen. These political differences are compounded by an absence of democracy and the failure of the Cameroon government to seek the consent of the Anglophone minority it governed, the existence of a climate of fear that stifles freedom of speech and of the press, the absence of a free and independent judiciary, disrespect for the human rights of Cameroonian citizens, and especially of the Anglophone minority. The chapter is a litany of bad faith, obduracy, deceptiveness, and half-backed ideas floated by the Biya republican chiefery to hoodwink the population and the international community into believing that the regime was resolving the Anglophone crisis. The end result was that since the powers that be in Yaoundé did not see it fit to seek a lasting solution to the Anglophone Question, the crisis has morphed into a frozen conflict that will undoubtedly flare up in the future when the present actors are no longer on the political stage.

Chapter twenty-one, The Force of Argument Versus the Argument of Force, focuses on Anglophone voices that raised the alarm that the status of the Anglophone minority in *La Republique du Cameroun* was neither tenable nor tolerable. The merger or reunification of Southern Cameroons and *La Republique du Cameroun* after a UN plebiscite in 1961 had not turned out to be the national fairy tale Foncha, Nfon Mukete, Solomon Tandeng Muna, and other One Kamerun enthusiasts had naively hoped. When President Ahmadou Ahidjo and his Prime Minister Paul Biya instituted their repressive republican chiefdom in Cameroon, began to assimilate Southern Cameroonians into *la République du Cameroun,* and to erase its identitarian specificity through their program of harmonization, Anglophones were alarmed. However, they dared not protest openly due to the climate of fear that reigned under the Ahidjo/Biya one-party republican chiefdom. The fall of the Berlin Wall in 1989 unleashed a wave of "democratization" that swept across Africa. Demonstrations, strikes, and widespread acts of civil disobedience forced dictators across the continent to liberalize their regimes and allow multiparty elections. Cameroon was no exception. Anglophones, led by teachers and lawyers took advantage of this political opening to decry their subaltern status in *la République du Cameroun* and call for political change. The hardline, politically obdurate republican chiefdom of President Biya, whose stock-in-trade is repression and rule by-decree, turned a deaf ear–and the muzzle of its guns– on the discontented Anglophones who were led by lawyers, teachers, and student leaders. This chapter describes and explains some of these Anglophone voices that were not heeded, leading to a crisis caused by the tyrannical regime's failure to manage political and cultural diversity. These unheeded voices ranged from All Anglophone Conferences in 1994 to the Consortium of Anglophone Civil Society, a group that was later declared illegal and banned.

Chapter twenty-two, The Kondengui Chronicles, focuses on one of the most salient revelations of the Anglophone Revolt of 2016–the militarization of the justice system of Cameroon through the creation of military tribunals. These tribunals, which violate the letter and spirit of the African Charter on Human and People's Rights, were theatres of the absurd, where parodies of justice played out–Anglophone civilians tried in military tribunals whose medium of communication was perfect French, a language they did not understand, for crimes they did not know, by prosecutors whose arguments they could not follow, before military judges whose judgments they could not understand. As the saying goes, *l'armée camerounaise n'est pas bilingue*. The Cameroon army–and its military tribunals–are not bilingual. Many Anglophone defendants, who do not speak or understand French, did not know what they were charged with and could not understand the proceedings of the tribunal. Some had no idea they had been convicted or the crimes of which they had been convicted until their lawyers found someone who could translate the outcomes of their cases for them after the fact. The standing rule was that criminal defendants who needed translators could hire court-approved translators–at their own expense. Anglophone civilians court-martialed in military tribunals included federalists, trade unionists, independentists, dissidents, separatists, journalists, lawyers, teachers, politicians, and ordinary citizens. The most prominent military tribunal was the *Tribunal Militaire de Yaoundé* (Military Tribunal of Yaoundé), where the military is prosecutor, judge, jury, and executioner.

Figure 1.3. Military Judges of the Yaoundé Military Tribunal after their Swearing in 2022

This chapter consists of the testimonies of Anglophone political prisoners who had been tried by the military tribunal, had been convicted and sentenced to long prison terms, as well as Anglophone men and women who had languished for years in pre-trial detention at the prison. Their writings were smuggled out of the overcrowded, highly insalubrious Kondengui Central Prison in Yaoundé, where political prisoners are incarcerated with other prisoners in overcrowded, inhuman conditions. In Kondengui, prisoners are not even guaranteed a place to sleep. Despite Kondengui Prison's violation of prisoners' human right of freedom of speech and expression–it is illegal to own a cellphone behind bars–these Anglophone political prisoners were able to sneak out hand-written accounts that give us a sneak peek of life in Cameroon's most notorious prison.

Voices of Anglophone Refugees and Internally Displaced Persons

One of the outcomes of the decision of the Biya regime to use violent military repression and scorched-earth policies to end Anglophone calls for political change was the displacement of hundreds of thousands of innocent men, women, and children from their towns and villages by the Cameroon military that was determined to crush Anglophone separatist Non-State Armed Groups (NSAGs). Chapter twenty-three focuses on two Anglophone groups–refugees and internally displaced persons who fled to Nigeria and other parts of Cameroon, respectively, to escape the atrocities and human rights violations of the Cameroon military, led by the Israeli-trained and equipped BIR, the paramilitary gendarmerie, and the police. Further movements of refugees and internally displaced persons were triggered by the exactions of Anglophone Non-State Armed Groups (NSAG) who attacked anyone suspected of being a blackleg (collaborator of the Cameroon government military). This chapter consists of first-person accounts written by refugees and internally displaced persons from their refugee camps in Nigeria and settlements in other parts of Cameroon. These narratives give us another dimension of the Anglophone crisis that is not reported by the media. Only international human rights groups have given the world an inkling of the magnitude of this ignored conflict.

In chapter twenty-four, Ayah Ayah Abine, a humanitarian worker, and his father, Paul Ayah Abine, an unceremoniously retired justice of the Cameroon Supreme Court, a former political prisoner, and a former Member of the Cameroon National Assembly for Akwaya, present a critically important aspect of the Anglophone Revolt–the humanitarian catastrophe that followed the massive repression that the Biya regime visited on Anglophone demonstrators, dissidents, and innocent, men, women and children in the Northwest and Southwest region. The son-father duo, who had been engaged in humanitarian activities, namely, operation of orphanages in Buea and Akwaya before the Anglophone Revolt, became the face of humanitarian intervention on behalf of the hundreds of thousands of refugees flooding into Nigeria, as well as the hundreds of internally displaced persons fleeing the fighting in the Northwest and Southwest regions. In this chapter, Ayah Ayah Abine introduces the Ayah Foundation and the humanitarian relief it brought to the innocent victims– and they are mostly women and children – of the senseless war of subjugation in the Anglophone Northwest and Southwest regions. He also talks about the legal troubles to which he and his father, as well as the Ayah Foundation were subjected, after false and defamatory accusations were leveled against them by Ernest Obama, a rabid pro-regime commentator on French language Vision 4 TV. Justice Ayah Abine, a former sitting justice of the Cameroon Supreme Court, ends the chapter with some personal reflections. He had been arrested at the beginning of the Anglophone Revolt, removed from the Court, and imprisoned in inhumane conditions, without charge or trial for almost eight months. His crime? Advocating for federalism in Cameroon (Foute, 2021). He was promptly retired from the Court without a pension. This apparently happened because Justice Ayah Abine had expressed the view that members of the Anglophone Civil Society Consortium who had been arrested for promoting dangerous federalist ideas should be treated in accordance with the law (Nkafu Policy Institute, 2019). That meant giving the detainees a fair trial and the legal presumption of innocence that prevailed in the English-speaking regions of

Cameroon.

Enter Brave Francophone Intellectuals

To the casual observer, African and non-African alike, the "Anglophone Crisis" or "Anglophone Problem" in Cameroon is a conflict between Anglophones and Francophones, Africans who had been colonized by the British and Africans who had been colonized by the French for a relatively brief period of about 40 years. From this perspective, these two groups of Africans are being divided by colonial languages, worldviews, and allegiances. This is the conflict of colonial cultures hypothesis. That assertion contains a grain of truth, but it is lacking in substantial truth. For starters, as we have seen elsewhere in this volume (Chapter 19), due to President Biya's strategic deployment of Cameroon's natural resources–and these are mostly in English-speaking former British Southern Cameroons–the British have always been staunch partners of the authoritarian, Napoleonic chefferie républicaine of Chief of State, President Paul Biya, and against the political aspirations of the English and Pidgin-speaking minority of Cameroon which, ironically used to be part of the British Empire. Chapter twenty-five features the writings and pronouncements of a number of prominent Francophone intellectuals: David Aboum à Tchoyi, late Christian Penda Ekoka, Professor Fridolin Nke, Jean-Marc Soboth, and Dieudonné Essomba, Their presence in this volume and heir writings challenge this clash of cultures hypothesis. Their non-partisan, no-non-communitarian writings and actions suggest that the Anglophone Problem is a problem of lack of democracy, tolerance, and frank dialogue between the French Cameroon government and the minority English-speaking communities of the former Southern Cameroons, now divided into the Northwest and Southwest regions. Incidentally, Francophones call the English-speaking Northwest and Southwest regions "le NOSO."

The fifth part of the volume presents legal analyses of two diverse issues of the Anglophone Question. In chapter twenty-six, Professor Ndiva Kofele Kale presents a historical and legal analysis of the French Cameroon government's authoritarian confiscation of the land of the native Bakweri of Hvako. These lands were first alienated by the German colonial administration and subsequently managed by the British as "enemy lands" after World War I. Despite the fact that the African Commission on Human and People's Rights had advised the Cameroon government to enter into negotiations with the Bakweri natives who own the land to peacefully settle the issue, true to character, the enigmatic President Biya had turned a thousand deaf ears to the pleas of the Bakweri people. Chapter 27 presents the second legal analysis. It is a "Trial Observation Report" of the Yaoundé Military Tribunal. It was written by Dr. Marina Brilman, a barrister from the Law Society of England and Wales, who was sent to observe the court-martial of two civilian leaders of the Anglophone Civil Society Consortium, Barrister Felix Nkongho Agbor Balla and Professor Fontem Neba of the University of Buea, before the French-only Yaoundé Military Tribunal. These leaders of the federalist Cameroon Anglophone Civil Society Consortium had been arrested in Buea, transferred to Yaoundé, and court-martialed at the military tribunal under terrorism and secession charges that carried the death penalty. The major conclusion of this report is that the trial of Anglophone civilian activists, students, lawyers, priests, and teachers in military tribunals was at variance with international law in multiple respects.

Chapter 28 is a metaphorical walk down memory lane. It presents the Anglophone press as a site of collective memory that has, over the years maintained and promoted Anglophone collective/corrective memory in the face of acute assimilationist pressures and tyrannical governance. The Anglophone press has over the years exposed attempts to deny the specificity of Anglophone culture and worldview. The epilogue is written in Pidgin English, the other side of the coin of Anglophone cultural specificity. It pays homage to a very expressive hodge-podge of languages that make Anglophone Cameroon a unique cultural space. Wata go leave stone. Man no die man no rotten!

Conclusion

The Anglophone Revolt against the assimilationist, Napoleonic, republican chiefdom, which Chiefs of State, Presidents Ahmadou Ahidjo and Paul Biya imposed on the multi-cultural nation of Cameroon, to the detriment of the politico-cultural identity, specificity, and economic well-being of the English and Pidgin-speaking minority territory of Southern Cameroons, officially began with the Buea Declaration issued by the All Anglophone Conference (AACI), in Buea, on April 2-3, 1993. This was followed by the Bamenda Proclamation, issued by the All Anglophone Conference (AACII) held in Bamenda from 29th April to 1st May 1994. The Chief of State, President Paul Biya, turned a dictatorial glare and a thousand deaf ears to the Anglophone calls for change, and resorted to authoritarian police and military means to subjugate the Anglophone cause once and for all. Charles Tilly's clever dictum, "War made the state, and the state made war" (1990), is applicable to the Anglophone Problem. World War I led to the partition of German Kamerun into French Cameroun and British Southern Cameroons, leading to the introduction of French and British colonial cultures on the former German territory. These historical and colonial events ultimately led to the creation of the Cameroonian state, and that state made war on Anglophone identitarian and cultural specificity. In this book, we have argued that the Anglophone problem is the result of the failure of the authoritarian, neo-Napoleonic, republican chiefs of Cameroon, Presidents Ahmadou Ahidjo and and Paul to manage the complications of the colonial and post-colonial biculturalism of Cameroon. The autocratic and bellicist posture of 92-year-old Chief of State, Paul Biya towards the Anglophones has weakened the State of Cameroon. The Anglophone crisis has consumed national resources that would have gone towards economic development and poverty alleviation. It has resulted in wanton destruction of public infrastructures and private property. It has decimated hospitals, schools and roads in the Anglophone regions and affected development in the rest of the country. The Anglophone crisis weakened the fabric of the nation, exposed the impotence of the rubber-stamp National Assembly, the utter lack of independence of the judiciary, the militarization of justice and criminal law, the entrenchment of the national security state, and the genesis of an oxymoronic, *tromp l'oeil* system of centralized decentralization.

The Way Forward

The Anglophone Question in Cameroon has morphed into an intractable "frozen conflict" due to the lack of foresight, governance by bureaucratic inertia and sheer political "slothmanship" of President Paul Biya and his *chefferie républicaine*.... It has been a long, bloody, and costly conflict in terms of human life, human dignity, and material resources. The tragedy is that it was all avoidable. The Anglophone Question has been a conflict between political geography and cultural geometry, to borrow the formulation of Dailey (2024). The Ahidjo-Biya Republican chieftaincy has been bent on military subjugation of the physical geography of Southern Cameroons, assimilating it, and dispersing it into the cultural geography of *la Francophonie* through political and cultural harmonization and uniformization. The Anglophone response has been marked by a geometry of resistance to subjugation and cultural assimilation. This has involved drawing new lines and reinforcing cultural connections and networks with Anglophone communities in the Diaspora and with entities in the Anglosphere. The Internet and its networked social media platforms extended and strengthened the cultural geometry of Anglophone resistance to repression, subjugation and assimilation. The nine-monthlong Internet ban in the English-speaking Southern Cameroons, and drastic measures like sentencing teenagers who shared a joke about Boko Haram on WhatsApp to 10 years in prison, failed to crush Anglophone resistance. Geometry trumped geography in the Anglophone crisis. The unwillingness of the Biya regime to negotiate in good faith–President Biya rejected any changes to the "form" of the over-centralized neo-patrimonial Napoleonic state– ultimately led to unnecessary bloodshed, human rights violations, and transformation of the Anglophone Question into a "frozen" conflict that can only be solved in the post-Biya era.

To resolve the Anglophone problem in the post-Biya era, we must make collective/corrective and cultural memory our ally rather than our adversary. The way forward is backwards. This means a return of sorts to the past–recognition of the federal identitarian, cultural specificity and autonomy of Southern Cameroons, as well as rehabilitation of the collective memory of Francophone Cameroon, *la République du Cameroun* starting with celebration of the independence of French Cameroon (January 1, 1960), and resurrection of the East Cameroon Parliament. Cultural co-existence or co-habitation is preferable to politico-cultural assimilation.

References

AGOA.Info (2019). Cameroon, CAR, Gambia, Niger see US AGOA status changes. https://agoa.info/news/article/15691-cameroon-car-gambia-niger-see-us-agoa-status-changes.html

Ambazoniagate: Barrister Nalova speaks of the NERA 10 and the Abuja Abduction, *Cameron Intelligence Report*, January 8, 2019. http://www.cameroonintelligencereport.com/ambazoniagate-barrister-nalova-speaks-of-the-nera-10-and-the-abuja-abduction/

Barkin, K. (2023). Otto von Bismarck, German Chancellor and Prime Minister, *Encyclopedia Britannica Online. Retrieved from:* https://www.britannica.com/biography/Otto-von-Bismarck#ref753725

Bastiat, F. (1998). *The Law* (2nd edition). Foundation for Economic Education.

Berman, N., Couttenier, M., Rohner, D. & Thoenig, M. (2017). "This Mine Is Mine! How Minerals Fuel Conflicts in Africa." *American Economic Review*, 107 (6): 1564-1610.DOI: 10.1257/aer.20150774

Cameroon Ministry of Defense (2023). CESSNA: *Avions de Surveillance et de Reconnaissance* (Intelligence, Surveillance and Reconnaissance aircraft (ISR) https://mindef.gov.cm/armee-de-l-air/

en/cessna/

Cameroon signs agreement with Russia in further boost to military ties (2022). *Radio France Internationale* (RFI). https://www.rfi.fr/en/africa/20220422-cameroon-signs-agreement-with-russia-in-further-boost-to-military-ties-wagner-ukraine

Commonwealth Human Rights Initiative (2017). Submission to the Commonwealth Ministerial Action Group on Cameroon. (19th September). Retrieved from: https://www.humanrightsinitiative.org/download/CHRI%20Submission%20to%20CMAG_Cameroon_Sep2017.pdf

Crawford, J & Spoerndli, M. (2019). Cameroon's Biya: Why the Swiss Won't Stop His Geneva Stays. Swissinfo.ch. January 4. Retrieved from: https://www.swissinfo.ch/eng/who-foots-the-bill-_cameroon-s-biya--why-the-swiss-won-t-stop-his-geneva-stays/44644510

Dailey, A. (2024). Ukraine's "Masterstroke" Kursk Offensive is About Geometry, not Geography. The National Interest (September 17). https://nationalinterest.org/blog/buzz/ukraine%E2%80%99s-masterstroke-kursk-offensive-about-geometry-not-geography%C2%A0-212768

Eko L. (2010). New technologies, ancient archetypes: The Boston Globe's discursive construction of Internet connectivity in Africa. *Howard Journal of Communications*, 21(2), 182–198.

Glencore's ex-head of oil charged with bribery offences by UK fraud agency (2024). *Reuters*. https://www.reuters.com/markets/commodities/glencores-ex-head-oil-charged-with-bribery-offences-by-uk-sfo-2024-08-01/

Foute, F. (2021). "The two Cameroons have still not been reunited." *The Africa Report*. March 4. Retrieved from: https://www.theafricareport.com/88389/the-two-cameroons-have-still-not-been-reunited-says-paul-ayah-abine/

Fukuyama, F. (2014). *Political Order and Political Decay: From the Industrial Revolution to the Globalization of Democracy*. New York: Farrar Strauss and Giroux.

Government of Switzerland (2019). Swiss facilitation process in Cameroon, Press release, 27.06. (Via Reliefweb): https://reliefweb.int/report/cameroon/swiss-facilitation-process-cameroon

Government of Canada, Office of the Minister of Foreign Affairs (2023). Statement on peace process in Cameroon. June 20th. https://www.canada.ca/en/global-affairs/news/2023/01/statement-on-peace-process-in-cameroon.html

Key.Aero (2018). Two Cessna 208BS Delivered to Cameroon. https://www.key.aero/article/two-cessna-208bs-delivered-cameroon

Kim, I. & Woods, J. (2016). Gas on the Fire: Great Power Alliances and Petrostate Aggression,, *International Studies Perspectives*, Volume 17, Issue 3 (August), Pages 231–249, https://doi.org/10.1093/isp/ekv004

Kindzeka, M. (2018). U.S Donates Military Aircraft to Cameroon. Voice of America Africa Service. https://www.voanews.com/a/us-donates-military-aircraft-to-cameroon/4391923.html

Leahy Act (2007, as amended). Limitations on Assistance to Security Forces. 22 U.S. Code § 2378d

Mbembe, A. (2001). *On the Postcolony*. Berkley: UCLA Press.

Nkafu Policy Institute (2019). Rt. Hon. Justice Ayah Paul Abine. Retrieved from: https://nkafu.org/experts/rt-hon-justice-ayah-paul-abine/

O'Grady, S. (2019). U.S. cuts some military assistance to Cameroon, citing allegations of human rights violations. *The Washington Post*, February 7. Retrieved from: https://www.washingtonpost.com/world/africa/us-cuts-some-military-assistance-to-cameroon-citing-allegations-of-human-rights-violations/2019/02/06/aeb18052-2a4e-11e9-906e-9d55b6451eb4_story.html

Mudimbe, V.Y. (1994). *The Idea of Africa*. Bloomington, Indiana University Press.

Portes, J. (1987). *Une Fascination réticente: Les Etats-Unis dans l'Opinion Française*, 1870-1914 (A reticent fascination, the United States in French Public Opinion 1870-1914). Paris: *Université de Paris 1 Panthéon-Sorbonne.*

Resolving The Anglophone Crisis: When Personal Interest Overrides General Good. *The Guardian Post (Cameroon).* https://theguardianpostcameroon.com/post/706/fr/resolving-anglophone-crisis-when-personal-interest-overrides-general-good-

Ross, M. (2012). *The Oil Curse: How Petroleum Wealth Shapes the Development of Nations,* Princeton University Press, Oxford.

Sahli, A.& Lattime, N. (2022). Cameroon Rejects Swiss Mediation in Anglophone Crisis. The Counterterrorism Group, https://www.counterterrorismgroup.com/post/cameroon-rejects-swiss-mediation-in-anglophone-crisis

Senate Foreign Relations Committee (2020). S.Res.292. A resolution calling on the Government of Cameroon and armed separatist groups to respect the human rights of all Cameroonian citizens, to end all violence, and to pursue an inclusive dialogue to resolve the conflict in the Northwest and Southwest regions (116th Congress, 2019-2020). https://www.congress.gov/bill/116th-congress/senate-resolution/292

Smith, B. & Waldner, D. (2021). *Rethinking the Resource Curse.* Cambridge University Press.

Turse, N. & Speri, A. (2022). Even After Acknowledging Abuses, the U.S. Continued to Employ Notorious Proxy Forces in Cameroon. *The Intercept*, March 9. Retrieved from: https://theintercept.com/2022/03/09/cameroon-military-abuses-bir-127e/

United States Foreign Relations Committee (2008). Petroleum and Poverty Paradox: Assessing U.S. and International Community Efforts to Fight the Resource Curse". Washington DC, U.S Printing Office. Retrieved from: https://www.govinfo.gov/content/pkg/CPRT-110SPRT44727/pdf/CPRT-110SPRT44727.pdf

United States v. Glencore International AG, Docket No. 22-CR-297 (May 24, 2022). United States Department of Justice, United States Attorney for the Southern District of New York. Retrieved from: https://www.justice.gov/criminal-fraud/united-states-v-glencore-international-ag

Wright, J., Frantz, E. & Geddes, B. (2015). "Oil and Autocratic Regime Survival". *British Journal of Political Science.* 45 (2): 287–306. doi:10.1017/S0007123413000252.

Wright, J. & Frantz, E. (2017). How oil income and missing hydrocarbon rents data influence autocratic survival: A response to Lucas and Richter (2016). *Research & Politics.* 4 (3): 2053168017719794. doi:10.1177/2053168017719794

FIFTEEN

The Nigerian Connection in the Anglophone Crisis

The Tension Between Human Rights and Authoritarian Rule

LYOMBE EKO

It was the most brazen, yet most secretive extraordinary rendition operation undertaken by the Nigerian Defence Intelligence Agency on Nigerian soil. On Saturday, January 6, 2018, 13 leaders of the Interim Government of the self-styled Federal Republic of Ambazonia, the name given to the English and Pidgin-speaking former British Southern Cameroons by its proponents, had a scheduled meeting at the Nera Hotel, 26 Alex Ekwueme Way, Jabi 240102, Abuja, Nigeria, at 5 p.m. Virtually all the Ambazonian leaders gathered for the meeting were professionals who had Cameroon citizenship. The majority were academics, professors and administrators in various Nigerian universities. They were either naturalized Nigerians, lawful permanent residents, or political asylees registered with the United Nations High Commissioner for Refugees (UNHCR). Twelve of the 13 Ambazonian leaders arrived on time for the meeting. Some were guests at the Nera Hotel. The 13th person, Atam Millan, a UN refugee emergency official resident in South Africa, had sent a message that his connecting flight from Lagos to Abuja had been delayed. The group decided to proceed with the meeting without Millan. Just as the meeting was about to begin, a group of heavily armed, uniformed agents of the Nigerian Defence Intelligence Agency or State Security Service a.k.a Department of State Service (DSS) or the Presidential Guard Brigade or all three, burst into the room, arrested the Cameroonians without a warrant, handcuffed and blind-folded them, and bundled them into waiting unmarked cars, to the astonishment of the staff and guests of Nera Hotel, as well as passersby on the street. The Cameroonians were taken to a secret, unknown location. The arrested leaders were:

1. Sisiku Julius Ayuk Tabe, President of the Ambazonia Interim Government (AIG) of the Federal Republic of Ambazonia. Professionally, he was Assistant Vice President and Chief Information Officer, American University of Nigeria (AUN), Yola, Adamawa State He was a lawful permanent resident of Nigeria.
2. Prof. Augustine Awasum, Department of Veterinary Medicine and Imaging,

Ahmadu Bello University (ABU), Zaria; lawful permanent resident of Nigeria and of the United States.

3. Dr. Henry Kimeng Tata, Associate Professor, Civil Engineering, Ahmadou Bello University, Katsina, Nigeria; lawful permanent resident of Nigeria.
4. Tassang Wilfred, exiled Secretary General, Cameroon Teachers' Trade Union (CATTU), and Coordinator of the banned Cameroon Anglophone Civil Society Consortium (CACSC). He was granted political asylum by the Nigerian government and refugee status by the UN High Commissioner for Refugees.
5. Dr. Fidelis Ndeh-Che, Managing Director, Quantec Technology Services, Ltd, Abuja, & Senior Lecturer and IT Specialist, American University (AUN) Yola, Adamawa State. Lawful permanent resident of Nigeria
6. Dr Cornelius Kwanga, Senior Lecturer, Economics, Umaru Musa Yar'adua University (UMYU), Katsina, Nigeria, lawful permanent resident of Nigeria.
7. Dr Egbe Ngu Ogork Ntui, Associate Professor, Structural Engineering, Bayero University, Kano; lawful permanent resident of Nigeria.
8. Barrister Eyambe Elias Ebai, exiled President, Meme Lawyers' Association, member African Bar Association; granted political asylum in Nigeria
9. Barrister Shufai Blaise Berinyuy, exiled activist with Northwest Lawyers' Association (Cameroon), granted political asylum in Nigeria.
10. Nfor Ngala Nfor, National Chairman of the banned separatist political entity, the Southern Cameroons National Council (SCNC); political asylee, registered with the UN High Commission for Refugees in Nigeria.
11. Dr. Ojong Okongo, former Nigerian university professor, naturalized Nigerian citizen, business owner in Nigeria.
12. Barrister Nsoh Nalowa Bih (the only female in the group). Recent law school graduate; logistics coordinator, lawful resident of Nigeria.

The 13th member of the Interim Government of the Federal Republic of Ambazonia who was supposed to be at the Nera Hotel Abuja meeting was Atam Millan. He was flying in from South Africa via Kigali, Rwanda, and Lagos. He was a former official with the UN Office for the Coordination of Humanitarian Affairs (OCHA). He worked as Monitoring and Evaluation Officer and Manager of the Emergency Response Fund. He was the Secretary General of the Ambazonian Governing Council. Atam Millan had been invited to speak as an expert on refugee issues given that hundreds of thousands of Anglophone refugees were pouring across the border into Nigeria after they were expelled from their villages by the Prefect of Manyu, Mr. Joseph Oum II in December 2017 (Falana, 2018). The Cameroon government had decided to use military means to crush demands for federalism and other changes in the English-speaking Northwest and Southwest regions. The heavy government repression of unarmed federalist demonstrators had led to a nascent armed resistance in Manyu, a county near the Nigerian border. The Cameroon government decided to clear 16 villages that were believed to harbor separatists. An official announcement on the radio, ordering residents of the 16 villages to vacate their homes with immediate effect caused panic and sent thousands of men, women and children fleeing into Nigeria (Sanni, 2021).

This was the Biya regime's attempt to use military force to solve the Anglophone federalist political problem once and for all.

The main item on the agenda of the meeting was how the Cameroonian community in Nigeria could work with the Nigerian National Commission for Refugees, Migrants, and Internally Displaced Persons (NCFRMI) and the UN High Commission for Refugees to resettle the thousands of refugees expelled from or fleeing the conflict in the English-speaking Southern Cameroons (the Northwest and Southwest regions). Atam Millan, the South Africa-based Cameroonian refugee emergency expert who was to speak at the Nera Hotel meeting, wrote that when he arrived in Lagos on Air Rwanda, and was trying to connect to Abuja on Peace Air, a local Nigerian airline, he was assisted by Barrister Nalowa Bih, who had recently graduated from law school in Nigeria. She acted like a logistics coordinator for the Interim Government of Ambazonia. She handled booking and paying for flights, securing the meeting venue at Nera Hotel, Abuja, booking rooms for the guests, and so on. Millan communicated to Nalowa Bih that his connecting flight from Lagos to Abuja was postponed to 6 pm with a scheduled arrival time of 7:10 pm. He was met at the Abuja airport by some Cameroonian friends. Their car was stopped by Nigerian police who claimed there was some irregularity with the registration of their vehicle and demanded a bribe to settle the matter. This incident further delayed Millan, who arrived Nera Hotel at 8 pm, three hours after the meeting was scheduled to begin. He checked into the hotel and asked about his colleagues only to discover that they had disappeared without a trace. Attempts to get in contact with Nsoh Nalowa Bih, who had arranged his connecting flight to Lagos, failed. He later learned from patrons at the bar of the Nera Hotel that Nigerian security forces had arrested a group of Cameroonians at the hotel earlier that evening. Sensing trouble, Millan left the Hotel and stayed with friends. The Nigerian security forces came back later looking for him, but he had checked out. Other Nigerian government agents came back to Nera Hotel for the medications of four of the arrested Cameroonians, made inventories of all their personal belongings and carted them away. Millan promptly alerted and retained a well-known Nigerian human rights lawyer, Femi Falana before he slipped out of the country. The Nigerian media soon picked up the story. Three days later, on January 8, 2018, Millan received a text from one "Mr. Patrick, ADGS, DSS, Assistant Director General of Service DSS" seeking to determine his location. The Nigerian authorities must have gotten his number from his disappeared comrades. Unbeknownst to Millan, his colleagues were being held incommunicado at a top-secret underground detention facility at the Nigerian Defence Intelligence Agency Headquarters in Abuja.

Legal Challenges to the Detention of the Nera 10

As soon as Atam Millan raised the alarm that his Cameroonian comrades had disappeared from the Nera Hotel in Abuja and that eye-witnesses had informed him that they were probably being held by the Nigerian State Security Service, a.k.a Department of State Service (DSS) – they were actually being held incommunicado at an underground detention facility at the Defence Intelligence Agency Headquarters in Abuja – he informed well-known Nigerian human rights lawyer, Femi Falana about the abductions before slipping out of the country. Falana immediately denounced the abduction and detention of the Nera 12, claiming that the arrest, which did not have a warrant, was unconstitutional and a violation of the rights of the detainees under the Nigerian Constitution, as well as a violation of the African Charter on Human and Peoples' Rights. He and a team of human rights lawyers demanded access to the detainees. The families of the detainees and their doctors also demanded access to them. When Nigerian intelligence ignored the call and even refused to admit or deny that it was holding the Nera 12 and was making plans to deport them to Cameroon, Falana and his team of human rights lawyers sued the Nigerian government in the Federal High Court of Abuja on January 26, 2018. They prayed the court to issue declarations to the effect that the arrest of the Nera 12 in Abuja and their detention at the Defense Intelligence Agency Headquarters in Abuja was an unconstitutional violation of their dignity and human rights under the Nigerian Constitution and the African Charter on Human and Peoples' Rights, ratified by Nigeria in 2004. They requested the High Court to issue an order directing the Nigerian government to unconditionally release the Nera 12 from illegal custody. They also prayed the Court to issue an injunction restraining the Nigerian government and its agents from further violating the fundamental rights of the Nera 12 without lawful justification. In response, the Nigerian government argued that the High Court lacked the jurisdiction to hear and determine the suit filed on behalf of the Nera 12 (Ayuk Tabe and Others v. National Security Adviser and Another, 2018).

Deportation of the Nera 10 to Yaoundé

Barely three days after Femi Falana and his team of human rights lawyers filed suit against the Nigerian government on behalf of the Nera 12, the Nigerian and Cameroon governments engaged in an act of extraordinary rendition. In effect, on January 29, 2018, three weeks after abducting and detaining the Nera 12 at the Defense Intelligence Agency Headquarters in Abuja, the Nigerian government handed over the detainees to the Cameroon government, which had sent a military aircraft to Abuja to pick them up. The Nigerian government handed the Cameroon authorities all but two of the Nera 12 detainees. Dr. Ojong Okongo, a former Nigerian university professor convinced the Nigerian government that he was a naturalized Nigerian citizen and business owner. The only female in the group, Barrister Nsoh Nalowa Bih, who was pregnant at the time of their arrest at the Nera Hotel, suffered a miscarriage while in detention and was taken to a hospital. These two were left behind when ten of their comrades were handed over to the Cameroon authorities at the Abuja airport and flown to Yaoundé for trial at the Military Tribunal where they faced the death penalty (Carsten and McAllister, 2018).

Human rights lawyer, Femi Falana (2018), found the deportations so scandalous that on February 3, 2018, he wrote an open letter to the Nigerian President, Muhammadu Buhari, asking him to "bring back the Naturalized Nigerians, Refugees and Asylum Seekers who were illegally arrested, detained and deported from Nigeria to Cameroon on Friday, January 26, 2018 by the National Security Adviser, Major-General Babagana Monguno (see Complete letter in appendix 15.1).

Figure 15.1. The NERA 10 who were arrested at the Nera Hotel in Abuja and handed over to the Cameroon government for court martial at the Yaoundé Military Tribunal without due process, and in violation of international law.

Falana's open letter stated inter alia:

> Twelve of our clients who are the leaders of the people of Southern Cameroons and who have been living in Nigeria for several years were assembled for a meeting at Nera Hotel, Abuja on Saturday, January 6, 2018 to discuss the challenges faced by the over 10,000 Cameroonians who have sought political asylum in Nigeria due to persecution and repression under the Paul Biya regime in Cameroon.
>
> But before the commencement of the meeting a team of armed security personnel invaded the venue, abducted our clients and took them away to an undisclosed place. The said abduction was reported by the Premium Times edition of Sunday, January 7, 2018.
> However, a representative of the Office of the United Nations Commissioner for Refugees in Nigeria was allowed to visit our clients at the request of the Ministry of Foreign Affairs. During the visit, the United Nations representative found that our clients were held in an underground cell at the headquarters of the Defence Intelligence Agency on the orders of the National Security Adviser.
> ...
> On account of the refusal of the National Security Adviser to allow access to our clients by their lawyers, relatives and doctors we filed an application at the Abuja Judicial Division of the Federal High Court on Thursday, January 25, 2018 for the purpose of securing their fundamental rights to personal liberty and freedom of movement.

> Notwithstanding the pending suit and the intervention of the Office of the United Nations Commissioner for Refugees, the National Security Adviser expelled our clients from Nigeria and deported them to Cameroon on Friday, January 26, 2018.
> ...we are compelled to urge Your Excellency to grant the following requests: Order the National Security Adviser to produce the missing 5 deportees and bring back to Nigeria our clients who have been illegally deported to Cameroon without any further delay (Falana, 2018).

President Buhari did not respond to Falana's open letter. The Nigerian government also did not officially acknowledge that it had deported the Nera 10 and 47 other Southern Cameroonian exiles, refugees, permanent residents, and asylum seekers living in Nigeria to Yaoundé, Cameroon. It is the Cameroon government's official media's celebration of the deportation that provided information of the affair to the world.

For its part, the United Nations High Commission for Refugees (UNHCR), denounced the deportations saying that most of the deportees had filed political asylum claims, while others had refugee status in Nigeria. Even though a UNHCR official had been allowed to meet with the Cameroonian detainees while they were in detention, its appeals to the Nigerian government to respect the asylum claims and refugee status of the detainees fell on deaf ears. After the deportation, the UNHCR accused Nigeria of breaching international agreements on political asylum (Agence France Presse, 2019). Deporting detainees who had filed suit in a Nigerian court of law challenging the constitutionality of their arrest and detention without a warrant was a demonstration of contempt against the rule of law in general and the High Court of Abuja in particular. This was compounded by the fact that Nigeria had no extradition treaty with Cameroon at the time of the extraordinary extradition of the Nera 10. The deportation was also a violation of international law because some of the deportees were political refugees who had been granted political asylum in Nigeria. The speculation is that the government of Nigeria had handed the Nera 10 and 42 other Southern Cameroons refugees to the Cameroon government for trial because Cameroon was collaborating with Nigeria to fight Boko Haram terrorists in the Lake Chad Basin. The Southern Cameroonians were mere pawns in a quid pro quo deal between Nigeria and Cameroon.

The Nera 10 case at The Federal High Court, Abuja

On March 1, 2019, four weeks after Nigeria deported the Nera 10 to Cameroon for trial at the Yaoundé Military Tribunal, the Federal High Court of Abuja heard the Nera 12's case against the Nigerian government. It was a moot case that demonstrated the powerlessness of the Nigerian judiciary in the face of a strong, "national security" executive. Nevertheless, the Abuja High court soldiered bravely on. The issue before the Court was whether the Federal High Court in Abuja had jurisdiction over the Nera 12 case and whether the Nera 12 had made a convincing case that entitled them to the relief they sought. In other words, the issue was whether they had argued convincingly that their arrest and detention was unconstitutional under the law in Nigeria. The Court ruled that it had jurisdiction to entertain the Nera 12 suit and ruled that:

1. The arrest of the Applicants in Abuja on January 7, 2018 at the Nera Hotel, Abuja by the armed agents of the Respondents without a warrant of arrest is illegal and unconstitutional as it violates the Applicants' fundamental rights to dignity of the person and personal liberty enshrined in Section 34 and 35 of the Constitution of the Federal Republic of Nigeria, 1999 ss Amended) and Article 5 and 6 of the African Charter on Human and Peoples' Rights…
2. That the detention of the Applicants since January 7, 2018 by the Respondents in an underground detention center at the Defense Intelligence Agency Headquarters in Abuja is illegal and unconstitutional as it violates the Applicants' fundamental rights to dignity of the person and personal liberty enshrined in Section 34 and 35 of the Constitution of the Federal Republic of Nigeria and Article 5 and 6 of the African Charter of Human and Peoples' Rights…(citations omitted).
3. That the detention of the Applicants since January 7, 2018 by the Respondents without access to their lawyers and family members is illegal and unconstitutional as it violates the Applicants' fundamental rights to fair hearing….
4. That the arrest of the Applicants on January 7, 2018 at Nera Hotel, Abuja by the armed agents of the Respondents is illegal and unconstitutional as it violates their fundamental rights to freedom of assembly and association…

Having found that the Nigerian Government had violated the fundamental rights of the Nera 12, the Federal High Court of Abuja ordered the Nigerian government to pay the Nera 12, the sum of five million naira (about US$12,500) as general damages and aggravated damages for the illegal violation of their fundamental right to life, dignity of person, fair hearing, health, freedom of movement and freedom of association. Furthermore, in order to underline the illegality of the arrest of the Nera 10, the High Court issued a "perpetual injunction restraining the Respondents (government) from further violating the Applicants' (Nera 12) fundamental rights in any manner whatsoever and howsoever without lawful justification" (Ayuk Tabe and Others v. National Security Adviser and Another (2018)).

The international media reported that the Federal High Court of Abuja had declared the arrest and deportation of Cameroonian separatists who had applied for asylum in Nigeria "illegal and unconstitutional" (Agence France Presse, 2019). Since the majority of the Nera 12 detainees had academic affiliations in Nigeria, the Nigerian academy hailed the ruling of the Abuja High Court declaring the arrest, detention and deportation of the Nera 12 and other asylum seekers an unconstitutional violation of the Nigerian Constitution and an infringement of the African Charter on Human and Peoples' Rights. Their understanding was that the Abuja High Court had ordered the Nigerian government to repatriate or bring back the Nera 10 deportees, six of whom were academics in various Nigerian universities. The university community and staff unions hailed the court ruling as a sign that the courts can still protect and defend the rights of Nigerian citizens. "The Academic Staff Union of Universities (ASUU) has promised to ensure that the ruling will be enforced" (Fatunde, 2019). As early as 2018, months after the Nera 10 were arrested in Abuja, the Academic Staff Union of Universities (ASUU) in Nigeria embarked upon a campaign on various campuses in Nigeria calling for the immediate release of the six academics deported by the Nigerian government to Cameroon in January (Fatunde, 2018). Nothing came of these efforts. The Nigerian academic community was being naïve and optimistic. They believed that the rights of academic freedom they enjoyed in Nigeria existed in Cameroon. More than that, they believed Nigeria could wave a wand and undo the Buhari-Biya extra-judicial, "extraordinary rendition" of the Nera 10 and the 42 other deportees and retrieve them from Cameroonian custody. The Nigerian academics were not aware that Cameroon was a hardline republican chiefery where the rule of one man, Paul Biya, took precedence over the rule of law. They were not aware that the Nera 10 civilians were in the clutches of the Yaoundé Military Tribunal, and that they had been charged with secession and terrorism, offenses that carry the death penalty. Needless to say, their efforts to persuade the Buhari administration to repatriate the Nera 10 to Nigeria proved to be an exercise in futility.

The Abuja High Court as Moot Court in the Nera 12 Affair

In the face of the Buhari-Biya *fait accompli* in the Nera 10 matter, the Nigerian legal and academic fraternity was left clutching at legal straws. Human rights lawyer, Femi Falana told the media that "Justice Chikere [of the Abuja High Court] had declared the deportation of the applicants illegal and unconstitutional, awarded (compensation) to each of them and ordered the federal government to ensure that they are brought back to Nigeria forthwith." The Nigerian government ignored the Abuja High Court decision. Expecting the Buhari government to undo its deal with the Biya regime, extract the deportees from the dock of the Yaoundé Military Tribunal, and return them to Nigeria to enjoy the fruits of their successful litigation was expecting too much. The Nigerian government ignored the Nera 10 Abuja High Court decision as it had ignored the previous 2002 High Court decision holding that the people of Southern Cameroons were a people who had a right of self-determination. The lack of action of the Buhari government essentially made the Nera 10 High Court Decision moot. International humanitarian law experts concluded that the Buhari government's treatment of the NERA 10 violated international law (See Taku appendix 15.2).

The One that Got Away: Nsoh Nalova Bih's Story

One member of the Ambazonia leadership who was arrested at the Nera Hotel, Abuja by Nigerian State Security Service agents was a lady by the name Nsoh Nalova Bih. She was a recent law school graduate, a lawful resident of Nigeria, and the logistics coordinator of the Ambazonia leadership group. After the group disappeared into the labyrinthine dungeons of the Nigerian Security Services, the Nigerian and Cameroonian governments agreed to carry out an extraordinary, extra-legal rendition of the arrestees to Cameroon, despite the fact that both countries did not have an extradition treaty and despite the fact that the lawyers of the detainees had filed suit in federal court seeking to have them produced in court. Fortunately, or unfortunately for Nsoh Nalowa Bih, she was pregnant at the time of the arrest. For one reason or another, the Nigerian security personnel were persuaded that she was a Nigerian citizen (which she was not). She was, therefore, not deported to Cameroon with her colleagues. She subsequently suffered a miscarriage during the detention and was given "bail" to seek medical attention. She was ordered to report to the police regularly. Her miscarriage in Nigeria may have spared her the miscarriage of justice that her colleagues underwent at the Yaoundé Military Tribunal. She ultimately escaped from Nigeria and wrote her story on Facebook, where it was picked up by some independent media outlets, including the Cameroon Intelligence Report (Ambazonigate, 2019):

> "My name is Nsoh Nalova Bih, I was 1 of the 12 Ambazonian activists who gathered at the Nera Hotel in Abuja on January 5, 2018. Here is MY STORY of how we were abducted, and why I was not taken to Cameroon with the Nera10 to face bogus terrorism charges.
> On that fateful day, we had gathered in Abuja to discuss the growing [Cameroon] refugee crisis in the Cross River State of Nigeria caused by the war that President Biya had declared on the people of Southern Cameroons. The group consisted of professors, lawyers, teachers: Sisiku Ayuk Tabe, Prof. Awasum Augustine, Dr Henry Kimeng, Deacon Tassang Wilfred, Dr. Fidelis Ndeh-Che, Dr Conerlius Kwanga, Dr Ogork Ntui, Eyambe Elias, SHUFAI Blaise, Nfor Ngalla Nfor, Dr OJONG & myself. We had barely settled down when a group of unidentified, heavily armed men appeared, handcuffed and blindfolded us, and took us to an unknown destination. All I could remember was that we drove for hours. When we arrived at our destination, all I can remember is that I was still with the 11 others. Our abductors then took us from the car, one after the other. I was searched and taken to a cell. This was a Friday. On Monday morning, a girl walked in and blindfolded me then took me to a dark room where I was questioned. I refused to answer her questions. I was fingerprinted, and my picture taken.
>
> Two weeks later, I was once again blindfolded and taken to a car, where I realized that I was with the other 11 male ACTIVISTS. I knew who they were despite the blindfold because I recognized them from their voices. When we got to our destination, we were told to remove our blindfolds, which we did. We were then ushered into a building that turned out to be the offices of the United Nations High Commission for Refugees (UNHCR) Nigeria. This was on January 18, 2018.
>
> Being at the UNHCR was a huge relief given that 4 of the abducted activists were legally recognized Refugees in Nigeria, while 6 others had their political refugee/asylum applications pending with the UNHCR. Coming of the UNHCR was thus a relief. UNHCR Nigeria assured us that they were working with the Nigeria government to secure our release. This was the first confirmation that the Nigerian government was behind our

abduction, although we still did not know why we were abducted.
On Jan 25, 2018, at about 4 p.m., I was again blindfolded and taken to a car, where I heard the voices of my friends again. We drove for quite a while before getting to our destination.

Upon arrival, we were asked to remove our blindfolds & behave. Only then did we realize we were on our way to Nnamdi Azikiwe Intl. Airport, Abuja. When Sisiku Ayuk asked where we were going, we were told "back home." We didn't know what home meant.

When we got to the airport, a Cameroun military plane was waiting for us. We realized we'd been abducted by the Nigerian military and held by the Defence Intelligence Agency. How could we fight back? They were heavily armed and looked ready to shoot anyone who resisted.
When we were ordered to board the plane, Dr. Ojong objected saying two of the 12 activists were of Nigerian descent, that is, he and myself. The Cameroon *Bataillon d'Intervention Rapide* (BIR) officers alighted from the plane and insisted that they had come to pick up 12 not 10 detainees. After hours of discussions, two of us were finally left behind while the 10 others were forced to board the plane. The Nigerian govt had just violated its own laws, while UNHCR Nigeria had failed in its mission to protect the vulnerable asylum seekers.

Dr. Ojong and I were taken back to the DIA and locked up until Feb. 20, 2018 when we were finally transferred to Asokoro police station. On Feb. 25, 2018, I had a miscarriage while in detention. I was 3 months and 2 weeks pregnant. It was due to this miscarriage that I was granted bail on a 1 million naira bond and had to be reporting to a Police Station.

Our abduction and the forcible/illegal transfer of 10 of us to Cameroon was a watershed moment that violated Nigerian law, international refugee law, and basic human rights. This travesty must be corrected with #Justice4Nera10 via their immediate and unconditional release."
Published in *Cameroon Intelligence Report* (8, January 2019).

The NERA 10 and African Human Rights Law

While the Buhari government turned a blind eye and a deaf ear to the appeals of the Nigerian human rights and university communities over the Nera affair, the Cameroon government celebrated the return of the Anglophone refugees and proceeded to court-marshal the Nera 10 and hundreds of other English-speaking Cameroonians at the Yaoundé Military Tribunal. Femi Falana made one last ditch effort to protect his clients from the harsh, hardline, military justice regime that Cameroon imposed on civilians that dissented from its autocratic, one-man rule. It is an established rule of the African Commission on

Human and Peoples' Rights that civilians should not be subjected to military justice and tried in military courts. Falana decided to take the Cameroon government to the African Commission on Human and Peoples' Rights. Stating that Cameroon was a signatory to the African Charter of Human and Peoples' Rights and United Nations Convention Relating to the Status of Refugees, Falana urged the commission to intervene urgently to end "the ongoing human rights violations of the applicants who were forcibly returned to Cameroon by the Nigerian authorities." The human rights lawyer added that:

> ...But in a demonstration of reckless impunity, the government of Cameroon pressured the Nigerian authorities to hand over the refugees. They were handed over to the Cameroonian security forces who forcefully took them away from Nigeria on Friday, January 26, 2018.
>
> On account of the illegality of the deportation, the government of Nigeria could not announce that the refugees had been expelled from Nigeria but the Government of Cameroon decided to celebrate the deportation and threatened to prosecute the deportees for terrorism.
>
> Nigeria has no extradition treaty with Cameroon. Hence, the deportation was carried out outside the ambit of the extradition laws of Nigeria and Cameroon and the African Charter on Human and Peoples' Rights
>
> The Applicants are not soldiers, but civilians. Even though they are not military men, the government of Cameroon has decided to try them before a military tribunal. The military tribunal to try the Applicants has since been constituted by the government of Cameroon.
>
> The Applicants have since been arraigned for terrorism before a military tribunal specially constituted for the purpose of persecuting them even though they have never engaged in terrorist activities in Cameroon.
>
> The government of Cameroon's treatment of the 47 returnees falls with the 'worst crimes' of the Rome Statute of the International Criminal Court, which in article 7 defines crimes against humanity to mean acts such as deportation, imprisonment or other severe deprivation of liberty in violation of fundamental rules of international law, torture and other similar acts that are committed as part of a widespread or systematic attack directed against any civilian population.
>
> The Commission should ask the government of Cameroon to immediately stop the mistrial of the 47 refugees and asylum seekers before a military tribunal and return them to Nigeria to rejoin their families (Falana, cited in Chioma, 2019).

The spirited submissions of Femi Falana did not persuade the African Commission of Human and Peoples' Rights to take the unprecedented step of intervening in the trials of the Nera 10 and the rest of the 42 civilian deportees from Nigeria who were being tried by the Yaoundé Military Tribunal. However, his attempt to get the African Commission on Human and Peoples' Rights involved in the military mistrials in Cameroon accomplished a very important goal–it exposed Cameroon's system of law and disorder, a system where the law is used to suppress human rights and human dignity, a system where civilians are tried in military tribunals, to the world. All this publicity shone a spotlight on the trials of the Nera 10 at the Yaoundé Military Tribunal where the English-speaking deportees were being tried entirely in French without the benefit of a translator. Femi Falana may just have saved the lives of the Nera 10 deportees. The Yaoundé Military Tribunal sentenced them to life imprisonment, rather than to death.

Lessons from the Nera 12 Affair: The Rule of Man in Nigeria and Cameroon

The Nera 12 affair demonstrated that both Nigeria and Cameroon have systems of the rule of man rather than the rule of law. The difference is only a matter of degrees. It turned out that the Abuja High Court ruling declaring the abduction and detention of the Nera 12 illegal and unconstitutional was the mootest of moot court decisions. Issuing an injunction on a Nigerian government that had already engaged in an act of extraordinary rendition and deported the Cameroonian detainees to a jurisdiction where they faced the death penalty was the legal equivalent of selling after the market had closed. By deporting the Cameroonian detainees without due process, while their case was still pending before the court was a demonstration of the Buhari government's contempt for the Nigerian judiciary and for the rule of law. The High Court's finding that the constitutional and human rights of the Nera 12 detainees had been violated was moot, given that they had already been deported to Cameroon. The Nera 10 were held incommunicado in the dungeon of the State Defence Secretariat (SED) in Yaoundé, and even though they were all civilians, they were court-martialed at the French-language-only Yaoundé Military Tribunal for a litany of charges ranging from secession and treason to terrorism. Some of these charges carried the death penalty. In August 2019, the official government mouth-piece, *Cameroon Tribune* reported tersely that the Yaoundé Military Tribunal had found the Nera 10 guilty of, among other crimes, "secession, committing act of terrorism, complicity to commit acts of terrorism, financing of acts of terrorism, revolution, hostility against the fatherland, armed rebellion, propagation of fake news, undermining internal and external security of the state, and non-possession of national Identity cards" (Emmanuel, 2019) and sentenced them to life imprisonment. They were also fined USD $422 million (Germain, 2019). In Cameroon, civilians charged under terrorism and secession laws are tried in the military tribunal. The *Cameroon Tribune* also reported that the Minister of Communication, René Sadi, who as Minister of Territorial Administration (Interior) had worked with Minister Atanga Nji, an Anglophone from Bamenda, in securing the deportation of the Nera 10 from Nigeria, issued a tweet that reflected the logic of the *chefferie républicaine*. In Cameroon, made-to-measure law and political longevity trump human rights. When the Yaoundé Military Tribunal handed down its judgment on the Nera 10 civilians, Sadi tweeted:

> *La justice de la République souveraine et indépendante, s'est donc prononcée. Le Gouvernement en prend acte (Cameroon Tribune, 2019).*
>
> The justice of the sovereign and independent Republic has spoken. The Government takes note of that.

It would be recalled that Atanga Nji who succeeded Réné Sadi as Minister of Territorial Administration – the first Anglophone to do so – is famous for declaring that "there is no Anglophone Problem in Cameroon." The belief was that the arrest, deportation and imprisonment in perpetuity of the Nera 10 and other Anglophone activists and federalists would nip the nascent Anglophone Revolt in the bud. That turned out to be wishful thinking. A new Ambazonia Interim Government led by Samuel Sako emerged in the United States and new armed factions – many trained, armed and funded via Nigeria emerged. The difficult terrain, dense forests and rivers along the porous, Cameroon-Nigeria border made it relatively easy to smuggle fighters, weapons and improvised explosive device technologies from Nigeria to the Southwest and Northwest regions, thereby leading to an intensification of the conflict. The new generation of Anglophone fighters is being born and bred in Nigerian refugee camps. The Nigerian government, prompted by the Cameroon government, has banned Southern Cameroonian refugees from celebrating the Ambazonian "Independence Day," October 1st in Nigerian refugee camps. A climate of fear reigns in those refugee camps. There is great fear that Nigerian security forces will arrest and deport refugees who celebrate the Ambazonia Independence Day or any other event not approved by the Nigerian and Cameroon governments.

Historical Background of the Nigerian Connection in the Anglophone Problem

The precolonial, colonial, and postcolonial histories of Nigeria and Cameroon are inextricably intertwined. This is because neighboring African communities knew few or no official borders until colonialism. The Nera 12 affair is a contemporary problem that is rooted deep in the history of both Cameroon and Nigeria. The Contemporary conflicts in Southern Cameroons and Northeastern Nigeria can be traced to historical events, notably the partition of German Kamerun in 1916 by the inaccurate, ambiguous, imperialistic colonial cartography of Simon-Milner and other Anglo-French agreements that disposed of German "enemy lands" during and after World War I, without regard to the interests of the African peoples on the ground. The British and the French partitioned that part of the territory of German Kamerun closest to the Nigerian border into strips of often noncontiguous territories that touched Lake Chad in the North and the Atlantic Ocean in the South but discontinuous in the middle. The partition was done without the slightest regard to the wishes or welfare of the Africans who inhabited those territories. The partition of German Kamerun was enshrined in international law by a Franco-British Declaration signed on 10 July 1919 by Viscount Milner, the British Secretary of State for the Colonies, and Henry Simon, the French Minister for the Colonies (commonly known as the "Milner-Simon Declaration"). It was a colonial horse-trading operation that enlarged the scope of French Equatorial Africa, buttressed, and ultimately enlarged the British colony of Nigeria. Edwin Ardener (1962), a British social anthropologist and expert on Southern Cameroons, described the territories that became British League of Nations Mandates in 1919 and United Nations Trust Territories in 1946 as follows:

> The British Mandate consisted of mere strips of territory on the Nigerian border, shaped like two penknife blades pointing at each other, the smaller down from the north, the longer up from the south. They did not touch however, the space between being occupied by the northern Nigerian town of Yola....

The UK did not wish to administer these "two strips" of former German territory as a stand-alone colony, they were treated as mere appendages designed to strengthen the border of Britain's Nigerian Protectorate and Colony (Ardener, 1962). These two "strips" of territory were thus indirectly administered through Nigeria and essentially became neglected, insignificant extensions of the British Nigerian Protectorate from 1919 to 1961 (Budi, 2019). The British saw these former German territories as "Nomanslands" (Callahan, 2004. p. 24), disposable burdens that could be easily absorbed into its Nigerian Protectorate. Nevertheless, British colonial administrators kept separate administrative, financial and legislative records for the Cameroons territories for purposes of making periodic reports to the League of Nations and the United Nations (Callahan, 2004). Southern and Northern Cameroons ultimately became two of the most backward and under-developed parts of the British protectorate and colony of Nigeria (Phillipson, 1959).

On 2nd August 1946, the realities of that part of the German Kamerun territory placed under British trusteeship was further complicated by the British government. Under the 1946 Order in Council Providing for the Administration of the Nigeria Protectorate and Cameroons, the part of German Kamerun placed under British trusteeship was further sub-partitioned into Northern and Southern Cameroons for administrative purposes. The Northern Cameroonian territories were used chiefly to bolster the Nigerian border and the political strength of the Northern rulers of British Nigeria to counterbalance the West and East. The United Kingdom saw the "strips" of German Kamerun "enemy territory" it had negotiated from France as spoils of war that could be used to bolster its colonial balance of power in Nigeria. Northern Cameroons reinforced the northern sultanate of Sardauna (Crown Prince) of Sokoto, Southern Cameroons to serve as counterweight attached to the Eastern Igbo-dominated region of Nigeria. Things did not work out because Southern Cameroonians chafed under the yoke of second-class citizenship and Igbo domination in the Eastern Region of Nigeria. Nnamdi Azikiwe's National Council of Nigeria and the Cameroons (NCNC) was not a big enough tent to hold them. They "seceded" in 1953, and Southern Cameroons obtained a modicum of autonomy while Northern Cameroons stayed in the Northern Region, thus creating a situation of imbalance of the Federation of Nigeria, where each region had its own House of Assembly and its own Premier. At independence in 1960, the Northern Hausa-Fulani Region was preponderant over the Western (majority Yoruba) and Eastern (majority Igbo) Regions. In the 1959 independence elections, Nnamdi Azikiwe's National Council of Nigeria and the Cameroons formed an alliance with the powerful Hausa-Fulani Northern People's Congress led by Amadou Bello, Sardauna of Sokoto. Amadou Bello preferred to remain Premier of Northern Nigeria. The Deputy leader, Abubakar Tafawa Balewa became Prime Minister while Nnamdi Azikiwe was left with the largely ceremonial position of President of Nigeria (Britannica, 2021). The Igbo saw this as an imbalance and an entrenchment of northern preponderance in the Nigerian federation. This perceived imbalance would bedevil Nigeria and lead to the coup d'état of January 15, 1966, which saw the assassination of both Northern Regional Premier, Amadu Bello and Federal Prime Minister, Abubakar Tafawa Balewa, and ultimately to the Nigerian Civil war. Indeed, the Igbo leader, Chief Col. Chukwuemeka "Emeka" Odumegwu-Ojukwu, the military governor of the Eastern Region of Nigeria and leader of the breakaway Republic of Biafra (1966-1970) blamed the "imbalance" of the Nigerian Federation that had been created by the British colonial administration.

The Past That Has Not Passed: The Atiku Citizenship Controversy

Fast forward to contemporary Nigerian politics. Opponents of former Nigerian Vice-President Atiku Abubakar never fail to bring up his "Cameroonian" roots at every election. The billionaire former leader of the People's Democratic Party (PDP) served as vice president from 1999 to 2007 during the presidency of Gen. Olusegun Obasanjo. He was born on 25 November 1946, when the Adamawa region was part of the Northern Cameroons Territory carved by the British out of German Kamerun territory it obtained during World War I. Though Atiku had been elected governor of his state and successfully ran as Obasanjo's running mate during the 1999 and 2003 presidential elections, during the 2019 elections, operatives from Buhari's camp claimed that Atiku was in fact not a Nigerian because he had been born in Cameroon. They claimed that he was a citizen by plebiscite, a second-class citizen of sorts, not a citizen by birth (Ukhuegbe, 2021). He lost the elections. Whether that accusation about his Cameroonian origins played a role in his defeat is unclear. Though a Federal High Court in Abuja has dismissed a suit challenging Atiku's Nigerian citizenship, and his fitness to be president of Nigeria, those challenges are launched in all national elections he is involved in (Abuh & Ochojila, 2022). Nevertheless, the very fact that his Nigerian nationality could be questioned in 2019, and again 2022 shows that the ghost of the British Northern Cameroons is still lurking in Nigerian politics, just as the ghost of British Southern Cameroons is at the core of the Anglophone crisis, which was triggered by perceptions of the second-class citizenship, and marginalization of English-speaking former Southern Cameroonians in the French-dominated Republic of Cameroon.

Incidentally, the Boko Haram Islamist terrorist insurgency, emerged from the northern-most part of the former Northern Cameroons territories, which had been carved out from German Kamerun in 1916, and attached to Northern Nigeria to bolster the power of the traditional rulers of the region. Northern Cameroons was administered indirectly (essentially neglected) by the British until 1961, when it was subsequently incorporated into the independent Nigerian federation via a questionable plebiscite. From 1961, Northern Cameroons became a neglected part of the Nigerian federation and has since been sliced and diced into a number of states. Nevertheless, some analysts argue that the Boko Haram terrorist organization took on an anti-Western, Islamist coloration that hides multiple economic and political grievances, namely, the northeast (former Northern Cameroons) has the poorest population in the country. The region is marked by low education rates, high unemployment, high underemployment, and people who lack the basic infrastructures: clean drinking water, basic health services, schools, electricity, and so on. Boko Haram emerged out of these circumstances as well as what Adibe (2014) has termed "a sense of alienation" and a "retreat from the 'Nigerian project - the idea of fashioning a nation out of the disparate nationalities that make up the country - and instead construct meanings in primordial identities, often with the Nigerian state as the enemy." With its blissful, verdant Paradise populated by springs of the choicest non-intoxicating wines and multiple virgins in the Hereafter, religion has become the refuge from alienation and poverty.

Thus, by an ironic twist of history, the German Kamerun territories that the United Kingdom acquired under provisions of the Treaty of Versailles and partitioned into British Northern and Southern Cameroons, have become centers of armed conflict. The poverty and economic deprivation of the British Northern Cameroons territories that were annexed and attached to the postcolonial Federal Republic of Nigeria, led to the emergence of the Boko Haram Islamist insurgency in these former German "enemy" territories. The Anglophone Revolt of 2016 in what was the former British Southern Cameroons represented a failure of British and United Nations decolonization policies in the former territory of German Kamerun.

The Biya Regime and the Anglophone "Non-Issue"

The Anglophone problem in Cameroon is a problem of postcolonial authoritarianism and neo-patrimonialism. After destroying the Federal Republic of Cameroon that brought together French Cameroon and the English-speaking Southern Cameroons in 1961, the Ahidjo/Biya regime created a highly centralized, authoritarian, Napoleonic republican chiefery that set out, with the help of France, to erase the cultural and identitarian specificity of English and Pidgin-speaking Southern Cameroons, and assimilate it into the French-language sphere, *la Francophonie*. As the Biya regime engaged in authoritarian denialism, declaring the Anglophone Problem a non-issue, something that was not worth discussing in the Cameroon National Assembly, it turned a deaf ear to international calls for a negotiated settlement to discuss the root cause of the crisis. It instead opted to use highly repressive measures, and military means to suppress the Anglophone Revolt. Both separatist movements like the Southern Cameroons National Council (SCNC) and federalist organizations like the Consortium of Anglophone Civil Society were banned for organizing peaceful demonstrations and ghost town strikes. The Consortium's president, international human rights lawyer, Nkongho Felix Agbor-Balla, and its Secretary General, Professor Fontem Aforteka'a Neba, were arrested in Buea, transferred to Yaoundé and held incommunicado in the dungeon of the SED. They were later brought before the Yaoundé Military Tribunal and charged with eight counts of terrorism and insurrection against the state, under a 2014 Law on Repression of Terrorism (Amnesty International, 2018). They were charged with "publishing false news...complicity with, and non-denunciation of terrorist acts," "non-denunciation of information and sources," and other vague charges brought by military prosecutors (Amnesty International, 2018). The Biya regime had decided to use military means to solve the federalist Anglophone political problem by subjugating the English and Pidgin-speaking regions once and for all. As the crisis degenerated into an armed conflict, the demands of the Anglophones morphed into a demand for self-determination and independence. The Anglophone Restoration war had begun. Anglophone fighters called themselves "restoration forces," because they claim their resistance was aimed at restoring the autonomy and sovereignty of the state of Southern Cameroons. That is the genesis of the Ambazonia Interim Government whose members were abducted at the Nera Hotel Abuja on January 6, 2018, leading to the Nera 12 Affair discussed above.

The Nigerian Connection: The Ambazonian Improvised Explosive Device (IED) or "Popcorn" War

The news was startling as it was unusual. On January 7, 2021, international news agencies and independent newspapers in Cameroon reported that the military convoy of the Senior Divisional Officer for Momo in the Northwest region had been attacked by a locally made roadside bomb, an Improvised Explosive Device (IED). Five military officers had been killed along with a government official, communications delegate, Becky Liwusi Jeme. Many other soldiers had been wounded in the attack. Leaked copies of the official military report of the attack soon appeared on Facebook and Twitter, along with images of a bombed-out Chinese-made armored car lying on its side like a fallen elephant. A blown-up, armored Toyota Hilux truck carrying troops also lay shattered in a ravine while another was badly damaged. A few days later, another IED blew up a military truck-full of soldiers near Kumbo, Bui division, killing and wounding more soldiers.

During the weekend of April 24, 2021, Ambazonian resistance groups posted dramatic videos of IEDs scoring direct hits and taking out Cameroon military vehicles full of soldiers in Alou, Lebialem, Ikiliwindi, in the Southwest region, and Bali and Bui in the Northwest region. Unofficially, 14 soldiers were killed by the IEDs, and scores were wounded that weekend alone. Reports and videos of other IED attacks in the Northwest and Southwest regions followed even as renegade Amba Boys engaged in all kinds of excesses and exactions against civilians who did not follow their orders. This was the beginning of the Improvised Explosive Device (IED), "roadside bomb" or "popcorn" phase of the Anglophone conflict in Cameroon. Ambazonian separatists (they call themselves restoration forces) started planting roadside bombs, which they call "popcorn," at strategic locations, and waited, camera in hand, for the Cameroon military vehicles to drive over or near the bombs and be blown up. Indeed, there was a macabre competition between Ambazonia restoration/independentist groups (Amba Boys) on which one will post the most dramatic videos of direct IED hits against the military of *La Republique du Cameroun*. The modus operandi has been the same - planting a roadside bomb, waiting patiently to record its devastating impact on Cameroon army convoys, and posting the video on social media. The "popcorn" war was an ominous turn of events. The Anglophone war that started in 2017 when the Biya regime opted to use brutal military repression to solve the purely political Anglophone Revolt, had entered a new phase. As early as 2019, there were reports of IED explosions in

Manyu, where the Anglophone resistance had begun but these attacks looked amateurish at best.

Improvised Explosive Device (IED) manufacturing technology seems to have diffused rapidly among the Ambazonian resistance groups. The transformation of the Anglophone conflict into a deadly IED war did not go unnoticed. In March 2021, the United Nations Office for the Coordination of Humanitarian Affairs (OCHA), which works in the English-speaking regions reported that the use of IEDs was prevalent in the Anglophone war and that at least ten incidents had been reported of IEDs detonated or dismantled during February 2021 alone (UNOCHA, 2021). Before that, in 2020, the United States Embassy in Yaoundé issued a security alert when these devices started being used to attack Cameroon military convoys in the Northwest and Southwest regions. International broadcaster, Al-Jazeera TV of Qatar, reported that since January 2021, the Amba Boys had carried out close to 40 improvised explosive device attacks against military convoys from Limbe on the coast to Bui in the Northwest region. Indeed, the number of Ambazonian resistance groups posting videos of their IED kills against the Cameroon army included: Southern Cameroons Defense Forces (SOCADEF) (attack at Ikiliwindi, Meme), Manyu Warrior (attack at Eyumojock), the Red Dragons of Lebialem (attack at Alou), the Bui Warriors (attack at Kumbo), the Bali Buffaloes (attack in Bali), the Fako Mountain Lions (attack in Limbe), the Kutaba Force (attack in Mezam) and the Ambazonia Marine Force (attack in Bambalang, Ndop, Ngoketunjia). That deadly, explosive technology of resistance and insurgency that first appeared in Iraq and had a devastating impact on American occupation forces, had been introduced to the Anglophone conflict. The Amba Boys, English and Pidgin-speaking independentists resisting attempts by the Biya regime to subjugate and forcefully assimilate them into *la Francophonie*, have become the latest inductees into the IED club. Some observers saw a foreign hand in this development. It is believed that the fingerprints of the Indigenous Peoples of Biafra (IPOB) and the Niger Delta Avengers of Nigeria (NDA) were all over the IED war in Southern Cameroons.

The Ambazonia Governing Council (AGovC)/Biafra (IPOB) Alliance

Fast forward to April 2021, the Anglophone crisis that started in October 2016 is noted for its violent movements, its zigzags, its strange bedfellows, and its moving one-step forward and two steps backwards. On April 9, 2021, the so-called Anglophone crisis took another plunge into uncertainty. This was in the form of an announcement of an "alliance" between the "symbolic states" of Ambazonia and Biafra. The simultaneous announcement was "broadcast" on Radio Biafra, the satellite station that serves as the mouthpiece of the Indigenous People of Biafra (IPOB, the Igbo), and the Ambazonia Communication Network, the Facebook and satellite mouthpiece of a Southern Cameroons faction, the Ambazonia Governing Council (AGovC) and its military wing, the Ambazonia Defense Forces (ADF). The ADF is one of the military factions that emerged from the Cameroon Anglophone Revolt of 2016, when the Biya regime opted to use military means to solve the Anglophone political crisis. The announcement was an earth-shattering leap in the dark. It was momentous enough to make historians and observers of African politics and crises pause in their tracks. It amounted to a regionalization of the Anglophone conflict.

In effect, the leader of the Indigenous People of Biafra (IPOB), Mazi Nnamdi Kanu; and the Leader of one of the factions of the Southern Cameroons struggle, the Ambazonia Governing Council (AGovC), Dr. Lucas Cho Ayaba said during their joint "world press briefing" that the intent of the Ambazonia Governing Council (AGovC)/Biafra alliance was to further the "quest for the independence of their respective nations." Radio Biafra reported on its website that: "It is on record that the two nations and groups, in October 2020, signed a MOU [Memorandum of Understanding] to work together and to strengthen their unity and cooperation in their quest for self-rule."

This statement and the supposed Memorandum of Understanding between the "symbolic states" of Biafra and an Ambazonian faction, the Ambazonia Governing Council (AGovC), explained a number of things in the Anglophone war. One of the most disturbing videos – among thousands of disturbing videos – to come out of the Anglophone war was recorded at a military medical facility in the Northwest region of Cameroon. A fatally wounded soldier of the French Cameroon army was giving his commanding officer information as a healthcare worker tried to stabilize him. The wounded man gasped for breath and said in halting French that his patrol had been ambushed by Amba Boys and, that his colleagues had been killed. He told them where their bodies were in a ravine. Most importantly, he stated that the ambush had been led by a "light-skinned [tein clair] Nigerian." This Nigerian connection was intriguing. In 2017, the then Military Commander for the Southwest region, General Donatien Melingui Nouma had told TV5 Monde that Ambazonian fighters were being trained by "white mercenaries," whose nationality he declined to disclose. In November 2020, the late Cardinal Christian Wiyghan Tumi, the Archbishop Emeritus of Douala, stated that all but one of the "Amba Boys" who had abducted him and the Fon of Nso while they were traveling from Bamenda to Kumbo were "Nigerians." The man of God spent 24 hours with his captors. That Nigerian angle again.

Revelation of the existence of a Memorandum of Understanding signed between a Southern Cameroons faction, Lucas Cho Ayaba's Ambazonia Governing Council (AGovC) and Biafra that had been signed in October 2020, and the Biafra/ AGovC alliance of 2021 gave credence to these anecdotes. The changing guerrilla tactics of the self-styled Ambazonia Restoration Forces also showed a new dimension in the senseless war that emerged from the Cameroon government's political mismanagement of the Anglophone Revolt of 2016. As the Cameroon military and the BIR (an army within) introduced new Israeli, French, and Chinese armored personnel carriers, drones, and more sophisticated weapons designed to strike knock-out blows against the Amba Boys, things changed on the ground. As the Cameroon army and the BIR made headway and overran many of the camps of the divided Ambazonia resistance groups engaged in fratricidal wars and killed their own "generals," a game changer was introduced into the conflict – the dreaded improvised explosive device (IED). In 2020, the United States Embassy in Yaoundé had issued a security alert when these devices started being used to attack Cameroon military convoys throughout the Northwest and Southwest regions. Some observers saw a foreign hand in this new tactic. Some believed that Nigerians (Biafrans, to be specific) had trained the Amba Boys in handling of explosives and manufacturing improvised explosive devices. Al-Jazeera TV, Qatar, reported that since January 2021, the Amba Boys had carried out close to 40 improvised explosive device attacks against military convoys from Limbe to Bui. This has led to heavy loss of life and military equipment. These attacks are often recorded by their perpetrators and posted on Facebook, WhatsApp, Twitter, and other social media. In a show of force, the Amba Boys blocked the highway from the border town of Ekok to Mamfe for two weeks. This essentially shut down one of Cameroon's economic lifelines with impunity.

The ADF/Biafra alliance led to a stalemate in the Anglophone war. Days after announcement of the Biafra/AGovC alliance, the Nigerian Consulate General for the Northwest and Southwest regions warned Nigerians living in the Anglophone regions–and the majority are Igbos – to be law abiding residents of Cameroon. Translation: "Don't get involved in the Ambazonia/Cameroon war." The Biafra/ AGovC alliance seemed to be driven by the logic of "my enemy's enemy is my friend." Nigeria has had a strong military alliance with the Biya regime, and both countries collaborated in fighting the Islamist Boko Haram terrorists in North-eastern Nigeria and North Cameroon. Interestingly, the U.S.-based Ambazonian Interim Government led by Samuel Sako has denounced the AgovC /Biafra alliance (Obi-Maduabuchi, 2021).

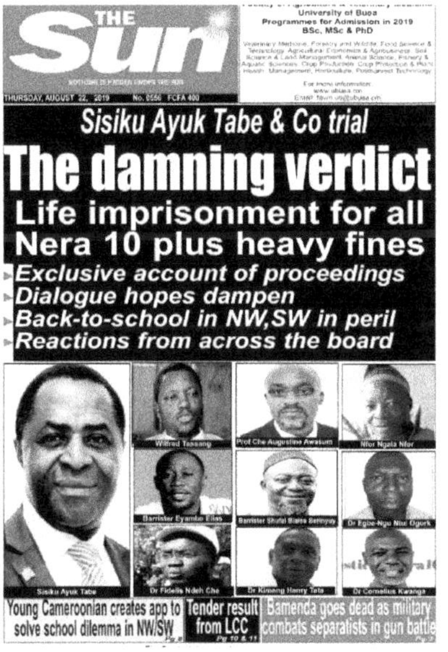
THE Sun

THURSDAY, AUGUST 22, 2019 No. 0556 FCFA 400

University of Buea
Programmes for Admission in 2019
BSc, MSc & PhD

Sisiku Ayuk Tabe & Co trial

The damning verdict

Life imprisonment for all Nera 10 plus heavy fines

- Exclusive account of proceedings
- Dialogue hopes dampen
- Back-to-school in NW,SW in peril
- Reactions from across the board

Sisiku Ayuk Tabe

Wilfred Tassang

Prof Che Augustine Awasum

Nfor Ngala Nfor

Barrister Eyambe Elias

Dr Fidelis Ndeh Che

Dr Kimeng Henry Tata

Dr Cornelius Kwanga

Young Cameroonian creates app to solve school dilemma in NW/SW

Tender result from LCC Pg 10 & 11

Bamenda goes dead as military combats separatists in gun battle

Figure 15.2. The damning verdict: Life Imprisonment for all Nera 10 plus heavy fines *The Sun*, August 22, 2019

The Ambazonian faction that signed the Memorandum of Understanding with Biafra was affiliated with Sisiku Ayuk Tabe, the imprisoned president of the Ambazonia Interim Government. Nigeria also has supplied Cameroon with military equipment to fight the Amba Boys in the Southwest, and deported other refugees from the Southwest and Northwest regions of Cameroon.

Ayaba Cho and his AGovC faction did not seem to be aware that the breakaway ethnocentric Republic of Biafra was led by ethnocentric military officer, Chukwuemeka "Emeka" Odumegwu-Ojukwu into a disastrous civil war (1967-1970). The war cost the lives of more than one hundred thousand soldiers, while close to two million civilians died of starvation caused by Nigeria's economic blockade of Biafra. The Nigerian civil war remains one of the bloodiest and most inhumane conflicts in African history. President Ahmadou Ahidjo agreed to Nigerian President, General Yakubu Gowon's request to participate in the economic blockade of Biafra in exchange for recognition of Cameroon's claims over the Bakassi peninsula. The Biafra/AGovC alliance is a very ominous development for the geo-strategic situation in the region. It seems to be the result of frustration on the part of the AGovC with the international community's failure to intervene to stop the crimes against humanity being perpetrated in Southern Cameroons by the Cameroon army and BIR. The AGovC /Biafra alliance is a counter-reaction to the inaction of the international community and especially the UN Security Council, four of whose members —France, the UK, China and Russia—have been bribed with natural resources by the Biya regime in Cameroon.

THE INDEPENDENT NEWSPAPER AT THE SERVICE OF THE PEOPLE

The Post

Wache Forever

Orange Cameroun Signs Partnership Agreement With University Of Douala

No. 02198 FRIDAY, JULY 16, 2021 PRICE: FCFA 400

AFTER BIAFRA-AMBAZONIA COALITION:

Nigeria Seals Anti-Secessionist Deal With Cameroon

Biya's envoy, HE Mbayu, and Nigeria's President Buhari exchanging pleasantries

Panic, Uncertainty Grip Nation As Ministerial Bombshell Lurks

DANIEL MUNA MEMORIAL CLINIC:

Ama, George Muna's Court Action Foils 'Board Of Directors Meeting'

Akere Muna Faulted For 'Rough Game'

Orange Cameroun Clears Air On Disgruntled Former Workers Defaming Company

MINSEC's BUSH-FALLING TEACHERS' LIST:

Witch-hunting Of Perceived Political Opponents Takes Lead

- *Staff Who Have Never Left Duty Posts, Country Implicated*
- *Escapee Inner Circle, Political Friends Shielded By Godfathers*

Crucial Role Of Contractors In Mismanaging COVID-19, Other Funds

Figure 15.3. Nigeria Seals Anti-Secessionist Deal with Cameroon, *The Post*, July 16 2021

The Nigerian connection in the Southern Cameroons conflict is probably the most significant connection. Nigeria and Southern Cameroons share a long, porous border that runs through multiple geographic zones: from dense forests, impassible rivers to rugged mountainous terrain. The people on both sides of the Cameroon Nigeria border have long ethnic ties that were not severed by colonial partitions. When the Anglophone Revolt began in 2016, and President Biya's hand-picked prefect for Manyu, Joseph Oum II transformed parts of the area into a war zone and expelled the inhabitants of 16 villages believed to offer aid and succor to Ambazonian insurgents, thousands of the displaced villagers crossed the Manyu and Akwaya rivers into the Nigeria states of Cross River, Akwa Ibom, and Taraba. In these states, the refugees were generally welcomed with open arms due to ethnic and cultural ties between peoples on both sides of the border. Historically, German Kamerun included parts of Southern Cameroons and Northern Cameroons, which became part of

Nigeria in 1961. When the Anglophone crisis began, the Nigerian National Commission for Refugees, Migrants, and Internally Displaced Persons (NCFRMI), worked with the United Nations High Commission for Refugees (UNHCR) to process, register and resettle Southern Cameroons refugees in Nigeria.

The human rights community, led by Barrister Femi Falana, defended Southern Cameroons asylum seekers, refugees, and residents whose human rights were violated by the Cameroon and Nigerian government. The President of the African Bar Association, Barrister Hannibal Uwaifo, wrote a strongly worded letter to the Nigerian Attorney General protesting the arrest and detention of Cameroonian refugees and asylum seekers in Abuja: "If the motive for these unlawful acts is to return the refugees to Cameroon, then Nigeria would be violating international Law that forbids Countries from returning refugees to the Countries they are fleeing from." Uwaifo also wrote to British Prime Minister, Boris Johnson, imploring him to intervene in Southern Cameroons to stop the massive human rights violations being perpetrated by the Biya regime on Southern Cameroonian civilians. The most publicized intervention of the Nigerian human rights community on behalf of Southern Cameroonians was the Nera 12 affair. Even the Nigerian courts have been sympathetic to the Southern Cameroons cause. In 2002, the Federal High Court in Abuja had ruled that the people of Southern Cameroons were a people who had the human right of self-determination. The Federal High Court in Abuja also ruled in 2019 that the arrest, detention and deportation of members of the Ambazonia Interim Government, the Nera 12, was unconstitutional, a violation of the Nigerian Constitution and the African Charter on Human and Peoples' Rights. For their part, the academic community, led by the Academic Staff Union of Universities (ASUU) undertook actions aimed at securing the six professors who were arrested and deported to Cameroon as part of the Nera 10. From the above summary, it is clear that the Nigerian civil society was very aware of the Anglophone crisis in Cameroon and took steps to defend and protect the rights of Southern Cameroonians in Nigerian territory.

The same cannot be said of the Buhari government. Knowingly and willfully rounding up Southern Cameroonian refugees, exiles, asylum seekers, political activists, and dissidents registered with the Nigerian National Commission for Refugees, Migrants, and Internally Displaced Persons (NCFRMI, and the United Nations High Commission for Refugees (UNHCR) and forcefully deporting them to face torture, life imprisonment or the death penalty in the country they fled was an unprecedented act of inhumanity. As the Federal High Court in Abuja held, the actions of the Nigerian government in arresting and deporting the Cameroonian exiles, refugees and asylees to their jailers, torturers, and persecutors – without due process of law – was an illegal and unconstitutional act that violated the Federal Constitution of Nigeria, and the African Charter on Human and Peoples' Rights. It was also a blatant violation of international humanitarian law. History will record that by doing the bidding of the authoritarian republican chiefery of President Biya of Cameroon, in order to maintain their partnership in the fight against the Boko Haram scourge, the Buhari government violated the human dignity of the Cameroonian refugees and exiles and used them as mere pawns in a struggle it was having a hard time containing. The extraordinary rendition of the Nera 10 is a stain on Nigeria, a country that used to have pretentions of having a system of the rule of law rather than the rule of man, one man!

References

Adibe, J. (2014). Explaining the Emergence of Boko Haram. Brookings Institute, Africa in Focus. Retrieved from: https://www.brookings.edu/blog/africa-in-focus/2014/05/06/explaining-the-emergence-of-boko-haram/

Abuh A. & Ochojila, A. (2022). Court throws out suit challenging Atiku's citizenship. The Guardian (Nigeria, February 22). Retrieved from: https://guardian.ng/news/court-throws-out-suit-challenging-atikus-citizenship/

Agence France Presse (2019). Nigeria court says extradition of Cameroon separatists 'illegal'. Retrieved from: https://news.yahoo.com/nigeria-court-says-extradition-cameroon-separatists-illegal-152332759.html

Ayuk Tabe and Others v. National Security Adviser and Attorney General of the Federation (2019). Suit No.FHC/ABJ/CS/85/2018, Federal High Court of Nigeria, Abuja Judicial Branch.

Britannica, T. Editors of Encyclopaedia (2021, May 7). Nnamdi Azikiwe. Encyclopedia Britannica. https://www.britannica.com/biography/Nnamdi-Azikiwe

Cameroon Tribune (2019). René Sadi, Tweet: Mincom Cameroon, August 20. Retrieved from: https://www.cameroon-tribune.cm/article.html/27493/en.html/sentencing-of-separatists-government-takes-note-of-military-tribunal

Carsten, P. & McAllister, E. (2018). UPDATE 2-Cameroonian separatist leader is deported to Cameroon from Nigeria, Reuters. January 29. Retrieved from: https://www.reuters.com/article/cameroon-separatists-nigeria/update-2-cameroonian-separatist-leader-is-deported-to-cameroon-from-nigeria-idUSL8N1PO5PN

Chioma, U. (2019). Falana drags Cameroon to African Commission over trial of asylum seekers, The Nigeria Lawyers (January 6). Retrieved from: https://thenigerialawyer.com/falana-drags-cameroon-to-african-commission-over-trial-of-asylum-seekers/

Emmanuel (2019). Sentencing of Separatists: Government Takes Note of Military Tribunal Judgment, *Cameroon Tribune, August 22.* Retrieved from: https://www.cameroon-tribune.cm/article.html/27493/en.html/sentencing-of-separatists-government-takes-note-of-military-tribunal

Falana, F. (2018). Open Letter to President Mohammadu Buhari, Sahara Reporters (February 4). Retrieved from: https://saharareporters.com/2018/02/04/falana-asks-buhari-bring-back-naturalized-nigerians-refugees-and-asylum-seekers-deported

Fatunde, T. (2019). Academics hail court rulings on deported lecturers. *University World News* (March 13).

Fatunde, T. (2018). Union to embark on action over detained academics, *University World News* (July 27). Retrieved from: https://www.universityworldnews.com/post.php?story=20180727135217169

Obi-Maduabuchi, I. (2021). Cameroon Separatist leader: We have no alliance with Nnamdi Kanu, IPOB. Today (August 7). Retrieved from: https://www.today.ng/news/nigeria/cameroon-separatist-leader-alliance-nnamdi-kanu-ipob-382284

Sanni, K. (2021). Cameroonian refugees in Nigeria pass 70,000 mark – UNHCR. *Premium Times,* (Abuja). December 6. Retrieved from: https://www.premiumtimesng.com/news/more-news/499384-cameroonian-refugees-in-nigeria-pass-70000-mark-unhcr.html

Ukhuegbe, S. (2021). Citizen by Birth Versus Citizen by Plebiscite, The Guardian (Nigeria), May 4th. Retrieved from: https://guardian.ng/features/citizens-by-birth-versus-citizens-by-plebiscite/

SIXTEEN

The French Connection in the Anglophone Crisis

Human Rights Rhetoric Versus Postcolonial Realities

LYOMBE EKO

The Anglophone Revolt of 2016 was like a volcano that had been gathering steam practically since the vague, ambiguous, UN-organized referendum of 1961. It rumbled during the General Certificate of Education (GCE) crisis of 1993, and especially during the All Anglophone Conference of 1993. Unfortunately, the Ahidjo/Biya regime was an autocratic regime that had a reckless and highly contemptuous disregard for the identitarian views, opinions and wishes of the muted, subaltern Anglophone minority. All calls for peaceful political change, namely, restoration of the autonomy, and respect for the cultural specificity of the English-speaking regions of Cameroon were met with authoritarian arrogance. A strike by Anglophone common law lawyers, Anglophone teachers, students and members of civil society was met with the extremely violent repressive measures that have been the trademark of the Biya regime since the 1984 failed *coup d'etat.* At the very outset of the Anglophone Revolt, on December 13, 2016, Honorable Joseph Wirba, Member of Parliament for Bui Division, in the English-speaking Northwest region, "subverted" a plenary session of the Cameroon National Assembly in Yaoundé by bringing up the massive government repression of demonstrating lawyers, teachers, students and members of the civil society in Buea, Bamenda and other towns. The unrest in English-speaking Southern Cameroons and the massive repression was not on the agenda of the National Assembly. It has never been on parliament's agenda. It is as if it never existed. Indeed, the eternal president (Speaker) of the Assembly, Cavaye Yeguié Djibril strenuously resisted any attempts by English-speaking parliamentarians to put the revolt on the agenda or attempt to discuss it. Hon. Wirba had taken the floor to speak on an entirely different topic when he suddenly delved into the Anglophone crisis that was shaking the country. Despite calls for him to yield the podium, Hon. Wirba stubbornly refused to stand down. He instead gave a fiery speech in which he decried the heavy-handed authoritarian repression that was going on in English-speaking Southern Cameroons, and issued a clarion call for Anglophones to resist the attempted Francophone subjugation. Wirba told the National Assembly: "*When the people will rise, even if you take the whole French army* [the "*partenaire privilégié*" of the brutal and repressive Cameroon military] *and add it to yours, you will never bring them down*." He quoted former American president, Thomas Jefferson, who wrote that 'when injustice becomes law, resistance becomes duty.' "The people of West Cameroon have a duty to resist." He concluded. To Hon. Wirba and many Southern Cameroonians, France was a *partenaire privilégié* of Paul Biya in crimes against humanity. France was seen as the villain of the Anglophone problem due to its historic assimilationist mission in English-speaking Cameroon and because it was the main funder of President Biya's architecture of repression–the Israeli-trained and armed *Bataillon d'Intervention Rapide* (BIR), an army within the Cameroonian army, trainer of the regular army, the para-military gendarmerie, and the police, that were carrying out a reign of terror in English-speaking Cameroon. The Cameroon government's architecture of repression and subjugation is French–its over-centralized administration with its unelected Napoleonic *préfets*, its cultural, political, and security apparatus, and its anti-riot equipment, arms, and military equipment are mostly made in France.

Exactly two weeks after Hon. Wirba had defied the President of the National Assembly and brought up the Anglophone crisis in parliament, the French international broadcaster, *TV5 Monde*, produced a news documentary on the dramatic turn of events in the Anglophone Revolt. In an effort to convince the international community that Cameroon was a bastion of stability in the unstable Central African region, and that the Anglophone Revolt was an internal disturbance commandeered from abroad, the Biya government sought to control messaging about its war of subjugation against the Anglophone minority. To this end, it granted the French/Francophone international television channel, *TV5 Monde*, exclusive access to the war zone in the Southwest. The *TV5 Monde* documentary was a dramatic narrative of events in what they called *la crise anglophone* (the Anglophone crisis). In effect, President Biya had opted for a military solution to the political crisis.

The TV5 Monde Anglophone War Diary

The *TV5 Monde* documentary gave the world the first comprehensive view of the emerging military situation of the so-called "Anglophone crisis" where the Biya government had opted to use military means to crush a revolt characterized by unarmed civil disobedience (strikes and ghost towns) as well as demonstrations in the former Southern Cameroons, now divided into two English-speaking regions. The killing of unarmed demonstrators in an attempt to nip the revolt in the bud had essentially poured fuel into the crisis that soon morphed into a shooting war in 2017. In effect, the program, "*Au Cameroun, carnet de guerre en 'Ambazo*nie'" (In Cameroon, War Diary in Ambazonia") (Fandio et al., 2017) confirmed the veracity of a video that had been posted on social media by a fledgling English-speaking resistance group, the Ambazonia Defense Forces (ADF), a group that had emerged in Manyu division, along the border with Nigeria. The ADF had posted a video of its self-styled "Commander-in-Chief," Lucas Cho Ayaba, a.k.a Ayaba Cho, an Ambazonian nationalist wanted by the Cameroon authorities for secession, treason and a host of other crimes that carry the death penalty, reviewing a rag-tag group of Ambazonian resistance fighters in the village of Da'adi in the remote Akwaya sub-division, near the Nigerian border.[1] Akwaya was known as "Mamfe Overside" because of its remoteness. Since Akwaya was separated from the rest of Cameroon by rivers that had no bridges, it was easier to access it from Nigeria than from Cameroon. Ayaba Cho had entered Akwaya from Nigeria. The commentary of the *TV5 Monde* documentary, which was reported entirely from the French/Francophone perspective, stated that:

> *Ce document a officialisé la création d'un groupe armé bien décidé à s'en prendre aux symboles de l'Etat du Cameroun dans cette partie du pays... Sur la désormais fameuse vidéo, on y voit aussi le drapeau de l'Ambazonie, sur fond bleu et blanc, avec treize étoiles. Un pays encore imaginaire, mais pour lequel les sécessionnistes ont déjà leur hymne. Une parade comme un défi lancé aux autorités camerounaises qui ont fait suivre ce rassemblement, minute par minute, grâce à un dispositif de surveillance aérienne comme le montre des photos que nous nous sommes procurées* (Fandio et al., 2017)
>
> This document [ADF video] formally confirmed the creation of an armed group that had decided to attack the symbols of the State of Cameroun in this part of the country...On the now famous video, one also sees the flag of Ambazonia, blue and white background with thirteen stars. A still imaginary country, which the secessionists have already given an anthem. A parade that was a challenge to the Cameroonian authorities which asked for this gathering to be monitored, minute by minute, through an aerial [drone] surveillance system, as shown by these photos which we were able to obtain.

The reporters then displayed French drone aerial surveillance images of the village of Da'adi, a clearing in the dense Akwaya forest, with the self-styled "commander-in-chief," Ayaba Cho, inspecting a guard of honor mounted by his ADF resistance fighters. The Cameroon army subsequently attacked and recaptured Da'adi and claimed that it had killed tens of secessionists in the process. The inhabitants of the village had all fled to Nigeria, leaving behind only two old and infirm women (Fandio, 2017). The French news report did not state which country the Cameroon government had relied on for the drone surveillance of the ADF and other Anglophone resistance groups. However, it unwittingly revealed the strategic partnership between France and the Biya regime in the human rights violations that were to become a major hallmark of the Anglophone conflict. Indeed, it was an open secret that France was providing the Cameroon army arms, operational and logistical support, including the latest drone surveillance capabilities within the framework of the pre-independence bilateral cooperation agreements that were first signed between France and *La République du Cameroun* in 1959, and amended by the Franco-Cameroon Defense Partnership agreement of 2009.

1 Anglophone separatists call administrative divisions "counties" and sub-divisions, "local government areas").

For his part, the then Cameroon military commander in charge of the Southwest region, where Da'adi is situated, General Donatien Melingui Nouma, told *TV5 Monde* that Ambazonian fighters were being trained by "white mercenaries," whose nationality he declined to disclose (Fandio, 2017). This raised the specter of foreign intervention, which the Ahidjo/Biya regime and French ambassadors in Yaoundé had feared since the reunification in 1961. In effect, as the well-documented litany of the Cameroon army's human rights violations and murderous rampages against civilians increased, the army of unemployed Anglophone youth decided to fight back. They created tens of resistance groups, with an alphabet soup of names in their localities. These groups included the Ambazonia Defense Force, the Southern Cameroons Defense Forces (SOCADEF), the Bambalang Marine Forces, the Black Hearts of Banga Bakundu, the Donga Mantung Self-Defense Group, Fako Action Forces, Gorilla Fighters, the Manyu Ghost Warriors, the Mountain Lions, the Ngoketundjia Defence Council, the Red Dragons, the Bui Warriors, the Seven Kata of Bafut, the Bali Warriors, the Tigers of Ambazonia, etc. These "restoration forces" emerged in response to Cameroon army massacres of unarmed demonstrators in Buea, Mamfe, Bamenda and other parts of English-speaking Cameroon. They called themselves restoration forces (RFs) in reference to their goal of restoring the sovereignty and autonomy of the State of Southern Cameroons as an independent nation of Ambazonia, which they felt had been taken away from them by the machinations of the international community and the treachery of France and the United Kingdom. These resistance groups are generally called "Amba Boys" by both their supporters and detractors. The daredevil Amba Boys, mostly unemployed Anglophone youth, some of whom were idle because of the school closures – and they included a good number of young women – had come to believe that there was nothing in Paul Biya's *La République du Cameroun* for them, and that they had nothing to lose by joining the resistance against the oppressive and dictatorial French *la Republique du Cameroun*, which treated them as second-class citizens. The Amba Boys had a mystical side to their resistance. They consulted "jazzmen" (traditional medicine men), who, they believed, had the power to fortify them through "odeshi," African mystical, occultic, and supernatural powers that made them impervious to the bullets of Biya's military. The phenomenon of *Odeshi* originated from the traditional beliefs and practices of the ethnic groups that straddle the Cameroon-Nigerian Border.

When President Biya declared war on the Amba Boys in November 2017, after they had attacked and killed elements of the Cameroon army in Agborkem-German, the Amba Boys procured some weapons from the black market in Nigeria. In order to obtain modern automatic weapons, these Amba Boys, Odeshi fighters, who believed they were spiritually fortified, carried out daring surprise attacks against forward positions of the Cameroon army, gendarmerie posts, and police stations in Manyu. The Amba Boys were armed with nothing but old, one-shot traditional hunting rifles, spears, machetes and knives. A good number of these Odeshi Amba Boys got killed but many others overwhelmed army and gendarmerie outposts and units, killed the officers, and seized their weapons. These ragtag resistance groups soon found themselves in possession of Israeli, French, Chinese, and Russian arms and ammunition. The most prized weapon was the AK-47 assault rifle. Several Anglophone deserters from the Cameroon army and the BIR trained the Amba Boys on how to handle weapons. That was the genesis of the Anglophone separatist resistance.

Thousands of unarmed civilian demonstrators, innocent villagers caught in the crossfire, suspected "Amba Boys," and "blacklegs" (persons accused of collaborating with the Cameroon military) have been killed. Hundreds of thousands have been displaced internally, and close to 100,000 have fled to Nigeria as refugees as the Cameroon army went on rampages and burnt down hundreds of villages that supposedly served as havens for Amba Boys (CHRDA, 2019; Hauchard, 2018). The Anglophone Revolt has not been the easy law enforcement exercise that President Paul Biya and the Cameroon army thought it would be when the military opened fire on Anglophone demonstrators in 2017. The Cameroon army has not been able to crush the "Amba Boys" since Biya declared war on the Anglophones in November 2017. The "Amba Boys" have exacted a heavy human toll on the Cameroon security forces. More than one thousand Cameroon soldiers, BIR, gendarmerie, police and other military personnel have been killed and thousands wounded. In fact, the Cameroon army became the largest supplier of weapons and ammunition to the Amba Boys. Most of the weapons were captured by the "restoration forces," but arms and ammunition have also been purchased from corrupt Cameroon army officials. The war escalated quickly. In an interview with the French News Agency (AFP), the Cameroon military commander for the Southwest region, General Donatien Melingui Nouma, admitted that: "In less than two weeks, there were attacks on the motorcades of the chief of staff [of the Cameroon army who was visiting the region] the governor [of the Southwest region] and me as well" (Hauchard, 2018).

The Franco-Cameroon Military Partnership Agreement of 2009 and the Anglophone Revolt

We have seen that post-Cold War demonstrations and agitations that started in the Anglophone regions of Cameroon spread to the rest of the country, leading to a modicum of political liberalization. One of the results was that the independent press, which had been subject to draconian licensing and pre-publication censorship under the Ahidjo/Biya regime, was suddenly free to publish without governmental permission, but at the risk of punishment after publication. The government allowed freedom of expression but did not guarantee freedom after expression (Eko, 2003). One of the hottest topics in the liberalized, French-language, independent media space of Cameroon was the controversial pre-independence cooperation agreements signed with France in 1959. For the first time since independence, the independent media spotlighted the financial provisions of these agreements, especially the French African currency, the CFA Franc. The independent press also commented on the military provisions that allowed France to intervene in African countries if the regimes they placed in power faced internal or external threats (Servenay, D. 2007). In response to widespread criticism of French economic, cultural, and military hegemony over its African postcolonies decades after independence, French President Nicolas Sarkozy launched an overhaul of the military provisions of the pre-independence agreements France had signed with its former colonies in Africa. The revised and updated Franco-Cameroon military cooperation agreement, called "*le Partenariat de Défense*" (the Defense Partnership), was signed in Yaoundé in 2009. During debates in the French

National Assembly on ratification of this defense partnership, the Sarkozy government told lawmakers that the partnership would reinforce the long-standing strategic partnership between France and Cameroon. The government told the French National Assembly that the partnership was important for French strategic interests in Central Africa:

> *...La France bénéficie d'un rang de partenaire privilégié...D'une certaine façon, ce pays est singulier: malgré ces facteurs de fragmentation, il connaît une stabilité remarquable, et une unité intéressante, qui repose en grande partie sur les forces armées... (Assemblée nationale,* 2011).
>
> France rises to the level of a privileged partner...In a way, this country [Cameroon] is unique: despite its factors of fragmentation, it has a remarkable stability, and an interesting unity which rests in large measure on the armed forces...

The French government entered into this military partnership because it recognized that the military was the bulwark of the authoritarian, kleptocratic, neo-patrimonial, republican chiefdom of Cameroon. Though the Franco-Cameroon partnership agreement of 2009 did not contain explicit provisions that granted France the right to automatically intervene and provide assistance to the government of *la République du Cameroun* for purposes of maintaining law and order in times of internal and external threats as the 1959 agreement had done, the partnership agreement permitted French military installations in Cameroon (*Assemblée Nationale*, 2011). This agreement paved the way for direct French logistical and financial involvement in the Anglophone crisis.

The French Logistical Base in Douala and the Drone Base in Garoua

A direct outcome of the hegemonic Franco-Cameroon Defense Partnership of 2009 was French military support for the Cameroon government as it struggled to repulse Boko Haram. This Islamist terrorist group had emerged in Northern Nigeria and spread its tentacles to the Lake Chad region that covers North Cameroon, Chad and Niger. That logistical support would also be extended to the war of subjugation of the Anglophone regions. The *TV5 Monde* documentary mentioned above demonstrated French logistical support for the Biya regime in the formerly autonomous Anglophone state of Southern Cameroons, which had reunited, on rather shaky legal grounds, with *La Republique du Cameroun* in 1961. In its report to the French National Assembly justifying the new defense partnership, the Commission on National Defense and the Armed Forces stated that the United States, Russia, China and the International community had made certain choices that resulted in a strategic balance of power in Africa. The outcome was that: *"Un équilibre de fait s'était institué pour reconnaître à la France un rôle de "gendarme" de l'Afrique francophone* (A de facto balance, which recognizes the role of France as the "gendarme" of Francophone Africa, had been instituted (*Assemblée Nationale*, 2011). The Commission noted that Cameroon was the center of this strategic balance of power in Central Africa and that it had received the highest amount of funding and "structural" military assistance from the Directorate of Security and Defense Cooperation (DCSD) of the Ministry of Foreign and European Affairs. This funding had covered the cost of supplying military advisers, training, equipment procurement, planning, logistical and operational support (*Assemblée Nationale*, 2011). The 2009 bilateral military partnership also authorized France to install a "*mission logistique*" (logistical mission) in the Douala Military Airbase 201. This military outpost operates under the auspices of the French embassy in Yaoundé. Its buildings, archives, documents and communications are inviolable and have diplomatic immunity. This military mission ensures air and sea transportation of military equipment and supplies to support French military missions in Chad and the Central African Republic (*Partenariat de Défense France-Cameroun*, 2011).

As we saw above, France is also involved in military aerial surveillance involving satellites and drones in Cameroon. In response to Boko Haram's terrorist activities in Nigeria, North Cameroon, and the Sahel region, President Barack Obama of the United States had authorized the United States African Command to install a drone base at the Garoua Airbase 301, adjacent to the Garoua Airport, to carry out intelligence gathering and surveillance of Boko Haram (Hammer, 2016). This was part of a Multinational Joint Task Force. One of its key projects is the so-called "*Pôle aéronautique national à vocation régionale* (PANVR) (National Regional Aeronautic Hub). France joined the United States and the UK on the drone project and continued to strengthen the Garoua Airbase 301, even after the United States pulled out its forces that were training Cameroonian soldiers in the wake of international condemnation of the atrocities and human rights violations of the French, Israeli, and American-trained Cameroon army, and especially the notorious, Israeli-trained commando unit within the army, the BIR. The BIR is known to have carried out human rights abuses, including the summary execution of women and children in North Cameroon. There is also ample evidence that the BIR tortured and carried out multiple extra-judicial executions of civilians, as well as the burning of whole villages in the Anglophone regions.

France participates in aeronautics and flight training as well as intelligence and surveillance gathering in aid of the Cameroon military (Assemblée Nationale, 2011; Hammer, 2016). Interestingly, the Garoua drone base was still being built when the Anglophone revolt broke out in 2016. Though the *TV5 Monde* French documentary did not state which country the Cameroon government had asked for assistance in carrying out surveillance on Anglophone resistance groups, it was an open secret that France was providing the Cameroon army operational and logistical support, including the latest drone surveillance capabilities within the framework of a military partnership agreement signed in Yaoundé in 2009. Though the new French partnership agreement with Cameroon did not contain the explicit permission granted to France to automatically intervene and provide assistance to the government of *la République du Cameroun* to maintain law and order in case of internal and external threats, as was the case with the 1959 agreements, the 2009 agreement had a few provisions that directly implicated France in the Anglophone crisis (*Assemblée Nationale*, 2011). As we saw in the *TV5 Monde* documentary on the Anglophone crisis, the French military uses its aerial surveillance assets from its military bases in neighboring Chad, Gabon, Cameroon, and elsewhere to monitor Anglophone separatist groups that are locked in a bloody insurgency with the BIR and other branches of the Cameroon military in the Northwest and Southwest regions. The Anglophone regions are thousands of kilometers away from the Lake Chad Basin, where Boko Haram is locked in a bloody conflict with the militaries of Nigeria, Cameroon and Chad.

Interestingly, when American Ambassador, Peter Barlerin, delivered two specialized C-208 CESSNA surveillance aircraft to the Cameroon military as part of U.S. commitment towards fighting the Boko Haram menace in North Cameroon, he told the Cameroon Minister of Defense, Beti Assomo, the Chief of Staff of the Cameroon Army, General René Claude Meka, and the Chief of Staff of the Air Force, General Calvin Momha, and other personalities present at the ceremony that the two aircrafts were not supposed to be used to carry out surveillance in the Anglophone Northwest and Southwest regions of Cameroon.

> Mr. Minister [of Defense] I know you have assured me several times that this equipment and assistance supplied by the United States will be used only in strict respect of the terms of our agreement. You have assured me that the equipment supplied by the United States will not be used for other purposes, in other conflicts. I would like to declare that we are aware that Cameroon faces difficulties in other parts of its territories. With respect to tensions in Anglophone Regions, we have consistently called for an end to violence and urged all sides to initiate a broad-based dialogue, without pre-conditions (Barlerin, 2019).

From this statement, it would appear that even though it had set up the drone center at the Garoua airport and that it had trained Cameroon soldiers on how to diffuse improvised explosive devices (IEDs), the United States military was not the source of the aerial surveillance images of the separatist Ambazonia Defense Forces that were broadcast by *TV5 Monde* in 2017. France, an active partner in the fight against Boko Haram in North Cameroon and Chad, did not have any qualms about diverting its military surveillance equipment and drones to the Anglophone separatist war in the Northwest and Southwest regions. The *TV5 Monde* documentary on the Anglophone war demonstrated Franco-Cameroon military cooperation in action.

As we will see later, when Paris-based Cameroonian illegal immigrant, Abdoulaye Thiam, aka Calibri Calibro confronted French President, Emmanuel Macron at the *Salon de l'agriculture* (Agricultural Fair) in Paris with allegations of crimes against humanity committed in English-speaking Southern Cameroons by the notorious BIR, as well as the French-trained, funded, and supported regular branches of the Cameroon armed forces, Macron had admitted that he knew of the atrocities and suggested that only genuine political dialogue could resolve the Anglophone problem. The impromptu human rights conversation between President Macron and Calibri Calibro brought to the fore the tension between France's historic cultural assimilationist policies, its humanitarian and human rights rhetoric, and its support for the Ahidjo/Biya republican chiefdom's bloody military subjugation of Anglophones and their identitarian specificity and autonomy in Cameroon.

Figure 16.1. French President, Emmanuel Macron

China is also a major supplier of arms, communications equipment, armored personnel carriers, and surveillance drones to the Cameron army. Suspicions of French, Israeli and Chinese logistical and surveillance support of the Cameroon army that was carrying out human rights abuses against Anglophones were confirmed months later when Ambazonian resistance forces in Bui, Northwest region, captured a French battlefield drone that had crashed in the territory they controlled (See image of captured drone).

Figure 16.2. Downed French drone

The French Ambassador and the Anglophone Crisis in Cameroon

While President Emmanuel Macron's encounter with Paris-based undocumented immigrant, Calibri Calibro, at the *Salon de l'agriculture* (Agricultural Fair) in Paris made international news headlines, his written correspondence to President Paul Biya was not as forthright. He couched his concerns over the Anglophone crisis in the highly restrained lingo of diplomacy. For their part, French ambassadors in Yaoundé had the task of explaining the official policy posture of France towards the Anglophone crisis to Cameroonians, and especially to skeptical Anglophones who were bearing the brunt of President Biya's war of subjugation. Most of the people of the English-speaking Northwest and Southwest regions of Cameroon were shocked by the callous indifference, arrogance and egoism with which the Biya regime, and especially ministers like Higher Education Minister, Jacques Fame Ndongo, Justice Minister Laurent Esso, Communications Minister Issa Tchiroma, Territorial Administration Minister, René Sadi, and their Anglophone subalterns, Prime Ministers Achidi Achu, Philemon Yang, Dion Ngute, and Atanga Nji, blithely ignored or flippantly dismissed the political, cultural, and identitarian concerns of the English-speaking lawyers, teachers, and other members of civil society whose deep historical grievances had burst into the Cameroonian political scene like lava from an erupting Mount Fako. The majority of the French-speaking community was ignorant of the history of Cameroon. Schools never taught the facts of the reunification of the two States of East and West Cameroon due to a very tightly controlled, politicized, educational curriculum, and a media regime geared towards propagating and promoting the assimilationist ideology of "harmonization."

Indeed, January 1, the official Independence Day of French Cameroun (*La Republique du Cameroun*), was jettisoned for May 20th, a national holiday created from thin air by President Ahidjo to celebrate his constitutionally questionable dissolution of the Federal Republic of Cameroon in 1972. Since French is the national, working language of the state of Cameroon and its repressive institutions, the reality is that the people in the French-speaking regions of Cameroon, the former *la Republique du Cameroun*, considered members of the Anglophone minority second-class citizens because of their geographic area of origin and their lack of mastery of the French language. In identitarian terms, Anglophones are the marginalized other (with a capital O) of Cameroon. Furthermore, the majority of Francophones were themselves living at the existential level. Large segments of the population lack the basic necessities: clean drinking water, schools, health care services, electricity, and roads were national problems. Like most other Africans, they were too busy struggling to survive in the highly corrupt, predatory, kleptocratic, *chefferie republicaine* (republican chiefery) of Cameroon to pay much attention to what politicians called, "*la crise anglophone*," and the Anglophone quest for autonomy and cultural identity came with it. People who are on the verge of existence do not think about abstract identitarian niceties like marginalization, linguistic and cultural specificity or political autonomy; they feel, and they feel hungry and angry as they strive to survive on a daily basis.

Ironically, Anglophones perceived the attitudes of Francophones as indifference and lack of concern towards their marginalization, as well as their cultural and identitarian concerns. As a result, English-speaking Cameroonians developed a certain level of resentment towards Francophones, France, and all things French. In a December 2016 "bilingual"[2] interview granted to Douala-based independent, mostly-French language,

2 In Cameroon, bilingual programs refer to peculiar political talk shows in which a French-speaking journalist asks questions to French-speaking and English-speaking panelists who respond either in English or in French depending on whether they are "Francophones" or "Anglophones."

Equinoxe Télévision, Cameroon Human Rights Lawyer, Barrister Nkongho Felix Agbor Balla, President of the Fako Lawyers' Association, a collective of self-described Common Law lawyers, told his audience that for minority Anglophones in Cameroon, "French is the language of oppression." By that, he meant that to Anglophones, oppression and tyranny come in French, that oppression speaks French. Though Cameroon is officially a bilingual state, the working language of the Cameroonian state and government is French. The three branches of government use French as their principal working language. The made-to-measure Constitution designed to maintain Biya in power in perpetuity and the repressive laws on which the highly centralized governmental institutions of Cameroon are grounded are African replicas of French politico-cultural and legal governmentality. The official language of the presidency is French. President Paul Biya has never read a national day speech in English in his close to 40 years in power. The Prime Minister's office, the National Assembly, the Senate, the Supreme Council of the Magistrature that is presided over by the President, military tribunals throughout the country, and civilian courts in 10 out of the 12 regions of Cameroon, the Supreme Court, government ministries, and all government parastatal organizations do business in French (with English translations now and then to suit specific purposes).

That means French is a tool for muting Anglophone identity, expressions and aspirations. In the Anglophone crisis, persons suspected of being anti-government, federalists, "secessionists," or of making anti-government utterances are arrested or issued summons in the French language, interrogated in French at the notorious interrogation chamber of the *Secretariat d'Etat à la Défense Nationale* (SED) in Yaoundé, tortured in French, prosecuted in French, tried in military tribunals whose only language is French, convicted in French, the judgments and sentences are written and read in French, and they are sentenced in French to a miserable existence in Francophone prisons. These Anglophone political prisoners often end up in the Kondengui Central Prison in Yaoundé or the New Bell Prison in Douala, where French is the language of incarceration and prison guards speak only French. French is the language of the Cameroon gulag. In Southern Cameroons the BIR and the Cameroon army burn village after village in French, suspected separatist fighters and civilians are summarily executed… in French. In Cameroon, life, and especially death, come in French. To Anglophones, French is the language of military subjugation and cultural assimilation, intimidation, exploitation, rape, and violence. French is the language of postcolonialism, of brutality and death. Even the climate of fear and the infrastructure of repression that reigns over Anglophones has a French coloration.

Cameroon's monolingual architecture of repression – the army, the Israeli-trained and armed "army-within-the army," the BIR, the navy, the air force, para-military gendarmerie, the police, and even prison warders – speak French, and French only – while carrying out a reign of terror and horrendous human rights violations in English-speaking Cameroon. They bark orders at their English-speaking victims in French; they torture their victims in French, they speak French when they rape, and they speak French when they pillage and burn village… after village… after village to ashes. Often, the last words their victims hear are French words. Since the BIR and members of the Cameroon armed forces speak no English – the oft-heard mantra of the Cameroon military is, *l'armée n'est pas bilingue* (the army is not bilingual). Military training in Cameroon is in French. It is carried out by French or French-speaking Cameroonian, Israeli, and American officials. The Cameroon government's architecture of repression and subjugation is made in France and sustained by France. Its over-centralized administration, over-dressed ministers, unelected Napoleonic governors, *préfets*, and *sous-prefets*, their wines, champagne and *haute couture* are all stamped "made in France," as are the tear-gas, water cannons, handcuffs, implements of torture, military transport trucks, armored personnel carriers and arms used to repress unarmed demonstrators and Anglophone separatists.

As a result of the assimilative and autocratic nature of the Ahidjo/Biya Napoleonic, republican chiefdom of Cameroon. Anglophones came to view French as the language of the postcolonial black-on-black oppressor, the language of subjugation, violence, and human rights violations. As such, the Anglophone Revolt gradually took on the coloration of resistance against Francophone and French hegemonic extension of the colonial *mission assimilatrice* (assimilationist mission) to English-speaking Southern Cameroons. These fierce anti-French sentiments were soon amplified on English language and Pidgin-English (Anglophone) social media platforms, particularly, Facebook, Twitter, and WhatsApp that were set up and maintained by Cameroonians. Social media groups in French and *Camfranglais* (a mixture of expressions from several Cameroonian languages, Pidgin-English and French that is spoken in the major Francophone towns) chimed in with anti-French and anti-Biya rhetoric as the Biya regime's political and military repression hardened, and the regime cracked down on the political opposition that was primarily made up of members of the Francophone Bamileke ethnic group. This large ethnic group originates from the Western region, which borders the English-speaking regions. Due to their ethnic connections with the Anglophones, the Bamileke are generally sympathetic to the Anglophones. As a result, propagandists of the Biya regime lump both groups together with the epithet "Les Anglo-Bami."

The Anglophone Revolt and "Anti-French" Ethos

Cameroon Anglophone sentiments towards France had evolved over the years from bemused neutrality towards French attempts to assimilate them into *la Francophonie* to a negative ethos as the corrupt, authoritarian machinery of the republican chiefdom that was the Biya regime, resulted in their repression, marginalization, and reduction into second-class citizens. When the revolt got underway, French-language schools (*écoles francophones*) in the English-speaking regions refused to participate in the strikes and demonstrations against Anglophone marginalization. They were immediately seen as accomplices and partners in the subjugation and assimilation of Anglophones. Anglophone strike enforcers descended on these schools and attacked them for failing to respect the Anglophone teachers' strikes, and for failing to observe civil disobedience measures, of which Monday "ghost towns," popularly known as "kontri Sunday," was the most potent. The arrival of these enforcers on motorbikes sent students scurrying in all directions in panic. That was the first manifestation of anti-French sentiments, which were ultimately extended to boycott French companies and products. The equipment and trucks of French timber companies that were harvesting the ancient tropical rain forests of the Southwest region were attacked and burned in Meme and Manyu divisions. Anglophone activists and militias soon banned the beer and other products of the French-owned brewery company, *Les Brasseries du Cameroun* in the Northwest and Southwest regions. *Brasseries du Cameroun* beer delivery trucks were attacked and destroyed in Bamenda, Limbe, and other places. Imported French water, wines, and spirituous liquors were also banned. Workers of *Supermont*, the French water-bottling company that operates near Ekona, were attacked despite the fact that the military sent a contingent of soldiers to protect the factory. Clashes between Anglophone separatists and Cameroon soldiers left casualties on both sides. Alarmed by these developments, the French diplomatic mission in Cameroon issued a travel advisory, warning French citizens against traveling to the Northwest and Southwest region, specifically to Limbe and Buea, where many French citizens living in Douala went on business and short weekend visits to escape the stifling heat and humidity of the port city of Douala.

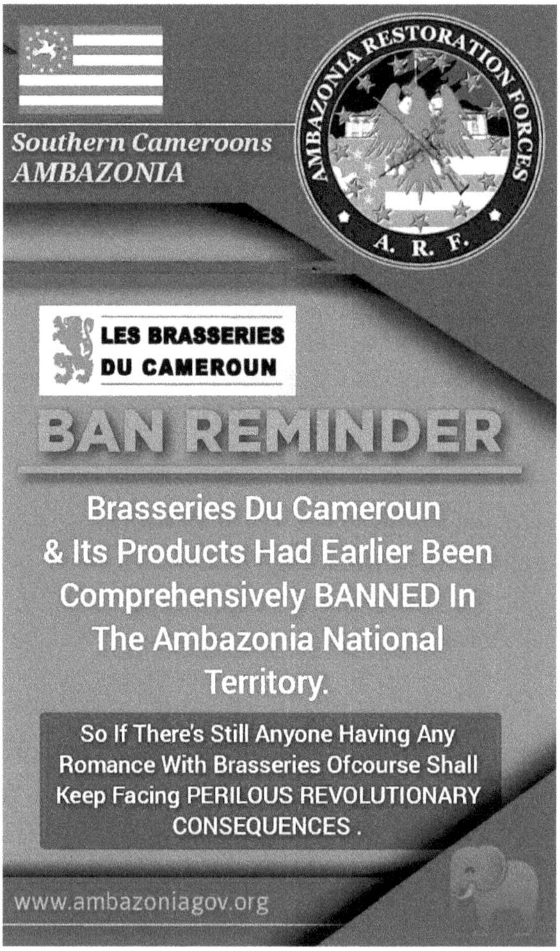

Figure 16.3. Pamphlet banning French products

Southern Cameroons in the Diaspora—particularly those in Brussels, London, Berlin, New York, Ottawa, Washington D.C, and Pretoria, South Africa—demonstrated in front of French embassies blaming France and its subalterns in Yaoundé for the atrocities being committed against Anglophones. The demonstrators called for a worldwide boycott of French goods. In the face of mounting anti-French sentiments and activities in the English-speaking Northwest and Southwest regions, the French Ambassador to Cameroon, His Excellency Gilles Thibault, visited the Northwest region to highlight French projects in that English-speaking region. He showcased French funding for a project at the Mbingo Baptist Hospital and visited the Fon or Chief of Ndop, whose cultural activities had been the beneficiary of French funding (Ambassade de France, 2017). Furthermore, Ambassador Thibault made known the position of France with regard to the Anglophone problem in a speech delivered at the French Embassy in Yaoundé on July 14, 2017 (Bastille Day, the French national day). Ambassador Gilles started his speech with the usual diplomatic courtesies and expressions of friendship and cooperation between France and Cameroon. In the middle of his speech, suddenly, and without warning, the ambassador switched to English, an unprecedented departure from the traditional French government requirement that all official speeches made by French government officials be made in the French language. The French Ambassador essentially addressed Cameroon Anglophones, a few of whom had been sent highly prized Bastille Day reception invitations:

> …it is more than ever necessary to give constant priority to dialogue after the tensions in the English-speaking regions. I wish to emphasize that the bilingual and multicultural nature of Cameroon is a tremendous asset in the context of globalization. And I hope that the Cameroonians will now fully take advantage of it. As far as I am concerned, I am proud that my country has never made a difference between English and French-speaking areas. For example, in the North-West where I just came back from, we contribute to the construction of health and vocational training centers, to the protection of the environment, as well as to the renovation of urban infrastructures and public spaces and last but not least, to the promotion of arts and culture. I would like also to tell you that I am pleased to receive a so warm welcome everywhere I go (*Discours prononcé par l'Ambassadeur de France*, 2017).

A few things stood out in this speech. The French ambassador called on the Cameroon government "to give a constant priority to dialogue," rather than the monologue of repression which it had engaged in since the Anglophone uprising began in October 2016. He stressed the importance of: 1) bilingualism, which the Biya government had only paid lip service to, 2) the fact that France had not discriminated against Anglophones as the Ahidjo-Biya government had done for more than 50 years, and 3) that France was fully engaged in the development of the English-speaking regions. The French Embassy posted a write-up and pictures of the ambassador's recent visit to the Northwest on its website.

Figure 16.4. French Ambassador to Cameroon, Christophe Guilhou

The French Ambassador could not have chosen a more auspicious occasion and a more high-powered audience to deliver his remarks to. Members of the audience included several big wigs of the government of *La République du Cameroun*: Hon. Ferdinand Ngoh Ngoh (Secretary General at the Presidency, who was believed to be the real president of Cameroon), and was the personal representative of President Paul Biya at the celebration, Ministers Issa Tchiroma Bakari (Communication), Louis Paul Motaze (Economy and Territorial Development), Joseph Beti Assomo (Delegate General at the Presidency in Charge of Defense), André Mama Fouda (Minister of Health), and Minette Libom Li Likeng (Minister of Posts and Telecommunications), who has shut down the Internet in the Northwest and Southwest regions, among others. The French ambassador's call to prioritize dialogue to resolve the crisis could not have come at a more opportune time. As the Anglophone uprising took a turn for the worse, the French ambassador demonstrated that Europeans were perhaps more sensitive to political pressure and human rights issues in English-speaking Cameroon than their Francophone subalterns. The question is whether the monolingual bigwigs of the Cameroon government who attended the reception at the French embassy understood the English part of the ambassador's speech. If press reports are anything to go by, they probably just ignored it. The official government media did not report the unprecedented event or the content of the ambassador's speech. The private Francophone media ignored the English part of the ambassador's speech (they either did not understand it or refused to report it for ideological reasons). Nevertheless, at least one Francophone newspaper, *Mutations*, fully reported the Ambassador's speech–including a translation of what he said in English.

The Franco-Cameroun Postcolonial Strategic Partnership and the Anglophone Question

The French Ambassador's visit to the Northwest and Southwest regions to highlight development projects funded by the French government as well as his speech in English, on Bastille Day, July 14, 2017, amounted to good public diplomacy in the Cameroonian context. It also seemed like a sea change from French political and especially cultural policy towards the English-speaking West Cameroon since the independence of *la République du Cameroun* in 1960, and reunification with the State of West Cameroon in 1961 to form the Federal Republic of Cameroon. However, Ambassador Thibault's claims of French impartiality in its dealings with French and English-speaking Cameroonians were clearly a misstatement of the facts, from a historical perspective. When he told the audience of dignitaries–in English no less–at the French National Day celebration at the French Embassy in Yaoundé that: "I am proud that my country has never made a difference between English and French-speaking areas" [of Cameroon]. At face value, the Ambassador's statement is a provably false counter-truth. As we show in Chapter 3, the historical record demonstrates that French postcolonial politico-cultural and policy conceptualized the English-speaking Southern Cameroons as a postcolonial prize, a territory to be assimilated into its African sphere of influence. In effect, the reunification of East and West Cameroon under legally and constitutionally ambiguous circumstances presented France with a golden opportunity to extend *la Francophonie*, the French zone of influence in Africa, West of the Mungo River, the physical feature that had historically separated French Cameroun from British Southern Cameroons. After the reunification in 1961, France launched a *mission assimilisatrice,* a concerted politico-cultural attempt to assimilate English-speaking Cameroon into the French African economic and cultural *chasse gardée*, the postcolonial *FranceAfrique*, as well as the global community of French-speaking nations and peoples, *la Francophonie.*

However, on second thought, Ambassador Thibault's statement had a gist of the truth because it is essentially a restatement of the denial of cultural and identitarian difference of English-speaking Cameroonians. That is to say, he was indirectly reiterating the French assimilationist policy. As stated by Michel Moreux, the French Consul in Buea in 1967, the French *mission assimilatrice* in West Cameroon was to ensure that the French language "impose itself…[facilitate] the generalized usage of our language, render it the everyday language among the Western Cameroon masses" (Moreux, 1967). Assimilation was the Francophonization of Southern Cameroons. Therefore, if France considered the Anglophone minority no different from the majority Francophone Cameroonians, it implied the muting and dispersal of Anglophone identitarian and cultural specificity in the Cameroonian nation. This policy had, for more than 50 years, gone by the name of harmonization. The problem is that harmonization amounted to the marginalization of Anglophones and the conferral of second-class citizenship status on them. It is precisely the muting and dispersal of Anglophone identitarian and cultural specificity that triggered the Anglophone Revolt of 2016. Indeed, Ambassador Thibault's statement had historical continuities. It was identical to the confidential instructions that the very first postcolonial French Ambassador to Cameroon, Jean-Pierre Benard, had given to Yves Robin, the French Consul in Buea, capital of Southern Cameroons, in 1962 (Benard, 1962). His task was to ensure that other English-speaking countries, particularly the United States, do not use their cultural proximity, their common connection to the English language, to ensure the maintenance of Anglophone identitarian and cultural specificity in West Cameroon.

> *…D'autres pays peuvent également porter un attention particulière à l'Etat de Cameroun Occidental…Les Etats-Unis…pourraient être tentés de s'intéresser*

> *plus particulièrement au Cameroun Occidental ou l'usage de la langue anglaise faciliterait l'implantation de leurs influence...Il conviendrait que vous suiviez attentivement toutes les tentatives faites en ce sens, qui tendraient ainsi à perpétrer le particularisme de l'ancienne zone britannique, et que vous m'en teniez régulièrement informé...(Bénard, 1962).*
>
> ...Other countries can also pay special attention to the State of West Cameroon. The United States could perhaps be tempted to interest itself, particularly in West Cameroon, where the use of the English language could facilitate the implantation of their influence. It would be necessary for you to closely follow any such moves, which would have a tendency to perpetrate the specificity of the former British zone, and to regularly keep me informed.

Ambassador Jean-Pierre Benard was particularly concerned about American influence that could come in the form of aid workers, technical assistance personnel and financing of economic projects in English-speaking West Cameroon. This would run counter to the French goal of diminishing Anglophone culture and identity for the purposes of assimilating the territory into *la Francophonie*. For the French, the Anglophone problem amounted to the maintenance of Anglophone identitarian and cultural specificity, a situation that would complicate French assimilationist objectives in English-speaking West Cameroon. The ambassador's worst fears came to pass. As a result of geo-strategic, Cold War realities, at the diplomatic level, the Ahidjo regime opened up to the United States and other Western countries. In the ten years that the Federal Republic of Cameroon existed, Buea was home to a number of diplomatic missions including the Consulate of the United States of America, the British Consulate and British Council, the French Consulate and French Cultural Center, the West German Consulate, the Consulate General of Nigeria, and the Swiss Agency for Technical Assistance (SATA). A number of countries sent aid workers to West Cameroon: The United States Peace Corps had volunteers in multiple fields ranging from education to cooperative development, the Swiss had technical aid workers, British Volunteers taught English at the Local Government Training Center, where local council workers were trained, the West German government also sent volunteers in multiple fields. The lingua franca of the mini-diplomatic community of Buea was English. In addition, missionary organizations in the United States and Europe sent missionary doctors, teachers, and preachers to West Cameroon. These Baptist, Catholic, Presbyterian, and other missionaries started schools, hospitals, and health centers. Churches were involved in all kinds of evangelistic and mission activities following the American evangelistic "crusade" model of Rev. Bill Graham that was popular in the 1960s and 1970s. All these activities consolidated and solidified the identitarian and cultural specificity of West Cameroon and solidified the place of West Cameroon in the global Anglosphere. Due to this cultural proximity, Anglophone Cameroonians turned to Lagos, Accra, Motown (Detroit), New York, Washington D.C., or London rather than Paris for media content and entertainment.

Furthermore, globalization, the interconnection of nations, cultures and peoples, made possible by the diffusion of American information and communication technologies, transistor radios, gramophones, cassette players, records, compact discs, computers, the Internet, word processors, cellular telephones, and social media platforms, spelled the doom of the French assimilationist mission in West Cameroon.

The All Anglophone Conference of 1993, whose Buea Declaration called for a return to the federal system of government and respect for the cultural and identitarian specificity of the former West Cameroon as a political entity, and the Anglophone Revolt of 2016 demonstrate that the French assimilationist mission did not work in West Cameroon. Worse, it created a generation of Anglophone Cameroonians who were bilingual enough to understand French postcolonial political, cultural, and economic hegemony in Africa to reject it.

The more things change, the more they stay the same

At the height of the Anglophone crisis, the French Minister of State attached to the Ministry for Europe and Foreign Affairs, Jean-Baptiste Lemoyne visited Cameroon on June 28 and 29, 2018. The French Foreign Ministry reported that Lemoyne met in Yaoundé with President Paul Biya and discussed the situation in Cameroon, particularly the crisis in the English-speaking "areas," economic relations, and cooperation between France and Cameroon. The minister then traveled to Buea, the capital of the English-speaking Southwest region. In Buea, he met with central government authorities, the unelected governor, Napoleonic *préfets*, mayors, and hand-picked "representatives of civil society," under military escort and very tight security. He did not speak with representatives of the striking lawyers, teachers or the Consortium of Anglophone Civil Society. Indeed, the visit was a stage-managed French-Francophone government public relations affair. The whole visit, including the welcome banner made by the Cameroon government, was in French. Unlike Ambassador Thibault, Mr. Lemoyne, who is a former strategic analyst for IBM Global Services and speaks perfect English, did not utter a word of English even though the banner indicated–ironically in French–that he was being welcomed by the people of the Southwest, who happen to be English and Pidgin speakers. The Lemoyne visit was intended to demonstrate that the Biya government was still in charge and underlined how tone-deaf, arrogant, and repressive the Cameroon authorities actually were. They had learned nothing from the Anglophone Revolt.

Conclusion

The Anglophone problem is made partly in France. It is a function of French cultural expansionism and assimilationism into Anglophone Cameroon. The fact is that after reunification, the French government policy of extending French culture to Southern/West Cameroon was a veritable *mission assimilatrice*, an assimilative mission whose aim was to extend the cultural geography of *la Francophonie*. The idea was that the Southern Cameroons was an easy, low-hanging fruit ripe for conversion by the French secular gospel, *la mission civilisatrice* (French civilizing mission). On the eve of the deliberatively vague and ambiguous reunification, it was the French–led by Ambassador Benard, who drafted a centralist federal constitution for the reunited Federal Republic of Cameroon that essentially transformed Southern Cameroons into a junior partner in the Francophone scheme of things. The subsequent abolition of the federal republic in 1972 and transformation of Cameroon into a ruthless, autocratic, neo-patrimonial, kleptocratic *chéfferie républicaine* run like an absolutist tribal fiefdom was done with the consent of Paris. The ambiguous reunification and subsequent abolition of the Federal Republic of Cameroon was in the French interest because it also sounded the death knell of the One Kamerun Movement, OK party, an Anglophone replica – in disguise – of the French Cameroun *Union des Populations du Cameroun* (UPC) party, which had been banned by the French for launching an anti-colonial war of liberation in French Cameroun. Ndeh Ntumazah, an English-speaker from Mankon, Bamenda, founded the One Kamerun Party and liaised with his Francophone comrades who had been declared "*maquisards*" (insurgents) in French Cameroon, to carry out their underground operations (Johnson, 1965). In 1962, just months after the reunification, Ndeh Ntumazah fled Cameroon to seek political asylum abroad (Asong & Chi, 2011). The reunification had denied the UPC and One Kamerun Party a base from which they could continue their insurgency against the postcolonial Cameroon government. Ernest Ouandié, leader of the UPC, had sought refuge in Kumba in 1958 until the British deported him and a few of his followers to Sudan after pressure from the French. After Cameroon gained independence in 1960, UPC rebels continued to fight the government of President Ahmadou Ahidjo, whom they considered a French puppet. Ernest Ouandié slipped back into Cameroon in 1961. Ahidjo invited French troops to help the Cameroon army "keep the peace" in the war against the UPC. This French intervention took place within the framework of the military provisions of the Franco-Cameroon bilateral cooperation agreement of 1959. French soldiers, led by General Max Briand, who had served previously in Algeria and Indochina, led the fledgling Cameroon army in conducting a brutal anti-UPC "pacification" campaign in the Bamileke territory of the West and elsewhere, that some researchers claim amounted to a litany of war crimes (Deltombe et al., 2011; 2016; Terretta, 2014). The French military and the fledgling army of the Federal Republic of Cameroun Cameroon army ultimately crushed the UPC and executed its leader, Ernest Ouandié, along with his comrades, Gabriel Tabeu, alias Wambo *le Courant*, and Raphäel Fotsing by firing squad in Bafoussam in 1971. Ironically, when the Anglophone Revolt began in 2016, and the Cameroon army and BIR began to execute the atrocious scorched-earth tactic that it had used in the war in Bamileke territory in the 1960s and 1970s, Anglophone civilians fled to Dschang, Bafoussam, and other Bamileke areas, as well as to Douala and Yaoundé. French cultural assimilation had led to gross human rights violations by the Cameroon army. History was repeating itself.

References

Asong, L. & Chi, S. (Eds., 2011). *Ndeh Ntumazah. a Conversational Auto Biography*. Mankon, Bamenda: Langaa RPCID.

Barlerin, P. (2019). Speech: Donation of Two C-208 CESSNAs. U.S. Embassy in Cameroon. Retrieved from: https://cm.usembassy.gov/ambassador-peter-balerins-speech-donation-of-two-c-208-cessnas/

Bayart, J-F. (1989). *L'Etat en Afrique* (The State in Africa) Paris: Fayard.

Betts, R. (1961). *Assimilation and Association in French Colonial Theory, 1890-1914.* New York: Columbia University Press.

Cameroon: Five People dead in roadside explosion (2021). *Vatican News*. Retrieved from: https://www.vaticannews.va/en/world/news/2021-01/cameroon-five-dead-explosion-separatists.html

Craig, J. (2021). Violence in Cameroon's Anglophone Crisis takes high civilian toll, *Al-Jazeera*, April 1. Retrieved from: https://www.aljazeera.com/amp/news/2021/4/1/violence-in-cameroon-anglophone-crisis-takes-high-civilian-toll?twitter_impression=true

Deltombe, T., Domergue, M. and Tatsitsa, J. (2016). *La Guerre du Cameroun. L'invention de la Françafrique* (The War of Cameroon and the Creation of Franceafrique) Paris: Éditions La Découverte.

Deltombe, T., Domergue, M. and Tatsitsa, J. (2011). « *Kamerun! Une guerre cachée aux origines de la Françafrique (1948-1971). (Kamerun! A Hidden war at the origin of Franceafrique)* Paris: Éditions La Découverte.

Hays, A. (2017). US troops train Cameroonians in counter-IED. United

States Department of Defense), Nov. 24. Retrieved from: https://www.defense.gov/Explore/News/Article/Article/1380300/cameroons-troops-learn-about-counter-bomb-operations/

Gaulle, Charles de. (1954). *Mémoires de guerre, l'appel, 1940-1942 (Memoirs of War, the Call, 1940-1942).* Paris: Plon.

Hauchard, A. (2018). *Au Cameroun anglophone, une «sale guerre» qui prend de l'ampleur* (In Cameroon, a "dirty war" that is expanding. France24. May 4. Retrieved from: https://www.france24.com/fr/20180504-cameroun-anglophone-une-sale-guerre-prend-lampleur

Johnson, W. (1965). The Cameroon Federation: Political Union Between English and French-Speaking Africa. In William Lewis (ed). *French-Speaking Africa*. New York: Walker and Co.

Mbembe, A. (2001). *On the Postcolony*. Berkley: UCLA Press.

Norwegian Refugee Council (2019). Cameroon Tops List of Most Neglected Crises. NRC 2019 Annual Report. Oslo: Norway. Retrieved from: https://www.nrc.no/news/2019/june/cameroon-tops-list-of-most-neglected-crises/

Pourquoi le Général Melingui Nouma a été Limogé! (Why General Melingi Nouma was fired) (2018). Cameroun Web. May 8. Retrieved from: https://www.actualite-cameroun.net/societe/ambazonie-voici-pourquoi-le-general-melingui-nouma-a-ete-limoge/

Terretta, M. (2014). *Nation of Outlaws, State of Violence: Nationalism, Grassfields Tradition, and State Building in Cameroon* (New African Histories). Athens, Ohio: Ohio University Press

SEVENTEEN

The Israeli Connection in the Anglophone Crisis

LYOMBE EKO

Introduction: Postcolonial Afro-Israeli Relations

The geographical names: Israel, Jerusalem, Bethlehem, the Holy Land, and others, have a deep psycho-spiritual resonance in the imagination of many Africans. This is especially true of countries where Christian evangelical missionary activities were part of the colonial, humanitarian, and "civilizing mission" of Western countries. In the British territories and protectorates of Africa, colonialism and missionary evangelism came with the Holy Bible, the King James version of 1611, with its archaic, ponderous, majestic, royalist cadences–and its 10 Commandments. Its commanding and authoritative narratives told marvelous tales of David and Goliath, Samson and Delilah, Moses and the liberation of the Children of Israel from the bondage of slavery in Egypt. The King James Bible spoke of the birth of Jesus Christ, the Messiah, in the little town of Bethlehem, the supernatural star that led the Three Wisemen who came from the "East" to Jerusalem seeking the Christ Child who had been born to be the "King of the Jews," the Christ that had been prophesied of old.

Figure 17.1. An African interpretation of the Resurrection of Christ at the Jesuit Hekima University College, Nairobi, Kenya (designed by Fr. Engelbert Mveng and executed by Stephen Lobalu, 1984)

Fast-forward to 1948. The State of Israel is proclaimed amid war with the Arab nations as the "National Home of the Jews" under David Ben Gurion (Tessier, 2009). Arab resistance and hostility towards the emergence of the State of Israel from the "Valley of Dry Bones" (Ezekiel 37), led Israel to seek new friends among the countries of Africa that were emerging from European colonialism. Enter Foreign Minister Golda Meir. The most iconic image of Israel in the newspapers of the newly independent African countries was Golda Meir, Israeli Foreign Minister from 1956-1966 and Prime Minister from 1969-1974; in the late 1950s, Golda Meir went on a safari to emerging Africa. She visited Liberia, Ghana, Nigeria, Kenya, Uganda, Zambia, etc. The King James version of the Bible and centuries of missionary activities had prepared the way for her by creating, in the minds of Africans who had undergone Catholic or Protestant missionary education, a religious and political befuddlement between the modern State of Israel of David Ben–Gurion, and the Biblical Kingdom of Israel of King David and his son, King Solomon. Furthermore, the long history of Western, Arabic, and Persian slavery and exploitation of Africa was, to a certain degree, analogous to Jewish enslavement in Egypt, discrimination and persecution in Persia, and the Holocaust in Europe. Christian missionaries and African Americans had created a deep analogy between Jewish slavery in Egypt and African slavery in America and the West Indies. The words of Moses recorded in the Hebrew Torah (Exodus 5): "Then Moses and Aaron went to the king of Egypt and said, The Lord, the God of Israel, says, 'Let my people go,'' inspired and became the title of a famous "Negro Spiritual" and civil rights anthem that diffused to Africa. Bible stories like David and Goliath (the Philistine giant), and Samson and Delilah (the Philistine temptress) were morality tales that pitted "God's people," the Nation of Israel, against the "Philistines" who worshipped false gods and were on the path to perdition. To average Africans, "Palestine" rhymed with "Philistine," the bad guys, the idol worshippers of the Bible.

Biblical narratives from the Torah (the Old Testament), along with the experience of slavery and colonialism, created a pseudo-spiritual and psychological connection, a "profound affinity" between Israel and Africa. This led to the "golden age" of relations between Israel and African countries that were gaining independence from Western colonialism (Ben Yosef, 2015, p.26). The wars between Israel and the Arab nations (the 1967 Six-Day War and the 1973 Yom Kippur War) were, in the eyes of many Africans, a rematch of the fight between David and Goliath, with Goliath, the Philistine, the perpetual, historical loser. This imagined psycho-spiritual connection–and religious beliefs are mostly emotional and psychological rather than rational–paved the way for interesting political relations between Israel and the newly independent nations of Africa. Foreign Minister, Golda Meir skillfully rode the crest of the wave of pro-Israel sentiments in many newly independent African countries. She presented the motivations for her Africa policy in her autobiography, *My Life,* (Meir, 1975)

> Like them, we [Israelis] had shaken off foreign rule; like them, we had to learn for ourselves how to reclaim the land, how to increase the yields of our crops, how to irrigate, how to raise poultry, how to live together and how to defend ourselves. [...] We couldn't offer Africa money or arms,

> but on the other hand, we were free of the taint of the colonial exploiters because all that we wanted from Africa was friendship. Let me at once anticipate the cynics. Did we go into Africa because we wanted votes at the United Nations? Yes, of course … But it was far from being the most important motive …. The main reason for our African "Adventure" was that we had something we wanted to pass on to nations that were even younger and less experienced than ourselves (p. 318–319).

Israel voted to isolate the Apartheid regime in South Africa. The Foreign Minister from the Holy Land was received with open arms. Thirty African countries recognized and established diplomatic relations with the State of Israel. Israel began to participate in the economic development of multiple countries and provided military and security assistance to these countries. Israel sent skilled technicians and experts to train Africans in the fields of education, agriculture, rural development and health. The Israeli government also provided training opportunities and scholarships for carefully selected African students to study agriculture, agronomy, water resource management, and other subjects at Israeli universities and training institutions.

Due to its Anglo-American English-language educational system, Southern Cameroons became a participant in post-colonial Israelo-African development cooperation. Israeli agronomists became advisers in the agricultural and plantation economy of the Cameroon Development Cooperation (CDC) and Pamol Plantations. In the 1960s and 1970s, a good number of agronomists working in these state-controlled agro-industrial corporations were trained in Israel. The blossoming relations between Israel and Africa came to an almost abrupt end after the 1967 Six-day War, when oil-rich Arab countries pressured the continent-wide Organization of African Unity (OAU) to break diplomatic relations with and boycott Israel or face diplomatic and economic consequences. Many African countries had no choice but to downgrade or sever diplomatic relations with Israel, for fear of reprisals from the Arab League and the Islamic Conference Organization. Nevertheless, Operation Solomon, the covert but spectacular Israeli military uplift of more than 14,000 Ethiopian Jews from war-torn, famine-stricken Ethiopia to Israel in 1991, went a long way toward restoring Israel's standing in Africa.

Aim of the Chapter

This chapter aims to survey, describe, and explain the role of the State of Israel and Israeli citizens, mostly former officers of the Israeli Defence Force (IDF), in creating, training, arming and supplying the *Garde présidentielle,* the personal praetorian guard of long-reigning authoritarian dictator, President Paul Biya, as well as the *Bataillon d'Intervention Rapide* or the Rapid Intervention Battalion (BIR), his private army within the Cameroon army. In terms of uniforms and munitions, both the *Garde présidentielle* and the BIR are mirror images of the Israeli defense forces. The chapter shows one of the greatest ironies of the Anglophone crisis, namely that Israel, the homeland of Jews, who have historically been the victims of genocide and crimes against humanity, knowingly and willfully partnered with the dictatorial Biya regime, in committing crimes against humanity in the

English-speaking Southern Cameroons. Nevertheless, Israeli human rights activists have taken the Israeli government to task for maintaining a decades-long relationship that goes way beyond "normal Israeli security exports being used for grave violations of human rights, but rather - a real intervention by the Israeli Ministry of Defense in the political life of another country in a neo-colonial manner," as Israeli lawyer and human rights activist, Eitay Mack, put it. This special relationship has involved Israel's "secondment" of retired Israeli Defense Forces officers to serve as international "securocrats," technical advisers for security and military affairs to the authoritarian president of Cameroon since the 1980s. As a result of this mutually beneficial relationship, retired Israeli military officials have, over the years, set up and equipped the national security apparatus of the Biya regime, including the creation of the Presidential Guard and the BIR. Israel has thus been very instrumental in propping up the dictatorial regime of President Biya, who has been president since 1982.

The Anglophone Revolt of 2016 and Biya's decision to use overwhelming military force – the Israeli-trained and armed BIR, as well as regular armed forces–to crush the purely political demands of the English and Pidgin-speaking minority in the Northwest and Southwest of Cameroon, created a rather delicate problem for Israel. Continued support of the BIR and the presidential guard amounted to Israel being a partner in crimes against humanity with the Biya regime.

The Problematic Israeli Connection in the Military and Security Sector in Cameroon

On August 1, 2018, the Israeli Ambassador to Cameroon, Ran Gidor, paid a courtesy call on Cameroon Minister of External Relations, Lejeune Mbella Mbella. He was accompanied by the powerful Israeli Finance Ministry Accountant General, Rony Hizkiyahu. The Israeli Accountant General was visiting Cameroon to appraise the projects the Israeli embassy in Cameroon was funding to prepare the bilateral cooperation budget between Israel and Cameroon. The Accountant General said his visit was intended to take the multi-dimensional cooperation between Israel and Cameroon in the domains of agriculture, technology, human resources, defense and security, to the next level. The main subject of the meeting was Israel's support for Cameroon's fight against terrorism, generally understood as the Islamist Boko Haram attacks in the Extreme North region. That innocuous expression, "defense and security," which was mentioned as one of the domains of "bilateral cooperation" between the State of Israel and Cameroon, is diplomatic speak, a verbal tree that hides the forest of intense and deadly military collaboration between Israel and the increasingly authoritarian, kleptocratic, republican chieftaincy of President Paul Biya. Interestingly, in their statements to the press, neither the Israeli Ambassador, Ran Gidor, the Finance Ministry Accountant General, Rony Hizkiyahu, nor Cameroon Minister of External Relations, Lejeune Mbella Mbella, mentioned a topic that was morally problematic and uncomfortable for the Israelis–President Biya's controversial and notorious BIR, and its crimes against humanity in the Anglophone Northwest and Southwest regions. In effect, the BIR, which is infamous in Cameroon because of its ruthlessness and human rights violations, was created by a retired Israel Defense Forces (IDP) official, Colonel Avraham Ravi Sivan, a former Defense attaché at the Israeli Embassy in Yaoundé, and later Technical

Adviser to President Paul Biya for Defense and Security affairs. The BIR is leading President Biya's attempted subjugation of the English and Pidgin-speaking minority in Cameroon. The question is how Israel came to find itself in this morally problematic situation where it has partnered with one of Africa's most brutal dictatorial regimes to the point where it has essentially become a partner with the Biya regime in crimes against humanity.

Figure 17.2. Vice Adm. Harry B. Harris Jr., commander of U.S. 6th Fleet, (left) speaks with retired Israeli IDF Col. Avi Sivan, military technical/security advisor to the president of the Republic of Cameroon (right) during a demonstration of Cameroon army special operations unit, *Bataillon d'intervention rapide* amphibious assault capabilities at Man O' War Bay, Southwest region. Credit: U.S. Department of Defense

Israeli Bilateral Medical Cooperation

Fast Forward to 2020. In February, the Embassy of Israel in Cameroon, the Italian Cooperation Agency, and the German Embassy in Cameroon organized an intensive emergency surgical training workshop for Cameroonian surgeons at the Yaoundé Central Hospital. A seven-person team consisting of six surgeons from Israel and one from Italy held four days of intensive emergency surgical training sessions for 73 Cameroonian medical professionals that included general surgeons, post-graduate surgery students, and specialized surgical nurses from all ten regions of Cameroon. The workshop was organized in collaboration with the Israeli Surgical Association and the World Society of Emergency Surgery. In addition, the Israeli surgeons performed life-saving surgeries in the Yaoundé Central Hospital and the *Hôpital Militaire de Yaoundé* (Yaoundé Military Hospital). In its report on the training session, the Embassy of Israeli in Cameroon stated that the justifications for the emergency surgical training session, the first of which had been held in 2019, included: "the crisis in the Extreme North, North West and South West regions of Cameroon" (Embassy of Israel in Cameroon, 2020). That oblique and innocuous reference to the Anglophone Revolt, the popular uprising in the English and Pidgin-speaking Northwest and Southwest, demonstrated Israel's morally complicated situation in Cameroon. That is because Israel is directly involved in the atrocities and human rights violations carried out in the English-speaking regions of Cameroon.

Figure 17.3. Israeli emergency surgeons and their trainees in Yaoundé (2020). Credit: Israeli Embassy in Yaoundé

The huge elephant in the room, the crisis that was conspicuous by its near absence, was the Anglophone Revolt. The Israelis were training surgeons to mitigate the direct effects of Israeli military involvement in Cameroon, specifically, the casualties sustained by the Israeli-trained BIR and other branches of the Cameroon armed forces in North Cameroon and especially in the Anglophone Northwest and Southwest regions, where the BIR and members of the elite presidential guard seconded to it, were suffering heavy casualties weekly. This included the loss of several high-level BIR officers.

17.4. Israeli diplomats meet the press in Yaoundé after their training course (2020). Credit: Israeli Embassy in Yaoundé

Cameroon-Israel Bilateral Security Cooperation and the Birth of BIR

Israel and Cameroon are the strangest of strange strategic bedfellows. Israel is a parliamentary democracy founded in 1948 by the survivors of Nazi Germany's Holocaust and

Russian pogroms. As such, it has a heightened sensitivity towards atrocities, human rights violations, genocide, war crimes, and crimes against humanity. Despite the fact that Israel has been accused of violating the human rights of Palestinian Arabs in East Jerusalem, the Occupied West Bank, and the Golan Heights, Israel is very sensitive about accusations of supporting dictatorial regimes, particularly those that commit crimes against humanity. Israeli activist groups regularly demonstrate and petition the Israel's Defense Export Control Agency, the Israeli Ministry of Defense, and the Israeli Supreme Court seeking to cancel arms export permits or halt Israeli arms shipments to authoritarian regimes in Africa, Asia, and Latin America if they feel these arms would be used to entrench dictatorships, oppress citizens and violate the human rights of minorities (Benn, 2014). For its part, Cameroon is an African country that has never experienced democracy since its independence from France in 1960 and its reunification with the former English-speaking British United Nations Trust Territory of Southern Cameroons. Cameroon is a harsh, highly centralized, authoritarian, neo-patrimonial, kleptocratic regime that is part of the French politico-cultural sphere of influence, *la Francophonie*. Its president, Paul Biya, is one of the longest-reigning presidents in Africa. He has ruled the country with an iron fist since he came to power in 1982 and crushed all political opposition and dissent in his 40 years in power. The Cameroon National Assembly is a rubber-stamp institution at the executive's beck and call. The judiciary is not independent since President Biya is the Chief Magistrate who appoints all magistrates and judges by decree and presides over the Supreme Council of the Magistracy. President Biya manages the country's oil and natural gas resources like his personal property.

Israel became a strategic partner of Cameroon almost by happenstance. Cameroon established diplomatic relations with Israel after Independence in 1960. Israeli Premier, Golda Meir, and President Ahmadou Ahidjo established bilateral cooperation focused on agriculture training. Due to their knowledge of the English language, many students from the English-speaking West Cameroon were trained in agronomy in Israel. These agronomists staffed the Cameroon Development Corporation and the PAMOL Plantations in Ndian. However, *la République du Cameroun*, under Muslim President, Ahmadou Ahidjo, was among the wave of African countries that broke diplomatic relations with Israel in the wake of the 1973 Arab-Israeli war, under pressure from the Arab League. Cameroon and Israel restored diplomatic relations in 1986, when Prime Minister Shimon Peres of Israel visited Cameroon. By happenstance, Mr. Peres arrived in Cameroon a day after gas emissions from Lake Nyos, a volcanic lake in the Anglophone Northwest region killed at least 1,500 people (Israel and Cameroon Renew Diplomatic Ties, 1986; Fomine, 2011). The Israelis were the first to send relief teams to help with relief efforts. The Nyos tragedy began an interesting strategic, diplomatic, and military relationship between Israel and Cameroon. This rather interesting visit of Israeli Prime Minister Shimon Peres to Cameroon, and the announcement of the reestablishment of diplomatic relations between the two countries was the consummation of sorts of the beginning of long-standing strategic, bilateral, defense, and security cooperation between Israel and Cameroon that emerged after an unsuccessful *coup d'état* against President Paul Biya in 1984, less than two years after he came to power. In effect, Cameroon's first President Ahmadou Ahidjo, the authoritarian "father of the nation," who had ruled for 22 years, resigned abruptly on November 6, 1982, and handed power to his "constitutional successor," Prime Minister, Paul Biya. Former President Ahidjo, moved to Nice, France for medical treatment. Ahidjo soon fell out with Biya, whom he had hoped to control from his Parisian retreat, over control of the government and the sole political party, the Cameroon National Union (CNU)—believing that Biya was weak and indecisive. On April 6th, 1984, the Republican Guard, which had been former president Ahidjo's hand-picked, mostly Northern praetorian guard, attempted to overthrow President Paul Biya in a *coup d'état*. The immediate reason for the mutiny was that President Paul Biya wanted to transfer officers from Ahidjo's northern region from the Republican Guard and replace them with officers and soldiers from his Beti-Bulu group due to frictions he was having with Ahidjo over the government and the presidency of the CNU. From his French residence, President Ahidjo expressed support for the coup. He told Radio Monaco: "if my supporters are involved in the coup, they will gain the upper hand, I think" (Lewis, 1984). President Biya survived the coup attempt and on 11 April 1984, dissolved the Republican guard. Former President Ahmadou Ahidjo was tried in absentia in a military court in Yaoundé and sentenced to death. From his Parisian "exile" he told the international media: "*Je reconnais humblement m'être trompé sur la personne que j'avais estimée, protégé, comblée et portée tout seul à la tête de l'État.*" (I humbly recognized that I was mistaken about the [nature of] the person that I esteemed, protected, and raised on my own to the summit of the State). Ahidjo soon became a persona non-grata in France, a country whose interests he had served assiduously as president of Cameroon. He was exiled to Dakar, Senegal, where he died in 1989 at age 65 and was buried by the State of Senegal.

The Israeli Defense and Security Connection

The Israeli connection refers to the role and place of the State of Israel, via approved former senior IDF officials which has seen a number of retired Israeli Defense Forces (IDF) officials serve as Technical Advisers for military and security affairs to the President of the Republic of Cameroon. The strategic security relationship between Israel and Cameroon began after the failed 1984 coup against President Paul Biya. The dissolution of President Ahidjo's mutinous "Northern" *Garde républicaine* left a major security vacuum that had to be filled. The shocked and shaken President Biya cast around for help in rebuilding a praetorian guard with trusted officers. There was no question of working with the French, the former colonial power, which had set up, trained and armed the dissolved Republican Guard. President Biya did not trust the French, who had picked and groomed Ahidjo as they had done in other African postcolonies. President Paul Biya was convinced that former president Ahmadou Ahidjo, who was receiving medical treatment in Nice, France, had ties with French intelligence, the *Service de Documentation Extérieure et de Contre-espionage–SDECE* (the External Documentation and Counter-Espionage Service). The Americans suggested he work with the Israelis, who had an unimpeachable security track record (Olivier, 2020). They had helped set up Singapore's army and security apparatus in 1965 (Oppenheimer, 2020). This security relationship between Israel and Cameroon was approved by the Israeli Prime Minister and Minister of Defense. The Israelis did not hesitate to take advantage of this economic and geo-strategic opportunity. Working with Cameroon would give them a friend at the United Nations, where they are often the subject of censure over the Palestinian Question and their ruthless suppression of Palestinian aspirations and uprisings. The Israeli Point man for the Cameroon mission was Colonel Avraham Avi Sivan, a distinguished former Israeli Defense Forces officer who had been one of the founders of the elite undercover IDF unit, Duvdevan, that was created to counter the Palestinian intifada (uprising). He was later seconded to the Embassy of Israel in Yaoundé as Defense Attaché. Col. Sivan went into business with another Israeli, Sami Meyuhas, who had been given Israeli Defense Ministry permission to export Israeli "security goods" (arms, ammunition, and communications surveillance equipment). Together, they laid the groundwork for the Cameroon mission. Sivan was appointed Special Technical Adviser to President Paul Biya for Security Affairs (Melman, 2010). The Israelis reported directly to President Biya and transmitted his orders to the Cameroon Delegate General at the Presidency for Defense. Avi Sivan came to be known as President Paul Biya's guardian angel. This turned out to be a very financially lucrative business for the former Israeli Defense Forces officers, turned licensed arms merchants, and Cameroonian bureaucrats and military officers involved (Freudenthal & Van Der Weide, 2020). The Israelis transformed the security apparatus in Cameroon. They created President Biya's praetorian guard, the *Garde présidentielle* to replace former President Ahidjo's dissolved French-styled Republican Guard. They dispensed with the flowing, colorful, French-style robes, kepi, swords, and other ceremonial accouterments favoring Israeli-style paratrooper berets, uniforms, and boots.

Figure 17.5. President Biya's Israeli-trained, and armed *Garde présidentielle* (20th May, 2019 march past)

The Israelis then installed various antennas and surveillance technologies enabling the interception of telephone and electronic communications in the capital Yaoundé and other cities (Olivier, 2020). All Israeli arms and ammunition shipped to Cameroon in the context of the military cooperation between the two countries have to be approved by the Israeli Defense Export Controls Agency (DECA). Israeli military officials serve as the Technical Adviser to the President of the Republic of Cameroon. These "securocrats" who report directly to the increasingly reclusive President Biya oversee the recruitment and train President Biya's personal praetorian *garde républicaine*, and its brutal, atrocity-prone elite BIR, which has an unenviable record of committing horrendous crimes against humanity in the Anglophone regions of Cameroon, including summary executions of civilians, burning of tens of villages, the savage killing and torturing of civilian demonstrators that has earned it the sobriquet "*milice bulu*" (militia of President Biya's Bulu tribe).

Figure 17.6. BIR Marching during National Day parade (May 20, 2018)

The "Israeli Unit," the Bataillon d'Intervention Rapide (BIR)

The Israelis soon created the BIR, essentially an "army-within-an army." It has no general staff and comprises three BIR stationed at Douala, Tiko, and Koutaba. These three battalions are the *Bataillon Spécial Amphibie* (BSA), the *Bataillon des Troupes Aéroportées* (BTAP) and the *Bataillon Blindé de Reconnaissance* (BBR) respectively. The Israelis were so influential and so successful that the Cameroon media and other units of the Cameroon army called them "mercenaries." In an article entitled, "Making a Killing: Israeli Mercenaries in Cameroon," Freudenthal and Van Der Weide (2020) write that Israeli citizens, mostly former senior officers of the Israeli Defense Forces (IDF), had, with the approval of the Israeli government, specifically the Ministry of Defense set up, recruiting, training and arming units of the military in Cameroon: 1) authoritarian President Paul Biya's personal, praetorian guard, the 2000 member *Garde Présidentielle*, and 2) the notorious, 6000-member BIR. They conclude that, "The BIR is known for the arduous training regime its soldiers go through and their access to superior weaponry. The BIR is also notorious for its ruthlessness" (Freudenthal & Van Der Weide, 2020). The BIR, which has also held training sessions with American soldiers since 2007, has been at the forefront of the fight against the Islamist terrorist group Boko Haram.

A succession of former Israeli Defense Forces (IDF) officers have had the official title of "Technical Adviser to the President for Security Affairs" in Cameroon. They report directly to President Biya and pass his instructions to the Cameroon Minister Delegate at the Presidency in charge of Defense. These Israeli officers/businessmen have included: Col. Avraham Avi Sivan, Brigadier General Erez Zuckerman, Mayer Heres, Eran Moas, and Brigadier General Baruch Menashe, aka Baruch MENA, a military communications systems specialist. The coupling of the Israeli security edifice and President Paul Biya's nearly 40 years of autocratic, neo-patrimonial, and kleptocratic rule transformed Cameroon into a national security state, where national security and draconian national security laws trump all rights. The military and security cooperation between Israel and the autocratic regime of President Biya, who celebrates 40 years in power in 2022, is a marriage of strategic convenience. The Israelis ensure the security and longevity of the Biya regime while Biya protects Israel's economic and geo-strategic interests. Eitay Mack, an Israeli lawyer and human rights activist who is critical of Israel's ties with authoritarian regimes, believes the Israeli government's position on the matter may be strategic. "Paul Biya is one of the most reliable friends of Israel in [the whole] African continent, ...The payoff is [for Cameroon] to support Israel openly in international forums...Cameroon is an important part of helping Israel to get legitimacy...It's all part of the geopolitical fight with the Palestinians" (Freudenthal & Van Der Weide, 2020).

Figure 17.7. BIR founder, Col. Avraham Avi Sivan with Presidential Guard and BIR trainee graduates at Man O' War Bay, Cameroon. Credit: U.S. Department of Defense

The leaked letter from Israeli Brigadier General Baruch Menashe, aka Baruch MENA, one of President Biya's Technical Advisers, is revelatory. The 2018 letter is addressed to the Cameroonian Minister at the Presidency in Charge of Defense (Defense Minister) Beti Assomo, ordering him to sign and cause to be broadcast on Cameroon national radio an announcement concerning the recruitment and training of 2600 elite commandos for the two military units under the control of the Israelis – the presidential guard and the BIR.

Freudenthal and Van Der Weide (2020) report that Israeli security collaboration in recruiting, training, and arming the BIR–and the presidential guard–was a lucrative venture. This is because both units are well-funded and widely believed to be financed through an off-budget account of Cameroon's national oil holding company, *the Société Nationale des Hydrocarbures* (SNH). As such, funding for the BIR and the presidential guard came indirectly from British, French, Chinese and other oil companies drilling in the Southwest Anglophone region of Cameroon. Nevertheless, while the Israelis are involved in the recruiting, training, command, and supply of weapons to the BIR and the presidential guard, the corporate structures through which they operate are deliberately opaque. However, the Israeli lawyer/activist, Eitay Mack, has identified several types of Israeli-manufactured weapons used by the BIR and the presidential guard. Israel apparently took a calculated decision to prop up an authoritarian regime in its national interest. This relationship is approved by the Israeli Prime Minister and Minister of Defense. All Israeli arms, ammunition, and equipment shipped to Cameroon in the context of the military cooperation between the two countries are approved and licensed by the Israeli Defense Export Controls Agency (DECA). Ultimately, the defense and security cooperation between Israel and the Biya regime was very lucrative for the former IDF officers who doubled as Technical Adviser to President Biya for security affairs as well as licensed arms merchants (Freudenthal & Van Der Weide, 2020).

Figure 17.8. Ex IDF Col. Avi Sivan, Israeli and American trainers of the BIR and presidential guard in Cameroon. The Americans ended the program when reports of the human rights violations of the BIR went viral on social media. The Israeli's continued the program. Credit: U.S. Department of Defense

Figure 17.9. The BIR hunting Ambazonian separatists in the Southwest region

Figure 17.10. An American Special Forces officer trains members of BIR in Man O'War Bay, Southwest Region

The BIR and the Anglophone Revolt in Cameroon

Israeli security is part of the architecture of repression of the autocratic Biya regime. Nowhere is this more evident than the atrocities and human rights violations visited on the minority English and Pidgin-speaking population in the restive Northwest and Southwest regions by the notorious BIR. In effect, as a result of the Ahidjo/Biya government policy of assimilating the English and Pidgin-speaking minority into the Francophone majority, and muting their cultural specificity, in the 1990s, the Anglophones demanded that the Biya government recognize their identitarian and cultural specificity, and restore their autonomy that had been extinguished by a constitutional sleight of hand in 1972. The Biya regime turned a blind eye and a deaf ear to the political pleas of the English speakers. In response to active French/Francophone majority governmental assimilationist policies and benign marginalization in the overcentralized, kleptocratic, authoritarian, neo-patrimonial, republican "chiefdom" of Cameroon, a movement of peaceful civil disobedience began in the English-speaking regions. In October 2016, the long-simmering Anglophone Question became a national crisis when minority English-speaking common law lawyers, teachers, students, and members of the civil society in the Northwest and Southwest regions went on strike demanding recognition of the cultural specificity and political autonomy of the two English-speaking regions. They organized peaceful demonstrations and constitutionally protected non-violent acts of civil disobedience.

The response of the Biya regime was massive repression. From the lap of luxury in his presidential suite at the InterContinental Hotel in Geneva, President Paul Biya let loose the Israeli-created, trained and armed special forces, the BIR and the regular military on unarmed civilian demonstrators and the civilian population of Southern Cameroons. They left death and wanton destruction in their wake. Hundreds of villages were burnt as punishment for hosting insurgents, hundreds of thousands of people fled to Nigeria, where they became refugees, and hundreds of thousands became internally displaced. The dictator had decided to impose a quick military solution on a long-standing political problem. President Biya's crackdown was an affirmative decision to violently suppress non-violent demonstrations by English-speaking common law lawyers, teachers, and students. Political demands by unarmed civilians in the Northwest and Southwest regions were met with brutal repression, targeted killings, arrests, imprisonment, beatings, and torture by the Cameroon armed forces, led by the brutal, Israeli, French, American, and Israeli-trained and armed BIR, the army, the gendarmerie, and the police (Amnesty International, 2018; Bensimon, 2018). On many occasions, members of the BIR recorded their torture, and summary execution sessions on video and posted them on Facebook and other social media. Some of these videos were featured on international broadcast channels.

Figure 17.11. BIR truck destroyed by the Red Dragons independentist group in Lebialem, Southwest region (2018)

Figure 17.12. Funeral of BIR Lt-Col. Maigari Alioum Brice, killed in action in Awing, Bamenda in 2019

Figure 17.13. Cameroon military casualties from the Anglophone War at the military morgue in Yaoundé (2019)

When the Anglophone Revolt began in 2016, the BIR was sent in to join the gendarmerie, the police and the regular army to quell the demonstrations and restore law and order. After the killing of dozens of unarmed protesters, the Ambazonia Defense Force was started and took up arms to resist the killings, atrocities, and human rights violations. When President Biya ordered the armed forces to crush the emerging independentist movement in November 2017, it was widely believed that the BIR, with its superior Israeli, Croatian, French and Serbian arms and ammunition, would crush the Anglophone separatist groups in a matter of days at most. That did not happen. Nearly five years later, the BIR and the rest of the Cameroonian army appear to be stuck in an expensive quagmire. Thousands of Anglophone civilians and separatists were killed, as have hundreds of members of the BIR, the regular military, the gendarmerie, and the police.

Figure 17.14. Israeli ammunitions captured from the BIR by Ambazonian separatist fighters (2019)

Things escalated in early 2021 when Anglophone separatist groups adopted the so-called "popcorn" war, the improvised explosive device (IED) war in collaboration with dynamite and weapons suppliers in Nigeria, Biya's ally, where everything is available on the black market, and everyone is on sale, including security and customs officials. Those killed include hundreds of BIR, including some high-ranking Officials of the elite corps. In January, they started targeting units of the BIR, the Cameroon army, and the gendarmerie in the Anglophone Northwest and Southwest regions. In August and September 2021, self-styled Ambazonia Restoration Forces carried out deadly and brazen attacks using IEDs against units of the BIR. In Kikaikilaki, Bui, an improvised explosive device blew away seven members of the BIR who were riding in an armored personnel carrier. The deadliest attack against the BIR occurred in Bamessing, Ndop on September 16, 2021–a unit of Ambazonia separatists that calls itself the Ambazonia Marine Force of Bambalang, Ndop, led by a fighter known as "General No Pity" coordinated with other Ambazonia "restoration" forces from Ngoketunjia, ambushed a BIR convoy at Bamessing, Sabga Hill. At what has become known as the Battle of Sabga Hill, separatists ambushed a BIR convoy. Using a combination of improvised explosive devices and a rocket-propelled grenade, the Amba Boys knocked out two Panthera F9 armored personnel carriers, killing 15 BIR soldiers on the spot. Images of Amba Boys jubilating in front of the burning Panthera F9 and dragging the bodies of the BIR went viral. The separatists captured the expensive Israeli Galil weapons and ammunition and posted videos and audio of the captured weapons online.

Figure 17.15. Unexploded BIR rocket that landed near a village and was captured by Ambazonian separatists

Figure 17.16. Screenshot of Ambazonia fighters displaying Israeli arms and ammunition seized from the BIR after the battle of Sabga Hill (September 16, 2021)

Figure 17.17. Screenshot of Amba Boy displaying Israeli-made weapons captured after Battle of Sabga Hill, September 16, 2021

The Israeli Disconnect: The Moral Dilemma of Israeli Involvement in the Subjugation of Anglophone Minority

Israel is one of the most fractious democracies in the world. Israelis differ over everything and over nothing. A salient bone of contention in Israel is the opaque Israeli arms export industry. According to the Stockholm International Peace Research Institute (SIPRI), Israel is among the top eight arms exporters in the World (Wezeman et al., 2021). Israeli weapons and ammunition are used widely in conflicts around the globe from Azerbaijan to South Sudan. Israelis are thus often conflicted over the opaque role of Israeli security and defense training and material (arms, ammunition, telecommunications and information and communication technology systems, etc.) in propping up dictatorial regimes and fueling armed conflicts in many parts of the world. The Israeli arms export industry is thus a contentious national security and national interest issue. Over the years, a small group of Israeli activists has challenged successive Israeli governments over their sale of lethal "security and defense" equipment to dictatorial regimes in Africa, Asia, the Middle East, and Latin America. In countries where there is no respect for human rights, authoritarian regimes use lethal Israeli technologies to suppress dissent, oppress their people, and violate human rights outlined in national constitutions and the Universal Declaration of Human Rights of 1948. Their rationale is that given the fact that Jews have been the victims of oppression, human rights violations, pogroms, and genocide, Israel is morally obligated to refrain from supporting or propping up dictatorial regimes that engage in the types of human rights violations and crimes against humanity to which Jews have been subjected in Europe and other parts of the world.

Israeli lawyer and human rights activist, Eitay Mack, and other activists have made it their duty to challenge and protest against Israeli arms shipments to dictatorial regimes in Africa, Asia, and Latin America, where these arms are used to prop up authoritarian regimes and violate human rights. These shipments are licensed by the Israeli Ministry of Defense in Collaboration with the Israeli Ministry of Foreign Affairs, which conditions the transfer of defense know-how and the provision of defense services on national security and foreign relations considerations, as well as international human rights obligations. While Eitay Mack and his colleagues have a global vision, in 2016, they turned their focus on Cameroon, where authoritarian President Paul Biya, who has been in power for close to 40 years, has a long-standing, mutually beneficial "defense and security" relationship with Israel. That relationship is unusual and deeper than simple arms shipments. In effect, as we saw above, since creating, training and arming the dictator's praetorian guard, *la Garde présidentielle,* and his elite "Israeli" military unit, the BIR. Mack and his fellow Israeli activists focused their critique of the use of the Israeli-trained and equipped BIR, as well as Israeli weapons and ammunition in Biya's attempt to subjugate the English and Pidgin-speaking minority in the Northwest and Southwest regions. In effect, at the outset of the Anglophone Revolt in 2016, the BIR was let loose on the civilian population of Southern Cameroons like dogs of war. The BIR and elements of the regular army and gendarmerie unleashed a wave of terror on unarmed civilian demonstrators and innocent civilians. Their scorched-earth policy left death and wanton destruction in their wake. Human rights organizations report that more than 5000 civilians were killed in the first two years of the conflict, more than 200 villages burned, 60,000 people fled to Nigeria as refugees, and close to one million others became internally displaced. Mack would later describe the Anglophone crisis in Cameroon as a "State Crime" (Mack, 2020).

Israelis Challenging the Role of Israel in the Anglophone Crisis

Eitay Mack and other Israeli human rights activists made revelations about the level and extent of Israel's partnership with the authoritarian Biya regime in the context of the Anglophone crisis. On February 7, 2018, Mack wrote to Racheli Chen, Head of the Israeli Defense Export Controls Agency (DECA), of the Israeli Ministry of Defense, regarding Israeli training and arming of the BIR in Cameroon. Mack asked DECA to apply Article 9 of the Israeli Defense Export Control Law, 5766-2007, and revoke, or suspend licenses to export Israeli arms, ammunition, and weapons to Cameroon (See appendix X). The activists also filed a petition with the Israeli Supreme Court asking the court to order DECA to cancel arms export licenses to the BIR under Article 9, citing the human rights violations to which the arms had been put in the Anglophone regions of Cameroon. The

Israeli Defense Export Control Law, 5766-2007 stipulates that when the Israeli Defense Export Controls Agency (DECA) takes into consideration the end-user or the end-use of Israeli arms and ammunition, "Reasons of state security, foreign relations considerations or international obligations will not constitute an argument against the licensing authority's decision under this section." In their petitions to DECA and the Israeli Supreme Court, Mack and his human rights activist colleagues argued that the relationship between the State of Israel and the Republic of Cameroon goes beyond mere supply of security services (arms and ammunition). Mack and his colleagues wrote presciently:

> ...In view of the crimes in which the BIR unit is involved across Cameroon, especially in the past year (2018) in the English-speaking provinces, and fearing that the grave political crisis in Cameroon may spiral out of control into a full civil war, I would ask that you freeze or cancel all security export licenses to the BIR unit, until one can make sure that it is possible to verify that its soldiers are no longer involved in severe violations of human rights, that the crimes which were committed are investigated and those responsible are brought to justice, and that the crisis in Cameroon is over... This case does not involve "normal" Israeli security exports being used for grave violations of human rights, but rather - a real intervention by the Israeli Ministry of Defense in the political life of another country in a neo-colonial manner. The Citizens of Israel, the State of Israel or the Knesset have never declared war on the residents of the English-speaking provinces of Cameroon, and have never voted to support the eternal reign of an aging dictator.

Figure 17.18. Eitay Mack & colleague demonstrating in Israel against Israeli support of the Biya regime's atrocities in Cameroon

In their article, "Making a Killing: Israeli Mercenaries in Cameroon," Freudenthal and Van Der Weide (2020) suggest that Mack's petition to the Israeli Defense Export Controls Agency (DECA) and the Israeli Supreme Court did not seem to have been unpersuasive. The Court issued a ruling but placed a gag order on it. This essentially means that Eitay

Mack is barred from revealing the content of the judgment. Nevertheless, the impact of the judgment was soon evident on the ground. With effect from 2019, newly trained members of the BIR were given Slovak and Serbian versions of the AK-47 assault rifle rather than the normal Israeli ACE assault rifles. Nevertheless, both units continued to wear Israeli paratrooper-style uniforms, berets, and boots. Apparently, the Israeli Supreme Court and Defense authorities had decided to stop or reduce the export of certain lethal weapons to the armed forces in Cameroon. The decision was too little, too late. The Cameroon armed forces were awash with Israeli weapons (some of which fell into the hands of the Anglophone independentists). Those weapons could be easily obtained in third countries licensed to produce them.

Conclusion

The Anglophone Revolt in Cameroon is a revolt against the tyranny of the dictatorial regime of President Paul Biya, who turned a blind eye and a deaf ear to calls for respect of the identitarian and cultural specificity of the English-and Pidgin-speaking minority in the former State of West Cameroon, whose territory was divided into the Northwest and Southwest provinces as part of a divide, conquer, and assimilate strategy. Biya's response to the Anglophone Revolt was to use military means to solve the purely political Anglophone Problem, which he had helped to create and which his authoritarian governance had exacerbated. Biya's long-standing defense and security collaboration with Israel provided him the military means to attempt to subjugate the Anglophones. Since the Anglophone Revolt broke out in 2016 in the form of strikes, civil disobedience (ghost town) and public demonstrations, Biya used two military units, the Israeli-trained and equipped presidential guard and BIR, to unleash a wave of terror on demonstrators, activists, students, and innocent, unarmed civilians in the English-speaking provinces. International human rights organizations and activists, including Israeli activists, report that more than 4000 civilians have been killed, close to 200 villages have been burned, more than 500,000 people have been internally displaced, and more than 60,000 people have fled to Nigeria as refugees. The world is indeed full of ironies. The Israelis, who are the world's most well-known victims of genocide, became partners in crimes against humanity with a fading African dictator who clung to power for four decades. However, since Israel is a democracy, Israeli activists were able to expose the strategic relationship between their country and the dictatorship in Cameroon. The Israeli government never responded officially to the petitions of the activists who wanted to put an end to Israel's shipment of arms and ammunition to the notorious military units of the Biya regime. The second irony is that the crimes against humanity that were visited on the Anglophone minority in Cameroon reached their apogee in 2018 when the president of the African Union was the post-genocide president of Rwanda, Paul Kagame. The inability of the African Union to go beyond tepid condemnation of the Biya regime's atrocities in Anglophone Cameroon and Kagame's silence over the crimes against humanity in Southern Cameroons was indeed deafening!

References

Amnesty International (2018). Cameroon: Anglophone Regions gripped by Deadly Violence. June 11. Retrieved from: https://www.amnesty.org/en/latest/news/2018/06/cameroon-anglophone-regions-gripped-by-deadly-violence/

Ben-Yosef, E. (2015). When Golda Meir Went to Africa, *Jean & Samuel Frankel Center for Judaic Studies Annual (University of Michigan) Vol. 2015*, pp. 25-27. Retrieved from: https://quod.lib.umich.edu/f/fia/11879367.2015.008/1

Benn, A. (2014). Who does Israel Sell Arms to? The Defense Ministry Won't Tell. *Haaretz.* January 9. Retrieved from: https://www.haaretz.com/who-does-israel-sell-arms-to-1.5309458

Bensimon, C. (2018). Cameroun: *La réponse répressive de Yaoundé envers les anglophones est incompréhensible.* Le Monde, June 20. Retrieved from: https://www.lemonde.fr/afrique/article/2017/06/20/cameroun-la-reponse-repressive-de-yaounde-envers-les-anglophones-est-incomprehensible_5148220_3212.html

Dougueli, G. (2015). *Cameroun: Biya Sous protection israélienne,* (Cameroon: Biya Under Israeli protection) November 19, 2015. Retrieved from: https://www.jeuneafrique.com/mag/276021/politique/cameroun-paul-biya-sous-protection-israelienne/

Embassy of Israel in Cameroon (2020). Emergency training Seminar, 2nd Edition:

During 4 days top Israeli surgeons trained Cameroonian doctors in Emergency surgery. February 5. Retrieved from: https://embassies.gov.il/yaounde/NewsAndEvents/Pages/Training-seminar-on-emergency-surgery.aspx

Fomine, F. (2011). The Strange Lake Nyos CO2 Gas Disaster: Impacts and The Displacement and Return of Affected Communities, *The Australasian Journal of Disaster and Trauma Studies* 1. Retrieved from: https://trauma.massey.ac.nz/issues/2011-1/fomine.htm

Freudenthal. E. Van Der Weide, Y. (2020). Making a Killing: Israeli Mercenaries in Cameroon. *African Arguments*, June. Retrieved from: https://africanarguments.org/2020/06/making-a-killing-israeli-mercenaries-in-cameroon/

Israel and Cameroon Restore Diplomatic Ties (1986). The Associated Press. August 27. Retrieved from: https://www.nytimes.com/1986/08/27/world/israel-and-cameroon-renew-diplomatic-ties.html

Israeli Defense Export Control Law, 5766-2007. Retrieved from: http://www.exportctrl.mod.gov.il/Documents/%D7%97%D7%95%D7%A7%20%D7%94%D7%A4%D7%99%D7%A7%D7%95%D7%97%20+%20%D7%A6%D7%95%D7%95%D7%99%D7%9D%20+%20%D7%AA%D7%A7%D7%A0%D7%95%D7%AA/Defense_Export_Contro_Law.pdf

Lewis, P. (1984). Cameroon Radio Says Attempted Coup has Failed. *The New York Times*, April 7, 1984. Retrieved from: https://www.nytimes.com/1984/04/07/world/cameroon-radio-says-an-attempted-coup-has-failed.html

Mack, E. (2020). State Crime in Cameroon. International State crime Initiative. http://statecrime.org/state-crime-in-the-cameroon/

Meir, G. (1975). *My Life.* New York: Putnam Press.

Melman, Y. (2010). Ex-IDF Top Officer Dies in Cameroon Helicopter Crash. *Haaretz* (Israel). Retrieved from: https://www.haaretz.com/1.5143112

The Associated Press (1986). Israel and Cameroon Restore Diplomatic Ties August 27. Retrieved from: https://www.nytimes.com/1986/08/27/world/israel-and-cameroon-renew-diplomatic-ties.

html

Olivier, M. (2020). *Cameroun: espionnage, troupes d'élite...quand Israël veille sur Paul Biya.* (Cameroon, espionage, elite troops...when Israel watches over Paul Biya). *Jeune Afrique,* January 30. Retrieved from: https://www.jeuneafrique.com/mag/886063/politique/cameroun-quand-israel-veille-sur-la-securite-et-les-interceptions-de-paul-biya/

Oppemheimer, S. (2020). A Life and Death Matter: How Israel Helped Singapore When it Needed it Most. Haaretz (Israel). March 16. Retrieved from: https://www.haaretz.com/israel-news/.premium-the-lion-city-and-the-start-up-nation-how-israel-helped-singapore-1.8676074

Tessier, M. (2009). *A History of the Israeli-Palestinian Conflict.* Bloomington, Indiana: Indiana University Press.

Wezeman, P., Kuimova, A., & Wezeman, S. (2021). Trends in International Arms Transfer (2021) Stockholm International Peach Research Institute Factsheet. March. Retrieved from: https://sipri.org/publications/2021/sipri-fact-sheets/trends-international-arms-transfers-2020

EIGHTEEN

The Resource Curse and the Anglophone Question

British Post-Brexit Partnership in Crimes Against Humanity in Cameroon

LYOMBE EKO

Treason and murder ever kept together, As two yoke-devils sworn to either's purpose, Working so grossly in a natural cause That admiration did not whoop at them; But thou, 'gainst all proportion, didst bring in Wonder to wait on treason and on murder; And whatsoever cunning fiend it was That wrought upon thee so preposterously Hath got the voice in hell for excellence.

Shakespeare, King Henry V, Act 2, Scene 2

Though those that are betray'd do feel the treason sharply, yet the traitor stands in worse case of woe.

Shakespeare, Cymbeline, Act 3, Scene 4.

We saw in Chapter 3 that the United Kingdom explored decolonization options for the much-neglected Trust Territory of British Southern Cameroons that it had seized from Germany as "enemy lands" during World War I and had administered indirectly through Nigeria since 1916. Despite the prevailing international political ethos of creating enabling environments for self-determination for colonized peoples, Britain excluded the possibility of independence for Southern Cameroons on the grounds that the territory would not be economically viable as an independent country. That conclusion was bolstered by a hasty, cursory survey of part of the economy of the territory by a British colonial official, Sir Phillipson, who the British government had assigned to study the economic viability of Southern Cameroons in 1959. Interestingly, the economic viability of Northern Cameroons, the other former German colonial territory that had also been apportioned to the United Kingdom in 1916, was not assessed since it was a foregone conclusion that Northern Cameroons would be incorporated into the independent federation of Nigeria. After surveying the emerging agricultural economy of the territory of Southern Cameroons – and it was grounded in a mixture of plantation agriculture inherited from German colonists after World War I, small-scale peasant farmer production of food crops for local consumption, and cash crops for export – Sir Phillipson noted that: "Southern Cameroons has been, and still to some extent is, one of the less developed, more backward areas embraced within the Federation[of Nigeria]" (Cited in Anyangwe, 2010, p. 556). This was not earth-shattering news given that the territories of Northern and Southern Cameroons had essentially been colonial backwaters governed indirectly as insignificant appendages to Britain's Nigerian Protectorate and Colony. The Phillipson Report (1959), therefore averred that the United Kingdom had failed in executing "the sacred trust" it had undertaken under the Treaty of Versailles of 1919 to administer the "enemy lands" (German territories) it had apportioned to itself, in agreement with France, as a League of Nations Mandate, and as a United Nations Trust Territory after 1946. The Phillipson Report (1959) arrived at a conclusion consistent with British decolonization without independence policy:

> As a completely independent state the Southern Cameroons, at its present stage of development, would not be viable. A further period of Trusteeship, if adequate, might afford the Southern Cameroons the time it needs to develop and test its financial strength" (Cited in Anyangwe, 2010, p. 575).

Northern Cameroons was economically even less developed than Southern Cameroons. The conclusion of the Phillipson Report became the basis for the official British policy of opposing the independence of Southern Cameroons. This campaign against Southern Cameroons independence was spearheaded by Sir Andrew B. Cohen, the UK representative to the United Nations Trusteeship Council. Cohen and other British diplomats used their influence in the fledgling United Nations to persuade other members of the United Nations to conclude that Southern Cameroons would not be an economically viable independent nation. The disunity, internecine political and regional divisions of the unsophisticated Southern Cameroons politicians, led by John Ngu Foncha, Dr. EML Endeley, Nfon Mukete, N.N Mbile, Solomon Tandeng Muna, Ndeh Tumazah and others, facilitated the British policy of decolonization without independence.

The Phillipson Report demonstrated the scope of British neglect of the Cameroons territories, the spoils of war the UK and France had seized from Germany after World War I, and dismembered haphazardly in line with their colonial balance of power and respective administrations. British and French Trust Territories were to be administered in the best interests of the peoples of the territory and prepared for self-determination. The most that Britain did was to dismember further the strips of German Kamerun territory that had been apportioned to it under the Anglo-French Milner/Simon Declaration of 10 July 1919 into two parts, Northern and Southern Cameroons, as pawns in its international balance-of-power diplomacy with its ally and rival France, as well the internal regional balance-of-power calculations in the emerging Nigerian federation. The United Kingdom paid no attention to the interests of the people being moved from German to British and ultimately to Nigerian sovereignty. The neglected, economically backward territory of Northern Cameroons was eventually split into several Nigerian states and became the hotbed of the Islamist Boko Haram insurgency in 2009, while the neglected Southern Cameroons, which had been annexed by French Cameroon in 1961 via a questionable UN plebiscite, erupted into the Anglophone Revolt of 2016. The Boko Haram insurgency in the former Northern Cameroons (today's northeast Nigeria and the Lake Chad Basin) and the unrelated Anglophone Revolt in Southern Cameroons, are history's revenge against the Anglo-French Milner/Simon Declaration of 10 July 1919, and especially British Machiavellian colonial policy in Nigeria and the Cameroons territories.

Aim of the Chapter

This chapter aims to describe and explain the British posture in the Anglophone Question in Cameroon in the post-Brexit era. The fundamental premise is that the Anglophone Revolt of 2016 in Cameroon coincided with the 1916 Anglo-French partition of German Kamerun and the 2016 Brexit vote in the United Kingdom over continued membership in the European Union. When the British voted to leave the European Union, Prime Minister Theresa May, and Secretary of State for Commonwealth and Foreign Affairs, Boris Johnson (who would later become Prime Minister in 2019) took the strategic decision of charting a new international trade course for the United Kingdom. This involved pivoting away from the European Union and opening or strengthening bilateral relations with non-European partners. One of these partners was *la République du Cameroun*, where the Biya regime was carrying out well-documented human rights violations and crimes against humanity in the former British Southern Cameroons, where common law lawyers and teachers had revolted against the marginalization, linguistic and cultural assimilation, and authoritarian governance of the neo-patrimonial, kleptocratic, republican chieftaincy of President Paul Biya, who had been in power for close to 40 years. Ironically, Southern Cameroons became an "Anglophone" territory because it had been a British League of Nations mandate from 1919 to 1946, and a British United Nations Trust Territory from 1946 to 1961. Despite the fact that the Biya regime's campaign of military subjugation of the English and Pidgin-speaking minority in the former British Southern Cameroons violated every tenet of the Commonwealth's democratic values, the African Charter on Human and Peoples' Rights, the Universal Declaration of Human Rights, as well as the laws of war, Cameroon continued to be a member in good standing in the British Commonwealth. Nigeria, Zimbabwe, Pakistan, and Fiji had been expelled from the Commonwealth for less serious human rights violations. The explanation for this British disregard of the horrendous human rights violations of the Biya regime in Anglophone Cameroon is that the regime strategically granted British companies exploration concessions in the rich oil and natural gas reserves of Cameroon which ironically, are located in the English and Pidgin-speaking Southern Cameroons, which Biya was trying to militarily subjugate, with horrendous results – more than ten thousand dead, 60,000 refugees crossing the border into Nigeria, and hundreds of thousands of internally displaced. By granting British companies these economic concessions, Biya succeeded in muting condemnation of his human rights violations, and dampening British support for its former Trust Territory and Mandate, the English and Pidgin-speaking former British Southern Cameroons. Clearly, post-Brexit Britain put its national interests above human rights. It preferred to become a partner in crimes against humanity with the repressive Biya in exchange for short-term economic gain.

When Natural Resources Trump Human Rights: The Anglophone Question in the Post-Brexit Era

One of the ironies of history is that Southern Cameroons, which the British government concluded would be economically non-viable as an independent state in 1959, and gladly gifted to France as, in President Charles de Gaulle's words, "*un petit cadeau de la Reine d'Angleterre*" (a little gift from the Queen of England) (Anyangwe, 2010, p. 735), suddenly became a valuable non-European economic opportunity – and a pawn – in French Cameroon and Post-Brexit British diplomatic and economic relations. On June 8, 2018, two years after the beginning of the Anglophone Revolt in Cameroon, the Right Hon. Liam Fox, British International Trade Secretary in the government of Prime Minister Theresa May, announced on Twitter that New Age (African Global Energy) Limited, a London-based, privately-held, oil and gas exploration and production company, had secured a significant deal to help develop Cameroon's Etinde Offshore block in the Rio del Rey Basin, offshore Southern Cameroons. Etinde is the name of a mountain in Fako, Southern Cameroons, where this project was scheduled to be located. Hon. Fox said the deal followed a May 2018 meeting between Baroness Fairhead and Cameroonian diplomats. On June 9th, 2018, New Age LNG signed a gas convention agreement (GCA) with the Cameroun Government, regarding building a Floating Liquefied Natural Gas (FLNG) project in the Etinde Offshore block. It was announced that the Floating Liquified Natural Gas project would be developed in conjunction with an upstream Etinde development which would include gas and gas liquid production facilities in Limbe, that would supply gas to customers in Douala and other parts of Cameroon (OilVoice Press, 2018).

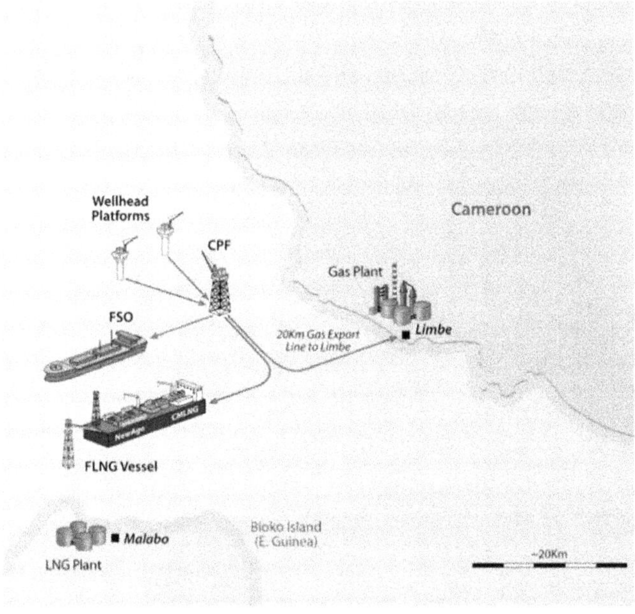

Figure 18.1. The New Age Etinde liquified natural gas project presented to the media in 2018. Etinde is the name of a mountain in Fako, Southern Cameroons

The Right Hon. Liam Fox presented the Cameroon project as part of a series of projects in many parts of the world that signaled the United Kingdom's return to the world stage as a global power unshackled from the European Union and its unelected bureaucrats in Brussels: "The [Etinde] project is of huge importance to the African country, who will be able to ramp up their gas export operation, in turn generating a huge revenue stream for the public treasury, whilst also helping to develop offshore infrastructure in support of future local power generation. There are strong reasons for the UK to be optimistic about our presence on the world stage and this series of deals, worth more than £1.9 billion, showcases Britain's world-leading capability in key sectors such as cyber security and life sciences as we leave the European Union" (International Visits Pay off for British Business, 2018). This was British post-Brexit hubris at its peak. Hon. Fox did not disclose that the Russian multinational energy behemoth PJSC Lukoil owned a 37.5% interest in the Etinde Floating Liquified Natural Gas (FLNG) project, as did Bowleven of Scotland. According to New Age, the final investment decision on the Etinde project was to be made in 2020, and the first production was expected in 2022.

The irony is that while Hon. Liam Fox was celebrating the signing of the deal for a future oil and natural gas bonanza in Cameroon, a separatist war was raging in the part of the country where most of the oil and natural gas of Cameroon are found. In effect, the Etinde offshore oil fields (named after Mount Etinde) are in English and Pidgin-speaking Southern Cameroons, which was once a British League of Nations Mandated Territory after World War I and later the British Trust Territory of Southern Cameroons after World War II. In 2016, the people of the region revolted against their oppression, assimilation, and marginalization by the French-speaking Cameroon government and majority French-speaking population to which they had been consigned by the British government and the United Nations in 1961. In effect, the so-called Anglophone crisis in Cameroon is one of the last unfinished items of World War I. The Anglophone Revolt, peaceful demonstrations and strikes led by lawyers, teachers, students, and ultimately, the general population in September and October 2016, were met with the most ferocious and violent repression. When the smoke from the guns and grenades of the Cameroon military cleared, scores of unarmed civilians lay dead in Buea, Kumba, Mamfe, Bamenda and other places.

Figure 18.2. Liam Fox, International Trade Secretary. Ignored human rights abuses in his dealings with the Biya regime

Indeed, while the Right Hon. Liam Fox was touting the blockbuster Etinde oil and natural gas agreement with the Republic of Cameroon, a nominally bilingual member of the British Commonwealth, Cameroonian and international human rights organizations, as well as the international media, including the BBC, were reporting that octogenarian president Paul Biya, who had been in power for almost 35 years at that time, had undertaken a war of conquest and subjugation against the English and Pidgin-speaking minority in the former British Trust Territory of Southern Cameroons. In effect, the common law lawyers and teachers of the English-medium educational system, along with the churches, which control most of the educational institutions and health services in the English and Pidgin-speaking Southern Cameroons, had revolted against the over-centralized, authoritarian, Napoleonic *chefferie républicaine* (republican chiefdom) of President Paul Biya, and especially its concerted actions to marginalize the English-speaking community, mute its identitarian and cultural specificity, and assimilate it into *la Francophonie*, the Franco-African political and cultural sphere of influence. In response, the Cameroon army, police, gendarmerie, and especially the Israeli-trained and equipped elite *Battalion d'Intervention Rapide* (BIR), unleashed a horrendous reign of terror in the English-and Pidgin-speaking Northwest and Southwest regions of Cameroon. Security forces became forces of law and disorder. They beat up lawyers and teachers in Bamenda, Buea, and other places. They also arrested and imprisoned hundreds of Anglophone teachers, lawyers, students, journalists, and activists. The federalist separatist agitation was suddenly transformed into a military conflict on September 22, 2017, and October 1, 2017 when the military, police, and gendarmerie, led by the Israeli-trained and equipped BIR, opened fire on unarmed civilian demonstrators that marched to Buea and set out to declare "restoration" of the sovereignty of their state of Southern Cameroons. Helicopter gunships fired fragmentation bombs on crowds in Buea, and soldiers fired on unarmed crowds in several towns: Mutengene, Ekona, Muyuka, Mamfe, and Bamenda.

The separatist Southern Cameroons National Council (SCNC) and the Consortium of Anglophone Civil Society, which were organizing peaceful demonstrations and ghost town strikes, were banned. The Consortium's president, international human rights lawyer, Nkongho Felix Agbor-Balla, and its Secretary General, Professor Fontem Aforteka'a Neba of the University of Buea, were both arrested in Buea, transferred to Yaoundé and held incommunicado in the dungeon of feared *Secretariat d'État à la Defense* (the State Defense Secretariat, popularly and fearfully known by its French acronym, SED). The Anglophone leaders were later brought before the French-language only Yaoundé Military Tribunal and charged with eight counts of terrorism and insurrection against the state, under the 2014 Law on Repression of Terrorism. This charge carried the death penalty (Amnesty International, 2018). Military prosecutors charged them with "disseminating fake news... complicity with, and non-denunciation of terrorist acts," "non-denunciation of information and sources," and other vague and overbroad charges brought (Amnesty International, 2018). The Law on Repression of Terrorism had been enacted in response to the Islamist Boko Haram terrorist activities in Nigeria and North Cameroon. The vague, over-broad and highly elastic Cameroon anti-terrorism law, which provides that the death penalty could be imposed on citizens who, either as individuals or as a group, carry out, abet, or sponsor terrorism, is routinely used to arrest and imprison journalists, activists and political opponents of the Biya regime. The law also criminalizes "incitement to rebellion," and "creating a general uprising in the country." Cameroon opposition parties, journalists, and international human rights organizations have condemned the law as an instrument of repression, and suppression of dissent and criticism of the excesses and corruption of the government (Johnson, 2014). Indeed, journalists were arrested, tried and convicted in the Yaoundé Military Tribunal for allegedly writing sympathetically about the Anglophone Revolt. Anyone suspected of having federalist, or autonomous tendencies that were at variance with President Biya's over-centralized one-man *chefferie républicaine* was thrown in jail. Hundreds of people were imprisoned when the Etinde Floating Liquified Natural Gas project was announced. Furthermore, in order to prevent Anglophone activists from using social media to organize strikes and demonstrations and to hide the atrocities of the rogue Cameroon army, Minister of Posts and Telecommunications, Mrs. Libom Lo Likeng ordered that the Internet be cut off from the English-speaking Northwest and Southwest of Cameroon in order prevent activists from using the Internet and social media to organize and present evidence of human rights violations by the Cameroon security forces to the world (See Chapter 10).

Emergence of An Anglophone Armed Resistance and International Condemnation of Human Rights Violations

The acts of extreme violence and human rights violations in the English and Pidgin-speaking former Southern Cameroons led to the emergence of a nascent Anglophone/Ambazonia separatist resistance known as the Amba Boys. In November 2017, a group of Amba Boys from the Ambazonia Defense Forces created by Lucas Ayaba Cho crossed the porous, poorly marked, and deeply forested border into Nigeria, procured weapons from the black market, attacked and killed five members of a Cameroon army patrol in Agborkem-German, Manyu. President Biya ordered the military to launch a scorched-earth policy in Southern Cameroons. The government appointed *préfet* (Divisional Officer) for Manyu, Mr. Oum II Joseph, issued a decree expelling the inhabitants of 15 villages in Akwaya, Eyumojock, and Mamfe sub-divisions, men, women and children, en masse. In the decree that was broadcast repeatedly on radio, Mr. Oum II ordered the expellees to "relocate to safer neighborhoods." The Cameroon army had declared these villages zones of war. He gave the villagers only hours to pack and set off on a journey to nowhere! Mr. Oum continued that those who did not leave their villages in a matter of hours would be treated as terrorists. Thousands of panicked men, women, and children left their villages and crossed the border to become refugees in Nigeria. Others in their thousands, ended up as internally displaced persons in other towns and villages. The Cameroon security forces, led by the Israel and American-trained BIR, moved in shortly thereafter. Their human rights violations included collective punishment, a scorched-earth policy of burning whole villages suspected of supporting armed separatists (sick, old, and infirm villagers who could not escape perished in the flames). They also engaged in kidnappings, rapes, and extra-judicial killings.

Enter the British Commonwealth Human Rights Initiative (CHRI)

By 2018, the atrocities carried out by Cameroon security forces in the former British Southern Cameroons had led to the death of more than 5000 people. More than 500,000 had become internally displaced persons, and the United Nations High Commissioner for Refugees reports had reported that more than 20,000 refugees had fled to Nigeria to seek safety and asylum. That number would rise to 60,000 (Center for Human Rights and Democracy in Africa & Raoul Wallenberg Center, 2019; Swiss Federal Department of Justice, 2018). The African Union, the United Nations, Amnesty International, Human Rights Watch, and other international human rights organizations appealed in vain for Cameroon to respect its international human rights obligations. The Commonwealth Human Rights Initiative (CHRI), an organization that works to promote human rights in the countries of the Commonwealth, along with a plethora of Commonwealth, international, and regional civil society groups, issued a joint "Submission to the Commonwealth Ministerial Action Group (CMAG)" in September 2018 urging the Commonwealth to put the Anglophone crisis in Cameroon on its agenda. The CHRI submission was a virtual laundry list of crimes against humanity perpetrated by the security forces of the authoritarian Biya regime against the Anglophone minority in response to their political demands that the French Cameroun government change its educational and legal policies and recognize the cultural and identitarian rights of the Anglophone minority. The submission noted the: "indiscriminate killings, arbitrary arrests, detention without recourse to justice, and torture in Cameroon. Amnesty International has reported that 20 protesters have been killed, and information from UN agencies and Cameroonian civil society indicate that as a result of the ongoing crisis, more than 411,000 have now been displaced, 128 villages burnt, and more than 1,000 individuals are in detention" (Commonwealth Human Rights Initiative, 2018). The CHRI added that in addition to the widespread reign of terror in the former British Southern Cameroons, the Biya regime had violated the right of freedom of expression of the Anglophone population by depriving them of Internet connections for months at a time: "The Government of Cameroon has blocked Internet connections and access to social media platforms. Between January 2017 and March 2018, the government shut the internet in Anglophone regions for 240 days. The government further passed repressive legislation that included the assertion that "irresponsible use of social media is punishable by law" (Commonwealth Human Rights Initiative, 2018). The CHRI also decried the fact that peaceful demonstrations by lawyers, teachers, and members of civil society had been harshly suppressed by the Cameroon security forces, resulting in deaths and injuries to unarmed civilians. "Protestors have been detained unlawfully, freedom of assembly, access to the internet and information constrained, and access to justice severely impaired" (CHRI, 2018). The Commonwealth Ministerial Action Group did not include the crisis in Cameroon on its agenda. Within a year, the atrocities mentioned by the CHRI had quadrupled.

The British Government and the Commonwealth Ministerial Action Group (CMAG) were unmoved by the spirited appeals of the Commonwealth Human Rights Initiative. It is not as if the Commonwealth was a stranger to the Anglophone Revolt in Cameroon. Just one month after President Biya ordered his security forces to crush the emerging

Anglophone armed resistance, and the military's scorched-earth policy began, Cameroon Anglophones took to the Internet and social media, and questioned how Cameroon could continue to be a member of the British Commonwealth when it was committing such horrendous crimes against humanity and shut down the Internet in the former British Southern Cameroons for nine whole months. They stated that Cameroon had violated the democracy, human rights and freedom of expression provisions of the Commonwealth Charter (2013), which states inter alia:

> We are committed to the Universal Declaration of Human Rights and other relevant human rights covenants and international instruments. We are committed to equality and respect for the protection and promotion of civil, political, economic, social and cultural rights, including the right to development, for all without discrimination on any grounds as the foundations of peaceful, just and stable societies
>
> ...
>
> We are committed to peaceful, open dialogue and the free flow of information, including through a free and responsible media, and to enhancing democratic traditions and strengthening democratic processes.

The crimes against humanity carried out by Cameroon security forces in the former British Southern Cameroons meant it had failed to abide by the values and human rights ideals of the Commonwealth that are also set forth in the Harare Declaration (1991) and include the promotion of:

> democracy, democratic processes and institutions which reflect national circumstances, the rule of law and the independence of the judiciary, just and honest government;
>
> fundamental human rights, including equal rights and opportunities for all citizens regardless of race, colour, creed or political belief...

Furthermore, the prolonged Internet shutdown in the former British Southern Cameroons by the government of Cameroon, a member of the Commonwealth, was a clear violation of the Commonwealth Cyber Declaration (2018), which affirms that "the same rights that citizens have offline must also be protected online" and commits members of the Commonwealth to: "limit the circumstances in which communication networks may be intentionally disrupted, consistent with applicable international and domestic law." While these declarations are not binding statements of law or legal obligation, English and Pidgin-speaking Cameroonians argued that with such blatant violations of the human rights values of the Commonwealth, Cameroon had no business being a member of that organization.

In 2017, the Law Society of England and Wales (2017) observed the trial of Cameroon Anglophone leaders Nkongho Felix Agbor Balla, Fontem Neba, and others (all civilians) at the Military Tribunal in Yaoundé. The observer of the Law Society of England and Wales found that the court martial of Anglophone civil society leaders, teachers, and students at the Yaoundé Military Tribunal, where they faced the death penalty under draconian, vague and overbroad anti-terrorism laws enacted in the wake of the emergence of the Boko Haram terrorist group in Nigeria in 2009. The militarization of the judicial system, the role of the military in the arrest, detention, torture, extra-judicial murder of Anglophone suspects, and court-martial of Anglophone civilians in military tribunals across the country amounted to massive violations of national, African Union, and international law. The observation report outlined the lack of independence of the judiciary, lengthy periods of detention without charge or trial in inhumane conditions at the Secretariat of State for Defense (SED), trial of English and Pidgin-speaking civilians in the Yaoundé Military Tribunal, whose official language is French, without benefit of translators, and so on. (See Chapter 27 for the entirety of the Trial Observation Report of the Law Society of England and Wales).

As a result of this violence and repression against English and Pidgin-speaking inhabitants of the former British Trust Territory of Southern Cameroons, *la République du Cameroun* became the Commonwealth country with the worst human rights. In response to the alarming situation in Cameroon and the trenchant criticisms of the Commonwealth's inaction, on December 15, 2017 the Commonwealth Secretary General, the Right Hon. Patricia Scotland, visited Cameroon. She framed her five-day visit in the context of Commonwealth-Cameroon relations, not necessarily as a mission to resolve the Anglophone Revolt. She couched the purpose of the visit in diplomatic language: "I am very much looking forward to my first visit to Cameroon as Secretary-General. As a valued member of our Commonwealth family, this visit will allow me to not only get to know the country and its people better but, more importantly, discuss concrete ways in which the Commonwealth can support Cameroon's efforts to address the pressing challenges it currently faces." After five days of meetings with President Paul Biya, his appointed Prime Minister, Philemon Yang, and Anglophone civil society members in Yaoundé and Buea, Scotland's visit did not achieve much. Indeed, it was a total failure. The opulent banquet in President Paul Biya's sumptuous palace, and the diplomatic platitudes mouthed by Biya and Scotland could not hide the palpable but visible specter of failure. President Biya, who was hell-bent on subjugating the Anglophones, did not commit to ending his war of subjugation of Anglophone Southern Cameroons. Next in line was Hon. Harriett Baldwin, the UK Minister of State for Africa at the Foreign and Commonwealth Office in the government of Prime Minister Theresa May. President Biya did not even bother to meet Mrs. Baldwin when she came calling in Yaoundé. He sent his appointed Prime Minister, Philemon Yang, to go through the motions of holding talks with her. It was all a façade because in 2017, Yang had gone to Kumbo in Bui Division, Northwest Cameroon, and echoed the hardline position of his master, Paul Biya. He told the traumatized people that there would be no compromise. Federalism (the only form of decentralization once popular among Anglophones) was out of the question. He was adamant that the government would not entertain any discussion on changes to the form of the over-centralized, corrupt, autocratic, Napoleonic system that had triggered the Anglophone Revolt. That was the end of the story.

The British did not offer even the most tepid statement of criticism of the atrocities and crimes against humanity being committed in the former British Southern Cameroons by Cameroon, a Commonwealth member in good standing. Fast Forward to the 2018 Summit of the Commonwealth Heads of State and Government in London. British Secretary of State for Foreign and Commonwealth Affairs, Hon. Boris Johnson, MP, made the rounds, visiting the heads of all the delegations. Thereafter, he commented on his individual meetings with the various Commonwealth dignitaries on his social media platforms. In his tweet about Cameroon, Johnson reports that he met with Cameroon's figurehead Prime Minister, Philemon Yang, at the ongoing Commonwealth Summit and "urged the need for urgent dialogue, decentralization, and respect for human rights in Anglophone Regions" of Cameroon. The tweet was accompanied by a picture of Boris Johnson and Philemon Yang.

Figure 18.3. Former Foreign Secretary and Prime Minister, Boris Johnson with Former Cameroon PM, Philemon Yang. Wishful thinking on the part of Johnson (2018)

The Resource Curse of Southern Cameroons: The Post-Brexit United Kingdom and the Biya Regime as Strange Economic Bedfellows

If Hon. Liam Fox was the international poster child of the amoral post-Brexit British Foreign trade and economic policy, which was guided not by long-standing international or Commonwealth humanitarian values or human rights norms, but by pure, narrow, British national, self-interest, the British High Commissioner to Cameroon, His Excellency Rowan James Laxton personified, for English-speaking Southern Cameroonians, the amorality and Machiavellianism of post-Brexit British policy in Cameroon. Indeed, High Commissioner Rowan James Laxton was a major actor in the Cameroonian version of what has come to be known as the African resource curse. This is the situation where African oil, natural gas and other mineral reserves attract the attention of multi-natural energy companies from the United States, Europe, China, and Russia. With the help of their governments and diplomats, these multinational companies enter into investment agreements with corrupt African authoritarian leaders. These deals, whose major beneficiaries are the corporations and their authoritarian kleptocrat partners, cause boom energy economies, decimate the agricultural sector and other sectors, without any tangible benefit to the people, who continue to wallow in extreme poverty, and lack the bare necessities of life – have no food security, no clean drinking water, no electricity, no schools, no health centers, no roads, and no hope (Ghazvinian, 2008). The former British Southern Cameroons (dismembered and renamed the Northwest and Southwest regions of Cameroon) is a paradigmatic case study of the resource curse–with a tragic, human rights twist, the so-called Anglophone crisis.

In effect, by an ironic twist of history, Southern Cameroons, one of the "mere strips" of territory that Britain and France had carved out of German Kamerun in 1916 as spoils of World War I, and used as bargaining chips, mere expendable pawns in the European colonial balance of power, turned out to have a lot of "natural capital" to use the expression of the World Bank (2011). That be agriculturally, oil and natural gas rich. It therefore turns out that the British government's conclusion in 1959, that Southern Cameroons could not be an economically viable independent country, were wide off the mark. The territory that the British colonial administration had rejected in 1959, as non-viable, was perceived in 2016 as a cornerstone of British post-Brexit trade policy due to its natural capital (reserves of oil and natural gas, forests, fisheries, cattle and other resources). Indeed, the territory is also of great interest to the governments of France, China, Russia, Israel, and their energy, national security and defense industries. Since the 1970s, these natural resources have been exploited by French and British companies in partnership with the neo-patrimonial Ahidjo/Biya regime, in a rather opaque, off-the-books manner. According to the World Bank, oil rents provided up to 10% of the country's gross domestic product (GDP) in 1985 but decreased significantly in the succeeding years due to fluctuating oil prices. However, as we saw earlier, there has been a renewed interest in the Cameroon energy sector since 2015. Resources from oil and natural gas produced mostly in the former British Southern Cameroons have been used to shore up the authoritarian regime and fund the lavish life-styles of President Paul Biya and the ruling elite. Specifically, the national energy company, *Société Nationale des Hydrocarbures* (National Hydrocarbons Company), commonly known as SNH, is the personal piggybank of President Paul Biya. It directly funds the notorious, Israeli-trained, and equipped BIR, which is infamous because of its human rights violations in North Cameroon and the rebellious former British Southern Cameroons. Western and Asian companies have also discovered another aspect of the natural capital of Southern Cameroons, its agricultural and forest wealth. The Cameroon Development Corporation, which was the emerging backbone of the Southern Cameroons economy in the 1950s, ultimately became the biggest employer in Cameroon besides the government. In the 1990s, under the International Monetary Fund and World Bank structural adjustment programs, the Cameroon government attempted to "privatize" segments of the vast agricultural plantations of the Cameroon Development Corporation, which operate on leased native land, without consulting the native landowners, in a somewhat opaque manner. Companies from France, Indonesia, Malaysia, and other countries expressed interest in these plantations, but they were deterred by legal action brought by the native owners of the land against the Cameroon government (see chapter 25 for Professor Kofele-Kale's analysis of that aspect of the Anglophone Question).

Indeed, President Ahmadou Ahidjo had abolished the Federal Republic of Cameroon and replaced it with the Republic of Cameroon, a highly centralized, Napoleonic system in 1972 in order to directly control the natural capital of Southern Cameroons. Since then, his successor, President Biya has used the country's natural resources as strategic tools of bilateral relations. In order to stifle criticism of his horrendous human rights record, President Biya granted companies from the permanent member countries of the United Nations Security Council - France, Britain, China, and Russia - oil, natural gas exploration and exploitation licenses, as well as concessions to extract other minerals. This fact essentially explains why the UN Security Council seemed paralyzed in the face of the vast human rights abuses of the Cameroon army and the BIR in the former Southern Cameroons. In addition, the autocratic neo-patrimonial regime signed national security agreements with Israel to create, train, and equip President Biya's personal praetorian guard, *la garde présidentielle*, as well as the army within the Cameroon army–the notoriously ruthless BIR. This has been a boon for the Israeli national security/defense industry complex. In exchange for British political and diplomatic support–or at least non-criticism–at the United Nations, the Commonwealth and elsewhere, British companies became the beneficiaries of concessions to Cameroon's natural resources. In this Machiavellian game of post-Brexit survival, the British turned a blind eye and a deaf ear to the atrocities and human rights violations of the Biya regime, and willingly became the economic bedfellows and partners in crimes against humanity of the bloody, authoritarian, neo-patrimonial Biya republican chiefdom.

Willful Diplomatic Blindness: British Partnership with the Biya Republican Chiefdom

The British–Cameroon political and economic partnership was publicly proclaimed in 2017 and 2018 by both countries while the Israeli-trained and equipped *Battalion d'Intervention Rapide* (BIR) and the regular Cameroon military was carrying out the most horrendous atrocities in the English and Pidgin-speaking former British Southern Cameroons. This partnership was publicly proclaimed by none other than the British High Commissioner to Cameroon, His Excellency, Rowan James Laxton. On July 23, 2020, Rowan James Laxton held a rare meeting with reclusive President Paul Biya at the presidential palace in Yaoundé. At the end of the short meeting, Laxton lowered his COVID-19 mask and read some prepared remarks to the press in French. He told the Francophone audience that he and President Biya had discussed the health situation in the world, notably the Coronavirus (COVID-19 pandemic). "I also conveyed my Government's thanks to the Head of State for his support of our conference on global vaccines, which took place in June 2020 in London, and the very generous financial contribution [$1 million dollars] that the Head of State made at that meeting, through his representative." Ambassador Laxton said he and President Biya had reviewed the security situation in the Far North, Northwest, and Southwest Regions of Cameroon. He said that he welcomed the measures that the Cameroon Government had taken and encouraged all parties in the conflict to go further to reestablish a durable peace and prosperity. He added that: "We talked about the economy and the way in which British companies can contribute towards achieving the President's 2030 [emergence] vision for Cameroon." Finally, they discussed several global challenges on which the UK and Cameroon are working together such as the Commonwealth and the 2021 United Nations Climate Change Conference (COP 26), which was due to take place in Glasgow (Productive Meeting with British High Commissioner, 2020). At the end of his remarks, an English-speaking reporter asked the Ambassador the substance of his meeting with President Biya, for the English-speaking audiences. Ambassador Laxton repeated his remarks in English, with an air of unease, looking instinctively at his prepared French text from time to time to ensure that his English remarks had the same substance as his comments in French. Strained and sanctimonious diplomatic niceties are the stock in trade of diplomats around the world, but the remarks of Ambassador Laxton were jarring, even stunning in the highly dramatic politico-cultural context of Cameroon, where the authoritarian President Biya had declared war on the Anglophone minority that had revolted against 60 years of cultural assimilation and five years of attempted military subjugation and human rights violations. It was unclear to English-speaking journalists what measures H.E. Rowan James Laxton was referring to when he said: "*j'ai salué les mésures prises par le gouvernement*" (I welcome the measures taken by the government) with respect to the crisis. H.E. Rowan James Laxton had apparently naively believed the handful of deceptive and misleading decrees issued by President Biya to give the world the impression that he was "solving" *la Question anglophone*, were worth the paper they were written on.

The fact is that Biya's measures were aimed at reinforcing the deeply entrenched, over-centralized, authoritarian, kleptocratic status quo. These *tromp l'oeil* measures included the decree creating the National Commission For the Promotion of Bilingualism and Multiculturalism, which had zero impact on the crisis or even the language policy of Cameroon, the decree creating the Emergency Humanitarian Assistance Program for the Northwest and Southwest regions, the decree creating the National Committee for Disarmament, Demobilization and Reintegration (DDR) (in the absence of a cease-fire), and especially a law granting the English-speaking Northwest and Southwest regions a fictitious "special status" (without consultation with the aggrieved English-speaking minority). These bad-faith unilateral measures that did not even pretend to address the root causes of the Anglophone crisis clearly did not assuage the deeply felt injustice and marginalization of the oppressed English and Pidgin-speaking population.

Somehow, Ambassador Laxton had missed all the reports of crimes against humanity committed by the Biya regime in the former British Southern Cameroons. He ignored the root causes of the problem. Indeed, the sanctimonious diplomatic platitudes pronounced by the British High Commissioner to Cameroon at the entrance of Paul Biya's Presidential Palace in Yaoundé, on July 23, 2020, reflected the Machiavellian character of post-Brexit British foreign trade policy. It was all about the role of British companies in Biya's "Emergence 2030." Indeed, as the elated diplomat basked in the glow of his meeting with the reclusive, authoritarian chieftain, who was probably the bloodiest president in the history of West Africa, the British diplomat seemed oblivious to the fact that Cameroon was going through what human rights organizations called "Cameroon 's Unfolding Catastrophe" (CHRDA & Raoul Wallenberg Center, 2019). The horrendous human rights violations in Anglophone Cameroon had been widely reported by the independent media in Cameroon as well as the international media, including the British Broadcasting Corporation, and condemned by the United Nations High Commissioner for Human Rights, and former

President of Chile, Michelle Bachelet. The United Nations had also expressed concern over the situation. In its 2019 report, the Committee on Economic, Social and Cultural Rights of the UN Economic and Social Council (2019) stated that it is also:

> deeply concerned by the widespread violence being witnessed in the North-West and South-West Regions, where most of the population belongs to the English-speaking community, and by reports that acts of violence leading to the destruction of hospitals, schools and entire villages in those Regions have been committed by non-State armed groups and by members of the State party's security forces

Besides the United Nations High Commissioner for Human Rights, the European Union, Canada, Germany, the United States Congress, and even the British House of Commons had discussed and condemned the human rights violations in English and Pidgin-speaking Southern Cameroons. At the height of the crisis, when prefectorial expulsions, the burning of villages, the murder of hundreds of civilians by the BIR, the Cameroon military, the para-military gendarmerie and the police resulted in a flood of refugees to neighboring Nigeria, as well as the massive internal displacement of hundreds of thousands of persons to neighboring French Cameroon (mostly Dschang, Bafoussam, Yaoundé and Douala) or to relatively safe Southern Cameroons towns – Buea, Limbe and Tiko – the international community began to pay attention. When the United States assumed the chair of the United Nations Security Council, it facilitated the holding of a so-called "Arria-Formula" meeting on the humanitarian effects of the crisis in Cameroon. The Arria-Formula is an informal meeting that allows the Security Council greater flexibility to be briefed about international peace and security issues. The meeting on the humanitarian effects of the crisis in Cameroon was officially organized by the Dominican Republic, Germany, the UK and the United States. Panelists included the UN Under-Secretary-General for Humanitarian Affairs Mark Lowcock, Secretary-General of the Norwegian Refugee Council, Jan Egeland, and Esther Omam Njomo, the Executive Director of Reach Out Cameroon, a local not-for-profit organization focused on the well-being of underprivileged groups such as women and children in Cameroon. The meeting took place on May 13, 2019. It was attended by all members of the United Nations Security Council and included other invited members of the civil society in the Northwest and Southwest regions of Cameroon. During the meeting, the UK Deputy Ambassador to the United Nations, Jonathan Allen issued a robust statement that was markedly different from the tepid, sanctimonious platitudes of the British High Commissioner in Yaoundé. Mr Allen told the Arria meeting:

> ...This is a man-made humanitarian crisis, a crisis caused by people not by nature, and that requires people to act to resolve it. We cannot talk about the humanitarian situation in Isolation. We must also talk about the political situation which underpins it.... The government of Cameroon has made a number of promises and proposals to resolve the underlying problems, and President Biya recently promulgated a new decentralization

> law paving the way for regional elections. This is a very welcome step. But we need to see greater implementation of the government of Cameroon's own proposals and greater trust building with local populations. The United Kingdom calls on the government of Cameroon to establish a credible political dialogue and make all efforts to resolve the crisis peacefully…We still have time to prevent this crisis from descending further into an intractable conflict but that time is limited and we cannot waste it. I reiterate the urgent need for the Government of Cameroon to act now to instigate a credible dialogue to tackle the situation and address the ever-worsening humanitarian crisis else I fear the Council will find itself discussing this issue more often (United Nations Security Council 2019).

By 2020, the urgency expressed in Ambassador Allen's statement had dissipated as the world moved on to other crises. Ambassador Laxton's statement after his meeting with President Biya in Yaoundé reflected a change in British attitude towards the Anglophone crisis in Cameroon. British national interests in the post-Brexit era trumped human rights considerations. It is no wonder that in its June 2020 report, the Norwegian Refugee Council (NRC) concluded that the Anglophone crisis had become an ignored international human rights crisis: "For a second year running Cameroon topped the list as the most neglected crisis on the planet in 2019….Three separate emergencies faced the African nation: an exacerbation of Boko Haram attacks in the north, a violent conflict in the English-speaking west, and a Central African refugee crisis. Ineffective conflict resolution, global news silence and a massive aid funding shortfall all contributed to the country topping this year's list" (Norwegian Refugee Council, 2020). The British High Commissioner in Yaoundé exemplified and reflected this global apathy and disinterest. To him, the Anglophone conflict was an afterthought, a minor concern that could not be allowed to cast a shadow on the lucrative economic relationship between the United Kingdom and the authoritarian Republican chieftaincy of President Paul Biya, whose repressive regime, continued its gross violations of human right, while remaining a member in good standing of the British Commonwealth.

The willful amnesia of the British High Commissioner meant he came across as being unaware of, or considered it of no importance, that the African Commission on Human and Peoples Rights had ruled in 2009, long before the Anglophone revolt, that the Biya regime had consistently and systematically violated human rights in the former British Southern Cameroons. This litany of violations included killing unarmed civilian demonstrators, arresting hundreds of lawyers, teachers, journalists, students, priests, and other members of civil society, and deporting them to French Cameroun, where they are detained for long periods without trial. Those who were "lucky" were tried before military tribunals whose language of communication is French – a language they did not understand – without the benefit of translators (Ngwang Gumne v. Cameroon, 2009). These French-language military tribunals routinely convicted and sentenced these Anglophone civilian political prisoners to lengthy jail terms that ranged from 10 years to life imprisonment, after parodies of trials that violated the elementary tenets of impartial justice and fairness, and due process of law. In Cameroon, military tribunals are part of the executive because they operate under the auspices of the *Ministre Délégué à la Présidence, Chargé de la Défense* (Minister Delegate at the Presidency in charge of Defense).

The cavalier and off-hand manner with which the British High Commissioner ignored the horrendous human rights violations and crimes against humanity visited on Anglophone Southern Cameroons (a territory that the Ahidjo/Biya regimes had divided into the Northwest and Southwest regions the better to conquer and assimilate it into the French Cameroun republican chieftaincy) stunned Anglophones, many of whom had been born under the British Empire. The large Anglophone population in the United Kingdom, the Republic of Ireland, Canada, Australia, and the United States were stunned into speechlessness.

18.4. British High Commissioner to Cameroon, His Excellency, Rowan James Laxton

The Cameroon government's official media outlets returned the favor. The banner headline in the government's mouthpiece, *Cameroon Tribune,* proclaimed: *Situation sanitaire et sécuritaire: Yaoundé et Londres en phase* (Health and Security Situation: Yaoundé and London in Synch) (Fig. 18.5). The front-page picture showed a masked Ambassador Rowan James Laxton meeting with President Biya at the presidential palace in Yaoundé. Another story in the same edition was headlined: *Situation sanitaire et sécuritaire: Accord Parfait entre Yaoundé et Londrès* (Health and Security Situation: Perfect Agreement between Yaoundé and London) (Djarmalla, 2020). These headlines referenced the two challenges facing the Biya regime: the COVID-19 pandemic, and the Anglophone Revolt. They informed the world that the British were in total agreement with Biya's attempted military subjugation of the Former British Southern Cameroons, and the crimes against humanity that resulted from the repression. The Cameroun government essentially proclaimed that the British government was its partner in crimes against humanity, was at least in agreement with the well-publicized human rights violations being perpetrated against the English and Pidgin-speaking minority that was once part of the British Commonwealth and used to pay allegiance to the British Crown before it reunited with *La République du Cameroun* in 1961. English-speaking Southern Cameroonians felt that the British had "sold" them again to French Cameroon in exchange for natural resources that ironically happened to be in their territory.

Figure 18.5. Perfect Agreement Between Yaoundé and London on Health and Security, *Cameroon Tribune*, July 24, 2020

His Excellency Rowan James Laxton's declaration of partnership with the Biya regime in front of the Etoudi Presidential Palace was one of the strangest political/diplomatic spectacles to take place in Cameroon since the Anglophone Revolt began in 2016. The British diplomat ambassador essentially turned a blind eye to President Biya's decision to opt for a military "solution," subjugation, as the means to resolve the long-standing politico-cultural and identitarian question of the role and place of the minority Anglophone population in the authoritarian, kleptocratic, republican chieftaincy of Cameroon. To the British Ambassador, the fact that Biya's attempt to subjugate Southern Cameroonians had resulted in a humanitarian catastrophe, was of no consequence in the lucrative bilateral relationship between the United Kingdom and Cameroon. Ambassador Rowan James Laxton paid no heed to the 240-day Internet shut-down in English-speaking Southern Cameroons, reports by international human rights groups including UK-based Amnesty International to the effect that the Cameroon security forces had razed hundreds of Southern Cameroons villages to the ground in a brutal scorched-earth campaign, that more than 5000 Anglophones had been killed by the murderous, Israeli-trained BIR, that more than 120,000 had fled as refugees to Nigeria, and almost one million had been internally displaced (Amnesty International, 2021). In the face of this humanitarian catastrophe, Ambassador Rowan James Laxton was concerned only about how British companies could do business with the Biya regime. He told the French Cameroun government media: "*j'ai salué les mésures prises par le gouvernement*" (I welcome the measures taken by the government). In the English version of his statement, he said, "I congratulated…I welcomed the measures that the government has taken."

The ambassador seemed to be blissfully unaware of the litany of human rights violations carried out by the Biya regime and reported extensively by the international media including the British Broadcasting Corporation (BBC Africa Eye, 2018), the Commonwealth Human Rights Initiative (CHRI), the UN Human Rights Commission, the United Nations High Commissioner for Refugees, the European Parliament, Amnesty International, Human Rights Watch, and multiple other human rights organizations which denounced the human rights violations and crimes against humanity perpetrated by the Israeli-trained and equipped BIR and other Cameroonian security forces in the former British Southern Cameroons. He did not seem to be aware of Biya's nearly nine-month-long Internet blackout in Southern Cameroons, and the international "#BringbackourInternet" social media campaign (Calis, 2017). Ambassador Rowan James Laxton essentially stated that he agreed with President Biya's decision to opt for a military solution to resolve the long-standing politico-cultural and identitarian question of the role and place of the minority Pidgin and English-speaking population in Cameroon. The repressive measures undertaken by Biya, against Anglophone Cameroon, and endorsed by the UK, had resulted in a humanitarian catastrophe.

In terms of the sheer number of citizens killed, the human rights violations perpetrated by the Biya regime in Anglophone Cameroon can be compared with the Gukurahundi atrocities, the murderous excesses carried out by President Robert Mugabe's special military unit, the North Korean-trained 5 Brigade between 1982 and 1988 in Matabeleland and the Midlands provinces of Zimbabwe. Mugabe sent the military to these areas ostensibly to quell an insurgency led by supporters of his political rival, Joshua Nkomo. However, these atrocities were actually aimed at crushing Mugabe's political opposition (Killander and Nyathi, 2015). Interestingly, though the Commonwealth had expelled Nigeria, Zimbabwe, Fiji, and Pakistan for less weighty human rights violations, it made no move to invoke its charter and numerous declarations or utter even the most tepid condemnations of the crimes against humanity perpetrated by the regime of President Paul Biya against English and Pidgin-speaking Southern Cameroons. In effect, in 1995, the Commonwealth Ministerial Action Group (CMAG) suspended military-ruled Nigeria from the Commonwealth for a 'serious violation of the principles set out in the Harare Declaration,' including the execution of political activist and writer Ken Saro-Wiwa and ten others in 1995. This suspension was a public declaration from the Commonwealth of Nations to the Nigerian government and the international community, condemning the undemocratic and human rights abuses which reverberated across the world (Nigeria Suspended from the Commonwealth, 1995). Nigeria was reinstated in 1999 after it returned to civilian rule. In 1999, Pakistan was suspended after a military takeover of the government. It was readmitted in 2004 only to be suspended again in 2007 after President Pervez Musharraf declared a state of emergency and sacked top judges. The suspension was lifted in 2008.

In 2002 Zimbabwe was suspended from the Commonwealth of Nations after electoral observers found the country's 2001 elections to be flawed and marred by politically motivated violence. Zimbabwe was suspended in 2002 for breaching the Harare Declaration. In 2003, when the Commonwealth refused to lift the suspension, Zimbabwe withdrew from the Commonwealth (Zimbabwe is suspended from the councils of the Commonwealth, 2002). In 1987, Fiji was suspended from the Commonwealth after the military, led by General Sitiveni Rabuka, overthrew the civilian government, deposed Queen Elizabeth as Head of State, and declared Fiji a republic. This occurred in the context of ethnic tensions between Indigenous Fijians and Hindi-speaking Indo-Fijians. Fiji was reinstated in 1997 after it adopted a republican constitution in line with the Commonwealth's shared principles of democracy and good governance. However, on September 1, 2009, the Commonwealth Secretary-General, Kamalesh Sharma, announced that the Republic of the Fiji Islands stood fully suspended from membership of the Commonwealth of Nations with immediate effect. Fiji's suspension occurred because the military overthrew the civilian government in December 2006, and the Commonwealth urged the military "to promote a return to constitutional democracy and to encourage a national dialogue aimed at tackling the underlying issues that led to this and past coups." The Commonwealth Ministerial Action Group (CMAG) urged the Fiji military regime "to reactivate immediately the President's Political Dialogue Forum (PPDF) process, facilitated by the Commonwealth and the United Nations, in a manner that was independent, inclusive, time-bound and without any pre-determined outcome, and that would lead to credible elections in the country by October 2010...failing which it would be fully suspended." Fiji did not comply and so was suspended (Fiji suspended from the Commonwealth, 2009). Fiji was reinstated in 2014 after parliamentary elections (BBC, 2014). In Cameroon, in the face of massive human rights violations in the former British Southern Cameroons, The British High Commissioner, His Excellency Rowan James Laxton, played the ostrich!

The Commonwealth and the Cameroon Human Rights Exception

History shows that the British Commonwealth of Nations has a track record of suspending member-states who violate its shared democracy, good governance, and human rights principles. However, Cameroon is the exception. The autocratic Biya regime escaped even the most tepid censure and condemnation from the British Commonwealth. We have seen that the Commonwealth Human Rights Initiative (CHRI), joined by multiple Commonwealth, international, and regional civil society groups (see list in the CHRI Submission in the appendix) drew the attention of the Commonwealth Ministerial Action Group (CMAG) to the well-documented human rights violations and crimes against humanity committed by the Israeli and American trained and equipped BIR and other units of the Cameroon military and security forces trained, armed and equipped by France, China, and the United Kingdom. The Commonwealth Human Rights Initiative (CHRI) and the international human rights community concluded unequivocally that the Government of Cameroon, a member of the Commonwealth, was in breach of the Commonwealth Charter, the Latimer House Principles, and the Harare Declaration. (Commonwealth Human Rights Initiative Submission to the Commonwealth Ministerial Action Group (CMAG) (2018). The Commonwealth Ministerial Action Group (CMAG) did not lift a finger. It did not add Cameron to its formal agenda as suggested by the CHRI. Nevertheless, the Commonwealth Secretary General, the Right Hon. Patricia Scotland, visited Cameroon in December 2017 and met with President Paul Biya, government officials, members of the Anglophone civil society in Buea, and even victims of the Anglophone crisis. Nothing came of the five-day visit. Two years later, the Chairperson of the African Union Commission, Moussa Faki Mahamat, the Secretary-General of the International Organization of *la Francophonie*, Louise Mushikiwabo, and the Secretary General of the Commonwealth, Patricia Scotland, undertook a tripartite visit to Yaoundé, Cameroon, from 26 to 28 November 2019, in order to exchange views with the national actors on the human rights situation in Cameroon, which is a member-state of the three organizations. The purpose of the meeting was to resolve the Anglophone crisis. At the end of their visit, the leaders of the three organizations mouthed the deceptive talking points of the Biya regime. They declared that they:

> welcomed the convening of the Grand National Dialogue which ushered

in a new dynamic and which recommended, inter alia, the acceleration of decentralization, the special status of the North West and South West regions, and the review of the education and legal systems, including the measures taken by President Biya to defuse political tensions" (Joint Declaration of the Tripartite Visit to Cameroon, 2019).

Figure 18.6. Chairperson of the African Union Commission, Moussa Faki Mahamat, the Secretary-General of the *Organization Internationale de la Francophonie*, Louise Mushikiwabo, and the Secretary General of the Commonwealth, Patricia Scotland, undertook a tripartite visit to Yaoundé, Cameroon, from 26 to 28 November 2019

The Grand National Dialogue turned out to be a sham that President Paul Biya did not even bother to attend. Its recommendation that the former British Southern Cameroons (the Northwest and Southwest regions) be offered a "special status" turned out to be nothing but deceptive rhetoric aimed at reinforcing the untenable, over-centralized Napoleonic status quo. Effective decentralization never took place. This is demonstrated by the fact that on August 10, 2021, five years after the Anglophone Revolt, the French Cameroon Minister of Decentralization and Local Development, George Elanga Obam, went to Buea to commemorate "the joint celebrations of the 10th edition of the African Day of Decentralisation and Local Development and the 4th edition of the African day of Civil Registration and Vital Statistics." There was no mention of "special status or federalism" in his speech. Despite this celebration of decentralization, the elected Buea Council does not even have the power to name its own streets in the age of GPS. The streets have no official names. That is the prerogative of another government ministry in Yaoundé, the Ministry of Town Planning and Housing. In 2023, sixty-two years after reunification, Yaoundé has not given Buea, Bamenda, Victoria (Limbe), Kumba, and other towns, the authority to name their own streets! As for reforming and decentralizing the educational and legal systems, nothing changed. If anything, they got worse. In 2020, Minister of Higher Education, Jacques Fame Ndongo dismissed Felix Nkongho Agbor Balla, a human rights activist and professor of law at the University of Buea Faculty of Law for setting an examination question on the Anglophone crisis, which the government considered "seditious" (Fatunde, 2020; Lawyers' Rights Watch Canada, 2020). Felix Nkongho Agbor Balla, had been arrested, jailed, and tried at the Yaoundé Military Tribunal under draconian, anti-terrorism laws for being one of the leaders of the Anglophone Civil Society Consortium (see Chapter 27.) Other Anglophone professors have faced a similar fate. The result was a climate of fear that chilled academic freedom at the Universities of Buea, Bamenda, Yaoundé, and elsewhere.

Erosion of the Rule of Law and Legal Protections in Southern Cameroons

The power of the courts in the Southwest and Northwest were further eroded as peaceful demonstrators and suspected sympathizers of federalism or secession were arrested, jailed for long periods without trial, or deported to Yaoundé for trial at the Yaoundé Military Tribunal. These points discussed by the Chairperson of the African Union Commission, Moussa Faki Mahamat, the Secretary-General of the International Organization of la Francophonie, Louise Mushikiwabo, and the Secretary General of the Commonwealth, Patricia Scotland, were recitations of the bad faith talking points put out by the Biya regime to deceive the international community, buy time to subjugate the former British Southern Cameroons and maintain the untenable status quo. The underlying issues of Anglophone marginalization, subalternity, and assimilation were never addressed. The Cameroon government actually reinforced its war of subjugation of the former British Southern Cameroons after this visit. None of the three organizations that visited President Paul Biya in Yaoundé did anything further. The war in Anglophone Cameroon took a turn for the worse as Anglophone separatists obtained more arms and developed improvised explosive device technologies that effectively neutralized Cameroon security force attacks and prolonged the conflict.

Post-Brexit British Transnational Corporate and Development Finance Capitalism in Cameroon

The British Empire was sustained by global trade. Britain no longer dominates world trade as it did in the 19th and early 20th centuries. Brexit, the process of British departure from the European Union that began when the majority of British voters decided in 2016, to leave the European Union single market and customs union, complicated matters. As the post-Brexit referendum UK–the UK officially left the European Union on January 31, 2020 – scurried about looking for trade partners to replace its European Union single market preferential trade partners, it jettisoned the human rights trappings of its global trade regime. The authoritarian republican chieftaincy of Cameroon was the first beneficiary of this "human rights waiver." The reason for the UK and the British Commonwealth's failure to follow its own precedent and treat the authoritarian, kleptocratic government of Cameroon as it had treated Nigeria, Zimbabwe, Pakistan, and Fiji when they violated Commonwealth norms is not hard to determine. Brexit had changed the human rights and good governance posture of the Commonwealth. The UK was in national survival mode and desperately needed trade and economic partners to fill the void created when it left the European Union. It soon deployed its model of international development finance capitalism to meet this perceived strategic need. With its natural capital–oil, natural gas, hydro-electric power, agricultural and forest resources–and they happened to be located mostly in Southern Cameroons–the Biya regime offered British government-owned investment funds, and British companies multiple investment and trade opportunities. Cameroon became an important component of Africa's post-Brexit British trade and economic policy. Human rights and good governance suddenly became less important than British national interests. The British embrace of the Biya regime despite its horrendous human rights atrocities against Anglophones in the former British Southern Cameroons, can be contrasted with the posture of the Trump Administration which decried the human rights violations and sent a letter to Congress informing it that he had decided to terminate the designation of the Republic of Cameroon as a beneficiary sub-Saharan African country under the African Growth and Opportunity Act (AGO) (see appendix XII).

London-based Perenco

The London-based, Anglo-French multi-national oil and natural gas exploration and production company, Perenco, which calls itself a leading independent oil and natural gas company, has been operating in Cameroon since 1993 in close partnership with Paul Biya's "national" oil company, *the Société Nationale des Hydrocarbures* (National Hydrocarbons Company, SNH). The exploration and producing operations of Perenco in Cameroon are based around concessions in Rio del Rey (Southern Cameroons), Moudi and Ebome, and elsewhere. These activities made Perenco the largest oil and natural gas producer in Cameroon with an operating area in the vast Rio del Rey and Douala basins, with oil and gas production of 51,000 barrels per day and 24 million m^3 of gas per day in 2018 (Perenco, Cameroon, 2018). It stores crude oil in floating offshore storage and offloading units, which are shipped to commodities traders, refiners, and other market players. Perenco's floating offshore natural gas projects power electricity stations in Kribi (Perenco, Cameroon, 2018). Perenco also partners with SNH, the Swiss conglomerate, Glencore and others. The notorious, Israeli-trained, and armed special forces, BIR, is funded directly by oil and natural gas revenues and operates as the protection force for the oil industry against pirates in the Gulf of Guinea and the Bight of Biafra in West Africa. Given this major British corporate stake in President Biya's oil and natural gas industry, the British High Commissioner had to protect British interest by kowtowing to the African republican chieftain and turning a blind eye to the former British Southern Cameroons.

British Transnational Corporate Capitalism in Cameroon

Bickering among the local subsidiaries of British transnational corporations doing business in Cameroon revealed the scope of British partnership with the kleptocratic Biya regime, and explains the Machiavellian posture of British High Commissioner, HE Rowan James Laxton, with respect to President Paul Biya. On July 3, 2020, Regulatory News Service (RNS), the news service of the London Stock Exchange, published a routine company press release entitled, "Victoria Oil & Gas Plc ("VOG" or the "Company") Termination of Agreement to Supply Gas to ENEO." This was the sort of material that interests international stock traders and investors in the United Kingdom, and perhaps the European Union. The press release informed the world that the British Company, "Victoria Oil & Gas Plc, had a wholly-owned African subsidiary, Gaz du Cameroun S.A. ("GDC"), an onshore gas producer and distributor with operations located in the port city of Douala, in

Cameroon. The release further stated that Victoria Oil & Gas was terminating its gas sales agreement with Actis Energy Cameroon Holdings, which is commonly known as ENEO Cameroon S.A. ("ENEO"), the Cameroon national electricity corporation. Victoria Oil & Gas stated that the reason for terminating its gas supply agreement with ENEO was that its subsidiary, Gaz du Cameroun S.A. ("GDC") had supplied natural gas to Actis Energy Cameroon Holdings (ENEO) since 2015 "despite ENEO's poor payment record," and that GDC had "made repeated requests in writing and in person to the senior management of ENEO to discuss a method of settlement of its burgeoning debt, which now stands at US$16 million receivables (US$9 million net to GDC) as at the end of June 2020." Victoria Oil & Gas concluded that: "as a result of this untenable situation, GDC served a notice of Event of Default on ENEO, pursuant to the signed binding term sheet on 2 June 2020. GDC has no alternative but to terminate the gas supply agreement with immediate effect…The Company will now rigorously pursue this unpaid debt via the legal channels available to it, including a penalty payment of three months' fees as a result of termination as per the signed term sheet." This very strong language and action suggested a scenario in which a British company, Victoria Oil & Gas, and its wholly owned Cameroon subsidiary, GDC were cutting off gas supplies to an inefficient, cash-strapped African national electric company, ENEO Cameroon, which had failed to pay its debts.

However, there was more to the Victoria Oil & Gas versus ENEO imbroglio than met the eye. While the decision by Gaz du Cameroun to suspend further supplies of natural gas to ENEO might look like a clash between a British company, and an inefficient Cameroon government utility that was having a hard time paying its bills to its creditors, that is not the case at all. In its much-publicized press release announcing the termination of its gas supply agreement with Actis Energy Cameroon Holdings (ENEO), Victoria Oil & Gas emphasized that the majority stakeholder (51%) of ENEO was actually a British investment company, Actis Group. Actis is a leading British fund manager previously owned by the Commonwealth Development Corporation (CDC) Group. The main role of Actis as a fund manager is to promote and manage funds invested in emerging markets on behalf of investors. Its single biggest investor is the CDC Group, which is itself wholly owned by the British government through its Department for International Development (DFID). Actis works with the CDC to manage DFID investments in Africa. Thus, through the Actis Group and the Commonwealth Development Corporation, the government of the United Kingdom and British taxpayers have a majority stake in Actis Energy Cameroon Holdings (ENEO). This disagreement was thus a business disagreement between two British entities in Cameroon. This unusual British majority ownership of natural gas and electricity utilities in the authoritarian, neo-patrimonial, kleptocratic, Francophone country whose president had been in power for 40 years and had a horrendous record of human rights violations is not inconsistent with British postcolonial, post-Brexit foreign policy. British international trade policy has always been driven by national self-interest rather than the norms, values, and niceties of human rights. The British posture in Cameroon is consistent with long-standing British foreign policy. In effect, the Commonwealth Development Corporation (CDC), the postcolonial development finance institution of the United Kingdom was founded in 1948 with the motto: "We support economic growth and deliver a return for the UK taxpayer." This policy has been given a note of urgency by British exit from the European Union. Today, the CDC describes itself as a public limited company "Our only share-holder is the Department for International Development (DFID)" (Our Company, 2020). Through ACTIS, the CDC, which is wholly owned by the DFID, invested $202 million US dollars in the Cameroon national electricity utility company ENEO in 2014, buying out the American company, AES, which had operated the Cameroon government's inefficient and unreliable national electricity corporation, *Société national d'éléctricté* (AES SONEL). The CDC/ACTIS investment also included two electric power plants in Kribi and Dibamba (CDC Invests Up to $20m in power in Cameroon, 2014).

What emerges from the much-publicized financial tussle between Victoria Oil & Gas of London and ENEO is thus the clash between two British corporate entities – a public company, and a British "governmental" international fund manager, in the Cameroon market. The Victoria Oil & Gas/Gaz du Cameroun suspension of gas supplies to Actis Energy Cameroon Holdings (ENEO) was because Victoria Oil & Gas had signed a gas sales agreement with ENEO in 2014 to supply natural gas to two power stations, which contributed 30 MW of electricity to ENEO's national grid (Victoria Oil & Gas, 2014).

This suspension of gas supplies to ENEO, did not come as a surprise to electricity consumers in Cameroon. ENEO is notoriously unreliable in supplying electricity to its close to one million customers in the country of 25 million people. To complicate things further for ENEO, the government of Cameroon, which owns 44% of the company, used the company to meet certain goals set by the International Monetary Fund (IMF) as part of a structural adjustment program called the "Extended Credit Facility Supported Programme." This program supported the financial inclusion of the small and medium-scale enterprises (SMEs) sector, mostly suppliers, in ENEO's business activities to ensure private sector-driven growth (ENEO Adopts Supply Finance Solution to Keep Cameroon's Lights On, 2018).

Actis Energy Cameroon Holdings (ENEO) and the Realities of the Cameroon Energy Market

We note above that Victoria Oil and Gas of London instructed its wholly owned Cameroonian subsidiary, Gaz du Cameroun, to stop supplying Actis Cameroon Holdings (ENEO) due to ENEO's failure to pay its natural gas bills in Cameroon. There are multiple reasons why Actis Energy Cameroon Holdings (ENEO), the beneficiary of investments from the Commonwealth Development Corporation (CDC) and the Cameroon government, was having problems meeting its financial obligations to Victoria Oil & Gas Plc/Gaz du Cameroun. ENEO's cash-flow problems were due in part to a lack of sufficient funding to invest in the improvement of Cameroon's anemic energy distribution infrastructure after the government imposed a politically motivated electricity tariff cap that prevented the company from raising prices (ENEO Adopts Supply Finance Solution to Keep Cameroon's Lights On, 2018). Many of ENEO's customers were also unable to pay their electricity bills on time for one reason or another. Furthermore, the poor service record and unreliability of ENEO's predecessors, the American-Cameroonian duo, AES *Société Nationale d'Electricité* (SONEL), left a residue of dissatisfaction, ill-will and hostility on the part of customers.

On July 20, 2020, Jean-Pascal Nkou, the Director General of the *Agence de Régulation du Secteur de l'Électricité* (Electricity Sector Regulatory Agency, ARSEL), the electricity regulator of Cameroon, went on Cameroon national television, CRTV, to talk about the persistent problem of the unreliability of electricity supplies in the country, and persistent outages due to load-shedding. Nkou stated that the major problem is that the electric power sector is faced with massive electricity fraud and power theft that had led to an emergency situation (ENEO, 2020). He said electricity fraud caused ENEO, whose majority owner was the British entity, Actis Energy Cameroon Holdings (ENEO), to lose more than 60 billion CFA Francs ($110 million US dollars) every year: "Fraud leads to more load shedding of entire neighborhoods, instead of the disconnection of isolated defaulting customers. Load shedding could, in some cases, cause social upheavals… 70% of honest customers suffer from the activities of 30% of dishonest customers or consumers…" (ENEO, 2020). According to Jean Pascal Nkou, electricity theft and fraud take the form of illegal connections to the electricity network, illegally using disconnected lines, or reprogramming electricity meters to falsify the amount of electricity consumed: "The result is a huge disequilibrium between the cost of electricity produced and supplied and the revenues obtained from the supply of that electricity. The amount of energy consumed is greater than the revenues collected for that supply. Regular clients suffer from poor service due to these fraudulent actions," Nkou concluded (ENEO, 2020). These fraudulent activities, which are carried out by persons outside ENEO with the connivance of some workers of the company, caused Actis Energy Cameroon Holdings (ENEO) to have the same problem of unreliable electricity supplies and consumer ill-will as its predecessor, AES SONEL.

The ARSEL Director General's claim that a full 30% of Actis Energy Cameroon Holdings (ENEO) consumers fraudulently consumed electricity is undoubtedly remarkable but not surprising. Cameroon is a country of the rule of man rather than the rule of law. The outcome is law and disorder where the law – and presidential decrees are the largest source of law in Cameroon – trump rights. In effect, ENEO is experiencing the impact of what Cameroonian economist, Célestin Monga (1996, p. 110-111) called the "anthropology of anger." Monga noted that in the face of authoritarianism, political repression, disrespect of the law on the part of the authorities, massive corruption, human rights violations, injustice, and misappropriation of public resources by agents of the kleptocratic republican chiefdom of Cameroon, many Cameroonians have developed a "life (saving) strategy of resistance" that includes the development of informal "sites of protest." These sites are "powerful vectors of collective insubordination." Government or public "property" is one of the "sites of protest," par excellence. Citizens who see that the ruling elite use their positions to misappropriate public funds and property, amass massive wealth through corruption, while disregarding the welfare of the people, "create counternarratives against the prevailing official discourse." Electricity fraud in Cameroon is a form of civil disobedience, a site of resistance against the ruling, neo-patrimonial kleptocracy. The idea is that if the ruling political elite, who live in areas with the most stable electricity and do not pay electricity bills, expect ordinary citizens to pay for unreliable electricity, which the "big men" get for free, it is unacceptable. Therefore, it is only normal for ordinary citizens to help themselves with this "public" resource. President Paul Biya is the perfect example of the regime's lack of transparency and accountability. The reclusive and out-of-touch President and his family spend months on end in the lap of luxury at the presidential suite of the British-owned Intercontinental Hotel in Geneva, Switzerland, while 40% of the people of Cameroon live under the poverty line, and most parts of the country have no electricity, no clean drinking water, no schools worth the name, and no basic health services. To the ordinary citizen, siphoning off "government" electricity becomes an act of resistance against Paul Biya's kleptocracy.

Actis Energy Cameroon Holdings (ENEO) did not bargain for or quite understand the politico-cultural realities and vicissitudes of the authoritarian neo-patrimonial regime of Cameroon, a simple country where everything is complicated by greed, corruption, abuse of power, and tribalism. For starters, ENEO is a statutorily semi-public utility in Cameroon. Despite the fact that the Commonwealth Development Corporation (CDC) owns the majority shares in ENEO, it has to work within the rule-by-decree framework of the Biya autocracy. The Ahidjo/Biya neo-patrimonial regime uses public companies to exercise political and ethnic patronage, and repress minorities, especially the English and Pidgin-speaking population in the former British Trust Territory of Southern Cameroons. The government shut off electricity, mobile telephony, and the Internet in the Northwest and Southwest regions at the onset of the Anglophone Revolt in 2016 and 2017.

Other British Corporate and Development Finance Capitalist Ventures in Cameroon

One of the most indelible and embarrassing images of the Biya presidency involved the luxurious presidential limousine. On 20th May 2016, President Biya's motorcade drove from the presidential palace in Yaoundé, to the ceremonial grandstand at the Boulevard du 20 Mai in grand pomp, led and flanked by military motorcycle escort riders in gleaming uniforms and expensive European motorcycles. The presidential limousine stopped at the grandstand. President Paul Biya descended and shook hands with the military's top brass as an officer barked orders to soldiers lined on either side of the grandstand. The president then walked towards the grandstand to take his seat among waiting dignitaries and members of the diplomatic corps. The presidential limousine, which was supposed to be parked at a designated location at the side of the grandstand till the end of the ceremony and parade, stood motionless in front of the grandstand. It had broken down. All attempts by the driver to restart the car proved futile. Members of the presidential guard rushed to the limousine and strained to push it out of sight as embarrassed government officials looked on helplessly. The official Cameroon government media, Cameroon Radio and Television (CRTV), which was covering the event live, panned away from the embarrassing image. Nevertheless, individuals in the crowd took pictures of the event and posted them on social media platforms, where commenters had a field day portraying the stalled limousine as the perfect visual metaphor of the Biya regime.

Figure 18.7. President Biya's stalled limousine, Boulevard du 20 Mai, May 20, 2016

Another limousine was rushed to the scene, and the president used it to inspect the guard of honor mounted by the Cameroon military. This was not the first time the presidential limousine had broken down (*Le Monde*, 2016). In response to this embarrassment, President Paul Biya acquired a Klassen Stretched Range Rover, a luxury, armored presidential limousine worth almost $1.5 million. This vehicle was unveiled at the National Day celebrations in 2018. Range Rover is, of course, a British automobile company that grants Klassen, a German manufacturer, a license to create "stretch," armored, luxury versions of its vehicles.

Figure 18.8. President Biya in his Klassen Stretched, armored, presidential Range Rover (unveiled 2018)

In 2018, two years after the start of the Anglophone Revolt and the massive human rights violations of the Biya regime in the former British Southern Cameroons, the Commonwealth Development Corporation (CDC) again invested €90m as part of a €1.26 billion financing program for the Nachtigal hydroelectric dam over the Sanaga river in Francophone Cameroon. Other Nachtigal project sponsors are *Electricité de France* (EDF), the International Finance Corporation (a member of the World Bank Group), and the Government of Cameroon (CDC backs transformational Nachtigal power generation project in

Cameroon with €90m investment, 2018). Additionally, the Commonwealth Development Corporation is invested in renewable energy in Cameroon through Cameroon Hydro, a division of the Africa Renewable Energy Fund managed by Berkeley Energy, a British multinational renewable energy investment company (Cameroon Hydro, 2020). The CDC is also involved in microfinance in Cameroon through Advans Cameroon, which Horus Development Finance manages (Advans Cameroon, 2020). Advans Capital is headquartered in Luxembourg. The CDC is also invested in Soproicam, a soya bean processing company in Cameroon through AFIG Fund II LP, which is managed by Advanced Finance and Investment Group. British development finance capitalism in Cameroon has no qualms about the human rights violations of its partner, the Biya regime. In June 2019, the CDC announced the launching of a new company, Gridworks, to invest over $300 million in long-term capital in electricity infrastructures and networks across Africa. ENEO will be one of the recipients of this new investment (CDC Launches new Company, Gridworks, 2019). In Cameroon, the interests of British corporate and Commonwealth development finance capitalism clearly trump human rights considerations.

Le Port Autonome de Limbe (The Limbe Autonomous Port)

In 1998, President Paul Biya signed a presidential decree creating four "autonomous ports" in Cameroon: Limbe, Douala, Kribi and Garoua. In 2020, he signed another presidential decree in French, modifying the 1998 decree and setting forth the statutes of *le Port Autonome de Limbe (PAL),* the Autonomous Port of Limbe, in the English and Pidgin-speaking, Southern Cameroons town that had been founded by British missionary, Rev. Alfred Saker in 1858 and named Victoria, after Queen Victoria of England (Nsangou, 2020). Biya's 2020 presidential decree once again ignored the cultural specificity of Victoria/Limbe. The people of the Southwest region were not consulted, and their input was not sought regarding the creation or management of this "autonomous port." The autocratic Biya regime demonstrated once again that it had learned nothing from the Anglophone Revolt of 2016. Ironically, after the signature of the presidential decree, Gaz du Cameroun, the wholly owned subsidiary of Victoria Oil & Gas Plc of London, was designated as the industrial partner of the *Port Autonome de Limbe.* As discussed earlier, Limbe had been chosen as the production and distribution center for the New Age LNG's Floating Liquefied Natural Gas (FLNG) project. In 2018, New Age LNG had signed a gas convention agreement (GCA) with the Cameroun Government to build the Floating Liquefied Natural Gas (FLNG) project in the Etinde Offshore block, off the coast of Limbe in Southern Cameroons. It was then announced that the Floating Liquified Natural Gas project would be developed in conjunction with an upstream Etinde development, including natural gas and natural gas liquid production facilities in Limbe. The plant was designed to supply natural gas to customers in Douala and other parts of Cameroon (Oil Voice Press, 2018). Victoria Oil & Gas/Gaz du Cameroun was selected to be in charge of the gas production and distribution facility at the *Port Autonome de Limbe.*

British Rare Earth Minerals Exploration in Cameroon

As rare earth minerals have become strategic natural resources used in the production of titanium metal as well as other chemical elements used in the global manufacturing of cell phones, electric cars, and tens of other products, the global search for these minerals has become a very competitive affair. Chinese and European companies scour the African continent, looking for commercial quantities of rutile sands that contain these strategic chemicals. The Central region of Cameroon has rich mineral sand deposits that include rutile and other rare earth minerals. On 30 December 2019, BWA Group plc, a British minerals exploration investment company specializing in rare earth exploration and mining, announced that its wholly owned subsidiary, BWA Resources (Cameroon) Limited, had been awarded an exploration license for rutile sands and related rare earth minerals in Nkoteng, an area covering 497 square kilometers. BWA Group plc was awarded a second rare earth mining exploration permit in Cameroon in January 2020 (Battersby, 2020). The Northwest region of Cameroon is also known to contain rare earth and other minerals. Exploration of that region has been halted by the Anglophone crisis and the resultant civil war.

Military Cooperation

Another concrete demonstration of the UK's strategic partnership with *La République du Cameroun*, despite its horrendous human rights record, was an agreement entered into between Marshall Aerospace and Defence Group (ADG) of Cambridge, UK, and the Government of Cameroon. Under the terms of the agreement, Marshall Aerospace and Defence Group was to provide aircraft maintenance, technical support, and training to the Cameroon Air Force's fleet of 3 American-made, C-130H Hercules aircraft, as part of a five-year contract approved by the *Ministre Délégué à la Présidence, chargé de la Défense* (Minister Delegate at the Presidency in charge of Defense), Beti Assomo. The agreement was signed in Yaoundé by Marshall ADG Sales Director, Matthew Harvey, and Brigadier General Jean-Calvin Momha, Chief of Air Staff of the Cameroon Air Force. Marshall ADG CEO, Alistair McPhee, said of the agreement: "We are delighted that the Cameroon Air Force selected our tender as the most competitive solution to deliver support to the operations of their C-130 fleet" (Marshall Group, 2020). Marshall ADG seemed to be completely oblivious to the fact that this was yet another strategic decision made by the repressive Biya regime to bribe the British government into turning a blind eye to the human rights violations in its former Trust Territory of Southern Cameroons. Marshall Aerospace and Defence Group (ADG) essentially became, with the full support of the British High Commissioner in Yaoundé and the British government, a cold-eyed, self-interested partner in crimes against humanity in Anglophone Cameroon. To the British, dubious but lucrative corporate business deals trump human rights responsibilities.

Conclusion

The Anglophone crisis in Cameroon is one of the last pieces of unfinished business from World War I. Historically, the British have a Machiavellian attitude towards Southern Cameroons, which was never a British colonial territory or protectorate. Britain came into colonial governance of these territories carved out of German Kamerun "enemy territories" after the defeat of the *Schutztruppen,* Germany's African colonial corps during World War I. The Cameroons territories were thus spoils of war. This partition of German Kamerun took place in the context of European imperial rivalries, balance of power, and compensatory diplomacy, whereby the victorious countries (Britain and France) granted each other territorial concessions in one geographic region of Africa in order to gain territories in another. Under British compensatory diplomacy, German Kamerun enemy lands which British and French armies had conquered, were essentially bargaining chips (Elango, 2015). The British conceded the lion's share (four-fifths) of German Kamerun to France in order to keep the French, who had colonized Madagascar, from demanding a share of German East Africa (Tanganyika) and German Southwest Africa (Namibia). The British Cameroons territories were thus mere territorial pawns in the Anglo-French geo-strategic, colonial chessboard (Elango, 2015). As a result of the prevailing Wilsonian ideal of self-determination, the British and French Cameron territories did not become direct colonial annexations as the British and French had wanted. Instead, the territories were transformed into League of Nations mandates under provisions of the Treaty of Versailles of 1919. The idea of the mandates was that the British and the French were required to act as disinterested trustees of the "enemy lands" they had conquered from Germany. Britain ended up with two "strips of territory" which did not even touch each other (Ardener, 1962). It further partitioned the territory into Northern and Southern Cameroons for purposes of administering them via Nigeria, to strengthen the border of its Nigerian colonial protectorate, as well as shore up traditional feudal Hausa-Fulani kingdoms in Northern Nigeria and create a semblance of regional balance with the South. As the UN Mandate came to an end in 1961, the British denied the people of the Cameroons territories the right of self-determination. Through flawed UN plebiscites, they succeeded in transferring Northern Cameroons to Nigeria's federation. Attempts to transfer Southern Cameroons to the Nigerian federation failed. Southern Cameroons leaders had "seceded" from the Eastern Region of Nigeria in 1953 in protest at the second-class citizenship they were relegated to in Nigeria. This resulted in the emergence of an autonomous Southern Cameroons, whose citizens voted to join *la République du Cameroun* in the 1961 plebiscite. The transfer of the Northern Cameroons territory from German colonial rule to British colonial rule and ultimately to Nigerian annexation, where it became a neglected, economically backward territory partitioned among multiple states, is the indirect cause of the Boko Haram crisis in Northern Nigeria. The transfer of Southern Cameroons from German colonial rule to indirect British colonial rule through Eastern Nigeria and ultimately to direct annexation by *la République du Cameroun*, where the Ahidjo-Biya regime engaged in a multi-prong strategy to assimilate the English-and Pidgin-speaking Southern Cameroonians into *la Francophonie*, ignoring the fact that the English-and Pidgin-speaking Southern Cameroonians had centuries-long linguistic and identitarian proximities with the Anglosphere.

British relations with its former UN Trust Territory of Southern Cameroons has been a series of engagements and disengagements, a veritable cascade of historical ironies, continuities and discontinuities. After the discovery of reserves of oil and natural gas off the coast of what used to be British Southern Cameroons, the governments of *La République du Cameroun* and France accelerated their policy of assimilating the English-and Pidgin-speaking Southern Cameroons into *la Francophonie*. This triggered an identitarian and cultural resistance on the part of the English and Pidgin-speaking Cameroonians for whom oil and other natural resources had become nothing but a curse. The resistance was led by lawyers, teachers, students, and churches. Given a choice between the English and Pidgin-speaking people of the former British Trust Territory of Southern Cameroons, and Biya's kleptocratic *la République du Cameroun*, which ironically had control of, and was using the natural resources of Southern Cameroons for its strategic survival, post-Brexit Britain chose to side with the oppressive Biya regime and overlook its gross human rights violations. This essentially made the Britain of Prime Ministers Theresa May and especially Boris Johnson, a partner in crimes against humanity with the Biya regime of *la République du Cameroun.* In effect, the post-Brexit United Kingdom and the authoritarian *Republique du Cameroun* have a symbiotic partnership that demonstrates an African reality - the natural resource curse. It is all about money and natural resources. Southern Cameroons is rich in natural resources – oil, natural gas, forestry, rare minerals, and other resources that President Biya personally controls. He uses revenues accruing therefrom in the most personal and extravagant manner. He strategically grants corporations from France, the United Kingdom, China, and Russia (all members of the United Nations Security Council), as well as his favorite European destination, Switzerland, and his national security partner, Israel, licenses to exploit these natural resources. The proceeds are used to fund an opaque Israeli-trained and equipped national and communications security apparatus made up of his praetorian guard, *la garde présidentielle*, and a brutal tribal army within the army, *le Bataillon d'Intervention Rapide* (BIR), special forces whose main task is to suppress political opposition of any kind and maintain President Biya in power for life. President Biya and his cronies live extraordinarily extravagant lifestyles. He spends months at a time at the British-owned InterContinental Hotel in Geneva, Switzerland, while more than 40% of Cameroonians languish in poverty. While oil and natural gas as well as agricultural and forestry products enrich President Paul Biya, his son, Frank Biya, and the political elite in Yaoundé through political and economic patronage, the people of the English and Pidgin-speaking Southern Cameroons, where these natural resources are found lack the basic necessities: clean drinking water, health centers, schools, roads, etc. For their part, the British need the oil, natural gas, and other business relationships with the kleptocratic republican chieftaincy of Cameroon to offset business lost in Europe due to its exit from the European Union single market and customs union. For the UK, it is Britannia über alles! This explains why the British have acted with steely disregard for the crimes against humanity committed in the former British Trust Territory of Southern Cameroons. Linguistic and cultural romanticism and sentimentality have no place in the geopolitical calculus of national interest. British national interest is, therefore, the driver of British partnership with the despotic regime in Yaoundé. It is a symbiotic relationship. The Biya regime needs the British stamp of respectability. The Biya dictatorship needs British support to maintain its membership in the British Commonwealth despite violating all the good governance tenets of the Commonwealth. But then, the British Commonwealth exists primarily to serve British interests. The Biya regime needed British support in the United

Nations Security Council to ward off calls for international intervention and sanctions against the regime and its henchmen. This explains why the British government and the British Commonwealth have essentially turned a blind eye and a deaf ear to the horrendous atrocities and crimes against humanity perpetrated by the Biya regime in the former British Southern Cameroons. Hon. Rowan James Laxton, became a participant in President Biya's bad-faith practice of deceiving the international community to fund its war against "terrorism," which was actually a genocidal "final," bloody, military solution – complete with crimes against humanity – to the justified political demands of the Anglophone minority in Cameroon (Roberts & Burton, 2020). The foreign policy of the post-Brexit government of the United Kingdom is characterized by the triumph of national economic self-interest over international norms of human rights.

British High Commissioner to Cameroon, Rowan James Laxton's sanctimonious celebration of the Biya dictatorship, while totally disregarding its crimes against humanity in the former British Southern Cameroons was clearly Machiavellian. Nay, the man had a whiff of Neville Chamberlain about him. After meeting President Biya, the elated and animated British ambassador sounded like British Prime Minister, Neville Chamberlain, who handed over the Sudetenland region of Czechoslovakia to Hitler on March 30, 1938, in pursuance of his infamous policy of appeasement. British High Commissioner, Rowan James Laxton's appeasement of Biya did not end the Anglophone crisis in Cameroon. It certainly was not in the long-term British national interest because it put British imprimatur on Biya's atrocities and alienated the English and Pidgin-speaking minority of Southern Cameroons. In an ironic twist, changing market conditions affected the viability of the Etinde FLNG project (Lewis, 2019). The COVID-19 pandemic and the Anglophone Revolt, which the government had transformed into a war of subjugation of the English and Pidgin-speaking minority of Southern Cameroons, got in the way. The resulting escalation of the Anglophone separatist conflict into a so-called "popcorn" or improvised explosive device (IED) war created enough uncertainty to make international investors in the Floating Liquefied Natural Gas (FLNG) project pause. By December 2021, the project had not taken off.

Epilogue

In December 2022, the British Foreign Commonwealth and Development Office issued its corporate report entitled "Human Rights and Democracy: the 2021 Foreign, Commonwealth and Development Office Report" (2022). The report surveys human rights priority countries ranging from Afghanistan to Zimbabwe. The report does not mention Cameroon at all. The human rights violations that started with the Anglophone Revolt of 2016 in the former British Southern Cameroons and continue in the present were conspicuously absent from the report. It is as if the the submissions of the Commonwealth Human Rights Initiative on the massive human rights violations in Cameroon were imaginary narratives conjured by ChatGPT or Bard. It is as if the killings in the Northwest and Southwest regions had stopped, as if the 40-year republican monarchy of President Paul Biya had become a shining example of democracy, as if the Anglophone refugees in Nigeria did not exist. With respect to the inconvenient Anglophone Problem in Cameroon, history will record that

British Foreign Secretary, James Cleverly, Minister of Human Rights, Lord Tariq Ahmad of Wimbledon, and the British Commonwealth, demonstrated a remarkable case of willful blindness. G.K Chesterton's apt aphorism: "It isn't that they can't see the solution. It is that they can't see the [human rights] problem." Business is business. In Cameroon, the Commonwealth's human rights principles were blurred by the allure of the dream of British corporations benefitting from President Biya's 2030 [emergence] vision for Cameroon. History will record that an African dictator with natural resources, and a willingness to kill to subjugate the territory in which those natural resources are located, and stay in power for life, made a mockery of the British Commonwealth and its high-sounding, selectively applied, "human rights" principles. Rendezvous with His Excellency Rowan James Laxton in President Biya's palace in Yaoundé in 2030 to celebrate the advent of the "emergence."

References

Actis Energy Cameroon Holdings (Eneo) (2020). Commonwealth Development Corporation. Retrieved from: https://www.cdcgroup.com/en/our-impact/investment/actis-energy-cameroon-holdings-eneo/

Advans Cameroon (2020). Commonwealth Development Corporation. Retrieved from: https://www.cdcgroup.com/en/our-impact/underlying/advans-cameroon/

Amnesty International (2021). Cameroon: Witness testimony and satellite images reveal the scale of devastation in Anglophone regions, July 28. Retrieved from: https://www.amnesty.org/en/latest/news/2021/07/cameroon-satellite-images-reveal-devastation-in-anglophone-regions-2/

Ardener, S. (2005). Ardener's "Muted Groups": The genesis of an idea and its praxis. *Women and Language*, Vol. 28, (2), Pp. 50-54,72.

Benard, J-P. (1962). Confidential letter No. 27 of 8 January 1962. French Embassy Yaoundé, Cameroon. Arria-formula Meeting on the Humanitarian Situation in Cameroon (2019). What's in

Blue: Security Council Report, Retrieved from: https://www.whatsinblue.org/2019/05/arria-formula-meeting-on-the-humanitarian-situation-in-cameroon.php

Battersby, R. (2020). BWA Group PLC: Update on Cameroon Exploration License. *Bloomberg*, February 6. Retrieved from: https://www.bloomberg.com/press-releases/2020-02-06/bwa-group-plc-update-on-cameroon-exploration-licence

BBC Africa Eye (2018). Cameroon Burning: The Unseen War (Video documentary). Retrieved from: https://www.youtube.com/watch?v=ct_SLnAGDuM

BBC (2014). Profile: Commonwealth of Nations: Timeline. September 26. Retrieved from: https://www.bbc.com/news/world-africa-16908628

Calis, T. (2017). Cameroon shuts down the Internet for 240 days. *Techtribes*. Retrieved from: https://techtribes.org/cameroon-shuts-down-the-internet-for-240-days/

Cameroon Hydro (2020). Commonwealth Development Corporation Retrieved from: https://www.cdcgroup.com/en/our-impact/underlying/cameroon-hydro/

CDC Invests Up to $20m in power in Cameroon (2014). Commonwealth Development Corporation (June). Retrieved from: https://www.cdcgroup.com/en/news-insight/news/cdc-invests-up-to-us20m-in-power-in-cameroon/

CDC backs transformational Nachtigal power generation project in Cameroon with €90m investment (2018). Commonwealth Development Corporation https://www.cdcgroup.com/en/

news-insight/news/cdc-backs-transformational-nachtigal-power-generation-project-in-cameroon-with-e90-million-investment/

Centre for Human Rights and Democracy in Africa (CHRDA) and Raoul Wallenberg Centre for Human Rights, "Cameroon's Unfolding Catastrophe: Evidence of Human Rights Violations and Crimes against Humanity in the Anglophone Regions of Cameroon" (2019). Retrieved from: Online and www.rwhrc.org

Djarmaila, G. (2020). Situation sanitaire et sécuritaire: accord parfait entre Yaoundé et Londres (Health and Security Situation: Perfect Agreement between Yaoundé and London). *Cameroon Tribune*. July 24. Retrieved from: https://www.cameroontribune.cm/article.html/33838/en.html/situation-sanitaire-securitaire-accord-parfait-entre-yaounde-londres .universityworldnews.com/post.php?story=2020052516062646

Djialeu, A. (2021). *Fridolin Nke convoqué une deuxième fois par la Sécurité militaire* (Fridolin Nke summoned a second time by military security). *Actu Cameroun* (July 30). Retrieved from: https://actucameroun.com/2021/07/30/fridolin-nke-convoque-une-deuxieme-fois-par-la-securite-militaire/

Fatunde, T. (2020). Law Lecturer's Dismissal Over Exam Question Raises Concerns. *University World News* (Africa Edition). May 26.

Foreign, Commonwealth and Development Office (2022). Human rights and democracy: the 2021 Foreign, Commonwealth and Development Office report," Retrieved from: https://www.gov.uk/government/publications/human-rights-and-democracy-report-2021/human-rights-and-democracy-the-2021-foreign-commonwealth-development-office-report#chapter-5-human-rights-priority-countries

Ghazvinian, J. (2008). *Untapped: The Scramble for Africa's Oil.* Boston, MA. HMH Books.

Joint Declaration of the Tripartite Visit to Cameroon (2019). The Commonwealth (November 28). Retrieved from: https://thecommonwealth.org/media/news/joint-declaration-tripartite-visit-cameroon

Killander, M., & Nyathi, M. (2015). Accountability for the Gukurahundi atrocities in Zimbabwe thirty years on: Prospects and challenges. <i>*The Comparative and International Law Journal of Southern Africa*, </i> <i>48</i> (3), 463-487. Retrieved August 12, 2021, from http://www.jstor.org/stable/26203994

Kingsley, P. (2019). Life in an Internet Shutdown: Crossing Borders for Email and Contraband SIM Cards. *The New York Times*. September 2. Retrieved from: https://www.nytimes.com/2019/09/02/world/africa/internet

Lawyers' Rights Watch Canada (2020). Cameroon: Dismissal of human rights defender Mr. Felix Agbor Nkongho from University of Buea: Joint Letter [to President Biya]. June 10. Retrieved from: https://www.lrwc.org/cameroon-dismissal-of-human-rights-defender-mr-felix-agbor-nkongho-from-university-of-buea-joint-letter/

Marshall Group (2020). Marshall wins 5-year support contract with Cameroon Air Force. Cambridge Network, May 4. Retrieved from: https://www.cambridgenetwork.co.uk/news/marshall-wins-5-year-support-contract-cameroon-air-force

Monga, C. (1996). *The Anthropology of Anger: Civil Society and Democracy in Africa.* Boulder: Lynne Rienner Publishers.

Norwegian Refugee Council (2020). Africa is home to nine of ten of the world's most neglected crises. Retrieved from: https://www.nrc.no/news/2020/june/africa-is-home-to-nine-of-ten-of-the-most-neglected-crises/

OilVoice Press (2018). New Age Signs Gas Convention Agreement with Cameroon Government. https://oilvoice.com/Press/17976/New-Age-Signs-Gas-Convention-Agreement-with-Cameroon-Government

Our Company (2020). Commonwealth Development Corporation (CDC). Retrieved from: https://www.cdcgroup.com/en/about/our-company/

"Productive Meeting" with British High Commissioner (2020). Presidency of the Republic. July 23. Retrieved from: https://www.prc.cm/en/news/audiences/4457-productive-meeting-with-british-high-commissioner

The Commonwealth Charter (2013). Retrieved from: https://thecommonwealth.org/about-us/charterCommonwealth Cyber Declaration (2018). Retrieved from: https://thecommonwealth.org/commonwealth-cyber-declaration

The Harare Commonwealth Declaration, 1991 (Issued by Heads of Government in Harare, Zimbabwe) 20 October 1991 https://thecommonwealth.org/history-of-the-commonwealth/harare-commonwealth-declaration

The Law Society of England and Wales Trial Observation Report – Cameroon (2017). Case of Nkongho Felix Agbor Balla, Fontem Neba and others Hearing 27 April 2017, Military Tribunal Yaoundé. Retrieved from: https://www.lawsociety.org.uk/en/campaigns/international-rule-of-law/news/cameroon-trial-observation-report

Lewis, I. (2019). Etinde Gas Export Project hangs in doubt. Petroleum Economist (June 11). Retrieved from: PJSC "Lukoil"

Ngwang Gunme v. Cameroon, Comm. 266/2003, 26th ACHPR AAR Annex (Dec 2008 – May 2009)

New Age Looking to Seal the Deal for Etinde Gas (2020). Offshore Energy Today (February 5). Retrieved from: https://www.offshore-energy.biz/new-age-looking-to-seal-the-deal-for-etinde-gas-supply-with-victoria/

Nsangou, A. (2020). Port autonome de Limbe (Limbe Autonomous Port: Laws Updated). *Cameroon Tribune*, May 7. Retrieved from: https://www.cameroon-tribune.cm/article.html/32291/fr.html/port-autonome-de-limbe-les-textes-mis

Perenco Cameroon (2018). *Perenco Subsidiaries*. Retrieved from: https://www.perenco.com/subsidiaries/cameroon.

Phillipson, S. (1959). Report of the Financial, economic and administrative consequences to the Southern Cameroons of separation from the Federation of Nigeria. Lagos: British Protectorate and Colony of Nigeria. OCoLC)654552976. Retrieved from: https://www.worldcat.org/title/financial-economic-and-administrative-consequences-to-the-southern-cameroons-of-separation-from-the-federation-of-nigeria-report/oclc/34571687

Roberts, C. & Burton, B. (2020). Cameroon's Government is Deceiving the West While Diverting Foreign Aid. Foreign Policy, November 22. Retrieved from: https://foreignpolicy.com/2020/11/22/cameroons-government-is-deceiving-the-west-while-diverting-foreign-aid/#

Stinson, N. (2019). UK signs £1.5Billion trade deal as Brexit Britain expands on world stage. *Express News.* June 9. Retrieved from: https://www.express.co.uk/news/uk/971445/brexit-news-eu-uk-trade-deals-liam-fox-cameroon-trade-deal-india-turkey

The Commonwealth Human Rights Initiative (CHRI) (2018). Submission to the Commonwealth Ministerial Action Group (CMAG). Retrieved from: https://www.humanrightsinitiative.org/download/1537957787Cameroon%20CMAG%20submission.pdf

The World Bank (2011). The Changing Wealth of Nations: Measuring Sustainable Development in the New Millennium. Washington D.C., The World Bank Group. Retrieved from: https://issuu.com/world.bank.publications/docs/9780821384886

United Nations (2019). Arria-formula Meeting on the Humanitarian Situation in Cameroon (2019). What's in Blue: Security Council Report, Retrieved from: https://www.whatsinblue.org/2019/05/arria-formula-meeting-on-the-humanitarian-situation-in-cameroon.php

United Nations Security Council (2002). Working Methods Handbook: Background Note on the "Arria-Formula" Meetings of the Security Council Members. Informal Non-Paper of 25 October 2002, prepared by the United Nations Secretariat. Retrieved from: https://www.un.org/securitycouncil/content/background-note#:~:text=The%20%22Arria%2Dformula%20meetings%22%20are%20very%20informal%2C%20confidential,facilitators%20or%20convenors)%20believe%20it

Victoria Oil & Gas Plc (2014). Major Gas Sales Agreement Signed with ENEO Cameroon. Retrieved from: https://www.gazducameroun.com/major-gas-sales-agreement-signed-eneo-cameroon/

NINETEEN

The Swiss Connection in the Anglophone Crisis in Cameroon

Human Rights versus Capitalist Rites

LYOMBE EKO

On Friday, January 19, 2018, the Spokesman for the United Nations High Commission for Refugees (UNHCR), William Spindler, informed the world of Africa's latest humanitarian tragedy, the refugee crisis in Southern Cameroons. Speaking at a press briefing at the *Palais des Nations*, the United Nations headquarters in Geneva, Switzerland, Spindler told the world that more than ten thousand refugees (mostly women and children) had crossed the border from Cameroon to Nigeria and that, "Thousands more are among the population of unregistered Cameroonians in neighbouring states." (UN High Commission for Refugees, 2018). The refugees from the English and Pidgin-speaking Southern Cameroons, had either been forcefully expelled from their villages by President Biya's hand-picked *préfet*, Oum II Joseph, who had declared 15 villages in Manyu Division anti-insurgency theaters, no-go military zones which they had been ordered to vacate. The Francophone préfet, Oum II, had decreed that all residents of 15 named Manyu villages "relocate to safer neighbourhoods of their choices in the hours that follow, failure of which they will be treated as accomplices or perpetrators of ongoing criminal occurrences registered on security and defense forces" (Oum II, 2017). The announcement was broadcast on radio and created panic in all villages in Manyu. In a matter of hours, the Cameroon army had descended on Manyu and streams of villagers were fleeing for their lives to the Nigerian border with anything they could carry. They were fleeing murder, rape, arbitrary arrests, abductions, torture and other human rights violations carried out by the infamous, Israeli-trained and armed special forces, the *Bataillon d'Intervention Rapide* (BIR), the regular Cameroon army and the gendarmerie of the then 84-year-old authoritarian dictator, President Paul Biya, who had been in power for close to 40 years at that time.

Spindler's press conference will probably go down in history as the most ironic press conference in the history of the United Nations High Commission for Refugees and of

Switzerland. In effect, the humanitarian crisis that the United Nations High Commission for Refugees was announcing to the world was masterminded and set in motion at the Intercontinental Hotel in Geneva, Switzerland, a few blocks from the UN's Palais des Nations in Geneva, Switzerland, where the press conference was taking place. The irony was completely lost on William Spindler, United Nations Diplomats, the Republic and Canton of Geneva, the Swiss Federal government, the Swiss press, the international aid industry and especially the indolent, complacent, and superficial international media. The facts that Mr. Spindler, the United Nations, the Swiss Federal government, the Republic and Canton of Geneva, the Swiss and the international media turned a blind eye and a deaf ear to were glaring and indisputable. On October 1st, 2017, the people of the English and Pidgin-speaking Southern Cameroons (renamed Northwest and Southwest regions, population, 8 million) came out en masse and symbolically declared "independence" from *la République du Cameroun* after 56 years of concerted Franco-Cameroun linguistic and cultural assimilation, marginalization, second-class citizenship, and identitarian erasure through and extreme political repression. This mass "declaration of independence" was a desperate measure in response to authoritarian President Paul Biya's refusal to entertain calls for dialogue and political change made by striking English-speaking common law lawyers, teachers, students, and civil society groups. In response to peaceful calls for change, the repressive, republican chieftaincy of President Biya swiftly shut down the Internet to forestall social media organizing, and unleashed its repressive military juggernaut, led by the Israeli-trained, equipped, and armed BIR, to crush and subjugate the English-and Pidgin-speaking minority once and for all.

Remote-controlling Human Rights Violations from Swiss Territory

This chapter aims to survey, describe and explain the role and place of Switzerland in the Anglophone Question and the Anglophone Revolt, which emerged from it. The central premise is that the kleptocratic, neo-patrimonial, authoritarian, republican chiefdom of President Paul Biya skillfully instrumentalized the economic gateways of Cameroon in physical space (seaports, airports and land borders) and cyberspace (telecommunications infrastructure and Internet border gateway protocols), as well as the nation's natural resources (primarily cocoa, coffee, timber, oil and natural gas, and rare earth minerals), as powerful attractants that transformed Switzerland, a nation with a legendary tradition of neutrality, humanitarian ideals, and uncompromising human rights rhetoric, into an uncritical, nay, hypocritical bulwark of the Biya regime, and a silent partner in its crimes against humanity in Southern Cameroons. This chapter demonstrates that since he came to power in 1982, President Paul Biya has been able to develop a mutually beneficial symbiotic relationship with the Swiss, whose country serves as his second home, whose hospitals and clinics served as his family's healthcare providers of choice, whose boutiques served as his wife and family's shopping venues of choice, whose international schools served as the educators of their child, Brenda Biya, whose multinational companies served as his commodities trading partners, whose charter airlines served as his principal means of international travel, and whose banks serve as his financial treasure stores. In exchange, Switzerland has had a privileged relationship with the Biya regime, and Swiss businesses have been granted access to and control of the strategic economic gateways and supply chains of Cameroon, as well as to its oil, natural gas, cocoa, forestry, and other natural resources. This hegemonic relationship and state of affairs would have been called a classic neo-colonial partnership between a European country and its "postcolony," to borrow the expression of Mbembe (2001, p.1), except for the fact that Switzerland was never a colonial power in Africa.

When Germany created Kamerun after the Berlin West African Conference of 1884-1885, the Swiss presence in the territory came in the form of the Swiss-German *Evangelische Missionsgesellschaft in Basel* (Basel Evangelical Missionary Society), the *Basler Mission* or Basel Mission, which began missionary work in German Kamerun in 1886. At the outbreak of World War I, British and French troops attacked German Kamerun. In September and October 1914, German missionaries, including those of the Swiss German Basel Mission, were interned by the Allies and held as prisoners of war until 1915 and ultimately deported to Switzerland and Germany (Nyansako-ni-Nku, 1982; Ndamukong, 2007). Missionaries from the Basel Mission returned in 1925 and focused their work in British Southern Cameroons, which was created after the Anglo-French partition of German Cameroon. The Basel Mission in Cameroon greatly influenced the historical development of English and Pidgin-speaking Southern Cameroons, leading to the founding of the Presbyterian Church in Cameroon (PCC), one of the major denominations in terms of religious membership, educational institutions (Presbyterian schools and colleges), Presbyterian Hospitals and other healthcare facilities, and professional training (Nyansako-ni-Nku, 1982). In the 1960s and 1970s, the Helvetas-Swiss Association for Technical Assistance (SATA), a non-governmental development assistance organization established an office in Buea, Southern Cameroons, and from there provided technical assistance in renewable natural resources, rural infrastructures (mostly village water projects) vocational training and culture with the aim of bringing about justice and solidarity through meeting the material and non-material needs of the people (Helvetas-Swiss Association for International Cooperation, 2010). Switzerland, therefore, has one of the oldest and longest-lasting international, non-colonial engagements in development in the English-speaking Southern Cameroons.

The Anglophone Revolt of 2016, which the Basel Mission-affiliated Presbyterian Church in Cameroon, together with the Roman Catholic Church in the English and Pidgin-speaking Southern Cameroons and the Cameroon Baptist Convention (CBC) supported in writing, was joined by teachers and students of Presbyterian schools and colleges. Teachers' and lawyers' strikes were followed by harsh government repression, which led to many deaths and compounded the disruption of some of the educational institutions and healthcare facilities that had been built over the years by the Basel Mission and its offspring, the Presbyterian Church in Cameroon (Nyansako-ni-Nku, 1982). Indeed, the Moderator or head of the Presbyterian Church in Cameroon, Rt. Rev. Fonki Samuel Forba was summoned to appear at the Buea High Court by a pro-government outfit, the Consortium of Parents, to answer charges related to the "non-resumption of schools." He was essentially sued for failing to order Presbyterian teachers and students to end their participation in the Anglophone Revolt and return to work as ordered by the Biya regime (Musa, 2017). Though the case was ultimately dropped, it was an early indication of the extent to which the government would go to crush the Anglophone Revolt.

Fast forward to 2018. When the Biya regime opted to use the military, led by the Israeli-trained and armed BIR, to subjugate the English and Pidgin-speaking community rather than engage in political discussions with it, Biya's cozy relationship with Switzerland came into the spotlight. Switzerland soon came to be known not so much for its historic missionary and humanitarian engagement in Southern Cameroons but for its mutually beneficial and lucrative, decades-long symbiotic relationship with the egotistical neo-patrimonial dictator, President Paul Biya. In effect, Switzerland is the favorite European destination, the second home of Paul Biya. For years, Biya has spent months on end in the lap of luxury at the Intercontinental Hotel in Geneva, Switzerland, while more than half of his country languished in abject poverty without clean drinking water, schools, health services, roads, etc.

Commandeering a Massacre in Cameroon from Swiss Soil

The greatest irony is that Switzerland will forever be inextricably linked to the human rights violations and crimes against humanity perpetrated by the Biya regime in Anglophone Cameroon. In effect, on that fateful day of the Anglophone symbolic declaration of independence on October 1, 2017, President Paul Biya was staying at his favorite European resort, the InterContinental Hotel, 7-9 Chemin du Petit-Saconnex, Geneva, Switzerland. That hotel is a stone's throw from the United Nations headquarters, the Palais des Nations in Geneva. From the lap of luxury in his Swiss presidential suite, Biya ordered a bloody crackdown on unarmed civilian protesters and demonstrators in the English-speaking region of Cameroon. A verbatim military report of the massacres sent to President Biya at the Intercontinental Hotel in Geneva was intercepted by Western intelligence agencies and leaked to Francophone Cameroon activists in Europe, who promptly posted it on social media platforms. The report described how civilians were shot and how helicopter gunships were used to fire fragmentation grenades on unarmed demonstrators. English translations are added below the original French. Note that 237 is the country code for Cameroon. The rest is the Cameroon security number from which the reports were sent to President Paul Biya at the Intercontinental Hotel in Geneva, Switzerland. The security report read in part (emphasis added):

- [01/10 à 16:33] +237 99104845: *Altercation armée au pont Satom à Mamfe contre une 50aine resent s brandissant leur gris-gris et tirant sur nous avec armes de chass. Bilan côté ennemi: 2 morts 5 arrêtés. Côté ami: RAS (Rien à signalé).*
- [01/10 à 16:33] +237 99104845: Armed clash on the Satom bridge in Mamfe against about 50 activists brandishing traditional medicinal charms and shooting at us with hunting weapons. Casualty figures: On the side of the enemy: 2 dead, 5 arrested. On the friendly side (Cameroun forces): Nothing to report.
- [01/10 à 16 :33] +237 99104845: *À Buea, les insurgés veulent prendre le palais du Gouverneur construit par les Allemands aujourd'hui avant 18h, car resent-ils, c'est leur capitale. Mais les FMO tiennent jusqu'à resent.*
- [01/10 à 16:33] +237 99104845: At Buea, the insurgents want to take over the Governor's Palace built by the Germans today before 6 pm, because they say it is

their capital but the military forces are holding firm up to the present moment.

- [01/10 à 16:33] +237 99104845: *Survol à basse altitude et largage des grenades F4 à partir des hélicos*
- [01/10 à 16:33] +237 99104845: Low altitude flight by helicopter gunships and dropping of F4 grenades [on the unarmed civilians] from helicopters
- [01/10 à 16:33] +237 99104845: *Dans le Nord-Ouest actuellement, la situation tourne au vinaigre. Le véhicule du préfet de Fundong vient d'être incendié. Plusieurs manifestants à Bamenda ont des grenades et des armes à feu.*
- [01/10 à 16:33] +237 99104845: In the Northwest the situation is turning sour. The vehicle of the prefect of Fundong has been burnt. Many démonstrators in Bamenda have grenades and fire arms.
- [01/10 à 16:33] +237 99104845: *Matériel récupéré: 02 pistolets artisanaux et 35 cartouches*
- 01/10 à 16:33] +237 99104845: Equipment retrieved: 02 locally made pistols and 35 cartridges.
- [01/10 à 16:33] +237 99104845: *Un Véhicule d'Intervention et de Dispersion (VID: Abraham) de la Gendarmerie mis hors d'état de fonctionner à Buea par les manifestants.*
- 01/10 à 16:33] +237 99104845: An Abraham Intervention and Dispersion Vehicle of the Gendarmerie damaged in Buea by the demonstrators. [Vehicle is made by Soframe, Alsace, France)
- [01/10 à 16:35] +237 99104845: *Point fait par un ami de la Semil*
- [01/10 à 16:35] +237 99104845: Clarification from a military colleague in SEMIL (Cameroun Military Security)
- [01/10 à 16:35] +237 99104845: *Vives altercations à Mutengene entre manifestants et FMO. Au moins 3 morts déjà enregistrés côté adverse. Déploiement des renforts gendarmerie par le COLEGION.*
- [01/10 à 16:35] +237 99104845: Serious altercations in Mutengene between demonstrations and Law Enforcement Officers. At least 3 dead recorded on the side of the adversary. Deployment of reinforcement by the commander of the gendarmerie legion
- [01/10 à 18:17] +237 99104845: *Buea 2... Akwaya 1...Kumba 3...Kumbo 4 prisonniers...Mamfe 2....Muyuka 2....Mutenguene 1*
- [01/10 à 18:17] +237 99104845: Buea 2...Akwaya 1...Kumba 3...Kumbo 4. Prisoners...Mamfe 2...Muyuka 2....Mutengene 1
- [01/10 à 18:17] +237 99104845: *On tend vers 20 morts depuis le matin quand même hein. Ils ne rigolent pas en face*
- [01/10 à 18:17] +237 99104845: We have about 20 dead since morning. The enemy is not laughing
- [01/10 à 18:17] +237 99104845: *Voilà le bilan actuel des morts par localité*
- [01/10 à 18:17] +237 99104845: These are the deaths by locality.

The clinical, military communication was confirmation that President Paul Biya had decided to employ deadly military force to solve a festering political problem, the so-called Anglophone Question in the English-speaking region of Cameroon. In effect, as commander-in-chief of the Cameroon armed forces, Mr. Biya had ordered his troops to open fire on unarmed civilians, who were demonstrating against what they perceived as their status as second-class citizens in the French-dominated *la République du Cameroun*. The Cameroon army reported on October 1 that 20 persons had been shot dead and more than 500 arrested (Amnesty International, 2018). That number rose as more bodies of the helicopter attack were found in the subsequent days. The irony is that the human rights violations taking place in Cameroon were masterminded from the InterContinental Hotel of Geneva, a mere 3-minute walk from the United Nations office in Geneva, where weighty matters of human rights and human dignity have been discussed since the founding of the United Nations Organization in 1948. The UN office in Geneva also houses the Office of the United Nations High Commissioner for Human Rights (OHCHR), and the United Nations High Commissioner for Refugees, Geneva is also the headquarters of the International Red Cross and Red Crescent Movement.

President Biya stayed in Switzerland until October 21, 2017, completely unmoved by the Anglophone Revolt and the resulting atrocities. He remained completely indifferent and impassive as whole Anglophone villages were burned to the ground, hundreds of people were killed, hundreds arrested, and thousands were fleeing to Nigeria. The Cameroon army's 20 helicopter gunship grenade attack against unarmed civilian demonstrators near German colonial Governor, Jesko von Puttkamer's castle in Buea, was a bloody affair that shocked Anglophones. The castle was a landmark that had been built in 1907 on expropriated native land with near slave labor. It was a landmark that was later converted to the West Cameroon Prime Minister's Lodge and office. It was the symbol of the state of West Cameroon. A giant Christmas tree was lit in front of the castle every Christmas season. That is why it became the rallying point of Anglophone demonstrators. The Buea attack left tens of demonstrators dead and hundreds wounded. Newspapers reported that the victims were buried at midnight in two mass graves (see newspaper front pages in Chapter 28). There were more deaths reported in Mutengene, Muyuka, Kumba, Mamfe, Bamenda, and other locations throughout Southern Cameroons. The Cameroon military atrocities of October 1, 2017 was the kick-off of Africa's latest atrocities, human rights abuses and crimes against humanity. The reason for all these horrendous atrocities was simple: One man, Paul Biya's megalomaniacal obsession with controlling the whole of Cameroon and using its resources as he saw fit, using oil and natural gas revenues – and they are mostly situated in English-speaking Southern Cameroons – to pay for the best security apparatus money could buy from the Israelis – his praetorian presidential guard and the notoriously violent Rapid Intervention Battalion. He also used these natural resources to bribe companies from member countries of the United Nations Security Council – France, the UK, China and Russia – to ensure that the Anglophone conflict would not be discussed at the United Nations and that the UN would not intervene to stop the bloodshed. According to its website, the Cameroon National Oil Company, la *Société Nationale des Hydrocarbures* (SNH) states that it "works in partnership with companies having well-established expertise, including subsidiaries of Gazprom [Russia], Glencore [Switzerland], Golar [Norway/

Bermuda], Sinopec [China], Lukoil [Russia], Grynberg [U.S.A], Noble Energy/Chevron [U.S.A], Bowleven [UK], Victoria Oil & Gas [UK], New Age [U.K.), Tower Resources [U.K.], Afex [U.S.A], Yan Chang [China] and Perenco [Anglo-French]."

Biya's Declaration of War Against Anglophone Federalists and Separatists

President Paul Biya's legendary authoritarian intransigence and refusal to dialogue with Anglophone civil society and seek a peaceful solution to the Anglophone Question greatly aggravated the situation. Less than two weeks after his return from his long Swiss vacation, on November 30, 2017, the President officially opted for a military solution to the Anglophone political problem. He declared war on Anglophone separatists and resistance at the Yaoundé Nsimalen International Airport upon his return from the fifth African Union - European Union (AU-EU) summit, which had taken place on 29-30 November 2017, in Abidjan, Côte d'Ivoire. The political crisis had been going on for over two months, while Biya blissfully vacationed at his favorite European destination, the Intercontinental Hotel in Geneva. Upon his descent from his chartered aircraft, President Biya read a short speech to the waiting gaggle of reporters (Crise Anglophone au Cameroun, 2017):

> *J'ai appris avec émotion l'assassinat de quatre militaires camerounais et de deux policiers dans le sud-ouest de notre pays...le Cameroun est victime des attaques à répétition d'une bande de terroristes se réclamant d'un mouvement sécessionniste...Toutes les dispositions sont prises pour mettre hors d'état de nuire ces criminels et faire en sorte que la paix et la sécurité soient sauvegardées sur toute l'étendue du territoire national*

> I learnt with emotion, the assassination of four Cameroun soldiers and two police officers in the Southwest region of our country. Cameroun is the victim of repeated attacks by a band of terrorists who claim to be a secessionist movement. All measures have been taken to neutralize these criminals and ensure that peace and security are maintained throughout the national territory.

On Sunday, December 3, 2017, the Minister of State at the Presidency in Charge of Defense, Joseph Beti Assomo, announced that the Cameroon army will promptly follow President Biya's orders to the letter: "Measures will be taken immediately for a process which will eradicate this inconvenient situation we are experiencing," he announced (Agence France Presse, 2017). Though the war was ostensibly aimed at separatists, in reality, the hardline regime arrested, jailed, tortured and even murdered Anglophone lawyers, teachers, professors, students, journalists, activists, and federalists. There was no room for dissent from the rigid, neo-patrimonial autocracy of Biya's republican chiefery. This was also the beginning of the scorched earth policy and the refugee crisis in Southern Cameroons that Mr. William Spindler, the Spokesman for the United Nations High Commission for Refugees (UNHCR), announced to the world. The situation worsened when a fledgling insurgency killed soldiers and gendarmes in retaliation. By 2018, more than 50, 000 Southern Cameroons refugees had crossed into Nigeria, and close to one million persons had been displaced internally in Southern Cameroons and French Cameroon. English-speaking Southern Cameroons refugees also started showing up in Spanish-speaking Equatorial Guinea, off the coast of Southern Cameroons, North Africa, European countries, as well as Panama, Mexico, and even the southern border of the United States, where they were the only English-speakers among the hundreds of thousands of refugees flocking the U.S. Mexico border. Five years later, the death toll had risen to thousands (including more than 1,500 Cameroon military and paramilitary gendarmerie personnel). More than 70,000 refugees had fled to Nigeria, while more than one million had become internally displaced.

The Biya Regime's Anti-Federalist Repression of Anglophone Civil Society in Cameroon

The Cameroon government's crackdown on Anglophone political dissidents was an affirmative decision to crush the non-violent demonstrations by English-speaking common law lawyers, teachers, and students. Political demands by unarmed civilians in the Northwest and Southwest regions were met with brutal repression, targeted killings, arrests, imprisonment, beatings, and torture by the Cameroon armed forces, led by the brutal, Israeli, and American-trained and armed Rapid Intervention Brigade (BIR), the army, the gendarmerie, and the police (Daoud, 2018). On many occasions, members of the BIR recorded their torture and summary execution sessions on video and posted them on Facebook and other social media. Some of these videos were featured on international broadcast channels. In order to silence Anglophone political and civil society dissent, on January 17, 2017, the Cameroon Minister of Territorial Administration, René Sadi, banned the activities of the separatist political movement, the Southern Cameroons National Council (SCNC) as well as the federalist Cameroon Anglophone Civil Society Consortium (CACSC), an umbrella organization of lawyers, teachers, professors, intellectuals, students, and human rights activists that had been created to address the human rights dimensions of the Anglophone uprising, promote peaceful dialogue with government officials, and discuss peaceful protests associated with the Anglophone revolt. The Consortium's president, international human rights lawyer and federalist, Nkongho Felix Agbor-Balla, and its Secretary General, Professor Fontem Aforteka'a Neba, were arrested in Buea, transferred to Yaoundé and held incommunicado in the dungeon of the State Defence Secretariat (SED). They were later brought before the Yaoundé Military Tribunal and charged with eight counts of terrorism and insurrection against the state, under a 2014 Law on Repression of Terrorism (Amnesty International, 2018). This law had been passed in response to the Islamist Boko Haram terrorist activities in Nigeria and North Cameroon. The vague, over-broad and highly elastic Cameroon anti-terrorism law, which provides that the death penalty could be imposed on citizens who, either as individuals or in a group, carry out, abet, or sponsor terrorism, is routinely used to arrest and imprison journalists, activists and political opponents of the Biya regime. The law also criminalizes "incitement to rebellion," and "creating a general uprising in the country." Cameroon opposition parties, journalists, and international human rights organizations condemned the law as an instrument of repression, and suppression of dissent and criticism of the excesses and corruption of the government (Johnson, 2014). Indeed, journalists have been arrested, tried and convicted in the Yaoundé Military Tribunal for "publishing false news," "complicity with and non-denunciation of terrorist acts," "non-denunciation of information and sources," and other vague charges brought by military prosecutors (Amnesty International, 2018). Furthermore, in May 2017, the head of the quasi-legal media watchdog, the *Conseil National de Communication* (National Communication Council), Peter Essoka, warned Cameroon journalists not to report on events that promote or advocate "secession or a return to federalism" in Cameroon (Kindzeka, 2017).

Anglophone Diaspora Protest to the Swiss Government

Even as President Biya assumed a Pharaonic posture of total indifference, nay, total lack of concern about the atrocities being perpetrated by his military in Southern Cameroons, Cameroonians living in Switzerland and other European countries organized demonstrations to coincide with his lengthy stays at the Intercontinental Hotel in Geneva, Switzerland. The first of these anti-Biya Geneva demonstrations took place in 2019. Since the horrendous and unprecedented human rights violations in Southern Cameroons were orchestrated by President Biya from the Intercontinental Hotel in Geneva, Switzerland, in November 2017, a collective of shocked English-speaking Southern Cameroonians in the Diaspora wrote an open letter to the Swiss government expressing its outrage over the turn of events and implicitly accusing Switzerland, the self-proclaimed land of human and peoples' rights, of hypocrisy, and of turning a blind eye to the atrocities of Paul Biya (see appendix XIV). Surely, Biya could not calmly and clinically decide to massacre unarmed, peaceful civilian demonstrators from the lap of luxury in the presidential suite in the Intercontinental Hotel, Geneva, Switzerland. How could a man who had declared war on peaceful Anglophone lawyers, teachers, students, and activists, a man whose troops had attacked the University of Buea, beaten and raped students, arrested, detained, tortured and killed thousands of unarmed civilians openly use Switzerland as his base of operations? How could a dictator whose record of human rights violations was equal to or even surpassed the worst of the worst – Ahmed Sekou Touré of Guinea, Denis Sassou Nguesso of Congo, Mobutu Sese Seko of Zaire/Congo, Idi Amin of Uganda, Mengistu Haile Mariam of Ethiopia, Robert Mugabe of Zimbabwe, Omar el Bachir of Sudan, etc., – be allowed to come and go as he pleased to Switzerland, the land of human rights and the Geneva Convention, and spend weeks at a time at the Intercontinental Hotel in Geneva while his Israeli-trained killers, the BIR were on the rampage, carrying out a scorched-earth policy in Southern Cameroons with impunity?

To the surprise of the English and Pidgin-speaking community, Ambassador Anne Lugon Moulin, head of the Sub-Saharan Africa and Francophone Division of the Federal Department of Foreign Affairs of the Swiss Confederation, responded to the Anglophone open letter with an open letter of her own. She acknowledged the open letter and wrote that:

> Switzerland firmly believes that the respect for human rights is an indispensable condition for genuinely sustainable social and economic progress in a

> manner that benefits every individual. As a country with several linguistic and other national minorities, Switzerland attaches great importance to the needs and rights...Further, the right to freedom of peaceful assembly and to freedom of association are a priority for Switzerland as they are, together with the right to freedom of expression, key prerequisites for any democratic society...Switzerland is concerned about the human rights situation in Cameroon. Through its Embassy in Yaoundé and in its bilateral contacts with Cameroon's authorities, we address human rights issues on a regular basis, including the complex situation in the English-speaking regions... (Ambassador Anne Lugon-Moulin, 2017).

The last part of Ambassador Anne Lugon-Moulin's open letter addressed the burning questions of the English-speaking Southern Cameroonians with respect to President Biya's interminable visits to Switzerland and his ordering human rights violations from there. She wrote: "President Biya's stays in Switzerland were either of a private nature or of official nature in the framework of multilateral conferences in Geneva." That was it. She did not address the hot potato question of Biya's ordering of human rights violations from Swiss territory. That absence was very conspicuous and highlighted Biya's unprecedented and problematic habit of leaving Cameroon, with its lack of clean drinking water, electricity, health services, schools, and food security, to live in the lap of luxury in the very expensive, British-owned Intercontinental Hotel.

President Paul Biya's Problematic Love Affair with Switzerland

Due to his very frequent, lengthy, and expensive stays at the presidential suite of the Intercontinental Hotel in Geneva, many observers concluded that President Paul Biya was either running Cameroon from Switzerland or had put the country on auto-pilot, secure in the knowledge that his Israeli-trained praetorian *Garde presidentielle* and the Israeli-trained and armed special forces, the BIR would crush any threat to his regime. The question that confronted the Swiss was why, knowing fully well that Biya had launched a bloody war of conquest and subjugation against the English and Pidgin-speaking minority in Southern Cameroons from his luxurious abode in Switzerland, a war that had resulted in horrendous crimes against humanity, why Switzerland continued to allow President Biya to return to Switzerland without any hindrance. How could a president, whose corrupt, autocratic and repressive regime contributes significantly to the flood of African migrants that head to Europe on a daily basis, be allowed to return to Switzerland, which is ostensibly a global defender of human rights and freedoms? According to SWI swissinfo.ch, the public service online news and information service of Switzerland – it receives 50% of its budget from license fees paid by all Swiss households and companies and 50% from a federal grant administered by the Federal Office of Communications (OFCOM) (About SWI, 2019) – President Biya's lengthy and embarrassing stays in Switzerland are not as simple as many people around the world thought. According to Crawford & Spoerndli (2019), Biya had spent more than 1645 days (a whopping four and a half years) on private visits abroad since he became president in 1982. His favorite residence was the Intercontinental Hotel in Geneva, Switzerland, which cost an estimated $40,000 per day – not counting private aircraft rental, food, medical care, entertainment and other expenses for the president and his large entourage.

Why did the Swiss continuously allow President Paul Biya to spend long periods in their country, knowing fully well that his regime was corrupt, authoritarian, kleptocratic, and a massive violator of human rights? Clearly, Biya's frequent trips to Switzerland were an embarrassment for Switzerland (Crawford & Spoerndli (2019). Why then did the lengthy stays continue? The answer is twofold: 1) the niceties of international diplomacy and diplomatic immunity, and 2) Swiss economic entanglements with the Biya regime and Swiss interests in the survival of the regime. When faced with the embarrassment of President Paul Biya's lengthy and expensive stays in their country, while a large proportion of citizens of his country wallowed in poverty and lacked the basic necessities of life (clean drinking water, electricity, health care, educational facilities, etc.), the first refuge of the Swiss was international diplomacy. According to the Swiss Federal Department of Foreign Affairs (FDFA), "Foreign heads of state can - in a private capacity - stay in Switzerland without the federal authorities being formally informed or involved in the visit..." (cited in Crawford & Spoerndli 2019). The Swiss diplomatic fig leaf was that as the head of state of a country with which Switzerland maintained cordial diplomatic relations, President Biya had a right to travel to Switzerland and to stay in Geneva – where many United Nations and other international organizations are located – for purposes of attending multilateral conferences (Crawford & Spoerndli, 2019). Nevertheless, the point remained that the Swiss Federal Department of Foreign Affairs ultimately had the "visa power," the sovereign right to grant or not to grant President Biya and his huge entourage visas to enter Switzerland. Indeed, though a Cooperation Agreement between the government of Cameroon and the Swiss Federal Council on the reciprocal abolition of visa requirements for holders of diplomatic and service passports of the two countries had been signed in Yaoundé on September 26, 2014, it was only in June 2021 that it was adopted by the Cameroon National Assembly and Senate, and sent to President Biya for signature and promulgation into law. The visa exemption also extended to family members of holders of the said diplomatic and service passports (Amabo, 2021). This law was clearly the *laissez-passer* that members of the ruling elite and their families needed to fly to Switzerland for vacations, medical care, and shopping since government hospitals were not worth the name, and the healthcare they provided left a lot to be desired.

Dragging the Swiss into the Anglophone Crisis: Fake News of the "Kidnapping" of Swiss and Italian Citizens in Southern Cameroons

Given the long, mutually beneficial, symbiotic relationship between President Paul Biya's neo-patrimonial republican chiefdom and Switzerland over the years, it is ironic that the Swiss were the first government that was used as bait to demonize Anglophone activists and federalists turned separatists as terrorists in international public opinion. *The* bait was manufactured fake news of the alleged "kidnapping" of Swiss and Italian tourists in Southern Cameroons. In effect, six months into the so-called Anglophone crisis, the first week of April 2018 saw the Cameroon military (BIR) and official media (CRTV and

Cameroon Tribune) fabricate a series of ironic events and even a prank worthy of an April fool's joke. The only problem is that this was not April Fool's Day (it was actually April 2nd), and the context was deadly serious. Then Cameroon Information Minister, Issa Tchiroma Bakary, who was notorious for his lack of candor, contradictory statements, and pompous proclamations, held a bizarre pseudo-event in Yaoundé that was broadcast on national television, Cameroon Radio and Television (CRTV) (Ross & Bavier, 2018). This was a press conference in which he essentially used Swiss and Italian embassy officials in Cameroon as mere props in a terrible political drama featuring subservient government ministers, and chest-thumping military officials. During the poorly staged event, the "honorable" minister announced to the world that 12 European hostages (7 Swiss and 5 Italians) had been rescued from "terrorists" in the scenic twin lakes region of Kupe Muanenguba in the Southwest region of Cameroon. He proudly announced that the Cameroon military had "neutralized" (killed) the terrorists who had taken the Europeans hostage. Tchiroma, who was joined by the Cameroon Foreign Minister, Mr. Lejeune Mbella Mbella, symbolically handed over the 12 "freed" European hostages to their respective embassy officials who were present at the pseudo-event. Tchiroma praised President Biya for his astute leadership and decisiveness and the Israeli-trained and equipped Cameroon special forces, the BIR, for their bravery and professionalism (Ross and Bavier, 2018). Western news agencies jumped on Tchiroma's story and flashed it around the world. The release of twelve European hostages in an African country fit the traditional template of Western journalistic reporting of Africa.

That was the official story until the "hostages" were freed from the clutches of Tchiroma and the authoritarian Cameroon government. As soon as they were no longer under the control and jurisdiction of the Cameroon government and its special forces, the so-called hostages quickly contradicted the official account. The tour operator, African Adventures, which had brought the tourists to Cameroon, promptly announced on its website that the Europeans had, in fact, not been taken hostage. The alleged "hostages" all stated that they had not been kidnapped. They said armed separatists had stopped them in the English-speaking region of Cameroon who checked their documents and let them continue on their merry way to Lake Muanenguba (Ross & Bavier, 2018).

Since this is an age of global social media, the separatist group that had allegedly "kidnapped" the tourists corroborated the story of the tourists. In an audio message posted on Facebook, a separatist group operating in Kupe Muanenguba told the world, in Pidgin English, that they had indeed stopped the European tourists who were visiting their area of control. The speaker said they had examined the tourists' documents and let them go since they had "no quarrel with the Europeans." The separatists said that they retreated to their mountain hide-out and from there observed soldiers from the notoriously brutal BIR, who are known in the English-speaking part of Cameroon as "mad dogs," arrive at the scene and stage a rescue that greatly frightened the tourists. The Separatist fighters said they did not engage the Cameroon army at that point because they feared the European tourists would be caught in the crossfire. They feared that the trigger-happy BIR would shoot the European tourists and blame it on separatists.

The Western news agencies quickly realized that they had been duped by a bad propaganda minister who wanted to divert attention from the human rights violations, set-backs and heavy losses the Cameroon military was experiencing in what was beginning to look like a military quagmire in the English and Pidgin-speaking Southern Cameroons. The news agencies quickly rectified the fake news, and some of them even quoted Dr. Cho Ayaba, commander of the separatist Ambazonia Defense Forces (ADF), who said his group does not kidnap foreigners (Ross & Bavier, 2018). This turned out to be a public relations disaster for the Cameroon government. This governmental fake news internationalized the Anglophone crisis like never before, gave Ayaba Cho an international platform, and painted Cameroon as an unsafe place to visit. Tchiroma's fake news backfired spectacularly. Even the government's mouthpiece, *Cameroon Tribune*, had a telling headline, "No gain for Cameroon," it blared. Officials of the Swiss and Italian embassies remained tight-lipped. They had been used as pawns by the Biya regime. However, they said nothing for fear of endangering their lucrative economic relations with the Biya regime. The Swiss had been dragged into the Anglophone Question against their will. As we see below, Geneva would soon become the European theater of the Anglophone crisis.

Figure 19.1. Swiss and Italian "hostages" in Kupe Muanenguba. The 12 "kidnapped" Swiss and Italian tourists pose with their BIR "rescuers"

Academia/Amnesia in Italy

The fake news event of the kidnapping of tourists was pregnant with irony for Switzerland and Italy. In effect, Biya's heavy-handed repression of peaceful, unarmed Anglophones who started demonstrating in 2016 for change; for a reduction of the burdens of the authoritarian, over-centralized, Napoleonic, colonial government of Cameroon, was post-marked and executed from Europe. As the Anglophone crisis began to spread and as Biya's repression intensified, they visited Italy and the Vatican from March 20-22, 2017. President Biya also met with the leaders of the CONFINDUSTRIA, the powerful association of Italian manufacturing and service companies, to "woo" Italian businesses to invest in a "stable" Cameroon (President Paul Biya woos Italian Investors, receives Gold Medal at Tor Vergata

University, 2017). To the consternation of Cameroonians who had chafed under the 35-year brutal, authoritarian, Biya republican chiefery, an Italian University, Tor Vergata University of Rome, stroked his already mountain-sized ego by giving him a gold medal. The official website of the Presidency of the Republic of Cameroon reported that "at the University of Rome Tor Vergata, the Presidential Couple was welcomed by Professor Gaetano MANFREDI, President of the Conference of Italian University Rectors (CRUI), and Giuseppe NOVELLI, Rector of the University of Rome Tor Vergata" (President Paul Biya woos Italian Investors, receives Gold Medal at Tor Vergata University, 2017). The award demonstrated that the academy was on the same page as the confederation of Italian industry. It certainly revealed the Italian university rectors' complete lack of awareness of, or total disregard for human rights in Cameroon. This was a supreme display of academic insularity, demonstrating that the word university sometimes rhymes with perversity. Antonio Gramsci, the influential Italian Marxist philosopher, journalist, and linguist who gave the world the word "hegemony," must have flipped in his grave. It certainly was an occasion for the Italians to curry favor with the authoritarian chieftain. There were many business opportunities and contracts to be had in Biya's Cameroon. The near-tragedy of the Swiss-Italian tourists who found themselves in the crossfire between Anglophone separatists and the brutal Cameroon government should teach the "learned" dons of Tor Vergata University in Rome a lesson on African realities that they did not learn from Italian history.

Figure 19.2. The amnesia of academia, President Biya arrives Tor Vergata University, Rome. (March, 2017)

The next stop was the Vatican, where President Paul Biya, the former Roman Catholic seminarian, visited Pope Francis and the Vatican Secretary of State, Cardinal Pietro Parolin. The Vatican issued the following tepid statement in response to the Catholic president's mounting atrocities in the Northwest and Southwest regions of Cameroon, which has a huge Catholic population, schools, and medical facilities:

> During the cordial discussions, the existing good relations between the

> Holy See and Cameroon were evoked, as was the important contribution the Church offers to the development of the country, especially in the fields of education and healthcare. Taking into consideration the peaceful co-existence and mutual respect between the various religious groups, attention was focused on the importance of promoting national cohesion, enhancing the richness of the various historic and cultural traditions of the country, with respect for human and minority rights (emphasis added) (Holy Sea Press Office Communiqué, 2017).

That tepid and vague statement is the only pronouncement that has come out of the Vatican in response to multiple atrocities perpetrated by the Catholic President against innocent civilians –including hundreds of thousands of Catholics, in the Anglophone Northwest and Southwest regions.

The biggest irony of the fake kidnapping of Swiss and Italian tourists and Biya's fondness for Switzerland is that the man loved the Swiss confederation but jailed anyone who was accused of being a federalist or having federalist tendencies in Cameroon. He had a permanent presidential suite at the luxurious Intercontinental Hotel in Geneva, where he stayed for long periods of time at the expense of Cameroon taxpayers and only occasionally visited his impoverished country, Cameroon, where millions of people do not have food security, clean drinking water, sanitation, healthcare, schools, decent roads, and so on. History will record that it was from the InterContinental Hotel in Geneva, Switzerland, that Biya unleashed his brutal repression and crimes against humanity that have led to hundreds of deaths and created a refugee crisis that has seen more than 20,000 refugees flee to neighboring Nigeria. The rest is history.

Figure 19.3. President Biya receives political gold medal at Tor Vergata University, Rome, Tor Vergata University Rome honoured Paul Biya while his army committed massive crimes against humanity in Anglophone Cameroon (March 2017)

Cameroonian Immigrants Invite Themselves to the Monied Streets of Geneva, Switzerland

The human rights violations galvanized Cameroonian immigrants, exiles and political asylees in Europe. Even as President Biya assumed a posture of total indifference, nay a reckless Pharaonic disregard towards the atrocities being perpetrated by his Israeli-trained military forces in Southern Cameroons, as well as towards the massive repression against the political opposition, Cameroonians living in Switzerland and other European countries organized demonstrations to protest against his lengthy stays in Switzerland while Cameroon burned. On Saturday, June 29, 2019, a crowd of Cameroonian immigrants, refugees and asylum seekers resident in Switzerland and nearby European countries gathered near the European headquarters of the United Nations and the Intercontinental Hotel in Geneva, capital of the French-speaking Republic and Canton of Geneva, Switzerland. Some of them had come out of the shadows, and the clandestine existence to which their undocumented status had consigned them, taking advantage of the power of numbers and the anonymity of the crowd (AFP, 2019). These Africans were in Geneva, a financial and diplomatic center at the heart of Europe, the land of human rights, political neutrality, and freedom–as well as opaque business and financial secrecy – to demonstrate against Switzerland's partner in crimes against humanity. This partner of Switzerland was none other than Africa's longest-serving kleptocratic dictator, Paul Barthélémy Biya Bi Mvondo, whose hardline republican chiefdom had launched a bloody war of conquest against the English and Pidgin-speaking minority in the former Southern Cameroons in 2017, triggering a refugee crisis that displaced more than one million people, including some demonstrators in the crowd. This repressive war of conquest was kicked off from the lap of luxury, the presidential suite at the Intercontinental Hotel, Geneva. It was an unofficial African drama being played out on the shores of Lake Geneva, one of the great cultural centers of Europe. The demonstrating Cameroonians who were led by one French-based immigrant, Robert Wanto, self-styled commander of the so-called Europe-based *Brigade Anti-Sardinard* (BAS, literally Brigade of Anti-sardine Eaters), were also demonstrating against the Biya regime's rigging of the 2018 presidential election, and the imprisonment of Maurice Kamto, leader of the opposition MRC Party, as well as a number of leaders of his party. The imprisoned leaders had dared to challenge the results of the 2018 elections, which observers had declared were neither free nor fair because they were a "master class in fake democracy" (O'Donnell & Gramer, 2018). The Brigade Anti-Sardinard (BAS) was a negative nomenclature of resistance against the common "bread and sardines" tactic used by President Paul Biya's political party, the ruling *Rassemblément Démocratique du Peuples Camerounais* (RDPC) to instrumentalize poverty for purposes of "encouraging" hungry voters to cast their ballots for Biya and RDPC candidates. In effect, during election campaigns, operatives of the ruling RDPC would go to villages where hunger and food insecurity are rampant. They would distribute a piece of French baguette and a can of Moroccan sardines to each villager who attended their rally. The elite ignore and even despise these citizens once the elections are over. The RDPC political operatives would then make the people who have "eaten" from them to promise to vote for them. The announced results are always the same, in the areas where bread and sardines are distributed, 95 to 99% of voters cast their ballot for Paul Biya and his ruling RDPC party.

The BAS demonstrations were taking place in Geneva, Switzerland, rather than Yaoundé or Douala because President Paul Biya was doing his favorite activities – spending a long, expensive stay at a presidential suite of the Intercontinental Hotel, Geneva, with its "magnificent view of Lake Geneva and Jura Mountains," as the hotel's advertisement states. Biya and his wife, Chantal, who are known for their fondness for the expensive, ultra-luxurious Intercontinental Hotel in Geneva, Switzerland, hired luxury aircraft and flew to Geneva, on multiple occasions, and occupy one whole floor of the hotel where he and his wife and their entourage would spend weeks at a time, and pay for their expenses in cash (*Wall Street Journal*, 2019). The Cameroonian demonstrators in Geneva held placards that read: "*Paul Biya Assassin, la Swiss complice*" (Paul Biya Assassin, Switzerland his accomplice), among others. In a bid to keep the demonstrators away from the Intercontinental Hotel, large numbers of Swiss riot police in full-riot gear created a cordon of riot police, anti-riot police cars, water cannons and barriers between the demonstrators and the luxury Intercontinental Hotel. When about 250 chanting, singing, and dancing demonstrators attempted to cross the Swiss riot police cordon, the riot police used tear gas, water cannons and stun grenades to disperse them (AFP, 2019; Cameroon President Leaves Geneva after Spate of Protests, 2019).

Figure 19.4. Unprecedented scenes of Africans demonstrating against a ruthless authoritarian President Biya in Geneva, Switzerland. Biya spent long periods of time in the lap of luxury at the Intercontinental hotel in Geneva, Switzerland, while supervising the killing of his people who were wallowing in poverty in Africa. Credit AFP

The unprecedented demonstration of African immigrants and refugees near the Geneva Intercontinental hotel in Geneva and the tough, heavy-handed measures taken by the police of the Canton of Geneva to crush it were unprecedented and highly embarrassing for Switzerland which considers itself the global center of human rights and political neutrality. Police spokesman Silvain Guillaume-Gentil told the media that officers had fired tear gas after a group of protesters attempted to break through police lines to reach the Intercontinental Hotel, where President Biya was residing (AFP, 2019). These unprecedented and embarrassing anti-Biya demonstrations in the streets of Geneva put the spotlight on Switzerland, and disturbed the genteel Swiss repose of the octogenarian president, who had been in power for close to 40 years at that time. These demonstrations also exposed the lengths to which Swiss law enforcement agencies would go to protect President Biya and members of his Israeli-trained and equipped praetorian guard, *la Garde presidentielle* who accompanied him, from vocal African demonstrators baying for the dictator's blood and demanding that he face charges for perpetrating crimes against humanity in Southern Cameroons. The Cameroon Minister of Communication, Réné Sadi, expressed the outrage of the Biya regime towards the Cameroonians who had organized and participated in the anti-Biya Geneva demonstrations "*Le gouvernement exprime sa réprobation totale face à ce spectacle ubuesque qui déshonore le Cameroun*" (The government expresses its total condemnation of this ludicrous spectacle that dishonors Cameroon, Foute, 2019).

Figure 19.5. Switzerland Supports the dictator Biya

President Biya's Presidential Guards and the Swiss Journalist

Former colonial metropolises of Paris, London, Madrid, Lisbon, and Berlin are often scenes of demonstrations by immigrants from African postcolonies that used to be administered and exploited from these European capital cities. These demonstrations usually take place when African authoritarian republican monarchs visit European capitals to sustain their autocratic regimes in power and protect specific European national or commercial interests. Switzerland was known as the favorite place where Africa's kleptocratic dictators stashed their loot, but President Biya had the record for length of residence in Switzerland. As President Biya's regime became one of the most autocratic and most corrupt hardline regimes in Africa, his Swiss visits became the subject of media attention and especially demonstrations by Cameroonian immigrants, refugees, and asylum seekers based in Europe. The demonstrations in Geneva, one of the great cultural centers of Europe, were unprecedented and newsworthy. European news agencies covered them extensively. Before too long, members of *la Garde présidentielle,* the Israeli-trained and equipped personal praetorian guard that accompanied President Biya on his long Swiss vacations, would clash with the Swiss press, which wanted to cover the African drama of resistance against authoritarianism that had invited itself and was being played out on the banks of Lake Geneva.

It all started on June 26, 2019, in front of the Intercontinental Hotel in Geneva. President

Paul Biya and his vast entourage are on yet another private visit to Switzerland. They are ensconced in their reserved presidential suite on the 16th floor. A demonstration against the president is organized on social media and planned for the 29th. A small group of demonstrators show up in front of the hotel. A journalist for the Swiss public broadcaster, *Radio Télévision Suisse* (RTS), Adrien Krause begins to record the demonstration. He is violently tackled, roughed up, knocked to the ground and pinned down by six members of President Biya's presidential security detail. They seized his bag, which contained his professional equipment, his wallet and his mobile phone. The items were later returned after Swiss government intervention. The Swiss reporter filed a complaint of assault against the six persons with the public prosecutor. After the assault, the Swiss government summoned Cameroon's ambassador in Bern, Léonard Henri Bindzi, and told him in no uncertain terms that the attack on the journalist was tantamount to an intolerable attack on freedom of expression: "such incidents are unacceptable, and that freedom of the press is protected and must be respected" (Cited in Cameroon President Leaves Geneva after Spate of Protests, 2019). After a review of the hotel's security camera footage, Swiss police arrested the six perpetrators of the attack. The Cameroon side advanced a defense of diplomatic immunity. The Embassy claimed that the six persons could not be charged criminally because they had diplomatic immunity. The Swiss government countered that President Biya had diplomatic immunity but that the immunity did not extend to his security detail. Ultimately, five unnamed presidential security guards and a female embassy worker were tried in court, found guilty of coercion, damage to property and illegal appropriation, and given suspended prison sentences that ranged from three to four months (Dethurens, 2021). The convictions meant they were subject to deportation and barred from re-entering Swiss national territory. The Cameroonians appealed the conviction and sentence at the Appeals Court, which rejected their immunity claims. Whereupon they appealed further to a Swiss Federal Tribunal, claiming once again that their actions were covered by diplomatic immunity and, as such, they were outside the ambit of Swiss justice. Before the Federal Tribunal, the issue was whether the Cameroon presidential security guards had diplomatic immunity in Switzerland. The Federal Tribunal answered in the negative, stating that since President Biya's visit was a private one, his presidential security guards were not acting in their official securitarian roles when they attacked the journalist. The Federal Tribunal stated that the reporter presented no danger to the president of Cameroon and ordered the security guards to pay the legal costs of the case. The court also ordered them to pay the journalist $3000 in damages (Dethurens, 2021). The protests against President Biya in Geneva and the arrest, prosecution, conviction, and sentencing of members of his presidential guard were all unprecedented. In Cameroon, members of the Israeli-trained and equipped military units – the presidential guard and the notorious BIR and other branches of the military and gendarmerie have the power of life and death over ordinary men, women and children. They arrest citizens, seize their cellphones and other personal property, jail them without trial, and even kill them with impunity. The most well-known case is that of Samuel Wazizi, a journalist from Buea, who was arrested and tortured to death in military custody. His mortal remains were never released to his family (Cameroon Journalist Samuel Wazizi died in Detention in 2020). Swiss legal action against members of the all-powerful presidential guard was simply unbelievable to many Cameroonians, who found out about it only on social media. The state-owned and controlled national media, Cameroon Radio Television (CRTV) and *Cameroon Tribune* (print press), censored the story about the anti-Biya demonstrations and the resulting trial and conviction of members of President Biya's Praetorian guard in 2019.

To Declare or Not to Declare Paul Biya "persona non-grata" in the Republic and Canton of Geneva

Pressure from Cameroonian immigrants, refugees and exiles demonstrating on the street around the Intercontinental Hotel, diplomatic, as well as local political pressure essentially forced President Biya to leave Switzerland just 12 days after his latest arrival, cutting short his planned weeks-long stay (Cameroon President Leaves Geneva after Spate of Protests, 2019). The French newspaper, *Le Point,* reported that inconvenient demonstrations and unprecedented incidents had caused Switzerland to "push President Biya towards the exit…to encourage Biya to leave" (Hamel, 2019). However, the dictator's departure did not quell the political storm that his most recent visit to Switzerland had spawned. On October 2, 2020, the Grand Council of the Republic and Canton of Geneva, one of the 26 cantons of the Swiss Confederation, was the scene of an unprecedented debate. In effect, Sylvain Thevoz, an elected member of the Grand Council, tabled an unprecedented motion for the Council to declare President Paul Biya of Cameroon a persona non grata in Geneva. Biya, whose lengthy, expensive, and controversial stays at the Intercontinental Hotel in Geneva had become a point of international political contention for a number of reasons. Biya, his wife, Chantal and his large entourage often took up whole floors in the Intercontinental Hotel where they lived lavishly in the lap of luxury, at the cost of millions of euros while more than two-thirds of Cameroonians languished in poverty and lacked the basic necessities of life. The debate focused on several facts–President Biya had launched and orchestrated the war of conquest against the Anglophone minority of his country from the confines of the Intercontinental Hotel in Geneva, an unprecedented anti-Biya demonstrations had taken place in Geneva. These protests had been crushed by the Swiss anti-riot police with tear gas and water cannons, resulting in mass and social media images that were highly embarrassing to the Swiss. Finally, media reports and litigation over the way and manner in which President Paul Biya's infamous, Israeli-trained presidential bodyguards had roughed up a Swiss journalist trying to cover anti-Biya demonstrations disturbed the Swiss, who have a long tradition of freedom of speech and of the press.

Sylvain Thévoz, co-president of the Geneva section of the Socialist Party and member of the Great Council of the Canton of Geneva, the legislative body of Canton, launched a petition against President Paul Biya, asking the Great Council to declare Paul Biya persona *non grata* in Geneva, and asked the Swiss Federal government to do the same. Though the petition received more than 15,000 signatures, the Great Council of the Canton of Geneva voted it down 27-43. The failure of the petition demonstrated that the Swiss were divided over President Paul Biya's long but inconvenient private visits to Switzerland. Sylvain Thévoz suggested that the outcome of the vote was affected by the Anglophone question in Cameroon. He said that though Switzerland is officially a neutral country, it has its own interests to take into consideration and defend in the international relations arena. He believed that the petition was not successful because it was brought up in a complex diplomatic environment in which Switzerland was trying to mediate between the Cameroon government and Anglophone separatists. In a television interview shortly after the vote, Thévoz said the Swiss Federal Department of Foreign Affairs wanted a very reluctant Biya to engage in peace talks with Anglophone separatists. Declaring him a persona non-grata would have complicated the situation. This line of thinking made no sense given that Biya's visits to Switzerland were classified as "private" and that he had no official contacts with the Swiss authorities or the Anglophone leaders despite Swiss claims that they were mediating between the Cameroon government and the Anglophone separatists (Petite, 2021).

A good number of Swiss politicians feared that declaring Biya a persona non grata in Geneva would have had international law and international relations consequences and compromised Swiss attempts to mediate in the Anglophone versus *la Republique du Cameroun* civil war in Cameroon. They said declaring President Biya persona non grata would have compromised Swiss neutrality and raised questions about their role as honest brokers in the negotiations. He said the petition had made some right-wing politicians uneasy because they believed that it was tantamount to interfering in the internal affairs of Cameroon. Thévoz added that though the majority of members of the Great Council of the Republic and Canton of Geneva had voted against the petition, the minority made it known that it was for human rights, the Geneva Convention, and against corrupt dictators who brought the fruits of their corruption and deposited or spent it in Switzerland. Swiss national interest, therefore, trumped the political interests of Cameroonian demonstrators and Swiss politicians who wanted President Paul Biya banned from visiting his favorite city in the world. For its part, the Cameroon Francophone press reported that the failure of the vote to "expel" Biya from Geneva was a victory for President Biya since the vote sent a message that he was still welcome in Geneva (Happi, 2020). The Swiss Federal Department of Foreign Affairs need not have worried that a very reluctant Biya would refuse to engage in peace talks with Anglophone separatists if he were declared persona non grata in Geneva. It would have compromised Swiss neutrality and raised questions about their role as honest brokers in the negotiations. The unprecedented and embarrassing –for Cameroonians – vote failed, but President Biya still failed to engage in peace talks with the Anglophone minority.

The 2021 Anti-Biya Geneva Demonstrations

President Paul Biya seemed to have been attracted to the spectacular views of Mont Blanc, Lake Geneva, the Alps and the Jura mountains. His favorite city, Geneva, Switzerland, offered those and more – banking and business secrecy, French haute coûture and haute cuisine. This was the idyllic location for long "private" vacations away from the sea of crushing poverty, dusty, muddy, pothole-riddled, over-crowded, chaotic, garbage-infested streets, unstable electricity, intermittent water supply, a feeble, anemic and near-non-existent healthcare system. Then there was the omnipresent Israeli-trained and armed presidential guard and BIR that transformed his presidential palaces in Yaoundé and his native village, Mvomeka'a, into veritable luxurious prisons. Geneva was a respite from the realities of the Republican chieftaincy over which President Paul Biya presided with absolute sway for forty years. Geneva, Switzerland, was so irresistible to Paul Biya that despite the humiliating demonstrations against his presence in Geneva, despite the conviction and suspended sentence handed down on five members of his presidential security, and an embassy staffer in Switzerland, despite the Grand Council vote in which more than a third of the members of the Council voted to declare him a persona non-grata, rumors started swirling in July 2021 that Paul Biya would be heading back to Geneva in the summer of 2021. Apparently, the COVID-19 pandemic and lockdowns had prevented him from returning to Geneva in 2021.

As soon as "news" that Paul Biya was heading back to Geneva in July 2021, his political opponents in Europe, the Brigade Anti-Sardinard (Anti-Sardine Brigade, aka BAS), set to work organizing demonstrations at the Intercontinental Hotel in Geneva, knowing fully well that Biya and his entourage would be there. BAS units in multiple European countries started organizing another anti-Biya protest action code-named "Operation Catcham" (Pidgin English expression for "operation catch him or arrest him"). The subject of this metaphorical collective "citizens' arrest" was, of course, President Paul Biya, who was expected to be at his favorite Swiss hideout, the Intercontinental Hotel in Geneva. Fearing that these demonstrations would lead to violence, the Swiss authorities closed off that part of the city and told the inhabitants to stay indoors and close their windows, possibly to avoid tear gas (Simon, 2021; Ben Ahmed, 2021). Fearing that the July 17, 2021 demonstrations and the planned "arrest" of President Paul Biya would lead to a repeat of the 2019 anti-Biya demonstrations that essentially shut down Geneva, and were violently dispersed by the Geneva police with tear gas, water cannons, and stun-guns – to the great embarrassment of Geneva and Switzerland (Simon, 2021). However, as the date of the demonstration approached, and as it became the major subject of discussion on social media platforms, the Republic and Canton of Geneva took a leaf from Biya's tried and true dictatorial book – it banned outright, the July 17, 2021 anti-Biya protest march that had been authorized to take place at the *Place des Nations Unies* (United Nations Place), a stone's throw away from the Intercontinental Hotel, Geneva, where President Biya and his entourage were ensconced. Florence Forget, spokesperson for the Department of Security told the media that:

> *La manifestation a été refusée ce jour en raison d'un faisceau d'indices démontrant un risque concret de débordements*
>
> The demonstration was banned today because there are ample indicators that there is a concrete risk of misbehavior on the part of the demonstrators) (Cited in Simon, 2021).

In order to justify the ban, the spokesman of the Geneva police, Jean-Philippe Brandt, told the media that 10 Cameroonians who had attempted to enter the Intercontinental Hotel by force had been arrested and were being investigated (Simon, 2021).

Since the ban on the previously authorized demonstration took immediate effect, despite the fact that its Swiss-Cameroonian organizers had appealed the decision of the authorities to ban the rally, the Cameroonian demonstrators resorted to techniques of defiance that had been honed by years of resistance against the brutal and repressive Biya regime in the streets of Douala, Yaoundé, Buea, and Bamenda. Civil disobedience and defiance were the main weapons of resistance that emerged in the 1990s. In his book, *The Anthropology of Anger*, Monga (1991) wrote that in the face of a kleptocratic, authoritarian, neo-patrimonial, tribalistic regime that was impervious to the sufferings of the people – a republican monarchy whose sole purpose was staying in power for ever – civil disobedience, incivility, and subtle acts of defiance against the overbearing State became the order of the day. By banning the previously authorized rally at the Place des Nations Unies in Geneva, the authorities of the Republic and Canton of Geneva seemed to have taken a leaf from the repressive playbook of Paul Biya – for purposes of protecting President Paul Biya and, by extension, their business interests in Cameroon. According to Paris-based magazine, *Jeune Afrique*, on Saturday the 17th of July 2021, the Cameroonian demonstrators, led by the anti-Biya Brigade anti-sardinards (BAS), proceeded with their demonstrations at the *Place des Nations Unies* in front of the United Nations compound despite the ban. They denounced the "genocide" in the English-speaking Northwest and Southwest. Carrying signs that read: *"La Suisse soutient le dictateur Biya," "Paul Biya : éternel dictateur," "Biya degage,"* "Stop the genocide of Cameroonians" ("Switzerland supports Biya the dictator, Paul Biya, eternal dictator, Biya buzz off!") in one hand, and mobile phones in the other to live-stream the event or record it for posting on social media, the demonstrators were ready to march from the United Nations headquarters to the Intercontinental Hotel where President Biya was ensconced in the lap of luxury. The angry demonstrators quickly found themselves face-to-face with a wall of police barricades and anti-riot officers in full anti-riot gear. This standoff ultimately resulted in a riot when the demonstrators attempted to move toward the Intercontinental Hotel. Some protesters threw eggs at the riot police, who proceeded to disperse the crowd with tear gas, water cannons, and plastic bullets (Simon, 2021; *Cameroun, Manifestation contre Paul Biya à Genève,* 2021).

Figure 19.6. Left, Cameroonians demonstrating against Biya near the Intercontinental Hotel in Geneva, Switzerland. Figure 19.7. Right, Swiss police blast water cannons to stop Cameroonian demonstrators from reaching the Intercontinental Hotel where President Biya was staying. Credit AFP

Videos and still images of the demonstration at the United Nations headquarters and its violent dispersal soon went viral on social media and traditional media. Despite the attempt by the authorities of the Republic and Canton of Geneva to avoid a repeat of the public relations disaster of the 2019 anti-Biya demonstration by banning the protests of 2021, the damage had already been done. The Swiss learned the hard way that in this day and age of the Internet and social media, there really is nothing hidden under the sun. The protests once again tarnished the image of Switzerland, as well as the Intercontinental Hotel, and did incalculable damage to the image of Cameroon.

Figure 19.8. Cameroonians demonstrators are stopped by Swiss police tear gas when they try to reach the Intercontinental Hotel where President Biya was staying with his wife and daughter, Brenda. Credit AFP

The Professor and the Autocratic Republican Chieftain

One of the leaders of the 2021 anti-Biya "Operation Catcham" (meaning Catch him in Pidgin English) at the Intercontinental Hotel in Geneva was Cameroon-American professor Patrice Nganang. A scholar, award-winning Francophone writer and professor of Cultural Studies and Comparative Literature at Stony Brook University (State University of New York). Nganang became one of the intellectual godfathers of the anti-Biya movement in the Diaspora because he was one of the earliest victims of the repressive Biya regime. He was an early voice for the respect for human rights at the start of the Anglophone Revolt in 2017. Indeed, the man made his name and reputation as an engaged intellectual in the early days of the Anglophone revolt in Cameroon. In effect, when the revolt began in November 2016, Nganang did what many Cameroonian and foreign journalists feared to do. He returned to Cameroon and, for 30 days, traveled extensively in the conflict-ridden Southwest and Northwest regions and saw firsthand the excesses of the Biya military occupation and the human rights abuses the Cameroon armed forces, led by the Israeli-trained and armed BIR, visited on unarmed English and Pidgin-speaking demonstrators and innocent civilians. This eye-opening safari into the tenebrous heart of the human rights violations of the Biya republican chiefdom would transform Nganang into one of the regime's fiercest critics. While in Southern Cameroons, he held discussions with human rights activist, Barrister Agbor Balla Nkongho, President of the Fako Lawyers' Association, a collective of self-described English-language "common law lawyers" in the Southwest region of Cameroon. Nkongho was also president of the Cameroon Anglophone Civil Society Consortium (CACSC), which the Cameroon government declared a threat to national security and banned. Nganang also met with university lecturers, leaders of the teachers' union, civil society, and students. From Buea, Nganang wrote a lengthy article for Paris-based *Jeune Afrique* magazine (Nganang, 2017). He noted that President Paul Biya had decided, without any qualms, to crush all Anglophone dissidents whom he labeled as "secessionists and terrorists." He revealed that as soon as Biya had made a public declaration of war against Anglophone dissidents in November 2017, his hand-picked appointed DO of Manyu Division, Oum II Joseph, had ordered the inhabitants of 15 named villages to vacate their homes, without specifying where they should go (Nganang, 2017). These Manyu villages are located in the general area where the nascent Anglophone resistance led by Lucas Cho Ayaba's Ambazonia Defense Force (ADF) had attacked and killed some members of the Cameroon military in retaliation for violent military attacks and killings of scores of unarmed civilian demonstrations on September 22 and October 1, 2017.

Professor Nganang also wrote that the Cameroon government had resorted to a scorched-earth military option to resolve a non-violent political problem in the so-called Anglophone zone. He reported that the Biya regime had shut down the Internet in the Anglophone regions to prevent the people from using social media to organize protests against its heavy-handed military repression. He wrote of the state of the English-medium schools, which more and more Francophone parents are preferring, as well as the mass migration of children from the English-speaking Southern Cameroons to make-shift "bilingual" schools in the French-speaking regions of Cameroon due to the crisis (Nganang, 2017). Nganang spoke of his visit with Mancho Bibixy, a radio personality in Bamenda who had led a so-called "coffin revolution," against the Biya regime's repression. He had been arrested and deported to the notoriously over-crowded Kondengui Central prison in Yaoundé, in French Cameroon in order to remove him from the jurisdiction of the English-language common law system of Southern Cameroons. He would ultimately be tried before the French-language only Yaoundé Military Tribunal and be sentenced to life imprisonment. Professor Nganang concluded that President Biya, who had never given a single speech or interview in English in his close to 40 years in power, had refused to dialogue with Anglophones. He wrote that Biya's military option would not succeed and that the Anglophone problem would only be solved when Biya was no longer president of Cameroon (Nganang, 2017).

Prof. Nganang's *Jeune Afrique* travelogue in the heart of the so-called Anglophone crisis quickly got him in trouble with the Biya regime. On December 8, 2017, barely three days after his travelogue was published in Paris, he was arrested at the Douala International Airport as he was about to board a flight out of the country. He was blindfolded, handcuffed, bundled into a police vehicle, and secretly driven to the capital, Yaoundé, where he was locked up at the notorious gendarmerie detention center in the Secretariat of State for National Security (SED) (*L'écrivain Patrice Nganang arrêté à l'aéroport de Douala*, 2017). He was subsequently charged with insulting President Biya on Facebook and threatening to shoot him. Nganang was also charged with entering Cameroon with two passports – one from Cameroon and one from the United States. Cameroon does not allow dual citizenship, though most government ministers, senior government officials, professional football players and their families carry second passports from other countries. The government seized Nganang's Cameroon passport and unilaterally revoked his Cameroonian citizenship without even a semblance of due process of law. After his arrest, there was an international hue and cry. The hashtag #Freepatricenganang became the focal point for a social media campaign on Facebook, WhatsApp and Twitter for the professor's release. Fortunately for him, he was saved by his American citizenship. The Trump administration intervened, and Nganang was released after 14 days in detention. The professor was declared a persona non-grata in the country of his birth (without even a court hearing), and promptly deported to the US on December 27, 2017. The irony is that Professor Nganang, a black African, was arrested in Cameroon, his country of birth, and deported to America by the government of Cameroon, the majority of whose ministers and /or family members have French, American and other European passports, as well as Swiss bank accounts. Prof Nganang's, arrest, detention, and deportation from Cameroon transformed him into one of the fiercest critics of the Biya regime.

This was not the first time Patrice Nganang had been arrested and detained by the Cameroon security forces. In 2014, he was arrested by the gendarmerie in Bonanjo, Douala, when the organization he founded, "Tribunal Article 53," (Article 53 Tribunal) organized the *Prix Bibi Ngota contre l'impunité en Afrique.* (The Bibi Ngota Prize Against Impunity in Africa). The name of Nganang's organization, Article 53 Tribunal, referred to the Court of Impeachment provided for under Article 53 (1) of the Constitution Cameroon. The Court of Impeachment, which has never seen the light of day, was supposed to have jurisdiction to try the President of the Republic for high treason and the Prime Minister, members of government and public officials of equivalent rank for conspiracy against the security of the state with respect to any acts committed by them in the discharge of their duties. Prof. Nganang created the *Prix Bibi Ngota contre l'impunité en Afrique* (The Bibi Ngota Prize Against Impunity in Africa) to recognize journalists who fight against "impunity." The award was named after Bibi Ngota, a journalist who was arrested by Cameroon security forces, and died in detention under very suspicious circumstances (Necedem, 2014). The inconvenient Bibi Ngota Prize award ceremony was banned by the *sous-préfet*, of Douala, Jean Marc Mbarga, on the grounds that the award ceremony posed a risk of a "serious breach of public order." The same reasons had been given when the ceremony was banned in Yaoundé in 2011 (*La Police arrête Patrice Nganang*, 2014). Furthermore, Article 53 Tribunal had incurred the wrath of the Cameroon government when its leader, Patrice Nganang had lodged a complaint against President Biya for high treason, high crimes, corruption, mismanagement, and incompetence (*La Police arrête Patrice Nganang*, 2014). In 2014, the gendarmerie had banned the inconvenient Bibi Ngota prize award ceremony and seized the prizes and other materials that were to be used in the ceremony, an event the authorities considered a provocative act of "rebellion." Professor Nganang, his fellow organizers, the award winners, and the journalists who were supposed to take part in that ceremony – and the winners happened to be English-language journalists – were arrested by the gendarmerie, taken to the gendarmerie station in Bonanjo, Douala and interrogated. They were released with a warning that if they dared to organize this illegal Bibi Ngota award ceremony in future, they would be arrested and charged with terrorism (Nganang, 2014). Two weeks later, the Cameroon Parliament passed Law No. 2014/028 of 23 December 2014 on the Suppression of Acts of Terrorism, which provides the death penalty for perpetrators of terrorist acts. This law essentially made political dissent a terrorist act in Cameroon. As we see elsewhere in this book, this law was the main weapon that the government used to arrest and prosecute Anglophone civilian dissidents and demonstrators at the Yaoundé Military Tribunal.

Patrice Nganang and "Operation Catcham"

Fast Forward to 2021. As a result of his run-ins with the Biya regime over the years, and especially after his detention in 2017, the arbitrary revocation of his Cameroonian citizenship, and his deportation to the United States, Professor Patrice Nganang engaged in active social media resistance against the Biya regime. He created a highly critical Facebook page that ridiculed the kleptocratic, republican, ethno-tribal chieftaincy of President Paul Biya. He presented the Anglophone war as a quagmire, a debacle for the French Cameroon army. He specifically reported the extensive human rights violations of the Biya regime in English-speaking Southern Cameroons. He amplified the atrocities of the Israeli-trained BIR and other branches of the Cameroon military and gendarmerie. He kept count of the number of dead or wounded Cameroon soldiers and even set up a social media fund to encourage Cameroon soldiers to desert the bloody conflict in Southern Cameroons. When the BAS began its online organization of "Operation Catcham" another anti-Biya demonstration scheduled in Geneva, Switzerland on July 17, 2021, Professor Nganang decided to travel to Switzerland and personally participate in the operation from within the entrails of the Beast, the Intercontinental Hotel in Geneva, where President Biya was staying. He booked a room online in order to be at the epicenter of the demonstration. Nganang told the Swiss newspaper, *Le Temps,* that one of the reasons he wanted to stay at the Geneva Intercontinental Hotel was to demystify the "enigma," that is, Paul Biya's love for the emblematic hotel that he had lived in for a total of about four years (Petite, 2021). The professor/activist flew from New York to Geneva, took a taxi from the airport to the hotel and proceeded to the reception desk to check-in. He said he was quite surprised at how "rather modest" the hotel was. He said he was expecting something as flashy as the Trump Tower in New York. That was not his only disappointment. He told *Le Temps* that checking into his room did not go as smoothly as anticipated. It took about an hour. He looked around and noticed the hotel lobby was full of President Biya's Israeli-trained security guards (Petite, 2021). They were fidgety and jittery, and kept looking in his direction. When the receptionist finally gave him the key to his room, he proceeded to the elevator. Swiss hotel security, Geneva police, and Biya's security guards surrounded him. They had apparently agreed that he would not be allowed to go to his room. A group of security men blocked his way and told him his room was not ready. He was not allowed to get into the elevator (Petite, 2021). He ultimately took a bus to another hotel. To his surprise, surreptitious images of him taken in the hotel lobby by the President's security detail and the hotel's video surveillance were sent to Cameroon where a local television station close to the Biya regime reported that Biya's security guards had foiled a "Machiavellian attack" by Nganang, "an activist and agitator" (Petite, 2021). Professor Nganang took advantage of his misadventure in Geneva to inform the Swiss that by continuing to welcome President Biya they were compromising their neutrality as mediators in the Anglophone crisis in Cameroon (Petite, 2021. The tragic irony of the situation is that President Biya loves Switzerland, a confederation, while arresting, jailing and killing English-speaking Cameroonians who called for a return to a federal system in Cameroon.

The Historical Ironies of the Anti-Biya Demonstrations in Geneva

The anti-Biya demonstrations by Cameroonian immigrants, exiles, and refugees in Geneva, Switzerland in 2019 and 2021 were incredibly ironic. History had come full circle! In effect, some of the mostly young Cameroonian demonstrators at the *Places des Nations* and in front of the Intercontinental Hotel in Geneva, had studied or received vocational training in schools started in Cameroon by Swiss German missionaries, or received medical care in health centers started by the Swiss-German *Evangelische Missionsgesellschaft in Basel* (Evangelical Missionary Society) that was commonly known as *Basler Mission* or *Basel Mission*. The Basel Mission first began its missionary work in Cameroon in 1886. These demonstrations were deeply ironic. The Swiss-German Basel Mission, which began missionary work in German Kamerun in 1886. The Basel Mission in Cameroon greatly influenced the historical development of Southern Cameroons, leading to the founding of the Presbyterian Church in Cameroon (PCC), one of the major denominations in terms of religious membership, educational institutions (Presbyterian schools and colleges), healthcare facilities, and (Nyansako-ni-Nku, 1982) professional training. The Anglophone Revolt of 2016 disrupted the educational institutions and healthcare facilities that had been developed by the Basel Mission and its offspring, the Presbyterian Church in Cameroon (Nyansako-ni-Nku, 1982; Ndamukong, 2007).

Missionaries from the Basel Mission returned in 1925 and focused their work in British Southern Cameroons, which was created after the Anglo-French partition of German Cameroon. The Basel Mission in Cameroon greatly influenced the historical development of English and Pidgin-speaking Southern Cameroons, leading to the founding of the Presbyterian Church in Cameroon (PCC), one of the major denominations in terms of religious membership, educational institutions (Presbyterian schools and colleges), Presbyterian hospitals and other healthcare facilities, and professional training (Nyansako-ni-Nku, 1982). In the 1960s and 1970s, the Helvetas-Swiss Association for Technical Assistance (SATA), a non-governmental development assistance organization established an office in Buea, Southern Camerons, and from there provided technical assistance in renewable natural resources, rural infrastructures (mostly village water projects) vocational training and culture with the aim of bringing about justice and solidarity through meeting the material and non-material needs of the people (Helvetas-Swiss Association for International Cooperation, 2010). Switzerland thus has one of the oldest and longest-lasting international, non-colonial engagements in development in the English-speaking Southern Cameroons.

The Swiss and the Anglophone Question in Cameroon

We have seen that the Swiss have had a long, historic relationship with Cameroon since the Swiss-German Basel Mission began missionary work in the German colony of Kamerun in 1886, in the aftermath of the partition of Africa at Bismarck's Berlin Africa Conference of 1884-1885. Fast-forward to 2019. The controversies caused by the unprecedented lengthy stays of President Paul Biya at the Intercontinental Hotel in Geneva, Switzerland, demonstrations by the Cameroon Diaspora, and violent repression of these demonstrations by the police of the Republic and Canton of Geneva, focused international attention on the fact that President Biya was masterminding human rights violations and crimes against humanity from Swiss territory caused Switzerland a lot of embarrassment. A Swiss federal government official, Ambassador Anne Lugon-Moulin, Head of the Sub-Saharan Africa and Francophone Division of the Swiss Federal Department of Foreign Affairs (FDFA), wrote a letter dated September 25, 2019, from Berne/Yaoundé, in response to a Collective of English-speaking Southern Cameroonians in the Diaspora. Ms. Lugon-Moulin stated that the FDFA was surprised and concerned by articles in Cameroonian newspapers regarding the "facilitation process led by Switzerland." She wished to clarify some things regarding that process. She said that "a majority of parties asked Switzerland to facilitate an exclusive negotiating process...The good offices of Switzerland are motivated by humanitarian considerations. In this context, Switzerland adheres to the principles of strict neutrality and discretion." Ambassador Lugon-Moulin emphasized the fact that the Major National Dialogue" announced by President Paul Biya was different from the facilitation process led by Switzerland, which was the subject of "ongoing confidential discussions with all parties... Switzerland's commitment is not motivated by any interest other than a peaceful resolution of conflicts and it engages in facilitation processes only as long as the parties judge it useful." This statement was in response to criticism that Biya's long stay in Switzerland and his economic links with Swiss companies made the Swiss a partner in his crimes against humanity. The question was why the Swiss government, which is a self-described champion of human rights, would continue to allow Biya, a human rights violator, to spend long periods of time in Switzerland, from which location he orders his soldiers and henchmen to transform Cameroon into a hellhole for innocent people.

Furthermore, official Cameroon government and pro-government media outlets gave the impression that Switzerland had given its blessing to President Biya's Major National Dialogue, which was essentially a government affair, a monologue created by the government, for the consumption of the government, the Francophone national audience, and the international community. Ambassador Lugon-Moulin acknowledged that President Biya did indeed have lengthy stays in Geneva, Switzerland on private visits and official multilateral conferences. She did not deny that he and his entourage were in Geneva during the period of the massacres. She however stated that, "I can assure you that Switzerland will continue to follow closely the human rights situation in Cameroon and promote the protection of human rights, including those of persons belonging to national or ethnic, religious and linguistic minorities, in the framework of its bilateral relations with Cameroon as well as on the multilateral level." Nevertheless, she did not mention that besides the Intercontinental Hotel in Geneva and Swiss banks, Switzerland had lucrative business interests in the agricultural sector in Cameroon, (cocoa beans for its chocolate industry), tropical wood and wood products, infrastructure (the Douala port), as well as commodities trading (primarily oil and natural gas). These were Biya's passport to Switzerland. It should be noted that in 2018, the Swiss Secretariat of State for Migration in the Federal Department of Justice, had produced a comprehensive report on the Anglophone Revolt in Cameroon entitled, "*Note Cameroun*: *Crise du Cameroun Anglophone*." The report highlighted the horrible human rights violations and the refugee problem that had been triggered by the human rights violations of the Cameroon military (Note Cameroun, 2018). This report did not cause Switzerland to limit Biya's visits to Switzerland despite Biya's continued refusal to engage in dialogue or to curtail his desire to use military means to solve an essentially political problem.

Conclusion

The tragic irony of the Swiss Connection in the Anglophone Question is that President Paul Biya loves Switzerland, a multi-lingual, multi-cultural confederation, while his government was a highly centralized, autocratic, neo-patrimonial republican chiefery that had launched a subjugation campaign against the Anglophone minority for purposes of maintaining absolute control of the natural resources of the Anglophone regions to maintain his regime in power. He loved Switzerland, a self-proclaimed champion of human rights, while his military, and especially his presidential guard and his Israeli-trained and armed BIR, carried out all kinds of atrocities and human rights violations – arresting, jailing, torturing and killing English-speaking Cameroonians who called for a return to a federal system in Cameroon. His hand-picked prefects and sub-prefects expelled thousands of villagers from their homes ostensibly to fight separatists. From the comfort of the Intercontinental Hotel in Geneva, President Biya ordered a scorched-earth policy that saw the burning of hundreds of villages in Anglophone Cameroon and triggered an unprecedented refugee crisis that the United Nations High Commission for Refugees, whose office is a stone's throw from Biya's suite at the Intercontinental Hotel in Geneva, has been managing for years. Biya violated human rights with impunity because the economic interests of Switzerland, France, Israel, the United Kingdom, Russia, and China trump human rights in Africa.

References

Amabo, E. (2021). Cameroon-Swiss federal Council: Visa Requirements Abolition in View. Cameroon Tribune, June 29. Retrieved from: https://www.cameroon tribune.cm/article.html/40833/en.html/cameroon-swiss-federal-council-visa-requirements-abolition-in%C3%A0-l-%C3%A9meute-%C3%A0-gen%C3%A8ve/2308019.

Andzongo, S. (2019). Paris Peace Forum: Paul Biya explains the background of the Anglophone crisis. *Business in Cameroon,* November 13. Retrieved from: https://www.businessincameroon.com/public-management/1311-9677-paris-peace-forum-paul-biya-explains-the-background-of-the-anglophone-crisis

Barry Callebaut and Cameroon Intensify Collaboration to Support Young Farmers (2019). Barry Callebaut, May 24. Retrieved from: https://www.barry-callebaut.com/en/group/media/news-stories/barry-callebaut-and-cameroon-intensify-collaboration.

Ben Ahmed, L. (2021), *Cameroun: Une Manifestation contre le President Biya tourne à l'émeute à Genève* (Cameroon: A demonstration against President Biya become a riot in Geneva). Anadolou Agency (Ankara, Turkey), July 18th. Retrieved from: https://www.aa.com.tr/fr/afrique/cameroun-une-manifestation-contre-paul-biya-tourne-

Cameroun: l'écrivain Patrice Nganang arrêté à l'aéroport de Douala (The Writer Patrice Nganang arrested at the Douala Airport). *Jeune Afrique* & AFP, December 7th. Retrieved from: https://www.jeuneafrique.com/500391/politique/cameroun-lecrivain-patrice-nganang-arrete-a-laeroport-de-douala/

Cameroun, Manifestation contre Paul Biya à Genève (2021). *Jeune Afrique*, July 18. Retrieved from: https://www.jeuneafrique.com/1204952/politique/cameroun-manifestation-contre-paul-biya-a-geneve/

Cameroon Journalist Samuel Wazizi died in Detention (2020) *Reporters Without Borders*, June. Retrieved from: Retrieved from: https://rsf.org/en/news/cameroonian-journalist-samuel-wazizi-died-detention.

Concern Grows for Women and Children (2018). United Nations High Commission for Refugees (UNHCR). January 18. Retrieved from: https://www.unhcr.org/en-us/news/briefing/2018/1/5a61b3bc4/concern-grows-women-children-fleeing-cameroon.html

Crawford, J & Spoerndli, M. (2019). Cameroon's Biya: Why the Swiss Won't Stop His Geneva Stays. Swissinfo.ch. January 4. Retrieved from: https://www.swissinfo.ch/eng/who-foots-the-bill- cameroon-s-biya--why-the-swiss-won-t-stop-his-geneva-stays/44644510

Crise anglophone au Cameroun : Paul Biya dénonce une « bande de terroristes (2017). Jenune Afrique and Agence France Presse. December 1. Retrieved from: https://www.jeuneafrique.com/498486/politique/crise-anglophone-au-cameroun-paul-biya-denonce-une-bande-de-terroristes/

Deca, K. (2020). Glencore Sues Cameroon's Sonara for FCFA 9.6 Billion. Afrikan Heroes. Retrieved from: https://afrikanheroes.com/2020/09/15/glencore-sues-cameroons-sonara-for-fcfa-9-6-billion/

Federal Department of Foreign Affairs (2018). Cameroonian delegation visits Switzerland to discuss plurilingualism, *Press Release*, June 1. Retrieved from: https://www.admin.ch/gov/en/start/documentation/media-releases.msg-id-71073.html

Foute, F. (2019). Cameroun: Yaoundé dénonce l'attitude "hostile et belliqueuse" des manifestants en Suisse (Yaounde denounces the hostile and bellicose attitude of demonstrations in in Switzerland. Jeune Afrique, July 1. Retrieved from: https://www.jeuneafrique.com/796826/politique/cameroun-yaounde-denonce-lattitude-hostile-et-belliqueuse-des-manifestants-en-suisse/

G'Nowa, O. (2008). *L'unique fille de Paul Biya fait ses études primaires en Suisse* (The only daughter of Paul Biya does her primary education in Switzerland). Cameroun Online, 26 September. Retrieved from: ttps://web.archive.org/web/20080926185233/http://www.cameroun-online

Helvetas-Swiss Association for Technical Cooperation (2010). Global Civil Society Database. Retrieved from: https://uia.org/s/or/en/1100001762

Happi, C. (2020). *Cameroun : Paul Biya reste le bienvenu à Genève.* (Paul Biya is still welcome in Geneva). *Actu Cameroun*, October 2. Retrieved from: https://actucameroun.com/2020/10/02/cameroun-paul-biya-reste-le-bienvenu-a-geneve/

Holy See Press Office Communique N. 170323e: Audience with the President of the Republic of Cameroon (2017). Thursday 23.03.2017. Retrieved form: http://press.vatican.va/content/salastampa/en/bollettino/pubblico/2017/03/23/170323e.html

Kindzeka, E. *(2017).* Cameroon Media Face Restrictions on Reporting, *Voice of America (VOA).* May 15th. Retrieved from: https://learningenglish.voanews.com/a/cameroon-media-face-restrictions-reporting/3849489.html

La police arrête Patrice Nganang (2014). Le Messager (Douala). December 9. Retrieved from: http://www.cameroon-info.net/article/cameroun-patrice-nganang-arrete-par-lapolice-a-douala-237642.html

Monga, C. (1996). *The Anthropology of Anger: Civil Society and Democracy in Africa.* Boulder, Co. Lynne Rienner.

Musa, W. (2017). Cameroon-Judiciary: PCC Moderator Goes to Court Monday. Cameroon Info Net (CIN). April, 19. Retrieved from: http://www.cameroon-info.net/article/cameroon-judiciary-pcc-moderator-goes-to-court-monday-287034.html

Necedem, A. (2014). Cameroun: la gendarmerie empêche la cérémonie de remise d'un prix international de la presse (The gendarmerie prevents the prize-giving ceremony for an international press prize). *Agence Ecofin.* December 9. Retrieved from: https://www.agenceecofin.com/evenementiel/0912-24974-cameroun-la-gendarmerie-empeche-la-ceremonie-de-remise-d-un-prix-international-de-la-presse

Nfor, N. (2020). *Paradise Lost? A Political History of British Southern Cameroons from 1916-1972.* Austin, TX, Pan African University Press.

Nganang, P. (2014). Cameroun-Douala: Comment Le Prix Bibi Ngota n'a pas été remis (Why the Bibi Ngota Prize was not awarded). Cameroon-Info.Net. Retrieved from: http://www.cameroon-info.net/article/cameroun-douala-comment-le-prix-bibi-ngota-na-pas-ete-remis-par-patrice-237675.html

Nganang, P. (2017). Cameroun: Carnet de Route de l'ecrivain Patrice Nganang en zone (dite) anglophone. (Cameroon: Travelogue of the writer Patrice Nganang in the so-called anglophone zone) *Jeune Afrique.* December 5, 2017. Retrieved from: https://www.jeuneafrique.com/499512/politique/cameroun-carnet-de-route-de-lecrivain-patrice-nganang-en-zone-dite-anglophone/

Note Cameroun: Crise du Cameroon Anglophone (2018). Departement Fédéral de la Justice, Secretariat d'État aux migrations (SEM). Switzerland. September 25. Retrieved from: file:///Users/LEko/Downloads/CMR-krise-anglophone-f.pdf

O'Donnell, J. & Gramer, R. (2018). Cameroon's Paul Biya Gives Master Class in Fake Democracy. Foreign Affairs. October 22. Retrieved from: https://foreignpolicy.com/2018/10/22/cameroons-paul-biya-gives-a-master-class-in-fake-democracy/

Oum II, J. (2017, December 7th). Communique No. C69/vIII/373. Communique. Mamfe, Southwest: Divisional Office Mamfe.

Petite, S. (2021). *Dans son hôtel genevois, Paul Biya choisit ses voisins de chambre (In his Geneva hotel, Paul Biya chooses guests of rooms near his), Le Temps (Geneva). July 23. Retrieved from:* https://www.letemps.ch/monde/hotel-genevois-paul-biya-choisit-voisins-chambre

President Paul Biya woos Italian Investors, receives Gold Medal at Tor Vergata University (2017). Presidency of the Republic. Retrieved from: https://www.prc.cm/en/news/travels-and-visits/2207-president-paul-biya-woos-italian-investors-receives-gold-medal-at-tor-vergata-university

Protocol Agreement Between the Barry Callebaut Group and the Interprofessional Cocoa and Coffee Council (2019). Barry Callebaut Group, Retrieved from: https://www.barry-callebaut.

com/en/group/media/news-stories/barry-callebaut-and-cameroon-intensify-collaboration,

Ross & Bavier (2018). European tourists were not kidnapped in Cameroon, tour operator says. Reuters, April 3, Retrieved from: https://www.reuters.com/article/us-cameroon-security/european-tourists-were-not-kidnapped-in-cameroon-tour-operator-says-idUSKCN1HB17T

Switzerland to Support Peace Efforts (2019). Presidency of the Republic. Retrieved from: https://www.prc.cm/en/news/audiences/3419-switzerland-to-support-peace-efforts-in-cameroon

UN High Commission for Refugees. (2018, January 18). UNHCR USA. Retrieved from https://www.unhcr.org/en-us/news/briefing/2018/1/5a61b3bc4/concern-grows-women-children-flee-ing-cameroon.html

Simon, S. (2021). La manifestation contre Paul Biya est interdite (The demonstration against Paul Biya is banned). *Tribune de Genève*, July 16. Retrieved from: https://www.tdg.ch/la-manifestation-contre-paul-biya-est-interdite-814825964739

Simon, S. (2021). *La manifestation contre Paul Biya tourne à l'emeut*e (The demonstration against Paul Biya become a riot). *Tribune de Genève,* July 17. Retrieved from: https://www.tdg.ch/la-manifestation-contre-paul-biya-est-en-cours-malgre-son-interdiction-364239910663

Sina, K. *(2018).* Bilingualism and Multiculturalism: Swiss Federal Delegate for Multilingualism Nicoletta Mariolini on a Five-Day Working Visit in Cameroon. *Cameroon Radio and Television (CRTV).* January 22. Retrieved from: https://www.crtv.cm/2018/01/bilingualism-and-multicul-turalism-swiss-federal-delegate-for-multilingualism-nicoletta-mariolini-on-a-five-day-work-ing-visit-in-cameroon/

Toronto Declaration (2021). The Southern Cameroons 2021 Leadership Retreat. *The Coalition for Dia-logue and Negotiation* (CDN). Retrieved from: https://business.facebook.com/CoalitionFDN/photos/pcb.450117513129608/450148596459833/?type=3&theater

TWENTY

The Swiss Dissonance

European Federalists, African Anti-Federalist Bedfellow

LYOMBE EKO

On Saturday, June 29, 2019, a crowd of Cameroonian immigrants, refugees and asylum seekers resident in Switzerland and nearby European countries gathered at the *Place de Nations*, the European headquarters of the United Nations in Geneva, the capital of the French-speaking Republic and Canton of Geneva, for a demonstration against their President, Paul Biya, who was lounging in the lap of luxury at the nearby Intercontinental Hotel (AFP, 2019). Some of the demonstrators had come out of the shadows and the clandestine existence to which their undocumented status in Europe had consigned them, taking advantage of the power of numbers and the anonymity of the crowd to vent their angst against the African dictator whose corruption and maladministration had caused them to become migrants. These Africans were in Geneva, Switzerland, a financial and diplomatic center at the heart of Europe, the land of federalism, human rights, political neutrality, and freedom – as well as opaque business and financial secrecy – to demonstrate against Switzerland's partner in crimes against humanity, their president, Paul Biya. The Cameroonian demonstrators held placards that read: "*Paul Biya Assassin, la Swiss complice*" (Paul Biya Assassin, Switzerland his accomplice), among others. Switzerland's "accomplice" was none other than Africa's longest-serving authoritarian leader, Paul Barthélémy Biya Bi Mvondo, an extreme exemplar of egotistical incarnation and personification of the state and power. Biya, a former Roman Catholic seminarian, was a hardline, ethnocentric, republican chieftain who had launched a bloody war of subjugation against the English and Pidgin-speaking minority in the restive, former Southern Cameroons in 2017. The scorched-earth atrocities and human rights violations of his security forces had triggered a humanitarian crisis that displaced more than one million people internally and created a flood of refugees that had sent more than 150,000 Anglophone refugees fleeing to neighboring Nigeria, Ghana, Equatorial Guinea, and as far away as Europe, Latin America and the United States. Some of the demonstrators in Geneva were either Anglophone refugees or friends and relatives of refugees.

Figure 20.1. Cameroon refugees and exiles demonstrate against President Biya and the United Nations at the *Place de Nations*, the European headquarters of the United Nations in Geneva (June 29, 2019)

Biya's repressive war of conquest had been kicked off from the lap of luxury at a posh and expensive presidential suite at the Intercontinental Hotel in Geneva. The anti-Biya demonstration was thus an unofficial African political drama being played out in the scenic Republic and Canton of Geneva, which the discontented Africans believed was a partner in Biya's crimes against humanity, because it was a beneficiary of the economic largesse of his kleptocratic *chefferie républicaine* (republican chiefery). Besides the Anglophone Crisis, the demonstrating Cameroonians represented a number of causes, the most prominent of which were, the Biya regime's rigging of the 2018 presidential election to give the octogenarian leader another seven-year term that essentially made him president for life. More than that, the Cameroonians were there to demonstrate against the massive post-election repression launched against the political opposition in Cameroon. This repression included the arrest and detention of Maurice Kamto and Mamadou Mota, leaders of the opposition *Mouvement pour la Renaissance du Cameroun* (MRC), as well as hundreds of members of their party. The imprisoned leaders had dared to challenge the results of the 2018 elections, which international observers had concluded were neither free nor fair. Indeed, one international commentator had called the elections a "master class in fake democracy" (O'Donnell & Gramer, 2018).

The Anti-Biya demonstrations were taking place in Geneva, Switzerland, rather than Yaoundé, Douala or even Gbea (Buea) because President Paul Biya was doing his favorite pastime, taking yet another lengthy, "short, private visit to Europe" (read, an extended, expensive stay at a presidential suite of the Intercontinental Hotel, Geneva, with its "magnificent view of Lake Geneva and Jura Mountains," as the hotel's advertisement states). Biya and his wife, Chantal, who are known for their fondness for chartered, luxurious presidential aircraft, the expensive, luxurious Intercontinental Hotel in Geneva, the luxurious and very expensive boutiques, beauty salons, and health clinics of Geneva, were decades-long clients of the British-owned hotel chain. They had a habit of flying to Switzerland on chartered luxury, presidential aircraft, occupying whole floors of the hotel at a time with their extended family and entourage. In true chiefly patrimonial style, a trip to Geneva and its luxuries were often used as occasions to reward regime stalwarts for loyal service to the president, his wife and family.

Switzerland has thus been a long-time beneficiary of President Biya's fondness for their country. The Organized Crime and Corruption Reporting Project (OCCRP) analyzed 35 years of editions of the government's sycophantic newspaper and mouthpiece, the *Cameroon Tribune*. It was found that, over that time, President Biya had spent at least four-and-a-half years on his "brief private visits" to Switzerland by 2015. This earned him newspaper titles like, the "roaming president," the "missing president," "the absentee president," and so on. (Freudental et al., 2018). Once in Geneva, Paul and Chantal Biya would spend weeks at a time at the Intercontinental Hotel and pay for their expenses in cash (euros) to obscure the provenance of the funds (Hinshaw & Parkinson, 2018). According to the Organized Crime and Corruption Reporting Project (OCCRP), most of those funds came from the *Société Nationale des Hydrocarbures* (SNH), the national oil company which President Biya uses as his personal slush fund (Freudental et al., 2018). The SNH also funds the Israeli-trained and armed *Bataillon d'intervention Rapide* (The Rapid Intervention Battalion, or BIR). As we shall see later, the SNH has a partnership with the Swiss commodities trading conglomerate, Glencore International AG of Baar, Switzerland. On May 24, 2022, the United States Department of Justice accused Glencore of bribing national oil company officials in Nigeria, Cameroon, Ivory Coast, Equatorial Guinea, Congo, and South Sudan to have profitable access to the oil and other natural resources (minerals) of these countries. Glencore International AG pled guilty to the charges. As we see below, American and British authorities charged that officials of the Cameroon National Hydrocarbons Company (SNH), and the national refinery, SONARA received bribes to have profitable access to oil and natural gas in Cameroon in furtherance of the interests of Glencore International AG (United States v. Glencore International AG, 2022). Other Swiss companies benefit handsomely from the close personal relationships of their CEOs with President Biya. For obvious reasons, the Swiss have not found President Biya's lucrative "Short private trips" to Geneva, Switzerland, problematic in any way, even when the president commandeered human rights violations against the English-speaking minority of Southern Cameroons from his sponsored presidential suite in Geneva, Switzerland (Crawford & Spoerndli, 2019). This is the background that triggered the embarrassing anti-Biya demonstrations in Geneva in 2019 and 2021.

The Swiss Confederation and its Authoritarian Anti-federalist Bedfellow

Since President Biya came to power in 1982, the Swiss Federal government and Swiss multinational companies have had a mutually-beneficial, symbiotic relationship with the over-centralized authoritarian, *chefferie républicaine* (republican chiefery) of President Biya, an anti-federalist who loves the Swiss confederation and its political, cultural, and economic benefits–and these are grounded on recognition of minority ethnic groups and their linguistic and cultural identities and specificities–but has gone out of his way to destroy federalism in Cameroon.

President Ahmadou Ahidjo and his French overseers changed the independent French *La République du Cameroun* to the ambiguous, bilingual, centralist Federal Republic of Cameroon to accommodate English-speaking Southern Cameroonians and Southern Cameroons was renamed West Cameroon in the process. The Anglophone problem is grounded in the old African natural resource curse. In 1964, French companies discovered huge oil and natural gas reserves in the Rio del Rey basin, in the territory of the State of West Cameroon. That information was kept secret from the leaders and people of West Cameroon. In a political sleight of hand designed to bring the oil and natural gas resources under the direct control of President Ahidjo and his cronies in Yaoundé, President Ahmadou Ahidjo violated the federal constitution and abolished the federation in 1972, through a referendum of dubious legality, creating a United Republic of Cameroon and splitting the state of West Cameroon into two provinces, the Southwest and Northwest provinces by decree. The authoritarian French Cameroon leader, Ahmadou Ahidjo soon imposed a highly centralized, autocratic African-style, *chefferie républicaine* (republican chiefery) with a Napoleonic administration complete with appointed proconsuls (governors,) prefects, and sub-prefects. That essentially ended the quasi-autonomous local government system of West Cameroon. These Machiavellian political moves also effectively transferred West Cameroon's oil, natural gas, and agricultural resources to the personal control of Ahmadou Ahidjo, and ultimately his successor, Paul Biya, and his tribal political cronies in Yaoundé. Reunification of Southern Cameroons and la *République du Cameroun* quickly turned out to be "lawful plunder" to borrow the expression of Bastiat (1998), who pointed out that "plunder is organized by law for the profit of those who make the law" (p. 7). In the post-reunification Cameroon, Southern Cameroons became the object of lawful plunder. Ahidjo-Biya, and their French overseers used legal plunder to take the wealth of Southern Cameroons – its natural resources – oil, natural gas, timber, state-owned agricultural estates, agricultural cooperatives, educational institutions, and so on, and gave them to a few, while throwing a few crumbs to a handful of Anglophone leaders now and then! Through political subterfuge, President Ahidjo imposed an unconstitutional referendum on May 20, 1972 that changed the form of the country from a federal republic to a centralized, authoritarian Napoleonic state, the United Republic of Cameroon, that engulfed the government and civil service of Southern Cameroons. This was a violation of Article 47 of the Federal Constitution of 1961, which had declared unconstitutional, any law aimed at changing the nature of the state. Additionally, he applied a divide-and-conquer strategy by splitting West Cameroon into two separate provinces, the Northwest and Southwest, via a presidential decree, and appointed governors to rule these provinces. President Ahmadou Ahidjo's controversial and unconstitutional referendum that eliminated the Federal Republic of Cameroon in 1972, and ushered in the highly centralized United Republic of Cameroon, and sowed the seeds of the Anglophone Revolt. Furthermore, Ahmadou Ahidjo's successor, President Paul Biya renamed the whole country, *la République du Cameroon* (the Republic of Cameroon), the original name of French Cameroon, via a presidential decree. These autocratic steps resulted in the abolition of the Federal Republic of Cameroon and West Cameroon's autonomous federal state and government.

Since the controversial Ahidjo/Biya anti-democratic referendum that eliminated federalism in Cameroon and created an over-centralized Napoleonic republican chiefdom, President Biya worked with his French allies to erase and silence the identitarian specificity of the Anglophone minority, and erect an over-centralized, Napoleonic-style regime that promptly confiscated the natural resources of the Anglophone region. The Swiss quickly became co-beneficiaries of the plunder of the Ahidjo/Biya republican chiefery. Clearly, the Swiss Confederation and the anti-federalist Biya regime are strange moral and philosophical but not political and economic bedfellows.

The Biya regime granted its Swiss partners the right to control and exploit the natural resources of Anglophone Cameroon, which he treated as his personal property – in exchange for hefty bribes paid to officials of the SNH and SONARA, according American and British authorities (*United States v. Glencore International AG*). In his extreme egoism, arrogance and intransigence, he refused to have a genuine political dialogue with the Anglophones, preferring to use military means to subjugate them once and for all, causing all kinds of atrocities and human rights violations and crimes against humanity. Faced with the moral philosophical choice between business interests and human rights in Southern Cameroons, the Swiss chose their economic self-interest, feigning neutrality, and forgetting that in a conflict between the oppressor and the oppressed, choosing to be neutral, while strengthening the oppressive machinery of the oppressor is to enable the oppressor and his oppression at best, or to give him carte blanche to oppress at worst. The Swiss did not cause the Anglophone crisis in Cameroon, they allowed it to happen. Thus, in a sense, the Swiss Federal government and the Republic and Canton of Geneva, have worked actively to undermine, undo and destroy the more than one-century religious and humanitarian endeavors of Swiss medical and other missionaries from the Basel Mission, Swiss aid and humanitarian workers have accomplished over the years in Southern Cameroons. The reason for this is simple–to be on the good graces of President Paul Biya who giveth. That was the only way for Glencore, SGS, Nestlé, and other Swiss multinational conglomerates to have control over the supply chain and economic gateways of Cameroon, and especially to be granted concessions to the natural resources of the Anglophone Southern Cameroons that the Biya regime is doing all in its power to subjugate.

Aim of the chapter

This chapter aims to survey, describe and explain the Swiss disconnection in the Anglophone crisis in Cameroon. Switzerland has a legendary reputation as the banker of authoritarian dictators, tax evaders, organized criminals, and traffickers of all sorts. It is therefore not surprising that President Paul Biya, who was one of Africa's longest-serving presidents and perhaps one of the continent's most hardline, authoritarian dictators, would be a client of the Swiss. As we have seen in Chapter 2, Biya, a republican chieftain who loved the Swiss Confederation but imprisoned federalists in his own country, had a very mutually beneficial relationship with the Swiss government, Swiss banks, and Swiss companies. Since the full extent of this symbiotic relationship is not known, thanks to legendary Swiss secrecy, this chapter will focus on the public economic, natural resources and logistical aspects of this relationship. Switzerland is a confederation with a very pronounced human rights ethic and rhetoric. Its embrace of and friendship with the anti-federalist, human rights-violating president of Cameroon caused cognitive dissonance in many circles in Cameroon, particularly among the Anglophone minority. The premise of this chapter is that since the late 19th Century, Switzerland has had a long, historical, religious (missionary) and humanitarian connection with Cameroon in general and specifically with the English-speaking Southern Cameroons. That connection started being frayed when the Swiss embraced President Paul Biya in order to have access to the natural resources of Southern Cameroons. It reached a breaking point when the Anglophones revolted against the Biya dictatorship in 2016, and the Swiss, through their legendary neutrality, took the side of the oppressor. This chapter explores Swiss federal responses to the Anglophone crisis and Biya's continued visits to Geneva. The last part consists of case studies that explore the problematic business and economic relationships between the Biya regime and Swiss multinational corporations in the cocoa and commodities (oil and natural gas) sectors, as well as their role in the control of the economic gateways, and business supply-chain infrastructure of Cameroon.

Paul Biya and His Symbiotic Economic Relationship with the Swiss: The Cocoa and Chocolate Sector

As we have seen in chapter 20, President Biya, a republican monarch who loved the Swiss Confederation but imprisoned federalists in his own country, had a very mutually beneficial relationship with the Swiss government and Swiss companies. Since the full extent of this symbiotic relationship is not known, thanks to the legendary Swiss secrecy, this chapter will focus on the public economic, natural resources and logistical aspects of this relationship. It also explores abortive Swiss attempts to mediate in the Anglophone crisis. Swiss mediation in the Anglophone conflict has failed because of the Biya regime's hardline refusal to dialogue with Anglophones, which dialogue will raise the issue of modifying the nature of the state to give Anglophones more autonomy and make Cameroon look a little bit like Biya's Switzerland. This is anathema to Biya, who is viscerally opposed to changing the form of the Ahidjo/Biya republican chiefery of Cameroon. An anti-corruption group calculated that in his more than 40 years in positions of power in Cameroon, first as Prime Minister of President Ahmadou Ahidjo, and as president after 1982, Biya spent more than a total of four years in Switzerland. This is unprecedented for a sitting president of any country. The fact is that Switzerland became Biya's home away from home for two reasons: His presidential security in Cameroon was airtight. After an attempted coup d'état in 1984, President Biya turned to the Israelis who took over the security and communications apparatus of the country, created a praetorian guard, *la Garde presidentielle*, and a special forces unit, the notoriously violent, infamous, human rights violating BIR patterned after Israeli special forces. The BIR, an army within the army, and the Presidential guard, were staffed by hand-picked officers from President Biya's Beti/Bulu ethnic group. Secondly, the legendary discretion and financial secrecy of the Swiss helped Biya and his tribal cronies to essentially transform the natural resources of Cameroon, mostly its oil and natural gas – and these were primarily in the English-speaking Southern Cameroons – into his personal slush fund. Switzerland, which is a confederation, is a curious choice for a president whose system of governance is a highly centralized, autocratic, Napoleonic, republican chieftaincy. But then, Switzerland offered Paul Biya what it has offered other African dictators from time immemorial–an opportunity to milk their poor countries dry in secret and with impunity. In effect, President Paul Biya has had a mutually beneficial symbiotic relationship with Swiss businesses. The symbiotic relationship between Switzerland and the kleptocratic Biya regime came down to this proverbial cliché: "follow the money."

On May 22, 2019, in the midst of the Anglophone crisis, with horrendous human rights violations and crimes against humanity being carried out in Southern Cameroons by the Israeli-trained and equipped BIR, the Swiss Ambassador to Cameroon, His Excellency Pietro Lazzeri, paid President Paul Biya a courtesy call. He was accompanied by Antoine de Saint-Afrique, CEO of Barry Callebaut, the world's leading manufacturer of high-quality chocolate and cocoa products (global sales, $7.1 billion). Cameroon is one of the largest cocoa producers in Africa. The *Société Industrielle Camerounaise des Cacaos* (Sic Cacaos), a subsidiary of the Swiss multinational chocolate manufacturer, Barry Callebaut, has operated in Cameroon as a buyer of cocoa beans from peasant farmers since 1949. It therefore has an interest in working with the Biya regime to ensure the continued flow of cocoa beans to its Cameroon-based roasters and grinders, as well as its chocolate manufacturing facilities in Belgium, France, Switzerland, and elsewhere. The next day Barry Callebaut reported that the multinational chocolate manufacturer and the government of Cameroon had "signed a letter of intent" to ensure the continued flow of cocoa grown by Cameroon farmers to Switzerland, and "to intensify the cooperation on sustainable cocoa farming, in particular, supporting the next generation of cocoa farmers. Barry Callebaut and the Cameroon government aim to support the next generation of cocoa farmers from Cameroon through the "New Generation" program–launched in 2012 by the Cameroon Cocoa and Coffee Interprofessional Council (CICC) to rejuvenate cocoa farms, introduce young Cameroonians to cocoa farming and lower the average age for cocoa farmers in Cameroon) by establishing access to family farm plots, training, inputs, financing and equipment acquisition" (Barry Callebaut and Cameroon Intensify Collaboration to Support Young Cocoa Farmers, 2019).

Cocoa farmers in Cameroon and elsewhere in West Africa are a dying breed, and because cocoa farming is a labor-intensive, low-paying, low-income activity, young people are not interested in replacing their parents and grandparents in the back-breaking work of cocoa farming. Barry Callebaut and other alarmed multi-national cocoa companies are promoting the emergence of the next generation of cocoa farmers to keep the raw material supply flowing to its factories. However, true to the over-centralized nature of the government in Cameroon, Barry Callebaut's New Generation program was carried out under the "patronage" and auspices of Mr. Luc Magloire Mbarga Atangana, Minister of Trade (Protocol agreement, 2019). This agreement did not mention the fact that the Anglophone war had decimated and greatly reduced cocoa and coffee production from Southern Cameroons. The Anglophone crisis was clearly secondary to these economic interests.

Swiss Holdings in the Oil and Natural Gas Sector in Cameroon

In 2020, while the global economy was being ravaged by the coronavirus (COVID-19) pandemic, Glencore, a Swiss multinational commodities (mostly oil and natural gas) trader, sued Cameroon's national refinery, SONARA at the High Court of Justice of England and Wales, through the Swiss company's subsidiary Glencore Energy UK Ltd, claiming €14.7 million euros, or $16.65 million dollars of unpaid bills. Glencore claimed that this amount was, for the most part, "penalties for late payments, in connection with contracts to deliver just over 1.6 million barrels of crude oil to SONARA between November 2012 and January 2015" (Deca, 2020). This suit revealed the tip of the iceberg of the relationships between Swiss multinational commodities trader Glencore, and the Biya regime in the oil and natural gas sector. This opaque business partnership had flourished under the radar for decades because President Paul Biya controls and uses the country's oil and natural gas sector as his personal property through the National oil company, *la Société Nationale des Hydrocarbures du Cameroun* (SNH) and SONARA.

Figure 20.2. Swiss Ambassador to Cameroon, Pietro Lazzeri meeting with Biya in Yaoundé

This litigation tore the veil of secrecy surrounding the Swiss role in the exploration and exploitation of Cameroon's oil and natural gas resources, which are mainly in the English-speaking Southern Cameroons but are controlled entirely by the Biya regime. In effect, in 2009, Glencore Exploration Cameroon, the Cameroon subsidiary of Switzerland-based multinational commodities (oil, natural gas, minerals) trader, Glencore PLC (GLNCY) and the state oil company, SNH, had signed multiple million-dollar oil exploration and production agreements in multiple offshore "blocks" including the Rio del Rey basin in the Anglophone Southwest region of Cameroon. Glencore Exploration Cameroon soon became one of the most prominent oil suppliers for the refinery, SONARA in Limbe. In addition, Glencore produces oil in landlocked Chad and pumps it via the Kome-Kribi pipeline to Kribi on the coast of Cameroon, where it is loaded at an offshore terminal. The commodities trader is an active player in the West African crude market. It is a regular marketer of Doba (Chadian) crude from the Kribi terminal in Cameroon (Glencore to halt output at Chadian oil fields, operations impacted by Covid-19, 2020). The existence of key natural resources (oil, natural gas, timber, and other products) complicated the Anglophone problem. Actually, it can be said that President Biya's downright refusal to negotiate a solution to the Anglophone problem was due to the natural resources. A return to federalism would mean Southern Cameroons would have a say in the exploitation of the natural resources in its territory, as well as the use of funds from these resources. Oil and natural gas have thus been a curse for Southern Cameroons, and Swiss companies were the Lords of the natural resource curse in Cameroon.

Figure 20.3. President Paul Biya meeting with Swiss Ambassador to Cameroon, H.E. Pietro Lazzeri (left) and Antoine de Saint-Affrique, CEO of Barry Callebaut in Yaoundé in 2019

The Glencore International AG Multinational Bribery Scandal

In many African oil and mineral-producing countries, rent-seeking ruling elite of autocratic kleptocracies often collude with international commodities (oil, natural gas, forest, agriculture, and mineral extraction) companies to further the interests of these companies while lining their pockets through bribery and corruption, while their people are mired in poverty and misery. This is one of the characteristics of what economists call the natural "resource curse." The fundamental premise is that in specific politico-cultural contexts, countries endowed with an abundance of natural resources, particularly oil, natural gas, and minerals, tend to be neo-patrimonial, kleptocratic, have less economic growth, more conflicts, and poor economic outcomes than countries that are less endowed with natural resources (Smith & Waldner, 2021; Wright & Frantz, 2017; Wright et al., 2015; Ross, 2012). In Cameroon, Swiss multi-national commodity (oil, natural gas, and minerals) traders are the Lords of the natural resource curse. The extent of Swiss involvement in the Cameroon natural resource curse came to light in a sordid multi-jurisdictional bribery and corruption case involving the oil operations of Glencore International AG and its subsidiaries in a number of African countries.

On May 24th, 2022, the United States Department of Justice announced that Glencore International AG of Switzerland, one of the world's largest commodities (oil, natural gas and minerals) traders had pled guilty in the Southern District of New York to violations under the Foreign Corrupt Practices Act (FCPA), while Glencore Ltd., pled guilty in the District of Connecticut to a commodity price manipulation conspiracy. The Department of

Justice announced that the United States Attorney for the Southern District of New York, had entered into a plea agreement with Glencore International, A.G. and Glencore Ltd, a subsidiary of Glencore International AG. The United States government had charged Glencore AG with bribing government and national oil company officials in multiple African countries, including Cameroon, Equatorial Guinea, Ivory Coast, Nigeria, and South Sudan, in furtherance of the interests and profits of the multinational company. In presenting the case, the United States v. Glencore International AG, and the Swiss company's guilty plea on May 24, 2022, the Attorney General of the United States, Merrick Garland, stated that: "The rule of law requires that there not be one rule for the powerful and another for the powerless; one rule for the rich and another for the poor. The Justice Department will continue to bring to bear its resources on these types of cases, no matter the company and no matter the individual." For his part, the U.S. Attorney for the Southern District of New York, Damian Williams, told the media:

> The scope of this criminal bribery scheme is staggering. Glencore paid bribes to secure oil contracts. Glencore paid bribes to avoid government audits. Glencore bribed judges to make lawsuits disappear. At bottom, Glencore paid bribes to make money–hundreds of millions of dollars. And it did so with the approval, and even encouragement, of its top executives. The criminal charges filed against Glencore in the Southern District of New York are another step in making clear that no one – not even multinational corporations–is above the law (U.S. Attorney, Southern District of New York, 2022).

Glencore International AG had pled guilty as charged on all counts and agreed to pay more than $1.1 billion in penalties and fines to the U.S. government and participate in a three-year compliance program of monitorship. Glencore also agreed to make a $39.6 million payment to the Brazilian Authorities for engaging in corrupt practices in Brazil. Furthermore, Glencore was ordered to pay the Swiss authorities almost $30 million as a result of a separate investigation into Glencore's activities in the Democratic Republic of Congo (United States v. Glencore International AG, 2022). These penalties looked like a mere slap on the wrist, considering that on February 15, 2022, the Glencore group released preliminary results for 2021 that showed earnings of $21.3 billion, up 84% from the previous year (Glencore plc 2021 Annual Report, 2022).

The UK's Serious Fraud Office (SFO) v. Glencore Energy UK

On the same day that the United States Department of Justice announced that Glencore International AG had agreed to plead guilty to violating the American Foreign Corrupt Practices Act (FCPA), and of a conspiracy to manipulate commodity prices, the United Kingdom's Serious Fraud Office (SFO), which had been investigating the Glencore group of companies, its officials, employees, agents and associated persons, announced that the SFO had charged Glencore Energy (UK) Ltd with seven counts of bribery in connection with its oil operations in Nigeria, Cameroon, Equatorial Guinea, Ivory Coast, and South Sudan:

> The SFO has charged Glencore with seven counts of bribery under the Bribery Act 2010, five substantive charges under Section 1 and two under the corporate failure to prevent bribery offence, section 7.
>
> The SFO's case is that Glencore agents and employees paid bribes worth over $25 million for preferential access to oil, with approval by the company.
>
> The SFO has worked in parallel with the US and collaboratively with the Dutch and Swiss prosecutors on this investigation.

The SFO stated that during a Westminster Magistrates' Court hearing, Glencore Energy UK Ltd had agreed to enter a guilty plea to all seven charges. The SFO's prosecution and the court's sentencing of Glencore were dealt with at Southwark Crown Court on Tuesday, 21 June 2022. Lisa Osofsky, Director of the Serious Fraud Office, said: "We won't stop fighting serious fraud, bribery and corruption, and we look forward to the next steps in this major prosecution" (Serious Fraud Office Charges Glencore with Seven Counts of Bribery, 2022).

Context of Bribery and Corruption in the African Oil Sector

In 2014, the National Resource Governance Institute noted that Swiss trading companies were the largest buyers of oil from the governments of Cameroon, Chad, Equatorial Guinea, Gabon, and Nigeria. In 2014, the National Resource Governance Institute presented the context and environment in which Glencore used bribery – directly and indirectly – to secure profitable business deals in Sub-Saharan Africa: "With respect to the petroleum sector specifically, Africa's producers lack many of the checks and balances needed to safeguard the public interest" (Gilles et al., 2014). There was "no public oversight, no transparency" in the process. It noted that there was "a lack of integrity in the selection of buyers and determination of the selling price, including detailed public disclosures on how the state's share of production is allocated and sold" (Gilles et al., 2014). First, sales occur in environments where corruption levels are high, and institutions are weak but where financing for development is urgently needed. The ten countries examined here perform poorly on measures of corruption and governance. This means the deals described above occur in environments where bribery, favoritism and other manipulations are common (Gilles et al., 2014). Glencore and other Swiss multinational commodities trading companies are the Lords of the African resource curse.

The Glencore Affair in Cameroon

In Cameroon, where the two National Oil Companies, the *Société Nationale des Hydrocarbures* (Nation Hydrocarbons Corporation, SNH) and the *Société National de Raffinage,* the National Refining Corporation (SONARA) have been the cash-cows of the Ahidjo/Biya regime, Glencore International's guilty pleas in the United States and the United Kingdom were embarrassing for the managers of these entities. Glencore had pled guilty to bribing and corrupting them to further its interests and profits. The United States Department of Justice charged that among other acts of corruption, Glencore bribed officials of National oil companies of Nigeria, Cameroon, Equatorial Guinea, South Sudan, Ivory Coast, and other countries in cash in connection with transactions involving state-owned and state-controlled entities: "Some of these corrupt payments were paid in cash that was dispensed from Glencore's offices in Baar, Switzerland or the Glencore UK subsidiaries' office in London, United Kingdom" (United States v. Glencore, AG, 2022).

As soon as the story broke, eminent, international anti-corruption activist, Barrister Akere Muna, former president of the Cameroon Bar Association, former vice chairperson of Transparency International, and former chairperson of the International Anti-Corruption Council (IACC), among other distinctions, wrote a strongly-worded letter to the *Commission Nationale Anti-Corruption* (the National Anti-Corruption Commission, popularly known as CONAC) to investigate SNH and SONARA to determine the officials of both state corporations that Glencore International admitted that it had bribed to advance its interests and profits in the oil sector. Such an investigation would be unprecedented given that neither the SNH nor SONARA, the opaque, cash-cows of the Biya regime had no parliamentary oversight, no transparency and no accountability, and were directly controlled by President Paul Biya and his long-term associate, Adolphe Moudiki who had been the Administrator and Director-General of SNH since 1993. Nevertheless, Moudiki was forced by the negative publicity generated by Glencore's confession that it had bribed officials of the SNH and SONARA, to respond to the allegations. He issued a press release on the SNH website that stated:

> The National Hydrocarbons Corporation (SNH) has been informed, through the press, that Glencore International AG and its subsidiaries have admitted to the American and British authorities that they have corrupted officials in several countries, including those of SNH in Cameroon... SNH is neither directly nor indirectly associated with such practices, which are strictly prohibited by its internal regulations. The American and British authorities have been contacted to provided information needed to substantiate these allegations (Moudiki, 2022).

Moudiki said he had asked the American and British authorities to provide evidence to support Glencore's guilty pleas and confession that it had bribed SNH and SONARA officials. This information should be readily available because the United States Department of Justice wrote that in Glencore's Defendant's Plea Agreement after it pled guilty to bribery and corruption, Glencore:

> ...made detailed factual presentations to the Offices [of the U.S. Department of Justice], producing a significant amount of documents located outside the United States to the Offices in ways that did not implicate foreign data privacy laws, collecting and producing voluminous evidence and information to the Offices, accompanied by translations of documents, and producing an analysis of complex trading activity conducted by the company's outside forensic accounting firm; in addition, the Defendant also provided to the Offices, all relevant facts known to it, including

> information about the individuals involved in the conduct described in the attached Statement of Facts and conduct disclosed to the Offices prior to the Agreement… (*United States v. Glencore International AG,* 2022, pp. 5-6).

In August 2024 Britain's Serious Fraud Office (SFO) announced that it had charged Glencore's former head of oil, Alex Beard, and five other former employees of Glencore at Westminster Magistrates' Court with conspiring to make corrupt payments to government officials and officials of state-owned oil companies in Nigeria, Cameroon, and Ivory Coast to benefit their company's oil operations in West Africa, in violation of The Bribery Act 2010 (Former Glencore Employees in Court, 2024). Under relentless pressure from the local media and anti-corruption organizations, Mr. Moudiki announced that some SNH managers and employees will appear before a UK court over suspected involvement in bribery offenses linked to Glencore (Atabong, 2024). By the first quarter of 2025, the identities of the SNH officials implicated in the Glencore bribery scandal had not been revealed.

Interestingly, Mr. Moudiki did not ask Glencore for the identity of the officials it had bribed. He also did not ask Glencore to provide the evidence it had provided to American and British authorities about the bribes it had paid to SNH and SONARA officials.

On its website, the SNH stated that it worked with commodities trading companies from around the world: Russia, China, the United States, France, the UK, and so on, in addition to the Swiss conglomerates: "SNH works in partnership with companies having well-established expertise, including subsidiaries of Gazprom, Glencore, Golar, Sinopec, Lukoil, Grynberg, Noble Energy, Bowleven, Victoria Oil & Gas, New Age, Tower Resources, Afex, Yan Chang and Perenco." The devil is in the details of the agreements – and they are not public – between SNH and these companies. The National Resource Governance Institute noted that in "Cameroon, Swiss (oil and natural gas) traders are leading customers of Cameroon's NOC, *Société Nationale des Hydrocarbures* (SNH). Swiss traders Glencore, Gunvor and Vitol together bought around half of the crude sold by SNH in 2013… these important transactions have escaped oversight due to opaque corporate practices and weak regulation." The point is that in Cameroon, as in other African oil-producing countries, contracts are "allocated through an opaque and discretionary process in an environment where the rule of law is weak and corruption widespread" (Gilles et al., 2014). The National Resource Governance Institute concluded that:

> Along with widespread opacity, the method for selecting the buying companies also creates governance risks. The opportunity to buy state-owned oil should be allocated through processes that are transparent, openly competitive and governed by clear rules so as to secure the best possible price and protect against problems like favoritism, patronage and bribery. This same logic applies to other valuable public assets like upstream licenses or government contracts (Gilles et al., 2014).

The Glencore case is complicated because the conglomerate played a dominant role in the Cameroon oil sector. It is an oil explorer and producer, seller of crude to the national oil refinery, SONARA, and buyer of oil from the SNH. Only time will tell whether Glencore or other Swiss multinational companies directly or indirectly funded President Paul Biya's lengthy stays at the presidential suite of the Intercontinental Hotel in Geneva, Switzerland.

La Société Générale de Surveillance (SGS) as Gateway and Supply-Chain manager of Cameroon

If trade, known in modern parlance as business, is the economic lifeblood of societies in our interconnected global society, and if air and seaports are the gateways to business in nation-states and territories, Cameroon's main gateway is the Port of Douala, its secondary gateways are the Douala International Airport, the Yaoundé Nsimalen International Airport, the ports of Kribi, Victoria/Limbe, Tiko, etc. One of the best-kept secrets of the Biya regime is that since 1987, a Swiss company, SGS has been the manager of the main economic gateways to Cameroon. Geneva-based SGS is the gatekeeper of business and, therefore, the main determiner of the state of the economy and revenues accruing from customs, excise and other taxes and fees levied and collected at these gateways. In effect, since 1987, SGS has specialized in oil, natural gas, and other commodities. SGS is the world's leading inspection, verification, testing, import and export certification company. SGS CAMEROUN SA is located in Douala, Cameroon. It provides inspection and testing services and confidence surveillance systems maintenance and monitoring. It is the key supply chain manager for Cameroon. SGS Cameroun SA is a subsidiary of the Swiss global company, SGS Group, which had since 1988 been a "preferred partner of Cameroon, working for the energization of the economy, facilitation of trade and putting in place infrastructures for the management of imports. It was also given the task of increasing and collecting customs duties under the auspices of the Ministry of Finance. SGS also offered the Cameroon government and economy strategic services in agriculture, oil and natural gas, petrochemicals, industry, and certification.

As the gateway through which Cameroon's imports are transited, SGS is responsible for ensuring conformity and inspecting, identifying, evaluating, and classifying goods imported to Cameroon. To this end, it issues import declarations, verifies import documents to evaluate imports and assess customs duties, secures customs revenues, reconciles customs duties and taxes due, and manages risk.

SGS performs the role of supply chain manager in multiple sectors of the Cameroon economy, including control and management of timber and wood products exports, issuing export declarations, collecting export taxes, identification and management of all vehicles and engines imported into Cameroon, scanning all containers off-loaded, and loaded in all ports, airports and in the hinterland, providing real-time image to customs, training of customs officers in imaging, scanning all import and export containers passing through customs, securing goods and facilitation of export procedures optimization of customs duties, capacity building and knowledge transfer. SGS carries out activities in agriculture, agrochemicals, biofuels, fertilizers, forestry products, inventory control, industry, petrol tankers and gas, and chemicals (SGS au Cameroun, 2021).

The Swiss and the Container Terminal at the Douala Port

In January 2019, a case in the *Tribunal Administratif du Littoral*, Douala (Littoral Administrative Court), *APM Terminals BV* (Denmark) and *Bolloré S.A* (France) versus the *Port Autonome de Douala* (Douala Autonomous Port) revealed another domain of Swiss political and economic clout in Cameroon. In effect, after more than 20 years of managing the container terminal of the Douala port, the French company Bolloré Logistics and its partner APM Terminals, a subsidiary of the Danish shipping conglomerate, A.P. Møller –Mærsk A/S, the world's largest shipping and logistics (supply chain company) suddenly found itself excluded from tendering for renewal of their management contract for the container terminal, which was to expire on December 31, 2019. They sued, claiming that the designation, in September 2019, of the Swiss company, Terminal Investment Limited (TIL) as their successor, with effect from January 2020, was irregular. Bolloré Logistics claimed that in 2017, the Port of Douala had extended its contract till 2023. Apparently, the Presidency of the Republic–and the president controls everything in Cameroon – had directed the Port of Douala to sign a contract for the renovation, modernization, management, and maintenance of the container terminal of the port to a different company, Terminal Investments Limited (TIL), a subsidiary of the Swiss shipping conglomerate, MSC Mediterranean Shipping Company SA of Chemin Rieu 12-14,1208 Geneva. President Paul Biya's friendship with Switzerland and his personal friendship with the Swiss Ambassador to Cameroon, Pietro Lazzeri, had won the contract for the Swiss.

The French and Danish companies that had lost the lucrative renovation, modernization and management contract immediately sued the Port of Douala for breach of contract and for unfairly eliminating them from the pre-qualification phase of the tendering process for renewal of its contract (Andzogo, 2019). Since the matter was being played out in two different theaters–the Presidency of the Republic and the Courts – the French also pulled their own strings and connections with President Biya. The CEO of Bolloré Logistics, Vincent le Breton, an old friend of President Paul Biya, who was his intermediary with the Macron administration, was not amused by Biya's cancellation of Bolloré's contract to renovate and manage the Douala Port's container terminal, and handing it to the Swiss. On 23 August 2019, Ferdinand Ngoh Ngoh, Minister of State and Secretary General at the Presidency, wrote a very urgent, confidential letter to the Director General of the Port of Douala, stating that on "Order from the PRESIDENT OF THE REPUBLIC," he was to stop work on finalizing the concessionary contract entered into with Terminal Investments until the Administrative Court of Littoral had decided the case. The letter found its way to social media platforms within hours. The Swiss were not happy with the developments. On October 28, 2019, the Swiss Ambassador, Pietro Lazzeri, held a meeting with President Paul Biya at the presidential palace in Yaoundé and delivered an undisclosed message from the out-going President of the Swiss Confederation, Ulrich "Ueli" Maurer, urging Biya not to renege on giving the contract to the Swiss consortium.

On 26 December 2019, the Administrative Tribunal of Littoral ruled in favor of Bolloré, holding that the Douala Port's decision to exclude *Bolloré S.A & APM Terminals BV* from the tendering process for renovating and managing the Douala container port had not followed the rules. The court then suspended the designation of a new concessionary or license holder for the container terminal of the Douala port. The management of the Port of Douala appealed the decision. During the appellate hearing in July 2021, the Autonomous Port of Douala, stated that the court was incompetent to try the case because the matter was outside its jurisdiction (Andzongo, 2019). The court rejected the submission of the port, holding that it was competent to hear and decide the case. This was a blow to the Biya administration, which had wanted to transfer renovation and management of the container services of the Port to the Swiss conglomerate, Terminal Investment Limited (TIL) in January 2020. The port management said it was not bound by the court's decision and appealed to the Supreme Court of Cameroon in Yaoundé. The matter was heard in the administrative branch of the Court. The issue before the Court was whether the Administrative Tribunal of Littoral erred when it issued an injunction to the Port of Douala to halt the transfer of the management of the container terminal of the port to Terminal Investments Limited of Geneva, Switzerland. The court answered in the Negative and affirmed the ruling of the Douala court (Andzogo, 2019). Interestingly, the authorities of the Port of Douala dismissed the ruling of the Court. They issued an official statement that the ruling of the Supreme Court would have no impact on the termination date of the concession of Douala International Terminals, the subsidiary of Bolloré. The management of the port stated that it was not going to reopen the call for tenders for a new concessionary because a Presidential decree of January 2019 gave it the power to manage the container terminal itself. This dispute opened a window to the Republican Chiefdom in Cameroon. The ports are controlled by the government's executive branch, which rules by decree. When it became clear that the Biya government wanted to hand over management of the container terminal of the Douala port to a Swiss company, Terminal Investments Limited, the move was resisted by Bolloré Africa Logistics and its partner, APM Terminals, which sued and won. However, the Port of Douala refused to recognize the Court's decision, stating that a presidential decree empowered it to delegate port management to third parties (Andzogo, 2019).

However, the COVID-19 pandemic and the global supply-chain bottlenecks and challenges that it caused led to drastic changes in the global container shipping business. In a *coup de théatre* worthy of Molière, on December 20, 2021, the French conglomerate Bolloré, whose subsidiary, Bolloré Africa Logistics, which had managed the Douala Port for more than 20 years, announced that its competitor, the Swiss shipping conglomerate, MSC Mediterranean Shipping Company SA, of which Terminal Investments Limited (TIL) is a subsidiary, had offered to purchase Bolloré Africa Logistics, which was locked in a legal battle with the Port of Douala for €5.7 billion euros (Assoko, 2021). This development essentially makes all the legal procedures brought by Bolloré over the transfer of management of the container terminal of the Douala Port to Terminal Investments Limited moot. Global market capitalism essentially accomplished what the Biya regime had wanted all along–transfer of the container terminal of the Port of Douala–and most of the supply chain of Cameroon–to MSC Mediterranean Shipping Company SA of Geneva, Switzerland.

Swiss Corporate Corruption in Cameroon and Other African Countries

The foregoing discussion demonstrates that due to its close, lucrative political and economic relations with the kleptocratic, neo-patrimonial republican chiefery of President Paul Biya, the Swiss Federal Government and the Canton and Republic of Geneva have essentially been partners in crimes against humanity in the Anglophone regions of Cameroon. In 2022, the United States Department of Justice revealed that the Swiss conglomerate, Glencore International AG's partnership with the Biya regime was grounded in bribery and corruption. This relationship exacerbated the resource curse in Cameroon. In effect, on May 24th, the United States Department of Justice announced that the United States Attorney for the Southern District of New York, had entered into a plea agreement with Glencore International, A.G., a Swiss multinational corporation, in which Glencore agreed to plead guilty to "Conspiracy to Violate the Foreign Corrupt Practices Act of 1977." The United States government charged Glencore with bribing government and national oil company officials in multiple African countries, including the SNH and the SONARA in Cameroon in furtherance of the interests of Glencore, a major commodities player in Cameroon and other African countries

Swiss Involvement: From Pilot Project in Pluriculturalism to Mediation in the Anglophone Conflict

Despite, or rather, because of the Swiss entanglement with the Biya regime, it was only natural that the Swiss would become involved in mediating the Anglophone Crisis. Biya was famous for his politics of deliberate deafness and very selective attention. He instinctively turned a deaf ear and ignored criticism from both friend and foe alike. He only paid attention to matters that directly and immediately threatened his regime and power. The Anglophone Revolt posed an existential threat to the Biya regime and shook it to the core. The regime looked into its bag of political tricks and tried everything from the cosmetic National Commission on Bilingualism and Multiculturalism to the parodic Grand National Congress and its decision to grant a so-called "special status"–and it was in reality, a reprise of the status quo–to the English and Pidgin speaking Southern Cameroons. The creation of the National Commission for the Promotion of Bilingualism and Multiculturalism paved the way for the Swiss involvement in the Anglophone crisis. On 22nd January 2018, the Swiss Federal Delegate for Pluriculturalism, Nicoletta Mariolini, began a five-day working visit to Cameroon. She and the Swiss Ambassador to Cameroon, Pietro Lazzeri, met with the President of the National Commission for the Promotion of Bilingualism and Multiculturalism, former Prime Minister, Peter Mafany Musonge, the Foreign Minister, Lejeune Mbella Mbella, and the de facto president of Cameroon, the Secretary General at the Presidency of the Republic, Ferdinand Ngoh Ngoh" (Sina, 2018). In an interview with CRTV, Nicoletta Mariolini essentially recommended a Swiss-style federal solution to the Anglophone Problem: "We have to preserve and protect the linguistic minorities and the representation of the language communities at the federal level. Multiculturalism can be reached only with a shared responsibility between the government and federation" (Sina, 2018). This was definitely not the message the Biya regime, which had arrested and jailed tens of federalists like Felix Nkongho Agbor Balla wanted to hear. In May 2017, the head of the *Conseil National de Communication* (National Communication Council), Peter Essoka, had warned Cameroon journalists not to report on "secession or a return to federalism" in Cameroon (Kindzeka, 2017).

The Swiss saw the visit of Nicoletta Mariolini as their contribution towards a resolution of the Anglophone Question in Cameroon. It was part of a pilot project between Switzerland and Cameroon whose aim was to "promote rights and social cohesion between the French-speaking and English-speaking linguistic communities in Cameroon, the development of public policies for the minorities and national dialogue on these issues" (Federal Department of Foreign Affairs, 2018). The next leg of the project involved a visit to Switzerland by members of the National Commission for the Promotion of Bilingualism and Multiculturalism. The Swiss Federal Department of Foreign Affairs (FDFA) described this visit, which took place from June 11 to 15, 2018, as "a study visit to Switzerland...with the objective of discussing questions linked to plurilingualism and multiculturalism (Federal Department of Foreign Affairs, 2018). If this Swiss-Cameroon multiculturalism pilot project was intended to pave the way for respect for the Anglophone minority, dialogue, negotiations and a return to federalism, it failed woefully. Either the Cameroonians did not do well in their studies or President Paul Biya did not want to discuss the root causes of the crisis and make the changes necessary to resolve the conflict. Paul Biya chose the status quo, thereby ensuring that nothing would come out of the Swiss-Cameroon, multicultural "pilot project." The Biya regime was just going through the motions. Nicoletta Mariolini's visit to Cameroon and Peter Mafany Musonge's visit to Switzerland did not achieve anything substantial, except perhaps to ensure that President Biya would continue to visit Switzerland and stay at the Intercontinental hotel in Geneva for long periods of time, while multiple conflicts were tearing his country. The failed pilot project on plurilingualism gave the Swiss the first taste of their partner, Biya's failed method of governance by deaf ear and intransigence.

Figure 20.4. Swiss Federal Delegate for Pluriculturalism, Nicoletta Mariolini meeting with Cameroon's Foreign Minister, LeJeune Mbella Mbella in Yaoundé, January 22, 2018

Though Paul Biya loved to stay in the Republic and Canton of Geneva, in the Swiss Confederation, for long periods of time, he had no intention whatsoever of taking lessons on democracy and federalism from his Swiss friends. This would put an unwanted spotlight on the country, and call attention of the wrong sort to its unprecedented relationship with

President Biya. Cameroonian immigrants, refugees and exiles would later hold unprecedented demonstrations in Geneva and cause Switzerland much embarrassment. If the Swiss realized President Biya was probably the most hardline African dictator of the post-Cold War era, they kept that realization to themselves. The facts show that Biya had no intention of changing his views or his kleptocratic republican chiefdom, even if it meant killing thousands of minority Anglophone civilians–and security personnel–destroying Southern Cameroons and sending hundreds of thousands of its people to refugee camps. He was using the Swiss pluricultural pilot study to buy time–in vain–to acquire Chinese weapons to crush the Anglophone separatists. Indeed, just one year after the charade of the Switzerland-Cameroon multiculturalism pilot project, President Paul Biya, in a surprising moment of candor, revealed the mindset of the Ahidjo/Biya regime, that is to say, his mindset with respect to the Anglophone minority. It was during an interview with Mo Ibrahim of the Mo Ibrahim Foundation, during the 2nd Paris Peace Forum that took place from November 11 to 13th, 2019 (Andzongo, 2019). In an unguarded, off-script moment, Biya made his most audacious statement on the Anglophone crisis. He declared in an unexpected moment of candor that German, French and British colonialism had bequeathed Cameroon a poisoned multilingual gift of sorts:

> *...une juxtaposition de culture et de civilisation qui rendent les choses assez délicates. Bon, on a tout fait pour mettre à égalité les deux langues, les langues anglaise et française. Mais, les mentalités, les systèmes scolaires, le système de la magistrature sont différents. Nous avons donc eu des conflits qu'on est en train de résoudre en ce moment, pour conserver à la partie de mon pays qui était sous colonisation britannique, un statut spécifique. On avait la possibilité de les [anglophones] intégrer directement dans le système francophone qui était celui de la majorité du peuple : 80%. Mais, je crois que les pays sont soucieux aujourd'hui d'affirmer leur identité et c'est pour ça que nous mettons sur pied un statut spécial qui reconnaît la spécificité de la zone anglophone, mais, elle reste dans l'intégrité territoriale du Cameroun* (Andzongo, 2019).
>
> A juxtaposition of cultures and civilizations that make things rather delicate; well, we first tried to put the two languages on an equal footing, the English and French languages. But the mentalities, educational systems, judicial systems are different. We then had conflicts that we are trying to resolve at the moment, to grant the part of my country [Southern Cameroon] that was under British colonialism, a special status. We had the possibility of integrating them directly into the Francophone system, which is the system of the majority of the people; 80%. But I think that countries are today conscious about affirming their identity that is why we are putting in place a special status which recognizes the specificity of the English-speaking zone, but it stays in the territorial integrity of Cameroon.

The "special status" turned out to be a deceptive and misleading parody of the status quo. The Cameroon civil war intensified, Biya continued to attempt to crush the separatists, who made an alliance with Igbo Separatists in Nigeria, acquired the technology to make improvised explosive devices, and carried out spectacular attacks against the Cameroon military, which they posted on social media. More separatists and soldiers were killed, more refugees crossed into Nigeria, and hundreds of thousands more Anglophones became internally displaced. The Swiss pedagogy on pluriculturalism had fallen on deaf ears.

Figure 20.5. Swiss Federal Delegate for Pluriculturalism, Nicoletta Mariolini meeting with Peter Mafany Musonge, President of the National Commission for the Promotion of Bilingualism and Multiculturalism (Bern, June 11, 2018)

From Pluricultural Study Tours to Swiss Mediation

After failing to crush the Anglophone separatists and subjugate the English and Pidgin-speaking Southern Cameroonians once and for all from 2017 to 2019, the Biya regime surreptitiously asked the Swiss to mediate between the two parties–while the war was still going on. This led to one of the most bizarre developments of the Anglophone conflict –the decision by both parties to allow Switzerland to play a vague and undefined role as a mediator of the conflict. After all, the Swiss had already been involved in the fruitless multicultural pilot project. They were not like the Americans who condemned the human rights violations of the Biya regime at every turn. The Swiss were also not the French, whom the Anglophones distrusted for joining forces with *La Republique du Cameroun* in an all-out attempt to assimilate the Anglophone minority into *la Francophonie*. Interestingly, the Swiss Federal government and the government of the Republic and Canton of Geneva, whose close diplomatic relationship and lucrative, symbiotic economic friendship with the neo-patrimonial Biya regime essentially transformed their country into Biya's second home, seem to have been blinded by their self-interest to the point of failing to see that Biya was using Switzerland to achieve its main goal. This was staying in power for as long as possible by crushing all attempts to change the highly centralized Napoleonic status quo. The Anglophone Revolt was a serious threat to the regime.

It appears that when the Swiss mediation efforts were announced in 2019, the three parties: the Biya regime, the Anglophones, and the Swiss Federal Department of Foreign Affairs, all had different understandings and expectations of the "mediation." According to the Presidency of Cameroon, His Excellency Pietro Lazzeri, the Swiss Ambassador to Cameroon, had a meeting with President Paul Biya on April 4, 2019. After the meeting, the Cameroon presidency reported that Switzerland had agreed to support the government's "peace efforts" in Cameroon, not to mediate between the Cameroon government and the separatists. The presidency further wrote that: "the Swiss Government will increase its humanitarian aid in Cameroon. This will target the population in the North-West and South-West Regions."

Figure 20.6. Screenshot of Presidency's announcement of Swiss "mediation" in the Anglophone conflict. Swiss Ambassador, Pietro Lazzeri meeting with President Paul Biya

The Swiss Ambassador to Cameroon was quoted as saying that: "We talked about the necessity and the needs of the civil population in terms of humanitarian aid. In this regard, the Swiss Confederation is supporting the authorities, but also we try to give our contribution in terms of humanitarian access. It is important that the population can get direct humanitarian aid in these two regions" (Switzerland to support Peace Efforts, 2019). Clearly, the Cameroon government framed the Anglophone crisis as an internal matter and that the Swiss had agreed to support the government's efforts to resolve it. It was the same old government policy of imposing a "reconstruction" of Southern Cameroons by force of arms on the rebellious Anglophone Northwest and South regions without resolving the underlying issues that triggered the Anglophone Revolt in the first place in 2016. There was no talk about the root causes of the problem, no talk of dialogue, no mention of mediation.

Southern Cameroons/Ambazonia and Swiss Government Statements on Swiss Mediation

On June 27, 2019, a group of eight self-described "Ambazonia liberation movements" whose address was 1250 Connecticut Ave, Washington D.C. USA, issued a press release in Geneva, Switzerland, announcing that it had made an offer to the Government of Switzerland to "set up a mediation process" aimed at resolving the political and cultural crisis in Cameroon and that the Swiss government had accepted to act as mediator between the Republic of Cameroon and Southern Cameroons/Ambazonia. The press release stated that Switzerland was an acceptable mediator to both parties but raised doubts about whether the Republic of Cameroon was "signing up to the Swiss-led Process in good faith." The independentist groups stated that despite uncertainty regarding the good faith of the Republic of Cameroon, they were "taking a leap in the dark to demonstrate their good faith." They indicated that they consented to including the Center for Humanitarian Dialogue (HD), the strategic partner of the Swiss Government, in the talks. The Southern Cameroons/ Ambazonia groups concluded they were satisfied that Switzerland had no "hidden agenda" in acting as a mediator between them and the Republic of Cameroon (Press Statements, 2019).

On the same day, the Swiss Federal Department for Foreign Affairs (FDFA) issued its own press release, which confirmed that: "At the request of the parties, Switzerland is acting as a facilitator in the crisis in north-western and south-western Cameroon…The Federal Department of Foreign Affairs (FDFA), working closely with the Center for Humanitarian Dialogue (HD Centre), is committed to finding a peaceful, lasting negotiated solution to the crisis in northwestern and south-western Cameroon. Switzerland was tasked by a majority of the parties with facilitating an inclusive negotiation process…between the Cameroon government and the political opposition…Facilitation is an instrument of Switzerland's traditional good offices. In this role, Switzerland can establish contacts and provide communication channels. Switzerland's good offices are open to all concerned parties who wish to participate in facilitation processes. Switzerland adheres to the principles of strict neutrality and discretion" (Federal Department of Foreign Affairs, 2019).

One Conflict, Three Perspectives

The Swiss Initiative was compromised from the start by the diverse perceptions of the parties with respect to the role of Switzerland in resolving the Anglophone conflict. What stands out from the three statements issued by the parties is their contrasting understandings of the Anglophone Question in Cameroon, and the role of the Swiss in resolving it. The content of the announcements of the "mediation" by the Presidency of Cameroon, the Southern Cameroons/Ambazonia separatist groups, and the Swiss Federal Department of Foreign Affairs demonstrated that all three parties were on "different wavelengths" with respect to the Anglophone crisis. The Cameroon government stated that the Swiss Confederation had "expressed its readiness to support national initiatives that can lead to lasting peace in Cameroon." This appears to refer to the failed Grand National Dialogue (September 30 to October 4, 2019), which Paul Biya did not even bother to attend, which turned out to be an exercise in futility. The Southern Cameroons/Ambazonia groups stated that the Swiss government had accepted to act as a "mediator" between the Republic of Cameroon and Southern Cameroons/Ambazonia. These suggested negotiations between the two parties on equal footing. For its part, the Swiss Federal Department of Foreign Affairs described the English and Pidgin-speaking or Anglophone former Southern Cameroons as mere cardinal points (north-western and south-western Cameroon), not the culturally and linguistically distinct geographic region of Southern Cameroons/Ambazonia that the English and Pidgin-speaking of Cameroon consider themselves. It appears that the Swiss framed the Anglophone conflict, for tactical reasons at least, as a conflict between the Republic of Cameroon and its "political opposition." This is a confusing choice of words given that the English and Pidgin-speaking Southern Cameroons (partitioned by the Ahidjo/Biya regime into the Northwest and Southwest provinces/regions) was not the official or unofficial political opposition in Cameroon. The official opposition party was John Fru Ndi's Social Democratic Front (SDF), along with Maurice Kamto's *Mouvement pour la Renaissance du Cameroun* (Cameroon Renaissance Movement, MRC). The 10,000-pound gorilla that was missing in the Swiss press release was a statement that the Biya regime had agreed to the mediation and would participate in it. Since these triple announcements in 2019, the Cameroon government has not officially confirmed or denied that it was participating in the Swiss mediation process.

Figure 20.7. Francophone Cameroonian cartoonist's view of Paul Biya's bad faith towards the "Swiss Mediation." Title: "This is why the "Swiss Mediation" (in red letters) does not gain traction." Biya, speaking to Anglophone separatists: "You have never taken a picture with a head of State, No? Ok Let's start by taking a selfie that we can send to the UN." "No cosmetics this time, reply the separatists" (Frontpage cartoon by Nyemb Popoli, published in *Le Popoli*, August 2, 2019)

The Swiss mediation turned out to be no different than the Swiss-Cameroon pluricultural pilot project. It never took off. Not one single meeting occurred between the Southern Cameroons/Ambazonian groups, the Swiss government and the Cameroon government. This cartoon by veteran Francophone cartoonist, Nyemb Popoli, captures the dilemma of the so-called "Swiss mediation." The cartoonist blames the failure of the Swiss mediation on President Paul Biya. He suggests that President Paul Biya's only intention of agreeing to Swiss involvement in the crisis was to crush and subjugate the Anglophone separatists. He was using the Swiss mediation efforts only as a publicity stunt designed to deceive the United Nations and the international community that he was doing something about the crisis. The official narrative of Swiss involvement in the Anglophone crisis put out by the presidency is not one of "mediation." It is simply a question of Switzerland providing humanitarian assistance to mitigate the human rights violations and calamitous humanitarian catastrophe unleashed on Southern Cameroons by his decision to use the military to subjugate the Anglophones and crush the revival of their identitarian specificity as an English and Pidgin-speaking people. The Cameroon government was never committed to the Swiss mediation. It just wanted to use it to buy time to purchase additional French, Israeli and Chinese equipment to crush Anglophone independentists. Through its politics of intransigence and deliberate political deafness, the Biya regime had once again skillfully used its partner, the Swiss, who were genuinely attempting to help find a solution to the problem–it was in their best interest to do so–to achieve his primary goal of resisting change and hanging on to power for as long as possible. The result was an impasse and an intensification of the conflict.

The Southern Cameroons Leadership Retreat & the Toronto Declaration

The non-commencement of the agreed-upon Swiss mediation between the Government of Cameroon and Southern Cameroonians was caused by the Machiavellian tactics of the Biya regime and the divisions of the Anglophone Resistance. The Biya regime engineered the splits in the Anglophone movement when it persuaded its partner in crimes against humanity, the government of General Mohammadu Buhari of Nigeria to arrest Ambazonian leaders resident in Nigeria - and most of them were legal political refugees and asylum seekers registered with the United Nations High Commission for Refugees - and deport them to Cameroon where they were tried at the Yaoundé Military Tribunal and sentenced to life imprisonment. This extraordinary rendition had made the Southern Cameroons/ Ambazonian groups suspicious of *La Republique du Cameroun* and Nigeria. However, the Anglophone Resistance soon splintered into multiple factions/armed groups that differed on political and sometimes military strategy on "Ground Zero" (Southern Cameroons). These different factions used social media - primarily Facebook, Twitter, and WhatsApp - as platforms to organize "drafts" (fundraising campaigns to support the Anglophone war effort), as well as open-market places on which political vitriol and personal and strategic differences were aired, often in very strident and hostile terms. Anglophone independentists often went hammer and tongs against federalists and unionists, whom they considered traitors, sell-outs and blacklegs. The Biya regime and the official media soon started using the excuse that it was not sure which faction to deal with in the splintered Anglophone community. The impasse was complete, while the war raged on in Southern Cameroons.

In response to this impasse, the Coalition for Dialogue and Negotiations (CDN), an international non-profit, non-governmental organization of Southern Cameroonians based in the United States, facilitated a Southern Cameroons Leadership Retreat in Toronto, Canada from October 29 to November 1, 2021. The aim was to enable all Southern

Cameroonian leaders and stakeholders–political, social, religious, civil society, women's, and youth groups–to unite and develop a common position in preparation for dialogue and negotiations with the Republic of Cameroon, whenever it agreed to come to the discussion table. The 30 groups represented at the Toronto Southern Cameroons/Ambazonia Leadership Retreat agreed to: "Work together to build trust, respect, tolerance, and courtesy as we work towards consensus. They stated that they "noted the Switzerland-led facilitation process and the lack of progress and commitment from the Government of Cameroon." At the end of the Leadership Retreat, the Southern Cameroonian Leaders resolved to, inter alia, "engage to improve the internationally-facilitated process by the Government of Switzerland, and commit to a multilateral mediation process as a viable way to achieve genuine resolution of the conflict... Engage in open communication with officials of the Swiss facilitation team and other international parties" (Toronto Declaration, 2021). The Southern Cameroons/Ambazonia leaders essentially resolved that the moribund bilateral Swiss mediation process, which was stymied by the intransigence of the Cameroon government, be enlarged into a multilateral process involving other countries. Only time will tell if this new-found Anglophone unity will last or if this new approach will bear fruit.

Conclusion

The Swiss are perhaps the most conflicted of all European countries with respect to the Anglophone Question in Cameroon. Since missionaries of the Basel Mission became involved in humanitarian and mission work in German Kamerun in 1886, the Swiss have been engaged in evangelization, education, healthcare, and development work in Cameroon in partnership with the Presbyterian Church in Cameroon. Their work has touched the lives of millions of Cameroonians and contributed to the country's development. However, the Swiss federal government and companies are now caught between Swiss religious and humanitarian values and their economic interests in Cameroon. The bankers of the world have chosen to be the bedfellows of what has been the most obdurate, hardline, kleptocratic regime in modern Africa, the Biya regime. Swiss discomfort with the atrocities and gross human rights violations of the Biya regime, a regime that has been good for business for the Intercontinental Hotel in Geneva, as well as for other businesses, is demonstrated by attempts by politicians like Sylvain Thevoz, an elected member of the Grand Council of the Republic and Canton of Geneva, one of the 26 cantons of the Swiss Confederation, who tabled an unprecedented motion for the Council to declare President Paul Biya of Cameroon, a persona non grata in Geneva. This demonstrates that a segment of the Swiss population has not closed its eyes to the human rights violations of Paul Biya despite Swiss economic partnerships with the Biya regime.

References

Amabo, E. (2021). Cameroon-Swiss Federal Council: Visa Requirements Abolition in View. Cameroon Tribune, June 29. Retrieved from: https://www.cameroon tribune.cm/article.html/40833/en.html/cameroon-swiss-federal-council-visa-requirements-abolition-in%C3%A0-l-%C3%A9meute-%C3%A0-gen%C3%A8ve/2308019.

Andzongo, S. (2019). Paris Peace Forum: Paul Biya explains the background of the Anglophone crisis. *Business in Cameroon,* November 13. Retrieved from: https://www.businessincameroon.com/public-management/1311-9677-paris-peace-forum-paul-biya-explains-the-background-of-the-anglophone-crisis

Atabong, A. (2024). Cameroon state oil firm says staff linked to Glencore bribes will face UK court. *Reuters*, August 3, 2024. https://www.reuters.com/world/africa/cameroon-state-oil-firm-says-staff-linked-glencore-bribes-will-face-uk-court-2024-08-03

Barry Callebaut and Cameroon Intensify Collaboration to Support Young Farmers (2019). Barry Callebaut, May 24. Retrieved from: https://www.barry-callebaut.com/en/group/media/news-stories/barry-callebaut-and-cameroon-intensify-collaboration.

Ben Ahmed, L. (2021), *Cameroun: Une Manifestation contre le President Biya tourne à l'émeute à Genève* (Cameroon: A demonstration against President Biya become a riot in Geneva). Anadolou Agency (Ankara, Turkey), July 18th. Retrieved from: https://www.aa.com.tr/fr/afrique/cameroun-une-manifestation-contre-paul-biya-tourne-

Berman, N., Couttenier, M., Rohner, D. & Thoenig, M. (2017). "This Mine Is Mine! How Minerals Fuel Conflicts in Africa." *American Economic Review*, 107 (6): 1564-1610.DOI: 10.1257/aer.20150774

Cameroun: l'écrivain Patrice Nganang arrêté à l'aéroport de Douala (The Writer Patrice Nganang arrested at the Douala Airport). *Jeune Afrique* & AFP, December 7th. Retrieved from: https://www.jeuneafrique.com/500391/politique/cameroun-lecrivain-patrice-nganang-arrete-a-laeroport-de-douala/

Cameroun, Manifestation contre Paul Biya à Genève (2021). *Jeune Afrique*, July 18. Retrieved from: https://www.jeuneafrique.com/1204952/politique/cameroun-manifestation-contre-paul-biya-a-geneve/

Cameroon Journalist Samuel Wazizi died in Detention (2020) *Reporters Without Borders*, June. Retrieved from: Retrieved from: https://rsf.org/en/news/cameroonian-journalist-samuel-wazizi-died-detention.

Concern Grows for Women and Children (2018). United Nations High Commission for Refugees (UNHCR). January 18. Retrieved from: https://www.unhcr.org/en-us/news/briefing/2018/1/5a61b3bc4/concern-grows-women-children-fleeing-cameroon.html

Crawford, J & Spoerndli, M. (2019). Cameroon's Biya: Why the Swiss Won't Stop His Geneva Stays. Swissinfo.ch. January 4. Retrieved from: https://www.swissinfo.ch/eng/who-foots-the-bill-_cameroon-s-biya--why-the-swiss-won-t-stop-his-geneva-stays/44644510

Crise anglophone au Cameroun : Paul Biya dénonce une « bande de terroristes (2017). Jenune Afrique and Agence France Presse. December 1. Retrieved from: https://www.jeuneafrique.com/498486/politique/crise-anglophone-au-cameroun-paul-biya-denonce-une-bande-de-terroristes/

Federal Department of Foreign Affairs (2018). Cameroonian delegation visits Switzerland to discuss plurilingualism, *Press Release*, June 1. Retrieved from: https://www.admin.ch/gov/en/start/documentation/media-releases.msg-id-71073.html

Foute, F (2019). Cameroun: Yaoundé dénonce l'attitude "hostile et belliqueuse" des manifestants en Suisse (Yaounde denounces the hostile and bellicose attitude of demonstrations in in Switzerland. Jeune Afrique, July 1. Retrieved from: https://www.jeuneafrique.com/796826/politique/cameroun-yaounde-denonce-lattitude-hostile-et-belliqueuse-des-manifestants-en-suisse/

Freudental, E.; Batchou, F.; & Tjat, G. (2018). Paul Biya, Cameroon's Roaming President. *Organized*

Crime and Corruption Reporting Project (OCCRP). February 18. Retrieved from: https://www.occrp.org/en/28-ccwatch/cc-watch-indepth/7653-paul-biya-cameroon-s-roaming-president

Glencore (2022). Annual Report, Glencore plc, retrieved from: tps://www.glencore.com/media-and-insights/news/2021-annual-report-of-glencore-plc#:~:text=The%20Group's%20strong%20 2021%20profitability,December%202020%3A%20%2435.4%20billion).

Gilles, A., Guéniat, M. & Kummer, L. (2014). Big Spenders: Swiss Trading Companies. African Oil and he Risks of Opacity. Natural Resource Governance Institute. Retrieved from: https://resourcegovernance.org/analysis-tools/publications/big-spenders-swiss-trading-companies-african-oil-and-risks-opacity

Helvetas-Swiss Association for Technical Cooperation (2010). Global Civil Society Database. Retrieved from: https://uia.org/s/or/en/1100001762

Happi, C. (2020). Cameroun : Paul Biya reste le bienvenu à Genève. (Paul Biya is still welcome in Geneva). Actu Cameroun, October 2. Retrieved from: https://actucameroun.com/2020/10/02/cameroun-paul-biya-reste-le-bienvenu-a-geneve/

G'Nowa, O. (2008). *L'unique fille de Paul Biya fait ses études primaires en Suisse* (The only daughter of Paul Biya does her primary education in Switzerland). Cameroun Online, 26 September. Retrieved from: https://web.archive.org/web/20080926185233/http://www.cameroun-online

Deca, K. (2020). Glencore Sues Cameroon's Sonara for FCFA 9.6 Billion. Afrikan Heroes. Retrieved from: https://afrikanheroes.com/2020/09/15/glencore-sues-cameroons-sonara-for-fcfa-9-6-billion/

Kim, I. & Woods, J. (2016). Gas on the Fire: Great Power Alliances and Petrostate Aggression, *International Studies Perspectives*, Volume 17, Issue 3 (August), Pages 231–249, https://doi.org/10.1093/isp/ekv004

Kindzeka, E. *(2017)*. Cameroon Media Face Restrictions on Reporting, *Voice of America (VOA)*. May 15th. Retrieved from: https://learningenglish.voanews.com/a/cameroon-media-face-restrictions-reporting/3849489.html

La police arrête Patrice Nganang (2014). Le Messager (Douala). December 9. Retrieved from: http://www.cameroon-info.net/article/cameroun-patrice-nganang-arrete-par-lapolice-a-douala-237642.html

Monga, C. (1996). *The Anthropology of Anger: Civil Society and Democracy in Africa*. Boulder, Co. Lynne Rienner.

Moudiki, A. (2022). SNH requests corroborating information from US and UK authorities, in Relation to the Glencoe Case. Retrieved from: https://www.snh.cm/index.php/en/

Musa, W. (2017). Cameroon-Judiciary: PCC Moderator Goes to Court Monday. Cameroon Info Net (CIN). April, 19. Retrieved from: http://www.cameroon-info.net/article/cameroon-judiciary-pcc-moderator-goes-to-court-monday-287034.html

Necedem, A. (2014). Cameroun: la gendarmerie empêche la cérémonie de remise d'un prix international de la presse (The gendarmerie prevents the prize-giving ceremony for an international press prize). Agence Ecofin. December 9. Retrieved from: https://www.agenceecofin.com/evenementiel/0912-24974-cameroun-la-gendarmerie-empeche-la-ceremonie-de-remise-d-un-prix-international-de-la-presse

Nfor, N. (2020). *Paradise Lost? A Political History of British Southern Cameroon from 1916-1972*. Austin, TX, Pan African University Press.

Nganang, P. (2014). Cameroun-Douala: Comment Le Prix Bibi Ngota n'a pas été remis (Why the Bibi Ngota Prize was not awarded). Cameroon-Info.Net. Retrieved from: http://www.cameroon-info.net/article/cameroun-douala-comment-le-prix-bibi-ngota-na-pas-ete-remis-par-patrice-237675.html

Nganang, P. (2017). Cameroun: Carnet de Route de l'ecrivain Patrice Nganang en zone (dite) anglophone. (Cameroon: Travelogue of the writer Patrice Nganang in the so-called anglophone zone) *Jeune Afrique*. December 5, 2017. Retrieved from: https://www.jeuneafrique.com/499512/politique/cameroun-carnet-de-route-de-lecrivain-patrice-nganang-en-zone-dite-anglophone/

Note Cameroun: Crise du Cameroon Anglophone (2018). Departement Fédéral de la Justice, Secretariat d'État aux migrations (SEM). Switzerland. September 25. Retrieved from: file:///Users/LEko/Downloads/CMR-krise-anglophone-f.pdf

O'Donnell, J. & Gramer, R. (2018). Cameroon's Paul Biya Gives Master Class in Fake Democracy. *Foreign Affairs*. October 22. Retrieved from: https://foreignpolicy.com/2018/10/22/cameroons-paul-biya-gives-a-master-class-in-fake-democracy/

O'Grady, S. (2019). U.S. cuts some military assistance to Cameroon, citing allegations of human rights violations. *The Washington Post*, February 7. Retrieved from: https://www.washingtonpost.com/world/africa/us-cuts-some-military-assistance-to-cameroon-citing-allegations-of-human-rights-violations/2019/02/06/aeb18052-2a4e-11e9-906e-9d55b6451eb4_story.html

Oum II, J. (2017, December 7th). Communique No. C69/VIII/373. Communique. Mamfe, Southwest: Divisional Office Mamfe.

Petite, S. (2021). *Dans son hôtel genevois, Paul Biya choisit ses voisins de chambre (In his Geneva hotel, Paul Biya chooses guests of rooms near his), Le Temps (Geneva). July 23. Retrieved from:* https://www.letemps.ch/monde/hotel-genevois-paul-biya-choisit-voisins-chambre

Protocol Agreement Between the Barry Callebaut Group and the Interprofessional Cocoa and Coffee Council (2019). Barry Callebaut Group, Retrieved from: https://www.barry-callebaut.com/en/group/media/news-stories/barry-callebaut-and-cameroon-intensify-collaboration

Reuters (2024). Former Glencore employees in court charged with bribery offences (2024). Serious Fraud Office, August 1, 2024. https://www.reuters.com/markets/commodities/glencores-ex-head-oil-charged-with-bribery-offences-by-uk-sfo-2024-08-01/

Ross & Bavier (2018). European tourists were not kidnapped in Cameroon, tour operator says. *Reuters*, April 3, Retrieved from: https://www.reuters.com/article/us-cameroon-security/european-tourists-were-not-kidnapped-in-cameroon-tour-operator-says-idUSKCN1HB17T

Ross, M. (2012). *The Oil Curse: How Petroleum Wealth Shapes the Development of Nations*, Princeton University Press, Oxford.

SGS au Cameroun (2021). SGS Group (Geneva, Switzerland). Retrieved from: https://www.sgs-group.cm/

Switzerland to Support Peace Efforts (2019). Presidency of the Republic. Retrieved from: https://www.prc.cm/en/news/audiences/3419-switzerland-to-support-peace-efforts-in-cameroon

Serious Fraud Office Charges Glencore with Seven Counts of Bribery (2022). UK Serious Fraud Office, May 24. Retrieved from: https://www.sfo.gov.uk/2022/05/24/serious-fraud-office-charges-glencore-with-seven-counts-of-bribery

Simon, S. (2021). La manifestation contre Paul Biya est interdite (The demonstration against Paul Biya is banned). *Tribune de Genève*, July 16. Retrieved from: https://www.tdg.ch/

la-manifestation-contre-paul-biya-est-interdite-814825964739

Simon, S. (2021). *La manifestation contre Paul Biya tourne à l'emeute* (The demonstration against Paul Biya become a riot). *Tribune de Genève,* July 17. Retrieved from: https://www.tdg.ch/la-manifestation-contre-paul-biya-est-en-cours-malgre-son-interdiction-364239910663

Sina, K. (2018). Bilingualism and Multiculturalism: Swiss Federal Delegate for Multilingualism Nicoletta Mariolini on a Five-Day Working Visit in Cameroon. *Cameroon Radio and Television (CRTV).* January 22. Retrieved from: https://www.crtv.cm/2018/01/bilingualism-and-multiculturalism-swiss-federal-delegate-for-multilingualism-nicoletta-mariolini-on-a-five-day-working-visit-in-cameroon/

Smith, B. & Waldner, D. (2021). *Rethinking the Resource Curse.* Cambridge University Press

Toronto Declaration (2021). The Southern Cameroons 2021 Leadership Retreat. The Coalition for Dialogue and Negotiation (CDN). Retrieved from: https://business.facebook.com/CoalitionFDN/photos/pcb.450117513129608/450148596459833/?type=3&theater

Turse, N. & Speri, A. (2022). Even After Acknowledging Abuses, the U.S. Continued to Employ Notorious Proxy Forces in Cameroon. *The Intercept*, March 9. Retrieved from: https://theintercept.com/2022/03/09/cameroon-military-abuses-bir-127e/

UN High Commission for Refugees. (2018, January 18). UNHCR USA. Retrieved from https://www.unhcr.org/en-us/news/briefing/2018/1/5a61b3bc4/concern-grows-women-children-fleeing-cameroon.html

United States Foreign Relations Committee (2008). Petroleum and Poverty Paradox: Assessing U.S. and International Community Efforts to Fight the Resource Curse". Washington DC, U.S Printing Office. Retrieved from: https://www.govinfo.gov/content/pkg/CPRT-110SPRT44727/pdf/CPRT-110SPRT44727.pdf

United States v. Glencore International AG, Docket No. 22-CR-297 (May 24, 2022). United States Department of Justice, United States Attorney for the Southern District of New York. Retrieved from: https://www.justice.gov/criminal-fraud/united-states-v-glencore-international-ag

U.S. Attorney, Southern District of New York (2022). Glencore Entered Guilty Pleas to Foreign Bribery and Market Manipulation Conspiracies. Retrieved from: https://www.justice.gov/usao-sdny/pr/glencore-entered-guilty-pleas-foreign-bribery-and-market-manipulation-conspiracies

Wright, J., Frantz, E. & Geddes, B. (2015). "Oil and Autocratic Regime Survival". *British Journal of Political Science.* 45 (2): 287–306. doi:10.1017/S0007123413000252.

Wright, J. & Frantz, E. (2017). How oil income and missing hydrocarbon rents data influence autocratic survival: A response to Lucas and Richter (2016). *Research & Politics.* 4 (3): 2053168017719794. doi:10.1177/2053168017719794

The Biya Republican Chiefery & The Impact of Resistance to Autocratic Denialism

TWENTY-ONE

The Force of Argument Versus the Argument of Force

Anglophone Calls for Change and the Biya Regime's Repression

LYOMBE EKO

The Anglophone struggle is, first and foremost, a conflict of ideas, views, principles, and values. The Anglophone governmentality and political posture were always dialogical, dialectic, and discursive. In the more than 150 years of being directly and indirectly in the Anglosphere and the British Commonwealth–Empire Day was a day of pomp and pageantry in Southern Cameroons–Anglophone Cameroonians had inherited a system of representative local self-governance, the liberal values of freedom of speech and expression, freedom of the press, freedom of assembly, freedom of religion, and above all the Biblical principle of speaking truth to power. Anglophones had also inherited a culture of tolerance of opposing views, open and robust discussion of public issues, independence of the judiciary, an adversarial judicial system, and presumption of innocence (the principle that accused persons are innocent until proven guilty, the burden of proof being on the prosecution). They had also inherited the principle that everyone is equal before the law. They also had a culture of tolerance, free multi-party elections, political alternance and respect for minority rights. This culture of freedom of expression was summed up by the popular slogan: "The force of argument, not the argument of force."

After the reunification of Southern Cameroons and *La République du Cameroun* in 1961, the Southern Cameroons Anglophone culture of civil liberties and freedom of expression clashed head-on with the post-colonial, authoritarian republican chiefery of French Cameroun. In effect, at independence on January 1, 1960, French Cameroun instituted a highly repressive Napoleonic administrative state with a civil law system characterized by rule-by-decree, as well as draconian French colonial laws that had been enacted to crush the anti-colonial insurgency of the *Union des populations du Cameroun* (UPC). Indeed, in the run-up to the United Nations-supervised plebiscite of 1961, during which the people of Southern Cameroons were given the undesirable choice between the Devil (Nigeria) and the Deep Blue Sea (*La République du Cameroun*), former Southern Cameroons Premier and Leader of the Opposition Party in the Southern Cameroons House of Assembly, Dr. EML Endeley, had warned Southern Cameroonians that the Cameroun Republic had:

> A system under which everyone lives in fear of the police and the Army. You will not be free to move about, you cannot lecture freely or discuss your political views in public; you must carry your tax receipt around your neck like a dog, and you can be arrested and flogged by the police and even imprisoned without a fair trial.
>
> ...
>
> Who amongst you will like to live in a country which lacks complete respect for human dignity and where you cannot speak out your mind freely or pursue your business in peace? (Cited in Tande, 2006).

By 1990, it had become clear that Endeley's prophecy had been fulfilled. Presidents Ahidjo and Biya had transformed Cameroon into a repressive, authoritarian, neo-patrimonial republican chiefery. The judiciary had no independence. The Supreme Council of the Magistracy, the top judicial body of the country, was presided over by President Biya, who appointed judges and magistrates by decree and maintained power indefinitely through a pseudo-multi-party system, a made-to-measure constitution, a rubber-stamp National Assembly, an appointed Senate, powerful military tribunals, and weak civilian courts beholden to the executive. Former Ugandan dictator, Idi Amin is reported to have famously said, "There is freedom of speech, but I cannot guarantee freedom after speech." In Cameroon, there was no freedom before, during or after speech. The post-Cold War atmosphere of "democratization and liberalization" allowed the Anglophone community to assert its identitarian and cultural specificity and call for change. Civil society groups, starting with the All Anglophone Conferences, followed by the Anglophone Civil Society Consortium, lawyers', teachers', and students' associations, resolved to challenge the status quo and resolve the Anglophone problem through dialogue. The fact that the Anglophone problem degenerated into a bloody armed conflict that cost thousands of lives and led to the internal and external displacement of almost one million people from the Anglophone Northwest and Southwest region was due to the extreme intransigence of the neo-patrimonial, republican chiefery of Cameroon, which countered the Anglophone force of argument with the argument of extreme force.

The main premise of this volume is that the Anglophone Question has historical, political, cultural, and religious roots. The genesis of the problem was European colonialism, the self-interests of the European colonial powers: Germany, and after World War I, France and the United Kingdom. These two countries had outsized influence on the League of Nations and the Treaty of Versailles of 1919, which put its imprimatur on the partition of the colonial spoils of war, the so-called "enemy lands," of German Kamerun into French Cameroun, and British Cameroons Mandated Territories. The British further sub-partitioned their share of the territory into Northern Cameroons and Southern Cameroons and used these strips of land as territorial and administrative pawns in their Nigerian colonial protectorate. For a treaty that set out to resolve the dislocations of World

War I and prevent further conflicts and population dislocations, the Treaty of Versailles sowed the seeds of World War II–and the Anglophone Problem in Cameroon. The botched decolonization of British Cameroons under the United Nations ultimately led to the Boko Haram Islamist insurgency in the territories of the former British Northern Cameroon and the Anglophone crisis in the former British Southern Cameroons. However, the leading cause of the Anglophone crisis was the creation of a hardline, authoritarian, postcolonial and post-reunification *chefferie républicaine* (republican chieftaincy) under autocratic *Chef de l'Etat* (Chief of State) President Amadou Ahidjo who ruled from 1960 to 1982, and his successor, President Paul Barthélemy Biya bi Mvondo, who came to power in 1982 and ruled for more than 40 years. Biya's decision to deploy overwhelming military force to subjugate the Anglophone minority, which tried to use the force of argument to defend its threatened cultural and identitarian specificity.

The historical record shows that as Cameroon became an increasingly despotic, post-colonial republican chiefery under the tutelage of France, the naïve, ambitious, and unsophisticated Anglophone Southern Cameroons politicians who had entered into the reunification with la *République du Cameroun* under the mistaken belief that reunification with French Cameroun would lead to equality between English and French-speaking Cameroonians, began to have second thoughts. They became alarmed when the leveling scythe of French and French Cameroon assimilation launched a program of "harmonization" that undermined their linguistic and cultural specificity, discriminated against them, and marginalized them. Former West Cameroon Prime Ministers turned Vice Presidents of a reunited Cameroon, John Ngu Foncha, Solomon Tandeng Muna, and other vociferous proponents of reunification with French Cameroun began to express doubts about the place of Anglophones in the over-centralized structure of the country... after they had been cast aside by the republican chieftain, President Paul Biya.

In the early 1990s, there was no Anglophone political or cultural platform through which the political and cultural grievances and aspirations of the English and Pidgin-speaking people of the former British Southern Cameroons could be expressed; Anglophone journalists communicated Anglophone identitarian and cultural specificity surreptitiously through independent newspapers, and coded discourse in the tightly-controlled state media, first Radio Cameron, then the Cameroon Radio and Television (CRTV) (Eko, 2003). Those surreptitious communication practices continued until the early 1990s, when Anglophone disappointment and disillusionment with the republican Chief of State, Paul Biya, who had been seen as a reformer when he had succeeded the authoritarian Chief of State, Ahmadou Ahidjo, in 1982, reached its apogee. This chapter contains a record of countless attempts by the Anglophone community to deploy the force of argument to resolve the causes of Anglophone discontent. The chapter includes the correspondence that former West Cameroon Prime Ministers, John Ngu Foncha and Solomon Tandeng Muna addressed to President Biya to express concerns at the marginalization of Anglophones and the failure of the Francophone majority to keep promises it had made to the Anglophones before reunification in 1961. They also bemoaned the total lack of respect for the identitarian specificity of the English-speaking minority in the Cameroon Republic.

The first part of this chapter is a catalog of Anglophone politicians and members of the civil society, assembled under the auspices of the All Anglophone Conference (AACI & AAC II) held in Buea and Bamenda respectively, to bemoan the suppression of their cultural and identitarian specificity, their political autonomy, and their natural resources. President Biya's proposed constitutional conference, called in response to demonstrations and widespread unrest, gave them the opportunity to gather and speak with one voice. The Buea Declaration of AACI and the Bamenda Proclamation of the AACII were veritable *cahiers de doléances* or catalogs of grievances addressed to President Biya, who "incarnated" the Cameroonian State and its institutions, as the official media told the people continuously. Both documents constituted a silent and symbolic crescendo of the force of argument of a people that were not being listened to by the Biya regime, which always brandished the argument of force and repression in response to any and all calls for change. The Cameroon security forces, led by the Israeli-trained and armed *Bataillon d'Intervention Rapide* (BIR), crushed all types of speech, both literal and symbolic (meetings, strikes, demonstrations, marches), with extreme prejudice.

President Paul Biya turned a blind eye and a deaf ear to the appeals of the Anglophones who sought a modicum of autonomy and recognition of their identitarian and cultural specificity. His answer was to assimilate the Pidgin and English-speaking minority, which had been part of the Anglosphere since the early 19th century, into *la République du Cameroun* and, by extension, *la Francophonie*. The three main bulwarks of Anglophone identitarian preservation in the former British Southern Cameroons–the churches, the legal and educational systems, resisted assimilation, harmonization, and marginalization, leading to the Anglophone crisis. This chapter also contains the declarations and pronouncements of Anglophone churches, lawyers, teachers, and other members of the civil society who resisted Francophone assimilation, marginalization, and autocratic repression.

Anglophone Political Leaders Deploy the Force of Argument: Open Letter from John Ngu Foncha and Solomon Tandeng Muna to President Paul Biya (1992)

Interestingly, it was the "One Kamerun" Anglophone leaders, Foncha and Muna, who had spearheaded Southern Cameroons' reunification with *la République du Cameroun*, led the resistance to Biya's republican chiefery, which had neither the name (Kamerun), the form (federalism), nor the freedoms and prosperity they had hoped would follow reunification. They had learned the hard lesson that hope is not a viable political strategy in periods of flux. They wrote this open letter in desperation:

> A call to the Head of State to save the nation before it is too late
> From: Dr. John Ngu Foncha (former Prime Minister of West Cameroon, former Vice President of the Federal Republic of Cameroon, former Chairman of the Kamerun National Democratic Party, former Vice President of the UNC, former Vice President of the CPDM, former Grand Chancellor of National Orders)
> &
> Hon. Solomon Tandeng Muna (former Federal Minister of Post and Telecommunications, Transport and Power, former Prime Minister of West

Cameroon, former Vice President of the Federal Republic of Cameroon, former Speaker of the National Assembly of Cameroon, former Chairman of the Cameroon United Congress)

Your Excellency,

AT this hour in the history of our nation, we the undersigned believe it is our moral and historic duty to address this call to you as the Head of State and the only person who can save the nation from the brink of DISASTER, DISUNITY and DISINTEGRATION.

WE feel it our duty because we took part in the great events that brought about the INDEPENDENCE and REUNIFICATION of our Nation. We can recall what was the spirit of the Foumban Conference 1961 and later on the Yaoundé Conference of 1966 that led to the birth of the Cameroon National Union (CNU) to whom the Cameroon Peoples Democratic Movement (CPDM) owes its existence.

IN all these Conferences that brought about important changes to the political life of our nation, dialogue, concertation and genuine consensus resulting in the signed documents were the only means by which we were able to bring profound changes and at the same time maintain National Unity.

TODAY we are at the verge of another important political change in the life of our nation, but unfortunately Cameroonians are divided, and the unity of our nation is threatened.

IT would have been better if this phase of another change in the political life of Cameroon would have been preceded by a National Conference. However, you selected the Tripartite Conference which if properly conducted, with genuine concern for our nation and have honesty some results generally acceptable to all Cameroonians should have come about. Today, nobody can honestly and truthfully say what was agreed on at the tripartite talks because the conference was dispersed before the two Committees reported to the General Assembly. Delegates left the talks without knowing what was finally accepted and without signing any document as evidence of any consensus that was arrived at.

TODAY, the parties which assisted at this tripartite are not even in agreement that the media degree and the electoral law, for convening the tripartite are the results of any agreement or consensus. Even the second tripartite that was supposed to take place before the elections has not even been mentioned.

WE have watched with consternation and awe as the government has taken upon itself to violate the very laws (electoral law) that it proposed and passed. A government or nation that does not obey its very laws is doomed. When a government is the first to break laws, how can the same government call other citizens to obey the law?

TODAY, the Cameroon nation stands divided, the government has had to lure parties to contest elections by promising monetary reward. Some parties have been reluctantly forced to participate at the 11th hour. The list of candidates has not even been published. There are calls for strike and ghost towns etc. The political and social atmosphere is therefore pregnant with possible conflicts, confusion, chaos and violence.

IT is in this regard that in order to save this Republic from impending disaster, we hereby call on the President of the Republic to:

Call off immediately the legislative elections fixed for the 1st of March,

Convene a Constitutional Conference made up of the political parties and delegates arrived at a preparatory meeting of all the parties. Programme the transition of Cameroon from the one party system to a democracy by holding first Municipal elections, the Legislative elections and ultimately Presidential elections.

WE believe your Excellency, that if you take the above steps, you will dissipate the dark clouds that are gathering and the impending storm that may tear apart our nation.

YOU have a duty to stop it and we pray that God Almighty may give you the wisdom and strength to take this important and historic decision.

Done at Bamenda, this 22nd Day of February 1992."

Dr. J.N. FONCHA, Hon. S.T. MUNA

Deploying the Force of Collective Argument: The All Anglophone Conferences (AAC) of 1993 and 1994

The most significant Anglophone gathering of that period were the All Anglophone conferences. The All Anglophone Conferences (AAC) of 1993 and 1994 that were held in Buea and Bamenda respectively, marked the beginning of the mass awakening of Southern Cameroonians to the intolerable injustices they suffered as citizens of a reunified Cameroon and laid the foundation for organized mass resistance against French Cameroon programs aimed at dominating, marginalizing, and assimilating them into *la Francophonie.* Interestingly, these conferences were convened by legal minds: Barrister Sam Ekontang Elad, Dr. Carlson Anyangwe, Dr. Simon Munzu, and Mr. Benjamin Itoe. Ironically, the All Anglophone conference (AACI) that was held in Buea in April 1993 was convened for the purpose of "preparing Anglophone participation in the National Debate on Constitutional Reform" which the Biya Government had undertaken to organize in May 1993. The Biya regime had been dragged kicking and screaming to make democratic concessions after being buffeted by the wind of change that was sweeping across Africa in the wake of the fall of the Berlin Wall in 1989 and the collapse of the Soviet Union in 1991. Though the Biya Constitutional "reform" conference turned out to be an empty, cosmetic, trompe-l'oeil exercise, it gave the Anglophones, who had hitherto been barred from expressing their politico-cultural and identitarian specificity by the repressive Ahidjo/Biya regime, permission to meet and formulate a common platform to present at the constitutional reform conference that had been announced in 1992 but postponed indefinitely.

Figure 21.1. The Ahidjo Cabinet With Biya as Prime Minister. Anglophone leaders rejected the over-centralized unitary regime that had abolished the federal system and with it, the autonomy of Southern Cameroons

The AAC conferences were historically important because they called for constitutional reforms that included recognition of the politico-cultural specificity of the Anglophone minority of the former federal State of West Cameroon. They were *cahiers de doléances* (registers of grievances) of sorts that declared the unitary state's imposition on Anglophone Cameroon in 1972 unconstitutional, illegal and a breach of trust. They demanded a return to federalism through a federal constitution and a federal system of government, as well as recognition of Anglophone cultural and identitarian specificity, restoration of the independence of the judiciary, civil liberties and due process. They called for an end to the international isolation of Anglophone Cameroon, which had ensued since the abolition of the federal republic. In effect, under the Federal Republic of Cameroon, there was an unofficial agreement that foreign dignitaries who visited Yaoundé also visited Buea. Dignitaries that visited Buea included Presidents Albert Bongo of Gabon (Bongo Square in Buea is unofficially named after him), Heinrich Lübke of West Germany, and Moktar Ould Daddah of Mauritania. Buea also hosted multiple consulates: American, British, French, German, Nigerian, and others, which moved away after the abolition of the Federal Republic of Cameroon, leaving only the Nigerian Consulate in Buea. The All Anglophone conferences issued a Buea Declaration (1993) and a Bamenda Proclamation (1994) demanding a return to the Federal system of government that had existed in Cameroon between 1961 and 1972. They said only federalism would safeguard the politico-cultural specificity of the English and Pidgin-speaking regions that were facing assimilation and extinction (Anglophone Crisis: Pioneer Southern Cameroons National Council Chair Dies, 2023).

The AAC conferences sounded the alarm that all was not well in the French-dominated, over-centralized, autocratic, *chefferie republicaine* of *la Republique du Cameroun*. The English and Pidgin-speaking minority essentially demanded respect for their linguistic, cultural, and governmental specificity, as well as the type of autonomy and self-governance they had enjoyed under the former West Cameroon. History shows that their political demands were met with repression. Discussion of federalism was banned in the official media, and civilian federalists like Barrister Nkongho Felix Agbor Balla and Professor Fontem Neba were arrested and court-martialed at the Yaoundé Military Tribunal (See Chapter 27). As the demands for change became more insistent over the years, and lawyers, teachers, students, members of the clergy, and other civil society actors organized strikes, ghost towns, and massive demonstrations, the Biya regime and its Anglophone surrogates like Atanga Nji denied that there was any such thing as an "Anglophone problem." These appeals were met with repression and bad-faith top-down measures aimed at cementing and solidifying the entrenched republican chiefery. The government sent the BIR, the regular military, the gendarmerie, and the police to crush demonstrators with extreme violence.

The All Anglophone conferences of 1993 and 1994 were occasions for Anglophones to air their collective, cultural and identitarian grievances and aspirations. They did so with eloquence. The crux of their submissions was a return to the Federal form of government, which they believed had been illegally and unconstitutionally abolished by the Ahidjo/Biya regime in 1972. The AAC I resorted to the power of argument when it wrote:

> TODAY, NO GROUP OF PEOPLE who freely chose to join a political Union would want to be treated as a captive people. In 1961 the people of Southern Cameroons through a United Nations-supervised plebiscite decided to enter into a political Union with the people of La Republique du Cameroun whom they considered as their brothers and fellow countrymen. They did so, by the grace of God, FREELY and without the involvement or participation of the people of La Republique du Cameroun. Their aspiration was to establish a unique Federation on the continent of Africa, and to evolve a bicultural society in which the distinct heritage of each of the partners to the union would flourish. We believed that such a lofty goal could be achieved. During these past thirty-two years, however, our common experience in the Union leaves us in no doubt that far from attaining theses ends; we have become a people with a problem.
>
> Our problem, which the intolerant and hypocritical attitude of our Francophone brothers would rather suppress, springs from a breach of trust on the part of Francophone leadership and from a lack of openness in matters of public interest. Within these thirty-two years, our Union accord has been violated. We have been disenfranchised, marginalized, and treated with suspicion. Our interests have been disregarded.
>
> Our participation in national life has been limited to non-essential functions. Our natural resources have been ruthlessly exploited without any benefit accruing to our territory or to its people. The development of our territory has been negligible and confined to areas that directly or indirectly benefit Francophones. Through manoeuvres and manipulations,

> we have been reduced from partners of equal status in the Union to the status of a subjugated people.
>
> ---
>
> We subscribe fully to the Voltairean dictum that: "I wholly disapprove of what you say, but will defend to death your right to say it". Our idea of freedom of expression and of the press leads us to believe in the open discussion of public issues that affect our lives. Our Francophone brothers suppress freedom of expression and practice censorship of the press. The democratic principle of majority rule the minority rights leads us to believe in the rights and freedoms of the minority. Successive Francophone-led regimes in this country have pursued a policy of assimilation aimed at wiping out our identity. Thus, our vision of a bicultural society has become an illusive, unattainable goal, and will remain so unless and until we devise a better framework within which this aspiration can find expression (See Complete AACI Buea Declaration in the Appendix).
>
> ...

The AAC then proceeded to list a series of introductory "Whereas" recitations" that included the following:

> WHEREAS since May 1972, we have patiently suffered numerous indignities, humiliations and injustices in respect of which we repeatedly cried out for redress;
> WHEREAS our several petitions, cries and calls for redress have been repeatedly and callously spurned without serious attention being given to them by successive Francophone-led governments;
>
> WHEREAS our Territory, its natural resources, its environment and our cultural heritage are in imminent danger of destruction...
>
> The All Anglophone Conference then issued the Buea Declaration (1993) which stated inter alia:
> 1) THAT THE IMPOSITION OF THE UNITARY STATE ON ANGLOPHONE CAMEROON IN 1972 WAS UNCONSTITUTIONAL, ILLEGAL AND A BREACH OF FAITH.
>
> 2) THAT THE ONLY REDRESS ADEQUATE TO RIGHT THE WRONGS DONE TO ANGLOPHONE CAMEROON AND ITS PEOPLE SINCE THE IMPOSITION OF THE UNITARY STATE IS A RETURN TO THE ORIGINAL FORM OF GOVERNMENT OF THE REUNIFIED CAMEROON.
>
> 3) THAT TO THIS END, ALL CAMEROONIANS OF ANGLOPHONE

HERITAGE ARE COMMITTED TO WORKING FOR THE RESTORATION OF A FEDERAL CONSTITUTION AND A FEDERAL FORM OF GOVERNMENT WHICH TAKES COGNIZANCE OF THE BICULTURAL NATURE OF CAMEROON AND UNDER WHICH CITIZENS SHALL BE PROTECTED AGAINST SUCH VIOLATIONS AS HAVE HERE ABOVE BEEN ENUMERATED.

4) THAT THE SURVIVAL OF CAMEROON IN PEACE AND HARMONY DEPENDS UPON THE ATTAINMENT OF THIS OBJECTIVE TOWARDS WHICH ALL PATRIOTIC CAMEROONIANS, FRANCOPHONES AS WELL AS ANGLOPHONES, SHOULD RELENTLESSLY WORK.

WE, THE PEOPLE OF ANGLOPHONE CAMEROON, CONVINCED OF THE JUSTICE OF OUR CAUSE AND RELYING FIRMLY ON THE PROTECTION OF THE ALMIGHTY GOD, DO HEREBY, IN SUPPORT OF THIS DECLARATION AND IN PURSUIT OF THE OBJECTIVES THEREIN SET OUT, MUTUALLY PLEDGE TO EACH OTHER, OUR LIVES, WELL BEING, PROPERTY, CAREERS AND FREEDOM. (Capital Letters in the original. See Appendix I for full Buea Declaration).

The All Anglophone Conference and the Buea Declaration of 1993 were met with President Biya's favorite negotiating posture–stony silence and massive deployment of the argument of force, the forces of law and disorder. The Anglophones created a Standing Committee that proceeded to develop constitutional proposals in the form of a draft federal constitution, which they submitted to the government and the general public in English and French for discussion. In the face of the deafening silence of the government, the Anglophones proceeded to organize the second All Anglophone Conference (AACII) in Bamenda one year later.

CAMEROON POST

STOP PRESS
Bundestag and American Congress Demand Fresh Presidential Elections in Cameroon

BUEA APRIL 2 - 3 1993 SPECIAL ALL ANGLOPHONE CONFERENCE

How Nice To Be Home Again

A PEOPLE'S RICH HERITAGE

WEST CAMEROON YESTERDAY

Figure 21.2. AAC: "Nice to be Home Again" *Cameroon Post*, April 2, 1993.

The Second All Anglophone Conference (AACII) & the Bamenda Proclamation (1994)

The second session of the All Anglophone Conference (AACII) took place in Bamenda from 29 April to 1st May 1994. This highly circumscribed conclave was held despite the heavy-handed, repressive measures of the Biya regime--BIR, police, gendarmerie, and military presence designed to prevent the meeting from taking place. The Bamenda conference was intended to evaluate how the Anglophone Standing Committee had implemented the mandate it had received from the All Anglophone Conference of Buea (AACI) in April 1993. Its terms of reference included instructions to submit a draft federal constitutional proposal, as well as other issues "concerning the People and the Territory of Anglophone Cameroon" to the Biya government (The Second All Anglophone Conference, Bamenda Proclamation 1994). The second session of the AAC congratulated the Standing Committee for officially drafting and submitting Anglophone constitutional proposals to the Cameroon Government in May 1993. These proposals came as a draft of the Cameroon Federal Constitution, which was subsequently released to the general public for discussion and comment in July 1993. The AAC II noted that the Standing Committee had published an official French translation of the AAC's Draft Cameroon Federal Constitution in July 1993 to make the Anglophone proposals accessible and more easily comprehensible to Francophone government officials, lawmakers, and the Francophone public. Furthermore, the Bamenda AAC noted that Anglophone officials have made efforts to educate Francophone government officials and the Francophone public about the content, spirit and purpose of the Anglophone Constitutional Proposals through appearances on Cameroon French language television programs. Finally, the AACII noted that it had "addressed several memoranda and resolutions to the government on the subject of constitutional reform and, in December 1993, addressed a formal request for audience to the President of the Republic in the hope that a meeting between the Head of State and officials of the AAC would provide the later the opportunity to obtain from the former the Government's official reaction to the Anglophone constitutional proposals." Anglophones essentially wanted to use Biya's proposed constitutional conference to renegotiate the terms and conditions of their reunification with Francophone Cameroun to address the constitutional violations that had led to Anglophone discontent and rectify those abuses. The AAC stated that it also engaged with the French Embassy in Yaoundé, given the influence of France on the Cameroon government.

The high-handed actions of the Cameroon security forces, in trying to prevent the holding of AACII probably hardened the resolve of the AACII attendees and may have influenced the subsequent tone and pronouncements of the conference. AACII dissolved the All Anglophone Conference and created an Anglophone Council in its place. The mandate of the Council was to "seek and secure Constitutional Talks between Anglophone Cameroon and Francophone Cameroun on the basis of the Draft Federal Constitution which was submitted by the Anglophone Standing Committee in May 1993." The Anglophone Council was given the following terms of reference:

> In its negotiations with Francophone Cameroun, the Anglophone delegation at the Constitutional Talks shall not accept any arrangement which does not envisage the restoration of an Anglophone Federated state within a Federal Republic of Cameroon in the recognition of the bicultural nature of Cameroon and under which citizens shall be protected as envisaged in the draft Federal Constitution against such violations and abuse as were catalogues in the Buea Declaration (AAC Bamenda Declaration, 1994)

The AACII issued a statement of regret that the Government of Cameroon had ignored its calls for negotiations. The sixth, seventh and ninth provisions of the recitation of "regret" contained independentist sentiments that should have made the Biya regime pause and consider the spirited submissions of the Anglophones:

> 6. Should the Government either persist in its refusal to engage in meaningful Constitutional Talks or fail to engage in such talks within a reasonable time, the Anglophone Council shall so inform the Anglophone People by all suitable means. It shall, thereupon, proclaim the revival of the Independence and Sovereignty of the Anglophone territory of the Southern Cameroons and take all measures necessary to secure, defend and preserve the Independence, Sovereignty and Integrity of the said Territory.
>
> 7. Following the Proclamation of the Revival of the Independence and Sovereignty of Southern Cameroons as provided for here above, the Anglophone Council shall, without having to convene another session of the All Anglophone Conference, transform itself into the Southern Cameroons Constituent Assembly for the purpose of drafting, debating and adopting a Constitution for the Independent and Sovereign State of Southern Cameroons.
>
> ....
>
> 9. In the event of the situation contemplated at paragraph (7) above, the Independent and Sovereign Southern Cameroons and the Independent and Sovereign Republique du Cameroun shall negotiate their peaceful separation on the basis of the Buea Peace Initiative and on such other terms as shall be mutually beneficial.

Taken together, the Buea Declaration and the Bamenda Proclamation of the All Anglophone Conference marked the kick-off of the visible, public face of Anglophone resistance to the status quo. The Biya republican chiefery turned a blind eye, a deaf ear, and guns from Israel, France, Serbia, Russia, the United Kingdom, Nigeria, and other jurisdictions towards the Anglophones. As a result, the Anglophone Problem soon became the Anglophone crisis that resulted in the arrest of federalists, lawyers, teachers, journalists, trade unionists, and other members of civil society. The conflict soon degenerated into a separatist war that resulted in the death of thousands of civilians, non-state combatants, and Cameroonian soldiers, police and gendarmerie. The authoritarian Biya decided to subjugate the Anglophone minority at all costs, rather than negotiate with it.

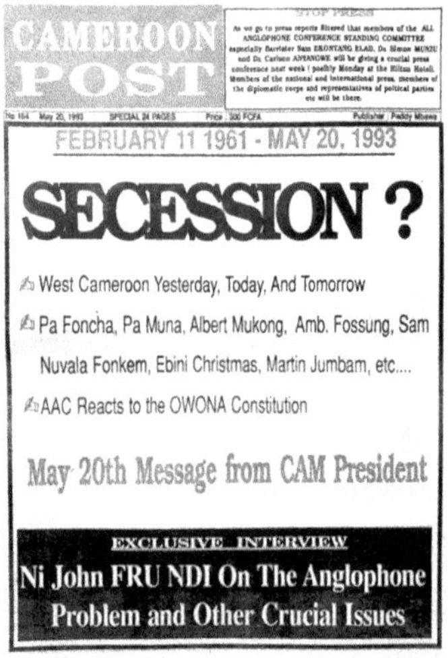

CAMEROON POST

STOP PRESS

As we go to press reports filtered that members of the ALL ANGLOPHONE CONFERENCE STANDING COMMITTEE especially Barrister Sam EKONTANG ELAD, Dr Simon MUNZU and Dr Carlson ANYANGWE will be giving a crucial press conference next week (possibly Monday at the Hilton Hotel. Members of the national and international press, members of the diplomatic corps and representatives of political parties etc will be there.

No 164 May 20, 1993 SPECIAL 24 PAGES Price 300 FCFA Publisher Paddy Mbawa

FEBRUARY 11 1961 - MAY 20, 1993

SECESSION ?

West Cameroon Yesterday, Today, And Tomorrow

Pa Foncha, Pa Muna, Albert Mukong, Amb. Fossung, Sam Nuvala Fonkem, Ebini Christmas, Martin Jumbam, etc....

AAC Reacts to the OWONA Constitution

May 20th Message from CAM President

EXCLUSIVE INTERVIEW

Ni John FRU NDI On The Anglophone Problem and Other Crucial Issues

Figure 21.3. *Cameroon Post* front page of May 20, 1993 summarizes the sentiments of Anglophones after AACI & II and the publication of a constitution that maintained the status quo

The Biya Regime's Non-Response "Response" and Foncha's Rejoinder

The Anglophone call for renegotiation of the structure and form of the country and a return to federalism, failing which, the former federated State of West Cameroons, the former British Southern Cameroons would become an independent country, transformed the Anglophone Problem into the Anglophone crisis. These clear and unequivocal independentist or separatist threats were acts of political resistance against cultural and identitarian assimilation and marginalization that would have made democratic states grounded on the consent of the governed to sit up and pay attention. They were alarm bells that signaled that all was not well in Cameroon. To the utter amazement of the Anglophone community and the world, these Anglophone expressions of disgruntlement and calls for political dialogue and change were viewed as subversive and secessionist, proverbial red flags to a bull for Biya, the republican chieftain, who incarnated the centralized Napoleonic, "one and indivisible" autocratic, neo-patrimonial State. In Biya's republican chiefery, "le vivre ensemble" (the desire to live together) is neither negotiated nor voluntary; it is a matter of compulsion and subjugation. The Buea Declaration and the Bamenda Proclamation, or rather the Biya regime's reaction to them, marked the beginning of the Anglophone crisis. The Biya government intransigently refused to entertain any discussion whatsoever of a change in the structure or form of the State of Cameroon. It resorted to repression, bad-faith half-measures, and delaying tactics in response to the bitter political grievances, trenchant critiques and calls for change detailed in the Buea Declaration and the Bamenda Proclamation of the All Anglophone Conferences.

True to its Napoleonic rule-by-decree system, on December 4, 1994, President Paul Biya signed a decree creating a Consultative Committee on Constitutional Reforms. Simon

Achidi Achu, an Anglophone baron of the regime, was appointed to head the commission. This was an act of window dressing aimed at giving the impression that Anglophones controlled the committee. The Consultative Committee on Constitutional Reforms. It turned out to be a trump l'oeil affair, an act of bad faith aimed at deceiving and misleading the Anglophone public while maintaining the status quo. Of the 58 members appointed by presidential decree, only 14 were English-speaking Southern Cameroonians. Before long, seven of the 14 later withdrew from the deliberation process in committee. Among them were former Southern Cameroons Prime Ministers, Foncha and Muna. There was no illusion that the Biya regime would heed the voices of the Anglophone civil society so eloquently expressed by the AAC's Buea Declaration and Bamenda Proclamations. Indeed, from the very beginning, it became clear that this would be a deceptive, misleading and bad faith attempt to entrench Biya's republican chieftaincy. It did not take long for the Anglophone participants to see that it was a charade; the lopsided membership and failure to include the Southern Cameroons question in the agenda of the meeting meant it was an act of window-dressing.

John Ngu Foncha, former Prime Minister of West Cameroon, former Vice President of the Federal Republic of Cameroon, former Chairman of the Kamerun National Democratic Party (KNDP), former Vice President of the UNC, former Vice President of the CPDM, former Grand Chancellor of National Orders, decided to withdraw from the meetings. He wrote a letter explaining why he and five other Southern Cameroonians had decided to withdraw from the Consultative Committee on Constitutional Reforms. Mr. Foncha's letter to the committee chairman, fellow Mezam native, Simon Achidi Achu, said in part:

> Mr. Ahidjo publicly stated to the people of Southern Cameroons during successive visits to that territory in 1960 and 1961 that unification would not mean annexation, that its modalities would be negotiated between representatives of Southern Cameroons and those of La Republique du Cameroun and that to render unification viable and useful; a flexible and federal form of the state which he qualified as unique and diverse, was envisaged… I can state here and now that the People of Southern Cameroons would never have voted in favour of unification if it had not been for the assurances given that the resulting union would take the form of a federation…The honourable S. T. Muna and I have often been accused of having allowed this situation [i.e. 'annexation of Southern Cameroons'] to come about. At this point in time, I do not feel the necessity–nor, I suppose, does the Honourable S. T. Muna– to defend myself against these accusations, unjust though they are. What is important is that the Good Lord who, in his infinite wisdom determines the affairs of each man and of each people, has preserved me long enough to have the opportunity of pleading before the Cameroon Nation for the correction of the wrongs which have been done, over the past three decades and more, against an unsuspecting and trusting people that I, acting in good faith and as a Cameroonian patriot, led into what I was assured would be a union of

equal partners, but which has since turned out to be an arrangement for the annexation, subjugation and domination of one of the partners by the other…

I responded to the invitation of the President of the Republic to attend this Committee in the confident expectation that the deliberations of the Committee would offer us the opportunity to correct the wrongs which I have referred above. For nearly two years, the people of Southern Cameroons whom I led into the union with *La Republique du Cameroun* have, through the All-Anglophone Conference- AAC (now the Southern Cameroons People's Conference-SCPC) carefully studied, responsibly formulated, and respectfully submitted to government, substantial constitutional proposals. These proposals are aimed at ensuring a better governance of the entire united Cameroon, while also putting an end to the annexation, subjugation and domination of one of our two territories by the other, thus restoring the spirit and intent of the union of 1961…In any event, in the proposals that have been submitted before us, I do not see any provisions at all which go in the direction of making even a token attempt to respond to the grievances of the Southern Cameroonian People…

Mr. chairman,
In the final analysis, the people of Southern Cameroons never participated in the elaboration and adoption of the supposed federal constitution of 1961 which was adopted by the National Assembly of La Republique du Cameroun on September 1, 1961, that is to say, one month before the birth of the Federal Republic of Cameroon. These same people never participated in drawing up the unitary constitution of 1972 which was imposed upon them in a nationwide referendum. Bearing this in mind, I had hoped that the present constitutional reform process would provide the people of Southern Cameroons the opportunity, for the first time since independence of our respective territories and the reunification of our fatherland, to contribute effectively to the elaboration and adoption of a truly Cameroonian constitution which responds to their aspirations as well… I feel distressed that the constitutional proposals put before this committee do not offer the opportunity for us, as a nation, to address our minds to, and resolve, the genuine and legitimate grievances of the Southern Cameroonian people in particular and the Cameroonian people in general. I feel all the more distressed that this should be happening under the chairmanship of a son of Southern Cameroons whom, I believe, is as sensitive as any one of us to the injustices which his People and their Territory have suffered in more than three decades. Today, he has been designated to preside over the completion of the process of annexation of that People and that Territory. For this, He shall tomorrow stand accused

> by his People, as I stand accused today. However, whereas in 1961 the bitter experiences of Southern Cameroons lay in the future that we could not predict, in 1994 we have behind us thirty-three years' worth of these experiences, with the prospect of more to come unless something is done now. In the light of these experiences, we have no reason in 1994 to repeat the mistakes of 1961.
>
> (Dr. John Ngu Foncha).

The Consultative Committee on Constitutional Reforms ignored the submissions of John Ngu Foncha, Solomon Tandeng Muna and the Anglophone community. It published the Cameroon Constitution of 18 January 1996, whose main distinction was that it cut and pasted parts of Article I of the French Constitution of 1958, which provides in part:

> *"La France est une République indivisible, laïque, démocratique et sociale....* Son organisation est décentralisée.
>
> France shall be an indivisible, secular, democratic and social Republic.... It shall be organised on a decentralized basis.
>
> For its part, the Cameroon Constitution of 18 January 1996 provides in relevant part:
>
> (2) *La République du Cameroun est un Etat unitaire décentralisé. Elle est une et indivisible, laïque, démocratique et sociale.*
>
> The Republic of Cameroon is a unitary, decentralized State. It is one and indivisible, secular, democratic and social.

The 1996 Constitution was supposed to reform the State of Cameroon but it acquired the opposite. It essentially entrenched the republican chiefery of the Chief of State, President Paul Biya. Some of the provisions of that constitution had not been implemented decades later.

From the Anglophone Question to the Anglophone Problem, to the Anglophone Crisis to the Anglophone Revolt: Political Discourses from the Center

As we saw in Chapter 1, the Anglophone war started on October 1, 2017, when President Biya was spending one of his habitually lengthy vacations at his presidential suite at the Intercontinental Hotel in Geneva, Switzerland. Eight weeks later, he formally declared war on what he called terrorists and secessionists.

> *J'ai appris avec émotion l'assassinat de quatre militaires camerounais et de deux policiers dans le sud-ouest de notre pays...le Cameroun est victime*

> *des attaques à répétition d'une bande de terroristes se réclamant d'un mouvement sécessionniste…Toutes les dispositions sont prises pour mettre hors d'état de nuire ces criminels et faire en sorte que la paix et la sécurité soient sauvegardées sur toute l'étendue du territoire national (Le Ched de L'Etat, le* Président Paul Biya, Airport de Yaoundé Nsimalen, le 30 novembre 2017).
>
> I learnt with emotion, the assassination of four Cameroun soldiers and two police officers in the Southwest region of our country. Cameroun is the victim of repeated attacks by a band of terrorists who claim to be a secessionist movement. All measures have been taken to neutralize these criminals and ensure that peace and security are maintained throughout the national territory.
>
> (President Paul Biya, November 30, 2017 at the Yaoundé Nsimalen airport upon his return from the fifth African Union - European Union (AU-EU) in Abidjan, Côte d'Ivoire.

This declaration of war meant that President Paul Biya had opted to use military force to solve the Anglophone Question, a political problem. This essentially meant that the assimilation of the Anglophone minority was no longer on the table. The new policy was subjugation. The first step of subjugation was denial of the existence of an Anglophone political problem. It was a law and order, natural security issue. To the republican chieftain, all political problems are national security problems that must be crushed by overwhelming military force.

One of the bizarre ironies of the Anglophone Crisis in Cameroon is that it was shaped and considerably worsened by the dogged determination of the Biya *chefferie républicaine*, which entrenched itself in arrogant and authoritarian cocoon of denial. According to the regime and its sycophants in the media, the Anglophone Problem did not exist; it was a creation of the figment of the imagination of terrorists and secessionists out to destabilize the regime. As such, there was no point discussing a non-existent problem in the National Assembly, the Senate or the official media. This was strange behavior, given that a parade of international diplomats passed through Yaoundé in search of a solution to the crisis. As soon as the Anglophone Revolt began in 2016, there has been a flurry of diplomatic activities and attempts to resolve this problem in venues as diverse as: the Nigerian Senate, the German Bundestag, the American Congress, the Canadian House of Commons, the British House of Commons, the European Parliament, the Commonwealth, the Francophonie, the African Union, the United Nations Special Representative for Central Africa, the United Nations Secretary General, António Guterres, the UN representative for the Central Africa region, Mr. Fall. on the Anglophone problem after a visit to Cameroon and by international human rights organizations like Amnesty International, the International Crisis Group, Committee to Protect Journalists, have put the problem squarely before the international community. From 26 to 28 November 2019, the Chairperson of the moribund African Union Commission, Moussa Faki Mahamat, the Secretary-General of the neo-colonial International Organization of *la Francophonie*, Louise Mushikiwabo, and the Secretary General of the colonial British Commonwealth, Patricia Scotland, undertook an unprecedented "tripartite" visit to Yaoundé, Cameroon. The impotent diplomatic waltz continued. The appeals of the American Ambassador, the French Ambassador, the British Foreign Secretary, the Pope's representative, and His Eminence Cardinal Secretary of State Pietro Parolin all fell on deaf ears. The Cameroon government continued to deny the very existence of the problem, despite the fact that President Ahidjo had recognized it and sent then Prime Minister Paul Biya, Dr. Mrs. Dorothy Limunga Njeuma, then Vice Minister of National Education, and Hon. David Abouem à Tchoyi, then Governor of the Northwest Province to try and resolve it.

Profile of Political Courage: Hon. Joseph Mbiydzenyuy Wirba, MP

The fire-brand Opposition Social Democratic Front (SDF) MP for Jakiri, Bui, Hon. Joseph Mbiydzenyuy Wirba, made history in the Cameroon National Assembly on December 16, 2016. On that occasion, the MP made an unprecedented speech that amounted to a catalog of grievances against the republican chiefdom of Cameroon. This speech resulted from the denialism of the Biya regime and its rubber-stamp National Assembly, whose Speaker, Cavayé Yeguié Djibril, steadfastly refused to acknowledge the existence of an Anglophone Problem, let alone discuss it. Hon. Wirba essentially forced the Anglophone problem on the National Assembly by saying:

> In this nation that you call yours, people can do what has been done to our children in West Cameroon. I call it West Cameroon because you will never take it out of our mouths again. Because that is a territory in which we believe in freedom. To go out on the street and demonstrate is a basic right for us. And that is why we are saying that there are two Cameroons that came together. If you are telling us like a State Minister stood here [Parliament] and told us that what happens in Cameroon is like dropping a few cubes of sugar in a basin of water. Who is the sugar and who is the water? I am asking the government bench of Cameroon. Who is? That you rape our children, my brother's daughter had been raped in Buea. I swear to you the government of this country...Does the President of this country know that the governors and the DOs (Biya's appointed Senior Divisional and Sub-divisional Officers) and all the administrators you have sent to West Cameroon are out there behaving exactly like a n army of occupation. Our people have no where to go. We have made all the efforts. Our ancestors and our forefathers trusted you to go into a gentleman's agreement that two people who consider themselves brothers could go to live together. If this is what you show us after 55 years, then those who say that we should break Cameroon are right. They are correct. The people of West Cameroon cannot be your slaves. The people of West Cameroon...you did not conquer them in war. If this is what you say we

should live in, I say, simply, No! It will not work. How do you have an army that is supposed to protect children step out there beat them and rape some? It is not heard of in any country. This is the 21st Century and anyone who does that should be willing to pay the price. We will exact it on you because you are making us believe that we went to the wrong place. What is there to say? I want the world to know and to have it on record that we have made efforts.

I have sat with [government] ministers and listened to them talk. The first one was the then Minister of Justice, Amadou Ali, ten years ago. And I took my time, drove from Kumbo to Yaoundé to tell him, "something is brewing out there," This thing that you are sending gendarmes to beat people up...there is pain in West Cameroon. Minister of Justice be very careful what happens there. And he turned round, looked at me and told me, Mr. Wirba, it is your people who chose to come here. He is alive, he told me. Last week I went to see the Minister of Higher Education, Professor Fame Ndongo, and I told him, the problems in Cameroon, the problems we have in West Cameroon, is the problem that will bring down Cameroon. If you do not handle it well, you will not know Cameroon as it is in a few months or in a few years. When people have had pent-up anger and pain, humiliation for over 50 years, when it bursts out, you will never be able to control it. What he asked me was simply, "*Qu'est-ce que vous allez faire*?" (What are you going to do?)

Because you have your army of occupation out in West Cameroon. When the people will arise, even if you take the whole of the French army and added it to yours, you will never bring them down. And we have no need for that! We don't have any need for that in the 21st Century. I was one of the believers in a unified Cameroon, and I want to tell this House that what has happened to those children in Buea University and in Bamenda has convinced me that the people who say Cameroon should go in two parts are correct. And there are more and more of us out there who now believe that it is the ultimate end. I listened the other night to an offer of a thousand jobs, an offer of two billion Francs for lay schools and I laughed at myself. Are my people slaves? So you now take them to be your dogs that you can beat and wound and maim, break their bones, then throw a piece of meat for them to fight over. It has to end. If we, the people of West Cameroon have to continue doing what we are doing is because we believe that the more is always the merrier. When you have more people, you have more chances of succeeding in life. If the more people who are the people of East Cameroon have proven to us that our blood means nothing, then it is time for us to say it will soon be over.

I want to give you a quote which I borrowed from the American liberators: "When injustice becomes law, resistance becomes a duty." (Thomas Jefferson). The people of West Cameroon have a duty to resist your oppression. I call it oppression because of what I have seen in the field.

Let me quote you another two instances. Three weeks ago there was an incident in Bangolan, which is a neighbouring village to Jakiri, where I come from. I don't know what it was all about but a gendarme officer was killed. The forces of law and order, under the instructions of the SDO of Ngoketunjia, moved into Jakiri and neighbouring villages and took away a hundred men, just beat them up, broke their bones, and just leave them there. And I went to that place where he took these people and I told him, "Mister, SDO (Biya's appointed Senior Divisional and Sub-Divisional Officers) you are going to release my people." He sent soldiers to me, and one of them told me. I told them. I am a representative of these people because I am a parliamentarian. And the young man turned round and asked me: "*et puis quoi*? *On n'est pas ici à Yaoundé*" (So what, we are not in Yaoundé here). And he drew a line on the ground to tell me, if you cross here, you will see the consequences. Unfortunately for him, I happen to be a descendant of the warriors of Nso, no body draws a line before me and I crossed and I told him "shoot me." I told the SDO release my people. In 12 hours, he released them. But some are still lying in the hospital. They beat and kicked a woman until she miscarried, a pregnant woman. And nobody can question this. That is the reason in this masterplan to finish our culture and our people. You have chosen that every single administrator and every single commander of the army is from East Cameroon. That is why they sit there and can kill the people without remorse. This has to end!

Mr. President, Mr. Speaker, I want to repeat this quote:
"When injustice becomes law, resistance becomes a duty." [Thomas Jefferson].

We the people of West Cameroon will resist you and if you want to take that territory by force, you will kill to the last man before you take it. And you can start from me today! It has to end. Somebody has to know that this is not how you treat a people. Fifty years is too long, 50 years is a very, very long time. And we come here and sit, just talking about the budget, you normalize murder, you normalize rape. Mr. Speaker, I am sorry to tell you that this is part of the resistance, you will hear me to the end [after Speaker Cavaye Djibril told him his time was up]. "When injustice becomes law, resistance becomes a duty." It is my duty to defend my people. You will not stop me because of lack of time [looking in the direction of the Speaker]. Or if you want to, you can call your brutal gendarmes to come and kill me here. I will not, I will not [after inaudible background noise in French]. I want you to hear this Mr. Speakerrrr!!! That my people are suffering, that the cube of sugar that was defined in this House... [turning to address Cavaye Djibril on the dais behind him] Are you just angry Mr. Speaker, that the person who was considered a slave has risen in the Master's house and is asking a question? Mr. Speaker, I am telling you this is part of my resistance. You will hear me to the end...Bring the brutal soldiers who raped our daughters to take me out of here. I will say it to my end. There's nothing you can do to me.

I am wondering whether His Excellency the President of the Republic knows that the governors and the DOs are behaving exactly, when they are posted to West Cameroon, as colonial masters. When they abuse people and insult them and do all they have done, we have to resist and we have to tell you our people will not be brought down because we came to this union as equal partners. Yes sir, I am done... and we will resist because this is part of our culture that we inherited. You people [Francophones) fear every administrator and every ruler. We [Anglophones] challenge our rulers, we take them to task and that is why they are accountable. Thank you very much."

Wirba's Letter of March 2017

Months later, he wrote this letter to his fellow Anglophone Members of the Cameroon National Assembly:

Hon. Wirba Joseph Mbiydzenyuy
MP. Bui South, Jakiri
Bui Division
28th March 2017

Honorable Members of Parliament,
The Representatives of
The People of West Cameroon
Right Honorable Members

Dear Colleagues,
SUBJECT: HISTORICAL MOMENT TO STAND TOGETHER FOR THE PEOPLE OF WEST CAMEROON
I have chosen this dark moment in our history to write to you from exile, following the vicious man-hunt to put me in chains and an attempt on my life, by a government that believes the people of West Cameroon are a lower cast of humans who must be kept in bondage and servitude. This is your moment in history in which all of you, without exception, must stand

together in the name of the suffering, oppressed and struggling people of West Cameroon! Our people have been mistreated humiliated, tortured, jailed, exiled and others killed; merely for peacefully asking for their basic fundamental rights, as a people with a distinct cultural heritage and a dignified way of life. They have endured systematic and traumatic abuse for over half a century and we all can testify that they have had enough! As the representatives of the people that you are, you have witnessed in each of your constituencies, the collective will and the dogged determination of our people to resist oppression in order to have a voice and a place in their own land. Our children and their teachers have been out of school for months! Our lawyers have been out of court for much longer! The general masses from every village to every town have joined the struggle to take back our freedom! Our brothers and sisters in the diaspora have fought and struggled along with the people in every way imaginable! The world has taken notice that our people are in bondage, and in various ways expressed support for them. You, their representatives, are the ONLY group left that has not supported the people in their desperate hour of need! YOU MUST STAND TOGETHER NOW AND JOIN YOUR PEOPLE IN THEIR STRUGGLE, OR FACE THE CONSEQUENCES OF INACTION AND SILENCE!

Honourable Members, this is the moment that you, representatives of the people of West Cameroon; from Boyo, Bui, Donga-Mantung, Fako, Kupe-Manenguba, Lebialem, Manyu, Meme, Menchum, Mezam, Momo, Ndian and Ngokitunjia, must stage a protest, in the name of our people, and walk out of the Cameroon National Assembly together! This is your historic moment to stand in solidarity with the people and save them from 56 years of slavery! If you lose this chance, our people and history will never forgive you!"

God is with us and He will bless and protect you all for standing up for His People!"

The fire-brand Opposition Social Democratic Front (SDF) MP for Jakiri, Bui, Hon. Joseph Mbiydzenyuy Wirba, again made history in the Cameroon National Assembly on the 19th of June 2018. The man made a spectacular, unprecedented re-entry into the august chamber and took the National Assembly to task for completely ignoring the costly Anglophone uprising, which has been dragging on since November 2017. Wirba who has emerged as a champion of the Anglophone cause, had been on the run for three months. As soon as he was recognized by the Speaker, Hon Cavaye Djibril, the fiery MP, took the podium and engaged in an animated shouting match with the Speaker, who attempted to silence him.

During the heated exchange, we learned that Wirba went underground and was "chased in the bushes" to use his own words because a warrant of arrest had been issued against him for championing the Anglophone cause in and outside of parliament. He said that while on the run, he had written twice to the Speaker requesting protection, but the Speaker had given a deaf ear to his pleas. Wirba challenged the speaker to tell the person who had issued the warrant for his arrest to come and arrest him at the National Assembly. The Speaker confirmed that a warrant of arrest had indeed been issued against Wirba, and asked the MP why he had gone underground: "au maquis." Cavaye declared that he would inform the issuer of the warrant of arrest that Wirba was back in the National Assembly.

Accusing Wirba of being a "maquisard" was an interesting accusation. During World War II, the "maquisard" were French guerilla fighters who resisted Nazi German occupation forces. In Cameroon, in the 1960s and 1970s, the name "maquisard" referred to anti-colonial UPC fighters (mostly Bamileke and Bassa) who fought against the French colonialists and the Ahidjo regime. Interestingly, when Biya came to power in 1982 with all kinds of hope and high expectations, he announced that henceforth, no one needed to go into the "maquis" to express his opinions. Thirty-five years later, Honorable Wirba did just that. Acquiescing to the arrest of an MP tarnished the image of the National Assembly. The Anglophone crisis had crashed into the Cameroon National Assembly and revealed it for what it really is: a moribund, sclerotic, rubber-stamp for Biya's dictatorship. The Speaker of the Cameroon National Assembly, Hon. Cavaye Djibril, did not seem to be aware that members of parliament have immunity. They cannot be arrested for what they say inside the House of Assembly. That is an ancient tradition that is sacrosanct in all parliaments around the world! We all know Hon. Wirba was not arrested in parliament despite the outstanding warrant against him. The reasons for that are simple. Even the blood hounds in Yaoundé know that arresting a member of parliament for defending his constitutions would be an unconstitutional violation of parliamentary immunity, human rights and freedom of expression. Hon Wirba, there is no denying that the man has guts. No one in the history of Cameroon has ever defied the old "Lion man" right in the "Lion's den!"

Hon. Wirba left the Cameroon National Assembly a free man. However, his life was never the same again. On November 18, 2018, a group calling itself the Hon. Wirba Support Team issued a press release announcing that the persecuted MP had safely arrived in the United Kingdom. The British government had apparently granted Hon. Wirba political asylum. His supporters claimed that he had been hunted by the Cameroon authorities since his fiery speech in the National Assembly in December 2016.

John Fru Ndi, Chairman, Social Democratic Front (Opposition Party)

> H.E. Paul Biya
> President of the Republic,
> Yaoundé, Cameroon.10th February 2018
>
> Mr. President,
> Once again, I am obliged to address myself to you in the supreme interest of our beloved nation, Cameroon. Following our last correspondence, I expected that given the urgency of things, you would have by this time extended an invitation for dialogue as was indicated in your last

mail. Unfortunately, there has been no such move on your part. I find it hard to believe that with the state of Cameroon in peril, our future uncertain, more so as my own "backyard" is burning, you still do not think it important for us to have meaningful dialogue and to work assiduously towards resolving this crisis. I understand that initial security reports, by some of your officers and administrators might have been misleading, reason why maybe you haven't scheduled for us to meet. It is necessary for me to bring to your attention that all such reports are done in bad faith and are a cover up by these officials, who are busy amassing wealth for themselves, justifying their poor judgement and masking their gross inability to manage the crisis. After more than three decades in politics I do have a proper understanding of what is at stake in this country. Disrupting the state of affairs for political gains or any form of recognition has never been my political vision or mission, even though in the past, a member of your Government accused me of such action. I believe in the protection and preservation of life. I told you before and I reiterate today, that I do not believe in coming to power or gaining fame by walking over the corpses of innocent Cameroonians, otherwise I would have opted for a civil war in 1992 following the Presidential Election debacle. I never took that option then, I am not ready to endorse it today.

Mr President, The fast deteriorating state of affairs in the two English Speaking regions warrants me once again to draw your attention to the need for prompt action dialogue on the Anglophone Crisis. An old English adage says a stitch in time saves nine. When this crisis began what was initially a trade union strike action and that could have very easily ended as such, rather morphed itself into a beguiling event of startling revelations. There has been a lot of talk and analysis on this crisis and we are all aware that there is a genuine Anglophone problem, very well known by you, most especially as rapporteur of the Ahidjo Commission on this issue. With all these revelations, we are compelled to act to save our country from the imminent woes and destruction that are staring at us. Everyday that passes, an innocent Cameroonian dies, a family is widowed, people go out of business, farmers can neither plant nor harvest their crops as all farming implements have been seized, villagers are on the run. This situation presages a future of hunger, malnutrition, famine and desperation.

Our refusal to face up to the realities of our country and facts of history is costing us tremendous economic, social and particularly in human lives. The line of division is growing deeper and deeper and as you are very aware, the rise in hate speech is steadily moving us towards a civil war. Those who are charged with the management of this crisis are failing and failing woefully. The protraction of this crisis should have signaled to you that the adopted line of action is not yielding the desired fruits and

thus the need to restrategize. Quite a lot of resources that should have been put to better use have all been diverted to military efforts and we are very far from an end point. No country has ever won a war against its people. The death of any Cameroonian, whether military or civilian, hurts me personally and is a loss to the nation. I condemn all forms of killings by both members of the armed forces as well as the children of this country, who have been pushed in to this predicament. Your declaration of war against your people, who are being murdered in cold blood by the unprofessionalism and recklessness of the forces of law and order, now being seen as a force of occupation.
Also, the killing of members of the Armed Forces, who have not been properly trained in counter insurgency techniques, not only exposes the security frailties of our country but equally leaves their families embittered. The military response to this crisis, from its beginning till date, only made a bad situation worse. It is imperative that I draw your attention to the continuous atrocities that are being carried out in this part of our country. Villages are being ransacked, businesses heavily looted, extortion of huge sums of money and their livelihoods and houses razed down with no consideration to human life and dignity. Women are being raped, the youth are being targeted, and local grain barns from the hard work of farmers are being burnt to ashes.

The anti-terrorism law, which was adopted to protect Cameroonians from extremist violence, has given a blank cheque for extra-judicial killings. Some politicians have taken advantage of this mayhem to witch-hunt and cause members of other political parties to be arrested and heavily punished on trumped-up charges. With all the havoc and carnage being fomented in this part of the country, more and more youths of the North West and South West Regions are being radicalised for the injustices they suffer. Cameroonians are seeking refuge in neighbouring Nigeria because they don't feel secure in their own country. Across the nation, we all live in fear and insecurity. Mr President, From the above, there is no way we can make any progress or get any positive outcomes under such circumstances. There must be an end to all this. To every dark cloud, there is a silver lining that lasting solutions can be found to resolve such crisis. We must face up to the realities of our history and correct the grievous mistakes that have been perpetuated in order to arrive at sustainable solutions. Frank dialogue is not a sign of weakness but an opportunity for us to start again and work towards a truly united Cameroon. I urge on you, to extend the olive branch for reconciliation. Let us give dialogue a chance in the supreme interest of the legacy of our fathers of reunification. We all have a responsibility to preserve the peace and justice of this nation and that job cannot be done by one person, but by all. Let us selflessly restore the lost confidence and hope in our beloved nation, so that her sons and daughters can safely return home to live in a country of smiling plenty. Let us finally reawaken the spirit of nationhood. That is our challenge and it is my fervent wish that we do so sooner than later. Examples abound of how dialogue as a political tool has saved other nations from eternal damnation. Nigeria was able to dialogue in order to heal its wounds of civil war, with General Ojukwu pardoned and reinstated. You were able to pardon Bello Bouba Maigari, Issa Tchiroma, Diakole Diassala amongst others following the abortive coup that almost had you killed. Today these people are ministers within your government. This is eloquent proof that you can pardon. Can all those arrested from the outset of the crisis be released in order to facilitate the process of dialogue and true reconciliation? You negotiated with Boko Haram for the release of captives. You are as well in the process of rehabilitating and reinserting these known Boko Haram terrorists. Can we for once treat all Cameroonians fairly and give them equal chances as one people?

Mr. President,
I am always available for discussions, though this has not been given any consideration so far. I avail myself, once again and extend to you my hand of fellowship in the interest of our beloved nation. Accept Mr. President, my esteemed considerations and best wishes.

Ni John FRU NDI, National Chairman

Discourses of the Church and the Anglophone Question

As has been noted, the Anglophone cultural and identitarian specificity was grounded on four pillars:

1. Linguistic specificity: The population of Southern Cameroons was mostly Pidgin and English-speaking. Pidgin was the lingua franca, the language of commerce and religion, while "proper" English was the official language of the Southern Cameroons government, and the educational system.
2. The legal profession, which was part of the Anglo-Saxon legal family, as comparative law scholars put it.
3. Religion: The Roman Catholic Church and two main Protestant denominations, the Presbyterian Church in Cameroon (PCC) and the Cameroon Baptist Convention (CBC). We saw in Chapters 1 and 2 how European missionaries introduced Christianity in the coast of Southern Cameroons. As part of their evangelistic mission, they established networks of primary and secondary schools, hospitals, and health centers in the Coastal and Grasslands regions of Southern Cameroons. The churches and their humanitarian missions created a unique English and Pidgin linguistic-religious culture.
4. The Anglophone legal profession: The Anglophone legal profession in Cameroon

> is part of the so-called Anglo-Saxon common law legal family. It inherited this tradition from the British Empire, which administered Southern Cameroons as part of its Nigerian colonial protectorate under a League of Nations Mandate and a United Nations Trusteeship agreement.

These four Anglophone cultural and identitarian pillars enabled Southern Cameroons to successfully resist 60 years of concerted efforts by French and Francophone Cameroon to assimilate and disperse the English and Pidgin-speaking minority into the exceptionalist Francophone cultural universal, *la Francophonie.* As the oldest identitarian cultural institutions in Anglophone Cameroon, the churches and their educational and medical institutions were custodians of the collective cultural memory and identitarian specificity of the English and Pidgin-speaking minority. As such, they played a crucial role in raising the cultural and identitarian consciousness of Anglophones in Cameroon. They did this through sermons, individual and collective statements, press releases, and, above all, a collective memorandum.

Memorandum of the Catholic Bishops of the Bamenda Provincial Episcopal Conference (BAPEC)

The most notable statement of grievances from the religious community came from the Roman Catholic Church in Anglophone Cameroon. Though a large proportion of Francophones–including President Paul Biya and most members of the ruling elite self-identify as Catholics, their allegiance was to the Biya regime. This essentially meant that in Cameroon, the Roman Catholic Church was split into an Anglophone Catholic Church and a Francophone Catholic Church. The Anglophone Roman Catholic Church provided the historical, cultural, and collective memory of Anglophone Cameroon. The Catholic Bishops of the Bamenda Provincial Episcopal Conference (BAPEC), which corresponds to the geographic region of the former Anglophone Southern Cameroons, penned a lengthy memorandum of grievances dated 22 December 2016, and addressed to fellow Catholic, President Paul Biya (See Appendix I for the full Memorandum). The Anglophone Catholic Bishops gave a summary of the political history of Cameroon and presented the Anglophone Problem as they saw it and lived it. They denounced the marginalization and assimilation of Anglophones, and essentially justified the Anglophone Revolt of 2016. They wrote as follows:

> **The Anglophone Problem**
>
> …No matter what some self-appointed elite and spokespersons for Anglophone Cameroonians as well as government Ministers say in public, the participation of various strata of the population and the growing popularity of separatist movements among young and older members of the Anglophone community demonstrates that there is an Anglophone Problem. There is a consciousness among Anglophone Cameroonians that all is not well and something needs to be done about their plight.
>
> The Anglophone Problem is:

- 1961 The failure of successive governments of Cameroon, since 1961, to respect and implement the articles of the Constitution that uphold and safeguard what British Southern Cameroons brought along to the Union in 1961.
- 1962 The flagrant disregard for the Constitution, demonstrated by the dissolution of political parties and the formation of one political party in 1966, the sacking of Jua and the appointment of Muna in 1968 as the Prime Minister of West Cameroon, and other such acts judged by West Cameroonians to be unconstitutional and undemocratic
  iii. The cavalier management of the 1972 Referendum which took out the foundational element (Federalism) of the 1961 Constitution.

1. The 1984 Law amending the Constitution, which gave the country the original East Cameroon name (The Republic of Cameroon) and thereby erased the identity of the West Cameroonians from the original union. West Cameroon, which had entered the union as an equal partner, effectively ceased to exist.
2. The deliberate and systematic erosion of the West Cameroon cultural identity which the 1961 Constitution sought to preserve and protect by providing for a bi-cultural federation.

The Catholic bishops' memorandum offered a reasonable way out of the emerging crisis: a frank, sincere and fraternal dialogue between Anglophones and Francophones on the matter of the institutional form of the state of Cameroon, the separation of powers between the executive, the judiciary, and the legislative, and recognition of Anglophone politico-cultural and identitarian specificity. Since hundreds of Anglophone demonstrators and federalists had been arrested in the Anglophone regions and deported to detention centers in Francophone Cameroon, the Bishops appealed to the president to ensure that the state "decide the destiny of the detainees according to appropriate judicial procedure." President Biya ignored the memorandum of the Catholic Bishops just as he had ignored the appeals of the All Anglophone Conference, politicians, political parties, Anglophone common law lawyers, teachers, and civil society groups. The eventual deepening of the crisis and the worsening of the human rights situation in the Northwest and Southwest regions demonstrated that the Catholic Bishops of the Bamenda Provincial Episcopal Conference (BAPEC) had grossly underestimated the obduracy of their fellow Catholic, President Paul Biya, and the rest of the Catholics who were at the helm of the State in Yaoundé.

Biya's Visit to the Vatican and the Vatican Secretary of State's Visit to Bamenda

Three months after the Catholic Bishops of the Bamenda Provincial Episcopal Conference (BAPEC) wrote their memorandum to President Paul Biya, the president went on an official visit to Italy and the Vatican. Though he had turned a blind eye and a deaf ear to the Anglophone Bishops of the former Southern Cameroons, the crisis in Anglophone Cameroon came up when he visited the Vatican on March 23, 2017. The Roman Catholic Church had, for over a century, been deeply involved in missionary educational and health service provision in Southern Cameroons. Church educational and medical institutions were being caught in the conflict. The Holy See, therefore, took the opportunity, after a meeting with Pope Francis, to subtly call on President Biya to respect the rights of the Anglophone minority. After a meeting with Cardinal Secretary of State Pietro Parolin and other authorities, the Vatican issued the following statement:

> During the cordial discussions, the existing good relations between the Holy See and Cameroon were evoked, as was the important contribution the Church offers to the development of the country, especially in the fields of education and healthcare. Taking into consideration the peaceful co-existence and mutual respect between the various religious groups, attention was focused on the importance of promoting national cohesion, enhancing the richness of the various historic and cultural traditions of the country, with respect for human and minority rights (Holy See Press Office Communique: Audience with the President of the Republic of Cameroon, 2017).

The Pope offered President Biya and his wife, Chantal, holy communion and blessed them. The president promptly ignored the entreaties of the Vatican. He rejected all calls for frank and open dialogue and the protection of the rights of the Anglophone minority. He would offer a "Grand National Dialogue" dominated by the elite of the regime. The President did not even bother to attend the meetings. The outcome was no different from the deceptive 1996 Constitution that had done nothing but entrench the status quo the Anglophones were dissatisfied with. The Roman Catholic Church proved powerless in the face of the obduracy and uncompromising posture of President Biya and his regime. Things just went from bad to worse. More and more Catholic schools, colleges, and hospitals got caught in the crossfire between Cameroon security forces and Ambazonian non-state combatants.

Figure 21.4 President Biya receiving communion from Pope Benedict XVI during the Papal visit to Cameroon in 2009

On January 30 and 31, 2021, Cardinal Pietro Parolin, the Vatican Secretary of State, described as an "ambassador of reconciliation," paid an official visit to Cameroon. He met President Biya in Yaoundé and was driven to the restive city of Bamenda under heavy military escort. He was accompanied by Ferdinand Ngoh Ngoh, Secretary General of the Presidency of Cameroon. Sensing that the Biya regime would use the visit for propaganda purposes, namely, to demonstrate that the Anglophone problem was over and that peace had returned to the Northwest and Southwest regions, Ambazonian separatist groups in the diaspora declared a "lockdown." They ordered everyone to stay indoors and boycott the mass that the Vatican Secretary of State was scheduled to preside over. The separatists believed that the Roman Catholic Church had not done enough to put pressure on President Biya to stop human rights in the Northwest and Southwest regions. The Church went ahead with the celebration at the Cathedral of Saint Joseph in Mankon. The cathedral was filled to capacity despite the intimidation of the separatists. Vatican News (2021), the official newsletter of the Vatican, reported that Archbishop Andrew Nkea Fuanya of the Metropolitan Archdiocese of Bamenda told Cardinal Pietro Parolin that:

> "Children have been used as bait for political reasons and for fighting. Many priests, religious, bishops and lay people of this province have been beaten, harassed or even killed in the conflict. And yet the Church continues to bring the message of the Gospel as a beacon of hope to a traumatized people."

Vatican News further reported that the Christians had come to attend the mass of the Cardinal, who had come to "sow seeds of peace" from far and near despite intimidation:

> The Secretary of State looked into the eyes of a suffering people, he set foot on soil bathed in the blood of hatred, and he offered words of reconciliation and peace, inviting everyone, without exception, to put aside all that stands in the way of the process of dialogue.

Despite pronouncements and sermons on peace and reconciliation, the 2021 visit of Cardinal Pietro Parolin, the Vatican Secretary of State, did not even begin to resolve the Anglophone crisis. The Francophone Catholic president of Cameroon ignored the peace overtures of the Anglophone Catholic Bishops, as well as those of the Vatican. The republican chieftain in Yaoundé was the Alpha and Omega of Cameroon and of the Anglophone crisis.

Voices from the Dungeons of the Chefferie Républicaine

One of the greatest paradoxes of human rights violations and crimes against humanity is that they always occur in plain sight or near institutions and centers designed to promote human concord and well-being. The torture chamber of the *Secretariat d'État à la Défense* (State Secretariat for Defense) in Yaoundé is a case in point. The State Secretariat for Defense is the headquarters of the *Gendarmerie Nationale*, an omnibus, notoriously brutal paramilitary security force that does everything from traffic control and internal security to military combat. The State Secretariat is located a stone's throw from the diplomatic representation of the European Union in Yaoundé, among other government buildings. The most poorly kept secret in Cameroon is that the Secretariat, commonly known by its French acronym, le SED, is one of the most notorious detention and torture centers in Cameroon. It is a location where security forces employ many different torture techniques on detainees (Freudenthal, 2019). When the Biya regime decided to use military force to crush unarmed civilian demonstrators in the English-and Pidgin-speaking former State of Southern Cameroons and subjugate it once and for all, it employed the most brutal repressive tactics. The "lucky" Anglophone demonstrators who survived the military attacks were arrested, beaten, tortured, bundled into over-crowded military trucks and deported from the English-speaking regions, where there was still a semblance of the rule of law, a common law presumption of innocence, and habeas corpus, to Francophone Cameroon where these rights are non-existent in the military tribunals that tried Anglophone political detainees. These deported demonstrators were locked up in overcrowded prisons and military detention centers. Those who were considered the ring leaders and organizers of the Anglophone protests were destined for trial before the French-language only Yaoundé Military Tribunal under draconian terrorism laws, which allow civilians to be tried in military tribunals. These tribunals have the power to impose sentences up to and including the death penalty. Anglophone Cameroonian jurists and international observers have raised serious questions about the applicability of military justice to civilians because these trials violate the African Charter on Human and Peoples' Rights (Brilman, 2017).

One of the major characteristics of the Anglophone crisis in Cameroon is, therefore, the surfeit of political prisoners. In the face of peaceful political dissent and street demonstrations, the regime resorted to hardline repression: mass arrests and mass warehousing of dissidents and political dissenters. Anyone who departed from the "Cameroon is one and indivisible" political mantra that the regime borrowed from the French Constitution, anyone suspected of harboring dangerous federalist ideas, anyone whose cellphone so much as contained content than any law enforcement officer found objectionable, seditious, subversive, and disrespectful of the Chief of State was subject to immediate arrest and incarceration. As soon as the Anglophone Revolt began, the Cameroon government put into practice a policy of arresting political activists, demonstrators, dissidents, members of civil society, lawyers, teachers, students, bike and regular taxi drivers, and so on, in the English and Pidgin-speaking Southern Cameroons, and deporting them to detention centers and prisons in French-speaking Cameroun. They ended up in different parts of the architecture of repression, torture, dehumanization, and death. The gulag of the *Chefferie républicaine* included: the academic-sounding but dreaded *Direction générale de la recherche extérieure*, the Directorate General for External Research, popularly known by its French acronym (DGRE), the infamous SED, the underground detention and torture facility at the Gendarmerie headquarters, the Secretariat of State for Defense, the interrogation and torture center at the headquarters of the *Division de la Securité Militaire* (Division of Military Security (SEMIL), or the Kondengui Prison in Yaoundé and Mfou, while others ended up in over-crowded, disease-infested prisons in Douala, Bafoussam and other places. Most were detained and tortured for years without trial.

Dead Men Talking: Roll Call from the SED Underground

One of the most shocking pieces of evidence of the inhuman treatment and detention of unarmed civilian demonstrators from the English-speaking Southern Cameroons came out of a cellphone video smuggled in and out of the dark dungeon of SED. Since detainees and prisoners are not allowed to have cell phones in the SED dungeon, prisons, or any other facilities where political prisoners are held in Cameroon, smuggling a cell phone into the dungeons in which political prisoners in Cameroon are kept was quite a feat. The cellphone video is not remarkable because of the extreme cruelty or the gruesomeness of its content. It is gripping because it shows a mock roll call of dehumanized human beings in the otherworldly, tenebrous existence of political prisoners in Cameroon: human beings deprived of their dignity and personhood, human beings plunged in the depths of depravity and misery simply because they called for political change in Cameroon (Freudenthal, 2019). In the four-minute video shot in 2018, Asah Patrick Ndango, who seems to have been the leader of the detainees in the dark cell, made a speech and carried out a parody of a roll call:

"My name is Asah Patrick Ndango," a man says in the wan light of the cell phone. The background is pitch-black.

> "I am speaking on behalf of 12 of us who were kidnapped by armed gangs and thugs of the Paul Biya regime and the government of *la Republique du Cameroun*. Since our abduction some six months ago, we have been held hostage at various hidden cells, under conditions only comparable to concentration death camps for the singular purpose to kill us. At the moment we are held in a bunker at the SED Gendarmerie headquarters in Yaoundé. If dying is the price that we must pay to guarantee our freedom, and to reestablish the independence of our country, then it is a price worth paying. Whatever you do and whatever you think, please do not be afraid. Fear will kill you faster than any bullet. Think and act according to the righteousness of your motives. The decay, the corruption, the uselessness of the Paul Biya regime and what has become of *La Republique du Cameroun* must never become us. We are a million times better than those. It is our individual and collective responsibility to forge this new nation that we all dream of. Southern Cameroons is my country, damn it! As of Monday the second [the month and year are not mentioned], to safeguard what we have been fighting for, we are beginning an indefinite hunger strike that we shall not stop even if it has to claim us, we are prepared for the ultimate sacrifice. Thank you."

Ndango then read the name of each Anglophone Southern Cameroonian prisoner in the pitch-dark dungeon and the person walked briefly into the wan light of the cellphone before disappearing into the tenebrous background: Joe Tamo, Ayuk Oteh Ayuk, Fonyuy Terrence, Tangem Thomas, Fabiano Deco, Angwan Benson, Tabe Edward, Kisob Bertin, Kechawa Silver, Kwalar Malvin… The prisoners then proceeded to "show" and describe the inhuman conditions in which they were being detained in the SED dungeon. Fortunately for the viewers, what they were describing was visible in the dim light of the cellphone. However, the following words stood out: "Look at the conditions, an asbestos pen that will surely give us cancer in six months…No windows, no light, no water. Just a hole for us to ease themselves." The political prisoners described their situation in the dark, over-crowded jail cell as being like that of animals. The video ended as it had started in the extremely dim light of the SED dungeon. The smuggled dungeon video went viral, but the political detainees were never heard from again.

Figure 21.5. Screenshot of silhouette of Asah Patrick Ndangoh at the "dungeon" of the SED, the Gendarmerie Headquarters in Yaoundé, where Anglophone political prisoners are held (2017, exact date unknown)

Fast forward to 2020. A detainee featured in the grotesque roll call at the SED dungeon, Rev. Tangem Thomas, a former Catholic monk and sheet metal worker from Nkambe, Donga Mantung, was not so fortunate. When the Rev. Brother Tangem fell ill in the dungeon, the Cameroon authorities ignored him and denied him medical care. His unknown and undiagnosed illness became so serious that he could hardly stand in the dark cell. He was finally taken to the Yaoundé Central Hospital and chained to his hospital bed. He died a few days later, his right hand still chained to his bed (see photo below). Anglophone political prisoners at the Kondengui Central Prison in Yaoundé held a demonstration when news of Tangem's death reached them (Fofung, 2020). That did not change their lot. The Center for Human Rights and Development (CHRDA) decried the inhuman conditions under which Tangem and other Anglophone political prisoners were held and criticized the failure of the Cameroon prison authorities to provide him proper medical care in the three years he was detained in the dungeon (Ndi, 2020; Fofung, 2020).

Many Cameroonians were disgusted by the medical authorities of the Yaoundé Central Hospital who would allow a very sick patient to be chained to his hospital bed and die in his chains. Of the 11 political prisoners featured in the grotesque SED video, one was released and escaped to Europe, while the other eight were dispersed to prisons holding Anglophone prisoners in the Yaoundé area.

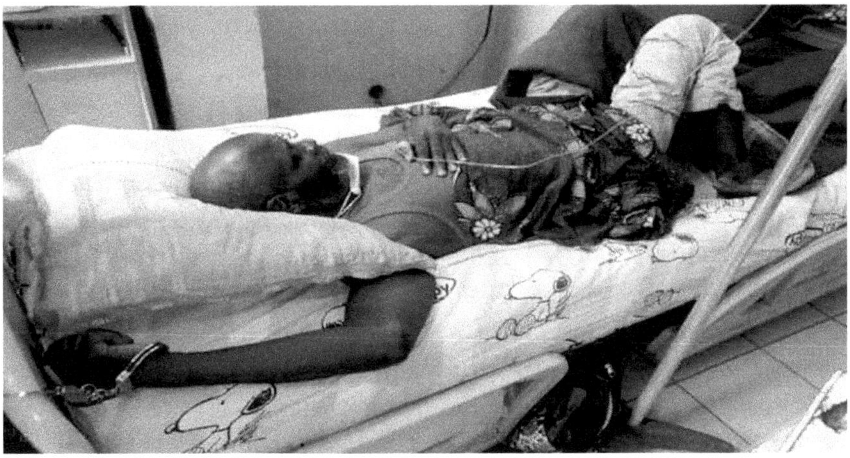

Figure 21.6. Tangem Thomas chained to his hospital bed at the Yaoundé Central Hospital, where he died in 2020 after three years of detention without trial

This video from the underground gave us a glimpse of the dungeon and torture chamber at the SED in Yaoundé. This was the first place of incarceration of Anglophone political detainees in French Cameroon. That was the "holding pen" for Anglophone federalists, separatists, deportees from Nigeria, as well as BIR and other military deserters awaiting trial before the Yaoundé Military Tribunal. Anglophone detainees who have been held at the SED include Justice Ayah Paul Abine, former Justice of the Supreme Court of Cameroon, Barrister Agbor Balla Nkongho, Professor Fontem Aforteka'a Neba, and journalists, Mancho Bibixy, Kingsley Njoka, Pen Terrence, Tsi Conrad, and Samuel Wazizi who was tortured to death by the Cameroon military, and his body was never released to his family, and hundreds of others. The most famous Anglophone detainees at the SED were the NERA 10, leaders of the separatist Ambazonia Interim Government led by Sisiku Julius Ayuk Tabe. They had been arrested on the premises of the NERA hotel in Abuja, Nigeria, in 2018 by Nigerian authorities, and became the subject of extraordinary rendition to Cameroon despite the fact that some of them were permanent residents, while others had official refugee status in Nigeria. The NERA 10 were ultimately tried at the Yaoundé military Tribunal and handed life sentences.

The leaders of the Anglophone lawyers, teachers, members of the civil society, and ordinary citizens who survived torture and lengthy detention in the gulags of the regime, were tried at the French language-only *Tribunal Militaire de Yaoundé* under harsh secession and terrorism laws. The practice of transferring political prisoners detained in English and Pidgin-speaking Southern Cameroons, which had inherited the Anglo-Saxon common law, with its presumption of innocence and its emphasis on due process, to the Francophone Napoleonic civil law jurisdiction with its presumption of the guilt of the accused, essentially eviscerated the power of the courts and the utility of common law lawyers in Anglophone Southern Cameroons. This was one of the reasons why Anglophone common law lawyers were at the forefront of the Anglophone Revolt in 2016. Furthermore, trying English and Pidgin-speaking civilian suspects in French-only military tribunals was a violation of due process of law and of the African Charter on Human and People's Rights (See chapter 27).

The Scorched Earth Policy and Cultural Institutions: The UNESCO Heritage Site of the Fon's Palace, Bafut

One of the characteristics of the brutal Anglophone war is that as early as 2018, the Cameroon army, led by the Israeli-trained and armed *Bataillon d'Intervention Rapide* (BIR), engaged in a scorched-earth policy. Any house, any village suspected of harboring, aiding or abetting Anglophone separatist/restoration forces was destroyed and reduced to ashes with extreme prejudice (CHRDA). Individuals similarly accused were "neutralized" or "deleted" to use the expression of Mr. Issa Tchiroma, former Minister of Communication. Traditional rulers, fons and chiefs, who the Cameroon government had transformed into "auxiliaries of the administration," were caught in the crossfire. Those who were seen to support the Cameroon military's atrocities against their people were targeted for capture, arrest, or even death by the Anglophone independentists, while those who were perceived to be sympathetic to the Anglophone separatist cause were treated harshly by the BIR and other branches of the military. The Fon of Bafut, Abumbi II–and the Bafut fondom–was one of the major fondoms in the West Cameroon House of Chiefs–found himself in a very delicate situation. The Bafut Palace Museum was listed on the UNESCO Register of World Heritage Sites because of the priceless art pieces it contained. The Cameroon military transformed the Bamenda/Bafut airport into a military base, while the Bafut separatist fighters, the "7 Kata," pledged allegiance to the Fon of Bafut. The Fon of Bafut tried to be neutral in the conflict that ebbed and flowed in his fondom. This did not endear him to the Cameroon security forces, which believed that the Bafut 7 Kata, a reference to Bafut men being excellent carriers and porters during the colonial era, sought refuge in the hallowed precincts of the palace after attacking the BIR and other security forces. The BIR invaded the Bafut Palace on at least two occasions in search of Ambazonian fighters. In response, the Fon of Bafut, Abumbi II, wrote a letter of protest to President Biya's appointed Governor of the North West region, protesting against the BIR invasions of his palace. He copied the Minister of Culture, key Western Diplomatic Missions in Yaoundé and the Bafut community around the world.

> Letter from His Majesty the Fon of Bafut Abumbi the Second
> 24th September 2019
> The Governor of the North West region,
> SECOND INVASION OF THE BAFUT ROYAL PALACE BY THE RAPID INTERVENTION BATTALION (BIR) ON THE 24TH OF SEPTEMBER 2019
>
> The Bafut Royal Palace is a UNESCO World Cultural Heritage Site. The Rapid Intervention Battalion (BIR), forcefully entered the Palace by climbing over the security enclosure walls build of stones and burnt bricks. The invasion was carried out under the cover of heavy and deafening armoured cars and machine gunfire at 1:00 p.m. on the 24 of September 2019.

1. Invasion of the upper section of the queens' residential Area

The soldiers destroyed and climbed over the burnt bricks walls connecting the houses of the upper section. They subjected Queens, young princes and princesses of the residential zone to brutal inhuman treatment. They searched the bedrooms, parlours, children's bedrooms and kitchens of all the queens of this residential quarter. Young children below the ages of five years were brutalized with the butts of guns and they sustained injuries. Property and money was taken away from the houses of all the Queens of this Upper Residential Section.

2. Invasion of the Lower Residential section of the Queens' Residential Area

The soldiers went here on the rampage, pulling notables out of the Queens' houses and torturing them, ordering others to prostrate while they carried away property and money from rooms of the queens.

3. Destruction and Desecration of three five-hundred-years old Takumbeng shrines.

The soldiers using axes destroyed five doors of the Takumbeng Secret Society buildings recently rehabilitated by the Government and the World Bank. The Takumbeng Secret Society belongs to princes and descendants of the eleven Royal Families of the Bafut Fondon. Having gained access into the Takumbeng Secret Lodges, they met the princes with jugs of native mimbo, achu, cooked chickens, eight cartoons of beer, each containing twenty-four cans of beer. They proceeded to destroy the native mimbo and achu, confiscated the beer and chickens, ordered all the princes to be prostrate while Prince Neba Ngu Christopher was shot six times. Prince Neba Ngu Christopher is under the medical care of an N.G.O called Doctors Without Borders operating at Saint Mary Hospital Bamenda. Prince Neba Ngu Christopher has very slim chances of surviving.

4. Looting of Museum Antiquities

The soldiers broke two rooms of the Bafut Palace Royal Museum and took away some antiquities. We are preparing an inventory of all the antiquities taken away.

5. General Trauma and Nervous shock in the Bafut Palace

After all these gruesome acts of the Rapid Intervention Battalion (BIR), the Royal Palace and the Bafut people are mourning and are in a state of shock and trauma.

6. Appeal

I wish to appeal to His Excellency the Governor and all relevant Government

Institutions of Cameroon to carry out an impartial and transparent investigation of the above barbaric acts in the Bafut Palace in particular and the cultural heritage of the Bafut people in general. Photos attesting to these barbaric acts are attached for your perusal.

Kind greetings

Signed

Fon of Bafut
Abumbi II

CC
Attorney General, Northwest Region
Minister of Culture
UNESCO
British High Commission, Yaounde
German Embassy, Yaounde
USA Embassy, Yaounde
National Human Rights Commission, Yaoundé
Amity Chambers c/o Suh Fuh, Ben Box 317 Bamenda
Bafut Development Manjong Branches

Conclusion

An alternative name for this chapter could be "milestones in the political tragedy of Anglophone Cameroon: Triumph of the argument of force." It chronicles the genesis, political highlights and principal actors of the Anglophone drama in Cameroon. All the spirited submissions of the Anglophones lead to an unmistakable conclusion–the Anglophone crisis in Cameroon is a political problem that could have been solved through political dialogue and compromise. Unfortunately, the argument of force took precedence over the force of argument–dialogue and compromise were not part of the vocabulary of the authoritarian republican chiefdom of Presidents Ahidjo and Biya. The Anglophone crisis and especially the bloodshed, atrocities and human rights violations that ensued from it were all avoidable. The decision of the Biya regime to use military force and extreme violence, the argument of force, to solve the political problem of the role, place, and political status of Anglophones in a post-colonial, reunified Cameroon transformed the political problem into yet another African humanitarian catastrophe.

The countdown to the Anglophone crisis began with the political submissions of the All Anglophone Conference (AAC) demanding a return to federalism and democratization in the light of the transformation of Cameroon into an over-centralized, hardline, authoritarian republican chiefdom. The plaintive calls of former West Cameroon Prime Ministers, John Ngu Foncha and Solomon Tandeng Muna, for a re-examination of the untenable situation of Anglophones in the assimilationist Francophone political steamroller or *la République du Cameroun fell on deaf ears.* Other milestones on the way to the Anglophone war include the brave, parliamentary resistance of Hon. Wirba Joseph Mbiydzenyuy, the appeals of John Fru Ndi, leader of the opposition Social Democratic Front (SDF), the eloquent but unprecedented memorandum of the Anglophone Catholic Bishops denouncing the lack of respect for the human rights, human dignity, and cultural specificity of Anglophones. The writers all condemn the massive arrest, incarceration and torture of Anglophone lawyers, teachers, students, protesters, demonstrators and ordinary citizens–many of them merely for being federalists– and the rape of female students at the University of Buea. The destruction by fire of hundreds of villages suspected of giving aid and shelter to Anglophone federalists and separatists, the flow of refugees to Nigeria and the arrest of Sisiku Ayuk Tabe and 12 members of the Interim Government of Ambazonia at the Nera Hotel in Abuja Nigeria, internationalized the conflict. The illegal extraordinary rendition of 10 of the Ambazonian leadership to Cameroon for trial demonstrated that the Buhari regime in Nigeria had no respect for the rule of law, due process of law, and international law. It was the rule of the state over the rule of law. The spirited but futile submissions of Barrister Femi Falana and his team demonstrate that despite the Buhari regime's contempt for the rule of law in Nigeria, as well as international principles governing refugees and asylum seekers, human rights lawyers worth the name refuse to keep silent in the face of the most egregious violations of human rights. The letter of the traditional ruler of Bafut, Fon Abumbi II, protested the reckless disregard that the Cameroon military, led by the Israeli-trained and armed *Bataillon d'Intervention Rapide,* showed for human rights and the cultural patrimony of Anglophone Southern Cameroons. The Anglophone War was a war against the Pidgin and English-speaking people of Southern Cameroons and their culture.

The tension between the force of argument and the argument of force in the Anglophone Question in Cameroon did not result in the triumph of might over rights as the Biya regime had hoped. The avoidable conflict left thousands of civilian and non-state combatants dead or wounded in Anglophone Cameroon. It also led to the displacement of more than a million people, of which thousands have become refugees in Nigeria, Ghana, South Africa, and other countries, and the bulk have become internally displaced persons in many parts of Cameroon. For its part, the Cameroon military and security forces ended up with thousands of troops dead or wounded. The Anglophone war has become yet another "frozen conflict," a stalemate reduced to sporadic attacks and counterattacks between Cameroon security forces and Ambazonian non-state combatants. The most visible and palpable reminder of the Anglophone Revolt that the military might of the Biya regime has not been able to crush is the Monday "ghost town strikes" in Anglophone Cameroon. This long-running act of resistance against the Biya republican chiefdom is testimony to the fact that the idea of freedom cannot be killed by force of arms. Only time - the post-Biya era will tell how this conflict will end. The world is waiting with bated breath. History shows that the abuse of power, that is to say, the argument of force, the force of arms, wears down power and debilitates force and arms. That is the lesson of the Biya regime's myopic posture towards the Anglophone Question in Cameroon.

References

Cardinal Parolin in Cameroon: 'Faith is greater than intimidation' (2021). Vatican News. February 2nd. Retrieved from: https://www.vaticannews.va/en/vatican-city/news/2021-02/cardinal-pietro-parolin-cameroon-bamenda-archbishop.html

Fofung, A (2020). Cameroon: Outrage as Anglophone detainee dies while chained to hospital bed. Pan African Visions. Retrieved from: https://panafricanvisions.com/2020/08/cameroon-outrage-as-anglophone-detainee-dies-while-chained-to-hospital-bed/

Freudenthal, E. (2019). Inside Cameroon's Bunker: Different guys had different torture techniques. African Arguments, May 7. Retrieved from: https://africanarguments.org/2019/05/inside-cameroon-torture-bunker/

Holy See Press Office Communique: Audience with the President of the Republic of Cameroon (2017). Communique N. 170323e, Thursday March 23. Retrieved from: http://press.vatican.va/content/salastampa/en/bollettino/pubblico/2017/03/23/170323e.html

Tande, D. (2006). The Cameroon Reunification Revisited (2): The Endeley Prophesy. Scribbles from the Den. Retrieved from: https://www.dibussi.com/2006/02/unification_rev_1.html

TWENTY-TWO

Kondengui Chronicles

Voices of Anglophone Political Prisoners in the Penal Den of Indignity

LYOMBE EKO

This volume has been a catalog of the transformation of the Anglophone Question in Cameroon from a philosophical, political, cultural and identitarian problem to a human rights crisis that cost more than ten thousand lives on the Anglophone side as well as on the side of the Cameroon military. The crisis also led to massive violations of human rights in the English-speaking Northwest and Southwest regions. Hundreds of Anglophone lawyers, teachers, students, clergy, and other members of the civil society who either participated in demonstrations or used media outlets to call for change, advocate for non-violent strikes (like ghost towns, sit-ins and other acts of civil disobedience, were rounded up, deported to Yaoundé and charged under the draconian Anti-Terrorism Law of 2014. In the face of this unrelenting mass arrest and deportation of suspected Anglophone federalists, separatists, secessionists and Southern Cameroons independentists, a good number of Southern Cameroonians of all political stripes fled to Nigeria and launched an "Interim Government of the Federal Republic of Ambazonia," led by Sisiku Julius Ayuk Tabe. The name "Ambazonia" was a neologism created from Ambas Bay, the bay in Southern Cameroon that stretched from Victoria (modern-day Limbe) to Bota. The Cameroon government was alarmed by this development. Its violent and uncompromising crackdown quickly spread to Nigeria, where, for historical reasons, there was a large Southern Cameroonian diaspora community. After all, the United Kingdom had administered British Southern Cameroons as part of Nigeria under post-World War I international peace settlements. The linguistic and cultural proximity and commonality between English-speaking Nigeria and English-speaking British Southern Cameroons made Nigeria a preferred place of refuge and exile for many Southern Cameroonian intellectuals and ordinary citizens fleeing the rampages of President Biya's Israeli-trained and armed *Bataillon d'Intervention Rapide* (BIR). Nevertheless, the fact that Nigeria had its own historic secessionist problem, the Biafra problem, over which it had fought the Biafra Civil War from 1967 to 1970, made Presidents Biya and Buhari natural allies against secession. Additionally, both countries were engaged in fighting the Boko Haram Islamist terrorist group in Northeastern Nigeria and Northern Cameroon. This chapter focuses on President Mohammadu Buhari's collaboration with the Biya regime to abduct and deport the leadership of the separatist Interim Government of Ambazonia and deport them to Cameroon to face trial at the Yaoundé Military Tribunal even though both countries do not have an extradition treaty and despite the fact that Nigerian courts were hearing challenges to the abduction and deportation of the Southern Cameroonians. The second part of the chapter shows one of the outcomes of the Biya regime's attempts to quash Anglophone voices calling for change as part of his grand strategy of maintaining his over-centralized republican chiefdom by subjugating the former Southern Cameroon and erasing its cultural and identitarian specificity. It also explores the outcome of the collaboration between the Biya and Buhari regimes in detaining and deporting the Nera 10 and other Southern Cameroon dissidents from Nigeria to Cameroon. It reproduces the declarations of some key Anglophone political prisoners who are serving lengthy sentences in the Kondengui Central Prison in Yaoundé for calling for political change in Cameroon, and for recognition of the linguistic, cultural and identitarian specificity of English and Pidgin-speaking Southern Cameroonians.

Interestingly, Nigeria, which did not have the best relations with Cameroon due to their territorial differences over the oil-rich Bakassi peninsula, developed a friendship of convenience that served the interests of both regimes. Despite the cultural and linguistic proximities between the peoples of Southern Cameroon and Nigeria–the British had governed English-speaking Southern Cameroon as part of the Eastern region of Nigeria from 1919 to 1960–the Nigerian posture towards the Anglophone problem in the Northwest and Southwest regions was driven by pragmatic self-interest. Nigeria was keen to maintain its partnership of convenience with the Biya regime to maintain their military cooperation in the fight against the Islamist terrorist group, Boko Haram, an offshoot of the Islamic State of Iraq and Syria (ISIS). Boko haram had launched a religious reign of terror in large swathes of impoverished northeastern Nigeria that corresponds roughly to the former British Northern Cameroons, which was, along with British Southern Cameroons, hewn out of German Kamerun in 1919 as part of the spoils of World War I.

The relationship between Nigeria and Cameroon was also a lucrative opportunity for the Nigerian "securicrats," the top bureaucrats of the national security apparatuses of both countries. Cameroon Anglophone political refugees and asylum seekers were rounded up from their hotels by Nigerian security forces. Chalsma Hotel, Otop Abasi Street, Calabar, Cross River State, and Nera Hotel, Abuja were two of the most well-known Nigerian hotels where Cameroonian refugees and asylum seekers were abducted and hastily deported to Cameroon. These extra-judicial, extra-ordinary renditions and deportations took place while Nigerian human rights lawyers were challenging these detentions and deportations as illegal under international and Nigerian law. By the time the country's slow, ponderous, and labyrinthine legal system could begin examining these matters, the courts were faced with a fait accompli. The detainees had already been deported to Cameroon. Southern Cameroons political refugees and asylum seekers who were abducted in Nera Hotel Abuja and Chalsma Hotel, Calabar, reported that suitcases full of cash exchanged hands between security officials of both countries as they were being transferred into waiting Cameroon military aircraft that had been sent to Abuja to pick them up for the rapid extra-judicial rendition to the Yaoundé Military Tribunal, without due process of law, and in the absence of an extradition treaty between the two countries.

The Cameroon deportees who had been arrested in Calabar and other locations in Nigeria included a handful of Anglophone members of the notorious Israeli-trained and equipped *Bataillon d'Intervention Rapide* (BIR), as well as other branches of the armed forces, who had deserted Cameroon and fled to Nigeria. A couple of BIR deserters who were interviewed for this book said they objected to being sent to fight their own people in their own villages. Others deserted after their colleagues had lost their lives fighting Southern Cameroons/Ambazonia separatist attacks against the BIR in places like Ekona, Kumba, Ndian, Manyu, Bali Nyonga, Bamenda, Ndop, Bafut, Nso, Oku, Babanki, Fundong, Wum and other locations in the Northwest and Southwest regions. Ironically, the BIR and other military deserters have not been tried openly at the Yaoundé Military Tribunal. They have been in pre-trial detention since their extraordinary rendition. In the next chapter, we reproduce verbatim, the narrative of a BIR deserter who was recruited by a security consultant in Nigeria to work for a security firm in an Arab country in the Middle East. Some Cameroon BIR, army, and Gendarmerie deserters were granted political asylum in several European countries.

The partnership between the Buhari regime of Nigeria and the Biya republican chiefdom of Cameroon meant that Southern Cameroonian activists, federalists, autonomists, separatists, and independentists–they were considered one and the same by both governments–were caught between the hammer of *la République du Cameroun* and the anvil of Nigeria. This considerably slowed down but did not defeat Southern Cameroons (Ambazonia) separatist ambitions. It pushed Ambazonian and Biafran separatists in Nigeria into each other's arms, under the logic of "my enemy's enemy is my friend" (See chapter 15, The Nigerian Connection). One outcome of this collaboration has been the importation of the technology of improvised explosive devices (IEDs) into the Anglophone conflict in Cameroon. These devices have continued to have a devasting impact on the BIR and Cameroon military. As late as December 2023, the Cameroon military was reporting casualties from IEDs (Ambazonia, Army Hunts Amba Fighters After Death of Five Troops, 2023).

The NERA Hotel (Abuja) Abductions: Voices of the Principals

On January 6, 2018, agents of the Nigerian State Security Services abducted 12 Southern Cameroonians, the symbolic leaders of the symbolic Southern Cameroons/Ambazonia Interim Government, who were meeting at the Nera Hotel in Abuja (see chapter 18, the Nigerian Connection). All of the abductees were either asylees, registered refugees, or lawful permanent residents of Nigeria. Some of them held dual nationalities. In blatant disregard of Nigerian and international law, Nigeria handed over these and 47 other Southern Cameroonians seeking refuge in Nigeria to the Biya regime without benefit of a court hearing. Lawyers for the abducted sued, claiming that the detention of the NERA 12 and others was a violation of the Nigerian Constitution. On Friday, March 1, 2019, the Federal High Court of Abuja, Nigeria, ruled that the abduction of the Ambazonians at Nera Hotel was an illegal violation of Nigerian Law, the African Charter on Human and Peoples' Rights, and the United Nations Convention of 1951 on the Status of Refugees. It ordered that the NERA 10, the Anglophone Pro-Independence leaders, and 47 others arrested in Gembu and deported to Cameroon be sent back to Nigeria. The Nigerian government ignored the court order. The Ambazonian separatist leaders were tried at the Yaoundé Military Tribunal and sentenced to life imprisonment. This section presents some voices from the NERA 10 saga.

Figure 22.1. Nera Hotel, Abuja, Nigeria, where Ambazonian leaders were abducted

Statement of Mrs. Lilian Ayuk Tabe, Wife of Jailed Ambazonian Leader, Sisiku Julius Ayuk Tabe

February 2018

I need to start by thanking God for all good things come from Him, even difficult moments too.

With every passing day we are becoming more and more worried about the whereabouts of Sisiku Julius Ayuk Tabe. The last three weeks have been a nightmare, for all his family and friends and the people of former British territory Southern Cameroons (hereafter referred to Federal Republic of Ambazonia), not knowing where he is.

I issue this statement because we have reason to be worried for my husband's life and safety and we know that the media, public, governments and organizations will pay attention.

Sisiku Julius Ayuk Tabe is a loving, caring, humble, and honest husband and father of my children. A trained and experienced computer engineer, he is calm and always desire to serve others and seek solutions toward improving human prosperity. These are the qualities that earned the confidence of Ambazonians who trusted him to lead legal and diplomatic efforts toward the independence restoration and international recognition of the Federal Republic of Ambazonia as a democratic and sovereign state.

My husband Julius is not a terrorist. He is not a criminal. Julius is an activist fighting for freedom, equality and justice in the land of our birth Ambazonia.

Julius and I last discussed on 5th January 2018, when he flew to Abuja ahead of a scheduled meeting with close members of the Interim Government of the Federal Republic of Ambazonia. The meeting, he told me, was to focus on the rising humanitarian need of Ambazonia refugees in Nigeria and indiscriminate killing, arrest, and destruction of property and businesses of unarmed citizens in our homeland by armed soldiers and paramilitary forces of *La Republique du Cameroun* and appointed government officials of President Paul Biya regime in Yaoundé.

In the evening of 5th January 2018, Julius had not returned home and was unreachable via phone. On the of 6th January 2018, after several inquiries and consultations, we received information that my husband Julius and eleven other leadership members of Ambazonia Interim Government were abducted by Nigerian Security Service during their meeting at Nera Hotel in Abuja. For three weeks, no single person, including Nigerian human rights lawyers Femi Falana and Abdul Oroh and family members of the abducted leaders including myself have neither seen nor heard from one of the abductees.

On 28th January 2018, the two lawyers defending my husband and 11 others issued a statement indicating that the Government of Nigeria extradited the 12 leaders to Cameroon. On 29 January 2018, Cameroon government spokesperson Issa Tchiroma Bakary announced to Cameroun's public and international community that 47 abductees in Nigeria including my husband Sisiku Julius Ayuk Tabe are in Cameroun's territory and under custody. Until the announcement, my children and I still had no information of Julius' whereabouts. Today is 31 January 2018, we have no proof that Julius and the 11 others are alive. And if they are alive, what are the charges against them and why have they not been allowed to talk to their families and to access legal due process under international law?

I did not choose to be born in Southern Cameroons. Sisiku Julius Ayuk Tabe and other 11 leaders did not choose to be born in Southern Cameroons either. Our children and grandchildren did not choose to be descendants of Southern Cameroons. More than 8 million of us within Ambazonia territory and worldwide did not choose to originate from Southern Cameroons. It is our land of birth, and our ways of life are shaped by our common culture and values. We will all die Southern Cameroonians.

Hear my cry and that of my children. Hear the cry of thousands of spouses, children and family members of those who have been killed, injured, kidnapped, detained and are missing. We appeal to the international community and governments to urge Mr. Paul Biya to produce video footages of Julius Ayuk Tabe and 11 others, grant access to lawyers and family members to meet them, and free them because they are not criminals. Our appeal equally applies to all other activists illegally detained in prisons and unknown locations across Cameroun territory.

I call on fellow women, Amnesty International, the United Nations, Commonwealth, and African Union to act swiftly and decisively by offering to mediate on finding a political solution to the independence restoration struggle of Southern Cameroons.

Hear our voices. We are not terrorists. We are Ambazonians. We are fighting for freedom, sovereignty, and human dignity for millions of Southern Cameroonians. Our birth rights have been suppressed, our liberties erased, our political, cultural and economic freedoms denied for more than half a century by the Governments of La Republique du Cameroun.

Mrs. Lilian Ayuk Tabe

Barrister Femi Falana's Open Letter to President Buhari on the Matter of the Nera 10

Nigerian human rights lawyer, Femi Falana, who was representing the NERA 12, sent an open letter to President Mohammadu Buhari of Nigeria, asking him to "bring back to Nigeria the naturalized Nigerians, refugees, and asylum seekers who were illegally arrested, detained and deported from Nigeria to Cameroon on Friday, January 26, 2018 by National Security Adviser, Major-General Babagana Mungano (retired)"

> Twelve of our clients who are the leaders of the people of Southern Cameroons and who have been living in Nigeria for several years were assembled for a meeting at Nera Hotel, Abuja on Saturday, January 6, 2018 to discuss the challenges faced by the over 10,000 Cameroonians who have sought political asylum in Nigeria due to persecution and repression under the Paul Biya regime in Cameroon.
>
> But before the commencement of the meeting a team of armed security personnel invaded the venue, abducted our clients and took them away to an undisclosed place. The said abduction was reported by the Premium Times [newspaper] edition of Sunday, January 7, 2018.
>
> In spite of the detailed report of the credible online news medium, the Police and the security agencies denied knowledge of the abduction of our clients. Consequently, all efforts made by the lawyers, doctors and family members of our clients to visit them in custody were frustrated without any legal justification. Even Mrs. Nalowa Bih who is pregnant was denied medical attention by the National Security Adviser.
>
> However, a representative of the Office of the United Nations High Commissioner for Refugees in Nigeria was allowed to visit our clients at the request of the Ministry of Foreign Affairs. During the visit, the United Nations representative found that our clients were held in an underground cell at the headquarters of the Defence Intelligence Agency on the orders of the National Security Adviser.
>
> On account of the refusal of the National Security Adviser to allow

access to our clients by their lawyers, relatives and doctors we filed an application at the Abuja Judicial Division of the Federal High Court on Thursday, January 25, 2018 for the purpose of securing their fundamental rights to personal liberty and freedom of movement.

Notwithstanding the pending suit and the intervention of the Office of the United Nations High Commissioner for Refugees, the National Security Adviser expelled our clients from Nigeria and deported them to Cameroon on Friday, January 26, 2018.

Although the National Security Adviser was ashamed to disclose the deportation of our clients from Nigeria the Government of Cameroon has celebrated the deportation and threatened to prosecute our clients for unspecified crimes. Thus, with the connivance of the National Security Adviser the Government of Cameroon has since held our clients in an undisclosed military custody in Cameroon.

Out of the 52 people who were expelled from Nigeria the Government of Cameroon has maintained that the National Security Adviser handed over to it 47 deportees. Up till now, the National Security Adviser has not accounted for the whereabouts of the remaining 5 detainees!

The National Security Adviser knew that two of our clients are naturalized Nigerians, six are refugees while 37 others are political asylum seekers who are entitled to be protected by the Federal Government of Nigeria. For the avoidance of doubt, the Office of the United Nations High Commissioner for Refugees in Nigeria drew the attention of the National Security Adviser to the legal obligations of Nigeria to respect the rights of our clients.

Under the National Security Agencies Act (Cap N74) Laws of the Federation of Nigeria, 2004 and the Immigration Act 2015 the National Security Adviser is not competent to arrest, detain and deport any alien or immigrant from Nigeria to any other country.

Since the Government of Nigeria has never violated the provisions of the United Nations Convention Relating to Refugees and the OAU Convention on Refugees by deporting refugees and asylum seekers to any country where they might be persecuted we are compelled to urge Your Excellency to grant the following requests: Order the National Security Adviser to produce the missing 5 deportees and bring back to Nigeria our clients who have been illegally deported to Cameroon without any further delay.

If the National Security Adviser is unable to bring back our clients to Nigeria he should be removed from office for such brazen impunity which has exposed Nigeria to ridicule before the comity of law abiding nations. The Federal Government should prevail on the Government of Cameroon not to persecute our clients to prevent the United Nations from sanctioning Nigeria for violating the provisions of the 1951 United

Nations Convention Relating to Refugees.

You will therefore agree with us that the arrest, detention and deportation of our clients from Nigeria to Cameroon by the National Security Adviser cannot be justified on the following grounds: Based on the appeal by Nigeria for a peaceful resolution of the political crisis in Cameroon the people of Southern Cameroons filed a suit at the Federal High Court to determine whether the people of Southern Cameroons are not entitled to self-determination within their clearly defined territory separate from *La Republique du Cameroun.*

By a consent judgment delivered by the Court on March 5, 2002, the Federal Government was directed to file a suit at the International Court of Justice to have a judicial confirmation of the human right of the people of Southern Cameroons to self-determination...

The Federal Government also undertook to take other measures as may be necessary to place the case of the people of Southern Cameroons for self-determination before the United Nations General Assembly and other international organizations.

Even though the suit has not been filed at the International Court of Justice the Federal Government has continued to recognize the human rights of our clients and other people of Southern Cameroons to self-determination."

Femi Falana, esq. Senior Advocate of Nigeria (Senior Advocate of Nigeria).

Figure 22.2. "How Nigerian gov't violated own laws, historical role by expelling separatists, *The Premium Times*, Abuja, Nigeria (Feb. 17, 2018)

Abduction and Extra-judicial Rendition of the Nera 10: A Legal Analysis

The abduction and extra-ordinary rendition of the Nera 10 from Abuja, as well as the abduction and extra-judicial deportation of other Cameroonian refugees and asylum seekers, including women and children, from Nera Hotel Abuja, Chalsma Hotel, Calabar, and other locations in Nigeria, to torture and detention centers, and ultimately the Yaoundé Military Tribunal, without giving the abductees and deportees due process of law, shocked the Nigerian and Anglophone Cameroon legal and human rights communities. Though there was no extradition treaty between Nigeria and Cameroon, what was shocking, from a rule of law perspective, was that the matters were sub-judice. Nigerian courts had been seized about the matter of the arrests and detention of the Cameroon political refugees by the Nigerian security operatives, but the Nigerian government demonstrated a wanton disregard for Nigerian and international law. The Anglophone Cameroon Common Law lawyers also found Nigeria's lack of interest in the niceties of international law, as well as its snubbing of the United Nations High Commission for Refugees (UNHCR) quite troubling. A Cameroon Anglophone Common Law luminary, Chief Charles Taku, a traditional Chief from Lebialem, Southwest region, and an international lawyer who specializes in International Criminal, Humanitarian, and Human Rights Law and Practice, penned a response to the abductions and deportations. Chief Taku, who represented clients as Lead Counsel at the International Criminal Tribunal for Rwanda (UNICTR), Special Court for Sierra Leone, the International Criminal Court (ICC), the United Nations Human Rights Committee in Geneva, and the African Court on Human and People's Rights in Arusha Tanzania, wrote the piece below entitled: "Unmasking Another International Conspiracy: Hail the Rule of Law." Barrister Taku's piece is instructive:

> "The judgment of the Nigeria Federal High Court in Abuja on March 1, 2019, declaring illegal and unconstitutional, the abduction and deportation to Cameroun of the President of the Interim Government of the Southern Cameroons/Ambazonia Sisiku Ayuk Tabe, members of the Interim Government and several Southern Cameroons refugees carries significant symbolic weight. The judgment has comprehensively determined the legal status of the abductees which was in controversy since Cameroun characterized them as terrorists on the account of alleged crimes committed against Cameroun from the territory of Nigeria; so, the Isa Tchiroma and the Court-martial alleged. The Federal High Court of Abuja Nigeria on the territory of which the crimes alleged in the court-martial were allegedly committed has decided that they are persons who were legally in the territory of Nigeria as refugees under the protection of international conventional law at the time of their abduction and deportation. They were not therefore terrorists nor did their presence and activities constitute terrorism to warrant their being characterized as terrorists to warrant abduction and deportation to face a court-martial. Even if they were terrorists, international law still outlawed the abduction and deportation without compliance with the municipal and international rule of law.
>
> This judicial determination settles a key issue in the subsequent case brought against the victims by Cameroun, the state to which they were

deported. The failure of the court-martial in Cameroun where the abductees are forcefully subjected over their objections, to take judicial notice of the Judgment of the Abuja Federal High Court will have bilateral relations and multilateral treaty obligations consequences on the two countries, in the short and long term. Nigeria and Cameroun are state parties to the 1951 United Nations Convention on Refugees and its Additional Protocol 1967. Both countries are state parties to the OAU 1969 Convention Governing the Specific Aspects of the Refugee Problem in Africa which came into force in 1974.

The refugee problem globally and in Africa is a matter of significant international emergency, if not a humanitarian crisis. Without the existing multilateral treaty regime to manage this humanitarian crisis, millions, of the world's vulnerable refugee population will be pursued across international boundaries and slaughtered by the murderous regimes and criminal squads from whom they fled in the search for protection. International law mandates state parties to the Refugee Convention to open their frontiers to allow refugees fleeing from wars, genocide, crimes against humanity and other life-threatening conditions to their lives to provide them protection. International law outlaws the abduction, deportation, rendition or the refoulement of persons who have sought refugee status to the countries from which they fled. Once the status of refugees is sought or obtained, the person concerned becomes a ward of international law under the Refugee Convention and its Additional Protocol. State Parties to the Refugee Convention are mandated to ensure compliance and indeed are obligated to submit periodic reports on compliance with their treaty obligations under the convention. Nigeria and Cameroun had a multilateral obligation to ensure that the refugee status of the abductees in Nigeria was respected and protected. Their mandate and responsibility are to the international community, since the 1951. The Refugee Convention has near world-wide membership. By engaging in criminal conduct to abduct and deport the victims to face a court-martial that applies the death penalty to Cameroun, Nigeria and Cameroun betrayed, violated and endangered the multilateral treaty regime and a protected international human rights value system.

The Federal High Court judgment provided an opportunity to Nigeria to explain to the world, the rationale and legality of the abductions. It is significant that Nigeria did not convince the court that the abduction and deportation was informed by any compellable reasons justifiable in municipal and /or international law. Nigeria did not convince the court of any legally justified reason to violate with impunity the Nigeria Federal Constitution (1969), its multilateral treaty obligations under the UN Refugee Convention and its Additional Protocol, the African Convention, the International Covenant on Civil and Political Rights and the Rome Statute. There is no compelling reason to explain why Nigeria mortgaged its reputation, its influence in Africa and its claims to lead and represent Africa as a world power at the UN Security Council to fulfil the dictatorial and criminal proclivities of a regime baying for the blood of millions of Southern Cameroonians. Hundreds of thousands of Southern Cameroonians have been deported by Cameroun from their ancestral home which are systematically torched as a deliberate government policy as senior military commanders and civilian government officials have admitted, across the border with Nigeria. The victims who at a great risk of a genocide sought international protections within the territory of Nigeria are living under continuing threat of abduction and assassination, after Nigeria provided support to Cameroun to pursue the commission of international crimes against them in the territory of Nigeria.

The answer as to what endeared President Mohammadu Buhari to place Nigeria at the centre of an unfolding genocide, rather than acting as a facilitator of negotiations and peace may not be answered in this one critical historic judgment. Yet the judgment has the merit of laying an enduring foundation for answers to be provided within the compelling injunction of history. The truth, it is said, will never die with those who thought they could imprison it with sheer political chicanery and stealth transborder corrupt operations. Truth is as stubborn as a rock. Nigeria and Cameroun are aware, and this is important, that the underlying cause of the war declared by Paul Biya as a proxy of France, are the resources within the territory of the Southern Cameroons. These minerals are the umbilical cord to the perennial Nigeria misadventure that has devasted the Niger Delta, its ecosystem, maritime resources, economy and human health. Time will reveal if there are a convergence of economic and hegemonic interests by the known yet, invisible political god fathers enforcing the genocide using Nigeria and Cameroun proxies.

I learnt from my years as a lead counsel at the Special Court for Sierra Lone, in the case of the Revolutionary United from for Sierra Leone (RUF)-Morris Kallon that minerals are the curse of Africa. That is why Central Africa Republic has never been at peace since independence despite its mineral rich capabilities. The Democratic Republic of the Congo is one case in point; so also, Burundi where abundant mineral resources have attracted the interest and wrath of neo-colonial economic and natural resource predators.

***

This judgment of the Abuja Federal High Court conveys an underlying message to the abductors that the abduction of Southern Cameroons leaders and citizens will have consequences that may potentially threaten peace and security in the Gulf of Guinea. That Nigeria has become a key ally of the state actor that declared the war of choice that have the capacity of igniting a conflagration in the Gulf of Guinea affecting its own citizens and interests on both sides of the borders, is a matter of profound concern.

The judgment is a municipal judgment on compliance by Nigeria with its multilateral treaty and constitutional obligations. Finding that Nigeria violated its municipal laws and treaty obligations, is an important contribution to international law. This judgment therefore must be served on the United Nations Secretariat, the United Nations High Commissioner for Refugees in Geneva, all the permanent and non-permanent members of the Security Council through their permanent representations in New York, all ECOWAS state parties through their diplomatic representations in Abuja, the EU state parties present in Brussels, the AU Commission, and give wide publicity.

This judgment negates the charge by Cameroun that the abductees were and are terrorists. Nigeria did not make this charge before and during the hearing. Nigeria should be concerned that persons found to be refugees by its own judiciary are facing a court-martial based on international and municipal violations of its own government. With this judgment, the blood of the abductees and other Southern Cameroonians will lay on the hands of Nigeria should they be further held in violation of this judgment or should they be executed pursuant to the court-martial.

International law mandates that any offence committed on the territory of Nigeria can be investigated and prosecuted by Nigeria failing which Nigeria can send the refugees to a third country willing to accept them but not to the country from which they fled and sought refuge in Nigeria. Will Nigeria submit itself to a court-martial in Cameroun to provide evidence of acts alleged in the charges before the court-martial that were allegedly committed in Nigeria? Does Nigeria recognize a court-martial for civilians which is international human rights jurisprudence has characterised as torture and thus illegal? Does Nigeria by the abductions give legal approval to the crime of abduction which criminalised under the Rome Statute which Nigeria is a state party? Is abduction of civilians not one of the crimes alleged against Boko Haram in which hundreds of thousands of Nigerian civilians have lost their lives? The Abuja High Court trial was an occasion for Nigeria to prove that abduction is legal when conducted by a state actor but illegal when carried out by non-state actors. Nigeria failed to prove this or even convince the court that this crime may be legal under such or other circumstances.

Nigeria under President Mohammadu Buhari tends to disobey court orders and indeed disobeyed the order of the Federal High Court in Abuja made by Justice Gabriel Kolawole dated December 2, 2016 ordering the release of Ibrahim el Zazaky the leader the Shiite Muslim Movement who was abducted by the DSS on December 13, 2015. The DSS alleged that he was detained at his own request for protection. The Judge was unpersuaded on the grounds that protective custody was unknown to law or National

Security Agencies Act establishing the DSS. Since December 29, 2015, Colonel Abubakar Malami former National Security Adviser of President Goodluck Jonathan has remained in jail despite court orders for his release.

However, in a suit brought by a constitutional lawyer Johnmary Jideobi praying the court to void the SAN [Senior Advocate of Nigeria] of the Attorney General of the Federation, Abubakar Malami for professional misconduct for advising the Federal Government to disrespect court orders, the Attorney General refused being held accountable for advising the Federal Government to disrespect court orders and that he was not informed about the detentions and so his advice was never sought in the cases....This defence by the attorney therefore begged the questions. If he was never informed how then did he enter appearance to defend the illegal actions of the Nigeria Government?

Africa, and African leaders should hail the Judgment of the Federal High Court of Nigeria in Abuja and pressurise Nigeria and Cameroun to execute it without delay. This judgment protects the municipal and international protections of refugees afforded by multilateral treaties and municipal constitutional provisions. The international multilateral treaty regime has been tested and proved to be critical in checking the excesses and exactions of the world refugee crisis and the humanitarian calamity that is rocking the conscience of humanity. In their imposed inhuman dungeons Sisiku Ayuk Tabe and the Ambazonia abductees represent the face of humanity at risk. This judgment protects that human value represented by Sisiku Ayuk Tabe. African leaders and the international community should applaud this judgment and pressurise Nigeria and Cameroun to obey and execute it.

This judgment should be a shock reminder to everyone, the powerful and the weak, that a refugee is a protected ward of humanity and the legal regimes emplaced to protect him or her attest to this fact. Abducting and deporting refugees to be court-martialed or placing them in harm's way tantamount to driving a sword on the collective conscience of humanity. This should not be allowed to happen without consequences.

I have a message for those responsible for the abduction and court-martial of civilian victims. Respecting this judgment may be the only opportunity for them to avoid placing their own poisoned chalices to their own lips. Babatoura Ahmadou Ahidjo, with the use of terror pursued nationalists who sought refuge in foreign lands but died a refugee himself in solitude in distant Senegal. The refugee status he imposed on others and pursued, abducted and killed or assassinated them was the status that protected and sustained him until he died. In 1968, Joseph Desiré Mobutu otherwise called Mobutu Sese Seko lured and murdered Pierre Mulele over strong world-wide appeals and condemnation. Mobutu died a miserable refugee in Morocco. The extensive empire he acquired through, murder, looting and plundering the mineral resources of his country is in ruins. The blood of the thousands he slaughtered to keep himself in eternal power still haunts the memory of him. His countrymen and women are even traumatised, turning his extensive empire into the memorial for his innocent victims.

This recorded history may already have extended a hand of invitation to the actors in the theatre of criminality and violations that the Federal High Court High Court in Abuja addressed in this judgment. Whether they will on their own volition abide by this judgment, is not known to me. However, this judgment is addressed to the collective conscience of Humanity represented by the multilateral treaty regime which the court found was violated. The multilateral treaty regime must demonstrate that it has teeth and that it must not condone or encourage the impunity of state violators of their treaty obligations, lest it wrongly encourages non-state actors. Nigeria itself has a refugee problem in far and distant lands, including Cameroun. It will be unfortunate if Nigerians allow their government to determine their fate through the legitimisation of the violations found in this judgment…

…The Abuja abduction of Sisiku Ayuk Tabe and others and their deportation to Cameroun requires a strong international legal intervention. It is a crime against the Rome Statute to which Nigeria is a state party. The unwritten underpinning of the Judgment indeed has this implication. It has violated the UN multilateral treaty regime and that of the AU.

Social media activism alone will not get this judgment executed, enforced. It will not rely on the judgment to pursue all international crimes and violations in which hundreds and thousands of civilians are systematically exterminated and civilian settlements, places of worships and hospitals are torched and reduced to rubble…. What cannot wait even for a minute are contributions intended for the collective good, the protection of victims, refugees, vulnerable categories and preventive and protective strategies."

The NERA 10's "Court Martial" Conviction and Post-Conviction Statement

On August 19, 2019, the French language-only Yaoundé Military Tribunal held a marathon session that ran from 1 pm to 5 am on the 20th of August. It appears the tribunal had orders from "above" to expedite the trial. At 5 am, when the defendants and lawyers on both sides were hardly awake and alert, the military judge, Jacques Baudouin Misse Njone, stood up, read out, in halting French, the 10 counts on which the tired and yawning, half asleep English-speaking Sisiku Ayuk Tabe and the rest of the NERA 10 deportees were charged. The Military Tribunal did not bother to translate the proceedings into English. Afterall, in Cameron, French speakers arrogantly declare that, *l'armée n'est pas bilingue* (the army is not bilingual). The judge of the Yaoundé Military Tribunal proceeded to convict all the defendants on all 10 counts, sentenced each of them to life imprisonment, and fined them the colossal sum of 250 billion CFA, despite the futile protestations, in English, of their lawyer, Barrister Eta Bissong to the effect that the trial was a gross miscarriage of justice. The trial was a parody of justice that was the logical result of a dialogue of the deaf. The parties *were* literally speaking different languages, and relying on different legal cultures, values, standards, and ethics. The Yaoundé military judges, the military prosecutor, and tribunal officials spoke French and applied a tropicalized version of the Napoleonic code, while the defense lawyer, an Anglophone, spoke English and made allusions to the Anglo-American common law, legal principles and rights. It was not clear that the drowsy defendants even understood all the charges against them. It was also not clear that they understood the verdict entered against them since it was all in French. They were also barely awake to know what was going on in the Military Tribunal. Depriving defendants who are facing the death penalty of sleep and passing judgment on them is a form of torture.

The next day, the NERA 10 defendants learned their fate from Cameroon Radio and Television (CRTV), the government broadcaster. Cameroon radio and television reported that the NERA 10 had been charged and convicted of the following crimes against the state, some of which carried the death penalty:

- Apology for acts of Terrorism,
- Secession
- Complicity to acts of terrorism
- Financing of acts of Terrorism
- Revolution
- Insurrection
- Hostility against the fatherland
- Propagation of fake news
- Internal and external attack on state security
- Non-possession of Cameroon national identity cards.

Since their extraordinary, extra-judicial rendition from Nigeria in January 2018, the conviction and sentence of the NERA 10 were foregone conclusions. In Cameroon's Napoleonic civil law system, accused persons are presumed guilty until proven innocent, and the burden of proof is on them, never on the prosecution.

Nevertheless, the NERA 10 were lucky that they were not sentenced to death. Such an outcome would have been highly embarrassing for Nigeria, whose Department of State Security (DSS) had abducted the defendants in Abuja and deported them to Cameroon. The Cameroon government believed that the abduction, deportation, trial, and conviction of the NERA 10 would be a fatal, crushing blow against the Anglophone Revolt (Teke, 2019). That ultimately turned out not to be the case. The judgment of the Abuja High Court holding that the deportation of the NERA 10 was illegal, had been ignored by the Nigerian government.

In response to the illegal deportation, kangaroo trial at the Yaoundé Military Tribunal, their conviction and sentence by that Tribunal, the NERA 10 signed and smuggled the message below from the Kondengui Prison in Yaoundé, where they are serving out their life sentences.

Figure 22.3. The NERA 10: Sisiku Ayuk Tabe, Nfor Ngala Nfor, Barrister Shufai Blaise Berinyuy, Tassang Wilfred, Barrister Eyambe Elias Ebai, Dr Egbe Ngu Ogork Ntui, Dr. Fidelis Ndeh-Che, Dr. Henry Kimeng Tata, Dr Cornelius Kwanga, & Prof. Augustine Awasum

Statement of the NERA 10 from the dungeons of Kondengui

An African proverb states that if a parent disciplines his or her child, that parent must not stop the child from crying. Doing so would constitute double punishment. It is in that spirit that the Cameroon prison authorities looked the other way when NERA 10 issued a statement from the depths of the political prisoners' quarters of Kondengui Prison in Yaoundé. Thou it is illegal to own and use cell phones in that prison, the Anglophone leaders were able to put out the following post-conviction message:

Message to the People of Southern Cameroons (Ambazonia) From Sisiku Ayuk Tabe and the Leadership in Detention

> "The August 20, 2019 pronouncement of a life imprisonment sentence by the *Yaoundé Tribunal Militaire* against us is a major push o our restoration quest and not a setback. This judgment was delivered long after the Federal High Court in Abuja, Nigeria had declared that our abduction on January 5, 2018 and subsequent deportation to Cameroon were illegal and in violation of international laws and her own national laws. This life imprisonment sentence is yet another demonstration of the socio-political, cultural and economic nightmare the Southern Cameroonians (Ambazonians) have suffered since 1st October 1961. This jail term there came not to retard but to justify and hasten our strides, as a people to FREEDOM. If anything, the LIFE IMPRISONMENT SENTENCE, should be seen as the last call divinely delivered to all doubting Thomases to join the fast-moving RESTORATION TRAIN.
>
> The pronouncement of a life imprisonment sentence on us by the *Tribunal Militaire* in Yaoundé amidst unbelievable irregularities, is a validation

of our self-determination and claim to a sovereign and free Southern Cameroons (Ambazonia). This despicable judgment should l leave each and every one of us with no other option than to unite and increase our resolve, fortitude and determination to complete the journey to Buea. Like one people, in a single voice aw se did in YAOUNDÉ, we pray you all to join us and tell French Cameroon that *it is all over.*

Before now, some have doubted what to do, what to stand for, what to believe and some had opted to take sides with the Yaoundé Regime. Should anyone still harbour doubts today? Like the barbaric slaughter of baby Martha Ngwa, the LIFE IMPRISONMENT SENTENCES on us shall prove to all Southern Cameroonians (Ambazonians) that irrespective of who you are, and what you stand for, we all are nothing but captives, waiting for the opportunity to be slammed such LIFE IMPRISONMENT SENTENCES for the fortunate ones, or outright butchering even on your beds.

It is therefore our call to each and every Ambazonian, anywhere and wherever you are, to, in whatever way you can, stand up and be counted. Our arrival in Buea has certainly been delayed, but it will come to pass. The truth and only the truth shall prevail.

Doubt not what you are already doing. Your sacrifices, your actions and prayers, are reflected in the *Yaoundé Tribunal Militaire* pronouncement of August 20, 2019 and the Lord God of Ambazonia does not miss out on anything. The pronouncement is a direct reflection of the disillusionment, panic and desperation looming over Yaoundé. Trust in everything you do, for the writing is flaring on the wall, Yaoundé is losing and losing woefully. It is now let to each and every one of us to step up everything we had done to come this far and Buea shall be ours in the days ahead. History has proven that no colonial master ever defeated the colonized people! What more, in this age when colonization has been declared a crime? La République du Cameroun has lost the war. As a people, with a history and international boundaries, we can look at them in the face as we did the *Yaoundé Tribunal Militaire* and say, *it is all over.*

Without cause, President Paul Biya declared war on us on November 30, 2017. Since then, in their genocidal and scorched-earth policy, their military has killed thousands of our people some as young as four months old baby Martha, burnt down over 250 of our villages ad communities, violated and abused our girls and women of their dignity, abducted and incarcerated over 3000 of our compatriots in their torture centers and caused over a million of our people to become IDPs and Refugees. The life imprisonment sentence on us is a reminder that Buea is our only destination. It is a call to all Ambazonians to rise up with renewed zeal and momentum to complete this historic task for posterity. We will sin against our children if we for any reason whatsoever, elect no to complete this struggle God called us to prosecute on their behalf.

We are winning and Buea is a reality. We implore you all to remain prayerful, determined, courageous, and committed to the struggle, and our Good Lord will see us through in no distant time.

Thank you all, Great People of Ambazonia for standing strong.

Signed by the NERA 10.

Missives from Political Prisoners at the Kondengui Prison

The Ambazonian leadership, the so-called Nera 10, were sentenced to life imprisonment by the Yaoundé Military Tribunal, which is the tip of the iceberg of the politico-military-judicial system of Cameroon, which is controlled tightly by the Napoleonic republican chieftain. There is no separation of powers of an independent judiciary in Cameroon President Biya is the Supreme Magistrate. As such, he is the President of the Supreme Council of the Magistrature. He appoints and dismisses magistrates and judges of both civilian and military courts by decree. Military justice, which is, in theory, a justice of exception, handles all cases related to the Anglophone crisis. The Yaoundé Military Tribunal, and the 10 regional military tribunals around the country are under the ambit of the Ministry of Defense, which itself is part of the Presidency, which appoints and dismissed judges. President Biya has been known to dismiss judges of the Yaoundé Military Tribunal in the middle of sensitive trials, and sometimes after they make rulings that the regime did not like (Tabot-Tanyi, 2023). The Yaoundé Military Tribunal essentially acts as judge, jury, and executioner.

A Journalist on Trial Pens Open Letter to the Yaoundé Military Tribunal

In an attempt to crush the Anglophone Revolt, the Biya regime criminalized Anglophone civilian dissent by bringing it within the ambit of very broad and elastic, anti-terrorism laws. The most notorious of these laws is the notorious Law No. 2014/028 of 23 December 2014 on the Suppression Acts of Terrorism. This law was applied to a whole spectrum of Anglophone speech. As we have seen throughout this volume, the dragnets of the republican chiefdom swept all views from Southern Cameroon federalists to Ambazonian separatists. Journalists were not spared from its broad sweep. We saw in chapter 11 that Samuel Wazizi of Chillen TV, Buea was arrested on accusation of aiding and abetting terrorism, was tortured to death, and his body disposed of. The Cameroon government admitted he had died in military custody one year after the fact.

Other civilian journalists, writers, teachers, lawyers, and students were also caught in the security dragnet of the republican chiefdom and its Chief of State. Journalist and writer, Penn Terence Khan, is from the English-speaking Northwest region. He was arrested in Bamenda, tortured, deprived of his basic human rights, and drained of his human dignity, like all the other Anglophones. He was deported to Yaoundé, tried before the French language-only *Tribunal Militaire de Yaoundé*, convicted, and incarcerated at the dreaded, over-crowded, den of dehumanization and disease, the Yaoundé Central Prison, which is popularly known as Kondengui. That is where Anglophone dissidents of all political stripes eventually end up–if they survive the gauntlet of dehumanization and torture of the gulag of the Biya republican chiefdom. This political prisoner experienced the Biya gulag of dehumanization from the inside and lived to tell the tale. Knowing full well that he was considered guilty of crimes against the State, and that his doom was sealed even before he appeared before the Military Tribunal, he bravely wrote an open letter to the Presiding Military judge, Col. Abega Mbezoa epouse Eko Eko.[1] The open letter is reproduced verbatim below:

> "Dear Madam President (Col. Abega Mbezoa epouse Eko Eko) and Government Commissioner (Prosecutor) Engono Thaddée) Tribunal Militaire de Yaoundé,
>
> As this process draws to its end, I think it is time for me to give you my final word before you pass your long-awaited judgement. Before your verdict, I wish to remark that:
>
> 1) The abduction, incarceration and trial that I have been subjected to before this Tribunal is political and challenges the fundamental basis [Constitutional] of this country, Cameroon.
>
> 2) Trials of civilians by Military Tribunals contravene the right to a fair trial by a competent, independent, and impartial court. Not being a member of the army or the owner of any military weapon, this trial has violated all my rights as guaranteed by the Universal Declaration of Human Rights (1945), the UN International Covenant on Civil and Political Rights, the African Charter on Human and People's Rights and even the fundamental rights to a fair trial as laid down in the preamble of the 1996 Constitution of the Republic of Cameroon.
>
> 3) I wish to emphasize that this trial has been illegal from the start. How else do you explain the fact that I was illegally abducted in Bamenda since January 16th, 2017 for acts allegedly committed there but put on trial before a Military Tribunal in Yaoundé instead of Bamenda? How do you explain the fact that throughout the trial, this court has shamelessly acted as Prosecutor and Judge at the same time? No fair-minded person can expect Justice from this type of charade trial. The Anglo-Saxon [Common Law] system of criminal justice that is supposed to be applied in the English-speaking Northwest and Southwest regions of this country demands that Justice should not only done, but it must be seen to be done, the principles for which I am prepared if need be to pay the ultimate price.
>
> 4) The charges against my person have all been trumped up charges with the court presenting no proof of any of the charges. The reason being that

1 Translation: Col. Abega Mbezoa spouse of Eko Eko. Her husband, Léopold Maxime Eko Eko (a Francophone from Biya's region, who has no relation to the author of this volume). He was head of the Cameroon Intelligence, agency, la Direction General de Renseignement Exterieur (DGRE). He masterminded the extrajudicial deportation of the Nera 10 from Nigeria to face trial at the Yaoundé Military Tribunal. Ironically, Léopold Maxime Eko Eko was arrested in March 2023, for being allegedly involved in the kidnapping, brutal torture, mutilation and murder of Francophone journalist, Martinez Zogo. He was held in detention at the Kondengui Central Prison, and had appeared before the Yaoundé Military Tribunal at the time of publication).

they do not exist. I am neither a terrorist nor a secessionist, but the political nature of the trial makes it possible for the court to slam the "Guilty Verdict" on me. If the term or word "Terrorism" is an attribute to people and individuals who decry societal injustice and inequality, then find me guilty again because these are the reasons for which I stand before you today. Where then is the justice that we seek?

5) No tribunal including the one over which you preside can solve the "Anglophone problem" in this country because it is a political problem. It requires political will rather than court cases for its resolution. That is why both the United Nations, the African Union and other international bodies or organisations have consistently advised the government of this country to address the Root Cause if she wants to solve the political imbroglio facing the country.

6) Madam President, no terrorist is a peace-loving person. I too and a few of my brothers locked up today have tried in our most modest, humble ways, to propose several solution-oriented projects to top government officials on how to appease the angry population. We have met and written to the prosecutor on the need for a peaceful solution to the crisis, the urgent need for the Executive branch that controls this trial remotely to seek ways of engaging the marginalized population in the much-awaited dialogue so as to settle this Anglophone marginalisation question once and for all, but it seems all cries have fallen on deaf ears. Dialogue is the best cure for the crisis rocking Cameroon today. Dialogue averted war in 1993 and it can still do that today.

7) Your Honour, the so-called Cameroon Anglophone problem is specific; it has nothing to do with developmental problems plaguing Cameroon as a whole. It is about the lack of institutional protections for the English-speaking minority, the cultural assimilation of the people and her identity. It is about the ongoing cultural genocide against the English-speaking minority. Throughout history, it has been the inaction of those who could have acted, the indifference of those who could have known better, the silence of the voice of Justice when it mattered most, that has made it possible for evil to triumph. I hope this message will be passed through you to the system that you represent, those that seek to kill the cause of justice and inequality for which I stand.

Cameroon is a state of law and can do better than this. Thank you Madam President and the Prosecutor of the Yaoundé Military Tribunal for giving me the opportunity to make these remarks.

The journalist who wrote this missive was Penn Terence Kahn. He was convicted of a slew of offenses under the 2014 Anti-terrorism Law and sentenced to 12 years imprisonment. He has been at the dreaded Kondengui maximum security prison in Yaoundé along with hundreds of other Anglophone political prisoners, lawyers, university professors, journalists, teachers, students and ordinary citizens who had either been on pre-trial detention or have been convicted under anti-terrorism laws since 2017.

In the Belly of the Beast: A Kondengui Political Prisoner's Diary

On July 22, 2019, there was a prison demonstration at the Yaoundé Central Prison, Kondengui. The riot, which was streamed life on the Internet by inmates, was a protest against the extremely inhumane and over-crowded conditions in which the Anglophone political prisoners, as well as political prisoners from the MDR and other prisoners, were being ware-housed in Kondengui. They demanded to be released. The demonstrators called attention to the very deplorable, inhumane conditions in which prisoners awaiting trial were remanded, sometimes for years, at the Kondengui Maximum Prison. In response to this worldwide negative attention being paid to Cameroon prisons, the Minister of Communication, Réné Sadi, issued a statement on July 23, 2019, stating that the Government of the Republic wished to inform international public opinion that well-known detainees had started an insurrection in the prison. It stated that the event started as an assembly of pretrial detainees from the Northwest and Southwest regions who had been jailed in the context of "security problems" perpetrated in those regions and wished to present their grievances to the high authorities of the State. Instead, the gathering had degenerated into a violent and seditious insurrection, insurgency and mutiny. He said the library, the ladies' sewing workshop and the office of the discipline master of the prison had been set ablaze. He said 179 prisoners had been arrested and were being interrogated. He said that despite the insurrection, the government "remains attentive to these detained compatriots and continues objectively and impartially to examine the case of these demonstrating detainees…with 'republican deliberation'. In the *chefferie republicaine*, justice delayed is not justice denied.

This prison riot and the government's response to it demonstrated that the overcrowded Cameroon prison system, whose population had been swelled by Anglophone pre-trial detainees, had serious problems. The following write-ups from some Anglophone political prisoners and pre-trial detainees who had been in detention for years awaiting trial, give us an inside look at the conditions of the over-crowded, poorly resourced Kondengui Central Prison in Yaoundé, which serves as both a full-fledged maximum-security prison as well as pre-trial center for hundreds of Anglophone detainees.

The Kondengui Prison: Seen Through the Eyes of An Anglophone Political Prisoner

The prison demonstrations of 2018 called attention to the state of the overcrowded, inhuman conditions in which pre-trial detainees and convicted prisoners are held at the Yaoundé Central Prison. An Anglophone civilian journalist and writer, Tsi Conrad, who had been incarcerated at the Kondengui Prison since 2017 for publishing "fake news" about the Anglophone problem in Cameroon, kept a prison diary in which he described, in great detail and unemotional terms, the stark, inhuman reality of Anglophone political prisoners on lengthy pretrial detention, as well as those who had been convicted by the Yaoundé Military Tribunal, under the draconian Anti-terrorism act. Excerpts of the handwritten and scanned documents were downloaded from a social media platform.

> "Prison Facilities:
>
> The Prison administration in Cameroon is under the Ministry of Justice. according to the Minister of Justice, Laurent Esso, the total prison population as of June 2022 including pretrial detainees and remand prisoners stood at 32,000 while the official prison capacity is 17,000 prisoners. The Pre-trial detainees /remand prisoners to the percentage of prison population stands at 58%. The population of female prisoners to the Prison population stands at 2.6% while the Juveniles or minors to the percentage of prison population stands at 2.6%.
>
> - The Total number of prisons in Cameroon is 79
> - The number of functional prisons in Cameroon is 70
> - There are no exclusively female prisons in Cameroon. Cameroon simply creates female wings in male prisons, and, in most prisons, the women do not even have a separate yard for outside activities, and they share the same yard with men. For example, in the Kondengui Central Prison, the women use the same yard for sporting and social activities as the men. They also are transported to court in the same prison vans with the men. In some cases, they even share toilet facilities like in the Yabassi prison. For example, the Yabassi Principal Prison, located in the Nkam division of the Littoral region of Cameroon awakens female prisoners at five o'clock in the morning to give them access to the bathrooms before the men. Thus, by implication, the women have no access to the bathrooms during the day. In Cameroon, the penitentiary administrators state that pregnant women and those with little children are not allowed in prison but this is not the case in reality. There are no special care measures for pregnant women, mothers with little children inside the prison, or minor children outside the prison. There are no provisions for menstruation and issues specific to the well-being of women inmates.
> - There also are no youth facilities or rehabilitation centers in Cameroon.
>
> **Types of prisons where Anglophones arrested in connection with the crisis are Incarcerated**
>
> In a typical situation, one would describe the types of prisons Anglophone detainees are locked up based on the personal stories and experiences of these detainees from arrest to final imprisonment. Most Anglophones detainees when arrested are first of all transferred to a local police station or a military/paramilitary gendarmerie security base. Some are first taken to a military barrack. It may be a newly created military barracks or a temporal military base set up in the area or zone of arrest because of the crisis. Anglophone detainees are detained in these facilities, which are not designed to hold prisoners, from a few days to months and

some stay there up to a year and more. Other are executed here. These first line of detention centers are noted for torture, brutality, and the worst kind of inhuman treatments. Human rights violations in these detention centers are at their peak. Here, interrogations are carried out and forced confessions are extracted using all available means of torture including but not limited to water boarding, shooting of the suspect with live bullets on their legs, to the infamous "*balancois*" where a suspect is hanged upside down on two poles and beaten with electric cables. They also use matchets, battens and electric cables to beat and lacerate the bodies and soles of the feet of suspects. Some Anglophones are forced to drink and eat their own waste in such centers. The suspects are always held incommunicado. No family members or lawyers are allowed in these torture centers.

After this first line of detention centers, most Anglophones are transferred to divisional or regional judicial police stations, military bases, or central police/gendarmerie stations. Here, more interrogations are carried out, sometimes including force. Some anglophones spend from a few days to months in these detention centers and sometimes some disappear. Pockets of information indicate extrajudicial executions take place here, and it's most probable that detainees are held incommunicado here too for long periods of time.

The third line of detention centers are the national detention centers in Yaoundé. Here we are talking about the infamous:

SED (*Secatariat D'etat a la Defense*),

DGRE (Direction General de Renseignement Exterieur),

DST (Direction de surveillance territoires),

SEMIL (securite Militaire) which is attached to the Ministry of Defense in Yaoundé.

Other detention centers include the DPJ, (Direction de Police Judiciare) and several police stations in Yaounde also act as detention centers.

In this network of detention centers, Anglophone are kept incommunicado from a few weeks to months and sometimes for more than one year. We know some Anglophone suspects who were detained at SED for one year four months and more. These detention centers have the most brutal forms of torture. Here interrogations are never carried out according to Cameroon law. Suspects are sometimes tortured to death. Some are taken out in the middle of the night and never returned. There is a high probability that most of those taken out in the night are killed because co-detainees never hear anything about them again. They just disappear into thin air. Anglophone journalist, Samuel Wazizi, disappeared in this network of torture centers. The government admitted that he had died in military custody but his body was never returned to his family and no one was prosecuted for his disappearance, torture and death.

The fourth line of detention centers are the prisons. With the conflict, most divisional prisons known by the French title "Prison principale", loosely translated as "Principal prisons" in the Anglophone regions have been shutdown and so most Anglophones are transferred to the regional or central prisons. Amongst the prisons hosting Anglophones, we have identified:

- The Kondengui Central prison Yaounde
- The Kondengui Principal Prison Yaounde
- The Bamenda Central prison
- The Douala Central prison Douala
- The Bafoussam Central Prison Bafoussam
- The Buea Central prison Buea
- The Kumba Central Prisons Kumba
- Foumban principal Prison
- Mbouda principal prison
- Ndchang principal Prison
- Tcholerie prisons North Region
- Yoko Principal prison in Center region
- Eseka Principal prison Littoral Region
- Mbalmayo principal Prison center region
- Mfou principal Prison center region

We have reliable information that some Anglophones are incarcerated in other prisons which we are not aware of. Due to the difficulty of communication, we fear that we have not been able to find everyone and so documenting their existence in the many hidden detention centers around Cameroon has been difficult.

1c) Inmate Population:

The inmate population in Cameroon as stated by the ministry of Justice in Cameroon stands at 32,000+ as of June 2022 with a prison capacity of 17,000. This inmate population includes pre-trial/remand prisoners.

- Remand inmates. The global pre-trial detainee population stands at 58% of the global inmate population making it (16,640). The prison population of the Yaounde Central prison Kondengui, stands at 4,500 inmates with about 3500 remand detainees making it 78% pre-trial inmates.
- The sentenced inmates stands at 48% of the prison inmate population making it (15,360). The sentenced prisoners of the Yaounde Central prison Kondengui stands at 1000 making 22% sentenced.
- The population of sentenced inmates arrested in connection with the anglophone crisis for six years is 37aking it 15%.

  2) Population of Anglophones arrested in connection to the crisis in

each prison

The population of anglophones arrested in connection with the crisis in each Prison is

- The Kondengui Central prison Yaounde - 275
- The Kondengui Principal Prison Yaounde - 35
- The Bamenda Central prison - 400+
- The Douala Central prison Douala - 200+
- The Bafoussam Central Prison - 70+
- The Buea Central prison - 700+
- The Kumba Central Prisons - 50
- Foumban principal Prison number not known
- Mbouda principal prison number not known
- Ndchang principal Prison number not known
- Tcholerie prisons North Region number not known
- Yoko Principal prison in Center region- 2
- Eseka Principal prison Littoral Region number not known
- Mbalmayo principal Prison center region- 1
- Mfou principal Prison center region number not known
- The Nkongsamba principal Prison – 5

The Kondengui Central Prison, Yaoundé which was constructed for 1000 inmates now hosts at least 4500 inmates. As such it is over–crowded and very difficult to run on a daily bases. The prison administration has therefore allowed an unofficial inmate or prisoner management structure which is run by inmates duly nominated by the prisons administration (the superintendent in charge).

The prison is divided into various quarters (living sections). Kondengui has 14 living sections. Each of these sections has a given number of cells.

The prison administration appoints inmates as "auxiliaries" to handle the day to day running and control of other inmates.

Problems plaguing the Cameroon Prisons

Lack of accurate data: There is lack of data from Cameroon prisons due to the bottlenecks of the government bureaucracy. The government cracks down on any individuals or organizations that try to investigate or decry the human rights violations happening in Cameroon prisons. Therefore, data is hard to find and research on prisons is not readily allowed. The prisons in Cameroon are relatively inaccessible to academia, professionals, and even policy makers, and as such there is little or no change of the situation in the prisons.

Overcrowding: Cameroon has 10 central prisons, One in each of its ten regions. The Kondengui central prison in Yaoundé is the most populated maximum security prison in the country. It was initially built for 1000 prisoners, but the statistics as of October 15, 2022 show a total of 4,567 (four thousand five hundred and sixty seven) inmates. It is overcrowded and stretched beyond limit. With inadequate prison infrastructure, the prison has plunged into chaos. The main drivers of these overcrowding are:

- Judicial laxity and failure to follow judicial procedures by magistrates and prosecutors
- Failure of the general judicial system which causes extended imprisonment terms especially for pre-trial inmates. Sentences inmates who suffer extended prison terms because of court delays, prison delays, missing judicial documents in the files of the prison Secretariat, inmate inability to pay heavy court fines, lack of awareness of release procedures. Some inmates spend extra time in prison because they did not know their date of release etc... these factors cause overcrowding

  Inadequate infrastructure to accommodate the incarcerated population.
- Corruption in the prisons causing the sales of prison bed spaces for money by the prison administration and designated inmate prison "auxiliaries" who handle such transactions on behalf of the prison officers....

Infectious diseases: Rule 24 of the Nelson Mandela Rules states that the healthcare of prisoners is the government's responsibility: The overcrowded nature of the Cameroon prisons makes it a hub for infectious diseases such as tuberculosis which is very common in the Kondengui prisons due to the availability of hard drugs, cigarettes and marijuana within the prison....The problem is that the period between diagnosis and quarantine may sometimes take months. Diseases like hepatitis and skin rashes are also common and easily spread. Elephantiasis is also common within the Kondengui Central prison.

Human Rights Violations: Assault: Assault in the prisons is at two levels. In Kondengui Central Prison, Yaounde, the first level of assault is from the prison officers (wardens). Wardens are regularly found beating or torturing inmates for several reasons. Sometimes it is because the inmate has broken the one or several of the internal rules of the prison like stealing from another inmate, fighting and inflicting bodily harm on another inmate, or sometimes just for the sake of imposing authority. These torture spans from simple lashes of the cane to brutally attacking the inmates to using battens and other harmful objects like sticks and wooden boards to beat the inmate. Sometimes inmates are chained for long hours to a pole. At other times one leg is lifted up and chained to one hand above the head so that the inmate stands on one leg and the other is stretched out for long for long periods of time. This is an extremely painful position to be in. Some inmates are also tortured by wardens in cases of homosexuality. Wardens also use solitary confinement to punish inmates and bring them untold hardship from a few days to several months.

Assault of inmates by other inmates: the structure and internal functioning of the prison leaves the possibility for the inmate auxiliaries to the administration to inflict pain and bodily harm on other inmates and get away with it. These auxiliaries to the administration who are inmates themselves have been given the authority to brutalize other inmates in the course of carrying out their duties. Sometimes, these auxiliaries go as far as lacerating their victims and they get away with it because they are protected by the administration. Other forms of human rights abuses like extortion of inmates by the prison administration is common. The prison administration sells bed spaces which are supposed to be free, to inmates. When you are detained or sentenced to prison, you need money to get a bed space. They also request you pay money before transferring you to a habitable loving section especially for pre-trial who do not want to be mixed with hardened criminals. Most VIP inmates (former government official accused of corruption) pay huge sums of money to be sent to VIP living sections. The auxiliaries to the prison administration have also been given the power to extort money from inmates in the name of "sanitary taxes" and "cell rights.: When an inmate is unable to pay the money, they made to clean the toilets, and sleep outside even during the rainy season.

Prison Feeding

The penitentiary authorities of the Kondengui Prison provide one meal a day for all the inmates. The food is interchanged between days with corn and beans and days with rice and soup. The quantity provided is inadequate to serve everyone given the overcrowded nature of the prison. Also the food is prepared very poorly so much so that only those who cannot afford to have their families provide them food from home eat prison food. Most of the food is eaten by those who inhabit the Kosovo quarters (the most populated living sections), and it still is not enough to go around to all of them. The food is cooked by prisoners in a kitchen located a few hundred meters outside the prison. The general sanitation conditions around the food are very poor. The pots in which the food is cooked and taken to the various living sections are very old, and are hardly washed properly. The food tastes so bad even a pig will refuse to eat it. Most people who eat this food develop health complications over time.

Anglophones arrested and detained in connection with the crisis do not eat food provided by the prison administration because it is poorly prepared and is inadequate. One will need to fight his way to be able to receive a spoonful of rice and soup or corn and beans without oil, salt or Maggi [seasoning] and the quantity is not even sufficient to keep a man for six hours.

The first Anglophones who were transferred to the Kondengui Central Prison, Yaoundé, after noticing this feeding problem, created a community of Anglophone detainees to able to survive. Management teams were set up to solicit food and medical support for the Anglophone detainees from good will donors and family members who could help. For almost seven years, this management teams have helped in keeping Anglophone political prisoners together and fed. They have saved the lives of hundreds of Anglophone detainees who have passed through Kondengui Central Prison as well as those still incarcerated. Anglophone detainees have a common meal of rice and groundnut soup prepared by Anglophone themselves for every Anglophone, every day. Nonetheless, with the dwindling resources available in the revolution [Anglophone Revolt], the Anglophone political prisoners in Kondengui Central Prison have experienced a fair a share of confusion, with Anglophones not being able to cook sometimes for weeks because of lack of food. However, we commend the good will of some Non-governmental Organizations (NGOs) and individuals who have been constant in their support and are very grateful for to them. We however do not also relent to say that, a few NGOs cannot carry the burden of feeding political prisoners. With our current number of 246 Anglophone political prisoners in Kondengui Central Prison, we need at least a bag of rice, groundnuts and other condiments daily to be able to provide a plate of rice for every Anglophones every day.

Prison Sanitation

Sanitation is very poor. The toilets are inadequate and poorly managed. A few toilet holes for thousands of prisoners in the various quarters. There is inadequate water supply and inadequate supply of first aid medication in the prison clinic. Corruption in the prison clinic necessitates that prisoners and detainees pay for basic medication which is supposed to be free. Many inmates suffer from skin rashes because they use dirty water. Many suffer from dysentery and have constant stomach issues because they are constrained to consume impure water from the water taps. The overcrowding in most of the living quarters leads to easy spread of disease.

Prison Cells and Prison Inmates

Inmates in the Kondengui Central Prison are divided into 14 different quarters. The population per quarter varies with quarters 8 & 9 hosting the most inmates (these two quarters are nicknamed KOSOVO). That name refers to the most dangerous and most populated living sections of the prison.

The 14 quarters are categorized in terms of the social status of the prisoners and detainees in society. It also reflects the ability of inmates to pay transfer fees and cell dues demanded by the inmates who are "auxiliaries" of the prison administration. These fees vary with each living section. For example, quarters 11,12 &13 are reserved for inmates who had high ranks in the administrative [government] and in society– Former General managers of state-owned cooperations accused of embezzlement and mismanaged of state funds, former senior divisional officers etc.… while quarter 14 is reserved only for former Ministers and Ministers of State, accused of mismanagement and embezzlement of State funds. These quarters are considered VIP quarters. These VIP quarters are less populated with cells hosting between 2-6 inmates each. Present and former inmates of the VIP section of the Kondengui prison include former Prime minister Ephraim Inoni, former Minister of Higher Education, Jean-Marie Atangana Mebara, Minister of Water and Energy, Basile Atangana Kouna, former Minister of Défense, Edgar Alain Mebe Ngo'o, former Director General of Cameroon Radio and Television (CRTV), Gervais Mendo Zé (he died in prison), former Director General of Cameroon Airlines, Yves Michel Fotso, former director of External Intelligence, Leopold Maxime Eko Eko, opposition leader, Maurice Kamto, his colleague Christian Penda Ekoka and many others.

Most inmates transferred to the Kondengui Central Prison are first sent to the Kosovo quarters which is super populated and crowded. Inmates who cannot stand the difficulty there then pay an unofficial transfer fee to the penitentiary officer in charge of transfers who then transfers them to another quarter which is less populated and crowded. This fee is illegal, but it is collected anyway.

The cells are of equal sizes throughout the prisons and quarters but the number of inmates in each cell differs as per the quarters. The cells measure 3m by 2m square each. Each cell is demarcated into fifteen (15) bed spaces with a central space in the middle of the cell which serves for additional bed space at night, for those who cannot afford to buy a personal bed space but can pay cell dues. This is for the regular quarters.

The Kosovo quarters (8&9) is made up of 26 cells each with a cell hosting at least eighty (80) inmates. Some cells in those two quarters host up to 100 inmates. With 15 bed spaces and an additional 15 spaces created at night at the centre of the cell by placing mattresses on the floor. We have at least 50 inmates who sleep outside of the cells. They find themselves in the yards, toilet corridors, clandestine shelves and around gutters. These two quarters alone host at least three thousand (3000) inmates. The situation is so bad, some inmates literally stand up to sleep or manage to squeeze themselves near garbage bins and urinaries (sic) where there are little or no restrictions. Unfortunately, these two quarters hosts at least 100 Anglophones political prisoners arrested in connection with the crisis.

When I was transferred to Kondengui prison on 23rd December 2016, I was first transferred to quarter 9 (Kosovo) which had a population of 1,800 inmates. I slept on the floor for two weeks. With the help of my family, I was able to pay the transfer fee (50,000frs CFA) to quarter 3 which was less crowded. I paid for a bed space (25000 frs CFA) and spent the first one year in a cell that had 34 inmates. Nineteen of those inmates squeezed themselves every night on mattresses on the floor. I then sought another transfer to quarter 1 which is less crowded and paid a bed space (25000fra CFA) in a cell which has 15 inmates. Every inmate has a bed space in my new cell. But the majority of Anglophones political prisoners live in the over-crowded quarters 8,9 and 3.

The peculiarity about the living sections is the living conditions and rules and regulations implemented there. The VIP quarters do not allow cigarette smoking and hard drugs consumption and trafficking. Homosexuality is practically absent in these quarters and other intense ills are limited. Stealing is heavily punished in these quarters too. These quarters are meant to host inmates who are relatively deemed responsible.

The most populated Kosovo quarter is essentially deemed to be a no man's land. All the ills prohibited and heavily punished in the VIP living sections are common in Kosovo. Although punished by the prison penitentiary, the inmate living conditions there are so deplorable that it makes it difficult to track down the perpetrators. The Kosovo quarters is most at times referred to as the real Kondengui, where we have the bad and the ugly. This is where inmates eat rats and cockroaches because of lack of food. The biggest crime and drug cartels of hardened criminals running illegal businesses worth millions of frs CFA are also in these quarters. It's a free for all and anything goes environment.

Living Conditions: The Water Situation

The Kondengui Central Prison, Yaoundé was initially constructed to host 1000 (one thousand) prisoners. Today it hosts over 4500 (four thousand five hundred) inmates, most of whom are pre-trial detainees. These inmates are divided into 14 different quarters (living sections). The living sections are called 'Quarters' and numbered as such from Quarter 1 to Quarter 14.

Each of these quarters has at least two water taps. Water runs from the main government water supply company, Camwater, but Quarters 1 and 3 have borehole water supply running from separate water taps. Nevertheless, there are frequent water shortages and cuts. The prison suffers at least 5 months of water shortage every year. In my almost seven years of incarceration, we have had to go through weeks of water cuts. Sometimes inmates go for days without water supply and the prison administration does nothing about it. Drinking water supplied by Camwater within the prison facility is not advisable to drink because the water is widely considered as impure. The pipes supplying the water are old and inmates who consume this water tend to suffer from frequent dirty water related ailments. Most prisoners tend to buy bottled water from vendors accredited by the prison administration. Most of these water vendors to the captive population are prison guards and penitentiary officers. For most prisoners who cannot afford a constant supply of bottled water, it's a nightmare especially when there are long water cuts.

Medical care

There is a prison clinic which admits patients whose cases are serious. Treatment is paid for by prisoners despite penitentiary laws which says the prison is supposed to take care of first aid and treatment of common diseases like fever and malaria. As such, there is a huge health care gap in which sick prisoners are left to die because they don't have money to buy basic medication from the prison clinic. Many die in the confines of their cells or quarters without treatment due to lack of money.

Nevertheless, there is one quarter dedicated for inmates suffering from contagious diseases like tuberculosis (Quarter 2). This quarter hosts inmates who have been diagnosed with contagious diseases and follow up on their cases is done by the resident medical doctor in the prison clinic. Most of these patients are sometimes neglected and left without their medications for months. Some end up dying as a result of neglect.

The Covid-19 Pandemic at the Kondengui Central Prison

The Advent of the Covid-19 pandemic caused untold hardship for inmates in the prison. These hardships are a result of the restrictive measures taken by the penitentiary authorities without due consideration of the welfare of prisoners. The covid 19 pandemic affected us as follows: a) The prison administration restricted prison visits for almost 3 years. Family members and friends could not pay regular visits like before. Prisoners were deprived of the right to family visits from March of 2020 to early 2023. B) The penitentiary administration permitted food delivery to inmates whose family members come to give them food after 6 months. This lasted for another 6 months. In March of 2021, visits were allowed within a restricted space and the time spent by a visitor was reduced to 5 minutes. C) The courts were grounded for several months after the outbreak of Covid 19. They only resumed duty 5 months later. That caused a long delay in the hearing of the cases of thousands of inmates. D) During the Covid 19 pandemic, inmates were not able to see their lawyers because lawyers were not allowed to pay visits to prisoners. Many inmates saw their lawyers only after they were called to court in August 2020. Many cases were not called to court for 5 months, so preparing for cases with the lawyers was practically impossible.

Within the first two months of the outbreak of the pandemic, at least 25 inmates died. The prison administration refused to declare the cause of their deaths and denied allegations that their deaths were linked to the

Corona virus. This caused panic and trauma among prisoners for months.

In April 2020, the Cameroun government in a calculated move to decongest prisons released a few hundred prisoners from prisons around Cameroon through a Presidential decree announcing a prison remission for certain offenses. Kondengui Prisons unfortunately did not release a significant number of prisoners and so the prison remained congested. In January of 2022, the Minister of Justice permitted normal visits to resume once every week (on Sundays). Inmates could receive their loved ones on Sunday for 30 minutes in the courtyard of the prison, which had been formally closed to visitors. This was an improvement but not a normalization of visits which used to be three times a week.

Types of Prisoners in Kondengui

The Kondengui Central Prison is host to all types of prisoners given the fact that it is Cameroun's biggest maximum security prison. It serves as a central prison for both the central region and Cameroun. The prison therefore has: a) Political prisoners and prisoners of conscience (Ambazonians and Opposition MRC party militants arrested for taking part in civil protests). There are about 500 inmates in this category. B). Economic prisoners arrested under the anti-corruption campaign, Operation Sparrowhawk in Cameroun. These prisoners are either accused of embezzlement and mismanagement of state fund or convicted of same by the Special Criminal Court. This group is made up of mostly former ministers, managers of state corporations, civil servants and civil administrators, resident in the VIP section of the prison. There are about 200 inmates in this category. C). Female prisoners arrested for diverse offenses including political offenses. There are about 250 women in this category in the Kondengui Central Prison. D). Minors. These are prisoners below the age of 18 who were arrested for diverse offenses. Some are students arrested for participating in Anglophone demonstrations. There are about 150 detainees in this category. E) Regular felons arrested for diverse offenses ranging from armed robbery to abuse of confidence, to murder, assault etc....

Anglophone political prisoners have been relatively very disciplined since 2016, when the first group of them arrested in connection with the crisis were deported to Kondengui. Nevertheless, the prison inadequacies and the very notion of Anglophone marginalization is present in the prison. Francophone inmates who are the majority have carried out targeted attacks against Anglophone detainees because of disagreements over events of the Anglophone crisis. Some Penitentiary officers have also orchestrated and planned attacks on Anglophone detainees using proxy hardened criminals serving long jail terms. Nevertheless, Anglophone detainees through their management teams and their various leaders incarcerated in the prison, have been able to strike deals to maintain peace and discipline within the Anglophone community. This greatly improved the level of discipline amongst Anglophones. Anglophones however are not completely left out of the prison crime problem. Some have been involved in illegal activities like drug trafficking and cigarette smoking and sales. No matter our short comings, the Anglophone community has never relented in its efforts to keep Anglophones away from such activities, and we are proud to say our record here shows relatively excellent marks on discipline.

Banned and Illegal Gadgets

The first illegal gadget in prison is the telephone. But because the Kondengui Central Prison does not make provision for inmate communication facilities, they are forced to unofficially allow the use of mobile phones within the prison (especially analog telephones). Android phones are completely banned but inmates still use them anyway. This however does not give inmates the rights to abuse their use of telephones. If you are caught using a telephone out of your bed space in the VIP quarters, the penitentiary officer has the right to confiscate it and never to be returned to you. In cases where a prisoner is suspected of using the telephone to carry out financial scams and other ills, the disciplinary office is allowed to carry out cell searches targeting the perpetrator. But due to corruption, most of the telephones confiscated by penitentiary officers are returned to the inmates in exchange for a handsome bribe. That is how phones are maintained in prison no matter how many search parties are organized to confiscate them. Besides, all the illegal substances and telephones are brought into the Prison through warders who are paid handsomely for the risk. Penitentiary warders caught bringing in illegal substances for inmates face the law of the state pertaining to the penitentiary staff.

Political Prisoners

A Political prisoner is widely considered as a person who is imprisoned because his actions or beliefs are contrary to those of his or her government. As such, a political prisoner will be someone imprisoned because they have opposed or criticized the government responsible for their imprisonment. In the Republic of Cameroon, political prisoners are those arrested for and charged with felonies/crimes against the state or the person of the President of the Republic of Cameroon (Paul Biya). They may also be referred to as prisoners of conscience. They are prisoners of conscience because their incarceration is a result of differences in political and social ideas. They hold opinions which are heavily cracked down on by the government in place.

To talk about Political prisoners in the Kondengui Central Prisons is synonymous with talking about prisoners arrested in connection with the Anglophone crises that is now dubbed the "Southern Cameroons/

Ambazonian independence struggle" by Southern Cameroons liberation activists and freedom fighters. However, we cannot leave out other prisoners considered as political prisoners because of the nature of their arrests and charges levelled against them. Here we will talk about the militants (members) of one of the opposition parties in Cameroun called the Cameroun Renaissance movement (MRC) headed by Professor Maurice Kamto. This set of prisoners were arrested for defying the government, and protesting in public, amongst other reasons, against the regime's handling of the crises in the two English-speaking regions. They insist on pushing the regime to abandon the military assault on Southern Cameroons independence freedom fighters and go for an all-inclusive dialogue as a means to solve the conflict. Also, after the presidential elections of 2018, Maurice Kamto of the MRC claimed to have won the elections while accusing the incumbent president Paul Biya and his government of rigging the elections in favour of the 90-year-old president, who had been in power for more than 40 years. These political prisoners heeded Maurice Kamto's call to carry out post-election protests asking President Paul Biya to step down and let the "president-elect" and presumed winner of the presidential election, to become president of the Republic of Cameroon.

A Female Political Prisoner's Perspective

My name is Gracious ANGOH.[2] I'm Cameroonian.

I was arrested in Buea on the 21st of September 2017. On this day, more than 20 armed men came to my job site at about 6:30 pm. They intimidated me with their guns, slapped me, took my handbag containing my purse, my phones and money, then took all the data processing accessories–computers and calculators– at my job site, handcuffed me and whisked me off to the police station at Ekona, where they asked me to identify some boys who were under arrest, boys I didn't know.

From here, I was driven to my house in the same condition, where my house was ransacked by the same men, who took along money amounting to four hundred and ninety-two thousand francs CFA in cash, and my phones with the sum of four hundred and fifty thousand francs CFA in my mobile money accounts. They also took away my personal identification documents in the house, and I have no idea where they ended up, since they were never handed back to me.

From here I was blindfolded and driven to an unknown destination where I was locked up still blindfolded for three weeks.

During the first week, I was asked to identify a group of boys said to be Ambazonians, then I was accused of sponsoring the said boys in question.

I explained to the interrogators that I operated a business which

2 Name altered to protect her from retaliation.

included money transaction (Mobile money), so my account was used by these guys to collect their money, but that I wasn't their sponsor.

After serious torture to enable me denounce these guys I did not know, I was hence transferred to the Judicial Police station where I was kept for two months behind closed doors and fed like a dog. I was later transferred to the Kondengui Central Prison in Yaoundé on the 1st of December 2017, where I am till today.

Communication with the Outside World from Prison is awfully difficult for me since my detention. I have prayed and hoped that the mystery of the false accusations which led to my arrest be solved. I have hoped to reacquire my dignity, so I can resume with normal life. Yet, no change so far. I am a single mother to a ten-year-old boy. My family is very poor, with no one to assist them financially or otherwise; so they have been unable to secure my release; though I must admit they have tried everything possible to get me released. My mother had to borrow almost two million francs CFA to secure my release. She paid the money to those who were supposedly in charge of my incarceration. Her efforts were futile, but the money was never refunded. Now I am counting on everyone, every single noble-hearted person out there, who reads this Post (my cry out for HELP) to say or do something at their best, so that I am released. My fear is dying here unjustly, like some useless animal. Of which I am not. I am barely a young woman and mother, who started off a small business to feed her family.

Thank you for liking and or commenting.

Fabiano Deco, Former Political Prisoner in Bamenda and Yaoundé

My Involuntary Journey Across the Cameroon's National Security Detention Network

I AM CALLED 'THE CHINESE' AND I AM A MEMBER OF THE ANGLOPHONE PARLIAMENT IN JAIL IN KONDENGUI

Note*: Fabiano Deco was one of those detainees featured in the infamous SED dossier discussed in the first part of this chapter. He tells us how he got caught up in the massive repressive machine of the Biya republican chiefdom.*

My name is Fabian V. Nouanwoh (aka Fabiano Deco). I am single and a talent promoter and radio animator/announcer (City FM Radio, Bamenda) I was kidnapped at Small Mankon, Bamenda, at my workplace (a Parifoot or football betting kiosk) on 15/06/17 @ 18:24. I am a Parifoot sales agent. One man approached me and said he wanted to validate a ticket, just when I was about to close, but I told him I can't reopen work again because I am late to go and deposit my sales [at the agency]. He insisted and I asked him if it was by force. Unfortunately for me I saw 5 others who then ca me with guns. They were all dressed in civilian clothes.

They carried me away and I left the money I had sold for that day in my drawer (78,8000frs). They took me to Judicial Police station Bamenda and I could only recognize a commissioner called Commissioner Ade, who is an Anglophone. Since I knew him I asked why they abducted me that way. He rather asked one police officer who had a green T shirt on which was written R.A.S.S. to take my phones. They took two phones from me, one Techno W5 and one Xtigi Mobile. About one hour later,

Commissioner Ade transferred me to the Public Security Police Station himself. Information about my arrest went to my brother Shingwa Henry, and he came looking for me the following morning. I narrated to him as above and sent him to go to Mr. Commander Ade and ask why he had ordered my arrest, but Commissioner Ade refused to reply and sent him away. They put me in a single room to sleep on bare tiles and gave an order after three days after that I shouldn't receive visitors, make calls or talk to anyone. Fifteen days later, one man came and called me out into and interrogation room with three, four-stars commissioners plus himself. He said I am a Biafran, a rebel, a terrorist, a secessionist, and they all fell on me and asked: why did I want to divide Cameroon?

The man in civilian clothes told me that due to what they had seen on my phone and my publications about Southern Cameroons on Facebook, I am having charges of terrorism, secession, rebellion and destabilization of the country brought against me. I asked him if talking about Southern Cameroons is a crime. He slapped me and told me he will send me to Yaoundé. He found a WhatsApp message which I forwarded about the singing the Southern Cameroons anthem for a singing competition and he asked why I had forwarded it and I told him 1 was running a radio talent show program called "Premier stars." I had sent the message due to the singing aspect of the program. I wanted interested contenders to apply. He forced me to write things which he wanted me to write, with threats from the other three. He then read one of my posts on Facebook that read: "Hon Wirba [Member of the National Assembly from Bui], is back, the second leg of this match seems to be bloody". He asked who is behind me as a sponsor to be writing all these things and why I had used the word "bloody". I told him I have no sponsor and that I am a free thinker. As for the word "bloody," I could have also used terrible, wonderful, crazy, funny, it was just a choice of words. He told me to apologize so that they release me, if I promise I will not write such things again which I did. He then left and three days later, I was transferred to the judicial police station, Elig-essono Yaoundé.

In Yaoundé I experienced the same conditions as in Bamenda. About 16 days later, I was called by another interrogator who was purely Francophone. He said he had gone through my phone and seen images of strikes /ghost town actions, which I had sent to people about Southern

Cameroons and bad things like that. I told him that when I highlight a picture to read on my phone online, it automatically downloads the picture into the phone. As for all those images he is talking about in my phone, they checked my phone and didn't find anything like that in Bamenda, and my phone had been with them for almost 46 days, so I didn't know anything about forwarding images of strikes. Moreso he could go to the streets or universities and check the phones of students, if he won't see images of what's happening in the Northwest and Southwest, even his phone will have one.

He shook his head and asked me if could identify three foreign numbers which were stored in my phone. I told him they were my friends with whom I had worked together, my boss at City FM radio and my bank account.

Things didn't change as per our living conditions in the cells at the Judicial Police Station Elig-essono Yaoundé. We were 12 Anglophones in number, and we started a hunger strike to ameliorate our conditions. We were rather transferred to an underground bunker [dungeon] at the Gendarmerie headquarters at the *Secretariat d'Etat á la Defense (SED)* where we succeeded to produce and smuggle out a video on 05/08/17 to tell the world how they were killing us slowly. Two months later, I was transferred, along with others to Kondengui Central Prison on 12/10/17. Till date that's where I am.

*Fabiano was never tried in a court of law for lack of evidence. He was released from the notorious Kondengui Central Prison along with about 40 other Anglophone youth caught up in the authoritarian dragnet of the Biya republican chiefdom, after a presidential decree. Fabiano Deco joined the throng of immigrants headed for Europe and arrived at a country where he lives a precarious existence "under the radar."

Conclusion

As we have noted throughout this volume, the Anglophone Question was caused by a lack of democracy and dialogue in Paul Biya's authoritarian, neo-patrimonial republican chiefdom, where the rule of man takes precedence over the rule of law. It is the result of an autocratic system of law and disorder where might is right. In Cameroon, the law takes precedence over rights and accused persons are considered guilty until proven innocent, the burden of proof being on them. This chapter presented the voices of the victims of Paul Biya's war of political, cultural, and above all, economic subjugation of the former British Southern Cameroon–for purposes of controlling its natural resources. The hundreds of political prisoners in his prisons, whether sentenced through French language-only show trials at the Yaoundé Military Tribunal, or awaiting trial for years at the notorious torture chambers of the SED, the overcrowded dungeons and human cages of Kondengui or Mfou Prison–the very system Anglophone lawyers, teachers and members of the civil society had demonstrated to be distanced from– the tens of thousands of refugees languishing in refugee settlements in Nigeria, and the hundreds of internally displaced persons in the Francophone and Anglophone Cameroon, represent a collective indictment of the political and legal system of the Biya republican chiefdom. The Anglophone problem demonstrates the lack of separation of powers in Cameroon and shines a spotlight on the cruel and tragic lack of independence of the Cameroon judiciary, where President Biya is the Supreme Magistrate who appoints and dismisses judges and presides over the Supreme Council of the Magistrature. The crisis exposed the lack of due process of law, the preponderance of law over rights, the superiority of military tribunals over civilian courts, and the court-martial of Anglophone civilians in French language-only military tribunals, which have a system of presumption of guilt rather than innocence. It is a system characterized by lengthy detentions without trial and incarceration of political detainees awaiting trial for political offenses in the same overcrowded and inhuman conditions as convicted criminals. The chapter also discusses the arrest of Sisiku Ayuk Tabe and 12 members of the Interim Government of Ambazonia, at the Nera Hotel in Abuja Nigeria, the detention, and extraordinary rendition, without due process, of these men, who were either legal residents in Nigeria or asylum seekers registered with the United Nations High Commission for Refugees, to Cameroon for trial at the Yaoundé Military Tribunal, demonstrated that Nigeria is, like Cameroon, a country of law and disorder. After all, there really is no extradition treaty between the two countries. The extraordinary, extra-legal rendition of Cameroonian political asylum seekers from Nigeria to Cameroon demonstrated that the Buhari regime in Nigeria had no respect for the rule of law, due process of law, and international law. Nigeria has a system of the rule of the state over the rule of law. The spirited but futile submissions of Barrister Femi Falana and his team of human rights lawyers, demonstrate that despite the Buhari regime's contempt for the rule of law in Nigeria, as well as international principles governing refugees and asylum seekers, human rights lawyers worth the name refused to keep silent in the face of these egregious violations of human rights.

Afterword

At the onset of the Anglophone Revolt, President Paul Biya signed a decree creating a Code of Military Justice. This decree created a military tribunal in each of the 10 regions of Cameroon. The decree granted the president the power to create more than one military tribunal in certain regions. Article 4 of the decree stipulates that in exceptional circumstances set forth in article 9 of the Constitution, serious threat to public order, to the security of the State, or terrorism, the Yaoundé Military Tribunal may exercise jurisdiction on the entire national territory." Additionally, the judges and investigating magistrates (prosecutors) of the Military Tribunal may be "either Military Magistrates or Civilian Magistrates." They are appointed by a decree of the President of the Republic" (Law No. 2017/012, 2917). Additionally, the Minister in charge of military justice, has the power to transfer military judges–and civilian judges drafted to serve in military tribunals–to other jurisdictions for a maximum of six months. In situations where a civilian magistrate presides over a case, the decree stipulates that he must be assisted by two military judges/assessors. Military Tribunals have the competence to judge all cases of terrorism, state security, cases involving firearms or armed robbery, and importation of military attire and equipment. The Yaoundé

Military is a jurisdiction of first and last instance. Its decisions cannot be appealed to the civilian Supreme Court. The President of the Republic and the Minister in charge of Military Justice (the Minister of Defence) can, at any moment, order the termination of cases before military tribunals at any stage of the proceedings (Law No. 2017/012, 2917). This decree essentially militarized justice in Cameroon, blurred the lines between military and civilian justice, brought the judiciary further under the ambit and control of the executive (the Republican chieftain), and eliminated the presumption of innocence. It essentially removed the biggest legal and constitutional issue in the history of Cameroon, the Anglophone Revolt, from the jurisdiction of the civilian courts. It was yet another nail on the coffin of the comatose common law system in the former Southern Cameroon (Northwest and Southwest regions). We have seen the Yaoundé Military Tribunal in the Trial Observation Report of Dr. Brilman of the Law Society of England and Wales (See Chapter 26).

In 2023, the country witnessed a case that was heard in a regional military tribunal, the Military Tribunal of Buea. In effect, the Buea-based Center for Human Rights and Democracy in Africa (CHRDA, 2023), which is headed by former political prisoner, Barrister Felix Nkongho Agbor Balla reported the story of a pregnant woman by the name, Kongnso Antoinette Gohla. She was arbitrarily arrested and tortured by one Chief John Ewome Eko, a Cameroonian soldier who is popularly known as Chief Moja Moja, who doubles as a traditional ruler of his village, near Buea. Kongnso Antoinette Gohla was arrested, tortured, and detained at the Buea prison in 2021. She gave birth in prison and stayed there with her baby until she was brought before the Buea Military Tribunal in 2023, after 16 months in pre-trial detention. She was formally charged with "failure to report terrorism" because she happened to be the former girlfriend of the dreaded separatist fighter, 'General No Pity' who operated in the Northwest region. The Buea Military Tribunal sentenced her to time served (16 months) and imposed a fine of 65,000CFA (about $110) (CHRDA, 2023).

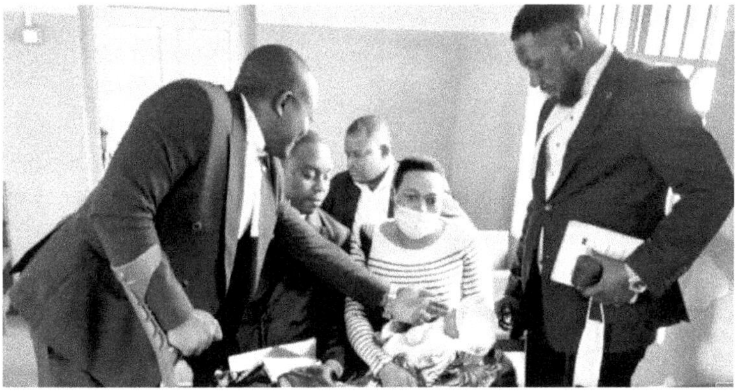

Figure 22.4. Kongnso Antoinette Gohla with her baby and lawyers at the Buea Military Tribunal (February 2023)

References

Ambazonia, Army Hunts Amba Fighters After Death of Five Troops (2023). Chinese News Agency (Xinhuanet). Retrieved from Cameroon Intelligence Report: https://www.cameroonintelligencereport.

com/ambazonia-army-hunts-amba-fighters-after-death-of-five-troops/

Ambazoniagate: Barrister Nalova speaks of the NERA 10 and the Abuja Abduction (2019). Cameroon Intelligence Report, January 8th. Retrieved from: https://www.cameroonintelligencereport.com/ambazoniagate-barrister-nalova-speaks-of-the-nera-10-and-the-abuja-abduction/

Fofung, A. (2020). Cameroon: Outrage as Anglophone detainee dies while chained to hospital bed. Pan African Visions. Retrieved from: https://panafricanvisions.com/2020/08/cameroon-outrage-as-anglophone-detainee-dies-while-chained-to-hospital-bed/

Freudenthal, E. (2019). Inside Cameroon's Bunker: Different guys had different torture techniques. African Arguments, May 7. Retrieved from: https://africanarguments.org/2019/05/inside-cameroon-torture-bunker/

Holy See Press Office Communique: Audience with the President of the Republic of Cameroon (2017). Communique N. 170323e, Thursday, March 23. Retrieved from: http://press.vatican.va/content/salastampa/en/bollettino/pubblico/2017/03/23/170323e.html

Presidency of the Republic (2017). Loi No. 2107/012 of 12 July 2017. Creating a Code of Military Justice. Retrieved from: https://www.prc.cm/fr/multimedia/documents/5695-code-justice-militaire

Tabot-Tanyi, A. (2023). Martinez Zogo Affair: Dismissal of two judges has opened up debates about poor delivery of justice. Cameroon Intelligence Report. Retrieved from: https://www.cameroonintelligencereport.com/martinez-zogo-affair-dismissal-of-two-judges-has-opened-up-debates-about-poor-delivery-of-justice/

TWENTY-THREE

The Human Victims of the Autocratic Republican Chiefdom

Anglophone Refugees and Internally Displaced Persons

LYOMBE EKO

> Always avoid violence. If you succumb to the temptation of using violence in your struggle, unborn generations will be the recipients of a long and desolate night of bitterness, and your chief legacy to the future will be an endless reign of meaningless chaos.
>
> Martin Luther King, Jr.
> Sermon at Dexter Avenue Baptist Church, Chicago, Illinois (1956).

We saw in chapter one that after a year of demonstrations by Anglophone lawyers, teachers and others calling for change, on October 1, 2017, crowds took to the streets to peacefully commemorate the symbolic "independence" day of Southern Cameroons. The Cameroon military, led by the Israeli-trained and equipped *Bataillon d'Intervention Rapide (BIR)*, the *Gendarmerie Nationale*, and police opened fire on the unarmed Anglophone civilian demonstrators in Buea, Kumba, Mamfe, Bamenda and other towns in the English and Pidgin-speaking Northwest and Southwest regions, killing dozens. In response, a fledgling Anglophone separatist, None-State Armed Group (NSAG), the Ambazonia Defense Force (ADF), led by Lucas Cho Ayaba, retaliated by attacking and killing six members of the Cameroon armed forces in Agbokem-German, Manyu, Southwest region, near the border with Nigeria. In November 2017, President Biya declared war on the separatists. Shortly thereafter, his government triggered the largest refugee flow between Southeastern Nigeria and Cameroon since the Nigerian Civil War (1967-1970), when refugees escaping the Biafran war crossed from eastern Nigeria to Cameroon. In 2017, President Biya succumbed to the temptation of violence. His decision to opt for a military solution to the Anglophone Problem rather than dialogue, triggered a flow of refugees going in the opposite direction. Thousands of Anglophone refugees started crossing into Nigeria from the Southwest and Northwest regions of Cameroon, headed mostly to a life of deprivation, hunger, poverty and suffering in United Nations High Commission for Refugees (UNHCR) settlements

(Unah, 2020).

Figure 23.1. Cameroon Anglophone Refugee Camp sign, Ogoja, Cross River State, Nigeria

Aim of the Chapter

From time immemorial, political prisoners, refugees, exiles, political asylum seekers, and internally displaced persons (IDP) have been the hallmarks of war, civil strife and conflict. The Anglophone Crisis in Cameroon is not an exception to that rule. This chapter aims to lift the veil on the refugees and internally displaced people that the atrocities and human rights violations of the autocratic republican chiefdom of President Biya spawned, like so much detritus, in its attempted military subjugation of the English and Pidgin-speaking, former Southern Cameroons, and its forceful assimilation into the highly centralized, megalomaniacal, neo-patrimonial, Napoleonic, *République du Cameroun.* President Paul Biya's attempts to use extreme military violence and political obduracy to solve the political problems between the English and Pidgin-speaking minority of Cameroon and the Francophone majority led to predictable consequences–thousands of deaths, human rights violations, refugees and internally displaced persons. In Francophone Cameroon political circles, the Anglophone refugee problem does not exist, just like the Anglophone problem does not exist. Anglophone refugees are never mentioned in official pronouncements and the official state media. For strategic and national interest reasons, France, the United Kingdom, China, Russia, Switzerland, Israel, Nigeria, and other countries that have an economic stake in the longevity of the authoritarian republican chiefdom of President Paul Biya, the Anglophone crisis in Cameroon quickly lost its salience in the international community, to the point where the Norwegian Refugee Council called it the most neglected international crisis in the world despite the massive atrocities and human rights violations that were taking place there (Cameroon tops list of neglected Crises, 2019). This situation was compounded by the splintering of Anglophone "resistance" in the Diaspora into contending factions headed by egotistical "presidents." This chapter surveys the origins of the Anglophone refugee problem from its genesis in 2017 to 2023. It is informed by the operational updates of the United Nations Office for the Coordination of Humanitarian Affairs (OCHA), which works with Cameroon refugees through the UN High Commission for Refugees (Nigeria) and its national partners, the National Commission for Refugees, Migrants, and Internally Displaced Persons (NCFRMI), and the State Emergency Management Agency (SEMA) of Nigeria. Thereafter, the chapter delves into the lived experience of two victim groups of the Anglophone crisis: Anglophone refugees in Nigerian refugee settlements and internally displaced persons in Cameroon. In effect, the violence of the Anglophone conflict also displaced more than one million Anglophones from their villages and towns in the Northwest and Southwest regions. These internally displaced persons ended up in areas of relative calm like Buea and Limbe in the English-speaking regions and Dschang, Bafoussam, Nkongsamba, Yaoundé and Douala in French-speaking Cameroon. This chapter gives a group of refugees and internally displaced persons an opportunity to tell their stories of what drove them to seek political asylum in Nigeria or leave their villages and settle elsewhere in Cameroon. The premise of the chapter is that Anglophone Cameroon refugees in Nigeria, and internally displaced persons (IDPs) inside Cameroon are just a miniscule and insignificant part of the business activities of the billion-dollar global aid industry. The Nigerian partner of the United Nations High Commission for Refugees, the NCFRMI, exemplifies the power, ostentation, and prestige of the billion-dollar international aid industry that led Graham Hancock (1989) to call its powerful high officials the "Lords of Poverty." The NCFRMI's website showcases the ostentation of its finely attired, jet-setting bureaucrats attending international conferences, wining and dining with their European and American peers, rather than the refugees and Internally Displaced Persons (IDPs) in whose name it makes its money at the national and international levels.

Indeed, the NCFRMI was nowhere to be seen during the Nera 10 affair. This was the scandalous violation of international law by the Nigerian State Security Service, which abducted Anglophone Cameroon political refugees and asylum seekers from the Nera Hotel in Abuja, the Chalmas Hotel in Calabar, as well as other locations and deporting them to the Republic of Cameroon torture centers, military tribunals, and overcrowded prisons without due process of law and despite the lack of an extradition treaty between Cameroon and Nigeria. The illegal but lucrative Nera 10 affair showed that Nigeria was a partner with the Biya regimes in violating international law. NCFRMI hypocritically lists non-refoulement (extraordinary and extra-judicial rendition) on its website as a violation of international law, knowing full well that the Buhari regime had extra-judicially deported the Nera 10, as well as hundreds of other Anglophone political asylum seekers and refugees–and their wives and children– to Cameroon to face torture, court-marshal, lengthy imprisonment, and death. For the Biya regime, Anglophone Cameroon refugees did not exist at all. The refugees and asylum seekers were considered "Biafrans," --the epithet some Francophones call Anglophones–– who had returned to their Nigerian "home." In Nigeria, the name Biafra was an epithet that recalled the bloody Nigerian civil war in which President Buhari had participated.

Genesis of the Anglophone Cameroon Refugee Problem

In September 2023, the United Nations Office for the Coordination of Humanitarian Affairs (UN-OCHA), the United Nations High Commission for Refugees (UNHCR) and its Nigerian government partner, the National Commission for Refugees, Migrants, and Internally Displaced Persons (NCFRMI) reported that, "Over 87,000 Cameroonian refugee men, women, and children are registered in Akwa-Ibom, Anambra, Benue, Cross River, Enugu, and Taraba States" (Cameroon Refugees in Nigeria, 2023). These refugees are English and Pidgin speakers from the Northwest and Southwest regions, who were driven from their homes either by the atrocities of the Cameroon military or the exactions of None-State Armed Groups (NSAG) in both regions in the context of the Anglophone crisis. Thousands of children have been born to Anglophone Cameroonians en route to or in UN refugee settlements in Nigeria. They know no other reality. The Nigerian government's policy of abducting key Anglophone political asylees and refugees–including those registered with the UN High Commission for Refugees–and handing them over to the Cameroon government, in violation of the international norm of non-refoulement, made Nigeria a clandestine transit point for many Anglophone refugees and political asylum seekers heading to other destinations. Many Anglophone Cameroon refugees, fearing for their safety after the arrest and extra-ordinary, extra-judicial rendition of the Nera 10 from Abuja and hundreds of others from Calabar and other locations to Cameroon, where they were detained in torture centers, were tried in the French-language-only Yaoundé Military Tribunal, given life sentences, and incarcerated in over-crowded, disease-infested prisons, moved from Nigeria to Ghana and ultimately to the Middle East, Europe, and the Americas.

The Cameroon Anglophone refugee exodus was triggered by the violent response of the Cameroon republican chieftain (the Chief of State) to the peaceful political demands for change made by lawyers, teachers, churches, students, and other members of the civil society in the English and Pidgin-speaking former Southern Cameroons, now split into the Northwest and Southwest regions of Cameroon. Francophones call these regions "le NOSO" (Willis et al. 2019). By 2023, the crisis had left more than 10,000 people dead–including more than 1000 Cameroon soldiers, BIR, gendarmerie, and police– and more than one million internally displaced.

The mass movement of Anglophones to Nigeria and parts of French Cameroon was triggered in November 2017 by Joseph Oum II, the Cameroon President's hand-picked Francophone *prefet* in Manyu Division in the English-speaking Southwest region. Francophones call the president's appointed *prefets* and *sous-prefets le chef de terre* (lord of the land). That means he is the all-powerful "president" of the region's administrative division or county. After the Biya regime decided to solve the problem through military means, Prefect Joseph Oum II issued a prefectorial decree expelling the inhabitants of 15 villages in Akwaya, Eyumojock, and Mamfe sub-divisions en masse (CHRDA, 2019). In the decree that was broadcast repeatedly on the local FM radio, Mr. Oum II ordered the expellees to "relocate to safer neighborhoods {sic)." (See Prefect Oum Joseph II's decree expelling the inhabitants of certain Manyu villages). The Cameroon army had declared the 15 villages theatres of military operation. Mr. Oum II gave the villagers only hours to pack their belongings and set off on a journey to nowhere! Oum ended by saying that those who did not vacate their villages would be treated as terrorists by the military.

The announcement struck the villagers of the named localities like a thunderbolt. It led to the familiar images the world has seen over and over again in areas of war and conflict around the world. Thousands of panicked men, women, and children carried bundles of whatever possessions they could on their heads and fled their homes. Women carried small children on their backs and held others by the hand. They quickly left their villages and headed for the Nigerian border, which had been ordered closed on the Cameroon side after clashes between the Ambazonia Defense Force (ADF), an Anglophone Non-State Armed group, and the Cameroon armed forces in Agbokem-German. The refugees soon formed a river of humanity that headed East towards the Manyu River, the border between Cameroon and Nigeria. Others headed North, South, and West to nearby villages and localities to escape the 15 "condemned" villages on the Cameroon government's list. Since the riverine border between Nigeria and Cameroon is porous even in the best of times, refugees used bush paths and canoes to hastily cross the Manyu/Cross River into Nigeria. Villagers from Akwaya, a virtually inaccessible place known as "Mamfe overside" because it was easier to get there from Nigeria than from Cameroon, moved en masse to Nigeria. Whole villages streamed across the border into Cross River State, Nigeria, Fortunately, for those early refugees, people on both sides of the Cross River had cultural affinities, and so were welcomed by their "kith and kin," who considered them "brothers and sisters."

Cameroon security forces, led by the notorious BIR, soon descended on the condemned villages. They set in motion a scorched-earth policy that amounted to collective punishment and left death and destruction in their wake. Whole villages suspected of supporting armed separatists were burnt to ashes. Sick, old, and infirm villagers who could not escape perished in the flames. The Cameroon military also engaged in mass arrests, summary executions, torture, and rape. As the Anglophone resistance spread, refugees also started flowing into Nigeria from Ndian, Akwaya, Donga Mantung, Nso, and Wum as the geography of military atrocities, collective punishment, and massive human rights violations was extended to all parts of the Anglophone Northwest and Southwest regions. The Cameroon government unleashed its military might on villages suspected of giving aid and succor to Anglophone None-State Armed Groups (NSAG) in both regions, sending their inhabitants fleeing for safety. According to the authoritative Buea-based Center for Human Rights and Democracy in Africa (CHRDA), within two years of the conflict, the Cameroon defense and security forces had attacked and burnt 206 villages in the Northwest and Southwest regions, killing thousands of people, displacing more than one million, who became internally displaced persons (IDPs) (CHRDA, 2019). By 2023, more than 87 thousand refugees had crossed into Nigeria, where they stayed either within Nigerian communities or in refugee settlements created by the United Nations High Commission for Refugees (UNHCR).

This massive military action and the mass expulsion of villagers were part of a strategy of military and political subjugation of English and Pidgin-speaking Southern Cameroons. In effect, at the onset of the military action in Manyu in 2017, Biya regime hardliners in the National Assembly, the ruling CPDM party, the official government media, and the state-affiliated private, tribal media outlets, all championed a military rather than a political solution to the Anglophone Problem. The main state-aligned private media was Vision4 TV, part of Jean-Pierre Amougou Belinga's *Consortium L'Anecdote* (Anecdote Consortium). The billionaire polygamist is a traditional chief, whom his semi-private Vision4 TV addresses as, "*l'homme d'affaire billionaire, Sa Majesté Jean Pierre AMOUGOU BELINGA, Chef Supérieur des Mvog Belinga*" (The billionaire businessman, His Majesty Jean Pierre AMOUGOU BELINGA, Supreme Chief of the Mvog Belinga) (Cameroun, *Sous le Thème Royal*, 2021). The ethno-political orientation of Vision4 TV and the Anecdote group, which includes newspapers, is due to the fact that His Royal Majesty, Jean Pierre Amougou Belinga is from the same Bulu/Beti ethnic group as President Biya. It is, therefore, no surprise that Vision4 TV was closely aligned with and served as a bulwark of the Biya regime. Ernest Obama, the former News Director of Vision4 TV and a commentator on the same channel, Jean Jacques Zé, revealed the thinking of the ruling elite on the escalating Anglophone crisis. Jean Jacques Zé declared on Vision4 TV that the Cameroon military "operations" in the Anglophone Northwest and Southwest regions were nothing but pest control measures, a *deratisation* or rat extermination exercise. Ernest Obama, sitting on the set next to Zé, nodded in agreement and added that President Paul Biya had been too lenient on Anglophones. These Vision4 TV "journalists" had essentially transformed the station into the Cameroonian equivalent of *Radio-Télévision Libre Mille Collines* (RTLM). This Rwandan radio station had fanned the flames of genocide by spreading dehumanizing hate speech against the Tutsi minority and calling for them to be exterminated like cockroaches (Three Media Leaders Convicted for Genocide, 2003).

Figure 23.2. Cameroon Anglophone refugees in Ogoja, Cross River State, Nigeria (2018)

The Rise of Anglophone Warlords

As the Anglophone Revolt degenerated into armed conflict due to the Biya regime's decision to use military means to solve the political problem, namely, the discontent of Anglophone Cameroonians, led by lawyers, teachers, churches, students and other members of the civil society, the None-State Armed Groups (NSAG) assumed a strident, separatist posture. They declared that they were fighting for a separate state they called Ambazonia. Warlords with exotic and exalted names like Field Marshall, General No Pity, General Die Man, General RK, General, Grandpa, General Cross and Die, General Mad Dog, General Ten Kobo, etc. emerged from all parts of the Northwest and Southwest regions. Each NSAG owed allegiance to and received funding from competing, fractious, Anglophone factions in the Diaspora, notably the United States, the United Kingdom and Canada. These NSAG often switched allegiances between a number of self-serving, power-hungry Ambazonia leaders in the United States and the leaders of the jailed Interim Government led by Sisiku Ayuk Tabe. The fractious nature of the separatist movement ironically made it difficult for the Cameroon military to crush the revolt because it became a metaphorical hydra with multiple heads. Before too long, these separatist groups became known in the English-speaking Northwest and Southwest regions by the sobriquet, "Amba Boys," a term that took an increasingly negative connotation as the NSAGs began to prey on villagers or villages to support the conflict. These imposed "liberation taxes" on business owners, arrested people and held them to ransom, and severely punished those whom they labeled as "blacklegs," anyone they suspected of collaborating with or giving information to the Cameroon military. They banned the sale and consumption of all beer produced by Les Brasseries du Cameroun, a French-owned brewery, as well as other brewers in Francophone Cameroon, including the Irish brewer Guinness. This disrupted the livelihoods of thousands of beer distributors, bars, nightclubs, and off-licenses. They kidnapped and killed Cameroon central government officials in the Northwest and Southwest regions and set fire to government buildings. They imposed a strict ban on education, to enforce the teachers' strike that had been called in 2016, and enforced Monday "ghost town" strikes in both regions. Whole villages were caught between the excesses and atrocities of the Cameroon military and the exactions and impositions of the Amba Boys. This reality triggered the exodus of Cameroonians into refugee camps.

Before the flow of Anglophone refugees to Nigeria and internal locations actually began, Anglophones in the Diaspora wrote open letters to the European Union and the Swiss Confederation, from whose territory President Paul Biya ordered the 1st October 2017 massacres, fore-warning them about the reality of a new African refugee crisis, but they gave a deaf ear to the pleas of the Anglophones (See attached letter in the appendix 2). European–French, Swiss, British– and Israeli economic and strategic interests trumped human rights considerations. It was months after the human rights atrocities had swept the Anglophone regions that the European Parliament passed a resolution condemning the human rights violations of the Biya regime (See European Parliament Resolution, Appendix 3). To make matters worse, the Cameroonian government closed the border with Nigeria. That did not stop thousands of Southern Cameroonians from seeking refuge in Cross River and other Nigerian states. The Cameroon Anglophone refugees were initially welcomed with open arms by Nigerians on the other side of the Cross River due to ethnic and linguistic affinities between Cameroonians and Nigerians on both sides until they overstayed their welcome. As we saw in chapter 20, on Friday, January 19, 2018, the Spokesman for the United Nations High Commission for Refugees (UNHCR), William Spindler, informed the world of Africa's latest humanitarian tragedy, the refugee crisis in the

Northwest and Southwest regions of Cameroon. Speaking at a press briefing *at the Palais des Nations*, the United Nations headquarters in Geneva, Switzerland, Spindler told the world that more than ten thousand refugees (mostly women and children) had crossed the border from Cameroon to Nigeria and that "Thousands more are among the population of unregistered Cameroonians in neighbouring states." Mr. Spindler seemed to be blissfully unaware that President Paul Biya had triggered the refugee crisis at the InterContinental Hotel, less than a mile from where he was holding his press conference.

Figure 23.3. Cameroon Anglophone refugee children in Nigeria studying on desks provided by Anglophones in the Diaspora

Nevertheless, the UNHCR, working with the NCFRMI, the Cross River State, and the State Emergency Management Agency (SEMA), dutifully set up several refugee camps for Cameroon Anglophone refugees in places like Ogoja, Ikom, Adagom, Boki, Amana, and other locations in Nigeria (Cameroon Refugees in Nigeria, 2019). The population of refugees in these camps increased rapidly as Cameroon security forces intensified their atrocities, and more civilians got caught in the crossfire between Cameroonian security forces and Anglophone None-State Armed Groups (NSAG). Despite the massive human rights violations of the Cameroon military, the burning of hundreds of villages suspected of hosting, aiding, or abetting None-State Armed Groups (NSAG) in the Northwest and Southwest regions, and the deaths of thousands of people in the Anglophone conflict in Cameroon, it remained one of the most neglected conflicts in the world (Cameroon tops list of most neglected crises, 2019). The reality is that China, France, Russia, Switzerland, the United Kingdom, Israel, and other powers that have strategic economic interests in Cameroon helped prop up the Biya regime, ignored or downplayed the conflict and became partners in the crimes against humanity that his authoritarian republican chiefdom was perpetrating.

Narratives from the Lived Experiences of Anglophone Refugees in Nigeria

This chapter was not in the original table of contents of this volume. Like refugees and internally displaced persons, it was an outcome of the crisis. The original focus was on the historical and contemporary aspects of the Anglophone Question in Cameroon. The material in this chapter essentially presented itself to the author. As we have noted throughout this volume, the Anglophone Question was caused by a lack of democracy and the megalomaniacal obduracy of Cameroon's authoritarian, neo-patrimonial republican chiefdom. President Biya is the perfect example of a regime of rule by decree in which the rule of one man, Paul Biya, takes precedence over the rule of law. The Anglophone problem is, therefore, the result of his autocratic system of law and disorder where military might is political right. As we saw in Chapter 22, in this regime, the president is the Chief Magistrate of the republican chiefdom, and military justice, which falls under the executive, takes precedence over civilian justice, which is traditionally under the purview of the judiciary. This makes the president the incarnation of the executive, the legislative and the judiciary–he wears the robe of the judge and the legislator's suit under his chiefly robes. In Cameroon's system of law and disorder, the Almighty State has absolute sway and control over the citizen, who is essentially the government's property. In this system, human dignity, human rights, justice, fairness, and individual privacy are non-existent. The citizen's person and belongings– including his or her home, cell phone, and vehicle–are subject to search at all times without the benefit of a warrant. Any text message, internet address, phone number or image in any cell phone may lead to arrest, detention, torture, and imprisonment. Being found in possession of these incriminating communications is tantamount to guilt and is therefore grounds for arrest, torture, imprisonment and execution (see Chapter 11 for a narrative of the murder of journalist, Samuel Wazizi while in Cameroon military detention).

In 2014, a bizarre case involving three Anglophone students, Fomusoh Ivo Feh, Afuh Nivelle Nfor, and Azah Levis Gob, revealed the extreme perversity of the Biya regime's oppressive justice system to the world. These three Anglophone high school students were arrested and detained at the infamous torture center at the Gendarmerie headquarters, the Secretariat of State for Defence (SED) in Yaoundé. Their crime? Sharing a sarcastic joke on their cell phones about the difficulty of getting a job, any job, in Cameroon without connections and good exam results. The joke said that even Boko Haram, the murderous Islamist terrorist group fighting in Nigeria and North Cameroon, now required prospective recruits to have good results in their exams. The Cameroon government did not think that joke was a laughing matter. After months in detention, the three students were tried at the infamous Yaoundé Military Tribunal and convicted of "non-denunciation of terrorist-related information" (failure to report terrorist-related information to the authorities). On November 2, 2016, they were each sentenced to 10 years imprisonment (McVeigh, 2017). Civil society and human rights organizations around the world were scandalized by the parody of justice. They condemned the detention, court martial, conviction, sentence, and imprisonment of the students as a violation of the right to freedom of expression. The Biya regime turned a deaf ear to appeals from Amnesty International and multiple other human rights organizations to free the students. After seven long years behind bars, the Cameroon

Supreme Court upheld their conviction for failure to report terrorist-related information to the authorities but reduced their sentence to five years imprisonment on December 16, 2021. They were released after serving a total of seven years in pretrial detention and in prison. The tragedy is that the joke shared by the students was lost on the Military Tribunal and the Supreme Court. It never occurred to the learned men and women of the law that the joke was the young student's critique of the lack of opportunities in Cameroon. This monumental misunderstanding might have occurred because the joke the students shared was in English, while the Yaoundé Military Tribunal and the Supreme Court are French-language-only institutions, which may not have grasped the subtleties of the joke. The students were essentially convicted of mentioning the name Boko Haram! This was a small but significant exemplar of the Anglophone problem in Cameroon. The fact is that in Cameroon, Anglophones suspected of being federalists, secessionists, or "terrorists" –or sympathizers of these groups–are considered guilty, prosecuted before military tribunals, and jailed for long periods of time. The burden of proof of innocence is always on the accused. The case of the three students who spent seven years in jail for a sarcastic joke is an indictment of the political and legal system of the Biya republican chiefdom.

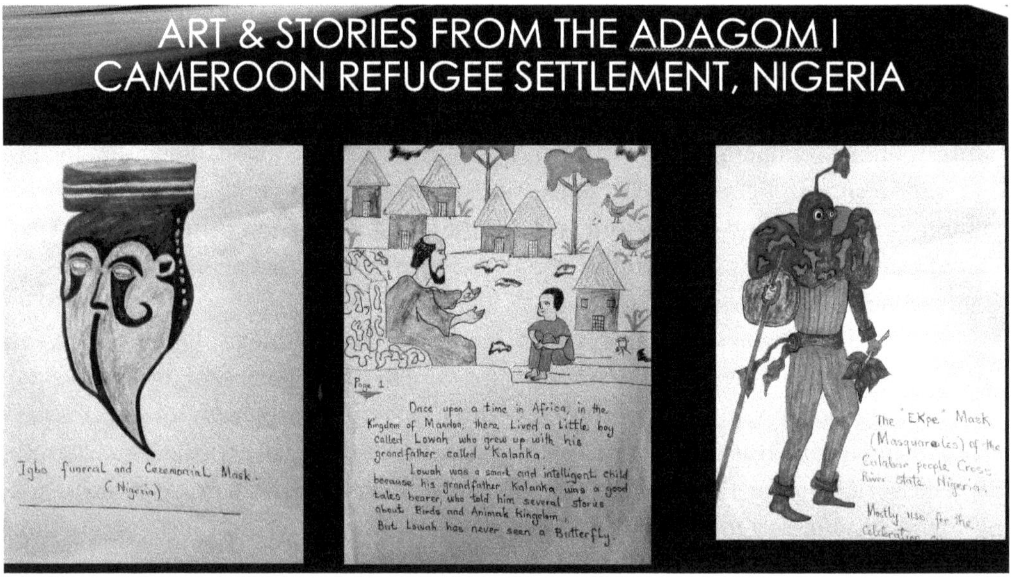

Figure 23.4 Art and Stories from Nigerian refugee camp

Voices From the Road to the Unknown: Stories of Escape to Nigerian Refugee Camps

At the onset of the Anglophone crisis, I decided to do my duty as an African intellectual who was born in Southern Cameroons, then part of the British Empire, to keep a record of the revolting and unspeakable atrocities and human rights violations that the autocratic republican chieftaincy of President Paul Biya was visiting on the place of my birth. I undertook this task because the victims of these crimes against humanity included my relatives, friends, and neighbors. My record of the happenings in Southern Cameroons took the form of a weekly Facebook post entitled "Chronicles of the Anglophone Problem." The entries were weekly summaries of the unfolding tragic events of the Anglophone Revolt. My goal was to record, for posterity, my revulsion at the duplicity and hypocrisy of Biya's international partners in crimes against humanity: Emmanuel Macron's France, Queen Elizabeth II, David Cameron, Theresa May, and Boris Johnson's United Kingdom, Benjamin Netanyahu's Israel, the Swiss confederation, the Canton of Geneva, Xi Jinping's China, Vladimir Putin's Russia, and Mohammadu Buhari's Nigeria. My *Chronicles of the Anglophone Problem* was also intended to be an expression of indignation at the powerlessness of the African Union, the United Nations, the European Union, the British Commonwealth and the *Organisation de la Francophonie* in the face of President Paul Biya's blatant violations of the United Nations Universal Declaration of Human Rights, and the African Charter of Human and People's Rights.

My Facebook page was followed by about one thousand people, a miniscule number by social media standards. Before too long, I received a friend request from someone named "Efasa Mote" who was based in Nigeria. That was clearly a pseudonym because it is a variant of Ehvarz'a Mote" (literally, Half-Person), the deity of the Hwakpe (Bakweri) people of Hvako (Fako) Division in the Southwest region. This person was probably a former student of the University of Buea, who was familiar with the Hvako deity, but how he wrote it indicated that he was not a native speaker of the Mokpe language. Efasa Mote wrote that he had contacted me on Facebook to ask for help for Anglophone refugee children, some of whom had been born in the bush and survived as their pregnant mothers escaped to Nigeria. In contrast, others had been born in Nigerian refugee camps. He said that Anglophone refugees (the majority of whom were women and children) were being stalked by hunger and the spectre of starvation. He said that though hunger was their constant companion, education was more important to them than food. Could I help them purchase some benches and exercise books that volunteer teachers (themselves refugees) could use to teach children the basics in the refugee camp? He attached pictures of children sitting on the floor in an overcrowded hall, with no space between them, and a teacher attempting to teach them. It appeared to be a jam-packed, one-room refugee preschool in which the children had no desks to sit on, books, or pencils. As an educator, that message and the images stopped me dead in my tracks. I decided to do some research. I checked the websites of the United Nations High Commission for Refugees (UNHCR, Nigeria) and the Nigerian National Commission for Refugees, Migrants, and Internally Displaced Persons (NCFRMI). All I found were bureaucratic public relations texts and pictures of the bureaucrats of UNHCR and NCFRMI attending international conferences in places like Geneva and New York, resplendent in their elegant and expensive clothes. Other pictures showed them celebrating World Refugee Day (June 20) in pomp, circumstance, and textile finery that could turn the heads of habitues of the French and Italian high fashion industry.

I was skeptical and told Efasa Mote that his request sounded like something that should be addressed to the United Nations High Commission for Refugees (UNHCR) and NCFRMI. I told him I was not in a position to feed and educate a whole refugee camp. His description of both organizations, as well as the State Emergency Management Agency (SEMA) of Nigeria, which seemed to be the administrator of Anglophone Cameroon refugee camps in Nigeria, was consistent with Graham Hancock's negative description of the international aid business as "Lords of Poverty" (Hancock, 1989). One of the pictures clearly showed an outhouse provided by the Norwegian Church Aid. Since Efasa Mote had said that many of the Anglophone refugees were former students, lawyers, teachers, and even a handful of soldiers who had deserted the Cameroon military rather than kill their own people, it occurred to me that these refugees could tell stories about the Anglophone Revolt and the atrocities, exactions, and crimes against humanity perpetrated on innocent civilians by the Cameroon military–led by the dreaded BIR–and Ambazonian Non-State Armed Groups (NSAGs), from their lived first-hand experience. I therefore made Efaso Mote a proposal. I would raise funds to buy a few benches for that refugee preschool. I created a GoFundMe account and used the proceeds to purchase the benches. Efasa Mote sent me receipts and pictures showing the benches and the children sitting on them. The next thing I did was to ask him if he could create a writing circle where refugees could get together, write down their stories and send them to me for future publication. I promised I would pay each writer a few dollars for every story I received. The refugees enthusiastically accepted my proposal. They created a refugee writing circle which they named, "Voices from the Wilderness." This was a take on the Biblical story of John Baptist, the herald of Jesus Christ, who ate locusts and wild honey in the desert.

The Anglophone refugees in Nigeria wrote their stories on paper, took them to an Internet café near their refugee settlement, and paid a small fee for Internet access. They typed the stories on Facebook Messenger and sent them to me as messages. Voices from the Wilderness was composed of an average of 17 members. The number of members varied because some of the writers would stay a little while in the refugee settlement, join the writing circle, contribute a couple of stories, and then move on to other countries. Some headed West to Ghana and further North to the Sahara Desert with the hope of reaching Europe via Morocco, Tunisia, or Libya. Others set their sights on the United States and Canada via Nicaragua, Panama, or Mexico. The Anglophone former soldiers, particularly the former BIR were soon contacted by recruiters looking to fill security and bodyguard jobs in the Middle East. That is how we lost two of our best refugee writers.

Facebook Messenger thus became the platform that members of the Voices in the Wilderness writing circle used to post their stories for me to download. They started posting their writings at the end of 2018. Each month, Efasa Mote would collect stories from each member of the writing circle, combine them and post them on Facebook Messenger for me to download. Apparently, word of the refugee writing cycle spread from the refugee camps to people in internally displaced settlements. Before long, a number of internally displaced persons contacted me asking if they, too, could write their stories for me for a little food money. I agreed to receive their stories too. I pay the sum of $11 (eleven dollars) per story. That was equivalent to 3000 Naira or 6000 CFA. The stories of Anglophone refugees in Nigeria and internally displaced persons in Cameroon reproduced below are a few of the tens of stories that I have received via Facebook, WhatsApp, Telegram, or my official university email.

Voices from the Wilderness

The flow of refugees from the Anglophone Northwest and Southwest regions to Nigeria was an alarming development given the dangers and hardships displaced persons are confronted with. They have to navigate multiple existential challenges ranging from survival in the forests: crossing rivers and waterfalls in the dense rain forest, ever-present hunger and thirst, encounters with wild animals like crocodiles, pythons, cobras, and monkeys; dealing with snake and scorpion bites, the sting of poison ivy, the bite of malaria-bearing mosquitoes, wasps, soldier ants, leeches, black flies, and ticks; swift river currents, typhoid fever, human predators, rape, violence, and exploitation of the weak and the helpless on lawless the borderlands between Cameroon and Nigeria. The story below was posted on my Facebook Messenger application by Efasa Mote, the coordinator of the Voices from the Wilderness refugee writing circle, a collective of writers from several refugee settlements in Cross River and other states of Nigeria. The writers wrote the titles and sub-titles. They mostly used pseudonyms due to the precarity of their status as refugees and fear of retaliation from Nigerian security officials who could send them back to Cameroon for any reason. These first three stories are refugee stories of escape from the atrocities visited on innocent Anglophone civilians by the Cameroon Military and Southern Cameroonian/ Ambazonian Non-State Armed Groups (NSAGs). In the first piece, the writer, OJ Boy describes his escape from Cameroon to Nigeria through the Korup National Park. He describes the devastation the conflict brought to humans and wildlife in the Korup National Park in the Southwest region.

The Korup National Park and Its Untold Stories, As Told by OJ Boy

The Korup Forest is widely known as the Korup National Park (KNP) or the Korup Reserved Forest (KRF). This reserve and wildlife conservation sanctuary is located in the Southwest region of Cameroon, precisely between the Ndian and Manyu forest zones. It ranges from Mundemba town right up to Ejagham land in Bajoh village. Some of the villages found in the Korup National Park are: Bareka-Batanga, Ikenge, Ngenye, Mofako, Bera, Esoki, Erat, Esokotan, Ikondokondo, Baro, Bajoh, just to name these. The Korup Forest has an escape route immediately you cross the Bajoh river in Obang land directly towards the border areas with Nigeria in Cross River State. It serves as a gateway of survival for many Ambazonian victims escaping from the murderous attacks of the Cameroun armed forces.

Escape Routes for Survival Through the Park

> My survival in this forest was a difficult and terrifying experience to recount. The routes are not clean and clear enough for people to just find their way out to their various destinations. You must struggle by following any track you find that appears better. It is dangerous to follow every track you meet in the park while moving. This is mainly because some of these little footpaths lead to areas where you will find rivers with big waterfalls, which are the natural habitats of crocodiles and pythons. These meandering trails cross each other because the movement of the forest guards and other park workers is facilitated by using compasses and GPS. They do not

move following straight lines. As a result of these confusing trails, all of us who ran and entered the KNP for refuge to escape the Cameroon army suffered for several weeks in the dark and dense tropical forest because we always missed our way and went in the wrong direction...

This dense tropical rainforest is very hilly. The topography is absolutely stony and coarse, making movement very difficult and tiring. Sometimes, we slept by the foot of several hills. On this course, struggling with the challenging environment, adaptability and nutrition remained an unending problem. From time to time, we had to search for some common forest fruits like "Monkey Kola," as it is commonly called and also eat another special fruit from a tree known as "Okoyon" by the Ejagham people of the Manyu division. This fruit tree bears reddish fruits in bunches that look like strawberries. The most dangerous experience I and my family encountered in the KNP was crossing rivers and streams in the forest. Many fast-flowing rivers always overflow their banks during the rainy season, and that was the period we found ourselves making use of this escape route from Cameroon to Nigeria. Though natural tides and heavy rainfall account for the overflowing waters, it is believed by the natives that the "water witchcraft spirits" of the local villagers are responsible for the overflowing of the bodies of water because they need human beings for their yearly sacrifices. In the area of the Korup National that was of interest to our movement, the German Development Service from Germany had only supported it with the construction of a modern hammock bridge across the Bake-Munaya River. It remains an undoubtful fact that we had to swim with the other rivers and big streams to get to the other side. In other rivers that cannot be crossed by swimming, we had to use small logs of wood from tree species that float on water and use forest ropes to make a local raft by tying the sticks together to form a platform on which we would sit and use another piece of stick as a paddle until we crossed the river. The season was not conducive to our movement. There were no dried or shallow waters to cross or food. We were living on wild fruits. We had plenty of edible fruits that sustained our daily living...

Sometimes, when we lacked energy, we picked a few eru [a wild forest vine that is a staple vegetable] leaves and chewed them to boost our energy banks. Amidst the ongoing conflict in the Northwest and Southwest regions of Cameroon, the Cameroon Government still has partial control of certain parts of the KNP, especially those axes of the forest that are close to town centers. Their control is unlike before. The conflict has scared away park workers, especially those attached to the Ministry of Forestry and Wildlife, who are predominantly Francophones. They too have escaped for safety to their hometowns and communities. The Ministry has grossly limited its activities and has witnessed acute shortcomings in managing this reserve forest. At first, when one entered the forest, one would meet at least a group of Forest Guards clad in their green uniforms at any distance of five square kilometers. They were there to ensure maximum protection of animal species and fishes in the waters and check other forms of exploitation in the park.

The internationally funded Korup Project ended in 2003. At the moment, the park is left with just a handful of workers while facing huge financial and logistical support deficits. At first, anti-poaching patrol brigades were spotted everywhere, destroying traps, arresting encroachers like hunters and seizing their guns. But today, a good number of these workers have retreated to towns and villages where KNP housing infrastructures are located or live as tenants in those communities. The most common areas where one can find forest guards are the KNP head office in Mundemba, Ndian, and the Nguti area office in Kupe Muanenguba, as well as the Eyumojock office in Manyu Divisions. These guards do not spend the night at their duty posts for fear of being attacked by the Amba Boys. They now move without their uniforms because many of their colleagues were attacked and killed in the forest by Amba Boys, and their Mark-4 guns were collected. So, they prefer to mingle with civilians to avoid being easily identified by the Ambazonian Freedom Fighters...

At Nguti, where the forestry office is located, one can take a look at what the Francophone forest guards do to secure their lives. At any drinking joint where the forestry guards intend to sit and relax, they politely call all the boys around the drinking spot, begging them to sit and share a drink with them. But if the boys hesitate, they use force to get them seated inside the bar with them. The boys have to be there until the forest guards are done with their drinking before allowing them to go. They are doing this because the guards know and have realized that whenever they sit together with the local Ambazonian civilians, their fellow Amba brothers, who are freedom fighters living in the forest, can never launch an attack on them because their loved ones and community people are there. Attacking the bar will endanger their lives. Many young men would quickly run away each time they saw these Francophone armed guards approaching from a distance to avoid being implicated as a blackleg sitting and wining with the enemies.

An interesting and dramatic scenario happened in Bakut village in the Ejagham area. There was a planned ambush by the Amba Boys on the forest guards. The moment the guards left the forest zone, the attack was launched; the panic-stricken fellows ran into the village, where each of them grabbed a child and gathered around the children, using them as human shields. The children were screaming, and the Amba Boys could not attack the Francophone forest guards because of the presence of the children. In the end, they let them go free and returned to the forest burning with anger. No child was injured due to this display of war-time intelligence. Entering the KNP illegally with the intentions of either hunting, trapping, fishing, timber exploitation, and harvesting non-timber products like eru and snails has never been an easy adventure. Even at a time like this, when the conflict is still ongoing, the risk factors are high. Before the outbreak of the crisis, the KNP engineers had long set up and planted hidden remote cameras all over the park. The purpose of these automatic GPS cameras is to pick images of hunters using their guns to shoot animals in the park. These kinds of cameras do not take images except when a gun is fired within a certain circumference. It immediately snaps and transmits the data to a radio reception center. Another type of cameras is hidden along the banks of strategic rivers with a huge fish population. This camera records every movement within a given distance, and the recorded data is sent to the office for examination. These cameras have caused the arrest, trial and imprisonment of several hunters, fishermen and other intruders. These technological restrictions have brought about a tremendous increase in the populations of many wildlife species. Once upon a time, in the Baro and Bajoh forest zones, herds of Elephants from the Park were rampantly invading the farms of villages. One day, the angry Chief of Baro village went straight to the forestry office at Nguti to complain with them...

The Forestry Delegate sent his agents to go down to the locus and bring him word. It was later established that there was massive destruction of the crops and farms of people of the said community. The Forestry Chief then issued a permit granting permission to the chief to shoot just one Elephant each time such an uncomfortable event occurred. The Chief returned smiling and broke the news to the Elephant hunters. With the law on his side, 19 stray Elephants were killed that year in Baro alone, while 4 Elephants went down in Bajoh with 3 in Abat village. Behold, the Forestry authorities did not allow the chiefs to take the tusks. They took them away and said it was state property. This is the lone legal advantage we have benefited so far since the creation of the Korup National Park engulfing our ancestral lands.

Korup National Park and the Anglophone Conflict

Immediately after the Cameroun-Ambazonia crisis started, all local hunters, elephant poachers, trappers, fishermen, et al., were very happy as the Francophone forest guards were no longer patrolling the interior parts of the Park. Hunters of all categories invaded the forest by night from all the neighboring communities and destroyed all the visible automatic cameras, thus giving them free access to this reserved forest. Within 10 to 13 months into the Struggle, the Amba boys in this area experienced a severe scarcity of food since everyone in these localities was running into Nigeria. Hunger was beating them day and night, and there was no money. They devised a remedial strategy, and an ordinance was enacted, signed, and sealed by the Amba generals stating that all exploiters in the KNP must be levied exploitation taxes upon entry into the Park for whatever reason. Particular emphasis was placed on timber, elephant poaching and harvesting of Eru. This new management climate by the Amba Boys brought in a lot of anarchy. Many people who tried to evade the taxes were immediately found guilty, and they were severely beaten and thrown into local Amba cells pending the payment of bail bonds and other fines.

Nigerian timber dealers reaped enormous benefits from this opportunity. The Amba Boys generated huge amounts of revenue from these routine cash collections from the forest users. On a sad note, the ordinary villagers are bitterly disgruntled on two fronts: when the Cameroun Government was controlling the park, they were restricted from using the forest, and today, with the new government by the Amba Boys, all they receive is flogging and jailing by the Amba Boys. The Korup National Park, created in 1986 by a Presidential Decree, is of immense importance to the Government of Cameroun in the domains of tourism and education. According to written history, the Korup Forest is one of the oldest forests in the world. It contains many varieties of wildlife and is a natural ecosystem that is the habitat of many unique species of animals, trees, birds, and many different springs, fountains and other flowing bodies of water. This historical forest attracted many researchers, scholars in academic tourism and other tourists at home and abroad, fueling Government coffers. Many reputed institutions of higher learning have been coming to KNP to carry out research programs in this forest. Research institutes like John Hopkins University are conducting research in the area of animal blood, most especially on primate species and the ape category. The KNP serves the Government of Cameroon educationally as a field research site for universities and students nationwide undergoing studies in disciplines like forestry, botany, and holistic natural resource management. Such students use this natural environment for research and other practical activities. It is extremely interesting to mention that some years back, the largest male elephant in West and Central Africa was found in the KNP. It was located by a group of German scholars. They caught the elephant and fastened a tracking device with a belt around the neck of the giant beast. It was connected to the Global Positioning System (GPS), which allows animal monitoring via satellite. The device had a manual bell attached to it, and it jingled as the elephant moved around the forest. The German scholars never wanted the animal to leave the park zone because it had become the cynosure of all eyes and the focus of all animal-loving tourists. The idea of a forest reserve and the creation of the KNP was not breaking good news but serious embarrassment for the natives of the Korup ethnic group in particular. Many villagers around the park were not happy as the park's limits were extending over time, swallowing their native lands. However, a few nice words of appreciation trickled from a small fraction of the natives. They were happy because, according to them, the KNP project disenclaved some of their communities by giving them earthen roads and access to electricity and water supply. The KNP project helped finance the building of traditional village halls in Mundemba and my native Baro village.

Baro village was well electrified by the KNP, and our people at the time enjoyed a good water supply with regular repairs and maintenance of the water facilities. Also, KNP constructed an excellent farm-to-market road from Ediangho village to Baro. On a somber note, the villages in the park proper are none other than the Korup villages of Erat, Ikondokondo 1 and II, and Akwasang. With the extension of the park came the villages of Esokotan, Ikenye, Esoki, and Mofako and their forests. Their forests have been grabbed, and they have very little land left to cultivate their own cash crops. They no longer have any access to their forests. As rural Africans whose livelihood and sustainability solely depend on farming, depriving them of their forests is a grave threat to their general well-being. Apart from the Ikondokondo people of the Korup ethnic group who were resettled between Mundemba and Fabe, all other affected villagers who were evicted from their native lands are yet to be resettled.

The human versus elephant conflict continues in Korup... All because of the laid down forestry laws in Cameroon declaring certain animal species as endangered and subject to protection, the elephants dwelling in the park as well as out of the park have become a great threat to human beings and their crops. These anti-poaching restrictions have caused an alarming increase in the number of elephants per square kilometer. They now encroach into the farms of natives in a manner most invasive and abusive. These destructive elephants will, in one night, eat a farm of plantain and bananas while smashing the entire farm. This usually happens during the rainy season, in the months of July and August. In the same line of destruction comes the chimpanzees. They love eating young plantain leaves and young palm fronds. It is their delicacy. The wild swine is also not left out. They go in to devour cocoyam and cassava farms. Thus, the relationship between the natives and the park authorities is as sour as lime juice.

The life of an elephant is valued more than a human being based on the degree of protection accorded to these beasts both in the law courts and the forest. Each time farmers complain about the damages they have suffered because of the illegal activities of elephants on their farms, their matter is not taken seriously. When an elephant kills a man, it is no news, but when a man kills an elephant, the long arm of the law begins to run its entire course. The whole system has broken down due to the crisis.

...The Korup National Park (KNP) has served and will save a lot of Southern Cameroonian victims of the brutal attacks from the Cameroun Armed Forces and as a safe escape route to the nearby Nigerian communities.

The original tensions between the natives of the villages taken over by Korup National Park and the Government made it easy for the Amba Boys to take over the Park and impose taxes on anyone entering the Park to hunt for bushmeat. Nigerian loggers have also benefitted by paying the Amba Generals to cut down giant trees for timber. Those who refused to pay the taxes imposed by the Amba Boys or disobeyed their orders were called "blacklegs," enemies working with the hated Government. Those who obeyed the Amba Boys or had connections with them were called "terrorists" by the Government and subject to being killed on the spot or arrested, tortured and sent to Yaoundé for military trial. All those animals that have been protected for decades are no longer safe. We, the ordinary villagers, were caught between the harsh killing machine of the Cameroon military and the merciless Amba Boys. We had no choice but to cross through KNP to enter Nigeria and head to the refugee settlement at Adagom, where we were registered as refugees with thousands of other helpless villagers. We are strangers here, but we are free from the atrocities of the Cameroon military and the harsh demands and flogging of the Amba Boys and their Generals.

Damned if You Are Seen to Work for the Government… or a Government Minister

The story of the devastation of Korup National Park due to the mismanagement of relations between the park and the villages whose lands and forests it swallowed, as well as the political intransigence of the Cameroon government, on the one hand, and the predatory activities of the Amba Boys on the other, demonstrated another aspect of the top-down, authoritarian, ethno-patrimonial, republican chiefdom of President Paul Biya. This put millions of innocent villagers across Southern Cameroon in a "damned if you support and damned if you do not support scenario." The villagers are caught between the bullets of the Israeli Tavor assault rifle, the bullets of the AK 47 assault rifle, and the hunting rifles of the Amba Boys. This next narrative presents why an Anglophone who had a business association with a Cameroon government ministe-r found himself in a refugee settlement in Cross River State, Nigeria. The story was posted on my Facebook Messenger by the "Voices in the Wilderness" writing project.

Who Saved My Life? – Alem

I am a typical Banya man from Menji in the Lebialem Division of the Southwest region of Cameroon. Though the school bells were ringing in my ears, I dropped out of technical school just after I had my CAP certificate in building and construction, and I joined others in the practice of this trade. I was born and bred in Menji some forty-five years ago and my father was a big cocoa and coffee dealer while my mother, who is still alive and lives in the US with my younger brother retired as a primary school teacher. After a couple of years as a builder working for other contractors in Menji, Mamfe, Kumba and Muyuka towns, I gained a lot of experience, and I moved up the ladder by becoming a contractor and recruiting others to work for me in different building and construction sites that I was engaged in. Though I made some money, marriage was like a thorn to my flesh because I enjoyed living a free life like that of a modern-day playboy.

I chose my friends carefully by avoiding those who hated my lifestyle and flocked with those who spent money on beer, women and went to the best nightclubs in Limbe and Douala. I enjoyed nightlife on weekends. That was when I came to realize that, to the ordinary man and woman, weekends are for laundry, but to me and my kind of friends, it is for leisure and adventure into the thighs of beautiful girls worth admiring. In Munyenge community in Muyuka subdivision, there I established ten hectares of cocoa and built my first house as a young man who is aspiring to reach higher heights based on the type of contracts that were awarded to me, ranging from classrooms to building little bridges and culverts in my area.

In 2019, I became the main contractor to a top politician and government official from my hometown of Menji. He is no other person than Hon. Minister Paul Elung [officially ELUNG Che Paul] who is the Deputy Secretary General of the Presidency of the Republic of Cameroon. Back at home, I was building one of his bungalows. This imposing structure stood out as the cynosure of all eyes as the architectural framework was state-of-the-art as compared to others. Because of this contract at hand, I had to move to Menji to follow up on this work and make sure that I delivered on time, as hard work is my motto, and luck has always been on my side. This project coincided with the heat of the Anglophone uprising and the enforcement of the declaration of the independence of Ambazonia [by Non-State Armed Groups].

Paul Elung is a politician and a staunch militant of the ruling Cameroon Peoples Democratic Movement (CPDM). This is the political party in power, which secessionists and Ambazonian guerrilla fighters see as their enemy. Anyone sympathizing with this party definitely finds themselves in hot water. Many such persons, including traditional rulers, had to flee from Lebialem to places like Yaoundé and Douala in Francophone Cameroon for safety.

My trouble started in 2022 when I was still in Menji building another house for Paul Elung. Being close to him and working for him as his head contractor attracted the interest of the separatist fighters in Lebialem. The Red Dragons under Field Marshal Oliver Lekeaka opened my file [investigated me] due to all kinds of accusations and high-profile allegations against me.

It was said that I was not just a building contractor but also a spy feeding Paul Elung in Yaoundé with information about the operations of the Red Dragons of Lebialem.

It was concluded that I was using my smartphone to carry out this treasonous assignment against the people of Ambazonia.

My death warrant was signed by Field Marshal Oliver Lekeaka, who ordered my arrest and immediate execution.

One day, while I was working at the new site, a group of dreaded and heavily armed young men arrested me and took me deep into the forest where I was supposed to be killed. They were six in number. Two of them stood against the decision to eliminate me and insisted that they should take me to their main barracks. When we got there, I was given a snake beating, and I was stripped naked and locked in a cell. The famous warlord, Field Marshal, who doubled in capacity as the Paramount ruler of Lebialem, had gone on a mission with some of his strong men only to return by 4:00 pm. On his way into the barracks, he asked with an angry voice if they had killed that blackleg whom they went to arrest in town.

The answer was, "No! But he is under our custody," replied the mission commander who led the group that came and arrested me.

Field Marshal then said they should bring out the idiot so that he could kill him by himself.

That was how I was dragged out of the cell.

I then stood naked before Field Marshal; I was afraid to have eyeball-to-eyeball contact with him. When I lifted my head, and he saw me clearly, he wept and called me by my name.

He was shocked to know that I was the one he wanted to kill based on what they had told him about me. He sought to know what I was doing with my phone and if that phone was used to transmit information to Paul Elung. I told him that the phone in question was with his men.

He asked them to bring the phone and ordered me to open it. I did so, and he went through the phone, read the messages and listened keenly to all my conversations with Minister Paul Elung.

There was nothing incriminating, and he gave orders that I should be taken back to the cell.

Later in the evening, he asked his men to bring me to his lodge. I sat there with him as naked as I was born. This man was my relative, and he had to spare my life. He told me that if he allowed me to go, fingers would be pointed at him for partiality and discrimination. As such, I have to be in the cell for at least two weeks. He brought some clothes and ordered his men to put water in a bucket for me to take a bath, and thereafter, they should give me food. I wasn't sent to the cell anymore. I slept in some other quarters.

Three days later, he met me "licking my wounds" and sympathized with me. He told me that the only way out is that he can't set me free outrightly. We must play smart because the next day, as early as five in the morning, he is going out on a mission with his men. So, early that morning, I should take a bucket to fetch water from a stream, and that is how I am going to escape death. I couldn't sleep; I was impatiently waiting for that time.

I did as he said, and daylight met me at the banks of the little stream about one kilometer from the barracks. I kept the bucket there, crossed to the other side, and started finding my way out of the forest. He had asked me if I could find my way out of this forest through safe tracks without bumping into those Cameroon soldiers who are always laying ambush waiting for him and his men. I told him that I was a villager and a forest man, and I would make it.

I set out as planned and I spent two days trekking in the forest until I crossed the finishing line into my compound in the village.

Everyone knew that I had been killed.

They were surprised to see me alive limping with wounds all over my body.

News of this incident reached Minister Paul Elung and he swore to get Field Marshal Oliver Lekeaka dead or alive. Lekeaka was declared most wanted.

Was I really safe?

I abandoned the Minister's building and ran back to Muyuka. And in July 2023, I left Muyuka to Ogoja in Nigeria where just like others, I am in dire need of a Refugee Identity Card.

This prima facie document would facilitate my movement through Colombia to Mexico in South America. When I get to Mexico, my younger brother would take it up from there.

As I conclude, I have already acquired my transit visa and all I am waiting for is the Refugee Identity Card.

Editor's Note: *The dreaded Ambazonian separatist warlord, Field Marshal Oliver Lekeaka was killed in July 2022 by one of his men, and the Cameroon military publicly displayed his decomposing corpse in several towns and villages as a warning to other Non-State Armed Groups (NSAG) (Kindzeka, 2022).*

Tale of The BIR Deserter

One of the earliest and most disturbing videos of the atrocities visited on unarmed civilian demonstrators in the Northwest and Southwest regions of Cameroon in 2017 was a video from Bamenda. It depicted a group of soldiers from the army-within-the army of Cameroon, the BIR torturing and beating a very frightened, groaning, unarmed civilian, with a heavy piece of two by four plank (see appendix for link to the video that is still on the Internet). Soldiers of the BIR took the video of the torture as a souvenir of their zealousness in protecting the Biya regime. The video ended up on social media platforms and went viral. The BIR was subsequently shown harassing and carrying out a mass arrest of frightened young girls, rough handling them, shoving them, herding them like cattle, and forcing them to sit tightly together on the ground like frightened chickens. This time, the event took place in Limbe, in the Southwest region. Again, the video was shot by one of the soldiers involved in the humiliating spectacle and posted on social media. This was just the tip of the iceberg of the extreme barbarity and inhumanity of the BIR, which Israeli military officials had created to prop up and protect the Biya regime after a bloody coup attempt on April 6, 1984. Members of the BIR considered themselves "commandos" who were "licensed" to kill innocent civilians with impunity. And they did so again and again in the Northwest and Southwest regions. Dissemination of the videos also showed that some members of that elite military corps were not comfortable with the excesses of their battalion that is why they made these human rights violations public. However, the BIR was not invincible. A good number of BIR soldiers and officers were killed in clashes with Ambazonian Non-State Armed Groups. At the same time, some members of the BIR who were from the Northwest and Southwest regions decided that they would no longer take part in operations against their own people, sometimes in their own villages. Many deserted to Nigeria and registered as refugees with the intention to continue on to the Middle East, Europe or the Americas. In effect, international "security brokers" had gotten wind of the availability of well-trained, English-speaking Cameroonian military men in Nigeria and recruited them for "security" jobs in the Middle East. Unfortunately, for some of these BIR deserters, who entered Nigeria as civilians, they were arrested by the Nigerian State Security Service and handed to the Cameroon military for hefty fees, without benefit of a court trial. A group of BIR deserters and their families were arrested at the Chalsma Hotel, 7 Otop Abasi Street., Calabar, and other locations, and handed over to waiting Cameroon military aircraft, without benefit of a court hearing. They were flown to Yaoundé where they were detained at the notorious torture chambers of the Secretariat of State for National Defense, which is popularly known by its French acronym, SED. They were subsequently transferred to the notoriously over-crowded Kondengui Central Prison. Sources say at least 10 Anglophone former members of the BIR have been in pretrial detention at Kondengui since 2018.

However, some members of the BIR got away. After they deserted, they slipped into Nigeria, registered as refugees in refugee settlements. Once they received their refugee identification or Temporary Protection Status identification card from the United Nations High Commission for Refugees (UNHCR), most of them moved to Lagos, Abuja, or Accra, where they were secretly recruited by agents of international security firms, provided travel documents, and sent to the Middle East or Europe. The narrative below was posted on my Facebook page in September 2021 by an unknown individual called "Massa Petro", a former BIR who deserted, slipped into Nigeria and stayed in a couple of refugee settlements before being recruited for a security job in the Middle East. He joined the Voices in the Wilderness writing circle in the refugee camps when he first arrived in Nigeria. He wrote the story below while waiting for his Refugee Identification Card from the UNHCR. It appears he slipped back into Cameroon and became a trainer of a number of Anglophone

Non-State Armed Groups (NSAG). The training Cameroon army and BIR deserters provided Ambazonian separatists in the Northwest and Southwest regions, explain in part why the armed resistance has lasted since 2017. Massa Petro vanished into thin air as soon as he received the Temporary Protection card at a refugee camp in Nigeria. He also vanished from Facebook. All attempts to reach him and get more writings from him were in vain. However, my sources at the Voices in the Wilderness refugee writing circle and the few Anglophone BIR deserters I had been introduced to on social media while writing this book, confirmed that they had met him and that he had been recruited into the international security business in the Middle East. The recruiters were on the lookout for former Cameroon BIR, Anglophone or Francophone, for security jobs. They valued the Israeli training they had received in Cameroon. Below are the three messages Massa Petro left on my Facebook Messenger in box in 2021. All attempts to discover his identity or reach him were fruitless. He just vanished into thin air.

BIR versus Boko Haram by Massa Petro

I am "Petro." My friends call me "Massa Petro" because they think I am solid as a rock when I play defence in football, like Peter in the Bible. I am native of xxx, a speaker of the xxx language from xxx Division of the xxx English-speaking Region of Cameroon…. I am not a good history student, but events around me have opened a book in my mind for the in-take of memorable moments in life as time goes on. I am proud to say that I was once an element [member] of Cameroon's *Rapid Intervention Battalion,* better known by its French name and acronym, *Bataillon d'Intervention Rapide* (BIR). I deserted work together with a handful of other Anglophone brothers in 2017. A good number of them are refugees and asylum seekers already living in the civilized world in places like Dubai, Germany, the United States and Italy. Unfortunately for me, I am still in Nigeria living in a refugee settlement. Will I make it in this life in Nigeria where things are getting so hard?

Without mincing words, I used to like my job as a trained commando who joined this elite force in 2008. We were well-equipped, well-trained and better paid than other units of the Cameroonian Armed Forces. We were the pride of President Paul Biya who went to bed without closing his gates because we were watching over the national territory. We quenched several unrest and uprisings in Cameroon, and Mr. Biya had confidence in our Israeli-drilled comrades. The regular army of Cameroon bitterly envied us in all aspects of military life. We were not military collaborators; there was always tension between elements and officers of both units at different levels and places, even in beer parlors. The regular army of Cameroon had its baptism of fire during the days of the Bakassi palaver between Cameroon and Nigeria in the 90s, and those days were gloomy and bloody as they were pregnant with all manner of uncertainties. The soldier's life was in the hands of his enemies and not himself.

We experienced real fire with the rise of the Boko Haram insurgency in the Far North Region of Cameroon. A counter-terrorism force was put in place, and the BIR was at the forefront alongside troops from Nigeria, Niger and Chad, to fight against Boko Haram. Boko Haram increased in strength every day because anti-Biya militia groups also joined them to destabilize the entire sub-region. We had first-hand confessions from those we arrested. My maiden march as an armed commando took me to the Far North of Cameroon in 2014 when President Paul Biya of Cameroon said, "we are here to declare war on Boko Haram." This declaration signaled the direct involvement of our combat unit of the Armed Forces. All was set; there was anxiety, but not without fear. Not just rumors, but I had watched disturbing videos of how Boko Haram militia slaughtered Chadian and Nigerian soldiers. These grave images were playing on my mind as I had never had an encounter with this group, and this was going to be the first confrontation.

When your name appears on the list of those to go fight Boko Haram for three months, you feel like dying before being butchered by those wild Boko boys. After my successful training, I was posted to Isongo in the West Coast area, near Limbe. Each time our comrades returned from the Far North, panic gripped the whole camp. It is not that we were not happy to see and receive the survivors, but many things were involved. This time around, you had the chance to watch live videos of actions in the battlefields from the smartphones of our comrades. I saw images of Boko Haram fighters with horribly looking faces with charms tied all over their bodies. These were believed to be potent bullet-proof charms. No matter what, my name was already on the list pasted on our notice board. I was bound to join my comrades to go to war for the love of my fatherland. Those soldiers who went to the Central African Republic for a UN Peace Keeping Mission returned home with huge amounts of money while we were facing death at every ticking of the clock.

Two hundred men from different BIR camps were airlifted from the Douala International Airport, and we landed at the Maroua-Salak Airport in the Far North Region of Cameroon. Salak, a village locality, served as our military base. We were going up on a mission to either relieve our comrades who had been there for about three months, or we were beefing the number of men with boots on the ground. Those whom we met alive were happy to see us. There was no turning back. Boko Haram has thousands of fighters, including women and children, and oftentimes, these categories of persons are used as involuntary or forced suicide bombers. That notwithstanding, there are those who willingly offer themselves to die in a bomb blast, dying for what they considered a just cause. They always target crowded places such as markets, and they hate churches with all the bitterness of their souls. At times, you'd find a brand-new motorcycle parked somewhere in the middle of the sandy grounds. Don't go for it, it has a bomb attached to it. Once you touch it, it explodes.... We had no time to cook, and we relied solely on bread and sardines for our daily food rations. You also never had to joke with your water bottle. Later, an American company was stationed in Maroua to produce highly nourishable biscuits, which complemented our bread and sardines. Surely, because of the food crisis, when Boko Haram shoots and kills either a civilian or Cameroonian army soldier, in most cases, they struggle to carry the dead body and run away with it. They'd butcher it and share it among their comrades, make soya [skewers], cook it and eat it with boiled cereals. That is why you'd always find fewer healthy corpses of enemy forces littering the sandy Sahel grounds. We always deeply mourn when a comrade falls in their midst because we know his flesh will surely be eaten by those cannibals. These people make poisonous videos of such events and share them on the Internet. After a few weeks of intensive fighting, one day, Boko Haram ambushed us in little groups and gave us a shocking attack in Kolofata, which left over 100 soldiers dead and I was fortunate to be counted among the survivors. But that was not the end of the war! Honestly, those of us who were alive did not have the morale to continue fighting. We had to retreat to base while Yaoundé was kept posted on the horrible incident. Our superior officers quickly called for backup. In my experience, fighting Boko Haram is just like fighting the entire forces of evil unleashed upon mankind, gathered in one big village. They devise unknown and unfamiliar strategies to counter our invasion of their hide-outs. They even use civilians in the villages they attack and conquer, as human shields. They always stand behind them while firing at us.

Regrettably, the casualties on our side have always been relatively high, but communiqués from Cameroon's Ministry of Defense have always lowered the figures in terms of soldiers who fall on the battlefields. There was a time when I was moved to the unit operating rocket launchers. I was new to this unit, but I had no option; we were at war. The comrade I worked with, a certain Onambele, was already an expert and I came in as an assistant. Boko Haram no longer saw ordinary bullets as a potential threat. We went to a particular open place, dug a new trench, filled several bags with sand and mounted them around the trench to a certain height of about 1 meter above the ground while allowing space in the middle to turn around and begin to fire the grenades at oncoming targets either on foot or in vehicles. My immediate responsibility was to watch his [Onambele's] back and sides standing right there with an automatic rifle; he was my commander, and I took orders from him.

One day, my commander was unwell after firing rocket-propelled grenades for over two weeks, killing scores of Boko Haram terrorists. He asked me to take his place in front of the trench while he went out to seek medical attention. Another comrade was sent to take my former position in the trench. After firing for a whole day carrying the launcher on my left shoulder, I automatically developed problems with my hearing; the left ear was blocked, and the right one was no better. I only had my eyes to use. I thought as much, was I permanently deaf, or was it just temporary? I could not hear anything again, and my comrade was laughing at me as I had never heard a single word that he spoke. It took some time for me to regain my hearing. There was a time when we killed them [Boko Haram] in great numbers. We were gladly under the command of Lt. Colonel Bouba Dobekreo.... Lt. Colonel Bouba Dobekreo is always at the forefront leading by example with his powerful rifle, demonstrating as a commander. This his unique military character kept our morale high as we took a posture to fight the enemy till the last man standing. He encouraged us to collect the enemy's materials each time we had the chance to safely do that.

When we come back from Boko Haram campaigns, our wives are always full of anxiety. Many are shocked to comprehend that their own husbands did not return. Oftentimes, the sad women would march straight to our Colonel's Office demanding to know the whereabouts of their husbands. "Your husband is still in the battlefield in the Grand Nord," says the Colonel. The women, with grieving hearts and mourning souls, would just understand that their husbands were dead, and they were now widows. They'd retire home in a mood so lamentable. At times, we broke that oath of secrecy and began to comfort them; we had knowledge of the truth, which can never be hidden forever. The fortunate women would receive their husbands with open arms and legs even if they were badly injured....

From a Soldier to a Civilian: Why I Deserted the BIR

I am now in a refugee settlement in Nigeria. Everyone in the settlement has surely heard my story, and most of them sympathize with me and pity me for my present living conditions, which do not reflect my previous status. I earned close to 300,000 FCFA per month as my basic salary. But when we go out for missions, the amount is worth the risk. There are those who look at me using different lenses, even if they do not empty their minds in my presence. There are flashbacks of reality in the way I when my conscience starts playing those military drumbeats, bringing shame and guilt as my closest companions. I surely do not owe them any detailed explanations relating to how and why I left my job and became a refugee. This disclosure would be weaponized against me. It is not uncommon in history, both past and present, to hear of soldiers who escape, leaving their comrades on the battlefields. Some go for good while others, especially in liberation movements, join the insurgents.

I am human and blood runs in my veins and aside from being a soldier, I come from a family of people, a tribe of people and a fellow from the English-speaking minority within the political contraption called Cameroon. An Anglophone in the Cameroon Defense Forces is purely an alien in the midst of so-called comrades or colleagues. Even with your eyes closed, you can still see the difference. Many of my Anglophone [BIR] brothers have disappeared during the heat of the Ambazonian crisis and no one knows a thing about them. There was a day when we went out after Amba Boys in a locality in Fako [Southwest region]. When we got to the community, we couldn't find the insurgents, so we gathered the folks to tell us what they knew about those boys and the reasons why they were sheltering them and feeding them. While we were talking to the people of that community, we asked them to sit on the ground, and one of them started speaking in French, telling the soldiers that he was not one of those supporting the Amba Boys, that he was a Bamileke man [from French-speaking Cameroon] and not an Anglophone. I got furious and greatly embittered. I just came from behind and gave him a shot in the head, and he died on the spot. None of my colleagues offered even a single word. Finally, nothing happened to the other civilians until we left the community. We all as human beings do pray for our days on earth to be longer and filled with livelihood satisfaction, prosperity and a better and brighter future for our children. I believe this angle should be every sane man's dream; if not, he could be considered a lower animal whose lives do not really matter... In my locality, chickens are in trouble during the Christmas period, and sheep are not safe during Muslim religious festivals... Do my people's lives really matter? Cows are taken to the slaughterhouse every day, but my people are slaughtered by their own Government. We have rendered many of them homeless, and we have forced them to leave their villages and communities and run into strange lands.

Then, I started to wonder aloud if our lives mean anything to politicians and even our own military hierarchy in Yaoundé. I decided that it was time to leave. While I was still at the refugee reception camp at Ikom, I enjoyed the solidarity of the people, and I rarely encountered moments where I felt ashamed of having left my job. They encouraged me and showed me lots of love and kindness. But here on the Settlement at Ogoja, some refugees do provoke me, calling me names such as run-away BIR, who is a run-away soldier, who is a typical example of a coward. They mock at me and tag me with all sorts of degrading names and scandalous titles. In the face of all these temptations, I try as much as I can to always maintain a civil temperament in order to contain their aggressive utterances. They looked at me, a former BIR, with bitterness because of what my battalion, the BIR had done to their homes, villages and family members in the Northwest and Southwest regions. Some of these words are very painful, but I have no choice but to endure their bitterness. After all, insults don't kill a man, but bullets do; they are mere civilians who know nothing about guns and what they do to humans. Their words keep piercing my heart like a Fulani man's sword. Some would say, if I were not a coward, then why did I abandon service and disappear into thin air? All these sets of biting questions have short answers which the ears of men may hear but with great shock and dismay.

There are many Amba Boys who come to this refugee settlement. They come in different ranks, from camps and for different purposes. And when they get to know that there is a BIR element here, they grow wild, and it is as if they should devour me with their bare hands. They see me as their enemy and wouldn't want me to get anywhere close to them. I am not the only Cameroon soldier who fled to Nigeria. I have identified a junior and younger colleague living at the refugee settlement…. Jones deserted work [the BIR] in Bamenda, out of annoyance and extreme anger. He was part of a team of BIR elements who went down to Widikum and killed scores of villagers alive in their homes. Jones is an indigene of that Widikum court area. Before his own eyes, he saw the carnage meted on his own people in several villages. Dying villagers were pleading for mercy in the language of his birth. Jones did what he did and had worked out his plan pretty well; he made up his mind to leave the BIR. He had the rare opportunity of appearing on the headlines of several tabloids when he shot and killed one of his superior officers, ran away into the forest with four pieces of AK-47s and automatically joined the Amba Boys. Jones became an Ambazonian fighter. But why did he not stay with them in the forest for long after a series of successful operations that he led against his former comrades? The short answer is commandership squabbles within the barracks. He was unanimously raised to the rank of Mission Commander. Many of the old fighters did not genuinely welcome the appointment. They never threw their weight behind this decision. They started scheming on how to get him out of the way. One day, a serious fight erupted in their barracks pitting Jones and another fighter. During this fight, he sustained a serious wound on his head which caused him to bleed profusely.

Since it was evident that his life was on the line and the brewing bitterness in the hearts of his brothers, the forest was no longer a place to be. Everything moved along the lines of jeopardy. Those who eyed his position hardly took orders from him and they were always picking faults and looking for the slightest opportunity to deal with him. Therefore, Jones chose the best option, which was to find his way to Nigeria since his wife and baby had already made moves in that direction. Jones is now a refugee registered with UNHCR with a family size of 4 persons. He is now a livestock farmer rearing pigs and goats and also fattening broilers for sale. His wife runs a provision store at the reception. But, when you take a close look at Jones' head, you'd see the scar borne of the injury he sustained during the senseless fight in the forest. He is an introvert and spends his time around his premises and with his family.

During my registration process at Ikom where we were camped, I never disclosed my identity to the immigration officer and the UNHCR staff. The questions were straightforward. They wanted you to tell them exactly what happened to you that caused you to flee from Cameroon and cross over to Nigeria. The immigration officer kept a firm gaze into my eyes all through the interview. It was ok by me, and I did not panic but softened my facial expression so that my countenance would depict someone who actually needed help. I did not carry my professional card nor my Cameroonian National Identity Card during this exercise for fear of the unknown. The officer asked to know from which part of Cameroon I came. I told him that I am from xxx Division in the North West Region. After staring at me for some time, he asked me to tell him the capital of the North West Region. I smiled and told him it is Bamenda, and he told me, "congratulations and welcome to Nigeria."

And at the end of the exercise when I sat in front of the UNHCR staff on duty, I knew that I had already crossed the bridge. Here, I was asked simple questions like my date of birth, place of birth, religion, marital status and level of education. That was how they issued me my printout, and I was successfully registered and handed a prima facie document commonly called "progress paper" or "fact sheet." And after two weeks, I was issued my refugee identity card. My wife is in xxx, Cameroon, with our three children living with my maternal aunt. I have a large plot of land there which I bought while I was still in service. Now that things have turned inside out for me, I have communicated and instructed my wife with whom all the documents are in her keeping, to put the land on sale and even advertise it on Facebook. I bought this piece of building plot for 2 million FCFA. I have been on my knees all this while pleading with my wife and aunt to sell the land. My legally married wife is willing, but my aunt is refusing to endorse the move for the transaction to commence. Honestly speaking, the value of the land has even tripled based on its strategic location. I intend to use part of the money to process my documents and travel to Dubai where I have gained employment in a security firm. While my wife would go into business in order to support our family. But here I am, marking time while my biological clock keeps its ticking pace undisturbed. I don't know what my aunt is up to! Things can never be the same again since i can't go home and be free to move about. The military would not spare me even for one second once they got to know that I was around. My pictures and bio-metric data are everywhere. What do I do at this juncture?

Training Ambazonian Insurgents in Akwaya and Beyond

I am a trained commando who had served in the Rapid Intervention

Battalion, better known by its French acronym, BIR. It is a dreadful wing of the armed forces of the Republic of Cameroon. This force is often referred to as "*les enfants de Paul Biya*" (the children of Paul Biya). Aside from carrying a gun, a soldier needs to be trained in the handling and maintenance of his weapon and, above all, fighting tactics, and to be disciplined. This is what often takes me to the forest to meet with the Ambazonian Freedom Fighters, not just to encourage them but to invest in them the wealth of skills I have acquired while I was a soldier with the BIR unit of the Cameroon armed forces. I have been to many Ambazonian military camps, particularly those along the border between Cameroon and Nigeria. I have encountered the good, the bad and the ugly in the hands of several armory commanders within these camps. But as an experienced soldier, I always calm the tides and cool the storms. At one time, I went to the Ejagham land on the invitation of General Die Man. Upon my arrival, the reception I had from a handful of the fighters was not the least cordial. The warmth of brotherhood was not there because of who I had been before, and the circumstances that led to me deserting the BIR remained largely unclear to many of them. In the midst of all this emotional display, General Die Man and his Commanders heartily welcomed me and hailed me for the brave decision I took to leave the circles of evil. They acknowledged my good work with the many Amba camps that I have visited. He told me to feel free and feel at home. It took some time for the other fighters to embrace my presence as one could read suspicion glittering in their eyes each time our sights collided. Yes! I came for a purpose and my mission must be accomplished. That was the first day and I took time to acquaint myself with the premises and then ask a few pertinent questions that would help me get along with them.

Immediately, I went down to work and did my best to repair their weapons, especially the Pump Actions and the other automatic rifles. I later gave them lessons and practicals on the various positions to take when confronting an enemy. I hilariously remember at one time, with a well-loaded AK-47 in my hands while I was in the training grounds with these fighters, I heard several voices coming from the fighters. They spoke in their native Ejagham dialect. Their faces were gloomy, and I immediately decoded that something was wrong somewhere. General Die Man kept smiling and he was looking at me while I gave orders commanding the fighters to take certain positions and postures before firing. Finally, he burst the bubble when he told them, "Petro, you see here is harmless; take him as your brother, and he has a lot to offer, and many have benefited from his simplicity". I now understood what was running on their minds. Their greatest fear was that I could turn around, change my mind and open fire on them. But that was far from being true. I have given up on the Cameroon army, and there is no going back. My feeding was well taken care of, including drinks like plain whisky, which they have in abundance. I ate lots of plantains, cocoyams, and fufu with different types of soups inhabited by bush meat. Some of the boys are professional hunters. They go out at night with their Dane guns and come back with plenty of game. The camp has a drug department. This is not a clinic but a department that is well stocked with cartons of cigarettes, packages of marijuana, thai and cayou, tramadol and several injectable drugs and syringes. Unfortunately, I do not take any of the above except alcohol. After spending two weeks with General Die Man and his boys who numbered thirty and five, I left in peace with enough pieces of bush meat, dried snails and bush mango and returned to the xxx Refugee Settlement. Some fighters were ordered to, and civilians loyal to the Amba camp opted to bear my load until I left the forest.

Many young men involved in the Ambazonian Struggle as fighters have passed through my hands in gainful ways. They have received short courses in guerrilla warfare lasting over thirty days. I drill them in several combat techniques. Just returning from Mavas in the heart of the Akwaya grassland, memories of this savannah landscape and its undulating topography and the freshness of its waters and the air you breathe, make me really wonder if that isn't where God dwells with His angelic beings. It is a very picturesque countryside with direct contact with nature, surely unalloyed. The pleasure is always mine while visiting. Away from the eyes of a tourist interested in the wild, you have to be careful while threading that beautiful country because of the presence of Cameroon military men moving about with their guns in search of Amba Boys. You may be doomed to meet with them. Between God and Satan, it depends on whose angels may save you from the hands of these heavily armed and bloodthirsty human beings.

The Grassland Vultures of Mavas gave me a heroic welcome when I entered into their presence. When I got their distress call, l quickly responded to the urgency of the call by Major General Omega who is the Supreme Commander of Amba Boys in the whole of Akwaya. Some of their supporters who live here in these Settlements contributed money and financed my redemption trip to Mavas. I was escorted by some fighters who were returning to base. The Vultures had fought hard, and the Cameroon military retreated to Besongabang and beyond before the close of the year 2021. Upon their return, they sent word to General Omega that they were back in Akwaya to deal with them. Therefore, General Omega must not go to sleep for surprises may come their way. This message to the Vultures is not a good one since their guns had developed faults and they are almost without ammunition. Then we were on the tracks already moving down to the barracks. You avoid talking because you have covered yourself with spiritual darkness. In fact, you forget about speech and use sign language while being vigilant enough with your eyes wide open scanning the bushes as far as possible. And your ears as alert as those of a bush fowl. When you carry this mystical vegetable rope on you, you don't talk. Once you utter a word, cough or sneeze, the darkness opens automatically, and you are visible to your enemy. I believed in this rope when on one of my trips to Mavas, we met a group of Cameroon military men on the road. They were coming in our direction. Before stepping out, I was cautioned that once I saw my enemy, I should not panic; let me increase my belief in the juju that I was carrying. And that was what I just did when those soldiers were approaching us. We stood by the roadside, and they came and passed just close to us. I understood all that they were saying in French. They were insulting their Colonel that he is there enjoying in his cozy office while they are here combing the forest searching for Amba monkey. It was all fun, but the rules of the day did not permit me to even smile. We stood there, and they all marched and went away.

My fear was that, as I have experienced in the field, I had some colleagues whose spiritual eyes are open. When we used to go after Amba Boys, especially when we took them by surprise, they were the ones who led the search, and many Amba Boys who were covered by this darkness were exposed by these guys, and we apprehended them and killed them. No matter how hard they pleaded, they had to go down. There was a day it happened like that, and my Commander ordered me to shoot the Amba Boy and kill him. I had no option but to open fire on him. I thought his head had exploded because I had fired more than one bullet. Nothing happened to the body of this young man. Seeing what just happened, those spiritual BIR elements ran towards him. The Amba Boy crawled to a nearby pond of water and disappeared therein. These BIR mystics stood around the pond and made several incantations, but the boy did not come out. Well, we left!

With these memories coming up in my mind, I moved thereafter, almost with my heart in my hands until we got deep into the forest, yet no one was mad enough to break the silence. It is on record that many fighters and civilians have been ill-fated over the years as they have lost their lives on these tracks, eliminated either by BIR elements or the regular army. Here, with each step you take towards Mavas, in particular, you may be heading to your grave. But I don't care, I believe through my efforts, there are trained fighters in this zone who always launch brutal attacks on Cameroonian military men who are stationed in these areas. News of a run-away BIR element did not take long to reach the ears of interested quarters in Akwaya like the BIR, the Gendarmerie Brigade, the regular army, and the Police post. They aligned the bravery of these boys with the training sessions I have been holding with them. Now, their greatest wish is that they want to get me dead or alive at all costs and there is a price money on my head. Their informants have detailed them that, I do live in xxx, precisely at the xxx Settlement. There are fighters who have never touched a gun before, even the ordinary Dane gun used for hunting.[1] Many of these youths were students before the conflict escalated. Many of them joined the Struggle for diverse reasons. But the point of convergence is the freedom and independence of Ambazonia. It is a great task to take them through this learning process. A soldier must be trained both physically and mentally. The Ambazonian freedom fighters are totally different from the Biafran freedom fighters. The latter has boys and men who are used to all kinds of arms. Many of them have been armed robbers for a very long time until armed robbery has become their profession. With the increase in the illegal circulation of guns in Nigeria, weapons are in the hands of many men and youths. They have a mastery in handling guns and confronting the Nigerian defense and security forces. But the Amba boys are premature.

I gave them serious orientation and started training the fighters as freshmen. I did this in a place designated as a shooting range. I'd mount targets and give them Dane guns to shoot at particular spots. I always prefer they lie flat with their bellies on the ground before shooting. Within a few days, they'd know how to place the gun on the right chamber of their chests and how to aim at their target, manage their breath and then shoot to kill. From Dane guns, after successful sessions with them, we moved to start using AK-47 assault rifles. It is the finishing touches but also the most technical phase of the training. I take them through several operations. How to open the gun, the most important parts to take note of such as the selector switch-how to keep it safe such that it cannot fire, semi-automatic for firing single shots and automatic for firing continuously. Here, I noticed that most of the fighters did not know how to keep their rifles safe from firing, and in the course of handling them, especially when moving, they fired by themselves. Here, i did receive fighters from other sub barracks. From Dane guns, we move ahead with the use of AK-47 rifles. It is easy to fire an AK-47 but difficult to shoot with precision. Your bullets may fly totally off target all the time. When this happens while in the battlefield, you are in a big seat. So, this phase of the training involves even the old fighters. I take them through several operations. I teach them how to open the gun and the most important parts to take note of, such as the selector switch.

1 Editor's Note: The Dane gun was a "colonial weapon." It originally referred to many brands of a type of single or double, long-barreled flintlock musket imported into West Africa in the 19th Century by Danish and Norwegian traders. This rifle was very popular with Europeans in British, French, Portuguese and Spanish colonial settlements, where it was used to hunt game and maintain security. In the Anglophone conflict, the term "Dane gun" refers to remnants of these European rifles, as well as all variants of it that are made by African blacksmiths for hunting. They were sometimes used in intertribal conflicts (Dillard, 1975).

I tell them that the selector switch on the rifle is a very tricky part of the machine in their hands. I explained to them using the gear lever of a vehicle as the selector switch while the accelerator is the trigger. Here, I noticed that even the old fighters did not know how to keep their rifles safe from firing and in the course of handling it either sitting down or moving, it fires by itself. Many have died or sustained series injuries. I also taught them how to unload and load their rifles. Sometimes, I organized little competitions to get the best gunmen. In these barracks, I also noticed that most arms dealers supply old and faulty weapons to the fighters. These guns have serious malfunctions. They kick and become hot too often when fired even briefly. Many fighters carrying such weapons to the battlefield hardly ever return alive. I make sure I service all the machines and encourage the armory commanders to pay attention to what I am doing because, in my absence, they'd do the same. I use pure engine oil to service the guns and test them to find out their degree of effectiveness. I also train them in tactics to overpower your enemy even if he is more armed than you are, you attack and deliver a deadly shot and withdraw. Here, they undergo lots of weapons training, how to lay ambush and wait for their enemy to approach. I equally give them a bit of commando training to improve their physical resistance and build their muscles. I also showed them techniques in close-range combat. I discouraged excesses in alcohol consumption and drug abuse. Everything should be taken with moderation. You have the weapons, and you have undergone some training. If you are not ambushed, do you know when to go to battle? They all turned and looked at me with frozen mouths. This again became a priority area for me to hit on before closing remarks.

In many if not all the camps that I worked with, their mission commanders hardly plan their attacks. I drilled them on mission planning and information gathering. The state of their guns and the wellness of the fighter and components that must be fine-tuned before thinking of going for an attack. The Ambazonian Interim Government and other people abroad have promised to put me on a steady monthly allowance of 100 USD for me to work in the capacity of a weapons inspector and consultant in the border camps. But unfortunately, they have never kept their word. I am doing what I am doing with no remuneration. I have never made up my mind to accompany fighters to the battlefield. I only stay back and pray for them. On my way back from this hectic trip, I was escorted by a special squad of fighters until I got to xxx, where I took a vehicle that went straight to the refugee settlement.

Refugees of the Anglophone Problem: Women and Children

News coverage of refugees and internally displaced people who are obliged to flee their homes or countries and head for the uncertainties of refugee camps always feature the real victims of war and unresolved conflict, women and children. The senseless conflict triggered by the Cameroonian republican chieftain's refusal to dialogue with the Anglophone community is not different. The violent crackdown on unarmed Anglophone civilians by the BIR, the Cameroonian army, and the *Gendarmerie Nationale* sent women and children fleeing into Nigeria. The story below was contributed by a refugee who is a nurse by profession. She fled Cameroon with her child after the atrocities of the Cameroon military brought tragedy into her family.

The Cameroon Anglophone Theatre Nurse in a Nigerian Refugee Camp

I am Angela. My father is an Ejagham man from Eyumojock, Manyu Division while my mother was from Meangwe 1 village in Toko sub-division of Ndian Division. I am the only female child of my parents. I attended my primary school in Government School Manja, a village near Mundemba. I was trekking from a neighborhood called Ghana Quarter in Mundemba to the said Manja school. In the morning, I will eat cassava and palm oil. In the afternoon, I will eat banana and pepper mixed with Ngakanga or Akwana and pepper. Akwana is our staple, it is best served with pepper. Its scientific name is Zandozoma [Xanthosoma]. On Saturdays, we would go fishing using our small fishing nets to catch crayfish, crabs, mudfish (catfish) and even tadpoles to make ends meet. I had a painful childhood in Mundemba. Oftentimes, I would go to the farm to look for foodstuff like Ibo Coco [Colocasia]. I would carry full on my head. When it rained, the drops fell on the Colocasia, mixed with its sap, and the mixture dropped down to my body; it started itching my whole body from the farm to the house. I would bath with hot water and rub palm oil all over my body to relieve the itch and go to sleep. The Oroko people were acutely under-scholarized at that time. Fortunately, in August 1987, I succeeded in the Common Entrance Examination and, equally, the First School Leaving Certificate Examination. It should be worthy of mention that I was a good athlete specializing in the 200-meter and 3000-meter races, the relay, high jump, long jump and handball. In that Government School Manja, I was an Oroko cultural dancer, winning many prizes. The teachers lived in the school campus. During school period, we would work for our teachers. We carried their planks and cultivated their farms. During harvest, they would ask us to close our eyes...

From a Theatre Nurse in Cameroon to a Refugee in Nigeria

After high school, I passed my General Certificate of Education Advanced Level (A-Level) examination with flying colors in the sciences. I enrolled in the Government School of Nursing in Mile One, Limbe, where I studied for three years and graduated as a State Registered Nurse. A few months after graduation, I started working in Banga Bakundu as a theatre nurse at the Banga Apostolic Hospital, putting in fifteen years of service.

Before this war started in early 2017, I had just two children as a single mother: Francis Mokoro, aged thirty-three years, and Ako Peace, aged 10 years old. Francis Mokoro was a final-year student at the University of Buea, where he was reading physics. At one time, he decided to visit me in Kumba during the heat of this crisis and shockingly, Mokoro my son was shot dead around my compound by the Cameroun soldiers. He died on the spot. I came out and fell on his warm body and asked the soldiers to just finish me too since they had killed my only hope. There was no response from the local administration. We finally buried him. Shooting continued everywhere. The Cameroun army burnt down several villages suspected of helping the separatists.

With this dangerous twist of events, we had to leave immediately. My only surviving child, my daughter, Ako Peace and I had to be on the move from Kumba to Mamfe for fear of the unknown. Here, we were looking for a means to enter Nigeria. We walked through the forest for a long distance with other refugees to escape the roadblocks of the heavily armed Cameroun soldiers who were stopping everyone, looking for any suspicious-looking male. I arrived with my daughter at Ebinsy near Ekok Road, where there was a crowd of refugees seeking to cross into Nigeria. The border was officially closed. Cameroun soldiers were trying to stop refugees from crossing into Nigeria. I saw soldiers catching female children and separating them from their parents. I saw them burying some dead female children who had been killed in the war, in one hole. I was terrified. I took my only surviving child and put her inside a big plastic bag, that is fondly called "Ghana must go" and zipped up the bag. I pleaded and negotiated with one driver to carry me across the border to Ikom, Nigeria. I was half dead and half alive contemplating if my daughter would die of suffocation in that bag. We had stayed in the forest for quite some time before hitting the road. We slept in the bushes under inclement conditions sucking bush mango and eating monkey sugar cane. I would go and catch crabs with my bare hands, even amphibians like frogs, to cook in a small tin pot. It was really not easy being in the forest. Many people died therein, not of gunshots but of multiple sicknesses and hunger.

My baby contracted malaria because of the mosquitoes that invaded us in the forest since we came without tents. I was afraid she might die since there was no available medication or healthcare attention. We survived by the grace of God and kanda stick [barks of medicinal trees]. We would cover ourselves with plantain leaves and sleep on old fallen tree trunks. The fear of snakes, scorpions and wild animals was dismissed. What was on our minds the most was the fear of "ekelebey" a word referring to the army troops of Cameroun. The Ambazonian fighters we met in the forest gave us lots of courage, assuring us they were with us. Gun battles would ensue for days on end between the separatists and government forces with heavy casualties on the side of the former. The driver bribed the soldiers, and they let our vehicle cross the border. When we finally got to Ikom, Nigeria, I quickly opened the bag and found my daughter alive; the bag had holes through which she could breathe. I begged for money from well-wishers and moved straight to the Adagom I Refugee Settlement at Ogoja. My baby girl fell sick for about three months. At the settlement, we slept at the open reception hall.

I am a hypertensive single mother with just one child. I sadly remembered the traumatic conditions in the forest and the great loss of my jewel, my son, Francis Mokoro, who was in his last year in Physics at the University of Buea, and had dreams of becoming an engineer. The Cameroun military had ended his life and dreams. While at Adagom, the United Nations High Commission for Refugees (UNHCR) gave me a tent to be sleeping with my daughter. Sympathizers from the homeland who knew me and how helpful I had been to them as a health care giver in different communities, always tried their best in terms of feeding me and my girl child. Later, I was moving about in search of a job to sustain myself and my daughter after my registration. The UNHCR brought the idea of a scholarship scheme abbreviated as DAFI. Only refugees who were twenty-eight years of age or younger were eligible for the scholarship to any of the designated universities. I am close to 50 years old, so I was not opportune to take the DAFI Scholarship[2] of 350,000 NGN (about $1000). I lamented and started working odd jobs around to support my family. Such as clearing and hoeing of farms for Nigerians who needed refugee labor. Here, I raised a little money and got recruited into the National Open University of Nigeria, where I am reading Public Health.

This is my second year at the National Open University of Nigeria (N.O.U.N). I am attending the Ikom campus. I am hopeful that after my third year, I will bag a B.Sc. in Public Health. My little daughter does trek for about four kilometers to get to her school. She is in form 1. She covers the same distance every day since I often would not get transport money to give her. When she returns from school, she is always tired and weary from hunger and the scorching Ogoja heat.

Hunger is like a demon that has taken permanent residence in my household. Could you imagine that the International Committee for the Red Cross recently gave us planting seeds like corn, rice and groundnuts. These seeds have been chemicalized, but what do we do? We wash off the seeds and eat them. That is what I am eating with my daughter. A few days ago, I had a running stomach, and I almost thought my end had come.

2 Editor's note: The DAFI is the Albert Einstein German Academic Refugee Initiative, a scholarship programme which offers qualified refugee and returnee students the possibility to earn an undergraduate degree in their country of asylum or home country. DAFI is organized by the UNHCR. See: https://www.unhcr.org/us/what-we-do/build-better-futures/education/tertiary-education/dafi-tertiary-scholarship-programme

There is too much hardship in the refugee settlement in terms of feeding. The UNHCR was giving us 7.200 NGN (about $10) per month, but it has dropped to 3.700NGN (about $5), and the payment is not consistent. Presently, my eyes are always paining me because I was exposed to too much tear gas in my locality. I cannot see as well as usual. Well, this is my story. When I see my son's age mates, I start crying and thinking about the past. Throughout that day, I'd be extremely sad, consoled by my daughter and only child.

When a Healthcare Worker is Accused of Treating the "Wrong Patients"

This next piece is by another healthcare giver, a State Registered Nurse (SRN) who was accused of providing health care to sick and wounded members of Non-State Armed Groups. She was faced with the most distressing choices that healthcare workers, who are trained to take care of the sick and wounded, are faced with in situations of war and conflict. She was literally caught in the middle of the armed conflict between the Cameroon military and Separatist, Non-State Armed Groups. The government accused her of using scarce state medical resources to treat separatist "terrorists." Obeying government orders not to treat sick and wounded members of Non-State Armed Groups also exposed her to reprisal from the Groups. As we saw in Chapter 14, healthcare facilities were caught between their professional ethics and obligation to treat all human beings, and the Cameroon government's policy of denying all medical care to sick and wounded separatists at all times, in all places, and at all costs, despite the provisions of the Geneva Convention and the international laws of war that call for respect for the sanctity of healthcare facilities and healthcare givers in times of war. The writer of this piece was a nurse who was driven into refugee status by the contradictions of the Anglophone crisis.

Birth Control Red Flags by Mireille

I am Mireille from Boki in the Akwaya forest zone. I have never lived in Nigeria before, but because I am from Dadi village, which has been tagged a separatist stronghold, I was forced to run away with my four-year-old son to Ikom, where we took refuge before coming to Ogoja in August 2018 to start a new life from scratch. Back at home, I was a Certified Nurse Practitioner in our local health center. As it always was the case back then, I was in trouble. The Cameroon military accused me of giving medical assistance to wounded and sick Amba Boys in the forest. The Divisional Officer of Akwaya further emphasized that I was usurping government medications meant for the treatment of law-abiding citizens to take care of terrorists who are sponsored by the white man's country to divide Cameroon into two with Ambazonia as the main item on the agenda. I was scared of those days, and I tried writing to the authorities of the Ministry of Health, requesting to be transferred either to Buea or Limbe. But all attempts to escape were futile and I packed little or nothing of what constitutes my belongings and took off. My job is gone, and I am no longer on the government payroll, based on a series of labor censuses carried out in our health sector by the Divisional Delegation of Public Health for the South West Region in Buea.

Here I am in the Adagom 1 Settlement in Ogoja scratching for a living. I haven't folded my arms waiting for men to pay my bills or put food on the table for me and my son. I am heavily supported by my kid sister, whom I sent to the United States to study, using my hard-earned salary as a civil servant. The returns of this gesture are now yielding better fruits. In the days ahead, she intends to move me from Ogoja Refugee Settlement to where my son and I would feel the warmth of life, leaving behind the desert of Ogoja.

As one who is enthusiastic about service to humanity, I have opened a small back-door pharmacy where I attend to refugees with manageable ailments. Unfortunately, since I am operating illegally, the National Drugs Enforcement Agency of Nigeria came after me and seized all my drugs, demanding that I present my license. I pleaded with them and lost a huge amount of money to free myself from detention for being in possession of questionable medications that I dispense. God has always been on my side!

Things are not the same as they used to be before. The UNHCR has stopped the free treatment of Refugees in health centers and hospitals. This has caused a lot of medical unrest as refugees are wailing in tears and utter despair and desperation. Young girls and women under this dispensation are quite fragile and on the danger list. As concerns contraceptives and family planning, there are many issues at stake that are begging for interventions. At the Adagom health center, young girls of school-going age were advised to put hormonal and copper coils on their arms to prevent unwanted pregnancies. This was done for free, and many of these girls and women went in for it, and pregnancy is not their portion. Well, some of them have been using this family planning method to go out there and indulge in rampant sex in the Refugee Settlement.

But what is traumatizing is that with this new medical policy, which is being enforced, there is danger looming within the female refugee population. Those who had this coil inserted into their arms as far back as 2018 would need to remove it after the stipulated period of time.

There are those who need to take this coil into their flesh as well.

Now, it was done for free. It is no longer free. To remove these old contraceptive coils now costs three thousand Naira (3000 Naira). Where is the Naira? This has a deterrent effect on the client. What about those who are looking up to this birth control method to avoid pregnancy?

The dangers are real and let us start counting our newborn babies and also the matrimonial problems that accrue as a result of the failure of this healthcare scheme.

Many of these young girls are alarmed and do not know how to go about it.

One Martin, who is a senior nurse here in this Refuge Settlement, is the one assisting in the removal of these coils from the arms of these young women. He is doing it for free.

Injections and natural birth control methods are relatively uncommon.

This is a glimpse of the medical tragedy which is about to consume us all.

Stories from Internally Displaced Persons (IDP) in Cameroon

News of the Voices in the Wilderness Refugee Writing Circle project in the refugee settlements of Nigeria soon reached internally displaced Anglophone populations in Cameroon. In early 2023, I received a message in my Facebook Messenger inbox. Saul, one of the participants in the writing project, which had been started at the end of 2019, decided that life in the Nigerian refugee camps was unbearable. He decided to run the gauntlet of Non-State Armed Groups (NSAGs) and the Cameroon Army and return to Mamfe. Though the violence had died down, the place was not livable. Many of the villages had been burnt and deserted. He therefore traveled to Kumba and crossed over to Loum, in Francophone Cameroon. From there he found his way to Douala, where his relatives had fled. Saul was a survivor. He said he was living in crowded situations with other Internally Displaced Persons who were struggling to survive. Would I like him to start an informal writing group there? He said he had met many desperate, internally displaced persons in Buea, Limbe and Francophone Cameroun. He said a little assistance from time to time would help them keep body and soul together. I responded that I would pay internally displaced writers the same amount of compensation I paid each refugee writer in Nigeria for each story, the equivalent of $11 (eleven United States dollars). The stories below were among the first batch that Saul sent me as soon as he had transitioned from a refugee in Nigeria to an IDP in Francophone Cameroon.

Saved from the BIR by Her Baby

My name is Mamun Manka Ngongben. I am from Wum town in the Northwest region of Cameroon. I'm a single mother. I was a student before all the happenings.

Just Like a Dream

I was taking care of my grandmother; news came that military soldiers from *La Republique*[3] will soon visit our areas to fight the Amba boys. We were like, are you really sure? But if that is true, they will detain only the boys, not the girls. It was not so serious because, according to CRTV news

3 "La republic" (or la République) is the short form of *La République du Cameroun*. It is an epithet that Anglophones use to differentiate themselves from French Cameroun. President Paul Biya imposed the name of French Cameroun, *la République du Cameroun* on the whole country, symbolically erasing Anglophones whose state was Southern Cameroons. The narratives in this volume describe the Anglophone conflict as a war between Amba Boys and la republic soldiers.

reports, only the Mamfe people were troubling the government. But even if they have to come and attack, it would be by night.

How it Started in Wum

One morning, about 9 o'clock, we heard gunshots, boom! boom !! boom !!!, I was in front of the house washing dresses. Everywhere, there was shouting, people were running, "La Republique soldiers have entered Wum!"

With that fear, I ran into the house to watch out first. Because I saw them a bit far, I came back out to carry my baby girl who was outside.

The Good Soldier

As I came out of the house, a very tall, black soldier man, pointed his gun at me and asked me in French, "Tu pas u? (where are you going?), Since I understand a little French, I immediately pointed at my baby. I came and carried my baby. I knew he would shoot me if I turned my back on him, so I said, "Sir, please don't kill me." He said, "No, just go inside and lock the door." Another thought came to me, that he wanted to set this house ablaze.

I said, I live with my grandmother; she is inside; please don't burn us alive, kneeling and begging. So, he told me confidentially, "No, no, I cannot do that; when you go inside, turn off your phone, and I will stand here for a while, okay?" I said, "Yes, sir," I went inside, peeping at him from the window. He stood outside for almost 15 minutes; his soldier friends were passing. Seeing him there, he would wave them on, saying nobody was inside. That is how I was saved that day. That same day, eight young boys and girls were killed in Wum.

Why I Ran for My Life

After the first attack, places were becoming normal after a month. I was still there with my grandmother until, one day, the military entered Wum again. We all, my sisters and my little brother, were inside the house hiding, sleeping flat on the ground, because everywhere outside were gunshots. I never knew who was fighting who. I went behind the door and added some heavy tables and chairs to keep it strong.

To our surprise, a military man only smashed the door with one leg, and the door was open. A huge, dark-complexioned soldier, whose eyes were red, whose face was marked and scarred like those Hausa [Northern] people commonly called Toupouri.

He saw me and motioned with his head that I should come. I knelt down, lifting my hands in the air, as I used to see in movies. That man had just used his ring on his finger to search the house, glancing around everywhere. If someone were hiding, the ring would indicate. That is how he picked all of us out.

Narrow Escape

The soldier man told us never to hide in the house again because they were about to burn down houses. Then he led us out another way, telling us never to return to the house until next week. We then ran into the forest. We climbed, non-stop, up a hill till the summit, where we stopped and slept in one hunter man's bush house.

Can you imagine that when the La Republic soldiers entered and checked around the village, they did not catch even one Amba boy? They had the guts to climb that hill to attack the Amba boys!

We must run down the valley without stopping, with my baby tied behind me. From then on, I struggled and came down to Douala, in the Littoral region, to meet my uncle, never to return home. I can't afford to suffer that kind of trauma again.

From Anglophone Businessman to Internally Displaced Person in Douala

My name is Enogene Oscar, alias "Young Money." I am a businessman based in Manyemen village. I am married and the father of four kids. I own an off-license bar, restaurant, and a small hostel where I lodge travelers. I also do cocoa business. From the look of things, before the Anglophone crisis and war started, I was one of the most successful business icons in the Nguti subdivision.

How It Started

AMBA Boys and their attacks have now become rampant. All of us are very familiar with the war because it was always very hot in Mamfe town. The Cameroon military always stopped in Manyemen, my village, to buy food, especially bush meat pepper soup, when they were going to Mamfe.

On my own part, I had always been calm, keeping quiet because I knew that if I made a single mistake, my shop and business would be attacked by Amba boys or la republic soldiers, so I am like a grasshopper when two cocks are fighting, you cannot dare come out to separate them.

Just Like Play

As military soldiers were passing on their way to Mamfe, one rascal boy from nowhere just started insulting and provoking them, saying, "wonna di go Mamfe, chop for last time, because na wonna die body we go carry go back Yaounde" [You people are going to Mamfe, eat for the last time because we will carry your corpses back to Yaoundé].

This provoked one of the La Republic soldiers, and in truth, there was a massive killing of La Republic soldiers at that time in Mamfe, when our boys were using just cutlass to cut their heads and hands. The soldier who was provoked gunned down the guy there and then. Everyone scattered and ran into the houses and quarters.

One Week Later

A week later, some of the village boys came to me and asked me to give them a sum of three million francs CFA so that they could go and prepare themselves and come back for revenge for the death of their brother and friend. I said, "I don't have money, and if I should have, I can offer them the sum of 500,000 Frs." They were very angry with me; at this point, they held me there and beat me up. They said that I was in support of the La Republic government to kill them when I was innocent. So, they told me that I was going to hear from them. I never knew what their plan was.

Rough Business Trip

I bought my cocoa products as usual and went to sell them in Kumba. As they were monitoring my movement without me knowing, they ambushed my motor vehicle carrying my goods. Immediately after we passed a village called Kokobuma, they stopped us with weapons and many deadly things blocking the road. Little did I know it was my village boys until I saw their faces. They didn't harm me or cause me any wounds, but they collected all my goods and cocoa and transported it into the thick bush. They gave me an imperial warning: if anybody in any case came to locate them on the charge of stealing, let me know that they would come after my life. I lost about 4.5 million CFA that day.

One Friday

One Friday, about three months later, this criminal group entered my village, Manyemen. They said they were back to complete their mission. That is when I knew that this was the beginning of sorrow. These boys went to Nigeria and fortified their bodies [with juju, charms, and talismans] and with my hard-earned money.

Jeopardy Season

This group did not come to fight La Republic soldiers again, as they said. They started stopping anything on the highway, cars, trucks, bikes, bicycles, businesses, and doing many other crooked things. Most often they would just post a written note on my door saying, "we need 500,000 CFA." At this juncture, if I report them to La Republic soldiers and if the soldiers go after them, then if some of them successfully run away and come to investigate and find out that I was the person behind the scenes who reported them to La Republic Soldiers, then I will be good as dead. So, I had to comply with their demands. On the other hand, if La Republic heard that I, Enogene Oscar, was giving Amba Boys money, then my name would have become Kondengui Life Prison [would have been arrested and jailed for life at the Kondengui Central Prison in Yaoundé]. So, I always played smart with the two parties to keep myself out of this deadly situation.

What Provoked Me

When the Amba boys started taking the upper hand in the crisis, whether they were good or not, we were just hailing them, for it is true what they say, "If you cannot beat them, join them." They gave the order that since La Republic government is our enemy country, they don't want to see any Brasseries mimbo (alcoholic drinks), Cameroon beer, even Guinness, anything from the French Cameroon.[4] Before this ban, my warehouses were already stocked with Cameroon beer. There was nothing I could do. I had to sell this beer to regain my money. Unfortunately, one day, a group of boys came into my off-license, bought food, and ordered Cameroon beer. Me too, I never knew them. As I brought them the Cameroon beer, they said, "So you are one of them who doesn't want to take our instructions, right?" They entered my warehouse and broke over 50 plastic crates of Kadji beer. I had to pay them 100,000 CFA to save my head.

When they left, I never wanted to cause myself or my family any harm by involving ourselves in any revenge, so we transferred to Douala to avoid problems. That is how I found myself in French Cameroon.

Internally Displaced Person's Narrative: The Cameroon Army's Sunday Morning Attack in Big Butu

I'm called Bokwe L., and my friend here is Badoma M. M. We are from Big Butu, which used to be one of the biggest villages in Meme Division in the South West region. It had a population of about one thousand three hundred inhabitants. But for five years now, life hasn't been the same again ever since the Ambazonia crisis visited us with several untold casualties. We used to live in harmony, always celebrating and sharing what Almighty God has blessed us with, such as rich soil, beautiful streams, a dense forest blessed with eru [a wild forest vine whose leaves are a widely consumed vegetable], good timber, trees, and animals of all species.

It was in 2018, in the month of March, when the Cameroon military launched an attack on us all in the name of searching for separatists and stating that we were harboring Ambazonia forces in our community. They claimed that the so-called Ambazonia forces were all children from that same village (Big Butu). They were punishing us for their activities. Even those who were not from our village, strangers who had migrated from the Northwest and neighboring Nigeria in search of greener pastures to

4 Editor's note: The Ambazonia Non-State Armed Groups banned the sale and consumption of beer brewed by the French and Dutch owned company Brasseries du Cameroun (renamed Boissons du Cameroun), as well as other alcoholic beverages brewed in Francophone Cameroun.

fend for their families back home, were affected. They were there because our village was a very hospitable place and welcomed all who served as workers in our coco farmlands.

Nevertheless, this attack was launched against us on Sunday morning. Some sources said the military started penetrating the area on Saturday at about 11 p.m. They penetrated our village from all the small and main roads leading to our community. Firstly, through Kumba town, passing through Matuw, and through the Kumba -Mamfe road, passing through Ikiliwindi. Their journey through Ikiliwindi was difficult since their armored cars and trucks broke down because of the difficult terrain. They had to trek what they called a "marche commando" (commando's march) until they arrived at our village at about 6 a.m. They waited until we had started going to church, and all of a sudden, we started hearing gunshots from all directions in the village. It was a total surprise. The whole village was all confused as no one wanted to be left behind to die in that manner. Several people were killed, starting from 0 age to the old. If you were caught, they either killed you with a bullet or their axe, or they tied you with your property in your house and burned you to ashes. There were several cases of old people who were burned in their homes since they had no strength to run and no one to help them. The entire village was burned to ashes, including villagers' coco that were ready to be sold to buyers. Our primary and newly constructed secondary schools, including the market and health center, were burned down. Dead bodies were found in every part of our community and even in the bushes. They were all decomposed as the military stormed and stayed in our village for one week, firing gunshots in the air, killing domestic animals, eating them, and stealing drinks and some foodstuff from people's stores. From that day till today, no one has ever wanted to return to the village because of that catastrophe. Though at first, we knew we were going to return, the fact that some villagers who started living in their farms so that they could work on their farmlands were still killed by the military who managed to make their way there to the farms.

We have been IDPs from 2018 till today (November 2023) in a town in which we never hoped to live. Life is so difficult here in Kumba because there are over 12 thousand IDPs here. This situation has given birth to other social ills like robbery, kidnapping, and raping of young ones. But we, however, pray to be safe so that we can one day return to our village and once again live the life we were living before.

Thanks for your time.

Conclusion

In this book, we have argued that the Anglophone problem is the result of the failure of the authoritarian republican Chiefs of State, Amadou Ahidjo and Paul Biya, to manage the complications of the post-colonial biculturalism of Cameroon. This chapter showed the outcome of the repressive and bellicist policies of the autocratic, 91-year-old Chief of State, Paul Biya, towards the Anglophone minority. It is a lengthy catalog of woe: thousands of dead men, women and children, and thousands more wounded; militarization of the judiciary and the court-marshaling of civilians; prisons full of political prisoners; almost one million internally displaced persons; almost one hundred thousand Anglophone refugees in Nigeria; hundreds headed for Europe through the Sahara Desert; the destruction of agro-industrial enterprises– the Cameroon Development Corporation, the Pamol Plantations–and above all, an eight million-strong Anglophone minority which chafes under the political, economic, cultural and autocratic domination of the Francophone majority. As a people, Anglophones have come to realize that they have never been heard and have resigned themselves to the reality that they will never be heard until the Biya republican chiefdom becomes history. As a result, Anglophones in Cameroon have withdrawn their consent to be governed by the authoritarian kleptocratic Chief of State. Biya's attempts to impose a top-down, centralized decentralization in total disregard of the federalist wishes of the Anglophone minority is the latest heavy-handed attempt to impose the will of the Chief of State on the Anglophone minority. The avoidable Anglophone crisis and resultant civil war have weakened the State of Cameroon. It has directed national resources towards the military and the infrastructures of repression like the BIR, it compromised the future of Cameroon. Since wars make nations and nations make war, as Tilly (1990) suggested, Cameroon will never be the same again. Anglophones feel that they have not been listened to. The deaths of thousands of innocent civilians, the displacement and transformation of more than one million others into internally displaced persons, and the movement of close to a hundred thousand refugees into Nigeria represent an indictment of historical proportions of the authoritarian Napoleonic Ahidjo/Biya republican chiefdom. The tragedy of it all is that it could have been avoided by dialogue and compromise. History will record that Anglophone lawyers, teachers, and students took to the streets because the Chief of State, President Biya, turned a deaf, contemptuous ear to their calls for change. Biya's refusal to recognize the identitarian and cultural specificity of the Pidgin and English-speaking minority in Cameroon sowed the seeds of the Anglophone crisis and its bloody outcome. This chapter presented the human cost of authoritarian intransigence and the rule of one man rather than the rule of law. The refugees and internally displaced persons featured in this chapter are just a few of the hundreds of thousands of innocent men, women and children caught in the senseless conflict. We have read narratives of Anglophone refugees in Nigeria from multiple perspectives. We have also read the narratives of internally displaced persons who fled from the Northwest and Southwest regions to Francophone Cameroon to escape the atrocities of the BIR, the Cameroon army, the para-military gendarmerie, and the police in both regions. The chapter also documented the fact that the movement of people both internally and externally was also triggered in part by the exactions of Non-State Armed Groups (NSAG), the so-called Amba Boys, who took advantage of the chaos, and breakdown of law and order brought about by the crisis, to impose a reign of terror, and exploit the poor and powerless people of the former state of Southern Cameroons.

References

Cameroon: Release of students sentenced for 10 years for sharing joke on Boko Haram is a great relief (2021). Amnesty International (December 27). Retrieved from: https://www.amnesty.org/en/latest/news/2021/12/cameroon-release-of-students-sentenced-for-10-years-for-sharing-joke-on-boko-haram-is-a-great-relief/

Cameroun: sous le thème royal OR/BLANC, Amougou Belinga et Mélissa Ronalde etoundi Nsoé se sont unis pour les qualités et surtout les défauts (Cameroon: under the royal theme of GOLD/WHITE, Amougou Belinga and Mélissa Ronalde Etoundi Nsoé were united in matrimony by their qualities and especially by their default (2021). *Vision4 TV* (November 20). Retrieved from: https://www.vision4.tv/cameroun-sous-le-theme-royal-or-blancamougou-belinga-et-melissa-ronalde-etoundi-nsoe-se-sont-unis-pour-les-qualites-et-surtout-les-defauts/

Cameroon Refugees in Nigeria-Operational Update September 2023 (2023). ReliefWeb, *United Nations* Office for the Coordination of Humanitarian Affairs (*OCHA*), Nov. 15. Retrieved from: https://reliefweb.int/report/nigeria/cameroonian-refugees-nigeria-operational-update-september-2023.

Cameroon tops list of neglected Crises (2019). Norwegian Refugee Council. June 4. Retrieved from: https://www.nrc.no/news/2019/june/cameroon-tops-list-of-most-neglected-crises/

Hancock, G. (1989). *Lords of Poverty: The Power, prestige, and corruption of the international aid business*. New York: Atlantic Monthly Press.

Christophersen, P. (1975). Some Special West African English Words. In Joey Lee Dillard, *Perspectives on Black English*, pp. 202–21. The Hague: Mouton.

Kindzeka, M. (2022). Cameroon Displays Separatist Leader's Corpse to Deter Rebels, Recruits. Voice of America (July 18). Retrieved from: https://www.voanews.com/a/cameroon-displays-separatist-leader-s-corpse-to-deter-rebels-recruits-/6663315.html

McVeigh, K. (2017). No laughing matter: Cameroon students face 10 years in jail for Boko Haram joke. *The Guardian* (September 21). Retrieved from: https://www.theguardian.com/global-development/2017/sep/21/no-laughing-matter-cameroon-students-face-10-years-in-jail-for-boko-haram-joke.

Médecins Sans Frontiers (Doctors Without Borders) (2019). Cameroon Refugees in Nigeria. January 25. Retrieved from: https://www.msf.org/cameroonian-refugees-nigeria

Oum II, J. (2017, December 7th). Communique No. C69/vIII/373. Communique. Mamfe, Southwest: Divisional Office Mamfe.

Three Media Leaders convicted for Genocide (2003). United Nations International Criminal Tribunal for Rwanda (March 12). Retrieved from: https://unictr.irmct.org/en/news/three-media-leaders-convicted-genocide

Tilly, C. (1990). *Coercion, Capital, and European States, AD 990-1990*. New York: Basil Blackwell.

Unah, L. (2020). Cameroon refugees struggle to cope with life of need in Nigeria. *Aljazeera,* March 8. Retrieved From: https://www.aljazeera.com/features/2020/3/8/cameroon-refugees-struggle-to-cope-with-life-of-need-in-nigeria

UN High Commission for Refugees. (2018, January 18). UNHCR USA. Retrieved from https://www.unhcr.org/en-us/news/briefing/2018/1/5a61b3bc4/concern-grows-women-children-fleeing-cameroon.html

Willis, R., McAulay, J., Ndeunyema, N. & Angove, J. (2019). Human Rights Abuses in the Cameroon

Anglophone Crisis: A Submission of Evidence to UK Parliament. University of Oxford, Faculty of Law.

TWENTY-FOUR

The Travails of Humanitarian Relief in the Midst of Crimes Against Humanity

The Case of the Ayah Foundation

AYAH AYAH ABINE & PAUL AYAH ABINE

On April 30, 2020, Ayah Ayah Abine, director of the Ayah Humanitarian Foundation, which had been working with Anglophone refugees in refugee camps in Nigeria, as well as with Internally Displaced Persons (IDPs) fleeing war in the Northwest and Southwest regions, received an official *lettre-convocation* (letter of summons) No. 000648/DGSN/SG/DP/SDEEF/SEEF/3 of 30 April 2020, from the Presidency of the Republic, General Delegation for National Security, Directorate of the Judicial Police, Sub-directorate of Economic and Financial Investigations. The letter of summons, which was written in French, the administrative and working language of the Cameroon government bureaucracy, stated that the summons was connected to a letter from the Secretary General of the Presidency, Ferdinand Ngoh Ngoh, concerning an accusation that had been made against Ayah Ayah Abine and others of financing terrorism (Anglophone separatists). Ayah Ayah Abine was ordered to report to the office of the Judicial Police, Sub-directorate of Economic and Financial Investigations for "interrogation as a suspect" at 11 a.m. prompt. He was informed that he had the right to be assisted by counsel of his choice during the interrogation.

As the saying goes, "no good deed goes unpunished." In the case of the Ayah Foundation, it was "no humanitarian acts go unpunished." In effect, since the Anglophone crisis started in Cameroon in 2016, the Ayah Foundation, which was founded and managed by Justice Ayah Paul Abine and his son, Ayah Ayah Abine, had been engaged in humanitarian work among Cameroonian refugees in Nigeria and IDPs in Anglophone and Francophone Cameroon. Since charity begins at home, these natives of Akwaya were the first humanitarian organization to help refugees who had fled to the Cross River State of Nigeria after the Anglophone armed resistance started in Manyu, and Akwaya became a war zone. Justice Paul Abine Ayah is a former justice of the Supreme Court of Cameroon who had fallen out with the regime. He was a former Member of the Cameroon National Assembly for

Manyu, who opposed amending the constitution to give President Biya the opportunity to have an indefinite number of terms in office. In 2017, while still a sitting justice of the Supreme Court, he was arrested and imprisoned without trial for eight months in Yaoundé for allegedly supporting a return to a federal system of government in Cameroon – but he was never formally charged. He was also dismissed from the Supreme Court without reason – and without his pension. Before the Anglophone Revolt of 2016, the Ayah Foundation operated orphanages in the Northwest and Southwest regions of Cameroon.

The legal trouble that Ayah Ayah Abine got into, and the summons he received from the judicial police originated from media allegations, and from a number of Anglophone lackeys of the regime, who had an axe to grind with the Ayah Foundation. In effect, on January 7, 2017, when lawyers, teachers, students, and members of the civil society of the English and Pidgin-speaking Northwest and Southwest regions took to the streets to peacefully demonstrate against Anglophone marginalization and second-class citizenship in *La Republique du Cameroun*, and demanded a return to the federal system, their movement was met with governmental repression. Leaders of the movement, including Felix Nkongho Agbor Balla, lawyer, federalist, human rights activist, and president of the banned Fako Lawyer's Association, as well as president of the banned Cameroon Anglophone Civil Society Consortium (CACSC), Prof. Fontem Neba, Secretary General of the Consortium, and others, were arrested in Buea. They were blindfolded and driven to the underground dungeon at the Gendarmerie Headquarters, the *Secretariat d'État à la Defense* (Secretariat of State for Defense) in Yaoundé and held incommunicado. On 20 January 2017, they were charged with "terrorism, hostility against the motherland, secession, insurrection, contempt of public authorities, and collective rebellion"; "incitement to civil war by bringing the inhabitants of the South- and Northwest regions to arm themselves against other citizens"; and "attempt[ing] to modify the constitutional laws, notably the federalist system, through violence." Though Agbor Balla and his English-speaking co-accused were civilians, they were charged in the French-language-only Yaoundé Military Tribunal because their alleged offenses fell under Law No. 2014/028 of 23 December 2014 on the Suppression Acts of Terrorism. They faced the death penalty if found guilty.

In a panel discussion on the arrest of the Anglophone civilian leaders, their trial before the Yaoundé Military Tribunal, violent suppression of the lawyers' and teachers' demonstrations, the xenophobic, pro-regime television channel, Vision 4 (its detractors call it Vision 4 Mille Colines, an allusion to *Radio Mille Colines* that fanned the flames of genocide in Rwanda in 1993 and 1994) used hateful dehumanizing language to refer to the Anglophone detainees. The hosts of the Vision 4 TV program, Ernest Obama and Jacques Ze, said the arrests, detentions, trials, and imprisonment of Anglophone federalists and separatists amounted to a « deratisation » or elimination of "rats" from the country. He stated that all Anglophones should be subject to systematic searches and seizures. After a formal complaint by the Cameroon Association of English-Speaking Journalists (CAMASEJ), the National Communication Commission (CNC), the governmental media watchdog that regulates media content and hate speech in Cameroon, suspended Obama from broadcasting for two months in December 2017. The CNC did not specify which hate utterances he was being punished for. Obama ignored the suspension. Vision 4 Television is an untouchable channel because its owner, Jean-Pierre Amougou Belinga, is part of the ruling elite and is funded to promote a pro-Biya ideology. Dehumanization of the English-speaking minority by reducing them to the level of rats did not result in any serious penalties for either Obama or Zé.

A couple of years later, Vision 4 Television took on an Anglophone institution. During a live broadcast, Ernest Obama accused the Ayah Foundation, a charitable and humanitarian organization whose employees, including Ayah Ayah Abine, traveled to refugee camps hosting Anglophone refugees in Nigeria on a regular basis to help provide food, drinking water, and other supplies to the refugees, of working with Ambazonia secessionists (popularly known as Amba Boys). Ernest Obama accused the Ayah Foundation on national television of buying, importing and supplying arms to "Amba" boys. The accusation was surprising because the Ayah Foundation had a good reputation for its humanitarian cause. All the children of its orphanage in Akwaya–and they were all girls–fled to Nigeria when the war broke out. Both Anglophone and Francophones contributed funds to the foundation to help refugees and internally displaced persons (IDPs).

After the Vision 4 accusation, support for the foundation dropped precipitously, and some of its projects were canceled. The Cameroon government blocked the bank accounts of the foundation as well as the private accounts of its leaders, Justice Paul Ayah Abine and his son Ayah Ayah Abine. The false and defamatory accusations of Vision 4 led to the freezing of the humanitarian organization's bank accounts. The Presidency of the Republic opened a criminal investigation into the activities and funding of the foundation. The Directorate of the Judicial Police, Sub-directorate of Economic and Financial Investigations, issued a letter of summons to Ayah Ayah Abine to report to the judicial police for interrogation. He was so shocked by the accusations and criminal investigation that he sued Obama and Vision 4 for criminal defamation. To the surprise of Abine and the Ayah Foundation, the case "disappeared" and never came up for hearing. A court official told the Ayah Foundation "Obama, can't/hasn't been identified." Meanwhile, Obama continued to appear on TV on a weekly basis, smearing Ayah and others. It took almost a year to "identify" Obama.

Aim of the chapter

In this chapter, Ayah Ayah Abine introduces the Ayah Foundation and the humanitarian relief it brings to the innocent victims – and they are mostly women and children – of the senseless war in the Anglophone Northwest and Southwest regions. He also talks about the legal trouble they and the Ayah Foundation have had after the false and defamatory accusations leveled against them by Ernest Obama of Vision 4 TV. His statement is followed by reflections on the Anglophone Question by former Justice Paul Ayah Abine.

The Ayah Foundation

The Ayah Foundation is a humanitarian organization with neither political nor religious affiliations. It is at the service of vulnerable persons around the world. Founded in 2017 by Ayah Ayah Abine, it began as a solo effort to improve lives but quickly grew into a foundation committed to taking people 'across the gap' of want into the realization of their full potential. Several affiliates of the Foundation existed decades before the latter saw the light of day. The first affiliate of the Ayah Foundation is Saint Valentine's Orphanage, founded by the Ayahs as far back as 1989. Through this orphanage, scores of orphan kids have been successfully groomed and raised into responsible adult citizens. The orphanage consists of two branches: the boys' orphanage situated at Governors' Street, Buea Town, and the girls' dormitory in Akwaya town, Manyu. As of this day, several milestones have been attained by children who went through this initiative. Several of them are university graduates. The boys' dormitory houses over 20 children while the girls' dormitory harbors over double that figure, although all the children in the Akwaya orphanage are currently refugees in Nigeria owing to the current 'Anglophone' war that engulfed most of Manyu and Akwaya.

In the late 1990s, the Ayahs, struck by the hardship of vulnerable people in the Anglophone regions of the country, founded PROPS Cameroon, which, over the years, has been an integral part of the lives of several underprivileged persons, especially rural women and peasants. As of today, so humbling but great is our pride to see our efforts yielding fruits as several benefactors from humble beginnings now fend for themselves. At the dawn of the year 2000, the suffering of the indigenes of Manyu Division was tear-jerking, with Akwaya subdivision being a special case. There was a need to unite the people under a legal umbrella to harmonize resources and foster community development. As a result, the Ayah Family formed the TOOLS and TOILS CIG, which empowers agricultural workers–men and especially women in the said area, thereby rendering them autonomous.

Later on, Ayah Ayah Abine, Managing Director and Overseer of St Valentine's Orphanage, PROPS CAMEROON, TOOLS and TOILS, etc., found it necessary to enlarge the scope of the decade-long humanitarian activities of the Ayahs by founding the Ayah Foundation. The Foundation brings together all the existing above-mentioned organizations under a single umbrella. The Ayah Foundation reaches out to all vulnerable persons, including the underprivileged and minorities. It meets the have-nots at their doorstep with much-needed relief to the best of its ability. So great is our joy, and so profound is our resolve to get individuals 'across the gap' that separates them from living a fruitful life.

The Foundation's Motivation

The Ayah Foundation strongly holds that nothing truly changes/happens unless a life is changed. We build partnerships with willing non-governmental organizations (NGOs), businesses, and other associations to facilitate our goal of finding lasting solutions to difficult situations and transforming lives and communities from what they currently are to what they could become tomorrow. Money raised by our foundation is used directly to impact the lives of vulnerable persons through volunteers and experts. When supporting other philanthropic endeavors, programs and projects developed by potential partners are financed directly. We are guided in our vision by this truism: Empowerment is liberating and life changing. The Ayah Foundation is inspired by a love for humanity. It is driven by the spirit of sacrifice and a profound understanding of the sacredness of life. It is guided by truth and justice, with a profound desire for a more equitable society. The Ayah Foundation exists to unite physical and moral persons of one mind in the service of humanity. We continually encourage all persons of goodwill to partner with or support us in our endeavors to permit us to impact more and more lives because living for others is a natural call.

Activities During the Anglophone Crisis

Scores of life-saving milestones have been achieved by the Ayah Foundation over the years, especially after the Anglophone crisis and the insecurity plaguing the English-speaking parts of Cameroon since 2016. This crisis resulted in the flow of an increasing number of refugees from these war zones to Nigeria. When fighting began between the Cameroon security forces and multiple groups of armed non-state actors, the workers and 40-plus children in the Ayah Foundation's Saint Valentine's Orphanage in Akwaya Town were caught in the crossfire. During a lull in the fight, the orphanage was evacuated, and most of its residents joined the crowd of refugees fleeing to Nigeria. According to the United Nations High Commission for Refugees, 70,000 Anglophone refugees crossed into Nigeria. Some of these refugees were our relatives. As a result, the Ayah Foundation went to Nigeria on ten different occasions to provide food and non-food relief to these refugees as they battle for survival in abject misery in a foreign land (Anglophone refugees receive aid from the Ayah Foundation (2018). The Foundation is equally very active in supporting refugee kids of school-going age in Nigerian schools in order to fill the gap caused by the years of school closures resulting from the war, which has had a devastating effect on their communities. So far, thousands of refugee kids have been provided with complete sets of school uniforms as well as scores of school supplies to enable them to foster their education. Thousands of refugee women have equally been empowered by the foundation to start small businesses. As members of the Ayah Foundation staff have gone in and out of Nigeria to assist refugees, they have encountered Cameroon security forces, Nigerian security forces and armed, non-state actors. Both Cameroonian and Nigerian authorities recognized that the Ayah Foundation is neutral in the conflict, though it sometimes had to overcome bureaucratic and security hurdles that prevented them from having access to some refugee settlements. The non-state actors sometimes prevented agents of the Ayah Foundation from passing through the territory they controlled. These challenging encounters were often resolved through communication. At no time did the Ayah Foundation, its agents or its volunteers coordinate its activities with or collaborate with either the Cameroon security forces beyond normal communication on security issues and bureaucratic interaction or with any of the many armed non-state actors that it encountered in Manyu and other parts of the Northwest and Southwest as it sought to render humanitarian assistance to refugees in Nigeria and internally displaced persons in Cameroon.

Working With Internally Displaced Populations

Within the country, the Ayah Foundation provides humanitarian assistance to scores of displaced persons in several regions. The Foundation has had projects in the Littoral, West, Center, Northwest and Southwest regions. Its officials and volunteers have, on numerous occasions, traveled to these regions, providing relief to victims of war and violence, especially to the most vulnerable, who happen to be women and children. The encounters with these displaced and suffering populations are always tear-jerking, as most victims have lost everything. The number of displaced men, women and children fleeing the war and taking refuge deep in the forest and the bush is extraordinary, and their conditions are often indescribable. Wounded civilian demonstrators feared going to the hospital or health centers for fear that the Cameroon military would enter the health facilities and arrest them (Amnesty International, 2017). Some wounded civilian demonstrators died of their wounds in the forest. Women delivered babies in the forest without the most rudimentary care, leading to many deaths of women and children during childbirth; hungry kids drank unclean water from streams full of dangerous microbes; young girls used leaves as pads during their menstrual periods; men scavenged and prepared half-cooked or completely uncooked stuff, along with insects and worms for their families to survive; children were covered with mosquito bites and leeches; men, women and children died of snake bites or drowned in the process of fleeing across swollen rivers within Cameroon or between Cameroon and Nigeria. These are some of the scenes we witness again and again on a regular basis in the bushes and even in towns where displaced people find themselves battling for survival. The urgency for immediate and undivided attention to the needs of these victims of war cannot be over-emphasized.

Figure 24.1. Ayah Ayah Abine with Anglophone Refugees in Nigeria (2017)

In the Littoral region, the Ayah Foundation runs a girls' dormitory wherein over forty displaced girls are housed and protected. Many were separated from their parents, and some of them lost their parents and siblings in the crossfire of the war. Some of them were rescued from human traffickers who took advantage of the war to snatch vulnerable children. In the Ayah Foundation dormitory, these girls are housed, fed, enrolled in school, and provided with school supplies, pocket money, and a safe environment. The follow-up is rigorous because these girls are vulnerable. The Foundation employs standby staff and security officials to monitor all the girls strictly. We hope their education is smooth and they graduate with good grades. The endpoint will be their empowerment and ability to fend for themselves.

Healthcare has been a major challenge and priority to the foundation. Scores of patients have been attended to by the health services of the Ayah Foundation. Some of its critically ill patients have been evacuated abroad for more specialized medical attention. Several cases can be cited. In October 2017, in the course of the ongoing war plaguing Anglophone Cameroon, several innocent victims were shot indiscriminately. Fourteen-year-old Median and Eileen were two of the most delicate cases we attended to. They were gravely wounded by shrapnel from bombs and grenades employed by security forces. The Foundation enlisted the help of specialists from the USA to attend to the former while it worked on a series of surgeries abroad. These actions ultimately saved both lives. Many other civilian victims of this war have had their lives saved and their health restored through the foundation's intervention. Several other medical cases, unrelated to the current insecurity plaguing the Anglophone zones, have equally been attended to by the foundation. These have included several cases of tumors and several hydrocephalus cases. We, unfortunately, lost some patients, including sick detainees, whose cases we followed up on and helped evacuate abroad for heart surgery. The dedication of the Foundation to healthcare for the vulnerable has been unaffected by these setbacks.

Figure 24.2 Ayah Ayah Abine with Cameroon Anglophone refugees in Nigeria (2018)

Ayah Foundation Orphanages

As mentioned above, the Ayah Foundation runs two orphanages: one in Buea, our base, and another in Akwaya, our hometown. The Buea Orphanage is currently called Saint Valentine's Center. Formally called St. Valentine's Orphanage, it was founded by the Ayah family in 1989. If hosts and brings up boys, scores of whom are today grown-ups, married men, responsible citizens, while others ply their trades abroad. Situated at Governor's Street, Buea Town, adjacent to the governor's residence, it is equally the seat of the

Ayah Foundation. The Orphanage in Akwaya is for girls, scores of whom are today grown-ups, responsible citizens, and married women with their own families. Unfortunately, the war plaguing our communities has shut down the site, with a majority of the girls in the orphanage unaccounted for to date. It is rumored that several are refugees in different refugee camps in Nigeria, although we cannot independently confirm this.

Work in Prisons and Detention Facilities

International human rights organizations like Amnesty International (2020) and national human rights groups have reported that prison and detention facilities in Cameroon are some of the worst in the world (Human Rights Watch, 2022). The Prisons are badly overcrowded, mostly by accused persons who spend years in pre-trial detention. The legal theory is that accused persons are guilty until proven innocent, and the burden of proof is on them. Many detainees die for lack of medical care or of malnutrition (Amnesty International, 2017). The families of detainees have to bring them food behind bars - sometimes for years, or they starve. Prisons and detention centers also hold prisoners of conscience and political prisoners who have fallen foul of the regime in one way or another. Hundreds of these prisoners are Anglophone demonstrators and their family members who were arrested in places like Buea, Bamenda, Limbe, Kumba, Muyuka, Mamfe, Banso, Ndop, Ndu, in the Northwest and Southwest regions and deported to prisons and detention centers in Bafoussam, Yaoundé and Douala. Some prisoners were tried and sentenced to lengthy sentences by the Yaoundé Military Tribunal, but the majority have been in pre-trial detention awaiting their day in court since 2017.

The Ayah Foundation does humanitarian tours to prisons and detention facilities yearly. The conditions of these centers and detention facilities are sometimes indescribable. Inmates in some detention facilities are assisted more than once a year. Notable among these detention facilities are the Yaoundé, Buea, Bamenda and Kumba prisons. On several occasions, we visit these prisons and support detainees in diverse ways, providing them with food and healthcare. Regarding healthcare, we make it a duty to see to it that prisoners are physically and psychologically healthy. Our field agents liaise with detainees and medical staff to provide the best healthcare possible to those in need within our means. These actions have kept most beneficiaries in detention healthy and alive, even in the most overcrowded situations.

Persecution

The Ayah family, in general, and the Ayah Foundation, in particular, have a long history of persecution by the government of the Republic of Cameroon. This dates as far back as 2008, a year that marked a turning point in the history of Cameroon. That year, Honorable Justice Ayah Paul Abine, father of Ayah Ayah Abine, a Member of the Cameroon National Assembly for the ruling Cameroon People's Democratic Movement (CPDM) party, was the lone parliamentarian to boldly oppose the constitutional amendments aimed at removing constitutional limitations to presidential mandates. The aim was to allow President Paul Biya to run indefinitely and serve unlimited terms as president of Cameroon. Regardless of the threats Paul Ayah Abine received from all quarters, he stood his ground, insisting that such a move was immoral and a betrayal to the people of Cameroon. Despite his opposition to the bill, an unknown individual in Parliament fraudulently voted on his behalf in his absence. This opposition to unlimited presidential terms was a crime worth punishing him for, with the death penalty if possible. Paul Ayah Abine later resigned from the ruling party and joined the opposition to try to build from the outside. In 2011, Ayah Paul Abine ran for the presidency of the Republic and came in fifth. This, to the government, constituted another offense punishable under their unwritten laws. In the meantime, Paul Ayah Abine became a Justice of the Supreme Court of Cameroon. He was the highest-ranked Anglophone justice in the land's highest court. When the Anglophone crisis broke out in 2016, the government saw it as an excellent opportunity to finally nail Ayah to the cross. On Saturday, October 21, 2017, unidentified armed, plainclothes security agents broke into the Ayahs' residence in Yaoundé without a warrant and asked Justice Ayah Paul to follow them to the Military Tribunal. If at all Justice Ayah had committed an offence, a special procedure is stipulated in the criminal procedure code for the judgment and impeachment of judges if need be. Sadly, all these laws were violated as Justice Ayah was dragged to the floor half-naked by the armed men who tried to kidnap him. If Ayah Ayah, Justice Paul Ayah's son, had not intervened boldly, asking in French that his dad be left to dress up, Justice Ayah would have been dragged to an unknown destination as the plan appears to have been. Justice Ayah was finally taken away without a warrant and dumped at the notorious and infamous underground dungeon and interrogation center of the National Gendarmerie Headquarters, SED, in Yaoundé. He was detained for over eight months, during which period he had multiple cardiac issues and almost grew blind from being held in near-total darkness. He was later released without any charges filed against him at the Military Tribunal or a civilian court.

Upon Justice Ayah's release, his son became the new target. On several occasions, as the President of the Ayah Foundation carried out his humanitarian activities for the benefit of vulnerable people, especially the victims of the ongoing war in the Anglophone regions, the government of the Republic of Cameroon repeatedly took offense at his humanitarian activities that benefited innocent people which the government and its agents wished would disappear in refugee camps and IDP settlements. On several occasions, the Ayah Foundation has been stopped from providing humanitarian assistance to prisoners arrested on account of the ongoing crisis. This has occurred in Yaoundé, Buea and Bamenda. Most glaring and abusive of all this government lawlessness and persecution of the Ayah Foundation occurred at the infamous Kondengui Prison in Yaoundé. In mid-2018, on one of the foundation's outreaches to that detention facility, the food and non–food items–bags of rice, garri (tapioca), canned fish, cooking oil, and so on–brought by the foundation were already in the premises of the prison when orders came from above for everything to be rejected, and so it was (Cameroon Concord News, 2019). The hungry prisoners and pre-trial detainees who are not fed by the prison service, who survive on minimal food and the charity of those on the outside, were denied the right to receive charitable donations of food. So, rightfully or wrongfully depriving persons of their freedom was not enough. They also had to be deprived of their basic right to food assistance from willing hearts. The foundation has equally been prevented from going across the border to Nigeria to attend to refugees on at least one occasion, an action aimed not only at punishing the beneficiaries of our humanitarian outreach, persons living in life-threatening conditions, but also a move aimed at frustrating the foundation since many of the girl children from its Akwaya orphanage disappeared in refugee camps in Nigeria. The irony is that in 2018, President Biya's appointed Governor of the Southwest region had attempted to cross into Nigeria to provide the refugees with some food items and tried to persuade them to return to Cameroon. The refugees were so alarmed at the prospect of a visit from a governor who had shown hostility towards Anglophones that they protested the proposed visit to the UN High Commission for Refugees, which persuaded the Nigerian government to deny the governor access to Cameroon refugee camps (BBC News Pidgin, 2018). Regardless of these challenges, the Ayah Foundation has remained committed and focused on its mission to save and/or empower as many lives as possible within the law for the greater good, so God Help Us!

Figure 24.3. Honorable Justice Ayah Paul Abine, father of Ayah Ayah Abine, a former member of the Cameroon National Assembly for the ruling Cameroon People's Democratic Movement (CPDM) party, former Justice of the Cameroon Supreme Court. He died in December 2024

The Case of Ayah Foundation Versus Obama and Vision 4

The climax of bad faith and ill-intentioned attempts to frustrate the work of the Ayah Foundation and even destroy the foundation itself occurred in 2020. We saw earlier that Ayah Ayah Abine received a letter of summons from the Presidency of the Republic, General Delegation for National Security, Directorate of the Judicial Police, Sub-directorate of Economic and Financial Investigations. The summons stated that the Secretary

General of the Presidency, Ferdinand Ngoh Ngoh, had received accusations that Ayah Ayah Abine was financing terrorism (Anglophone separatists). Ayah Ayah Abine was ordered to report to the office of the Judicial Police, Sub-directorate of Economic and Financial Investigations for "interrogation as a suspect." He was informed that he had the right to be assisted by counsel of his choice during the interrogation. This was because, in January 2020, some paid Anglophone surrogates of the regime came up with some very dangerous accusations against the Ayah Foundation (Malplat, 2020). The public was shocked to hear our accusers tag the Ayah Foundation with false, dangerous and outrageous accusations of being "a terrorist organization used by separatists to buy guns abroad, import them into the country and supply to separatists' fighters championing the independence of the former Southern Cameroons." Since then, and contrary to all existing laws, rather than demand that our accusers show proof of their accusations, the government of the Republic of Cameroon has been at the Foundation's neck with multiple interrogations, asking the accused to prove their innocence rather than asking the accusers to prove the truthfulness of their crazy accusations.

On February 19, 2020, the president of the Foundation, Ayah Ayah Abine, was summoned to the Gendarmerie Headquarters at the Secretariat of State for Defense (SED) to answer questions based on these false and defamatory accusations. Ayah Ayah Abine showed up at the SED two days following the summons. During the two-day interrogation, he was asked questions on several issues unrelated to the buying of guns, after which he was asked to go home. After the interrogation, Ayah Ayah Abine revealed on December 7 that he had filed a complaint for defamation against its accusers: Success Nkongho, journalist Ernest Obama, activist Frankline Njume, Vision 4, *Anecdote* newspaper and the pro-regime social media platform noted for propaganda and disinformation, Ma Kontri Pipo Dem (MKPD) for defamation, blackmail, and propagation of fake news at the Yaoundé courts, but strangely, the complaint disappeared in the bureaucracy of the *gendarmerie nationale*. Defamation is a criminal offense prosecutable by the *procureur general* (state prosecutor), but the government did not seem to want to prosecute the accusers of the Ayah Foundation because they were its informants. The Ayah Foundation then filed a second complaint, this time through a private summons, which took weeks to be validated by the authorities (Bisong, 2020). Immediately after the legal department approved the complaint and sent it to court for the hearing to commence, the Yaoundé Judicial Police, which is subordinate to SED, summoned the president of the Ayah Foundation for questioning on the same complaint for which he had been summoned and interrogated for four hours at the Gendarmerie headquarters at the SED in Yaoundé. Once again, no question was related to the buying of arms; instead, Ayah Ayah Abine was informed that he was suspected of financing terrorism and money laundering, with state authorities holding firm on the fact that monies received by the foundation and its president could be funds used to fund the ongoing war in the Anglophone regions of Cameroon. It turned out that a repentant former Ambazonian activist, Success Nkongho, who was once on the government of Cameroon's "most wanted list" for arrest or elimination, had filed a complaint at the National Gendarmerie accusing Ayah Ayah of financing terrorism (Azohnwi, 2020). Ayah Ayah Abine would once again ask interrogators and the authorities a simple question: "On whom does the burden of proof lie?

On he who accuses or on the accused?" According to all existing national and international laws, isn't the accuser the one to provide evidence to substantiate his accusations? This false accusation demonstrates the major difference between the Common law system in Anglophone Cameroon, where the accused is innocent until proven guilty, and the burden of proof is on the accuser, versus the Francophone civil law system in Yaoundé, where there is no presumption of innocence, and the accused is considered guilty until proven innocent - the burden of proof being on the accused. The matter continues to drag on in court. The authorities stated that they could not "identify" the journalist Ernest Obama, a popular personality who presented the news on TV on a daily basis, for purposes of defamation. They had not been able to do so for ten months. The Ayah Foundation expects its accusers to show proof of their very dangerous, malicious, and damaging accusations. So far, they have not provided evidence to support their dangerous accusations. The Ayah Foundation states that if they do not get justice in Cameroon, they will seek justice at the African Court of Justice or the African Commission on Human and People's Rights.

Reflections of Justice Paul Ayah Abine, Retired Justice of the Cameroon Supreme Court

> ON BIYA'S BELLICOSE LANGUAGE
> January 16, 2019
> CONCRETING BELLICOSE LANGUAGE
>
> Mr. President has persisted in his bellicose language of neutralizing 'war mongers.' Preparations are openly building up to the full-scale prosecution of the war. It is rumored that it will all start as early as in two weeks …
>
> We of the Ayah Foundation have found 'civilian camps' in the heart of the virgin equatorial forests. We have seen 'civilian camps' on cocoa farms; under eucalyptus trees; in perforated bushes.
>
> We of the Ayah Foundation have seen villages burnt down without the slightest suggestion they were camps, even less, war mongers' camps.
>
> We have seen unarmed persons, even the demented, gunned down in cold blood.
>
> We know, like everyone else, that the terms 'war mongers,' terrorists, 'secessionnistes' are NOT written on anyone's face.
>
> All this leads us to ask some questions:
>
> 1 In this new war of NEUTRALIZATION, what special equipment have the belligerent forces acquired that will enable them to distinguish, in a trice, in the heat of fighting, between combatants and noncombatants; between 'Amba military camps' and civilian sanctuaries; between friend and foe…?
>
> 2 If any such sophisticated equipment they now have, have they been morally re-educated to avoid civilian facilities and their life-saving necessaries?

3 If not, is it now a war of the TOTAL extermination of a certain people?

I Do Remember My Teacher: Make Hay While the Sun Shines.

January 3, 2019

MORE KILLINGS AHEAD

Before his abduction and captivity, Ayah Paul Abine had, on at least ten occasions, called for and strongly recommended dialogue to resolve the Anglophone Crisis. He did not relent after his release and subsequent to the formal declaration of the Anglophone War. Ayah graphically painted the picture of the somber effects of war!

As if to vindicate him, in the prosecution of the war, unarmed Anglophone civilians dressed in red have been killed on occasions as if for the fun of it. On other occasions, it has been the turn of those in black. On others yet those in blue and white! The killers even turned their guns against the demented (mad).

EVEN THE DEMENTED!

In the currency of the war, scores of villages have been burnt down, some entirely, at times with human beings burnt alive in their houses – some in their sleep. In the currency of the war, foodstuffs have been burnt to ashes to secure the demise of the survivors of the guns! And we have seen the photos of both cash and food crops destroyed for fatal effect in the long term.

In the currency of the war, innocent Anglophones have been rounded up and taken away – no-one can vouch today if all are still alive or as to their whereabouts: many are languishing in dungeons. Thousands are battling it out with animal predators in the wild even as we write. Thousands more have relocated to foreign lands internally; and many more to Nigeria principally. These temporary survivors have had to fend for themselves for months before some even just smelt any relief supplies.

In all these situations of a merciless war, clearly out of the ordinary, the Cameroonian Authorities have consistently and sadistically praised the army for their 'efficiency and professionalism!'

NO COMMENT!

AND NOW!

In his 'address to the nation' on December 31, 2018, Mr. President did issue an ultimatum to the Anglophones to surrender UNCONDITIONALLY or be 'NEUTRALIZED'!

Going by the prosecution of the war in the past, it is tantamount to a call for more indiscriminate killings and the wanton destruction of property! It is a call for the callous killing of the very people Mr. President said voted him into office just three months back at as much as 89% in some places!

WHERE WITHER?
UNFORTUNATE!
SO SO SAD!

ON THE KONDENGUI PRISON REJECTION
January 10, 2019
NO-ONE CAN…

In our endeavors to alleviate the suffering of thousands of Anglophone refugees, both internally and externally, the Ayah Foundation has suffered several setbacks. The Cameroonian Government has prevented us in the past from bringing minimum survival items to detainees at Kondengui Prison, (including the Kondengui Central Prison), the gendarmerie headquarters – (SED), the Bamenda Central Prison, and to refugees in dire need in Nigeria (we were stopped at Ekok).

We have also been threatened to be shot dead if we did not stop building tents for babies born on leaves in the forests without shelter… We have been threatened with blackmail if we did not stop taking food and even hygienic pads to women/girls in the bushes…

When some stronger nations began to threaten that, preventing basic items from reaching persons in distress owing to war, it was a crime against humanity; the government then embarked on a smear campaign to cripple the Ayah Foundation. It even went into collusion with some international humanitarian organizations with recognized emblems to reject working with the foundation or to cut off any existing links.

Not only did these reprehensible acts fail to cripple the Ayah Foundation, but a divine booster saw the light of day when Professor Maurice Kamto came out powerfully to campaign for the funding of the Ayah Foundation, pointing out our determined and regular presence on the ground. It became abundantly clear that, like no one can hold back the wind, the Ayah Foundation was untenable!

Preventing us from taking food to Anglophone prisoners at Kondengui Central Prison today, January 10, 2019, is only a reminder to the international community that, as the Olitis so aptly put it, 'You don't kill a snake till you have cut off the head.' Furthermore, it provides but more corroborative evidence of crimes against humanity for process at the appropriate time!

NO ONE CAN STOP THE WIND FROM BLOWING!

Eight years after fleeing Amba threats:
Kake I Bongwana Chief returns to palace, calls for unity, peace...

Health benefits of apple

The Guardian Post
SUNDAY

Justice Ayah Paul Abine
Thousands bid farewell to incorruptible judge, political icon, rights defender

This World, This Life

Ebolowa:
Four kids from same family die of suspected food poisoning

20-year-old Cameroonian stabbed to death in Italy

At least 10 women killed in 27 days in Cameroon – Report

Douala:
Man sends wife packing for bleaching her skin

Figure 24.4. The Right Honourable, Mr. Justice Ayah Paul Abine died in Buea on 25 December 2024. A large number of lawyers dressed in their official regalia held a procession during his funeral service

References

Amnesty International (2020). Cameroon: Prisons at risk of becoming "epicenters of the pandemic." Press Release of May 5. Retrieved from: https://www.amnesty.org.uk/press-releases/cameroon-prisons-risk-becoming-epicentres-pandemic

Amnesty International (2017). Cameroon: Inmates packed like sardines in overcrowded prisons following deadly Anglophone Protests (October 13). Retrieved from: https://www.amnesty.org/en/latest/news/2017/10/cameroon-inmates-packed-like-sardines-in-overcrowded-prisons-following-anglophone-protests/

Anglophone refugees receive aid from Ayah Foundation (2018) *Journal du Cameroun*. Retrieved from: https://www.journalducameroun.com/en/anglophone-refugees-receive-aid-ayah-foundation/

Azohnwi, A. (2020). Cameroon – Anglophone Crisis: Ayah Ayah Abine Expected at Gendarmerie Headquarters Friday After Thursday's 'Baptism of Fire," Cameroon-Info-net. February 20. Retrieved from: http://www.cameroon-info.net/article/cameroon-anglophone-crisis-ayah-ayah-abine-expected-at-gendarmerie-headquarters-friday-after-thursdays-baptism-363576.html

BBC News Pidgin (2018). Anglophone crisis: Why Cameroon refugees for Nigeria deny goment assistance, July 6. Retrieved from: https://www.bbc.com/pidgin/tori-44727812

Bisong, N. (2020). Ayah Foundation Sues One for Defamation. *The Sun*. January 17. Retrieved from: https://thesuncameroon.cm/index.php/2020/01/17/ayah-foundation-sues-one-defamation/

Human Rights Watch (2022). Cameroon: Routine Torture, Incommunicado Detention. Retrieved from:

https://www.hrw.org/news/2019/05/06/cameroon-routine-torture-incommunicado-detention

Malplat, C. (2020). The risky business of aid in anglophone Cameroon. Agence France Presse/ Yahoo News. Retrieved from: https://news.yahoo.com/risky-business-aid-anglophone-cameroon-112147309.html.

Cameroon Concord News. (2019). Southern Cameroons Crisis: Kondengui prison authorities reject humanitarian aid from Ayah Foundation. January 4. Retrieved from: http://www.cameroonconcordnews.com/southern-cameroons-crisis-kondengui-prison-authorities-reject-humanitarian-aid-from-ayah-foundation/

TWENTY-FIVE

Francophone Voices of Resistance Against War and Human Rights Violations in the Anglophone Regions

LYOMBE EKO

To the casual observer, the "Anglophone Crisis" or "Anglophone Problem" in Cameroon is often seen as a conflict between Anglophones and Francophones, Africans who had been colonized by the British versus Africans who had been colonized by the French. From this perspective, the Anglophone conflict is yet another example of African post-colonial subjects who are unable to rise above imposed colonial ideas and mentalities. This conceptualization of the problem has a gist of the truth but is ultimately rather simplistic. At the onset of the Anglophone Revolt in 2016 and 2017, media personalities and public figures aligned with the Biya regime immediately began a campaign of group vilification against Anglophones. Jean Jacques Zé, a journalist of the pro-Biya, Vision 4 Television station owned by Jean-Pierre Amougou Belinga, described Cameroon military attacks, arrests, torture and killings of unarmed civilian demonstrators and suspected insurgents in the Northwest and Southwest regions as nothing but "*dératisation*" (extermination of rats). Sitting beside Zé on the set was Ernest Obama, the News Director of Vision 4 Television. Obama shook his head in agreement with Zé and added that President Paul Biya had been too lenient with Anglophones. Members of the Anglophone minority community and, especially members of the Cameroon Union of English-Speaking Journalists, raised a hue and cry, accusing Zé and Obama of hate speech. Nevertheless, on September 21, 2017, the National Communication Council, a governmental watchdog organization with the power to suspend newspapers and journalists who misbehave, issued a long list of punitive sanctions against media outlets and journalists who had published damning investigative reports of corruption by governmental officials. The Chairman of the CNC, veteran Anglophone journalist turned censor-in-chief, Peter Essoka, did not so much as lift a finger against Zé, Obama, or Vision 4 Television. On September 22, 2017, in an interview on the Cameroon Radio and Television (CRTV) national station in Yaoundé, Biya-appointed Francophone Governor, Bernard Okalia Bilaï of the Southwest region, used dehumanizing language to describe the Anglophone Revolt. The "honourable" governor called Anglophones dogs. He told the audience: "Let everyone go to his family, to his village and chain his dog. If these dogs continue to go out into the street and bite, that is to say, to destroy, they will encounter the security forces." Those kinds of utterances were common in the official media, private newspapers and television stations funded by and aligned politically, ideologically, and culturally with the Biya regime. That dehumanizing tribal rhetoric notwithstanding, to limit Francophone responses to the extremist utterances of Ernest Obama, Jacques Zé and others with a tribal or regional bent of mind would be overly simplistic and misinformed. British, French, and, to a lesser extent, German colonialism left their mark on Cameroon and Cameroonians, to be sure. The very nomenclatures of the territory Cameroon/Cameroun/Kamerun are British, French and German derivatives of the name, *Rio dos Cameroes* (River of Prawns) that Portuguese explorers had given up to the Wouri estuary in the 15th century. The English and Pidgin-speaking Southern Cameroons had been anchored to the Anglosphere for centuries, and especially during the era of the slave trade and 19th century colonialism, before it became the League of Nations Mandate, British Cameroons, under provisions of the post-World War I Treaty of Versailles of 1919. As for French Cameroun, it too was anchored in the Anglosphere until 1919 when it became French Cameroun, a League of Nations Mandate governed by France as an appendage of French Equatorial Africa.

These relatively brief, 40-year colonial experiences under Britain and France made their mark on the peoples of both territories, to be sure. Language is, after all, the gateway to cultures and worldviews. However, the issue goes beyond language. Politically, the governmentality (mentality of governance) of the English and Pidgin-speaking Southern Cameroons was loosely based on the British bi-cameral parliamentary system. The territory had a system of indirect rule with a Premier, a House of Assembly that paralleled the British House of Commons, and a House of Chiefs that paralleled the British House of Lords. Southern Cameroons also had an independent judiciary. It was a system of checks and balances. The territory had a system of local government and an educational system composed of Native Authority (NA) Schools and Mission schools, which were set up for the most part by American and European Catholic and Protestant missionary societies. For its part, French Cameroun was ruled directly by France as part of French Equatorial Africa. It inherited the highly centralized, unicameral, Napoleonic rule-by-decree system, which mimicked French secular republicanism with its trenchant anti-clericalism, a system where the law triumphed over individual rights.

Though these different governmentalities complicated the reunification of English and French-speaking Cameroon, they were not the leading causes of the Anglophone Revolt. The historical record shows that the Anglophone Revolt came about because the Ahidjo/Biya regime mismanaged the merged inherited colonial systems of governance, justice, and education. As we have seen in Chapters 4, 5, & 9 of Volume I, the Ahidjo/Biya regime set out to mute and erase the cultural and identitarian specificity of the English and Pidgin-speaking Southern Cameroons soon after the reunification of the two territories in 1961, through a policy of assimilation and "harmonization." More than that, Ahidjo instituted an authoritarian, neo-patrimonial, kleptocratic republican chiefdom that seized the natural resources (mostly oil and natural gas) in the territory of the English and Pidgin-speaking

Southern Cameroons, and essentially transformed the revenues they generated first into Ahidjo's political slush fund, and subsequently into President Paul Biya's neo-patrimonial slush fund that handsomely enriched his family, clan, tribe and friends when he became president in 1982. Furthermore, the regime split Southern Cameroons into geographically tautologous Northwest and Southwest regions. All calls for change by both Anglophones and Francophones are met with brutal repression. The regime uses massive repression to create a climate of fear that silences both Anglophones and Francophones. It can therefore, be argued that the Anglophone problem was brought about by poor governance, greed, autocracy, and a lack of democracy.

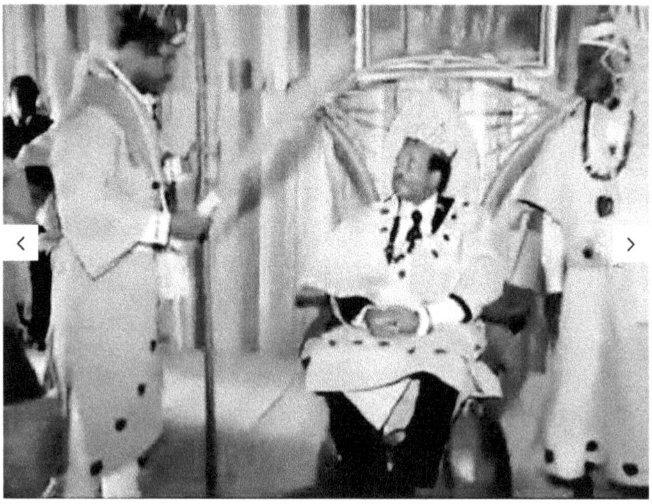

Figure 25.1. The Republican Chief of State sitting on a tribal throne in his native region, Mvomeka'a

Figure 25.2. Celebrating Chief of State, President Paul Biya, the Republican Chief in his home region

LE CRY N Infos

naja TV

Hebdomadaire bilingue d'informations générales

Directeur de Publication : Jérôme Ekoto

PAUL BIYA

Le messie du peuple camerounais

Face aux ennemis de la République, l'armée Camerounaise reste parée.
Sous les ordres directs du Chef des forces armées S.E Paul BIYA, les responsables des différents etats majors se distinguent par leur intégrité et leur efficacité afin de permettre aux Camerounais de dormir et vaquer paisiblement à leurs occupations.
En cette periode de fin d'année, les destabilisateurs et les malfrats n'ont qu'à bien se tenir.

Page 9

COMMUNE DE METET

La jeune commune dévoile son charme

L'éxécutif Communal de Metet tient à redonner une nouvelle urbanisation à cette cité par la recherche du bien-être commun.

Le Cryon Infos du 010 décembre 2021 · N°084

Figure 25.3. Chief of State, President Paul Biya, The Messiah (Savior) of the People of Cameroon. *Le Crayon Info* (pro-government newspaper), December 10, 2020

Enter Francophone Intellectuals

When the Biya regime opted to use the military, especially the Israeli-trained BIR to suppress the Anglophone Revolt with extreme violence and prejudice, a number of thoughtful, fair-minded, Francophone Cameroonian intellectuals who had studied in France, and especially in multi-cultural or federalist countries like Canada, Switzerland, the United States, and Germany, were appalled because they saw the problem for what it was, authoritarian repression and human rights violations that that were contrary to the Universal Declaration of Human Rights, the African Charter on Human and Peoples' Rights, and other humanitarian creeds. It was also a negation of cultural diversity. This chapter presents the voices and views of a select group of French-speaking or Francophone writers, journalists and statesmen with respect to the Anglophone Question, and especially the happenings of the Anglophone revolt of 2016. It is made up of case studies and of the writings of Professor Fridolin Nké of the University of Yaoundé 1, who got into serious trouble with Cameroon's State Security, personified by the Commander of the Military Security Division (SEMIL) of the Ministry of Defense. We also hear from Professor Ambroise Kom, University of Yaoundé, Université des Montagnes, and Eleanor Howard O'Leary Endowed Chair in Francophone Studies, College of the Holy Cross, Worcester, Massachusetts. We also present verbatim, the writing of Jean-Marc Soboth, former president of the Francophone Cameroon Union of Journalists, who as early as 2010, presented a clear and succinct analysis of the Anglophone problem. The prescient analysis of two distinguished Cameroonian Statesmen, David Abouèm à Tchoyi, former appointed governor of the Southwest and Northwest provinces, former minister of education and Secretary General at the Presidency of the Republic. This is followed by a write-up from the late Christian Ekoka Penda, a visionary who was a technical adviser at the Cameroon presidency. At the onset of the Anglophone Revolt, Christian Penda Ekoka wrote a 7-page manifesto stating that the call for federalism was not a call for secession and that the crisis was an opportunity to revitalize the institutions of the country. This was the beginning of a sad political journal that led him to prison and an untimely death. The chapter ends with a write-up by another visionary, former civil servant, economist, and media pundit, Dieudonné Essomba, who bravely expressed views on the Anglophone problem that were breaths of fresh air. He was a regular invitee who bravely expressed his views as a guest on the popular independent television station, *Equinoxe*. His appearances were cancelled from time to time under pressure from the powers that be, until he was declared persona non grata on the channel and retired from the civil service in retaliation for his views. All persons featured in this chapter wrote in French. Their writings have been translated by the author.

Figure 25.4. President Biya on the front cover of *Geminal*: Surpassed, of the past and passive. December 2, 2016.

Francophone Intellectual Resistance to Human Rights Violation in the Anglophone Northwest and Southwest Regions: The Fridolin Nké Affair

One of the most public and most dramatic cases of Francophone intellectual opposition to the Biya regime's attempt to violently subjugate the Anglophone minority involved Professor Fridolin Nké, a Francophone professor of philosophy at the University of Yaoundé 1. Prof. Nké, who had written a book entitled, *Paul Biya: Chroniques de la Fin* (published in English as "Biya's End and the Future of the Nation") was in the bad books of the regime. In 2021, Professor Nké wrote a Facebook post calling on the Cameroon army to disobey orders to shoot innocent Anglophones in the former British Southern Cameroons (the Northwest and Southwest regions). He was promptly summoned to appear before Colonel Joël Émile Bamkoui, commander of the dreaded Division of Military Security (popularly known by its dreaded acronym, SEMIL) for interrogation on charges of inciting insurrection and mutiny in the defense and security forces in time of war. Bamkoui had written that the Anglophone Revolt was, like the Boko Haram Islamist terrorism in North Cameroon, nothing but criminality born of organized crime and "corruption." (*Retraite du redoutable Emile Bamkoui*, 2022). Knowing that he faced torture and death at the hands of the military security and intelligence, Professor Fridolin Nké refused to present himself at the feared Division of Military Security (which is known for being a notorious torture chamber). He was summoned in writing a second time. He refused once more to present himself to the interrogators, and instead lodged a complaint against the dreaded SEMIL Commander, Colonel Joël Émile Bamkoui, with the Yaoundé Military Tribunal, the Presidency of the Republic, the Ministry of Defense, Western embassies in Yaoundé, and even the United Nations (Djialeu, 2021). Colonel Joël Émile Bamkoui, who was described by French magazine, *Jeune Afrique*, as being "trigger happy," had been court-marshalled at the Military Tribunal in Yaoundé, for shooting a police inspector, Hervé Michel Ndjifon Mapouro to death. He was given a symbolic sentence for involuntary manslaughter and before long, was promoted to the post of Commander of Military Security (Intelligence) in Yaoundé (Mawel, 2022).

The professor's tactic was that giving the matter the widest national and international publicity would prevent the Biya regime from quietly eliminating him. Nevertheless, even some of his colleagues turned against him. One of them was his former professor, Joseph Ndzomo Molé, who accused him of not taking responsibility and facing the consequences of his public declarations. Prof. Fridolin Nké wrote an open letter to his former professor and posted it on Facebook for all to see (Nké, 2021). The widely–shared letter was entitled:

> *J'assume : j'ai demandé aux soldats de ne pas obéir aux ordres illégaux et illégitimes*
>
> (I Admit it: I asked [Cameroonian] soldiers not to obey illegal and illegitimate orders)
>
> *Réponse à mon enseignant, Pr Joseph Ndzomo Molé, qui m'a reproché d'avoir refusé de déférer à la convocation du Colonel Joël Émile Bamkoui, Commandant de la SEMIL (Division de la Sécurité militaire, Ministère de la Défense).*
>
> (Response to my teacher, Prof. Joseph Ndzomo Molé, who reproached me for refusing to honor the summons of Colonel Joël Émile Bamkoui, Commander of SEMIL, the Military Security Division, Ministry of Defense).
>
> Response to my teacher, Prof. Joseph Ndzomo Molé, who reproached me after my publication yesterday, in which I stated that agents of the SEMIL [*Sécurité militaire* or Military Security) sent by Colonel Émile Joël Bamkoui were in the process of identifying my residence, you claimed that I was not consistent when I refused to report to the offices of SEMIL. You mobilized the Socratic method to reproach me for not assuming my responsibilities as a philosopher, of betraying the discipline, and you have predicted that I will soon die.

Professor, Socrates died more than two millennia ago. History has evolved, evolved a lot. History will continue to change... The philosopher is not an immaculate venerated figure in the imaginary museum of criticism, much less a sacred relic that is presented as an offering to brigands, thieves, and brutes to satisfy filthy pleasures...

....

If I refused to honour the summons of Monsieur Joël Émile Bamkoui, to present myself at the Division of Military Security, it is because that is not the court that should judge me. If it were someone else at the SEMIL who summoned me, I would have gone. It is not an institution that summons me, like the Gendarmerie or the Police, as you claim; it is a mythical personality of popular bloody tales with whom I have a major disagreement, who is reputed to have a lugubrious nature (that is what they say, I know nothing of it: they say he exists without living. Finally, I doubt what they say of him up to his very existence).

Professor, contrary to what you say, I take responsibility for my acts. I denounced the torture of civilians at SEMIL; I have denounced the war in NOSO (Northwest and Southwest regions) and I accept the consequences. I will not show that I am responsible for my statements by legitimating excesses and abuse of power....In the face of a dirty and unjust war like that which was launched in the NOSO (Northwest and Southwest), not against a foreign power but against our brothers and sisters, if one is indifferent to these screams, to these cries and groans of our soldiers and our compatriots of West Cameroon, we lose the dignity which makes us humans. It seems immoral to me that a philosopher worth the name can seek refuge in the history of philosophy to justify crimes, to support a barbarism, in order to sing a partisan patriotism."

I admit: I asked the military to disregard the orders they receive on the battlefield and in the gendarmerie stations [in the Northwest and Southwest regions].

And know that even when I ask the military not to carry out illegal and illegitimate orders, I remain a Republican [believer in republicanism as opposed to monarchism]. And as a Republican [believer in republican values] I do not submit myself neither to judicial gangsterism nor to State banditry...

Pour terminer, Prof.

Vous me prédisez un funeste sort : « à ce rythme, il ne mourra pas à soixante-dix ans comme Socrate»! Sachez d'abord que, généralement, les hommes de chez nous (en Afrique je veux dire) ne vivent pas vieux. Ensuite, en tant que penseur radical, je suis né trop vieux et mourir à un âge trop avancé serait un calvaire intenable pour moi. Je dois ruiner toute ma prolifique vie maintenant, de peur qu'elle ne prenne des rides malsaines du vieux temps.

To conclude, Professor,

You predict for me a fatal lot: "at this rate, he will not die at age 70 years like Socrates"! Know first of all that, generally, people at home {by that I mean Africa) do not live to old age. Furthermore, as a radical thinker, I was born too old and to die at a very advanced age would be an untenable cross for me to bear. I must ruin all my prolific life now, for fear that it might develop the unhealthy wrinkle of olden days.

Philosophiquement vôtre!
Philosophically yours, Fridolin NKE

Figure 25.5. BIR Torture Video, Bamenda (January 13, 2017). A number of Francophone intellectuals stood against the militarization of the "Anglophone Crisis" and against torture

Figure 25.6. BIR Torture, Bamenda (2017)

Prof. Fridolin Nké's strategy of publicly exposing an attempt to silence and erase him for being outspoken against repression in the English-speaking regions of Cameroon did not work. On September 20, 2021, a rather bizarre video was posted on the professor's Facebook page. It featured the professor standing in a red, ornate office, the official portrait of President Paul Biya in the background. A male voice in the background orders him "vas-y!" (carry on!). Looking furtively in the direction of the voice, the frightened-looking university don proceeded to say that he was in a "very delicate situation," that he was in the office of Colonel Joël Émile Bamkoui, Commander of SEMIL, the Military Security Division of the Cameroon Ministry of Defense: "and I have already received three huge blows, one from him [Colonel Bamkoui] and from his agents. I am here against my will because I had a matter in a company, I was asked to go there. When I went there, I was arrested and brought here. It is Col. Bamkoui who has ordered me to do this live [Facebook] stream against my will. We had a discussion on the army and the war in the NOSO [Northwest and Southwest]. The voice of Col. Bamkoui interrupted him from the background, "we will have a debate. I reiterate this, I am in his office…" The professor essentially told the world that he had been kidnapped and brought before the dreaded SEMIL commander, Col. Joël Émile Bamkoui for interrogation against his will.

The voice of Col. Bamkoui in the background orders him to say: "I am making this live Facebook stream from his office."

"I was arrested and brought here, and I am being made to do this video by force from Col. Bamkoui's office…" said the professor looking to his left in the direction of the voice of Col. Bamkoui.

"But I told him, and I reiterate this, that I am against the war in the Northwest and Southwest…. I am against the death of Cameroonians; I reiterate this and no one can convince me to be in favor of this war…. It is imperative that we stop this war… you slapped me. Instead of debating with a philosopher, they slap him…we must stop this war, we must stop this war. I say this in his office…" The professor said emphatically!

"Say that I am the one who ordered you to do this live presentation," the voice of Col. Bamkoui ordered in the background. The professor did what he was told and added that Cameroon was one country with two parts of Cameroon, Southern Cameroons and East Cameroon, and that we cannot force unity through war. He said this was a political matter and that he wanted to convince Col. Bamkoui who was in front of him.

"I tell all Cameroonians that I am prepared for everything. If I leave here, dead or alive, I am ready for everything…"

Figure 25.7. Prof. Fridolin Nke's Facebook post of his protest t-shirt: STOP KILLING IN NOSO. NOSO is the French acronym for the Anglophone Northwest and Southwest regions (July 2021)

Figure 25.8. Facebook screenshot of Prof. Fredolin Nké doing a forced live Facebook stream from the office of the Director of Military Security, Col. Joël Émile Bamkoui on September 20, 2021.

Later that day, Prof. Nké posted a message on his Facebook page: "Hold Paul Biya and Beti Assomo (Minister of Defense) responsible for everything Bamkoui does to me. I have been released and am in the hospital." It appears this bizarre episode was designed to show the general public of Cameroon that the professor could not defy a summons to appear before the all-powerful Commander of Military Intelligence with impunity. It was a clear triumph of law and power over rights. Col. Joël Émile Bamkoui showed the professor that he could not escape the long arm of Cameroon's military security intelligence. Cameroonians were stunned by what became known as the Fridolin Nké affair. Everyone expected the recalcitrant professor to turn up dead as had been the case with journalist Samuel Wazizi. Professor Nké was not murdered, perhaps because of the publicity his dissidence had caused. However, to everyone's surprise, in June 2022, a presidential decree announced that Colonel Joël Émile Bamkoui, Commander of SEMIL, the Military Security Division of the Ministry of Defense, would be retired from the armed forces with effect from April 3, 2023, the day after his 58th birthday, as per military regulations. Apparently, the regime did not appreciate this public, social media display of the raw power of the republican chiefdom over a citizen who opposed the regime's war of subjugation of the English-speaking regions of Cameroon. In November 2023, Professor Nké resurfaced, informed the world that he was still alive, and that he had written two books critical of the Biya regime.

The Felix Nkongho Agbor Balla Affair (University of Buea) and Prof Ambroise Kom

Professor Fridolin Nké of the University of Yaoundé I was not the only Francophone Cameroonian academician who rose up to resist the climate of fear under which Anglophone and Francophone professors and intellectuals were forced to ply their trade. The Biya regime's violent and highly repressive response to Anglophone lawyers, teachers, and churches' call for recognition of their cultural and identitarian specificity further complicated the situation of Anglophone intellectuals and reduced their freedom of speech and expression in general, and their academic freedom in particular. In 2020, the long-serving Minister of Higher Education, Jacques Fame Ndongo, who is also the keeper of the ideological orthodoxy of the regime, dismissed Barrister Felix Nkongho Agbor Balla, a human rights activist and professor at the University of Buea Faculty of Law for giving his students an examination question which the government considered "seditious" (Fatunde, 2020; Lawyers' Rights Watch Canada, 2020). Barrister Felix Nkongho Agbor Balla's examination question was: "*The Anglophone crisis since 2016 was caused by lawyers' and teachers' strikes. Assess the validity of this statement.*" The University of Buea authorities quickly sent the question to the security forces and to the Ministry of Higher Education in Yaoundé. The dismissal of Felix Agbor Nkongho can be contrasted with the reception he was accorded by the United States Congress (see appendix XX).

Figure 25.9. Free Agbor Balla Poster. Barrister Felix Nkongho Agbor (Balla). Dismissed from his post as instructor at the University of Buea for asking a question about the Anglophone Revolt

The summary dismissal of Barrister Felix Nkongho Agbor Balla from the University of Buea over that examination question stung Anglophone and Francophone professors in Cameroon. However, due to the insecurity of academic tenure in Cameroon–the minister of higher education and the president can dismiss any faculty member at any public university at any time, for any political reason or no reason– academicians reacted with a deafening silence. Venerable Cameroonian Francophone intellectual, professor, Ambroise Kom, who lived and taught in the United States, away from the toxic academic climate of fear in Cameroon, promptly wrote a seven-page open letter to the Minister of Higher Education, Jacques Fame Ndong (Kom, 2020). In the letter entitled, "*Lettre ouverte à Jacques Fame Ndongo, mon frère*" (Open letter to Jacques Fame Ndongo, my Brother), Professor Kom took the minister to task for violation of academic freedom, and for transforming state universities into institutions of ideological indoctrination:

> *Le traitement que subit aujourd'hui Felix Agbor Balla Nkongho* de l'Université de Buea ne peut en aucune manière me laisser indifférent et je me sens obligé d'interpeler mon collègue et frère Jacques Fame Ndongo,

pour lui rappeler, au cas où ils lui auraient échappé, quelques principes élémentaires des franchises universitaires et des libertés académiques....

The treatment to which Felix Agbor Balla Nkongho of the University of Buea is subject today cannot in any way leave me indifferent and I feel obliged to interpellate or call out to my colleague and brother, Jacques Fame Ndongo, to remind him, in case he has forgotten them, of certain elementary principles of the franchises/rights of universities and of academic freedoms...

...la liberté académique est la structure fondamentale de l'Université, qu'elle n'est pas faite pour le plaisir des enseignants mais pour le bien-être de la société au profit de laquelle ils exercent leur métier.... l'Université de Buea fut enfantée en 1993 par césarienne dans une indescriptible chienlit. Après plus de soixante ans d'indépendance, nous aurions pu donner, me semble-t-il, une identité à nos universités de manière à nous éviter la honte des errements actuels.

...that academic freedom is the fundamental structure of the University, that it is not established to please lecturers but for the good of society on whose behalf they carry out their professions.... the University of Buea was born in 1993 through a caesarian section in an indescribable chaotic situation. After more than sixty years of independence, we should have been able to give, it seems to me, an identity to our universities in a manner that spares us the shame of current mistakes.

Sans vouloir entrer dans les détails de l'affaire Felix Agbor Balla Nkongho, il est difficile de comprendre que le Ministre de l'Enseignement Supérieur mette un enseignant d'Université sur la sellette, non pas parce qu'il est accusé d'incitation à la haine raciale/tribale, d'injures, de diffamation, de négationnisme ou de harcèlement sexuel, mais pour un banal sujet d'examen donné aux étudiants, sujet portant sur une question d'actualité nationale : «The Anglophone crisis since 2016 was caused by lawyers' and teachers' strikes. Assess the validity of this statement. /La crise anglophone a été causée depuis 2016 par une grève des avocats et des enseignants. Évaluez la validité de cette déclaration ». À se demander si l'Université de Buea n'est qu'une école de formation des cadres du parti ou si elle se confond désormais à la CRTV (*Cameroon Radio and Télévision), à Cameroon Tribune*, à tous ces appareils idéologiques d'État ! Le *Chancelier ou le Recteur est-il devenu le ministre de l'Administration Territoriale ou le Ministre de la Communication, Porte-parole du Gouvernement ?...*

Without going into the details of the Felix Agbor Balla Nkongho affair, it is difficult to understand that the Minister of Higher Education takes

> a lecturer to task, not because he is accused of incitement to racial/tribal hatred, insults or defamation, of denial [of the Holocaust] or of sexual harassment, but for a simple examination question given to students, a question that concerns national current affairs...One has to ask whether the University of Buea is nothing but a school for training cadres of the party [the ruling CPDM] or it is henceforth equated with the CRTV (Cameroon Radio and Television), with *Cameroon Tribune* [the official government newspaper], with all the ideological apparatuses of the State! The Chancellor or the Rector has he become the Minister of Territorial Administration or the Minister of Communication, the spokesman of the government?
>
> ---
>
> *Tout compte fait, il est évident que dans notre pays, l'université n'est qu'un instrument du pouvoir au même titre que les autres appareils idéologiques d'État. Tout est mis en œuvre pour que les sbires du régime y occupent des positions privilégiées....*
>
> *Rester silencieux face au traitement qu'on fait subir à Felix Agbor Balla et à la forme de plus en plus hideuse que prend notre enseignement supérieur reviendrait à accepter d'être complice en oubliant ou plutôt en enterrant les valeurs cardinales qui m'ont permis de faire une exaltante carrière d'enseignant ici et ailleurs...*
>
> All things considered, it is evident that in our country, the [State] university is nothing but an instrument of power at the same level as the other ideological apparatuses of the State. Everything is done to ensure that the henchmen of the regime occupy positions of privilege there...For me to remain silent in the face of the treatment to which Felix Agbor Balla is being subject and the more and more hideous form that our higher education is taking would be equal to accepting to be an accomplice, [to] forgetting or burying the cardinal values that have enabled me to have an exalting teaching carrier here and elsewhere.

Professor Kom lamented that the old practice of government-appointed university administrators monitoring the lectures and examination questions of professors in state universities, forwarding material they considered objectionable to the national security authorities, and punishing professors who departed from the ideological strictures of the regime, were being applied. Professor Ambroise Kom's admonitions and pleas for academic freedom fell on deaf ears. Other professors at the University of Buea who were suspected of secessionist sympathies were dismissed by ministerial decree. It should be recalled that Barrister Felix Nkongho Agbor Balla, had been arrested, jailed, and tried at the Yaoundé Military Tribunal for being one of the leaders of the Anglophone Civil Society Consortium (see chapter 5 and 26). Other Anglophone professors have faced a similar fate. The result was a climate of fear that chilled academic freedom at the Universities of Buea, Bamenda, Yaoundé, and elsewhere.

Germinal

Accueil | Notre époque | Manières de voir | Notre opinion | Rebonds | Le dossier | Culture | Environnement | Micmacs | Contact

Lettre ouverte à Jacques Fame Ndongo, mon frère

Lettre ouverte à Jacques Fame Ndongo, mon frère

Lundi, 11 Mai 2020 19:02 Clics: 17039 Ecrit par Pr Ambroise Kom

Note des utilisateurs: / 0

Mauvais Très bien NOTE

Pr Ambroise Kom Pr Jacques Fame Ndongo

Ce n'est pas sans pincement au cœur que je prends aujourd'hui la plume pour écrire à quelqu'un envers qui, pour avoir entretenu d'intenses et fructueuses relations professionnelles pendant de nombreuses années, j'éprouve pas mal de respect. Certes, c'est sur fond de suspicion que ma relation avec le collègue **Jacques Fame Ndongo** commença au début des années 1990. À l'époque, Célestin Monga et moi, avions organisé le retour au Cameroun de Mongo Beti dont l'exil n'avait que trop duré. Fame Ndongo, auteur d'une thèse sur l'œuvre de Mongo Beti mais aussi conseiller en communication du prince, se positionna du côté de ceux qui percevaient l'initiative comme un geste de sédition. Ce qu'il fit savoir dans une interview imaginaire qu'il publia dans le journal *Le Patriote*, attribuant à Mongo Beti une sévère critique de Mme Frances Cooke, alors ambassadrice des USA au Cameroun, soupçonnée de collusion avec les partis d'opposition. Plus tard, Mongo Beti fit la connaissance de l'ami Jacques Fame Ndongo lors d'une cérémonie organisée par les Services Culturels de l'Ambassade du Canada à l'occasion de la sortie

du numéro 42 de *Présence Francophone* contenant un important dossier sous ma direction sur l'œuvre du romancier, publié avec le concours financier de ladite ambassade. Lorsque Fame Ndongo se présenta pour lui demander un autographe, Mongo Beti ne put se contenir et l'agressa verbalement, à haute et intelligible voix, jetant alors un froid glacial dans la salle du très diplomatique banquet. J'avais pourtant mis les organisateurs en garde contre ce genre d'incompatibilités mais ils m'avaient répondu que la diplomatie c'était aussi un jeu d'équilibrisme !

Par la suite, je ne reverrai **Jacques Fame Ndongo** qu'après sa nomination au poste de Ministre de l'Enseignement Supérieur (Minesup) puisqu'entre temps, j'étais parti aux USA dans les conditions que je raconte dans *Université des Montagnes. Pour solde de tout compte* (2017). D'avoir gardé un pied à l'Université de Yaoundé où je dispensais des enseignements des 2è et 3è cycles m'obligeait à revenir régulièrement au pays où, par ailleurs, je travaillais ardemment à l'éclosion de l'Université des Montagnes (UdM). Raison pour laquelle je me permis, en compagnie de l'ami **Fabien Nkot** d'aller à la rencontre du nouveau Minesup pour négocier les conditions de l'évolution de l'UdM à laquelle Maurice Tchuenté, son prédécesseur, avait donné naissance.

Pendant dix ans, de 2005 à 2015, j'ai travaillé assez étroitement avec le frère Jacques Fame Ndongo. Sans entrer dans les détails, j'ai accompli pour lui et pour le compte du Minesup, des missions informelles auprès de la Banque mondiale à Washington. Ce qui avait abouti à des réunions stratégiques avec les experts de la Banque mondiale au Minesup sous le regard médusé des proches collaborateurs du Ministre qui ne comprenaient pas à quel titre j'étais invité. En plus de m'intégrer dans des groupes d'études au Minesup tel que celui sur le « *Plan Directeur de la Recherche* », le Ministre Jacques Fame Ndongo interviendra énergiquement lorsqu'après le départ du collègue André-Marie Ntsobe du décanat de la Faculté des Lettres de l'Université de Yaoundé 1, son très zélé successeur, **Daniel Abwa**, entreprit de me rayer de la liste des enseignants. Alors que je m'y étais toujours préparé et m'apprêtais à accepter cela de bon cœur, j'eus la très agréable surprise d'entendre Abwa dire qu'il avait renoncé à son funeste projet parce que le Ministre Fame Ndongo, mis au parfum de son initiative, lui avait demandé de lever le pied. D'après les informations en sa possession, les cours que je dispensais et les services que je rendais aux étudiants et à l'Université de Yaoundé se comparaient très avantageusement, malgré mes va et vient entre les USA et le Cameroun, à ce que pouvaient offrir mes collègues qui étaient sur place à Yaoundé. Jamais, je n'avais entendu pareil compliment d'une autorité camerounaise. L'appréciation se confirmera par la lettre d'appui qu'il me donnera lorsque je décidai d'organiser à l'Université de Yaoundé 1 en 2009 un colloque en hommage à

FLASH INFOS

News

LA UNE

Germinal

Paul Biya, un homme dépassé, du passé et du passif

Figure 25.10. Screenshot of Prof. Ambroise Kom's Open Letter to Prof. Jacques Fame Ndongo, Minister of Higher Education, protesting the dismissal of Felix Agbor Nkongho (Germinal, 11 May 2020)

Francophone Perspectives on the Anglophone Problem: Politicians and Media Pundits

Outside academia, a number of Francophones courageously expressed their views on the Anglophone crisis despite the silence imposed by the regime, and climate of fear that reigned in the country over the issue. In this section, we publish the views of President Paul Jean-Marc Soboth, journalist, writer, and former president of the Cameroon Union of Journalists, David Abouèm à Tchoyi, former appointed governor of the Anglophone Northwest and Southwest regions, Christian Penda Ekoka, former technical adviser at the Presidency of the Republic, and Dieudonné Essomba, economist, former civil servant, and courageous media pundit.

Jean-Marc Soboth

Jean-Marc Soboth (Former President, Society of Cameroonian Journalists)

Truths (That We Refuse to Hear) And Lies About the Anglophone Problem in Cameroon.

September 7, 2010.

Dear All,

I present my homage to Everyone, specifically to my professor of *Introduction to Law and Legal Systems* at the University of Yaoundé (1986-1987), Professor Carlson Anyangwe, I would like to make, by way of contribution to the discussion, the following development which reflects the level of knowledge which I have of the Anglophone Question–having covered the AAC I & II at Buea and Bamenda, and having done multiple interviews, including of notables like John Ngu Foncha, at Foncha Street , and Solomon Tandeng Muna at Ngyembuh [his village in Momo division]...When I was chief of the political service of the newspaper, *Le Messager* in 1995, the *Anglophone Question* led me to win an award at the Yaoundé Hilton Hotel.

I beg the indulgence of all here present. I would like to indicate that I don't know everything on the issue...According to historians (including Victor T. Levine in his book, *The Cameroons from Mandate to Independence),* President Ahidjo showed some reticence with respect to Southern Cameroons joining the former French Cameroon, which had become independent the previous year (1960), before the reunification plebiscite (1961). Ahidjo subsequently delayed talks sought by Southern Cameroons nationalists, which talks finally took place in Foumban, under the patronage of his friend Njoya Arouna, and of the Sultan and Bamum King in July 1961.

Ahmadou Ahidjo was suspicious of the fact that Anglophones, who had a culture that was more respectful of individuals, was reputed to be a bit too uncertain about issues of human rights in the judicial process. Given that the bloody repression of members of the UPC [*Union des Populations de Cameroun*] was in full swing and that the Anglophone leaders criticized it without mincing words and by additionally extending hospitality to Francophone militant nationalists. The UPC, which had done most of the work of sensitization about the idea of reunification, had set up a last-ditch headquarters in Kumba. Its militants regularly escaped the genocidal spectacle of the French Army in French Cameroun (hundreds of thousands killed) and found themselves in Southern Cameroons, where the French army did not have the right to pursue these "maquisards" or resistance fighters.

For Ahmadou Ahidjo, the activism of Anglophone nationalists at the UN for reunification was aimed, in the long-run, at strengthening the UPC opposition in French Cameroon–we now have proof that that he rejected the idea of a territorial association with the Island of Fernando Po for the same reasons. Ahidjo had invested all his energies and his resources of the state in the Northern part of the country, named Northern Cameroons for demographic, political, religious and ethnic reasons. But according to

Levine, this region, which was more heavily populated than the South, was too influenced by the traditional emirates of North East Nigeria–notably the Shehu (Emir) of Yola, whose influence continued until his recent death, on the grand Lamibe or Chiefs of the North Cameroon, which he personally installed. Clearly, the religious rulers who controlled this region determined the outcome of the plebiscite, a vote to join Nigeria. After this failure, in a rage confirmed by his aides (source: interview with the late Ambassador Mojamadou Haman Dicko), immediately seized the International Court of Justice, claiming of massive fraud perpetrated by the British administration during the elections. The counsel for Cameroon raised, among other complaints, the fact that the election itself was illegal...

Having lost in the North and having no illusion on the verdict of the International Court of Justice, Ahidjo, "in national mourning," finally went to the Foumban talks, with the support of French advisers, according to a recent video.

In effect, in the Southern Cameroons region, enthusiasm for reunification had been substantially dampened long before the plebiscite of February 1961. The leaders of Southern Cameroons feared henceforth the extension into their territory of the murderous French across [the river Mungo] from them. They began to entertain the idea of a sovereign state to the exclusion of both neighbors [Nigeria and *La Republique du Cameroun*]. All those who were moulded in the forge of the NCNC (National Council of Nigeria and Cameroons), created by the father of Nigerian independence, Dr. Nnamdi Azikiwe–E.M.L Endeley, John Ngu Foncha–agreed for the first time to request the UN for a 'time of reflection." This platform came after years of political disagreement born of the abandonment of the ideology of reunification by the Bakweri Prince, Dr. E.M.L Endeley...

This fabulous project, which was the subject of popular songs, could have resulted, at a minimum in a third alternative, besides those imposed by the UN as a straight jacket., namely: 1) obtain independence by automatically joining Nigeria, or 2) by automatically joining the former French Cameroun. The alternative was radically rejected by the UN. Only the two UN alternatives were of necessity available to voters as options.

The philosophical basis of a federal state was thus laid at Foumban on the basis of a choice dictated by a dilemma, and after the fact, by the joy of "reuniting with our brothers after more than forty years of separation," after the moving words of a popular song composed on the occasion and was sung in public primary schools. Southern Cameroons renounced the more substantial advantages offered by the Nigerian state during the elections–in constituencies like Kumba, supporters of the option to join Nigeria, led by Dr. Emmanuel Endeley, won the election. In the federal constitution of 1961, the Anglophone leaders paid attention to the essential: this part of Cameroon was entering a state of equality under constitutional law, excluding any eventual imposition of the demographic majority Francophones on the minority Anglophones, at least from the point of view of a possible revision of the economy and the fundamental federal law. The new "independent" state committed itself to stay away from numerous international groupings such as the Commonwealth of Nations and la Francophonie. There again, the joint agreements were not adhered to.

It appears that it is the discovery of oil by the French [in Southern Cameroons] that led Ahmadou Ahidjo to begin to centralize the system in order to install a unitary totalitarian state. First step the forced one-party state of September 1966; all Anglophone and Francophone political parties "agreed" to fold and join the Cameroon National Union (CNU), the ancestor of the Cameroon Peoples Democratic Movement (RDPC/CPDM).

Second step: the referendum of 20th May 1972, organized for the forceful transformation to the unitary state, annexing subsidiarily, the parliamentary system of Southern Cameroons, thereby violating the constitutional provision that forbade revision of the Federal Constitution through an electoral procedure that would drown the Anglophone minority.

Some writers claim that strong-headed persons like Bernard Fonlon clearly warned Ahidjo against such a constitutional violation that was fatally unpopular in the former West Cameroon. Ahidjo did it, nevertheless. While this development allowed Ahidjo to hand over to the French multinational company, Elf, among others, control of the offshore resources on the coast of Southern Cameroons–and this filled [secret] numbered bank accounts in tax havens, according to the writer Mongo Beti–it above all led to the systematic destruction of the historic, moral, cultural, linguistic, and administrative infrastructure of this part of the country. This change allowed Ahidjo to impose, as a national holiday, not a national event or an event of national patriotic significance (the reunification of "independence") as is the case with countries around the world, but a ludicrous date (May 20th), which is simply the birthday of the First Lady, Germaine Habiba Ahidjo.... The calendars of that era showed "Reunification" in October and "Unification" on May 20th. To end this confusion, October 1st disappeared as if by magic from future calendars.

This process, it must be recognized, has remained essentially unknown to the Francophone public which, paradoxically believes it knows everything, and the Anglophone citizen is relegated to second class status. Minor or subsidiary positions like vice president of the Republic and later Speaker of the National Assembly, institutionally destined for Anglophones, were progressively emptied of content in the unitary presidential state. Nevertheless, through an inept presidential decree of 1984, President Paul Biya definitively erased the traces of the patriotic act of February 1961with removal of the word "united" in the official name of the country and removed the second yellow star from the flag, which represented the patriotism of this people who could never be part of this territory if they wished. The former Cameroon under French administration was called *La Republique du Cameroun*. Since 1984, we are back to *La République du Cameroun*, by a symbolic name, thanks to President Biya. A whole symbol.

By so doing, the subtle and vague process of "uniformization" continued with an attempt (failed) to transform the Anglophone high school leaving diploma, the General Certificate of Education (GCE) into the traditional French Baccalauréat, the "exportation" to the Anglophone zone, of the highly opinionated culture of arrogance, lack of civility, brutality, injustice, and disdain for the human rights inherited from French colonial direct rule, the monopolization of commanding positions in Anglophone regions by Francophones–preferably by persons who were not conversant with the "Anglo-Saxon" culture–even refusal of all dialogue and ignorance of all legitimate demands for change. During an All Anglophone Conference (AACI in Buea), the patriarchs of the reunification, John Ngu Foncha and Solomon Tandeng Muna, solemnly asked for forgiveness from their people for having allowed themselves to be fooled and to have been deceived in the process. THIS WAS A HIGHLY UNPRECEDENTED ACT (capital letters in the original). John Ngu Foncha had frankly confided to me in Bamenda, all his bitterness at having never been listened to on this matter, he who had believed he could offer advice to solve the problem.

Because it had at least become apparent in October 1992 [after the stolen presidential election victory of John Fru Ndi, Chairman of the Social democratic Front (SDF)] for those who still had doubts, that it is absolutely forbidden for an Anglophone, in the current state of affairs, to hope to lead *La République du Cameroun* in a "*territoire* « français » d'Outre-mer!" (a "French" Overseas Territory).

The Six Facets of the "Anglophone Problem"

David Abouèm à Tchoyi
Former Governor of the Southwest and Northwest Provinces
Former Minister of Higher Education
Former Secretary General at the Presidency.

Six facets of the Anglophone Problem come to mind:

1. Criticism of the centralized State
2. The transfer of centers of decision to Yaoundé, far from the people and their problems.
3. The non-fulfilment of commitments with respect to the equitable treatment of institutional, legal, and administrative cultures and traditions…inherited from former colonial administrations

4. The non-fulfilment of solemn promises made during the referendum campaign
5. Change of the name of the State: Replacement of: "The United Republic of Cameroon" with "*La Republique du Cameroun*".
6. The non-fulfilment of bilingualism in the public sector even though the Constitution makes French and English two official languages of equal value.

I will briefly review these different facets;

Figure 25.11. David Abouèm à Tchoyi former Governor of the Southwest and Northwest Provinces, Former Minister of Higher Education, Former Secretary General at the Presidency

1. Critique of the centralized State

Having been despoiled of important functions that the State of West Cameroon exercised autonomously, a number of compatriots of this part of the country developed a deep feeling of nostalgia, unhappiness, frustration and discomfort. This feeling has increased over the years following the installation of the Unitary State. It is not simple nostalgia for an imaginary era that has more or less passed. It is comparison of the quality of public governance practiced since 1972, and that which existed in the federated State of West Cameroon that systematically leads a large number of actors to assail the former and regret the latter, which many want reestablished. This feeling is real even among those who did not experience the self-government of West Cameroon as a federated State.

One can find fault infinitely with the conclusions of the Fumban Conference of July 1961. It is fair to recognize that it gave a lot of power to the federated States in a number of important domains that they were allowed to manage autonomously. The federated States had broad and exclusive competence over important matters like the Interior, Penitentiary Administration, Decentralization, Rural and Community Development, Agriculture, Cattle Rearing and Fisheries, Public Works, Cooperatives, Primary and Nursery Education, Energy, Water, Lands and Survey, Natural

Resources, federal finances, etc. Each federated State had its public service which it managed sovereignly. That of West Cameroon was managed with the aid of the Public Service Commission, a sort of Superior Council of the public service, which was charged with ensuring the objectivity and of appointments and promotions, as well as respect of ethical principles in the management of careers.

The management of natural resources by the future federated States was particularly sensitive in July 1961. In separate meetings, John Ngu Foncha, Solomon Tandeng Muna and Augustine Ngom Jua affirmed that this was the subject of acrimonious discussions with the delegation of *la République du Cameroun* at Fumban, and also in separate discussions with President Ahidjo. They did not want that agreements signed previously with France should be applied to the Federated State of West Cameroon. According to them, it was also within the framework of the sharing of revenues from the exploitation of certain natural resources (mines and petroleum specifically that they demanded and obtained the agreement that the people of each Federated State be explicitly mentioned in the text of the Federal Constitution of 1961.

Cameroon was considered a constitutional curiosity, with a strong presidential regime without counterweights at the federal level, but a classic parliamentary regime at the level of the Federated States. In East Cameroon, classic parliamentarism did not function despite constitutional provisions of this State, due to the unification of political parties and the fact that Ahidjo continued to exercise a daily influence on the management of public affairs in this part of the country, which he already led as President of *la République* before the Reunification. We recall the resignation letter of a former Prime Minister of East Cameroon, Vincent de Paul Ahanda, in which he stated that President Ahidjo did not allow him to carry out his responsibilities.

But in West Cameroon, parliamentary democracy was fully functional, within the framework of the Constitution of this State. Elections were organized by an independent electoral commission created by a federal law of November 1961, the first in a French-speaking country. Through its composition, the method of appointment of its members and its procedural rules, it was truly independent of the Executive and the Legislative. Its Chairman, Justice T. Asonganyi confirmed this to me during a meeting in Bamenda.

The government had to be vested with power by the State assembly before it entered into function and it was responsible to parliament. Parliament, made up of two chambers–House of Assembly and the House of Chiefs–guarded its prerogatives. President Ahidjo himself, despite all the authority he had, realized this several times, notably in 1966. After legislative elections organized that year, Foncha's KNDP party won the highest number of seats in the House of Assembly. But its leader, J.N. Foncha, until then Vice President of the Federal Republic, and Prime Minister of West Cameroon, could not hold these two functions due to a recently voted law. President Ahidjo decided to replace him with honorable S.T. Muna, whom he thought was more federalist than the KNDP deputy leader, Augustine Ngom Jua. But parliament sent him a firm message stating that it refused to vest a government led by a minority party with power. Ahidjo was forced to appoint Augustine Ngom Jua, Vice President of KNDP, whose autonomist tendencies irritated him, to this position.

Conflictual incidents soon occurred. At first between the Prime Minister and the Federal Inspector of Administration for the region of West Cameroon. –today we would call him governor– whom he considered as being in his territory. Then between the Police, a federal force placed under the authority of the Prime Minister, and the Gendarmerie Nationale, a federal force, with which the police almost came to an armed confrontation. Actors and witnesses of these incidents are still alive.

Frustrations

The fact that all this was eliminated without being replaced, at a managerial level, by something better or even just as good, generated frustrations and demands whose effects we are still experiencing today. Appointments to the upper administration and the para-public sector, for example, were no longer apparently rational, and the Anglophones felt marginalized. Whereas up to now, everything had been done on the spot in West Cameroon, henceforth, it became necessary to go to Yaoundé to "chase files." Our compatriots of that part of the national territory came with the conviction that the functionaries–civil servants–were in the service of the public. They were shocked by the welcome reserved for them by the public officials who, despite the bilingual nature of the State, were obliged to jabber in barely intelligible French, which often resulted in laughter and jeers.

2. Transfer of Centers of decision-making to Yaoundé

Centers of policymaking, that were formerly close to the people and their problems, were all transferred far from them, to be concentrated in Yaoundé. Consequences: a hyper centralization, exasperating delays, multiple inefficiencies in public administration, the absence of accountability of the leaders towards the people whom they had a mission to serve. Two illustrative examples:

The government decided to centralize, at the *Parc National de Matériel de Genie Civil (the National Pool of Civil Engineering Equipment,* PNMGC), in Yaoundé, all civil engineering equipment owned by public works subdivisions, in the headquarters of the regions and certain divisional headquarters. All the working equipment of the former Public Works Department (PWD) of West Cameroon was thus transferred to Yaoundé, where it was put on rent by the PNMGC. Now, the workers of PWD, knew the seasons well, and started road repairs two or three rains before the start of the dry season, in order to solidify the road surfaces. They tried to do the same thing the year after this centralization. When they requested to rent the equipment from PNMGC, including equipment that belonged to them as a matter of priority, a few months earlier, they were told that the equipment was being used in other construction projects, that the equipment transporters were in disrepair, that the documents that encumbered their expenses had not been released by the Ministry of Finance, or other reasons.

In the face of the deplorable and worsening state of the road network, the people threatened to revolt noisily. One had to go right up to the president of the Republic, after having knocked on all doors without success, in order for the beginning of a solution to be found for this problem, which was becoming explosive. Oh, the joys of Centralization!

Second example: Transfer of the management of water supply systems managed by municipalities to the *Société Nationale des Eaux du Cameroun* (SNEC), the National Water Corporation. This decision taken by the government was not even explained to the people. However, these water supply systems had been funded and built by the municipalities and village communities, with or without the assistance of external partners. Taking over the management of these water systems without having invested a single franc, the first decision of SNEC took, was to reduce the number of water-taps or fountains. In the city of Kumbo, the revolt almost became a riot. The CNU mayor of the city explained in vain that the pipelines had been funded by the people themselves, and that they paid their bills regularly to the council, that it was dangerous for the people to deprive them of drinking water, nothing came of it. A slogan spread like wildfire: "Beware of the snake, it has come to bite and kill." An ironic play on the word SNEC. These angry people were accused of "rebellion against the established authority." It became necessary to go all the way to the government for a solution to be found to a problem of water-taps in communities in the hinterland. Oh, the joys of centralization! Cases of a similar nature and other subjects of discontent became numerous. It was of course, not a matter of the malicious wish of the central power, but a clash of two administrative cultures: one with an instinctive centralizing reflex, and the other, functioning by nature on the principle of giving responsibilities to different hierarchical levels of organizations [local governance].

It is interesting to note that Francophone populations who were going through the same effects of hypercentralization, did not react in the same manner. Another matter of culture. In effect, and our Anglophone brothers could understand without difficulty, Francophones do many things without even realizing that they inconvenience, and not at all out of malice. Take the example of the names of administrative divisions.

During the creation of regions in 1962, the administrative divisions formally known as "Bamileke region" and "Bamoun region" were joined together to form the administrative region known as "West." Rightly so because it was the West of East Cameroon. But the territorial west of the Federal State was West Cameroon, rightly called West Cameroon. During the transformation of the regions into provinces in 1972, the Western region became the Western province while West Cameroon disappeared. Our country is thus the only country in the world where the Northwest and Southwest are contiguous! But then, as our teachers taught us, between the Northwest and the Southwest is the West.

To better understand what our Anglophone brothers feel, let us reverse the situation. In 1960 (sic), Southern Cameroons becomes independent. They negotiate the conditions of reunification with Francophone Cameroon. This reunification takes place on 1st October 1961. During the negotiations, Cameroon francophone gets a guarantee that the federal form of the State shall never be changed. An article of the Federal Constitution of 1st September 1961 sanctions this guarantee. The federal State is nevertheless ended on 20th May 1972, and a unitary state is instituted. From Kribi to Ndikiniméki, from Batouri to Tibati, from Poli to Kousséri, people are henceforth obliged to travel to Buea to follow their files [do business with the government]. They are required to express themselves in English. Faced with haughty and mocking government officials who are quick to ridicule them, even those who have never studied English are obliged to jabber an unintelligible camfranglais. Who could honestly state that Francophones would be satisfied with such a situation to the point of taking pleasure in it and being silent?

3. Failure to respect solemn promises made during the referendum campaign.

The promises made during the campaign for a "yes" vote and which persuaded a good number of voters to vote "yes" on 20 May 1972 were hardly kept. This was notably the case with acceleration of development which, in these two regions, was supposed to result from savings made from eliminating the institutions and organizations of the federal States. The mandatories or agents of the CNU party effectively promised the paving of road, the construction of dams, the urbanization of towns, development of frontier areas, etc. I was personally present when some of these speeches were made, since I was part of the team of the Political Secretary of the CNU and the Federal Minister of Territorial Administration (I served as director of territorial organization in this ministry).

4. The non-respect of commitments concerning the equitable consideration of the institutional, juridical, administrative cultures and traditions inherited from colonization.

Whether we want it or not, British colonization, just like French colonization, produced institutional, political, administrative, managerial, and other cultures and traditions. It also shaped ways of reasoning and ways of life. It was therefore necessary to take into consideration, in an equitable manner, despite the end of the Federal State, of this double heritage of Anglo-Saxon and French systems. The State of Cameroon committed itself to this.

Thus, on the eve of the installation of the unitary State, political rhetoric placed heavy emphasis on the bilingual and pluricultural State. It was emphatically affirmed that the positive elements of our double colonial heritage would enrich the positive values of our multisectoral traditions, the invigorating lifeblood of our march towards progress. The *Conseil National de l'Enseignement Supérieur et de la Recherche Scientifique* (National Council for Higher Education and Scientific Research), as well as the *Conseil National des Affaires Culturelles*, (National Council of Cultural Affairs) organized in 1974, contributed to the definition of this new Cameroon. It was also one of the main commitments made by President Ahidjo to S.T. Muna and J.N. Foncha when he consulted them on the immediate creation of a unitary State before making his speech of 6th May 1972. These two former vice presidents of the Republic confirmed this during discussions at their residences. In the eyes of some communities of the Northwest and Southwest, this commitment was not respected.

Francophone citizens often reproach their Anglophone brothers of their tendency to refer, in a quasi-obsessive manner, to their Anglo-Saxon heritage, as if it is colonial heritage which should structure relations between communities which had for a long time been united by multiple links before even colonization. At the same time, they resort with delight to "their" French colonial heritage. Our Constitution, our institutions, our administrative organization, our system of decentralization, our financial regime, the vast majority of our legislative and regulatory laws...originate from the French colonial heritage. Often, we engage in mere transpositions, some of them to the point of photocopying, as was the case with the creation of the *Observatoire National des Elections* (ONEL), the National Observatory of Elections.

...

Nevertheless, we could have been able–and we are still able to–to capitalize on this multicultural heritage to give our country norms that are more appropriate and of better quality. Our Code of Criminal Procedure, does it not give eloquent proof?

This penchant for institutional imitation forced protest movements like the Cameroon Action Movement to claim that Francophone Cameroon continued, by proxy, French colonization of West Cameroon. Emerging in 1979, and probably based abroad, this movement distributed many tracts in Cameroon, most of which were posted in Canada and the United States. These tracts denounced pell-mell (confusedly) the marginalization of Anglophones, who were treated as second-class citizens, the Frenchification of Cameroon, with little regard for the equality of the dual colonial heritage, the transformation of the National Assembly into a mere rubber-stamp, in contrast to what was the case in West Cameroon, excessive centralization, the multiplicity and complexity of procedures, abandonment of the pre-unification developmental priorities of West Cameroon, consequently leading to a slowing of development in this part of the country, etc.

Conscious of the impact of these messages, which used many communication platforms, President Ahidjo sent to Bamenda and Buea, high level delegations made up of members of the government, the Political Bureau and the Central Committee of the CNU [the ruling party]. Their mission was to present the facts and truth, give explanations to the people, warn them against the harmfulness of such messages, and reduce tension. He then put in place a high-level ad hoc committee to reflect on the Anglophone Problem. Only three members of the committee are still alive: His Excellency. Paul Biya, then Prime Minister, Mrs. Dorothy Limunga Njeuma, then Vice Minister of National Education, and myself [David Abouem à Tchoyi] then Governor of the Northwest Province.

....

Recognized at that period as real by the highest authorities of the State, could the Anglophone Problem have magically disappeared? Certainly not! Moreso since certain occurrences had added to an already complex situation.

5. Changing of the name of the State: Replacing "United Republic of Cameroon" with "Republic of Cameroon."

When it became independent, the former state under French tutelage took the name, "*République du Cameroun.*" It is with *la République du Cameroun* ([LRC] that Southern Cameroons negotiated the conditions of reunification. After reunification, *la République du Cameroun* became the federated state of East Cameroon, and Southern Cameroons became the Federated State of West Cameroon. Changing the name of the State in 1984–abandonment of the United Republic and return to the *République du Cameroun* was seen in many quarters as a mere phagocytosis [annexation] of the former West Cameroon by the former East Cameroon. The more pessimistic saw in this name change, a manifest desire to make disappear, down to the level of symbols, the contribution of the former West Cameroon to the Reunification and construction of a greater nation.

This name change caused the emergence, in numerous compatriots in the Northwest and Southwest, the sentiment of belonging to a "distinct entity," of which the people, had sovereignly chosen to join their brothers and sisters of another "entity," from which they had been separated, in order for the two entities to live in harmony and equality. To the extremists, not only was it necessary to resist this "annexation" but also to make this "entity" continue to exist through a name that recalled the history of this part of the national territory. The name "Ambazonia" seemed to meet this need.... But the name Ambazonia was not unanimous. Hence a return to "Southern Cameroons."

6. The non-application of bilingualism in the public sector despite the fact that the Constitution provides that French and English are official languages of equal value.

Of the six facets of the Anglophone Problem recalled above, which of them is not susceptible to a solution? None! Absolutely none. What then should be done?

History has given Cameroon a sublime challenge, that of building from the unique journey of their country, a united state capable of serving as a model of the integration of diverse colonial heritages and multi-sectorial traditional values. If it succeeds, it can be a model, even a reference for all Anglophone, Francophone, Hispanic, and Portuguese-speaking countries of Africa. It could therefore be the example of African unity. This challenge can be met, it must be met. This can only be done in humility, dialogue, consultation, and cordial understanding. Neither the power of numbers, nor military force can accomplish this task. In effect, opinions are like nails the more one hammers on them, the more one entrenches them.

Let us not make a mistake. Let us above all, not make the mistake of minimizing this problem. We run the risk of bitter setbacks, or it will be our children and grandchildren who will suffer the consequences.... Let us not wait for our fellow citizens who are ill at ease and who complain about their unhappy situation, to one day, out of despair, seek external support.

We negotiate with criminals to free hostages! Let us discuss with all fellow citizens who have the need to do so, to free Cameroon from the threats to peace, stability and security.

...

Let us listen to all the children of the fatherland. Without prejudices, as the President of the Republic said in his message of 31 December 2016 to the Nation. Let us offer every one of our compatriots the framework for discussion and consultation to tackle our problems without taking positions and resolve them with sincerity and truth.

What is going on with the lawyers and teachers is going in the right direction. But let us not limit ourselves to what constitutes appearances, mere symptoms. Let us approach the Anglophone problem in all its complexity and depth. With courage and determination, let us come up with satisfactory and convincing solutions. All citizens of our country will benefit from it. For peace is justice. For the good of the Nation. For the health of the fatherland.

David Abouèm à Tchoyi
Consultant
Former governor of the Southwest and then the Northwest,
Former Minister of Higher Education;
Former Secretary General at the Presidency.
(2017)

The Manifesto of Christian Penda Ekoka, Technical Adviser, Office of the President Republic of Cameroon (February 28, 2017)

In 2017, Christian Penda Ekoka, Technical Adviser, Office of the President of Cameroon, President Paul, Biya, was moved by the senseless violence and intransigence, wrote an open diagnosis of the problem and posted it on Facebook. The incident came across as the action of an adviser who was frustrated because Biya had refused to take his advice. He therefore called the nation to witness that he had diagnosed the problem and offered solutions that were not listened to by President Biya, to the detriment of the country. Penda Ekoka was ultimately removed from his position for not toeing the official line, according to which the Anglophone Problem did not exist. He gravitated to the opposition Movement for the Rebirth of Cameroon (MRC). He was arrested along with the party's leader, Maurice Kamto and jailed at the notorious Kondengui prison. After six-months in prison, he and Kamto were released after the intervention of French President Emmanuel Macron. Penda Ekoka took ill shortly after his release and died. His diagnosis of the Anglophone Problem gives us the view of someone inside the system, someone who dissented from the official, misguided policy. His premise was that the Anglophone Revolt was more than an Anglophone Problem, it was indicative of a national malaise. As such, it presented a "historic opportunity to reexamine our current institutions for an inclusive leadership."

Figure 25.12. Christian Penda Ekoka (second from left in Green t-shirt) in Kondengui Prison, Yaoundé with Maurice Kamto and others

Uprisings in Bamenda and Buea are indicators of a more profound national malaise

A moment comes, which comes but rarely in history, when we step out from the old to new, when an age ends, and when the soul of a nation, long suppressed, finds utterance...

Jawaharlal Nehru (Tryst of Destiny, speech to the Indian Parliament, August 15, 1947).

The current crisis in our Anglophone Southwest and Northwest regions is the expression of the soul of a people, which without doubt reminds us of the above declaration of the Indian nationalist, who became Prime Minister on the eve of the independence of India, 70 years ago. In effect, it is not about Anglophone demands, it is also about the demands of Francophones, which express a national malaise for several reasons.

Firstly, when the knell tolls in Bamenda, Garoua, Maroua, Bertoua, Bafoussam or anywhere in Cameroon, "...never ask to know for whom the knell tolls, it tolls for thee." That was the warning of the American writer, Hemingway regarding the death or suffering of a human being, no matter where he may be because he or she is part of humanity.

Secondly, more than an Anglophone problem, the recent uprisings in Bamenda and Buea are indicators of a more profound national malaise, resulting from the institutional leadership and structure of governance of our country whose architecture was flawed from the beginning. In the light of its experiments in the past 50 years, our institutional framework for the management of public affairs appears not to have been designed to respond to the needs and aspirations of the people.

What is called the Anglophone Problem is a specific aspect of a bigger national problem that could be defined as a genetic default of a system of public governance that is not responsive to the needs and preoccupations of citizens, Anglophones as well as Francophones.

By comparing our country to a human body, we can say that the emergence of boils on any part of the body is symptomatic of an infection of the entire body, and its proper treatment would require treating the cause of the disease...a tainted state architecture...the current imperfections can be traced to the original process of formation of our State. The disease has lasted for so many years with consequences evident in terms of lack of access of the people to basic services and infrastructures such as drinking water and public hygiene, electricity, public transport, health care, education, housing; the deliquescence of public corporations which live on endless subventions without prospects of autonomy, the moribund state of several public enterprises and institutions such as the Economic and Social Council, the National Investment Corporation, the National Hydrocarbons Corporation, the Douala Stock Exchange, Cameroon Telecommunications

Corporation (Camtel), the Agency for Regulation of Public Services, etc.

A total and transparent dialogue, not Piecemeal Solutions

Whatever its outcome, the current negotiations initiated by the government will only address some facets of the problem. With regard to the structural nature and scope of the malaise that involves different political, civil, religious, educational, legal, etc. stakeholders, it is absolutely necessary to adopt a broad, long-term perspective to attain a durable and credible solution. This demands a comprehensive, constructive and holistic approach. Otherwise, the problems will reemerge. "Law and order" is not a default effective response to people's complaints and concerns that can only be taken into consideration through a responsible and constructive dialogue, underpinned by good faith and the open mind of the parties involved, in a bid to attain consensually and mutually agreed solutions – and not imposed ones.

In this context, it should be clearly acknowledged that the case of the Supreme Court Judge, Paul Ayah and others [who were arrested and imprisoned for months without trial], do a disservice to the cause of our democracy. We should therefore stand up for a state that protects its citizens' rights and freedoms of expression, and not one that terrorizes them. Any piecemeal, partial or non-inclusive approach that will not fail to reduce the issue to a bureaucratic transaction, that will not fail to be seen as patchy and cosmetic, sadly reminding most of us of the sad scenario of Foumban in 1961, that has gone down in history as a deceitful, a sort of zero-sum game, whereby for one party to win, the other has to lose, or for one party to fatten, the other has to starve...

Any piecemeal approach means not doing so, and will result in omitting the most serious questions, such as: how best to organize a balanced distribution of political power for inclusive wealth? How best to design a system of transparent democratic governance that promotes development? How to organize a political system that ensures an efficient allocation of resources, whereby the Public Service socials or managers are accountable before the people? How to build a nation whose main goal is to ensure freedoms and rights of the citizens in their pursuit of happiness? How to design and organize a Public Service that is devoted to the service of the community and not become its predator?

The Role of the Media: The media is an indispensable instrument that should remain free and independent for the effective accomplishment of its role in the society, and not become a tool of manipulation by or propaganda for any special interest group's benefit, at the expense of the general interest...The media should avoid becoming propaganda agents for some special interest groups, which would force them to disinformation and misinformation, for instance in accusing the Anglophones of being a band of barbarians ready to massacre Francophones, with the obvious consequences of nurturing inter- community hatred and tribalism

Under leadership of its first Head of State, Amadou Ahidjo, the historic process of creation of the Cameroonian nation was grounded on a grand design of a highly centralized state, bordering on a totalitarian state. From the beginning there was a clear intention to emasculate the rights and liberties of the people. In keeping with this scheme of things, there emerged a culture of an oppressive State, which explains the number of abuses still observed today in this domain. In effect, if a State is not conceptualized to recognize and preserve the fundamental human rights of all its citizens, how could it be otherwise with those who have a different historic makeup, Anglophones for instance?

At the dawn of the independence of African countries, this process was observed in other countries which did not have a linguistic problem. It generally led to a hyper-presidential regime characterized by a heavy personalization of power at the summit of the State, and elimination of counter-powers, as well as the appearance of myths, values and behaviors associated with the nature of such power, thus the emergence of a cult of personality. Different developments in the post-independence life of our country followed this logic, notably, transformation of the multiparty system into a one-party system, transformation of the federal State into a unitary, totalitarian state, massive concentration of powers in the hands of the Head of State, the concomitant elimination of the legislative and judicial powers, perpetuation of a hyper-centralized colonial administration, whose goal was not the emancipation of the people but their enslavement, and their submission to the colonial authority, symbol of order and security...a top-down decision-making structure that despised the wishes of the people, and creation of a corollary dependence of the people on the State, while simultaneously choking their initiatives aimed at freely forging their destiny.

...In short, and more serious, these developments gave rise to the image of a vampire State in which a handful of people sucked the blood of their fellow citizens

We must avoid creating confusion among the people, federalism does not undermine and does not call into question the commitment of the founding fathers' policy of "unity in diversity," contrary to the current system of highly centralized government, as the negative consequences demonstrate. The oft-stated call, "Cameroon is one an indivisible" [copied from the French Constitution] can only be justified in the face of secessionist demands. Only systems of government that are highly decentralized or have federalist systems are naturally inclined to reinforce the capacity of citizens and local communities to become the principal agents of their development or the main actors of their lives,

> It is our moment of expression and stock-taking, it is a decisive moment for our country, and we must frankly face it, and neither go into denial nor procrastination, if we want to obtain lasting solutions to the current malaise. We owe it to the young and to future generations. We must take advantage of the events of Bamenda and Buea as a "blessing in disguise", as an opportunity to reexamine the performance of our State in order to construct an institutional infrastructure of governance of public affairs that will stand the test of time, which will free our country from violence and corruption, etc.; this will make coherent the structures of the State and the vision of our founding fathers, "Unity in diversity."...we must not be afraid to question our system of public governance, and our system of leadership in order to improve...our State in its present form and structure, is more of a liability than an asset. Hence the need for a critical and true assessment of our public affairs, leadership, and governance... Constitutions are not carved in stone. The only permanent thing is constant global change. Forward thinking and pro-activity are the best guides for avoiding the brutal and unwanted consequences of these changes...

Professor Patrice Nganang, who we have seen in Chapter 20, was one of the most vocal critics of the Biya regime's war of subjugation against the Anglophones. His arrest and imprisonment in Cameroon became international news. A resolution was tabled in the US House of Representatives to censure Cameroon for the arrest of Prof. Nganang, shutting down the Internet in the English-speaking regions of Cameroon, violation of freedom of speech and expression and atrocities against demonstrators in the English-speaking regions of Cameroon (see appendix XXI).

Figure 25.13. The Anglophone Revolt Book by Professor Patrice Nganang that was banned in Cameroon

The Biya Regime's Response to the Anglophone Revolt: A Chronology of Political Window Dressing

One of the characteristics of the Biya republican chiefery is its penchant for top-down rule-by-decree. Since the abolition of the Federal Republic of Cameroon, and partition of the State of Southern Cameroons into the Northwest and Southwest provinces/regions without the consent of the people of Southern Cameroons, Biya has turned a deaf ear to the entreaties of the minority Anglophones. His main interest was the oil and natural gas in the territory. Interestingly, instead of listening to the Anglophones and trying to address their grievances, he ignored them, refused to dialogue with them, only to come up with, and impose often inappropriate and badly-timed solutions to Anglophone grievances by decree. This was government by indecision, procrastination, and postponement. Biya's main preoccupation was to maintain the unconstitutional form of the Cameroon State that he and President Ahidjo had maneuvered into being in 1972 and 1985, as well as his 1996 French-style Jacobin "decentralized" constitution, which had been promulgated without the input and consent of the governed, and certainly without the knowledge, participation and input of the Anglophones. As we have seen, Biya did not even bother to implement his decentralization for twenty or more years after the Constitution was adopted in January 1996. Instead, he undertook a series of unilateral counter-measures that obfuscated and worsened the Anglophone Problem. At the onset of the Anglophone Revolt in 2016, President Biya first ignored the problem, then sent the BIR and the regular military to crush it while he was ensconced at his presidential suite at the InterContinental Hotel in Geneva, Switzerland. In Chapter 1, we posted an excerpt of the report that was sent to him on October 1, 2017, while he was in Geneva. The list of counter-measures President Biya took to obfuscate, confuse, delay, and ultimately crush Anglophone demands for a return to federalism are a textbook of Machiavellian bad faith governance by deception. These measures have not succeeded in solving the Anglophone Problem because none of them address the underlying issue of authoritarian governance without the consent of the governed. This brings to the fore a calculated exclusion of dialogue with the Anglophone minority, and lack of respect for its politico-cultural specificity.

Dieudonné Essomba is a Cameroonian economist, statistician and media pundit. A commentator and visionary former civil servant who, from the onset of the Anglophone Revolt in 2016, bravely expressed views on the Anglophone problem that were breaths of fresh air. He wrote eloquently on Facebook about the need to reform and federalize the Cameroonian state as a solution to the Anglophone Problem. He became a regular invitee on the popular independent television station, Equinoxe, where he bravely expressed his views on federalism as Anglophone federalists like Felix Nkongho Agbor were being rounded up, tortured, court-marshalled, and jailed. Essomba's appearances were cancelled from time to time under pressure from the powers that be, until he was retired from the civil service in retaliation for his views and declared persona non grata on the TV channel by the government. He continued expressing his views on social media platforms, which the government could not ban. The write-up we reproduce here was written in 2018. It is entitled:

L'Etat Unitaire Ne Peut Pas Résoudre Le Problème Anglophone

(The Unitary State Cannot Resolve the Anglophone Problem) (2018).

No one can say that he was not warned: The unitary State does not have the means to put an end to the Anglophone Crisis. From the start, we said so and we persist in saying so, despite the reproaches, because it is the truth. Some people intermingle ideological stances with patriotism., even if these stances can destroy a State. A State is not a magical divinity which defines by itself ethereal rules on the basis of specųlations, but an institutional instrument which a community sets up for itself and which has to be useful to it. Every State that does not respect this rule ends up dying and that is exactly for this reason that States die. Even the powerful USSR which we thought was eternal is dead, because its leaders imprisoned the State, which is an operational instrument, in an ideology that is sclerotic and antagonistic to humanity.

Cameroon is in danger of death, exactly because its leaders and their ideologues have imprisoned the State in worldviews obtained from books, which are reeled off in the face of major problems. Cameroon was born as a very fragile nation, as a result of its initial form of an "ad hoc" federation. Put otherwise, formerly colonized States which are created as federations on the basis of a merger of two colonial entities that had walked different paths or were managed differently. In Africa, there are five countries in this same situation:

1. Tanzania was made into a federation with on the one hand, the continental territory of Tanganyika, and on the other the Island of Zanzibar.
2. Nigeria to which was joined Northern Cameroon
3. Ethiopia, which was made up of the Ethiopian Empire, which was never colonized, and its coastal frontage that was colonized by Italy, Eritrea.
4. Sudan, made up of two territories, the Arab and Muslim North, and the South, black and Christianized. Since these two territories were managed differently, a fact which made the South to demand a separate independence. It was by promising the South a federalist system that managed the specificities of the two territories that Sudan became independent.
5. Somalia, composed of a British colony and an Italian colony.
6. Cameroon, which gained its independence with a Francophone Cameroon, to which Southern Cameroons was joined under a federal system.

These are the six African countries that had this type of coupling at independence. But we realize that of the six countries, only two have maintained this initial system and resisted the temptation to suppress the federation. First of all, Tanzania which was able to maintain the autonomous government of Zanzibar. Then there is Nigeria, which federalization was generalized and extended to Northern Cameroon, which became two States. Even though there were secessions in Nigeria, they have never affected this former part of Cameroon.

On the contrary, the four other federations gave in to the temptation to suppress federalism with the hope of erasing the historic divisions. In all of these countries, this attempt had led to terrible wars of secession. And of the four wars of secession, three resulted in independence. The only remaining one is the Anglophone secession in Cameroon. One must add that these are the only secessions that have succeeded in Africa since independence! How can we explain the success of secessions in ad hoc federations? The reason is found in the intrinsic fragilities of such groupings.

The Scope of Secessions: An exhaustive study of 200 secessionist movements show that the vast majority involve less that 2% of the population, which makes them rather controllable. But when a secession includes more than 5% of the total population, it becomes totally incontrollable by the central government. In effect, secession places the State in a terrible scissors effect: on the one hand, it prohibits the contribution of the rebel zone in the national production, destroys productive infrastructures and paralyzes activities. The contribution of the rebellious zone disappears from the gross national product. On the other hand, secession forces the State to transfer vast resources from elsewhere to ensure security, reconstruct destroyed infrastructures and ensure the presence of the State.

When secession involves more than 5% of the population, the scissors effect becomes intolerable and ends up putting the government on its knees.

Nostalgia For An Autonomous Nation

These secessionists rely on a past autonomy, real or imagined, but more or less grounded on irresistible nostalgia. The people always have in mind that they had lived or are expected to live in an autonomous political entity which could take just and adequate decisions without asking anyone. The Centralized State by building schools, hospitals and roads, imagines that it is integrating them, when it is only demonstrating paralysis...The central government bothers them by mentioning completed projects, when they themselves could carry them out without the mediation of a central power, which in addition does not seem legitimate to them. The persistence of the central government in defining their way of life, their needs and above all, mentioning its achievements, only sharpens the sentiment of oppression. They end up comparing the central government to the Devil himself end imputes on it, all the evils, thus becoming deaf to anything good and reasonable.

The International Dimension:

Born of colonial history, they base their demands on the same colonial references as the States that they fight. In contrast to secessionist movements whose causes are endogenic, and which can be considered the "internal affairs" of a State, some secessionist movements seem to be more like a form of continuation of colonial history, on the same level as our countries, makes them the direct responsibility of the Western powers and the United Nations. Thus, if the Casamance or Cabinda take up arms, they do so by relying on local specificities, while the secessions cited here speak of colonial action which enabled the incoherent fusions without ensuring their viability. On the whole they appeal to the international community and the United Nations to come and dismantle a yoke that they had created and which, in any case, does not work and will never work. This international dimension thus makes the international community aware of these kinds of secessions.

It is this explosive combination which transforms all these federations put together colonial groupings into intrinsically fragile entities whose tendency is to split as soon as one tries to change the rules.

The solution to the Anglophone problem ought to be arrived at from this context. They must be based on the following fundamental principles:

1. The Anglophone secession will never end as long as Cameroon is a unitary State and that the word "unitary" appears in the constitution. In effect, this word alone summarizes the absorption of a community which has a historic legitimacy and signals a final conquest. It is a warmongering word.
2. The State of Cameroon does not have the political, economic, financial and diplomatic means to militarily end the Anglophone secession, nor even contain it in the context of a unitary State because with 20 percent of the population, it is too big to be controllable.
3. The administrative decentralization proposed by the government cannot be a solution to the Anglophone crisis. In effect it is just a reorganization of the unitary State which lengthens the confiscation of the autonomy of Southern Cameroons, when it is this autonomy that should be restored. Moreover, besides, procrastinations over decentralization, the loss of time, the multitudes of obstacles are a sign that the elite of the unitary State is incapable of liberating power and enough resources to satisfy the Anglophone thirst for autonomy. At the end of the day, it is hard to see how it [decentralization] can be applied in the Anglophone regions, with armed groups that are spreading like a generalized cancer and are becoming more and more aggressive.

At the end of the day the only solution to the Anglophone Problem is simply a return to the federation, and we here condemn the autism [lack of awareness] of our stubborn and obtuse elite who are incapable of understanding a good message. Because, from the beginning, it was clear that the solution was to extend federalism to all the regions, rather than suppress the initial federation. By doing so, the State would have killed two birds with one stone.

On the one hand, it could have presented this federalism as the end of its own project of national unity, that is to say, Cameroon was not against the federal system but had evolved to arrive at a federalism adapted to our local realities and more appropriate to her diversity.

On the other hand, it would have enabled the State to drown the most dangerous variety of Anglophone specificity, because it is essentially colonial and thus pertinent in the eyes of the international community, in other specificities founded on local referents. And from this point of view, the two Anglophone regions could not have been opposed if the government had had the intelligence to render in time, political autonomy to the other regions.

Cameroon is in danger of death. It does not have the means to militarily crush the Anglophone secession and it must take note of that once and for all.

As in all secessions, the first victim will be the army, then the regime itself. Because that is how it is with all secessions. From the very beginning, the government believed because it is about a minority, it has the means of crushing it easily and force it to remain in the unitary State. It is a major parallax error that is difficult to escape. For example, the powerful imperial army [of Ethiopia] that had defeated Italy at Adwa could never believe that the little Eritrea could stand up to it. The same is true of Sudan.

Unfortunately, a secessionist war is not an ordinary war. It is the refusal of a community to be part of a whole, and that cannot be resolved through military means. The army flounder and begins to fracture and the economic machine is paralyzed. The weakened system develops sources of tension and war which leads to the collapse of the central government. Finally, the international community intervenes to put an end to the wreck, and consecrates, through a referendum, the secession.

This is clearly what is going to happen in Cameroon. And necessarily, fatally if we continue to follow the foolishness of this irrational and ruinous war. And when the Anglophones leave, then Cameroon will realize that it should have federalized the country, and to anticipate such events in future. It will end up federalizing the remainder of the country.

What Should Be Done?

We are lucky that for the moment, the secession is just beginning, that the majority of the Anglophone elite look favorably on the federal state, and that this elite still has influence. But that will not last indefinitely. Secession gains adherents every day. The word "Ambazonia" which was mysterious, has become a common name known by all. No one thought the State was vulnerable, but we have seen its desacralization, with a Ministry of Defense surrounded by generals who are attacked and governors stalked. The State is present only in the major urban centers, where the administrative authorities tremble in terror.

People who were able to arm themselves, barely two years ago, who feared any [presidentially appointed] sub-prefect or any [gendarmerie] station commander, cannot put down their weapons. And if they could not be prevented from being armed, they cannot be disarmed after the fact. It is a perfectly useless battle that must be abandoned.

What should be done now is to speak of federalism and ensure that a good proportion of Anglophones adhere to the federal project. You cannot attract them without compensating them with federal autonomy. In other words, a decentralization in which the rights of the regions are inscribed irrevocably in the Constitution in an infrangible manner. Before negotiations, the government must accept and proclaim the federal form of the state. It is the configuration of this federation that should be the subject of negotiations.

The decision of the government not to negotiate with secessionists is good, but on condition that it opens the way for federalists and negotiates with them. That is the only way of getting Cameroon intact out of the Anglophone quagmire.

One more time, the unitary state cannot solve the Anglophone problem and it's no use insisting. It is not for love of Cameroon, or Biya himself that this irrational position should be maintained.

In five or 10 years, when this problem, which will not quench will have taken a dangerous, incontrollable turn, I would like people to say, "One more time he was correct."

Conclusion

Many people who are not well acquainted with the Anglophone Question in Cameroon dismiss it as a post-colonial aberration, an African conflict over European languages. The claim is that Africans from the former German colonial territory of Kamerun, which happens to have been partitioned into British Cameroons and French Cameroun during World War I, are fighting over English and French, the languages of the colonialists. While it is true that the Anglophone Question is unfinished business from World War I and the Treaty of Versailles of 1919, the conclusion that the Anglophone Question is a clash between Cameroonian speakers of English and Cameroonian speakers of French is very simplistic. The Anglophone Question, defined as the role and place of the minority English and Pidgin-speaking peoples of the former Southern Cameroons in the post-colonial

Cameroon, is actually a problem of the deceptive muting, suppression and submergence of the democratic, multi-party, parliamentary system of the State of West Cameroon, into the over-centralized, neo-patrimonial, Napoleonic, Ahidjo/Biya republican chiefdom of *la Republique du Cameroun*. This was the prelude to confiscation of the natural resources of Southern Cameroons by the repressive, kleptocratic regime in Yaoundé.

The dictatorial suppression of the cultural and identitarian specificity of the English and Pidgin-speaking minority of Cameroon, confiscation of the natural resources of their region, and violation of their fundamental human rights of freedom of speech, expression and assembly, seemed normal to most members of the Francophones political class, and even some Anglophone elite with whom they shared the loot. French Cameroon attempts to erase the last bastions of Anglophone specificity, the English-medium educational system and the "Anglo-Saxon," common law system, triggered the Anglophone revolt of 2016. Francophone intellectuals who had been generally indifferent to the Anglophone problem soon began to see that it is a human rights problem that goes against the Universal Declaration of Human Rights and the moral philosophical underpinnings of French and Francophone education. Francophone intellectual heavyweights have begun to demonstrate a profound understanding of the Anglophone problems. The Francophone intellectuals featured in this chapter demonstrated an acute sense of humanism in the face the unspeakable human rights violations of the Biya regime in what they call the NOSO (Northwest and Southwest. These are men of good faith whose advice, if listened to, would have solved the problem long ago. Unfortunately, President Biya is politically tone deaf and listens only to the intellectuals of the stomach who have created an invidious echo chamber around him.

References

Andzongo, S. (2019). Paris Peace Forum: Paul Biya Explains the background of the Anglophone Crisis. Business in Cameroon, November 13. Retrieved from: https://www.businessincameroon.com/public-management/1311-9677-paris-peace-forum-paul-biya-explains-the-background-of-the-anglophone-crisis

A Second Look at Cameroon's Anglophone Special Status (2023). International Crisis Group, Briefing No. 188 (March). Retrieved from: https://www.crisisgroup.org/africa/central-africa/cameroon/b188-second-look-cameroons-anglophone-special-status

Bernand, C. (2006). The Right to be Different: Some Questions about the "French Exception." In Kathleen Perry Long (Ed). *Religious Differences in France*. (p. 201-219). Kirksville, Mo, Truman State University.

Mawel, A. (2022). *Cameroun: Émile Joël Bamkoui, le maître-espion de Paul Biya, poussé vers la sortie? Jeune Afrique* (23 June). Retrieved from: https://www.jeuneafrique.com/1356551/politique/cameroun-emile-joel-bamkoui-le-maitre-espion-de-paul-biya-pousse-vers-la-sortie/

Creation of a National Committee for Disarmament, Demobilisation and Reintegration for ex-fighters of Boko Haram and Armed Groups in the Northwest and Southwest (2018). Presidency of Cameroon. Retrieved from: https://www.prc.cm/en/news/press-releases/3178-press-release-creation-of-a-national-disarmament-demobilization-and-reintegration-committee-for-ex-fighters-of-boko-haram-and-armed-groups-in-the-north-west-and-south-west-%20regions

Djialeu, A. (2021). *Fridolin Nke convoqué une deuxième fois par la Sécurité militaire* (Fridolin Nke summoned a second time by military security). *Actu Cameroun* (July 30). Retrieved from: https://actucameroun.com/2021/07/30/fridolin-nke-convoque-une-deuxieme-fois-par-la-securite-militaire/

Fatunde, T. (2020). Law Lecturer's Dismissal Over Exam Question Raises Concerns. University World News (Africa Edition). May 26. Retrieved from: https://www.universityworld-news.com/post.php?story=2020052516062646#:~:text=The%20dismissal%20of%20a%20university,number%20of%20the%20country's%20academics.

Head of State's Message to the Nation (2019). Major National Dialogue. Retrieved from: https://www.nationaldialogue.cm/

Kom, A. (2020). "*Lettre ouverte à Jacques Fame Ndongo, mon frère*" (Open letter to Jacques Fame Ndongo, my Brother). Germinal, May 11, 2020. Retrieved from: https://germinalnewspaper.com/index.php?option=com_content&view=article&id=546:ecrit-par-pr-ambroise-kom&catid=29:maniere-de-voir&Itemid=53

Laurence, J. & Vaisse J. (2006). Integrating Islam: Political and Religious challenges in Contemporary France. Washington D.C., Brookings Institution.

Nké, F. (2021). *J'assume : j'ai demandé aux soldats de ne pas obéir aux ordres illégaux et illégitimes* (I Admit it: I asked [Cameroonian] soldiers not to obey illegal and illegitimate orders)

Presidential Couple in France for Peace Forum (2019). Presidency of the Republic Cameroon. November 10, 2019. Retrieved from: https://www.prc.cm/en/news/travels-and-visits/3922-presidential-couple-in-france-for-peace-forum

Renan, Ernest (1882). *Qu'est-Ce Qu'une Nation*? (What is a Nation and Other Political Writings. Paris: Calman Levy.

Retraite du redoutable Emile Bamkoui: Les succès du célebre colonel de Paul Biya (2022). Cameroun-Web. Retrieved from: https://www.camerounweb.com/CameroonHomePage/NewsArchive/Retraite-du-redoutable-Emile-Bamkoui-les-succès-du-c-l-bre-colonel-de-Paul-Biya-666908

UN High Commission for Refugees. (2018, January 18). UNHCR USA. Retrieved from https://www.unhcr.org/en-us/news/briefing/2018/1/5a61b3bc4/concern-grows-women-children-fleeing-cameroon.html

TWENTY-SIX

Asserting Permanent Sovereignty over Ancestral Lands

The Bakweri Land Litigation Against Cameroon

NDIVA KOFELE-KALE

INTRODUCTION

Land and natural resource issues, particularly the dispossession of an indigenous people[1] of the lands they have historically owned and occupied, are issues of fundamental nature that implicate all the existing international human rights.[2] The 'Scramble for Africa' (a period roughly between the 1880s and the start of the First World War during which Europe's major powers staked their territorial claims on the African continent) witnessed countless instances of land expropriations without consultation or compensation. By the time the scramble ended, Africa had been partitioned into spheres of influence under the hegemonic control of Great Britain, France, Germany, Italy, Portugal, Spain and Belgium—who among them acquired thirty new colonies and 110 million subjects.[3] Partition and colonization left behind a trail littered with millions of landless people pushed out of their ancestral

1 To bring some order to the multiple definitions of "indigenous people" floating around, the Special Rapporteur of the U.N. Sub-Commission on Prevention of Discrimination and Protection of Minorities offered this definition: "indigenous communities, *people* and nations are those which, having a historical continuity with pre-invasion and pre-colonial societies that developed on their territories, consider themselves distinct from other sectors of the societies now prevailing in these territories, or parts of them they form at present non-dominant sectors of society and are determined to preserve, develop and transmit to future generations their ancestral territories, and their ethnic identity, as the basis of their continued existence as peoples, in accordance with their own cultural patterns, social institutions and legal systems." *See* Jose R. Martinez-Cabo, The Study of the Problem of Discrimination Against Indigenous Populations, U.N. ESCOR, Sub-Comm'n on Prevention of Discrimination and Protection of Minorities, U.N. Doc. E/CN.4/Sub.2/1986/7/Add.4, p. 379 (1986)("U.N. Sub-Commission Report").

2 *See* Erica-Irene A. Daes, *Relevant Legal Standards and Materials Concerning Indigenous Lands and Resource; see also Indigenous peoples' permanent sovereignty over natural resources: Preliminary report of the Special Rapporteur, Erica-Irene A. Daes, submitted in accordance with the Sub-Commission resolution 2002/15,*E/CN.4/Sub.2/2003/20, 21 July 2003.

3 *See* Thomas Pakenham, *The Scramble for Africa* (1992).

lands to make room for colonial agricultural and commercial needs. Sara Berry who has studied this aspect of colonial occupation notes that:

> The military and administrative officers who fanned out across Africa in the 1890s and early 1900s, using force or the threat of force to impose European rule, claimed far-reaching authority over the land of their newly acquired domains. Specific legislative instruments varied from one colony to another, but they conveyed a common message. From Senegal to Malawi, French and British authorities claimed that "right of conquest," all "vacant and ownerless" land belonged to the colonial state. Often judged "vacant and ownerless" on the basis of cursory inspection or none at all, vast tracts of land were then sold to European buyers, or awarded to private concessionaires who promised to "develop" the land by exploiting its mineral and forest resources.[4]

Because indigenous communally-owned prime real estate was expropriated, almost always by force, and generally without compensation, for the benefit of the white settler population,[5] it set the stage for frequent confrontations between the dispossessed Africans and the colonial authorities and white settler populations.[6]

Germany which came late into the colonial race as well as the land grabbing spree more than made up for this tardy entry as can be seen from the ruthless efficiency with which she gobbled up some of the most desirable lands in German South-West Africa (now Namibia) and Kamerun (present day Cameroon).[7] The arbitrary and uncompensated

4 *See* Sara Berry, *Debating the land question in Africa,* Paper Presented at the World Bank, Washington, D.C., March 27, 2002. Available at https://www.jstor.org/stable/3879518

5 This insatiable appetite to claim 'native' land as Crown was very much evident in the Belgian Congo, German South-West Africa and British Rhodesia to mention the most notorious instances of colonial land grabbing. *See e.g.,* Alois S. Mlambo, *'Land Grab' or 'Taking Back Stolen Land': The Fast Track Land Reform Process in Zimbabwe in Historical Perspective,* 3 HISTORY COMPASS 1 (2005); Adam Hochschiled, KING LEOPOLD'S GHOST—A STORY OF GREED, TERROR AND HEROISM IN COLONIAL AFRICA 1, 70-71 (2006); Catherine Coquery-Vidrovitch, LE CONGO AU TEMPS DES GRANDES COMPAGNIES CONCESSIONAIRES, 1898-1930 (1972), Jean Surat-Canale, FRENCH COLONIALISM IN TROPICAL AFRICA, 1900-1945 (1971) and William H. (Lord) Hailey, AN AFRICAN SURVEY (1956).

6 In colonial Kenya British settlers appropriated for themselves 12,000 square miles (31,000 Km2) of coveted Kikuyu lands nestled in the salubrious central Highlands. The dispossessed Kikuyu then tried to take back these ancestral lands under white settler occupation, the ensuing struggle led to an uprising that claimed the lives of an estimated 70,000 Kikuyus in what became known as the Mau Mau Rebellion. For an excellent account of this tragic history, *see* David Anderson, HISTORIES OF THE HANGED: THE DIRTY WAR IN KENYA AND THE END OF EMPIRE (2005), Caroline Elkins, IMPERIAL RECKONING: THE UNTOLD STORY OF BRITAIN'S GULAG IN KENYA (2005), Wunyabari O. Maloba, MAU-MAU AND KENYA: AN ANALYSIS OF A PEASANT REVOLT (1998), Ngugi wa Thiong'o, A GRAIN OF WHEAT (1967) and Jomo Kenyatta, FACING MOUNT KENYA (1962).

7 Kamerun was a German Protectorate from 1884 to 1915 when German rule came to an end following their defeat at the hands of the French and British. Thereafter a condominium was established and provisionally administered by the victorious powers. An agreement to end the condominium was reached in 1916 and the old German protectorate was then partitioned between France and the United Kingdom with France receiving four-fifths of the area. When in 1922 the territories became mandates of the League of Nations,

alienation of some of the most fertile Bakweri land[8] was strongly resisted by this group, the reclamation of which has remained a major point of contention since then. This Article focuses on the century old struggle[9] to reclaim and assert permanent sovereignty over ancestral lands seized from this group, by force and without compensation, for the benefit of private German commercial interests. The particular focus of the Article is the recent litigation brought against Cameroon by the Bakweri Land Claims Committee (BLCC)[10]

French and British control over their respective zones was confirmed. *See* LEAGUE OF NATIONS COVENANT, art. 22. Following the replacement of the League of Nations Mandate arrangement with the United Nations Trusteeship system, the two Cameroons automatically become Trust Territories under the provisions of Chapter XII of the Charter of the United Nations. *See* TRUSTEESHIP AGREEMENT FOR THE TERRITORY OF THE CAMEROONS UNDER BRITISH ADMINISTRATION, approved by the General Assembly of the United Nations on 13 December 1946. U.N. Doc. A/296 (28th April 1947), 118 U.N.T.S. 120 (1947). During the mandate and trusteeship period, Cameroons under United Kingdom Trusteeship authority was administered as part of the Southern Provinces, then of the Eastern Provinces, and finally of the Eastern Region of Nigeria. In 1960 Cameroons under French Trusteeship gained its independence from France and the following year the other Cameroons achieved its independence by joining the French-speaking Republic of Cameroon. The reunification of the former Trust Territories gave birth to the Federal Republic of Cameroon which in 1972 morphed into the United Republic of Cameroon and since 1984 the Republic of Cameroon. All the expropriated land under discussion was in the British sector.

8 The Bakweri occupy the south-eastern slopes of Mount Cameroon in the former British sector of the old German Protectorate. When they entered their present territory as early as 1750 and perhaps even earlier, the area was unoccupied. *See* Edwin Ardener, COASTAL BANTUS OF THE CAMEROONS 24 (1956); *see also* Edwin Ardener & Shirley Ardener, KINGDOM ON MOUNT CAMEROON: STUDIES IN THE HISTORY OF THE CAMEROON COAST 1500-1970 (1996). Their continuous presence in this area satisfies the Rapporteur Martinez-Cabo's test of "historical continuity," meaning "the continuation for an extended period reaching into the present of one or more of the following factors:" 1. occupation of ancestral lands, or at least of part of them; 2. common ancestry with the original occupants of these lands; 3. culture in general, or in specific manifestation (such as religion, living under a tribal system, membership of indigenous community, dress, means of livelihood, lifestyle, etc.); 4. language (whether used as the only language, as mother-tongue, as the habitual means of communication at home or in the family, or as the main preferred, habitual, general or normal language); 5. residence on certain parts of the country, or in certain regions of the world; 6. other relevant factors. *See* U.N. Sub-Commission Report, *supra* note 1.

9 *See e.g.*, Petition of the Bakweri Land Committee, Cameroons under British Mandate, 18 AFRICA 30 (1948); Petition of the Bakweri Land Committee to the Trusteeship Council, U.N.O. Dec. T/PET.4.3, Report of the Trusteeship Visiting Mission, 1949; Petitions from Bakweri Land Committee. Summary of the Findings and Recommendations of the Investigating Officer and the Preliminary Observations of the Nigerian Government (1949); *see also* P.M. Kale, Memorandum submitted to the Secretary of State for the Colonies as a member of the Delegation of the National Council of Nigeria and the Cameroons, PAN AFRICA (October-November 1947).

10 BLCC is the predecessor to the Bakweri Land Committee (BLC) which was organized in 1946 by Bakweri traditional rulers, notables and elites, with its principal mission of reclaiming all Bakweri lands that had been expropriated by the Germans in the 19th century. Indeed, in its very first letter on this subject dated 18 June 1946 and was addressed to the colonial administration, BLC served notice of its determination to lead the struggle for restitution of ancestral Bakweri lands. The letter informed the Resident, Cameroon Province that "the nature and functions" of BLC are as follows to: (a) "continue to exist as long as Bakweri people lived"; (b) "be in charge of all land in the Victoria Division which virtually belongs to the Natives;" and (c) to adjudicate "any complaints whether how trifling, which have anything to do with the land" in question. *See* Letter to The Resident Cameroon Province, Ref. No. 3. B.L.C./2/1 of 16th June 1946 (copy on file). This was but the first in a long series of petitions, memoranda, and statements that BLC sent to the colonial authorities in Nigeria, the Colonial Office in London, and the United Nations Trusteeship Council in New York. After independence in 1960 and the reunification of the two Cameroons in 1961, the BLC (and its successor BLCC) continued the campaign for restitution and compensation through another spate of

in the African Commission on Human and Peoples' Rights.

1) The Bakweri Seise the African Human Rights Commission

In October of 2002, the Bakweri Land Claims Committee, on behalf of the Traditional Rulers, Notables and Elites of the indigenous minority Bakweri peoples of Cameroon, cited the State of Cameroon before the African Commission on Human and Peoples' Rights[11] (the highest human rights tribunal in the continent) for violations of various provisions of the African Charter on Human and Peoples' Rights[12] ("Banjul Charter"), more specifically for violating Bakweri rights over ancestral land occupied by a State-owned agro-industrial corporation, the Cameroon Development Corporation (CDC). BLCC sought a declaration from the Commission to the effect that (1) lands occupied by the CDC are Private Property as defined in positive law[13] belong to the Bakweri; (2) the Bakweri be fully involved in the CDC privatization negotiations to ensure that their interests are effectively protected following the privatization of this corporation; (3) ground rents owed the Bakweri people dating back to 1947 be paid to a Bakweri Land Trust Fund for the benefit of the dispossessed indigenes; (4) the Bakweri acting jointly and severally be allocated a specific percentage of shares in each of the privatized companies; and (5) BLCC be represented in the current and all future policy and management boards as was the case in colonial times.[14]

The action was filed eight years after a Presidential Decree announced the privatization of the CDC and after the Bakweri had failed to secure assurances from Government that the sale of the CDC would not adversely affect their rights over ancestral lands. At its 33rd session in May 2003, the African Commission on Human and Peoples' Rights ("Commission") took the extraordinary step of addressing an "Urgent Appeal" to the Cameroon's President, Paul Biya, to "suspend the alleged detrimental alienation of the disputed Cameroon Development Corporation (CDC) lands in the Fako Division,[15] pending a decision on the matter before the African Commission."[16] At its 36th Ordinary Session the Commission reached

---

memoranda, position papers, and petitions to successive Cameroonian Governments. Sometime in 2000 the leadership of BLC decided to change the name of this organization to the Bakweri Land *Claims* Committee, by adding "claims", to better convey its central mission, the reclamation of expropriated Bakweri lands.

11 The action was filed pursuant to Articles 55, 56 and 58 of the African Charter of Human and Peoples' Rights and was listed as *Communication 260/2002: Bakweri Land Claims Committee vs Cameroon.*

12 *See* AFRICAN CHARTER ON HUMAN AND PEOPLES' RIGHTS, OAU Doc. CAB/LEG/67/3/Rev.5; *reprinted at* 21 I.L.M. 58 (1982). Adopted by the Organization of African Unity on June 27, 1981; *entered into force* October 21, 1986.

13 *See* Ordinance No. 74-1 of 6 July 1974 to Establish Rules Governing Land Tenure *as amended by* Ordinance No. 19/83 of 20 November 1983 ("1974 Land Tenure Law").

14 *See* Bakweri Land Claims Committee, Communication Under Articles 55, 56 and 58 of the African Charter on Human and Peoples' Rights Concerning Violations of Land Rights of an Indigenous Ethnic Minority in Cameroon, 4 October 2002 ("BLCC Memorial") (copy on file).

15 A division is an administrative unit under the command of a Senior Divisional Officer. There are roughly 54 divisions in Cameroon and Fako Division is in the South West Province, one of two English-speaking provinces out of the ten provinces in the country. The South West and North West provinces were part of the former Cameroons under United Kingdom Trusteeship. The other eight provinces are French-speaking and were the former Cameroons under French Trusteeship. *See* note 7 *supra*.

16 *See* African Commission on Human and Peoples' Rights, Urgent Appeal to H.E. President Paul Biya, May 2003 (copy on file).

a decision: (a) declaring the case inadmissible for non-exhaustion of domestic remedies as required under Article 56(5) of the Banjul Charter,[17] but in view of the grave human rights issues raised by BLCC on behalf of the indigenous Bakweri people; (b) offering to avail its good office, through the Rapporteur of the *BLCC vs. Cameroon* Communication, to the contending parties, with a view to enabling them resolve the matter amicably;[18] and (c) referring the recommendation for an amicable settlement to the Assembly of the Heads of State and Government of the African Union for approval.[19]

The parties were subsequently notified that the Commission's Eighteenth Annual Activity Report, which incorporated the decisions pertaining to the BLCC case, had received the imprimatur of the African Union.[20] With this endorsement the way was now open for both parties to enter into negotiations under the auspices of the Commission with a view to resolving amicably this long-standing land problem. Thus came to a close one of the most compelling chapters of a post-colonial campaign waged by an indigenous group to reclaim ancestral lands unlawfully expropriated while their country was under colonial occupation. Between 1946 when the United Nations Trusteeship Committee first vetted this matter and when the Commission was seised of this complaint, a small, determined and politically astute minority people made clever use of non-violent methods of protest, petitions and remonstrations to vindicate their group rights to land they have traditionally owned or otherwise occupied or used since time immemorial.[21]

2) Significance of the Bakweri Land Case

Communication No. 260/2002: BLCC v Cameroon, as the matter was listed in the docket of the Commission, was a case of first impression as it was the first time that the Commission had been seised of a complaint by an indigenous minority group relating to title over land once considered *terra nullius* (unoccupied land). *BLCC v Cameroon* presented the continent's highest human rights body with a rare opportunity to pronounce on one of the most contentious but unresolved issues from Africa's painful colonial past. The case itself and the Commission's handling of it have raised some interesting doctrinal issues that continue to provoke debate in scholarly circles and in the jurisprudence of several international tribunals. At the core of the complaint and the Commission's decision is the issue relating to the enforcement of human rights, especially land rights, in post-colonial

17 *See Bakweri Land Claims Committee vs. Cameroon*, African Comm. Human & Peoples' Rights, Comm. 260/2002 (2004).

18 *See* Letter to BLCC Counsel from the African Human Rights Commission, Ref.: ACHPR/COMM/2 of 25th January 2005 (copy on file).

19 *Id.*

20 *See* Letter to BLCC Counsel from the African Human Rights Commission Ref. ACHPR/LPROT/COMM 260/CAM/NGL of 3rd February 2006 (copy on file).

21 For this history of unrelenting protest and remonstrations, see *e.g.*, Petition of the Bakweri Land Committee, Cameroons under British Mandate, 18 AFRICA 30 (1948); Petition of the Bakweri Land Committee to the Trusteeship Council, U.N.O. Dec. T/PET.4.3, Report of the Trusteeship Visiting Mission, 1949; Petitions from Bakweri Land Committee. Summary of the Findings and Recommendations of the Investigating Officer and the Preliminary Observations of the Nigerian Government (1949) and P.M. Kale, Memorandum submitted to the Secretary of State for the Colonies as a member of the Delegation of the National Council of Nigeria and the Cameroons, PAN AFRICA (October-November 1947).

countries making the slow transition from single-party authoritarian rule to multi-party democracies. But this case has a value apart from and equally important as the issues of land expropriation without proper consultation or compensation that it raises. It also confronts issues relating to the appropriate forum where human rights violations of this nature can be properly handled. Furthermore, it addresses questions relating to the receptiveness of domestic courts to cases of this stripe, where the State is the respondent, and the proper standard to be used for determining whether a complainant has satisfied the exhaustion of domestic remedies requirement? In relatively simple language, the Bakweri land case sought to find out: whether victims of human rights violations, of the kind this group has endured, should be required to comply with the exhaustion of domestic remedies rule in a State where the rule of law is still in gestation and where the judiciary is neither independent nor impartial?[22] And whether, it can be said, in a context such as this, that an effective remedy exists which complainant could avail itself of? More importantly, what forum is open to a complainant in a politically charged[23] case, which involves lands leased to a *State-owned* corporation and from which the respondent State has for over forty years been receiving ground rents meant for the landowners; and where the prospect of losing this steady source of revenue is clearly not lost on respondent State; and where it is evident that the property respondent State intends to privatize would not be as attractive to potential investors if stripped of the rich, fertile lands it occupies; and where the private landowners are required to vindicate their property rights in a court system that hardly meets internationally-accepted norms of independence, impartiality and fairness?

It is our view that, in the circumstances just described, insisting that such a complainant must exhaust all domestic remedies is tantamount to a denial of his right to seek redress for the harm done. To avoid this predictable outcome the exhaustion of local remedies rule should be given its broadest interpretation possible in order to (a) level the playing

22 In its 1999 Human Rights Report on Cameroon, the United States Department of State described Cameroon's judiciary as one that "cannot act independently and impartially, since all judges and magistrates are directly nominated by the President." The Report goes on to observe that *"politically sensitive cases never are heard."* *See* U.S. State Department, 1999 Country Reports on Human Rights: Cameroon (Feb. 23, 2000) [Emphasis added]. Available at https://1997-2001.state.gov/global/human_rights/1999_hrp_report/cameroon.html] Two years later the situation had not changed as the 2001 edition of the same Human Rights Report notes: "Corruption and inefficiency in the courts remained serious problems. Justice frequently was delayed or denied before reaching the trial stage.... *Political bias often brought trials to a halt or resulted in an extremely long process, punctuated by extended court recesses. Powerful political or business interests appeared to enjoy virtual immunity from prosecution; some politically sensitive cases were settled with a payoff and thus never were heard."* *See* U.S. State Department, 2000 Country Reports on Human Rights: Cameroon (March 4, 2002) [Emphasis added]. Available at www.state.gov/gldr/rls/hrrpt/2001/af/8285.htm

23 The Bakweri land question falls in this category of cases for at least three reasons: First, because it implicates the crown jewel of a Privatization Program that Government is determined to see through. Secondly, it pits the Bakweri people against a Prime Minister and Head of Government as well as an Assistant Secretary-General at the Presidency, both of whom are Bakweri, but, not being elected officials, hold their offices at the pleasure of the President. Finally, it places Government in a face off with a politically-conscious minority tribe that has refused to stay quiet and watch its ancestral lands being sold to non-natives. This is not the kind of politically-sensitive litigation that a judiciary firmly under the control of the President of the Republic would like to handle and it is a contest which plaintiffs are not likely to receive a fair hearing. For a confirmation of this view, *see* The Herald (Courts in Cameroon are not free and cannot render judgments when the government is standing and watching over magistrates' shoulders.)

field for both parties—the defenseless citizen whose fundamental human rights have been violated and the powerful State responsible for the violation; (b) preserve the right of individual petition now entrenched in all international human rights instruments; and (c) give true meaning to the principle of equality-of-arms upon which all human rights contests are anchored.[24]

The Article will discuss the Bakweri case against Cameroon from its inception to the Commission's final decision. Part I will present an historical background of the Bakweri land problem and the reasons behind the decision to commence legal action against Cameroon at this time. This case history is followed in Part II by a presentation of the case itself beginning with the Bakweri claims followed by a discussion of Cameroon's Preliminary Objections together with complainant's response to these objections. Part III discusses the Commission's decision taken at its 36th Ordinary Session which held from 23rd November to 7th December.[25] Finally, in Part IV the Article will re-visit the exhaustion rule, in the context of human rights claims, brought against States where the court system does not enjoy the kind of independence from the executive branch that is implied in the local remedies rule.[26] While not quarreling with the soundness of this rule, the Article will however question its rigid application in this case while advancing a plea for a much more flexible and nuanced approach in future cases that come before the Commission.

A. Historical Background to the Bakweri Land Litigation

The lawsuit initiated by BLCC was one of David-and-Goliath-like proportions and its origins can be traced back to the period when Cameroon was a German Protectorate[27] but the immediate cause was the July 1994 Presidential decree[28] in which the State of Cameroon announced that the Cameroon Development Corporation, the crown jewel of Cameroon's economy,[29] was among fourteen state-owned companies earmarked for privatization or sale

24 Equality of arms is an essential element of fair hearing, a principle guaranteed in all human rights instruments. *See* e.g., Article 10 of the Universal Declaration; Article 14(1) of the ICCPR; Article 6(1) of the European Convention; Article XXVI of the American Declaration; Article 8 of the American Convention; Article 20(1) of the Yugoslavia Statute; Article 19(1) of the Rwanda Statute; and Articles 64(2) and 67(1) of the Rome Statute of the International Criminal Court. The equality of arms principle requires both parties in a trial be treated in a manner ensuring that they have a procedurally equal position during the course of the trial, and are in an equal position to make their case. The Human Rights Committee has stated that a fair hearing requires a number of conditions, including equality of arms, respect for the principle of adversary proceedings and expeditious procedure. *See Morael v. France*, (207/1986), 28 July 1989, Report of the HRC, (A/44/40), 1989, at 210. It requires that the State as well as the complainant is afforded a reasonable opportunity to present its case, under conditions that do not place it at a substantial disadvantage *vis-à-vis* the opposing party. *See* European Court judgments in the cases of *Ofrer* and *Hopfinger*, Nos. 524/59 and 617/59, Dec. 19.12.60, Yearbook 6, p. 680 and 696; *see also Kaufman v Belgium* (1986) 50 DR 98, EcmHR 15.

25 *See Bakweri Land Claims Committee vs. Cameroon,* Comm. 260/2002, African Comm. Hum. & Peoples' Rights.

26 *See Panevezys-Saldutsikis Railway Case (Estonia v. Lithuania)*, P.C.I.J., Ser. A/B, No. 76, at 18 (1939).

27 For an excellent account of that period, *see* Harry R. Rudin, GERMANS IN THE CAMEROONS 1884-1914: A CASE STUDY IN MODERN IMPERIALISM 111-112 (1938).

28 *See* Decree No. 94/125of July 14, 1994

29 In its heyday the corporation accounted for 65 percent of the export tonnage and 55 percent of the export earnings of former British Cameroons. It ran hospitals and clinics, schools and community centers and

to foreign private entrepreneurs. This would have meant the alienation of approximately 400 square miles (104,000 hectares) of land which the Bakweri have traditionally owned or otherwise occupied or used. Because the transfer of two-thirds of their total land area into private hands ran the real risk of extinguishing forever native title rights and interests in this land,[30] the Bakweri decided not to take this lying down. In a hastily summoned Assembly of Traditional Rulers, Notables and Elites, the Bakweri serve notice of their resolve "to pursue this matter in all international for a available to [them] including, if necessary, the United Nations until [they] are vindicated."[31]

The land in question was forcibly, arbitrarily, and illegally, in contravention of all the principles governing land tenure among the indigenous Bakweri, seized from the Bakweri landowners between 1887 and 1905 during the period of German colonial occupation and handed over to private German companies and individuals.[32] This large scale expropriation of private property would later be condemned by the British colonial authorities and the United Nations General Assembly[33] and in a Report submitted to the Trusteeship Council by a Visiting Mission sent out to the then British Southern Cameroons in November 1949. The Report states in its paragraph 63:

> That these customary principles in the strictest sense– particularly the prohibition against absolute alienation– were contravened at least in the early stages of German development of the Territory is apparent from events after 1884. During the German administration of Kamerun, some 460 square miles of land in the Victoria and Kumba Divisions were alienated by the German Government to plantation companies, missions, and

---

provided a wide range of social services for employees and non-employees. The corporation's labor force of over 17,000 was second only to that of the Government. *See* Willard R. Johnson, THE CAMEROON FEDERATION: POLITICAL INTEGRATION IN A FRAGMENTARY SOCIETY 97 (1970); *See also,* Sanford H. Bederman, Plantation Agriculture in Victoria Division, West Cameroon: An Historical Introduction, *Geography*, vol. LI, no. 4 (November, 1966) at 354-356; ____________ & Mark Delancey, The Cameroon Development Corporation 1947-1977: Cameroonization and Growth, in AN AFRICAN EXPERIMENT IN NATION-BUILDING: THE BILINGUAL REPUBLIC OF CAMEROON SINCE REUNIFICATION 251-278 (Ndiva Kofele-Kale, ed. 1980); Edwin Ardener, Shirley Ardener & W.A. Warmington, PLANTATION AND VILLAGE IN THE CAMEROONS: SOME SOCIAL AND ECONOMIC ISSUES (1960); Piet Konings, PLANTATION LABOUR AND ECONOMIC CRISIS IN CAMEROON, 26 DEVELOPMENT & CHANGE 525-549 (1995); ____________, Privatisation of Agro-Industrial Parastatals and Anglophone Opposition in Cameroon, 34 J. COMMONWEALTH & COMP. POL. 199-217 (1996); Simon Joseph Epale, PLANTATIONS AND DEVELOPMENT IN WESTERN CAMEROON, 1885-1975: A STUDY IN AGRARIAN CAPITALISM (1985).

30 *See* Bakweri Land Committee, Memorandum of the Bakweri People on the Presidential Decree to Privatize or Sell the Cameroon Development Corporation, Buea: July 27, 1994 (copy on file).

31 *See* Bakweri Ancestral Lands Shall Not be Alienated without the Consent of the Natives: Submission of Counsel for the Bakweri: Buea, Thursday, August 18, 1994 (copy on file).

32 The two leading German firms that dominated plantation agriculture in the protectorate were Woermann and Jantzen und Thormalen. *See e.g.* William H. (Lord) Hailey, AN AFRICAN SURVEY 775 (1945) (Fifty estates, about 258,000 acres in all, were alienated to German private individuals); *see also* Cyprian F. Fisiy, THE DEATH OF AMYTH SYSTEM: LAND COLONIZATION ON THE SLOPES OF OKU, MOUNT CAMEROON (1992) (Places the number of German-owned estates on the eve of World War 1 at 58).

33 *See* U.N. Document at 189, ¶16.

> individuals. Available records of the methods by which this was done are not complete, but on the whole, the evidence that is available suggests that during the first 12 years of the occupation, there was no regular procedure, and that land was taken by whatever means seemed most convenient in each locality concerned– whether by purchase at small sums from local chiefs, or by simple expropriation. The German Government in turn sold estates into private hands or in a minority of cases, granted leases. The United Kingdom Authorities have pointed out, however, that demarcation of Crown Land was never done systematically nor did a Land Commission ever deal generally with all unoccupied land in Kamerun. When land was required for plantation purposes, the Commissioner was convened; if any claims were established the owners would be compensated by the planter or plantation company, this compensation being set off against the purchase price paid to Government. If the owners were actually settled within the area, they would be required to move to reserves outside the area, on the basis, under an agreement of 1904, that 'apart from land built and farmed upon by natives each hut is to be given six hectares.'[34]

The dispossession and expropriation of Bakweri land met with stiff resistance[35] from the Buea people who in the end lost out to the superior German military might. As punishment for their resistance, the Bakweri were forcibly relocated to 'native reserves' (*"reservats"*).[36] However, with the help of some foreign missions, notably the Basel Mission,[37] the Bakweri were able to protest directly to the German Imperial Government in Berlin about their inhumane treatment at the hands of the local German colonial administration. Although Berlin attempted some corrective measures to ease the plight of the Bakweri, these were aborted at the outbreak of the First World War in 1914.

1. From Private German Estates to State-owned CDC Plantations

In the years before the First World War, these alienated Bakweri lands were developed into large plantation estates by their German owners. After the war ended, these plantations were put up for auction but an embargo on bidding was placed on the ex-enemy nationals. However, since they were the only buyers who showed any interest, the legislation which

34 *See* U.N. Trusteeship Council [TCOR], Report of the U.N. Trusteeship Council Visiting Mission to the Cameroons Under United Kingdom Trusteeship, U.N. Doc. T/461 (Nov. 1949) at 189, ¶63.

35 The extension of German control in the Cameroon mountain area met its first serious resistance from the Bakweri of Buea when in 1891 an expeditionary force sent against was routed and its German commander, Gravenreuth, killed. In a second expedition three years later the Buea people were defeated, made to pay an indemnity and forcibly relocated to native reservations. For an account of this epic battle from the eyes of a Bakweri chronicler, *see* Paul Monyongo mo'Kale, A BRIEF HISTORY OF THE BAKWERI (1939); *see also* Kingdom on Mount Cameroon, *supra* note 8.

36 *See* Germans in Cameroons, *supra* note 27, at 111-112; *see also* Charles Kingsley Meek, LAND TENURE AND LAND ADMINISTRATION IN NIGERIA AND THE CAMEROONS 405 (1957).

37 *See e.g.*, Plantation and Village, *supra* note 29, at 313.

had prohibited the acquisition of these estates by ex-enemy subjects was repealed.[38]As a result, most of the estates were repurchased by their former owners with the assistance of the German Government.[39] Following the outbreak of the Second World War in 1939, these plantations were again sequestrated and declared enemy property[40] and vested by the Nigerian Government in the Public Custodian of Enemy Property for the duration of the war.[41] When the war ended, the British Colonial Government bought back all the erstwhile German estates from the Custodian of Enemy Property at a cost of £850,000 sterling. Under pressure from the Bakweri people through their agent, the Bakweri Land Committee (which had kept up the fight for the return of all expropriated Bakweri lands, carrying it all the way to the United Nations Trusteeship Council),[42] the British Colonial Government, which was administering Cameroon under the League of Nations Mandate system, declared these ex-enemy property as "Native Lands"[43] and placed them under the custody of the Governor of Nigeria to hold in trust for the Bakweri people. The lands were subsequently leased in 1946 to a newly created statutory corporation, the Cameroon Development Corporation, for a period of 60 years with effect from January 1947, to administer and develop these lands until such time that the inhabitants of the territory people were capable of managing them without outside assistance.[44]

The CDC was created as a public corporation (without private shareholders) to operate on a commercial basis but with broad socio-economic objectives which, in partnership with Government, would develop the rich and fertile lands of Fako Division for the common benefit of the inhabitants of the British Cameroons. By the terms of the 1947 lease the CDC was required, and it agreed, to pay ground rents to the landowners. Throughout this leasehold, the corporation set aside each year a sum of money as rent for the use of Bakweri lands. However, in breach of the terms of the lease, the rents were paid into the public treasury rather than to the local councils in Bakweri land.

2. Bakweri Reaction to the Privatization of CDC

Shortly after the presidential decree of July 1994 announcing the privatization of CDC became public, the Bakweri addressed a Memorandum, signed by 125 Bakweri Chiefs, Notables and Elites,[45] to Cameroon's President voicing their opposition to the privatization exercise for fear that it would adversely affect their rights to their ancestral lands occupied

38 *See* Ex-Enemy Immovable Property Ordinance No. 22 of 1924.

39 *See* Land Tenure and Administration, *supra* note 36, at 355.

40 *See* Ex-Enemy Lands (Cameroon) Ordinance, No. 38 of 1946, §4; and Ex-Enemy (Likomba Estates) Ordinance, No. 22 of 1947.

41 *See* Land Tenure and Administration, *supra* note 36, at 355.

42 *See e.g.*, Petition of the Bakweri Land Committee, Cameroons under British Mandate, 18 AFRICA 30 (1948); Petition of the Bakweri Land Committee to the Trusteeship Council, U.N.O. Dec. T/PET.4.3, Report of the Trusteeship Visiting Mission, 1949; Petitions from Bakweri Land Committee. Summary of the Findings and Recommendations of the Investigating Officer and the Preliminary Observations of the Nigerian Government (1949); *see also* Plantation and Village, *supra* note 29, at 316-317.

43 *See* Land and Native Rights Ordinance, Laws of Nigeria, 1958, Cap. 96 at §3.

44 *See* Cameroon Development Corporation Ordinance, No. 39 of 1946 (copy on file).

45 *See* Bakweri Land Committee, Memorandum of the Bakweri People on the Presidential Decree to Privatize or Sell the Cameroon Development Corporation, Buea: July 27, 1994 (copy on file).

by the CDC plantations. As no acknowledgment was received to that Memorandum, a second petition dated 3rd March 1999[46] signed by some 360 Bakweri traditional rulers, notables and elites, and a third petition by non-Bakweri bearing over 100 signatures, were again sent to Cameroon's President.[47] The second petition was subsequently endorsed by 139 Bakweri in North America and other parts of the world, by their letter dated 1st October, 1999 addressed to the President of the Republic.[48] Amidst this flurry of memoranda, BLCC also contacted the International Monetary Fund and the World Bank, the main sponsors of the Privatization Program in Cameroon, advising them of the need to resolve the explosive land issue before going through with the privatization of CDC.[49] BLCC also sent out a *caveat* emptor to prospective buyers of CDC assets to alert them of the unresolved land problem and to invite them to convince the Government of Cameroon to fully involve the Bakweri landowners in the ongoing negotiations.[50]

On 4 October 2000, some three months after a written request for a meeting, the Prime Minister and Head of Government finally met with a delegation of BLCC leaders to discuss issues relating to the privatization of the CDC and other related matters. Also present at this meeting was the Assistant Secretary General at the Presidency. During their discussions, the BLCC delegation voiced Bakweri support for privatization and expressed the hope that the exercise "will be carried out in a transparent and impeccable manner and that it would result in increased productivity, profitability, poverty alleviation and greater economic and social prosperity for the nation and its people."[51] These leaders also reiterated the position of the Bakweri people on the land question: that the lands now occupied by the CDC are private native lands, so declared before independence by the British Colonial Administration, and contained in the German Land Register or *Grundbuch*.[52] The BLCC delegation left this meeting guardedly optimistic that a resolution to the Bakweri land problem was in the horizon. Subsequent Government action would jolt them from this dream-like state and dash any hopes that an end was in sight because less than two years after the breakthrough meeting with the Prime Minister, Cameroon unilaterally decided, without bothering to notify the BLCC leadership, to privatize the Tole tea estates of the CDC. Equally noteworthy is the fact that the Cameroon Government did not respond to Bakweri demands to be consulted over the fate of their ancestral lands nor did it rescind

46 *See* Bakweri Land Committee, Memorandum Dated 3rd March 1999 to H.E. Paul Biya Concerning the Privatization of the Cameroon Development Corporation (CDC), Buea: March 3, 1999 (copy on file).

47 *See* Letter from Concerned Cameroonians Regarding the IMF Sanctioned Privatization of the Cameroon Development Corporation (CDC), October 19, 2000 (copy on file).

48 *See* Letter of Support for BLCC Addressed to President Paul Biya of October 1, 1999 (copy on file).

49 *See* Letter to the Managing Director of the I.M.F. on Privatizing the CDC without the Consent and Participation of Native Landowners Carries Grave Risks Especially to Potential Investors: June 16, 2000 (copy on file).

50 *See* An Open Letter to All Prospective Buyers of CDC Plantations, October 12, 2000 (copy on file).

51 *See* BLCC Letter to H.E. Peter Mafany Musonge, Prime Minister and Head of Government, 30th October 2000 (copy on file).

52 This national land register contained "detailed information on all land transactions and interests in land, including but not limited to, each land parcel's location, dimensions, and name and address of the legal owner(s) and relevant cadastral information such as coordinates and bearings." *See* Ambe Njoh, PLANNING RULES IN POST-COLONIAL STATES 85 (3001).

Decree No. 94/125 of 1994 privatizing CDC. It is against this backdrop that the Bakweri through their accredited agent, BLCC, cited Cameroon before two international human rights bodies for violation of Bakweri land rights.

PART II. THE BAKWERI FACE OFF THE STATE OF CAMEROON

A. Procedural History

BLCC's first petitioned the United Nations Sub-Commission on the Promotion and Protection of Human Rights (formerly the U.N. Sub-Commission on Prevention of Discrimination and Protection of Minorities)("U.N. Sub-Commission") in August 2001 pursuant to ECOSOC Resolution 1503[53] citing Cameroon for violating the land rights of the Bakweri people by seeking to sell CDC plantations on those lands without involving the indigenous landowners. On the 8th of July 2002 by a letter from the Governor of the South West province, who was writing on instructions from Cameroon's Minister of External Relations, BLCC was informed of the U.N. Sub-Commission's decision to discontinue further consideration of the matter.[54]

The letter from the Governor gave two reasons for this decision.[55] These were that "petitioners did not fully exploit local avenues available to solve the problem and the Cameroon judicial system was deemed competent to handle the petition;" Second, that "the Commission commended government's position on the issue and encouraged government's efforts in her "continuous willingness to resolve once and for all, this matter of Bakweri Lands."[56] The second reason given was a significant development in the BLCC struggle to reclaim expropriated Bakweri lands as it was the first and only time Cameroon acknowledged the existence of a Bakweri Land Problem and expressed a willingness to

53 *See* ECOSOC Resolution 1503 Concerning the Procedure for Dealing with Communications Relating to Violations of Human Rights and Fundamental Freedoms, E.S.C. Res. 1503, U.N. ESCOR, 48th Sess., Supp. No. 1A at 8, U.N. Doc. E/4832/Add.1 (1970).

54 BLCC would subsequently receive a letter dated 17th June 2004 from the Secretary of the African Commission and attached to it was a copy of a "Confidential decision relating to Cameroon" adopted by the Working Group of the United Nations Sub-Commission on Prevention of Discrimination and Protection of Minorities ("U.N. Sub-Commission") on February 12, 2002. This decision was in relation to a complaint submitted by BLCC in August 2001 to the U.N. Sub-Commission under the '1503 Procedure'. The Working Group on Situations to which this matter was referred concluded thus:

> "*Noting* the complexity of this long-standing issue,
> *Considering* that local domestic remedies have not been exhausted and that the matter should be addressed through a national judicial process,
> *Welcoming with appreciation* the exemplary reply received from the Government of Cameroon,
> 1. *Encourages* the Government of Cameroon to continue pursuing on-going efforts in this regard,
> 2. *Decides* to discontinue consideration of the matter,
> 3. *Requests* the Secretary-General to communicate this decision to the Government of Cameroon." *See* Letter to BLCC from the Secretary of the African Human Rights Commission Ref.: ACHPR/COMM/2/NGL of 17th June 2004 (copy on file).

55 Since the U.N. Sub-Commission's rules of procedure do not allow Petitioners (BLCC) to be served with a copy of the Government's Response nor to be present during commission deliberations, a right only extended to States Parties, BLCC surmises that the reasons contained in the Governor's letter were actually the arguments advanced by the Cameroon Government.

56 *See* U.N. Sub-Commission, Confidential decision relating to Cameroon of 17th June 2004, *supra* note 54.

see this matter satisfactorily resolved. Cameroon did not, however, follow through on this pledge despite repeated reminders from BLCC.[57]

Left with no other choice, BLCC decided to petition the African Commission on Human and Peoples' Rights pursuant to Articles 55, 56 and 58 of the Banjul Charter. At its 32nd Ordinary Session held from 17th to 23rd October 2002, the Commission considered the complaint and decided to be seised of it. On 4th November 2002 pursuant to Rules 113 and 117(4) of the Commission's Rules of Procedures, the Commission fixed the time limits for filing written pleadings on admissibility and informed the parties and invited them to file their submissions with the Commission.[58] Cameroon submitted its Memorial on Admissibility on 31st January 2003 and BLCC filed its Memorial on 3rd February 2003 and on 4th March forwarded a Reply to Cameroon's Memorial on Admissibility. On 8th May Cameroon filed Preliminary Objections claiming among other things that the matter was not ripe for hearing since BLCC had not exhausted all available domestic remedies. The Commission agreed to hear oral pleadings on admissibility at its 33rd Ordinary Session which held from 15th to 29th May 2003. A decision on admissibility was deferred to the next ordinary session to afford complainant sufficient time to file a Response to respondent State's preliminary objections.

In the meantime, at complainant's request and in conformity with Rule 111 of the Commission's Rules of Procedure which authorizes the Commission to take provisional measures pending the final outcome of a dispute before it, the Chairman of the Commission sent an urgent appeal letter to the President of Cameroon urging him to direct respondent State to cease and desist from any further alienation of the disputed land pending a

57 Barely six months after informing the U.N. Sub-Commission that discussions were under way with the Bakweri, Respondent quietly disposed of Tole Tea Estate in Complainants' heartland; entered into contract with a phantom South African company (Brobon Finex Pty Ltd.) which the South African Government attests does not exist (*See* Certificate from the South African Registrar of Companies and Close Corporations of 13th November 2003) and in which, contrary to Respondent State's assertions during the 35th Session of the African Commission, the share capital of the company formed to manage the plantations, *Cameroon Tea Estate*, has been apportioned, to the total exclusion of the landowners while *granting a lease of 70 years to the operating company with all ground rent payable to Respondent. See* Bakweri Land Claims Committee Submission on Admissibility, February 4, 2003, pages 7-9, 15, footnote 15 (copy on file).
Respondent State also failed to acknowledge receipt of, and continued to flout, the Commission's May 2003 Urgent Appeal to President Biya taken under Rule 113(3) of the Commission's Rules of Procedure, to halt further alienation of Bakweri ancestral lands under lease to the Cameroon Development Corporation ("CDC") pending a final resolution of this dispute. It did so by openly courting foreign investors and putting up for sale the remaining CDC plantations. Furthermore, Respondent State continued to ignore BLCC's repeated overtures to have this matter resolved amicably as evidenced in letters Complainants addressed to the Minister of State in charge of Territorial Administration and Decentralization and to the President of the Republic himself. *See* BLCC Correspondence with President Biya. Finally, Respondent State supported attempts by local law enforcement authorities to persecute and silence BLCC leaders; tacitly encouraged the creation of a rival organization—the Bakweri Cooperative Union of Farmers Real Estate Corporation-- to speak for the Bakweri, encouraging and financing this fake organization to tie up the BLCC leadership in the local courts through nuisance law suits in an effort to discredit BLCC before this Commission as not being the authentic and accredited voice of the dispossessed Bakweri people.

58 *See* Letter to Counsel for BLCC from the Secretary of the African Commission, Ref: ACHPR/COMM/2 of 4th November 2002 (copy on file).

final decision of the Commission.[59] Complainant filed its Response to respondent State's preliminary objections on 23rd August 2003. The Commission heard oral submissions from both parties at its 34th and 35th Ordinary Sessions held in November 2003 and June 2004, respectively. A decision was rendered at the close of the Commission's 36th Ordinary Session in November-December 2004.

B. Bakweri Claims

In its October 2002 communication before the Commission, BLCC made three principal assertions against Cameroon. First, BLCC claimed that Cameroon, by its acts and omissions, violated Article 21 of the Banjul Charter which enjoins States Parties from impairing the inherent right of all peoples to enjoy and utilize fully and freely their wealth and natural resources and guarantees their right to adequate compensation for lands expropriated by the State. Second, BLCC claimed that Cameroon had breached its obligations under Article 22 of the Banjul Charter which protects the right to economic, social and cultural development and obligates States Parties to ensure the exercise of this right. Finally, BLCC asserted that Cameroon was in breach of Article 7(1)(a) of the Banjul Charter which stipulates that "Every individual shall have the right to have his cause heard [which includes]... the right to an appeal to competent national organs against acts violating his fundamental rights as recognized and guaranteed by conventions, laws, regulations and customs in force."

1. Discussion of the Bakweri Claims

1) Article 14 Violation

This article provides that *"the right to property shall be guaranteed. It may only be encroached upon in the interest of public need or in the general interest of the community and in accordance with the provisions of appropriate laws."* BLCC's complaint alleged that Bakweri peoples' right to private property and their right not to be deprived of it arbitrarily had been violated by the Government of Cameroon. The complaint pointed out that the lands occupied by the CDC were repurchased from the Custodian of Ex-Enemy Property by the British colonial administration and declared private native lands long before Cameroon became an independent nation in 1960. Support for this position comes from a report of the supervisory authority when Cameroon was administered as a United Nations Trust Territory. On 9 June 1948 while forwarding to the U.N. Secretary General a Petition from the Bakweri people, the United Kingdom government made the following observations:

> [T]hat all [the repurchased ex-enemy] lands had been declared native lands and had been placed under the control of the Governor of Nigeria to be administered for the use and common benefit of the natives; that the Nigerian government had repurchased 14, 851 acres of plantation land for the benefit of the natives, and that the Cameroon Development

59 *See* Bakweri Land Claims Committee vs. Cameroon, Comm. 260/02, African Comm. Hum. & Peoples' Rights, 16-17 ("Commission Decision").

> Corporation had been set up to administer and develop the plantations until such time as the Bakweri people were competent to manage them without assistance....[60]

The complaint admits that the issue of the quantum of legal rights the Bakweri retained when their lands were acquired by the British administering authorities has been raised in some circles: whether title to these lands passed to the British Crown through the Governor of Nigeria or remained with the indigenous land owners. This issue, BLCC asserted, was expertly handled by Dr. C.K. Meek, the foremost authority of his time on land law in British colonial Africa, in his 1957 study on land law in colonial West Africa.[61] Meek opined that in situations such as this, existing titles were never extinguished. As he put it "*where the Government had itself assumed the position of landlord, it had done so only to protect native interests: the vesting of land in the Governor had not implied a transfer of ownership of the land of the territory to the Governor but had merely conferred on him a power of supreme trusteeship. Nor did it affect the existing titles, whether community or individual.*"[62] Meek was in no doubt that Bakweri title to these lands was never extinguished and that the Governor of Nigeria held them in trust for the indigenous landowners: "*Indeed, the United Nations at its 6th meeting of the Council in March 1950 states that increased effort should be made to explain to the Bakweris that Ex-Enemy Lands had in fact reverted to them and that ownership was now legally vested in them.*"[63]

Meek's conclusion reflects the weight of legal opinion that indigenous title to land was a right predating the colonial state and not dependent for its existence upon treaty or statutory law. These antecedent rights and interests survived the change of sovereignty, in the Bakweri case, the change from the British Crown to the Cameroon State.[64] This position, BLCC argued, is consistent with the view that the colonial territory was not *terra nullius* (land belonging to no-one) at the time of European settlement. In the landmark case of *Mabo v. Queensland,65* and most recently in *Bennell v. State of Western Australia66,* the High Court of Australia rejected the doctrine of *terra nullius* as repugnant and inconsistent with historical reality.

According to the BLCC complaint, that the CDC-occupied lands are private lands and Bakweri title was never extinguished finds confirmation even under Cameroon's own 1974 Land Tenure Act.[67] This law classifies lands that were entered in official German land registers, the Ground Book or *Grundbuch*, as private property. BLCC pointed out that as

60 *See* 18 AFRICA [Journal of the Royal African Society] 307 (October 1948).

61 *See* Land Tenure and Administration, *supra* note 36.

62 *Id.* at 355-356. (Emphasis added).

63 *Id.* at page 407 (Emphasis added).

64 *See Amodu Tijani v. Secretary of Southern Nigeria* 1 [1921] 2 A C 399, 407, 410; *Oyekan v. Adele* [1951] 2 All ER 785. *See also* T. Olawale Elias, BRITISH COLONIAL LAWS: A COMPARATIVE STUDY OF THE INTERACTION BETWEEN ENGLISH AND LOCAL LAWS IN BRITISH COLONIAL DEPENDENCIES (1962) and T. Olawale Elias, NIGERIAN LAND LAW AND CUSTOM (1951).

65 *See Mabo v. Queensland (No. 2)(1992) 175 CLR 1 (Mabo (No. 2).*

66 *See Bennell v. State of Western Australia* [2006] FCA (19 September 2006).

67 *See* 1974 Land Tenure Law, *supra* note 13.

many as 23 German plantations met this description and were entered in the *Grundbuch.* These are the plantations that were subsequently re- purchased by the British colonial administration from the Custodian of Enemy Property in 1946, declared as Native Lands, and then leased to the newly-created statutory corporation, the CDC.[68]

The 1974 Land Tenure Law takes great pain to distinguish between "National Lands" and Private Land. The former are lands which "are not classed into the public or private property of the State and other public bodies[69].... which the State can administer in such a way as to ensure rational use and development,"[70] and can be "allocated by grant, lease or assignment on conditions to be pursued by decree."[71] Private Lands, on the other hand, guarantee their owners the right to freely enjoy and dispose of them. Part II, Article 2 of the Land Tenure Act identifies 5 categories of land subject to the right of private property. These are: "(a) Registered lands; (b) Freehold lands; (c) Lands acquired under the transcription system; (d) Lands covered by a final concession; (e) *Land entered in the Grundbuch*."[72]

It should be noted that before land could be entered in the Ground Book it had to be mapped and demarcated. The CDC-occupied lands were surveyed before being registered in official records as private property and all this took place prior to the entry into force of the 1974 Land Tenure Law. Since these lands were only *leased* to the CDC, only the true owners, i.e., the Bakweri, reserve the right under the Land Tenure Act to dispose of these lands. Consequently, the sale or privatization of the assets of CDC should not, in principle, include the lands on which these plantations stand. The position of the Bakweri on this point has not wavered in 50 years. In their 1999 Memorandum to Cameroon's President, the Bakweri insisted that "upon Cameroon attaining independence, the role of the State in continuing to act as trustee over Bakweri lands, effectively ended. Existing contracts, e.g., the original 60 years granted by the Governor General of Nigeria, should be allowed to run its full course. Any subsequent extension of that lease by a Government of Cameroon, however called, is invalid, as the trustee relationship terminated when Cameroonians assumed political independence and were not subject to control by a foreign imperial power."[73]

2) Violation of Article 21

The first paragraph of Article 21 provides that "*All peoples shall freely dispose of their wealth and natural resources. This right shall be exercised in the exclusive interest of the people. In no case shall a people be deprived of it.*"74 BLCC's complaint alleged that the process of

68 *See* Letter Ref. No. 020/Y.2.5/MINUH/10/B.042 from the South West Provincial Chief of Service Lands attesting to the fact that the private property contemplated in the 1974 Land Tenure Law is indeed "ex-enemy lands." (copy on file).

69 *See* 1974 Land Tenure Law, Part III, §14(1), *supra* note 13.

70 *Id.* at §16(1).

71 *Id.* at §17(1).

72 *Id.* Part II, §2 (Emphasis added). In a letter Ref. 020/Y.2.5/MINUH/10/B.08 to the Secretary General of BLCC, the South West Provincial Chief of Service Lands confirmed that "*all ex-enemy lands of former West Cameroon are recorded in the Grundbuchs.*" [Emphasis added] (copy on file).

73 *See* Memorandum dated 3rd March 1999 to H.E. President Paul Biya Concerning the Privatisation of the Cameroon Development Corporation (CDC) at 6 (copy on file).

74 Banjul Charter, *supra* note 12, art. 21.

extinguishment set in motion by Decree No. 94/125 severely undercut the group's Article 21 right to exercise permanent sovereignty over their ancestral lands. They further complained that Respondent State ignored their repeated requests for a full and complete public disclosure of the terms of the sale or the lease of Bakweri lands to foreign purchasers. In this and in other respects, Decree No. 94/125 is in clear breach of a trust responsibility by the Cameroon Government (that is, of undivided loyalty to the Bakweri landowners who are the real beneficiaries) or, at the very best, an abuse of the State's power to control or dispose of lands held in sacred trust for an indigenous minority people relying on the authority of *Guerin v. The Queen.*[75] In that case, the Supreme Court of Canada held the Crown in breach of a trust or, at a minimum, fiduciary duties with respect to the manner in which the Crown disposed of reserve lands held by it for the use and benefit of an indigenous Indian tribe. *Guerin* involved the voluntary surrender by the Musqueam Indian Band to the federal Crown, "in trust," of some of its reserve land for the purpose of lease to a private club. The Crown subsequently concluded a lease on terms that were not authorized by the Indians and were less advantageous to them. BLCC asserted in the complaint that just as the Bakweri had agreed to the British colonial government's proposal to lease their land to the CDC on terms which clearly recognized their reversionary rights, any subsequent attempt by the successor government to lease this land to another party must be on terms acceptable to the Bakweri.

BLCC further argued that the contemplated extinguishment of Bakweri land rights equally violates the second paragraph of Article 21 (2): *"In case of spoliation, the dispossessed people shall have the right to lawful recovery of its property as well as to an adequate compensation."76* The privatization of CDC and with it the likelihood of transferring Bakweri private lands to third parties was being carried out without any discussion about fair compensation to the Bakweri, the principal stakeholders. BLCC pointed to the Commission's own jurisprudence which traces the origin of the rights contained in Article 21 of the Banjul Charter to the period when the continent was under colonial domination; a period:

> *during which the human and material resources of Africa were largely exploited for the benefit of outside powers, creating tragedy for Africans themselves, depriving them of their birthright and alienating them from the land. The aftermath of colonial exploitation has left Africa's precious resources and people still vulnerable to foreign misappropriation. The drafters of the Charter obviously wanted to remind African governments of the continent's painful legacy and restore co-operative economic development to its traditional place at the heart of African Society.*[77]

For the BLCC this reminder clearly was lost on Cameroon who, faced with the opportunity to right a historical wrong– one traceable to a period when the territory was under

75 *See Guerin v. The Queen [1984] 2 S.C.R. 335.*

76 Banjul Charter, *supra* note 12, art. 21(2).

77 *See The Social and Economic Rights Action Center for Economic and Social Rights v. Nigeria*, Comm. No. 155/96, ¶56, African Comm. Hum. & Peoples' Rights [Emphasis added].

foreign domination-- chose instead to behave no differently from its German colonial predecessors!

BLCC urged the Commission to follow the jurisprudence of the Inter-American Commission and the Inter-American Court and rule that the Bakweri be indemnified in an amount sufficient to remedy the entire scope of the adverse consequences that have resulted from the century-old expropriation of their most valuable asset, land. BLCC reasoned that the award of compensation would also be upholding both the letter and spirit of the Cameroon Constitution which proudly proclaims "*the right guaranteed every person by law to use, enjoy and dispose of property. No person shall be deprived thereof, save for public purposes and subject to the payment of compensation under conditions determined by law.*"[78]

BLCC based its demand for just compensation on several provisions relating to compensating victims of human rights abuses found in other regional human rights instruments as well as the jurisprudence of these regional tribunals. It pointed to the 1969 American Convention on Human Rights whose Article 21 parallels the Banjul Charter's Article 21. Article 21 of paragraph 2 of the American Convention reads: "*No one shall be deprived of his [her] property except upon payment of just compensation, for reasons of public utility or social interest, and in the cases according to the forms established by law.*"*79* BLCC also drew the Commission's attention to the case law of the Inter-American Commission on Human Rights where the question of compensation for State violation of the right to property, a right which the Inter-American Commission has described as an "inalienable right," has been addressed. For instance, in *Haydee A. de Marin et al.*,[80] the Inter-American Commission found Nicaragua in breach of its duty under the Convention for "depriving the petitioners of their property without any form of compensation or for no reason of public utility"[81] and recommended that the Government of Nicaragua return the confiscated properties to their legitimate owners and pay the injured parties the amounts owed in damages and compensation for the time the properties in question were held in usufruct.[82]

The Inter-American Court of Human Rights has also tackled the issue of remedies for human rights abuses. In the landmark case of *Velásquez Rodríguez*,[83] the Court articulated for the first time a framework for calibrating the type of reparations and compensation that may be awarded by the Court to victims of human rights violations and the criteria to be applied in making these assessments. In that case, the Court showed a marked preference for restitution although it left the door open for other forms of relief, such as outright

78 *See* Law No. 65 of 96-06 of 18 January 1996 *to amend* the Constitution of 2 June 1972, Preamble.

79 *See* AMERICAN CONVENTION ON HUMAN RIGHTS, O.A.S. Official Records OEA/Ser.K/XVI/1.1, Doc. 65 Rev. 1, Corr. 1, January 7, 1970, 9 I.L.M. 101 (1970). Signed at San Jose, Costa Rica on November 22, 1969, *entered into force on* July 18, 1979, Art. 21 (2).

80 See Haydee A. de Marin et al., Case No. 10.770, Inter-Am. C.H.R. 293, OEA/ser. L/V/II.85, doc. 9 rev. (1994)(Annual Report 1993).

81 *Id.*

82 *See also Carlos Martínez Riguero, Case No. 7788, Inter-Am. C.H.R. 89, OEA/ser. L/V/II.76, doc. 9 rev. 1 (1987)* (Annual Report 1986-1987) (Compensation recommended for Nicaragua's wrongful confiscation of the dividends earned on shares owned by the complainant).

83 *See Velásquez Rodríguez Case, Compensatory Damages (Art. 63(1) American Convention on Human Rights)* Judgment of July 21, 1989, Inter-Am. Ct. H. R. (Ser. C), No. 7 (1989).

compensation in cases where restitution is not possible. Velásquez Rodríguez also called for flexibility in the application of these criteria and on a case-by-case basis so as to "arrive at a prudent estimate of the damages, given the circumstances of each case."[84] Using this formula, the Court proceeded to award 'moral damages' to the Velásquez Rodríguez family as indemnification for the psychological harm it had suffered as a result of the disappearance of their loved one.

3) Violation of Article 22

Article 22 of the Banjul Charter stipulates that:

> 1. All peoples shall have the right to their economic, social and cultural development with due regard to their freedom and identity and in the equal enjoyment of the common heritage of mankind. 2. States shall have the duty, individually and collectively, to ensure the exercise of the right to development.[85]

The BLCC complaint asserted that the privatization of CDC without first resolving the underlying land problem poses a serious threat to the right of Bakweri people to their economic, social and cultural development. The Bakweri, the complaint pointed out, have for close to a century been confined to a space less than one-third the size of the land they occupied prior to German colonization. The large-scale agro-industrial development that has been taking place on the other two-thirds of their lands has benefited all Cameroonians and not the Bakweri exclusively. While other minority groups in Cameroon have been able to exercise continuous dominion over their ancestral lands, the bulk of Bakweri ancestral land has always been under non-native control, first German and now the State of Cameroon. And while these other ethnic groups have been left to develop their ancestral lands without external interference, that has not been the Bakweri experience.

It will be recalled that the total area of Fako Division where the Bakweri have traditionally lived is roughly 838 square miles. Two hundred square miles of this consist of rocky barren hilly slopes, another 30 square miles of mangrove swamps or bogs which are unsuitable for cultivation leaving approximately 588 square miles of arable land. Out of this total land area, existing settlements (towns and villages) take up no more than 100 square miles while the CDC plantations occupy some 400 square miles or approximately 60 per cent of the total arable land. Missions and other commercial interests take up about 50 square miles, leaving barely 38 square miles of arable land for the indigenous peoples of Fako Division.[86]

84 *Id.*

85 Banjul Charter, *supra* note 12, art. 22.

86 *See* BLCC, Communication under Articles 55, 56, and 58 of the African Charter on Human and Peoples' Rights Concerning Violation of Land Rights of an Indigenous Ethnic Minority in Cameroon 1, 9-10 (October 4, 2002) (copy on file); *see also* His Majesty's Government, REPORT BY HIS MAJESTY'S GOVERNMENT IN THE UNITED KINGDOM OF GREAT BRITAIN AND NORTHERN IRELAND TO THE GENERAL ASSEMBLY OF THE UNITED NATIONS ON THE ADMINISTRATION OF THE CAMEROONS UNDER UNITED KINGDOM TRUSTEESHIP FOR THE YEAR 1949 304 (1950) (Places the total area of land

Extending this already heavy concentration of non-natives on private Bakweri land, BLCC argued, would undermine the group's Article 22 rights in three ways. First, it would irrevocably alter existing land holding arrangements and the pattern of natural resource exploitation in Fako Division. As a result, future generations of Bakweri who have been deprived of, and denied access to, their ancestral lands, will never know or appreciate what it means to own land in close proximity to fellow culture-carriers and on territory where their ancestors once farmed, fished and hunted. Secondly, the confinement of the total Bakweri population in Fako Division to less than 40 square miles of territory would in the not-too-distant future trigger a forced exodus of Bakweri to other parts of Cameroon in search of available land for their agricultural and other development needs. Finally, as these Bakweri begin to move in large numbers to other parts of Cameroon, carries with it the risk of exporting the social tensions that have historically blighted settler-native relations in Fako Division.[87]

4) Violation of Article 7(1)(a)

BLCC's fourth claim against Cameroon boiled down to the process by which the respondent State chose to extinguish Bakweri land rights which they contend violates Article 7, paragraph 1(a) of the Banjul Charter.[88] The approach adopted by Cameroon, BLCC argued, was discriminatory, without due process of law and totally lacking in fundamental fairness in many respects. Although the Bakweri made representations to the highest decision-making organs of the State-- the President and Head of State and the Prime Minister and Head of Government—respondent State simply refused to meet face-to-face with Bakweri leaders; to include proper representation of the Bakweri stakeholders in the negotiations on the sale or privatization of CDC despite repeated calls for their inclusion; and to provide adequate notice and an opportunity for the accredited agents of the Bakweri people, the BLCC, to be heard.

BLCC pointed out that respondent State's "No-Talk" policy was in stark contrast to the solicitous attitude shown the Bakweri by the British colonial authorities when the decision to create the CDC was taken in 1946. Recognizing that this decision was directly related to the petition of the Bakweri Lands Committee to the Trusteeship Council in 1946, the British Government made sure that the Bakweri were fully consulted and gave their consent before the proposal to create the CDC was put into effect.[89] Respondent State, according to BLCC, refused to do for its *own citizens* that which the colonial administration was only too eager to do for them when they were a *subject* people, i.e., consult and seek their approval on how best to develop *their* lands. Rather, Cameroon chose to ignore the pleas and representations from the Bakweri or treated them with indifference.

originally occupied by the Bakweri at 634 square miles).

87 *Id.*

88 *Id.* art. 7(1)(a).

89 This entry in U.N. Trusteeship Council Document No. 1/182 attests to this point: "*The proposal to acquire the ex-enemy owned plantations by the Nigerian government from the Custodian of Enemy Property at a cost which will be in the neighbourhood of £850,000 [Eight Hundred and Fifty Thousand pounds sterling] and their declaration to be Native Lands was welcomed by the Bakweris.*"

C. Cameroon's Response to the Bakweri Claims

In its submission of January 31, 2003, Cameroon raised seven preliminary objections relating to admissibility, six of which were later dismissed by the Commission. Respondent State's first objection was to challenge BLCC's *locus standi* to bring a claim against the State of Cameroon. It argued that the author of the communication, i.e., Counsel for BLCC, failed to offer proof that he is the victim of a violation of the Banjul Charter or that the victims on whose behalf the communication had been submitted were unable to speak for themselves. Finally, Cameroon objected on *locus standi* grounds that since the author was not himself a victim of the alleged harm complained of and since the violations were neither serious nor excessive, the author should have but failed to marshal evidence of the alleged violations. This is what Cameroon had to say on this point:

> [T]he author mentions 'the probable transfer of Bakweri private lands to a third party,' and the fact that 'the privatization of the CDC without prior resolution of the crucial land problem constitutes a serious threat to the rights of the Bakweri people...'; in other words, the damage that will make the group on whose behalf the author is speaking a victim is merely probable and not real. The Commission cannot entertain virtual or potential violations of the Charter but only violations that have actually occurred.[90]

As its second objection, Cameroon asserted that the object of the communication was vaguer as it interchangeably spoke of the violation of the "right to own land in Cameroon," "the dispossession of indigenous peoples of lands that they have historically owned and occupied," and "the violation of the right of an indigenous ethnic minority in Cameroon to own land." Cameroon's third preliminary objection was simply another version of the second, that the communication was improper as the author deliberately remained imprecise about the actual illicit act for which the State of Cameroon is blamed whether it is privatization or sale.

Cameroon's fourth preliminary objection attacked the form of the complaint for containing language respondent State found objectionable. Respondent State took offense with references in the communication to the country's judicial system, references which in respondent State's view cast suspicions and aspersions on the judiciary. Respondent State was equally offended with the description of Cameroon's Prime Minister and the Assistant Secretary General at the Presidency as unelected and appointed officials who constitutionally owe their respective offices to the President of the Republic and who therefore serve at his pleasure. Cameroon found these statements to have "strip[ped] them of any legitimacy to represent the Bakweri...." warranting the application of the rarely used[91] Article 56(3) of

90 *See* Respondent's Reply Memorial on Admissibility, ¶1 (copy on file).

91 *See Ligue Camerounaise des Droits de l'Homme vs. Cameroon,* African Comm. Hum. & Peoples' Rights, Comm. No. 65/92 (not dated) which is perhaps the only communication the Commission has declared inadmissible for offending the letter and spirit of Article 56, paragraph 3 of the Banjul Charter which provides, in pertinent part, that communications relating to human and peoples' rights filed with the Commission will not be considered if "written in disparaging or insulting language directed against the State concerned and

the Banjul Charter to declare the communication inadmissible. On the mistaken reliance on *Mpaka-Nsusu Andre Alphonse vs. Zaire92,* Cameroon advanced as its fifth objection that the matter was *res judicata* and could not be entertained by the Commission since a sister international tribunal (the U.N. Sub-Commission) had already heard the matter on its merits.

Cameroon's most substantial preliminary objection was the failure of complainant to exhaust local remedies since all the actions taken by BLCC did not correspond to the remedies mentioned in the Banjul Charter. More importantly, complainant had not even bothered to seise the local courts. BLCC, respondent State insisted "must give the Cameroonian courts the opportunity to examine the BAKWERI (sic) case instead of hiding behind the total suspicion cast on the entire judicial system in order to evade it and transform the Banjul Commission into a court of first instance."[93] Cameroon objected to the admissibility of the communication on the ground that there is no provision under Cameroonian law that excludes any form of appeal against acts of the executive branch.[94] Relying on the *Velasquez Rodriguez* case,[95] Cameroon argued that "it must not hastily be concluded that a State Party to the convention has neglected to act in compliance with its obligation to provide effective local remedies."[96] Accordingly, BLCC, Cameroon reasoned, should not be allowed to transform the Commission into a court of first instance as this would be tantamount to rewarding complainant for its failure to respect the rule of exhaustion of local remedies; a rule which "implies legal action brought before the courts and not just political actions."[97] Admitting the BLCC complaint would, in respondent State's view, amount to affording complainant uncalled-for favoritism since it had made no effort between the time the privatization decree was announced and the commencement of this action to take any action against the State of Cameroon before local courts. Domestic courts "cannot be avoided on the basis of subjective suspicions or because of allegations that it is a politically charged case or a politically sensitive case," Cameroon insisted.[98]

D. The Commission's Decision on Admissibility

In its decision on admissibility taken at its 36th Ordinary Session in November-December 2004, the Commission rejected all but one of Respondent State's preliminary objections. It however upheld the Cameroon's objection concerning BLCC's failure to exhaust all available domestic remedies before seising the Commission. In rejecting Respondent State's

its institutions…." In declaring *Ligue Camerounaise* inadmissible, the Commission focused on four statements it found to offend paragraph 3 of Article 56. These were: "Paul Biya must respond to crimes against humanity;" "30 years of the criminal neo-colonial regime incarnated by the duo Ahidjo/Biya;" "regime of torturers;" and "government barbarisms."

92 *See Mpaka-Nsusu Andre Alphonse Vs. Zaire,* Comm. 15/88 (not dated), African Comm. Hum. & Peoples' Rights.

93 *See* Respondent's Rejoinder Memorial of 5th May 2003, at 3 (copy on file).

94 *Id.* at 2.

95 *Velasquez Rodriguez, supra* note 83.

96 *See* Reply Memorial, *supra* note 90.

97 *Id.*

98 *Id.*

locus standi objection that BLCC does not have standing to bring the matter before the Commission, it was noted that the complainants (including the counsel representing them) are all Bakweri and hence victims of the violation. Furthermore, BLCC was the accredited representative of the Bakweri with authority to speak for them as backed by a resolution adopted by the custodians of the Bakweri lands, i.e., the traditional rulers and notables.[99]

These factual considerations aside, the Commission went further to reject Respondent State's restrictive interpretation of the *locus standi* requirement noting that it was never meant "to imply that only victims may seize the African Commission. In fact, all that Article 56 (1) demands is a disclosure of the identity of the author of the communication, irrespective of him/her being the actual victim of the alleged violation." The *locus standi* requirement, the Commission took pains to point out,

> [I]s conveniently broad to allow submissions not only from aggrieved individuals but also from other individuals or organisations (like NGOs) that can author such complaints and seize the Commission of a human rights violation. The existence of direct interest (like being a victim) to bring the matter before the Commission is not a requirement under the African Charter. The clear rationale here for allowing a broad gateway for complaints under the Charter is the practical understanding, in Africa, that victims may face various difficulties impairing them from approaching the African Commission.[100]

All these factors, the Commission noted, were present in the case at bar:

> [T]he complainants are themselves Bakweri, who allege violation of their ownership of historical lands, and their counsel himself and the BLCC have been duly authorized, by a resolution of chiefs, to further the interests of the Bakweri, which fact has not been denied by the Respondent State.[101]

Without straying from the drafters intent behind Article 56(1) of the Banjul Charter, the Commission drove home the point that any complainant before the Commission "may be represented, through express consent or by the self-initiative of the author who speaks for him/her, irrespective of the fact that it is known to the Commission that one is soundly capable of representing oneself."[102] While BLCC had *locus standi* and is entitled to bring this communication before the Commission because of a direct interest in the matter, that need not always be case.

Having disposed of the *locus standi* problem, the Commission next turned its attention to respondent State's objection that BLCC failed to present a *prima facie* case because the "communication is unclear, interchangeably spoke of various matters, and is improper as it

99 *See* Commission Decision, *supra* note 58, ¶46.
100 *Id.*
101 *Id.*
102 *Id.*

remained deliberately imprecise about the illicit acts."[103] Having meticulously examined the original complaint and its supporting documents, the Commission observed that "contrary to the Respondent State's objections, it is evident in the file that the Complainant is indeed clearly alleging the alienation of the Bakweri Lands, which was triggered by the Presidential Decree No. 94/125 of 14th July 1994 where the Government of Cameroon listed the Cameroon Development Corporation (CDC) which is situate on Bakweri lands."[104] The Commission then concluded that BLCC's allegations were sufficiently clear to be taken up by the Commission.

The Commission summarily rejected respondent State's objection that the BLCC complaint describes Cameroon's judicial system in language that could be considered insulting within the meaning of Article 56(3) of the Banjul Charter. The Commission, however, found nothing in the various submissions of the complainant to warrant the invocation of Article 56(3) of the Charter to justify declaring the complaint inadmissible on the grounds that it was written in disparaging or insulting language.

> The Complainant can allege, among others, and as it did with a view to be exempted from exhausting local remedies, that the president of the Republic wielded extraordinary powers so as to influence the judiciary and that the judiciary is impartial and lacked independence. This would be nothing but a mere allegation depicting, as it perceives it, the complainants comprehension of the offices that it thought would not provide it with any remedies as the African Commission would demand. Whether the allegations are true is another matter. At best, the Respondent State may, if it so wishes, employ other means to acquaint the African Commission that the situation is indeed otherwise. The African Commission notes, however, that such a rebuttal is not necessary for purposes of examination under Article 56 (3).[105]

To Cameroon's objection that the U.N. Sub-Commission had settled the matter and the Commission should not therefore barred under Article 56(7) of the Banjul Charter to re-litigate it, the Commission disagreed with both Cameroon's assessment of the facts as well as its interpretation of the Commission's jurisprudence on this issue.[106] In rejecting this objection, the Commission agreed with complainant's submission that the U.N. Sub-Commission did not decide on the merits of the case so as to warrant the discontinuance of the consideration of this matter by the Commission as Article 56 (7) commands.[107] The Commission went on to shed light on the principle behind the requirement under this provision of the Charter and to educate future litigants as to the meaning of two principles embraced in Article 57(7), i.e., *non bis in idem* and *res judicata*. The goal of Article 57(7),

103 *See* Reply Memorial, *supra* note 90.
104 *See* Commission Decision, *supra* note 58, ¶47.
105 *Id.* ¶48.
106 *Id.* 49-53.
107 *Id.* ¶52.

the Commission noted, "is to desist from faulting Member States twice for the same alleged violations of human rights."[108] The *non bis in idem* rule or the Principle or Prohibition of Double Jeopardy, deriving from criminal law:

> [E]nsures that, in this context, no state may be sued or condemned for the same alleged violation of human rights. In effect, this principle is tied up with the recognition of the fundamental *res judicata* status of judgements issued by international and regional tribunals and/or institutions such as the African Commission.
>
> The parties before the African Commission have not disputed the fact that they were the very same parties at loggerheads before the UN Sub-Commission disputing the same issues as before the African Commission. They both, however, admit that there has been no final judgment on the merits of their dispute by the UN Sub-Commission. The contents of the excerpts of the letter reproduced in paragraph 47 above have not been contested either, thereby buttressing the fact that the matter was not conclusively dealt with by the UN Sub-Commission. This means that the provision of Article 56(7) incorporating the principle of *ne bis in idem* does not apply in the present case as there has been no final settlement of the matter by the UN Sub-Commission.[109]

It is against this backdrop that the Commission ruled that Cameroon's request to have the BLCC communication declared inadmissible under the provisions of Article 56(7) was untenable.

The Commission, however, agreed with the arguments put forward by respondent State on the issue of the nonobservance of local remedies. The Commission took note of the fact that the exhaustion of local remedies requirement under Article 56 (5) of the Banjul Charter should be interpreted liberally so as not to close the door on those who have made at least a modest attempt to exhaust local remedies.[110] That said, it then took on BLCC for not even attempting to submit the matter before respondent State's courts: "as can be seen from the set of facts adduced before the African Commission by both parties in writing and orally, the complainant, not even once, has seized any local or national court. For this, it explained that the courts are not independent and are likely to decide in favour of the Respondent State whose President has a say on their appointment."[111] The fact that a complainant "strongly feels that it could not obtain justice from the local courts does not amount to saying that the case has been tried"[112] in those courts, the Commission held. Such assertions are no more than subjective assessments which cannot form the

108 *Id.*
109 *Id.* ¶¶52-53.
110 *Id.* ¶55.
111 *Id.*
112 *Id.*

basis of a finding by the Commission that there are no effective domestic remedies which complainant can take advantage of to resolve the dispute.[113] The exhaustion rule imposes on the complainant an affirmative duty "to take all necessary steps to exhaust, or at least attempt the exhaustion of local remedies"[114] and her doubts about the effectiveness of those remedies are not enough to absolve the complainant from this duty.

The Commission warned that a dangerous precedent would be set if a complainant appearing before it is allowed to end run the exhaustion rule solely on the basis of its subjective assessment of "the perceived lack of independence of a country's judicial system."[115] This would have the effect of forcing the Commission to take over the role of the domestic courts and transforming itself into a court of first instance, a "court of convenience when in fact local remedies remain to be approached." In taking this position the Commission appeared to have strayed somewhat from its own jurisprudence which frowns on a rigid mechanistic application of the rule.[116] The Commission did not, however, break any new ground and would appear to have shied away from taking on the role of a court of first instance that many scholars and observers of the human rights situation in Africa have hoped it would do.[117]

PART III. REVISITING THE EXHAUSTION OF DOMESTIC REMEDIES DOCTRINE

It is well-established in international law that before resort to an international tribunal to redress a grievance against a state for injury on its national that person must first exhaust all available domestic remedies, unless, of course, such remedies are clearly inadequate

113 Clearly complainant's subjective judgments could have been subjected to an empirical investigation which is provided for in Article 58 of the Banjul Charters. The Commission was naturally reluctant to embark on this exercise which would have entailed a thorough investigation of the Cameroonian judicial system since it did not judge the allegations of judicial incompetence as violations as requiring an in-depth study. *But see e.g., Finnish Ships* arbitration where the arbitrator, Judge Bagge of Sweden, undertook a thorough survey of British sources of authority before applying a strict test of the local remedies rule. British legislation provided that certain claims for compensation should be referred to an Admiralty Transport Arbitration Board whose decision could be appealed on questions of law to the ordinary courts. Finnish shipowners, confronted with an adverse Board decision, took no appeal to the courts but requested their government to espouse their claim and proceed against the British government on the ground that Britain had incurred responsibility in international law by requisitioning the ships without subsequently paying compensation. At issue was whether the shipowners' failure to appeal the points of law amounted to a nonobservance of the local remedies rule. *Finnish Ships Case (Finland v. United Kingdom),* 1934, 3 R. Int'l Arb. Awards 1484, 1498-1505.

114 *Id.*

115 *Id.* ¶56.

116 In its jurisprudence, the Commission has always cautioned against a mechanical application of the domestic remedies rule particularly in "cases where it is impractical or undesirable for the complainant to seize the domestic courts in the case of each violation." *See e.g., Free Legal Assistance Group et al. vs. Zaire,* African Comm. Hum. & Peoples' Rights, Comm. No. 25/89, 49/90, 56/91, 100/93 (not dated), ¶3; *but see International Pen vs. Sudan,* African Comm. Hum. & Peoples' Rights, Comm. No. 92/93; *Kenya Human Rights Commission vs. Kenya,* African Comm. Hum. & Peoples' Rights, Comm. No. 135/94; *Alfred B. Cudjoe vs. Ghana,* African Comm. Hum. & Peoples' Rights, Comm. No. 221/98. *See also* UN Human Rights Committee Communication No. 192/85, *S.H.B. vs. Canada.*

117 *See e.g.,* Nsongurua J. Udombana, *So Far, So Fair: The Local Remedies Rule in the Jurisprudence of the African Commission on Human and Peoples' Rights,* 97 A.J.I.L. 1, 16 (2003).

or their application is unreasonably prolonged.[118] Support for this rule was provided by the Permanent Court of International Justice in the *Interhandel Case (Switzerland vs. United States)* where the Court noted that the "rule that local remedies must be exhausted before international proceedings may be instituted is a well-established rule of customary international law."[119] Both the Banjul Charter and the jurisprudence of the African Commission also recognize this rule. Article 56 (5) of the Banjul Charter requires the pursuit and exhaustion of domestic remedies before Commission proceedings may be instituted. The Commission has also articulated three pragmatic reasons why the requirement to exhaust domestic remedies is a necessary first step before international proceedings are engaged.[120] The first of these is the need to "give domestic courts an opportunity to decide upon cases before they are brought to an international forum, thus avoiding contradictory judgments of law at the national and international level."[121] Secondly, that a government against whom a complaint has been brought "should have notice of a human rights violation in order to have an opportunity to remedy such violation, before being called to account by an international tribunal.... The exhaustion of domestic remedies requirement should be properly understood as ensuring that the State concerned has ample opportunity to remedy the situation of which applicants complain."[122] Finally, the requirement of prior exhaustion of domestic remedies before seising the Commission is intended to ensure that the Commission does not become a "tribunal of first instance for cases which an effective domestic remedy exists."[123]

For a point which was an essential element in BLCC's case for the admissibility of the complaint before the Commission, it is important to enquire why[124] complainant did not even "attempt the exhaustion of local remedies"[125] before seising the Commission. BLCC instead tried to discharge this burden by claiming to fall within one or more of the admitted

118 *See generally* Restatement (Third) of the Foreign Relations Law of the United States §713, Comment and Reporters' Notes (1987).

119 *See The Interhandel Case (Switzerland vs. United States)*, [1959] I.C.J. Rep. 6, 26-27. For a recent discussion by the World Court of the local remedies rule, *see Case Concerning Elettronica Sicula, S.p.A (ELSI) (United States v. Italy)*, 1989 I.C.J. 15, 28 I.L.M. 1111.

120 See *The Social and Economic Rights Action Center for Economic and Social Rights v. Nigeria*, African Comm. Hum. & Peoples' Rights, Comm. No. 155/96, ¶¶37-39.

121 *Id.*

122 *Id.*

123 *Id.*

124 This enquiry is warranted even though the Commission did not find any of the reasons advanced by complainants sufficiently convincing to declare the communication admissible.

125 Based on discussions the author had with BLCC's Secretary General at the early stages of this litigation, it would appear that there was some concern within the leadership of BLCC on the effect of a negative judgment on the morale of the Bakweri people and whether such a decision would not weaken their resolve to continue with the land reclamation fight. The announcement of the privatization of the CDC had galvanized the Bakweri and re-energized BLCC as never before and the group's leadership did not want to lose this momentum. They were of the view that submitting to the local courts was far too risky convinced that the courts were already biased against their cause. The Government was also doing everything possible to buy-off Bakweri Traditional Rulers, almost all of whom but for a few dissidents like Chief Moka Endeley of Buea, were members of the BLCC Board of Trustees. A spilt in their ranks, it was felt would send a bad signal to the rank-and-file and put paid to the Bakweri struggle. *See "Editorial: Biya Appeases Bakweri Chiefs,"* The Herald of January 22, 2003.

exceptions to the exhaustion rule. BLCC justification for the nonobservance of the exhaustion rule hinged on this threshold question: where it is clear that the local courts are totally subservient to the executive who has taken the decision being challenged, is complainant required to exhaust domestic remedies? In response, BLCC offered three reasons why under these circumstances it should be excused from complying with the requirements of this rule. First, that the Cameroonian courts are notoriously lacking in independence as there is no real separation between the executive and judicial branches of government. The second reason was the inadequacy of the system of judicial protection given that the courts are over-burdened and corrupt. And the third, complainant's expressed fears that justice would not be done in this case because of judicial bias.

Article 15 of the International Law Commission's Draft Articles on Diplomatic Protection[126] which deals with the exceptions to the local remedies rule identifies five different circumstances in which local courts offer no prospect of redress. Only one of which, Article 15(a), concerns us here. Article 15(a) provides that "local remedies do not need to be exhausted where (a) there are no reasonably available local remedies to provide effective redress, or the local remedies provide no reasonable possibility of such remedies."[127] In the Commentary to this article, the draftsman offers the following *inter alia* as instances when the requirement of exhaustion of local remedies may be dispensed with: (a) local courts are notoriously lacking in independence; (b) there is consistent and well-established line of precedents adverse to the claimant; and (c) the respondent State does not have an adequate system of judicial protection.[128]

1. The Subordination of the Judiciary to the will of the Executive

Support can be found in judicial decisions for the view that where the local courts have proved to be notoriously lacking in independence, a complainant can be excused from seeking redress in that court system.[129] This is one of the grounds BLCC invoked for justifying the non-exhaustion of local remedies. BLCC explained that the legal and political context in which justice is administered in Cameroon allows the President to wield extraordinary powers at the expense of the judiciary. This subordination of the judicial branch to the will of the presidency goes back to the origins of the origin of the republic. In stitching together the basic law of the land, the constitutional draftsman set out to create an "*imperial presidency*"[130] by making this institution the font of a vast array of judicial and non-judicial powers. As a result of this deliberate constitutional engineering appointment to and removal from high office under this scheme is by Presidential decree. The President

126 *See* I.L.C., DRAFT ARTICLES ON DIPLOMATIC PROTECTION, REPORT OF THE I.L.C., 55th Sess. (2003), G.A.O.R., 58th Sess., Supp. 10 (A/58/10), p.76.

127 *Id.*

128 *Id.* at 79.

129 *See Robert E. Brown Claim* 2 I.L.R. 66; 6 R. Int'l Arb.Awards 120 (1923) (The country's President threatens to suspend Chief Justice from office in the event of his failure to uphold the right of the executive and legislative branches of government to override the Constitution); *Velasquez Rodriguez Case, supra* note 83, at 304-309.

130 *See e.g.*, Mbu Etonga, *An Imperial Presidency: A Study of Presidential Power in Cameroon*, in AN AFRICAN EXPERIMENT IN NATION BUILDING: THE BILINGUAL CAMEROON REPUBLIC SINCE REUNIFICATION 133-158 (Ndiva Kofele-Kale, ed., 1980).

appoints the Prime Minister and other members of Government (Article 10).[131] However, none of these executive officers exercise any independent authority since their authority is merely delegated. The prime minister who is the head of government has been described by one publicist as someone who functions only as a "subordinate to assist the President in the exercise of *his* executive power. He is not a co-beneficiary with the President and his appointment in charge of any departments does not imply an abdication by the President of his power over those departments."[132] In this system of a single unified Executive, arguably, the last word on domestic remedies whether of an administrative or legal nature in the Cameroonian context is the President of the Republic.[133] Presidential decisions carry a kind of *res judicata* effect on other state institutions and organs.[134]

Building on this first argument, BLCC submitted that the lack of an independent or impartial judiciary severely compromises the competence of any domestic court in handling the case at bar. Pointing out that the one striking feature about Cameroon's judiciary is its total lack of independence since it is under the firm control of the President of the

131 Article 10, paragraph 1 provides: "The President of the Republic shall appoint the Prime Minister and, on the proposal of the latter, the other members of Government. He shall define their duties. He shall terminate their appointment. He shall preside over the Council of Ministers." Article 27 delegates to the President the power to legislate texts outside a range of subjects that fall within the legislature's competence. Outside this range of activities, the President virtually has *carte blanche* to enact legislation on just about anything. Interestingly, this delegation of legislative competence to the Executive is unaccompanied by any built-in safeguards to check against presidential excesses. *See* Law No. 06 of 18 January 1996 to amend the Constitution of 2 June, 1972 ["1996 Constitution"]; *See also* Ndiva Kofele-Kale, LEGISLATIVE POWER IN CAMEROON'S SECOND REPUBLIC: ITS NATURE AND LIMITS 65-66 (1999).

132 *See* Imperial Presidency, *supra* note 130, at 136. [Emphasis in original]

133 Although the Constitution provides for a separation of powers among the three branches of government, in reality the Executive overshadows the other two branches. This is how the U.S. State Department describes Executive power in Cameroon: "The 1972 constitution as modified by 1996 reforms provides for a strong central government dominated by the executive. The president, without consulting the National Assembly, names and dismisses cabinet members, judges, generals, provincial governors, prefects, subprefects, and heads of Cameroon's parastatal (about 100 state-controlled) firms; obligates or disburses expenditures; approves or vetoes regulations to implement newly enacted laws; declares states of emergency; and appropriates and spends profits of parastatal firms. The president is not required to consult the National Assembly. *The judiciary is subordinate to the executive branch's Ministry of Justice*. The Supreme Court may review the constitutionality of a law only at the president's request." Available at https://1997-2001.state.gov/background_notes/cameroon_9912_bgn.html [Emphasis added].

134 It is at this level that some nine years ago the Bakweri victims of uncompensated land expropriation lodged their petition for presidential relief.

Republic.[135] Judicial officers owe their appointments to the President (Article 37(3))[136] and serve at his pleasure. This power of appointment and removal is like a sword of Damocles dangling over the heads of judges, ready to descend the moment one of them steps out of line. In theory though, the President is assisted by a Higher Judicial Council in the appointment of members of the bench and officials of the legal department. It is this body, sitting-in-council, that decides the fate of all judicial officers from judges, magistrates, procureurs of the republic down to senior court registrars. However, this organ which is responsible for all appointments, promotions and dismissals in the judiciary is completely under the control of the President who appoints the majority of its members and presides over all its meetings.

The supremacy of the Presidency and its dominance of the judiciary, BLCC argued, has given rise to a peculiar form of *de facto* Executive 'preemption' of decision-making by subordinate state organs, regardless of whether there is an actual conflict between them or not.[137] Presidential 'preemption' of decision-making at all levels and in all areas, judicial as well as non-judicial, operates in much the same way as an ouster clause which bars "the ordinary courts from taking up cases placed before the special tribunals or entertaining any appeals from the decisions of the special tribunals."[138] After examining the legal effect of "ouster" decrees in that *Ken Saro-Wiwa et al.*, the Commission concluded that they tend to "render local remedies non-existent, ineffective or illusory" because they create a "legal situation in which the judiciary can provide no check on the executive branch of

135 The Human Rights Committee was among the first international human rights tribunals to observe that Cameroon's judicial fails to meet internationally-accepted norms of independence. After reviewing Cameroon's 1994 periodic on the state of human rights in the country, the Human Rights Committee ("HRC") questioned "*the independence of the judiciary; in particular, the composition of the Supreme Council of Justice does not seem such as to guarantee respect for this principle*." Note that the members of this council are appointed by the President who presides over its deliberations! The HRC then recommended that "*measures should be taken, if necessary in the form of a constitutional reform, to guarantee the independence and impartiality of the judiciary, in accordance with article 14, paragraph 1, of the Covenant*." *See* Concluding Observations of the Human Rights Committee, Cameroon: 18/04/94, ¶¶14 and 24 (Emphasis added). Five years later, when considering Cameroon's third periodic report, the HRC again observed that Respondent still had not addressed all the concerns it expressed in its previous concluding observations on the second report of 1994. *See* Concluding Observations of the Human Rights Committee, Cameroon: 04/11/99, ¶2 [Emphasis added]; *see also* discussion in note 22 *supra*.

136 "The President of the Republic shall guarantee the independence of judicial power. He shall appoint members of the bench and of the legal department. He shall be assisted in this task by the Higher Judicial Council which shall give him its opinion on all nominations for the bench and on disciplinary action against judicial and legal officers...." *See* Law No. 65 of 96-06 of 18 January 1996 *to amend* the Constitution of 2 June 1972, Article 37(3).

137 This *de facto* preemptive authority is peculiar for two reasons. First, because it is *implied* since the Constitution is noticeably silent on the exercise of such authority. Second, because the underlying constitutional objective of the preemption doctrine is to avoid conflicting regulation of conduct by various official bodies that might have some authority over the same subject matter. In the Cameroon scheme, however, presidential 'occupation' of the judiciary and the legislature has nothing to do with jurisdictional conflicts. Rather, it reflects the wide range of powers – legislative as well as judicial – that the Constitution confers on the President.

138 *See International Pen, Constitutional Rights Project Interights on behalf of Ken Saro-Wiwa Jr. and Civil Liberties Organization vs. Nigeria*, African Comm. Hum. & Peoples' Rights, Comm. No. 137/94, 139/94, 154/96 and 161/97 (not dated).

government."[139] The involvement of Executive branch officials in the Bakweri land matter is not entirely dissimilar to that described in *Ken Saro-Wiwa* but in the former, as a result of *de facto* presidential override of the functions of the courts, the judiciary has been reduced to impotence, incapable of playing its traditional role of providing a check on the executive branch. In practice, a presidential preemption ousts the jurisdiction of the ordinary courts thus depriving complainants of effective domestic relief. It should be noted that complainants were seeking a declaration from the Government of Cameroon that lands registered in the Imperial German land registers (*Grundbuch),* occupied by CDC since 1947, and defined as Private Property under Cameroon's 1974 Land Law belong to the Bakweri. However, such an acknowledgment that would bind respondent State could only come from the authority that issued the 1994 CDC Privatization Decree in the first place or given on its instructions. That authority being none other than the President and Head of State. Although the President chose not to make such a declaration between 1994 and the filing of the complaint before the Commission, he could have, in theory, be compelled by court order to do so. But such an order, BLCC submitted, was not likely to come from a court system that is under the President's total control and whose judges are personally appointed, promoted or removed, by him.

2. The Inadequacy and Unpredictability of Judicial Protection

Local remedies need not be exhausted where the respondent State does not have an adequate system of judicial protection. BLCC argued that there is in Cameroon an implied power of discretion built into the judicial system. As a consequence, justice is exercised in a discretionary manner through a process of *de facto* ousting of the jurisdiction of courts. This procedure manifests itself through legal decisions made by ministers and law officials completely by-passing the courts.[140] In theory as in practice, the President is the Supreme Magistrate with the power to delegate some of his executive and, by extension, his judicial powers to subordinate officials who act in his name.[141] Where justice has been found to

139 *Id.*

140 Hardly a week goes by that the popular press fails to report on this "annoying interference." In an article entitled *Criminal Law: A conflict of systems*, Asong Ndifor, senior editor of *The Herald*, offers these examples: "During the trial of SCNC activists in Bamenda in 2001 the legal department wrote to magistrate Abenego Bea instructing him on how to handle the case. He repudiated the instruction and passed his judgement according to the evidence he had. He was later given a punitive transfer to the legal department in Buea. There is also the recent case where a Buea high court ruled that John Niba Ngu should be reinstated as general manager of the Cameroon Tea Estate but the South West legal department rejected the ruling and refused to order execution of the judgement." *See The Herald*, Monday 16-17 June 2003, page 8. In the Monday, August 11, 2003 edition of *The Post* newspaper, the Minister of Justice and Keeper of the Seals is reported to have "ordered that all pending matters concerning Beneficial Life Insurance Company be withdrawn from court. This order is contained in a submission filed by the Southwest Attorney General.... The Attorney-General stated in his submission that 'we have instructions from the Hon. Minister of State in Charge of Justice and Keeper of the Seals, that all pending matters in court, whether criminal or civil, touching and concerning the parties in this case be withdrawn from court.'" *See Minister Orders Withdrawal of All Beneficial Life Cases, The Post* No. 0495 of Monday, August 11, 2003, page 2.

141 Article 10(2) of the 1996 Constitution provides: "The President of the Republic may delegate some of his powers to the Prime Minister, other members of Government and any senior administrative officials of the State, within the framework of their respective duties." *See* Law No. 65 of 96-06 of 18 January 1996 *to amend*

be discretionary, the African Commission has not hesitated to declare the Communication admissible in order to give Complainant a forum denied them in the home state to be heard.[142] The issue in *Constitutional Rights Project* was a provision in the Robbery and Firearms (Special Provisions) Act which conferred on the State Governor the power to confirm or disallow a conviction for violations of this law by a Special Tribunal. The Commission described the Governor's power as "discretionary extraordinary remedy of a nonjudicial nature" and ruled that "it would be improper to insist on the complainants seeking remedies from sources which do not operate impartially and have no obligation to decide according to legal principles."[143] As a consequence, any remedy provided through this source would be neither adequate nor effective.

It is well-documented that the domestic courts are overburdened with a backlog of cases that will take years to clear. For instance, a 1996 World Bank Report put the number of cases pending before the Supreme Court at 3,000 in 1996[144] [*unofficially* the number is 4,343 as of June 2003]. Incidentally, it is the same year that a representative of Cameroon appeared before the African Commission, at its 20th session in October 1996, urging the Commission to overturn its decision on admissibility in the case of *Annette Pagnoulle (on behalf of Abdoulaye Mazou) v Cameroon*[145] on the ground that Mazou had not exhausted his domestic remedies! The Mazou case had been pending in Cameroon's Supreme Court for four years when this incredulous appeal was made in 1996.[146]

Aside from *Annette Pagnoulle* which the Commission declared admissible, after having concluded that Mazou's remedy was unreasonably prolonged, BLCC also referred the Commission to a case currently before it, *Victims of Post-Electoral Violence in the North West Province v Cameroon.*[147] This case had languished in the Supreme Court for five years

---

the Constitution of 2 June 1972, Article 10(2). For instance, sometime in February 2002 the Minister of External Relations represented before another international body that Government was favorably disposed towards a friendly settlement of this matter. This undertaking was clearly meant to signal Government's preference for a non-judicial resolution. Complainants in good faith relied on this stated preference for a resolution through dialogue to their own detriment. The Minister of External Relations Foreign Minister, an official with no independent authority and whose authority is merely delegated, could not have taken such a binding obligation without explicit directives from the presidency. However, the effect of this executive branch official's decision was to preempt other organs of government, including the courts, from looking into the Bakweri land question.

142 *See Constitutional Rights Project vs. Nigeria,* African Comm. Hum. & Peoples' Rights, Comm. No.60/91 (not dated).

143 *Id.*

144 *See* WORLD BANK REPORT NO. T-6928-CM TECHNICAL ANNEX TO THE MEMOMORANDUM AND RECOMMENDATION, MAY 22, 1996, ¶ 25, p. 6. (The Bank commented on the slowness of the judicial process and observed that in 1996 3000 cases were pending at the Supreme Court.). The Bank, it will be recalled, is the main underwriter of Respondent's privatization program which directly affects the disputed Bakweri lands.

145 *See* Annette Pagnoulle (on behalf of Abdoulaye Mazou) v Cameroon. Comm. 39/90, African Comm. Hum. Peoples' Rights.

146 Yet in entering this plea, Cameroon's agent, who was the one possessing superior knowledge about the court's case load, should have known about its huge backlog; and, as an officer of the court, was duty bound to disclose to the Commission how overburdened the Cameroon courts were at that time.

147 *See Victims of Post-Electoral Violence in the North West Province v Cameroon*, Comm. No. 272/2003, African Comm. Hum. & Peoples' Rights.

with no relief in sight before the complainants decided to seise the African Human Rights Commission. [148]

Corruption also contributes to the inadequacy and unpredictability of judicial protection offered by the local courts.[149] Cameroonian courts have been routinely dismissed by expert observers as well as the general public[150] as corrupt where justice is for sale usually to the highest bidder and to barons of the regime. These observations have been made by the highest ranking state official responsible for the judicial, none other than Minister of Justice and Keeper of the Seals.[151] Even the President of the Republic has weighed in in this debate in his 1999 New Year's Address to the Nation. After lamenting the scourge of corruption which has now spread to all sectors of Cameroonian society, the President next turned his attention to "judicial and legal officers whose task is precisely to ensure respect for the rules governing our society." As regards this branch of government, the President observed that "*[t]here are still many cases where justice is not rendered as it should. That is to say with dispatch and impartiality, in strict conformity with the laws and procedures in force. This should not be tolerated.* Even though I would want to believe so, the majority of our judicial and legal officers are upright, the deviant practices observed may lay the institution open to suspicion...." (Emphasis added).

148 Then there was the case of *Mukong v Cameroon*, which was declared admissible by the HRC after the Cameroon Supreme Court failed to take any action for two years. *See* Communication No. 458/1991, U.N. Doc. CCPR/C/51/D/458/1991 (1994).

149 A 1996 World Bank Report called attention to problems with the administration of justice in Cameroon which it described as "manifold. ... Judgements are often rendered in contradiction to the law; parties adopt dilatory *measures*; delays in dealing with cases are long (e.g., there are 3,000 cases pending at the Supreme Court); the Office of the Clerk of the Court operates in a very rudimentary fashion and is the source of substantial delays; the bailiff system operates haphazardly and there is much interference with the work of bailiffs; registering a mortgage is a difficult proposition." *See* WORLD BANK, TECHNICAL ANNEX TO THE MEMORANDUM OF RECOMMENDATION (REPORT NO. P-6928-CM) ON A PROPOSED CREDIT IN THE AMOUNT EQUIVALENT TO SDR 8.8 MILLION TO THE REPUBLIC OF CAMEROON FOR A PRIVATE SECTOR TECHNICAL ASSISTANCE PROJECT, MAY 22, 1996, at p. 6, ¶25.

150 For instance, three out of ten Cameroonians polled by Gallup International for Transparency International's 2003 Global Corruption Barometer, singled out the judiciary as the institution from which they would like to eliminate corruption if they were given the opportunity. The July 2002 Gallup survey polled 30,487 people in 44 countries on the following question: "*If you had a magic wand and could eliminate corruption from one of the following institutions, what would your first choice be?*" The institutions enumerated including among others, the courts, the customs, educational system, medical services, police, etc. Thirty-one percent of the Cameroonian respondents picked out the courts as their first choice with the police coming in a distant second being singled out by only 13.7 per cent of the respondents. In only two other countries did the majority of the respondents single out the court system: Indonesia (32.8%) and Peru (35%). Available at https://www.transparency.org/en/gcb/global/global-corruption-barometer-2003

151 While admitting that the Cameroon judiciary is corrupt, Justice Minister Amadou Ali tries to place the blame elsewhere: "*la corruption existe parce qu'elle est entretenue par des corrupteurs, dont beaucoup se recrutent, malheureusement, dans le monde de l'entreprise (...) Parce qu'ils veulent a tout prix gagner leurs procès, des chefs d'entreprises approchent des magistrats et leur font des offres alléchantes, les amenant ainsi a rendre des décisions qui, si elles arrangent leurs commanditaires, donnent de la justice camerounaise, l'image d'une justice inapte à soutenir le dévéloppement de l'entreprise et insécurisante pour les investissements.*" *See* Le Messager, no. 1519/vendredi 06 juin 2003, page 5 [Emphasis added].

3. Presence of Bias

Faced with a consistent and well-established line of precedents adverse to a complainant, the requirement of exhaustion of local remedies may be dispensed with.[152] In the *Robert E. Brown* case, an international arbitral tribunal held that local remedies were ineffective because the domestic courts had been "reduced to submission and brought into line with a determined policy of the Executive to reach the desired result regardless of the constitutional guarantees and inhibitions."[153] At least one publicist has is of the view that the *Robert E. Brown* case "illustrates the well-established principle that where the executive branch dominates the courts, judicial remedies against executive action need not be pursued."[154]

In its written pleadings and oral submissions BLCC drew the Commission's attention to a pair of judicial decisions directly related to the Bakweri land claims that convinced complainant that it was not likely to receive fair treatment in the local courts. The first was a court judgment intended to resolve a management crisis which had embroiled one of the recently private CDC estates and which the provincial attorney general summarily overturned. The second was the local court's treatment of a nuisance lawsuit brought by an organization which had the backing of prominent Bakweri politicians and high ranking State officials that claimed to be the authentic representative of the Bakweri on the land question and not BLCC.

a. The Cameroon Teas Estate Management Crisis

Secret negotiations between the Cameroon Government and a phantom South African outfit, Brobon Finex Pty Ltd.[155] and its Cameroonian subsidiary, Cameroon Tea Estates (CTE), to dispose of the Tole tea estates which sit on 454 acres of prime Bakweri land months before the BLCC action was filed.[156] As a matter of fact the sale was consummated[157] the very month BLCC seised the African Commission. However, legal developments in the aftermath of this sale gave BLCC reason to believe that any action taken before a Cameroonian court would likely produce an unfavorable result. Briefly, Mr. John Niba Ngu, a former General Manager of CDC and former Minister of Agriculture and the man who had brokered the CTE deal with Government was appointed General Manager of the company

152 *See Panevyzys-Saldutiskis Railway Case, supra* note 26; *S.S. "Lisman,"* 3 R. Int'l Arb. Awards 1769, 1773; *S.S. "Seguranca"*, 3 R. Int'l Arb. Awards 1861,1868; *Finnish Ships Arbitration, supra* note 108, at p. 1495; *X. v. Federal Republic of Germany,* 1 Yearbook of the European Convention on Human Rights 138 (1956); *X. v. Federal Republic of Germany, X. v. Federal Republic of Germany,* 2 Yearbook of the European Convention on Human Rights 342, 344; *X. v. Austria,* 3 Yearbook of the European Convention on Human Rights 196, 202.

153 *See Robert E. Brown Case, supra* note 129, at 198.

154 *See* David R. Mummery, *The Content of the Duty to Exhaust Local Judicial Remedies*, 58 A.J.I.L. 389, 403 (1964).

155 An investigation ordered by the Secretary General of the Bakweri Land Claims Committee to establish the true identity of Brobon Finex failed to come up with any evidence that this company was registered in South Africa or anywhere else in the world. *See* Without a Trace: On the Trail of the Elusive Brobon Finex, A BLCC-USA Investigative Report (October 2003) (copy on file).

156 *See* Statement by the Bakweri Land Claims Committee (BLCC) following the announcement on the Privatization of the Tea Estates of the Cameroon Development Corporation, 5th June 2002 (copy on file).

157 The Brobon Finex/Cameroon convention was touted as the very model of privatization. It would later turn out to be nothing more than a sweetheart deal designed to enrich a few high-ranking, well-connected barons of the regime who conveniently chose to hide behind a South African corporate shield.

in October 2002. Barely three months later Ngu was relieved of his position by the board of directors of Brobon Finex, the majority shareholder of CTE, and replaced by his deputy. On January 8th 2003, John Ngu sought and obtained injunctive relief from the Fako High Court in the South West Province by way of an *ex parte* order[158] temporarily suspending his dismissal and reinstating him as the "*legally appointed General Manager*" of CTE. Two days later, the Procureur General of the South West Province ("SW Procureur General"), the judicial officer charged in the High Court Order to lend support to bailiffs and process servers executing the order, issued countermanding instructions *overturning* the ruling! Because this highly unorthodox conduct by a judicial officer failed to draw a rebuke from the Minister of Justice and Keeper of the Seal, BLCC concluded that there by the grace of God go the Bakweri land case.

The management feud in CTE was a simple commercial dispute, a purely civil matter pitting two private litigants that could have been, and was temporarily resolved by a properly constituted court pending a full hearing on the merits. Yet, the State found it necessary to step in to block its execution. The dismissed general manager was not asking anything extraordinary from the court, only that his business associates should be compelled to respect the internal law of their company: that as an appointee of the CTE Board of Directors, only that board and not the Board of Directors of Brobon Finex, even though it holds the majority shares in CTE, can lawfully dismiss him as the general manager.

What court observers had expected of the SW Procureur General, that as Government's lead lawyer, faced with an *interlocutory* ruling the execution of which, in his judgment, could have serious immediate and irreparable consequences on the public order, was to do one of three things. He could have asked the same trial court that issued the offending order to lift it. Or, to the extent he was convinced that there was trial court error with respect to the manner in which the *ex parte* order was made or that the order completely ignored a compelling public interest that had to be protected, then he had the option of appealing the ruling in the Court of Appeals. Given the *provisional* nature of the high court order, the SW Procureur General was still left with a third option– this, from a procedural standpoint, would have been his first option– which was to ask to be joined as a necessary party so that when the matter eventually came up for hearing on the merits he would then be able to argue the State's interest (after all, his client, the State, is a 35 percent shareholder of CTE). The SW Procureur General decided not to pursue any of these options. The option the provincial attorney chose was the one option that was *not* available to him, that of *disobeying* a High Court order regardless of how repugnant he may have found it to be! The SW Procureur General's attempt to subvert the judicial process was a wake-up call for BLCC that the local courts would not be able to protect their interests.

It is important and necessary to situate the SW Procureur General's action of overturning a court order in the CTE management crisis, to understand how Complainants'

158 Like all court rulings in Cameroon, the High Court order carried the following instructions to law enforcement officials: "WHEREFORE the President of the Republic of Cameroon commands and enjoins all Bailiffs and Process Servers to enforce this Ruling, *the Procureur General and the State Counsel to lend them support* and all Commanders and Officers of the Armed Forces and Police Forces to lend them assistance when so required by Law." [Emphasis added]

confidence in the domestic court was bad shaken. First, the feud within CTE management was directly related to the CDC privatization exercise. This exercise cannot be separated from the Bakweri land question because the two are linked symbiotically. First, BLCC had publicly registered its opposition to the CTE deal and called on the Cameroonian parties to renounce it and denounce their phantom South African partners. Second, the land in dispute is in Fako Division, in the jurisdiction of the SW Procureur General. Complainants' action for a declaratory judgment declaring the lands as private Bakweri property would have required the filing of a writ in the Fako High Court. This is the same court whose order temporarily staying the dismissal of the general manager of CTE was unilaterally set aside by the SW Procureur General. Finally, the SW Procureur, as Respondent's lawyer would have been expected to appear before this court to defend Respondent's interest in this matter. This would have set the stage for a lawsuit in which the highest ranking judicial officer in the province, standing in for the Minister of Justice and Keeper of the Seal, would have been the defendant, prosecutor and judge in its own cause. If the court ruled in a manner displeasing to the SW Procureur General, he would as he did in the CTE case, simply instruct law enforcement officers not to enforce the judgment.

b. The Bakweri Cooperative Union of Farmers Lawsuit

Sometime in September 2003, the Bakweri Cooperative Union of Farmers (BCUF), a real estate and housing association,[159] brought a law suit in the Fako High Court against *Mola* Njoh Litumbe, the Secretary General of BLCC. Simultaneously with the filing of this action, counsel for plaintiff submitted a written complaint to the provincial attorney general, claiming that he had received, in his words, "*firm instructions from the Presidency of the Republic*," to lodge a report, requesting that BLCC officials be investigated and charged with perjury, impersonation, among other thins, for carrying out activities in Cameroon without benefit of a certificate of registration.[160] Acting on this complaint, the provincial attorney general authorized the judicial police to commence a criminal investigation of BLCC officials, beginning with its Secretary General.[161]

In the September 2003 action, plaintiff was asking for a declaratory judgment to the effect that BCUF, and no other corporate group, was the only legitimate organization to hold brief for the indigenous Bakweri people on all matters pertaining to their ancestral

159 The "Bakweri Cooperative Union of Farmers, BCUF", it was later revealed is in fact an imposter organization that had misappropriated the name, identity and assets of the original BCUF. This information became public when the real BCUF, upon discovering that it was a plaintiff in a lawsuit that its board of directors had not authorized, petitioned the SW Procureur General to investigate the misappropriation and illegal use of its corporate identity by this group. The real BCUF, it is worth pointing out, is a union of twenty-six *cooperative societies* representing thousands of small-scale farmers in Fako Division, created fifty-three years ago. The imposter BCUF, on the other hand, is a real estate and housing association owned by thirty-one *individuals* and was registered barely two years ago to engage in speculative real estate ventures. When the attorney general for the South West province failed to take any action, the owners of the real BCUF then petitioned the Minister of State for Agriculture. Following a ministerial inquiry, the registration certificate of the imposter association was revoked and firm instructions were given to ensure that the order revoking its status receive the widest publicity possible.

160 *See* Letter to the Procureur General for the South West Province of 25th October 2003 (copy on file).

161 *Id.*

lands. Although BLCC was not named as a defendant in the suit, its Secretary General was. And although he was never served with notice of the pending action (he was out of the country when it was filed), the Fako High Court went ahead, in his absence, to hold an *ex parte* hearing on plaintiff's motion for a declaratory ruling. These procedural defects notwithstanding, the trial judge delivered a default judgment in which he declared BLCC– a party that was not before the court and that was not named as a defendant in the original complaint-- an illegal organization and then ordered it disbanded![162]

Less than two hours after the order "disbanding" BLCC was read in open court, counsel for plaintiff was observed distributing copies of the *unsigned* bench order to the press and the general public. It would take another week before the *signed* and *official* opinion was ready for release![163] The judgment raised many questions. First, how was it possible that BLCC, who was not named as a defendant in the action, would suddenly find itself disbanded by a local court, one month before its Counsel was due to appear before the African Human Rights Commission? Second, where and how did Counsel for plaintiff BCUF stumble on a copy of a high court judgment minutes after it was delivered? Who could have given him access to this privileged court document that had not yet been deposited in the court's registry? And what was Counsel's haste in rushing to the media with this order? Complainants believed that the criminal investigation of BLCC officials, the nuisance lawsuit and the order disbanding BLCC were all part of a plan hatched by agents of Respondent (either acting on instructions or *sua sponte*) to use the local judicial authorities to discredit the *bona fides* of their organization.

PART IV REPRISE

The exhaustion of domestic remedies was never intended as a "rule of public police which States must treat as sacrosanct" as Judge Eysinga noted in his dissent in the *Railway Case.* [164] The African Commission on Human and Peoples' Rights has also ruled against a too literal and mechanical application of the exhaustion rule, stressing that where it proves impractical or undesirable for a complainant to seise the domestic courts then resort to the rule is unnecessary. This flexible approach in the application of this rule was very much evident in the Commission's decision to admit the complaint in *Association Pour la Sauvegarde de la Paix.*[165]Despite the complainant's failure to exhaust domestic remedies, but given the number of States against whom the complaint was lodged, the Commission proceeded to waive this procedural bar in the higher interest of protecting human rights.

In a similar vein, the European Human Rights Court has also recognized the need to apply the exhaustion rule with some degree of flexibility and without excessive formalism.[166] These cautionary words are intended to ensure that the exhaustion rule does not become an unjustified impediment to access to international remedies, itself a right under

162 *See* Judgment of the Fako High Court [signed version] (copy on file).
163 *See* Judgment of the Fako High Court [unsigned version](copy on file).
164 *See Panevezys-Saldutiskis Railway Case, supra* note 26, at 37 (dissenting opinion).
165 *See Association Pour la Sauvegarde de la Paix au Burundi v. Tanzania, Kenya, Uganda, Rwanda, Zaire and Zambia*, Comm. 157/96, African Comm. Hum. & Peoples' Rights.
166 *See Akadivar et al. v. Turkey*, (1996) Eur.Ct.H.R., Reports 1996-IV.

international human rights law as the Inter-American Court acknowledged:

> [T]he rule of prior exhaustion must never lead to a halt or delay that would render international action in support of the defenseless victim ineffective. This is why Article 46.2 of the [American] Convention sets out exceptions to the requirement of recourse to domestic remedies prior to seeking international protection, precisely in situations in which such remedies are, for a variety of reasons, ineffective.[167]

While one has no doctrinal quarrel with the conceptual basis of the local remedies rule, it is the linear focus on its application that is cause for concern. This rigid focus on going through the domestic courts ignores other equally important aspects of the exhaustion rule.[168] Because the right to individual petition, captured in Article 58 (7) of the Banjul Charter, holds such a prominent place in international human rights law, any restrictive interpretation of the exhaustion rule would end up not protecting this right. The insistence that individuals seeking to assert their rights as global citizens, by appealing *directly* to this Commission, *must* first go through the national court system even when it has been demonstrated that that system lacks independence, amounts to a preference for a formalistic approach that is totally at odds with the protection of the human rights enshrined in the Banjul Charter. Putting form over substance also leaves victims of human rights abuses in Africa defenseless against the all-powerful States. Any procedural system must be viewed a nothing but a means of attaining justice; and justice cannot be sacrificed for the sake of mere technicalities.[169]

A one-dimensional approach to the exhaustion rule creates an imbalance between individual complainants and respondent States in favor of the latter. It makes it possible for the respondent State to avoid addressing the merits of a complaint alleging human rights violations through a well-timed objection to the nonobservance of *domestic legal remedies*. Thus, outside the well-known exceptions to this rule, such an objection is enough to deny an individual complainant who alleges State violations of Charter guaranteed rights from having his complaint heard on the merits. The right to individual petition includes the principle of procedural equality of the parties. This procedural equality of arms (*egalité des armes*) is essential to any jurisdictional system of protection of human rights. It is for international rights tribunals like the African Commission to redress this imbalance in order to preserve the principle of procedural equality. Since the case law of the African

167 *See Velásquez Rodríguez Case,* Preliminary Objections, *supra* note 83, ¶93.

168 The rule also talks of providing respondent government with notice of a human rights violation in order that it can remedy the violation prior to being haled before the Commission. The fear of contradictory judgments of law at the national and international levels is obviated in this case because Complainants, after waiting nine years for presidential action to no avail, are now before an international tribunal whose decision the Cameroon Constitution guarantees will be respected. Since the Constitution recognizes the supremacy of international law over domestic laws, there is no reason to fear that the Commission's decision will not be given *res judicata* effect by the national courts.

169 *See Dismissed Congressional Employees/Peru, Report No. 52/00, Cases 11.830 and 12.038,* Inter-Amer. Comm. Hum. Rights, June 15, 2001.

Commission is in a constant process of progressive development, a jurisprudential construction of Article 56(5) that would have the effect of putting the parties on an equal footing and not create the appearance of protecting only respondent states to the clear detriment of individual is necessary.

To assist in this process of reconstructing the Banjul Charter's exhaustion rule and rethinking its application in the African context where judicial independence is more in theory than practice, we suggest that a narrow or restrictive interpretation of the rule should be avoided for three reasons. First such an interpretation does violence to the plain language of the rule; second that a restrictive interpretation does not accord with international law and third, because a broad construction of the rule is favored by jurists and publicists. We suggest also that in applying the exhaustion rule, courts should weigh and balance the relative harms to the parties if the rule is waived. Human rights tribunals should not allow themselves to be stampeded by powerful States into treating the exhaustion of domestic remedies as an unbendable rule out of fear that relaxing it will transform these tribunals into courts of first instance. This specter of international human rights tribunals being 'flooded' with an untold number of 'frivolous' complaints overstates the case. As one publicist notes, the effect, if not the intent, of States haled before these tribunals is to make access to them all but impossible for defenseless victims of human rights abuses whose "domestic courts are not able to serve as defenders of human rights" and who "cannot afford to 'oil the palm' of the judge" in order to get their case "heard on time or at all."[170] A little more flexibility in the application of the exhaustion rule is not likely to add to a court's workload nor will it have the apocalyptic effect on its procedural architecture that State parties claim to dread.

1. A Narrow Interpretation does Violence to the Plain Language of Article 56(5)

A quick perusal of the published decisions of the African Commission will reveal that in the majority of cases Respondent State's first line of attack is to raise the exhaustion rule to deny admissibility.[171] The usual reason given is the need to avoid transforming the Commission into a tribunal of first instance.[172] Latching on to this rationale, respondent states frequently interpret the domestic remedy to which Article 56 (5) of the Banjul Charter refers to mean only remedies sought from courts of a *judicial nature.* It is submitted that this rigid interpretation of the exhaustion of local remedies rule does violence to the plain language of Article 56(5). Under international law, the appropriate starting place in treaty interpretation is the text of the treaty. This textual approach to treaty interpretation is mandated by the rules of interpretation prescribed by the 1969 Vienna Convention on the

170 *See* So Far, So Fair, *supra* note 117 at 16.

171 *See* Reply Memorial of the State of Cameroon in the BLCC v. Cameroon communication ("the Government of Cameroon *will concentrate on the question of the exhausting of local remedies,* which has been discussed at length by the Complainants.") [Emphasis added]

172 *Id.* ("In addressing this question, and contrary to the Complainants' claims, the Government of Cameroon is not in any way trying to use *technicalities* to prevent the Commission from examining the case submitted to it. It is simply trying to preserve the integrity of the Charter's procedural system, by ensuring that its "flexible" interpretation does not encourage the Complainants to undertake subjective and abusive proceedings.") [Emphasis in original].

Law of Treaties. Article 31 of the Convention provides that: "[a] *treaty shall be interpreted in good faith in accordance with the ordinary meaning to be given to the terms of the treaty in their context and in light of its object and purpose.*"[173] What then is the plain and ordinary meaning to be given to the language of Article 56(5) of the Banjul Charter?

Article 56(5) states: "Communications relating to Human and Peoples' rights referred to in Article 55 received by the Commission, shall be considered if they: .... 5. Are sent after exhausting local remedies, if any, unless it is obvious that this procedure is unduly prolonged."[174] There is nothing ambiguous in the language of Article 56(5) that would warrant dispensing with the plain language rule. Article 56, paragraph 5 makes no mention of limitations to the local remedies that must be exhausted. While it is commonly understood that local remedies would include recourse to the courts, however, on the face of it Article 56(5) does not limit domestic remedies to only those that can be obtained in the court system. Nor does it expressly exclude from local remedies those provided by legislative or executive authorities. Accordingly, the plain and ordinary meaning of this provision should be given effect as it expresses the intention of the framers of the Banjul Charter.

Following the textual approach to treaty interpretation favored by the Vienna Convention, when a tribunal is called upon to interpret a treaty, such as the Banjul Charter, it must proceed on the assumption that the intention of the framers of this instrument is expressed in the words of the document which it has to interpret. In the instant case, it must be presumed that the intention of the framers with respect to the exhaustion of local remedies rule is clearly expressed in Article 56(5).[175] Therefore, any attempt to restrict the meaning of "local remedies" to only those "*sought from courts of a judicial nature*" must be rejected because such is not the expressed intention of those who drafted Article 56(5) of the Charter.

Furthermore, the Vienna Convention's rules of interpretation prefer an interpretation that conforms to the object and purpose of the instrument. A narrow reading of Article 56(5) clearly jeopardizes the objectives of the Charter. In this wise, provisions of human rights law should be liberally construed to accomplish the purposes of the international bill of rights in general and the Banjul Charter in particular. The phrase "*after exhausting local remedies*" has little inherent meaning and can be construed narrowly or broadly, therefore only a broad construction will ensure the effective protection of the guaranteed human rights under the Banjul Charter.

2. A Restrictive Interpretation not in Accord with International Law

A narrow reading of Article 56(5) does not accord with generally accepted rules of international law which recognize not only judicial remedies but also any *administrative*

173 *See* VIENNA CONVENTION ON THE LAW OF TREATIES, 1155 U.N.T.S. 331, U.N. Doc. A/CONF.39/27 (1969). Signed at Vienna, Austria on May 23, 1969; *entered into force* on January 27, 1980, in accordance with Article 81(1), art. 31.

174 Banjul Charter, *supra* note 12, art. 56(5).

175 *See* Comments of Sir Eric Beckett on the Report of M. H. Lauterpacht (of the Second Commission of the Institute of International Law) on the Interpretation of Treaties, 43-1 Ann. Inst. D. Int'l 437-38 (1950).

domestic remedy that may provide redress in the circumstances of the case.[176] As was stated in the *Ambatielos Case,*[177] the phrase "local remedies" should be interpreted broadly, including "the whole system of legal protection, as provided by municipal law," not only the courts and tribunals but also "the use of procedural facilities which municipal law makes available to litigants."[178]

3. *Broad Construction Favored by Other Tribunals and Scholarly Writings*

The less restrictive interpretation of the exhaustion rule is favored by the European Court of Human Rights[179] as well as the Inter-American Court of Human Rights, particularly in its judgments in the so-called *Honduran cases.*[180] Leading publicists have also embraced a broad construction of the local remedies rule. The Brazilian jurist and President of the Inter-American Court, Antonio A. C. Trindade, who has written extensively on the exhaustion doctrine, takes the view that a rule created and applied in matters of diplomatic protection should not apply *mutatis mutandis* to human rights cases:

> [T]o claim that the local remedies rule should be applied in human rights protection exactly as diplomatic protection, to claim that the content or scope of the rule is not affected by contextual values or *ordre public* in respect of the protection of the rights of the human person and not of the state, is to close one's eyes to reality. Generally recognized rules of international law, besides undergoing an evolution of their own within the contexts in which they are applied, necessarily undergo, when enshrined in human rights treaties, some adjustment, dictated by the special character of the object and purpose of those treaties and by the generally recognized specificity of the international protection of human rights.
>
> This is the lesson drawn from the experience accumulated in this domain; progress in the international protection of human rights has been made possible in the last decades, as well as in relation to the operation of the local remedies rule, by an awareness of the specificity of this *droit de protection* (which calls for an interpretation of its own), by a proper understanding

176 *See The Interhandel Case (Switz. v. U.S.), Preliminary Objections,* 1959 ICJ REP. 6, 27 (Mar. 21).

177 *See Ambatielos Case (Greece v. United Kingdom),* 1951, 12 R. Int'l Arb. Awards 91, 120, 122.

178 *Id.; see also Finnish Ships Case, supra* note 112, 1498-1505.

179 *See Klaas v. Germany,* 18 Eur. H.R. Rep. 305 (1994 (where the Court stated that the "national authority" referred to in Article 13 of the European Convention may not necessarily be a judicial authority).

180 Beginning with its eleventh Advisory Opinion of 1990 and Judgments in the *Velasquez-Rodriguez,* the *Godinez Cruz* case, and the *Fairen Garbi and Solis Corrales* case, the Inter-American Court began expanding the interpretation of the local remedies rule as a condition of admissibility of international petitions or communications under the American Convention. It did so by going beyond the generally recognized exceptions of undue delays and denial of justice and by tackling the issues of distribution or shifting (between complainants and respondent states) of the burden of proof with regard to the exhaustion and the express or tacit waiver of the local remedies rule. *See* Antonio Augusto Cançado Trindade, *"Thoughts on Recent Developments in the Case-Law of the Inter-American Court of Human Rights: Selected Aspects,"* Proceedings of the 92nd Annual Meeting of the American Society of International Law, 192, 193 (April 1-4, 1998).

> of the basic premises underlying the mechanisms of protection and by faithful pursuit of their object and purpose.[181]

A faithful pursuit of the object and purpose of the Banjul Charter calls for an interpretation of the exhaustion of domestic remedies rule in such a way that would not allow the State to prevent its' citizens from enjoying their fundamental human rights. It is in this light that one publicist has criticized the rule in *Cudjoe v. Ghana* for being "too dogmatic,"[182] and, as a renowned publicist notes, "remedies may be available whatever the constitutional status of the agency taking the measure concerned. The test remains that of the reasonable possibility of an effective remedy."[183] A student of this Commission's jurisprudence has observed that despite its wish not to be transformed into a tribunal of first instance, the Commission has increasingly found itself replacing national mechanisms for judicial remedies. This role has been imposed on the Commission by the "*lack of independent national judiciaries, and massive human rights violations that overwhelm domestic remedies.*"[184] The Commission has thus become the last hope for the defenseless victims of human rights violations in Africa.

4. A Weighing and Balancing of the Relative Harms to Both Parties if Rule is Waived

The application of the local remedies rule requires a balancing of the relative merits and burdens the rule places on the parties. This much is implied in a flexibility approach to the exhaustion rule.[185] Since the Commission's own jurisprudence lays much emphasis on a contextual analysis, the application of the exhaustion rule in a given case must take cognizance of the nature of that country's system of providing judicial protection including situations where the Head of State exercises both executive and *de facto* judicial powers. The Commission [should?] probe the extent to which presidential powers are far more extensive than those enjoyed by even the higher judicial bench. It is within the context of each country's specificity or peculiarity that the Commission should interpret and apply the local remedies rule in determining the admissibility of a communication.

The goal of this weighing and balancing exercise is to determine which party stands to lose the most from the application of the rule. For this exercise to be fruitful, the Commission must ascertain whether: (a) complainant has provided the respondent State with adequate notice of a human rights violation in order that it can cure the problem prior to being haled before the Commission;[186] (b) respondent State's insistence on the exhaustion of

181 *See* A.A. Cancado Trindade, *Book Review: C.F. Amerasinghe, Local Remedies in International Law (1990)*, 86 A.J.I.L. 626, 636 (1992).

182 *See* So Far, So Fair, *supra* note 117, at 27.

183 *See* Ian Brownlie, PRINCIPLES OF PUBLIC INTERNATIONAL LAW 500 (5TH ED. 1998).

184 *See* So Far, So Fair, *supra* note 117, at 16. [Emphasis added]

185 *See* Duty to Exhaust, *supra* note 154, at 401-401.

186 As Judge Hudson pointed out in his dissent in the *Railway Case*, the requirement to exhaust domestic remedies is "not a rule of procedure" nor "merely a matter of orderly conduct.... [rather] it is a part of the substantive law as to international responsibility, i.e. State-to-State responsibility." It follows, therefore, that "if adequate redress for the injury is available to the person who suffered it, if such a person has only to

domestic remedies is pled in bad faith[187] as a ploy to buy time; (c) respondent State operates a court system that is notoriously slow and overburdened where cases are tied up for years before being called up;[188] (d) the judiciary is structurally separate and independent from the executive branch or whether the latter exercises inordinate control over the former.[189]

CONCLUSION

Although the African Commission on Human and Peoples' Rights never got to the merits of *BLCC vs. Cameroon,* having declared it inadmissible for nonobservance of the domestic remedies rule, it is still necessary not to lose sight of the wider significance of the case. It raised an interesting doctrinal issue with respect to the exhaustion of domestic remedies rule. It posed the question whether remedies that call for observance by a complainant must be only those provided by courts? But what if it is clear that the local courts are totally subservient to the executive who has taken the decision being challenged, is complainant required to exhaust domestic remedies? The first question has been answered in the affirmative by the Commission's decision in *Alfred B. Cudjoe v Ghana*[190] but it is not at all clear from the Commission's own jurisprudence that the second question has been resolved. Under *Cudjoe* domestic remedies, within the meaning of Article 56 (6) of the African Charter, refer only to remedies provided by courts. For the rule of *Cudjoe* to work it must assume a truly normal functioning judiciary not one where justice is dispensed in a discretionary fashion and where bias has already been shown toward the complainant.

---

reach out to avail himself of such redress, there is no basis for a claim to be espoused by the State of which such a person is a nation. Until the available means of local redress have been exhausted, no international responsibility can arise." *See Panevezys-Saldutiskis Railway Case, supra* note 26, at 45 (dissenting opinion).

187 The harm to a complainant when the demand for exhaustion of local remedies is not done in good faith is three-fold. First, it risks wrecking irreparable damage to the complainant's Charter protected rights. Second, it forces a complainant with a well-founded claim to go through the motion for the sake of satisfying this technicality. Third, complainant is forced to spend time and scarce financial resources. A complainant may end up marking time at the same judicial spot especially where there are long delays in the disposing of cases in Respondent State's courts. A most instructive example is *Victims of Post-Electoral Violence in the North West Province v Cameroon* filed by Interights of London in July 2003 on behalf of a group of Cameroonians whose property was destroyed in Bamenda in 1992 in the wake of a presidential election whose results were contested by supporters of the opposition candidate. The original case had been languishing in the Supreme Court for almost five years until it was mercifully rescued by the African Commission. During this time the written pleadings were misplaced or mysteriously disappeared at least six times. *See Victims of Post-Electoral Violence in the North West Province v Cameroon,* Comm. 272/2003, African Comm. Hum. & Peoples' Rights.

188 It would be a real mockery of the exhaustion rule to require a complainant to work her way through a notoriously slow judicial system just to give respondent State the satisfaction of having complied with it believes is the local remedies requirement.

189 The purpose of the exhaustion of domestic remedies requirement is to give national courts an opportunity to decide upon cases before they are brought to an international forum. This would avoid contradictory judgments of law at the national and international levels. But the rule also speaks to the need to provide the State with adequate notice of a human rights violation in order that it can remedy the violation prior to being haled before this Commission. This notice can be presumed when the alleged violation is open and notorious. Clearly when a Government has knowledge, actual or constructive, of a complained violation and fails to remedy it, it cannot retreat to the position that because the alleged victims did not submit themselves before the law courts, access to an international tribunal should be denied them. *See Social & Econ. Rights Action Center for Econ. & Soc. Rights vs. Nigeria,* Comm. No. 156/96, African Comm. Hum. & Peoples' Rights.

190 *See Alfred B. Cudjoe v Ghana,* Comm. 221/98, African Comm. Hum. & Peoples' Rights.

Where that assumption cannot be sustained then the exhaustion of local remedies requirement should be waived in order to allow victims of human rights abuse to seek redress for those wrongs in a neutral and, arguably, impartial international tribunal.

TWENTY-SEVEN

Trial Observation Report-Cameroon

Case of Nkongho Felix Agbor Balla, Fontem Neba and others Hearing 27 April 2017, Military Tribunal Yaoundé

MARINA BRILMAN

I. Introduction

1. The Law Society is a professional body representing more than 166,000 lawyers in England and Wales. Its aims include upholding the independence of the legal profession, the rule of law and human rights around the world. The Law Society has consultative status with the Economic and Social Council of the United Nations since 2014.
2. The Law Society has been closely monitoring the situation in Cameroon following reports of the suppression of public protests and alleged excessive violence used by police forces against lawyers and others at the end of 2016. The subsequent arrest and detention of lawyers and civil society leaders have contributed to our concerns. On 13 February 2017, in a letter sent to authorities in Cameroon (see Annex A), the Law Society expressed its concern about the fact that the lawyer Nkongho Felix Agbor Balla, Fontem Neba, and others – all civilians – had been charged with offences carrying the death penalty and were being tried by a military tribunal. In a subsequent letter of 25 April 2017, the Law Society informed the authorities in Cameroon of its concern regarding the prolonged pre-trial detention of the defendants.
3. These concerns were the primary reason for the Law Society to carry out a trial observation at the hearing that took place on 27 April 2017 in the case against Nkongho Felix Agbor Balla, Fontem Neba and others at the Military Tribunal of Yaoundé. This specific hearing was regarded as an important moment in the proceedings, because a bail application would be discussed as well as - possibly - the merits of the case.
4. The aim of the trial observation was to impartially assess whether procedural guarantees, established in international and regional human rights law, were being complied with. The main objective was, therefore, to ascertain whether rules of due process were being respected and whether the accused were receiving a fair trial.
5. The International Human Rights policy adviser of the Law Society represented the

Law Society during this trial observation and at meetings held with officials and others. Meetings were attended together with a representative from the Bar Human Rights Committee of England and Wales, and the American Bar Association. At the hearing, representatives from the diplomatic missions of the United Kingdom, the United States of America, and Canada were present, as well as representatives of the field office of the United Nations Office of the High Commissioner on Human Rights (OHCHR), based in Cameroon.

6. This report reflects exclusively the observations made and conclusions reached by the representative of the Law Society. The observations only regard the hearing that took place on 27 April 2017. Therefore, no conclusions can necessarily be drawn on the compliance with procedural guarantees during hearings that took place prior and subsequent to that hearing.
7. In addition to the observations made regarding the hearing, reference is made to the historical background of the situation in Cameroon and to the previous stages in the proceedings against the defendants. The facts observed during the trial will be assessed by reference to international and regional human rights standards, as well as domestic law. However, since the Law Society representative is not a qualified lawyer in Cameroon, domestic law is interpreted literally and taken at face value.
8. In order to report impartially on the hearing and to obtain a better understanding of the local situation, meetings were sought with both parties to the proceedings, before and after the hearing, as well as with other officials. Meetings were held with members of the defence team, the *Commissaire du Gouvernement* (State Prosecutor at the Military Tribunal of Yaoundé), and the President of the Military Tribunal of Yaoundé. With the defence team, information relating to the circumstances prior to the arrest of the defendants was discussed, the previous stages of proceedings, the conditions of detention of the defendants, as well as submissions made during the hearing on 27 April 2017. At the meeting with the President of the Military Tribunal, the domestic law applicable to proceedings at the Military Tribunal was discussed. The Law Society thanks all these persons and authorities for their time and willingness to meet with us. The Law Society is especially grateful to the President of the Military Tribunal for her explanation of the jurisdiction of the Tribunal over certain types of offences. This was very helpful to understand the military jurisdiction in Cameroon. The Law Society also thanks the *Commissaire du Gouvernement* for agreeing to meet with us. Unfortunately, he informed us that he could not discuss the substance of the case or the proceedings without prior authorisation from the Minister of Justice or the Minister of Defence. He suggested that we should obtain such an authorisation and return to his office.
9. The Law Society also sought to visit Nkongho Felix Agbor Balla and Fontem Neba at the *Prison Principale de Yaoundé* where they are being detained. We obtained a permission from the *Commissaire du Gouvernement*, so that entry to the prison was given. We were received by the Registrar of the prison, but were not allowed to meet with the defendants. As the prison Registrar explained, there are three different regimes: one for counsel of the defendants, who are allowed to visit their

clients during working hours, if their name is on the list of counsel displayed at the entrance of the prison. Another regime for family members and friends, who are allowed to visit the prisoners with permission of the *Commissaire du Gouvernement*. And, finally, there is a regime for international visitors or observers, who must have authorisation from the Minister of Justice or the Minister of Defence.

10. The Law Society sought authorisation from both the Ministry of Justice and the Ministry of Defence to visit the defendants in prison and to speak with the *Commissaire du Gouvernement* about the case. We were told that the Minister of Justice would meet with us, but that he was in another meeting. After waiting for two hours and returning to the Ministry in the afternoon, we were instead received by the Director of a department for criminal and penitentiary matters, which forms part of the Ministry of Justice. He told us that a distinction should be made between a request to visit a prison – which fell under his jurisdiction – and a request to visit a particular prisoner – which is decided upon by the authority under whose jurisdiction the prisoner is being detained (in this case, the Ministry of Defence). The Law Society thanks both the prison Registrar of the *Prison Principale de Yaoundé* and the Director of the department for criminal and penitentiary matters of the Ministry of Justice for receiving us, but we regret not being able to visit the defendants in prison or speak to the *Commissaire du Gouvernement*. The latter would have allowed us to obtain the view of the Prosecution, which would have constituted a valuable contribution to this report. The Law Society also sought to meet with the President of the national Bar Council, but we understand that he was not in Cameroon at the time of the hearing.
11. This report was sent to the Government of Cameroon, the *Commissaire du Gourvernement* of the Military Tribunal in Yaoundé, the President of the Military Tribunal in Yaoundé and her Assessors, as well as the defence team. Due to the time constraints in publishing this report before the next hearing, that was supposed to take place on 24 May 2017, it was impossible to include the responses of the parties and authorities in the final report. However, any response received after its publication will be published alongside this report on the Law Society website, if the person or authority who provides it consents to such publication.

II. Historical background

12. The territory now known as Cameroon was a German colony from the mid 1880s until 1914. After World War I, the League of Nations granted mandates to France and Britain to administer the territory, with the latter responsible for administering two regions in the North West and South West. In 1960, the French part of the territory gained independence and *La République du Cameroun* was constituted. In 1961, following a plebiscite, the majority of inhabitants of the English-speaking regions voted to become part of the independent Cameroon, rather than Nigeria, under a federalist system. An amendment of the Constitution in 1972 abolished the federal system and the country became a "Unified Republic". Article 1(2) of the Constitution that is currently in force, lastly amended in 2008, establishes

that: "[t]he Republic of Cameroon shall be a decentralized unitary State" and that:

> "[t]he official languages of the, Republic of Cameroon shall be English and French, both languages having the same status. The State shall guarantee the promotion of bilingualism throughout the country. It shall endeavour to protect and promote national languages."

13. In Cameroon, two legal systems exist. In the French speaking regions, the civil legal system applies and, in the English-speaking parts, common law is used. For a few decades, a Government project has been under way, which intends to "harmonise" laws and to allegedly reform the criminal code and the criminal procedure code. Some Cameroonian lawyers have expressed their concern that such harmonisation could be construed as the establishment of a civil law system in the whole country, including the North and South West regions where common law is currently used.
14. The English-speaking inhabitants of Cameroon are a numerical and linguistic minority and many feel marginalised, because of an apparent lack of political representation and participation in public life. We understand that most important positions are held by French speaking Cameroonians and that many administrative matters are exclusively dealt with in French, also in the English-speaking regions. This seems problematic, since many English-speaking Cameroonians do not understand French (and vice versa, many French speaking Cameroonians do not understand or speak English).
15. Since 2015 and the beginning of 2016, common law lawyers held meetings to discuss their concerns about the marginalisation of the common law in the North and South West regions. The conclusions of these meetings, as well as recommendations made by the lawyers, were allegedly sent to the Government, but no response was apparently received. From October to December 2016, lawyers, teachers, and other civil society actors held protests in the English-speaking North and South West regions, particularly in their respective capital cities of Bamenda and Buea. The protests were held because French speaking teachers and legal officers, who had been educated in the French educational and civil law systems, were carrying out functions in the North and South West regions at English speaking schools and acting in cases regarding accused who are English speakers. More generally, these protests seemed to reflect a growing dissatisfaction with the marginalisation of English-speaking Cameroonians and the apparent lack of recognition of the educational and common law system applied in these two regions. At the end of 2016, the Cameroon Anglophone Civil Society Consortium (CACSC) was established to act, among other things, as an interlocutor for the Government in Yaoundé.
16. The protests were met with allegedly excessive force by the police. We understand that the police used teargas during a protest that took place in November 2016 in Bamenda and that many of the protesters were beaten and injured. We have heard reports that approximately 100 persons were arrested since November 2016, some of whom were released and others still remain in detention. We understand

that arrests were carried out arbitrarily, without an arrest warrant, and without informing those arrested which offences they had been charged with. The Law Society has also received reports of ill-treatment, mostly beatings, of those arrested by police officers in the first few hours after the arrests. It has also been alleged that, following those beatings, a number of those arrested gave statements to the police without the assistance of a lawyer.

17. The Law Society understands that some lawyers have gone into hiding or exile and that others are not able to travel because their passports have not been returned after their arrest or because they fear detention. Two of those lawyers reported to us that a group of lawyers had assembled in Buea and had not yet started protesting, when officers from the police training school, without name tags and in plainclothes, appeared and flogged the lawyers. The police officers carried batons and guns and were apparently overseen by a police commissioner who was in uniform. The lawyers were protesting in their robes and wigs were ripped off. Several lawyers were beaten and wounded. Other lawyers who were travelling to Buea for the protests were stopped on the road, flogged by police officers, and had to abandon their vehicles. The national press reported that Barrister Walters Abadem was arrested in Buea and transported by police officers to Yaoundé (The Post, 28 April 2017). He is being detained at Kondengui prison, but is currently in a hospital in Yaoundé after suffering from a back problem. We have no further information on this case, but will monitor his situation.

18. We understand that at the end of 2016, meetings took place between members of the National Assembly, the Minister of Justice, Bar Council members, civil society leaders from the North and South West, and lawyers in order to resolve some of the issues that gave rise to the lawyers' concerns. Unfortunately, these meetings were not successful in the sense that no measures were apparently taken to address those concerns. We understand that no statement was made by the Bar Council or its President in support of its members in the Anglophone regions. However, we have heard reports, and established at the hearing on 27 April 2017, that some civil law lawyers support their common law colleagues, including by providing legal representation for them and others who have been arrested.

19. As part of the protests, "ghost towns" have been declared by the protesters, which are specific days during which shops and businesses are closed and lawyers and teachers are on strike. We understand that these "ghost towns continue, although some have protested against them. The national press has reported that some of these protesters were in fact state agents, but the official Cameroon newspaper, the "Cameroon Tribune", alleges that people in the regions no longer wish to strike, because it negatively affects their economic situation.

20. On 17 January 2017, the Government took several measures to address the protests. It banned the CACSC, shut down the internet (this shutdown was limited to the English-speaking regions), and Nkongho Felix, Agbor Balla and Fontem Neba were arrested (see Law Society letter of 13 February 2017, Annex A). On 20 January 2017, they were charged with "terrorism, hostility against the motherland,

secession, insurrection, contempt of public authorities, and collective rebellion"; "incitement to civil war by bringing the inhabitants of the South- and Northwest regions to arm themselves against other citizens"; and "attempt[ing] to modify the constitutional laws, notably the federalist system, through violence". We understand that all those who were arrested were charged with similar offences. These offences are included in Law No. 2016/007 of 12 July 2016, relating to the Penal Code (the "Criminal Code"),[1] and fall under the jurisdiction of the military tribunal pursuant to Law No. 2014/028 of 23 December 2014 on the Suppression Acts of Terrorism (the "Terrorism Law"). The Law Society understands that the inhabitants of the South and North West regions differ in their views and demands. Although almost all of those arrested have been charged with secession, we understand that most are advocating for a return to a federalist system or merely a decentralisation of administrative and other functions to the regions.

21. On 23 January 2017, the President of Cameroon created a "*Commission nationale pour la promotion du bilinguisme et du multiculturalisme* (CNPBM)", consisting of 15 members who were appointed on 15 March (Cameroon Tribune, 27 April 2017). On 30 March 2017, the Minister of Justice and Keeper of the Seals announced that certain measures would be taken, such as the inclusion of a Common Law Section as part of the Supreme Court and National School of Administration and Magistracy (ENAM), and the recruitment of more Anglophone teachers at ENAM, as well as court officers. At the same time, it was announced that the "harmonisation process" of various laws would continue. In April 2017, the internet shutdown was lifted. According to the Cameroon Tribune, the internet shutdown had been ordered to stop the Cameroonian diaspora from using the internet to destabilise institutions and spread false information. Although these measures taken by the Government are a positive sign, it remains to be seen to what extent they effectively address the concerns that gave rise to the protests by members of the legal profession in 2016.

III. Previous stages of the proceedings

22. Nkongho Felix Agbor Balla and Fontem Neba were arrested on 17 January 2017. We understand that neither of them was shown an arrest warrant upon arrest nor were they informed of the charges against them. On 20 January 2017, the *Commissaire du Gourvernement* at the Military Tribunal of Yaoundé ordered their preventive detention, as well as that of Mancho Bibixy, without indicating a specific length of time in an *Ordre de mise en jugement direct*. This order submits the accused directly to the jurisdiction of the Military Tribunal for judgment. The first hearing before the Military Tribunal in Yaoundé was scheduled to take place on 3 February 2017, but was adjourned to 13 February 2017. During the hearing of 13 February 2017, the defence challenged the absence of adequate interpretation from French into English and the Prosecution alleged that it had yet to finalise its list of witnesses,

1 See, for example, the Criminal Code: Section 111 (Secession), Section 112 (Civil War), Section 113 (Insurrection), Section 158 (collective resistance).

so that the proceedings on the merits could not begin. The defence team allegedly submitted a bail application for consideration at the next hearing on 23 March 2017, but at that hearing the prosecution requested for the case to be joined with a case against 25 other defendants. The defence argued against such a joinder on the basis that the circumstances and arrests occurred at different times and in different places.[2] On 7 April 2017, the Military Tribunal decided to join the cases. The Law Society has not seen a written order, decision or judgment confirming the joining of the cases. The case was adjourned to 27 April 2017.

IV. Trial observation

A. *Location and Courtroom*

1. 23. The Military Tribunal of Yaoundé is situated close to the centre of Yaoundé, Cameroon's capital city, in a military compound. There are two adjoined buildings, one of which houses the courtroom and the other, the offices of the *Commissaire du Gourvernement*, Registrar, and President of the Military Tribunal. International visitors have to hand in their passports temporarily to obtain visitors' badges.

Figure 27.1. Tribunal Militaire sign

24. The lay-out of the courtroom is as follows: the President of the Military Tribunal, who presides over the proceedings in this case, and two Assessors sit on a platform at the front of the room, to the right is the prosecution (as well as, in this case, lawyers for the civil party). To the left is the defence. There are two wooden boxes (open structures) with seats for two persons each, where – in this case - the accused stand. There are a few rows of seats next to the boxes, which we understand

2 Criminal Procedure Code, Section 6 refers to that "[a] joint trial shall be obligatory in the case of indivisible offences and optional in the case of related offences".

are for witnesses. In this instance, military officials and some lawyers were seated there. Behind a wooden partitioning are benches, in two rows, for the public. The defendants were first seated, with their prison guards, in one of the rows before being moved to the boxes.

25. There is no air-conditioning or ventilation in the courtroom. Doors are open at the side and back of the courtroom, making it very hot. There are no microphones so that it was, at times, very difficult to hear what the parties and the President are saying. This was exacerbated by people talking in the public gallery, which is located at a short distance from the parties and judges. Consequently, some parts of the proceedings were inevitably lost on those sitting in the public gallery, who depended on the level of volume and articulation with which each speaker made his or her submissions.
26. The President of the Military Tribunal and her Assessors are all serving military officers in uniform. The President of the Military Tribunal has the rank of Colonel. The defence team is made up of 15 persons, almost all of them are former Presidents of the national Bar Council. They are French and English speakers, trained in the civil and common law legal systems and distinguishable by their robes. The prosecution is lead by a military officer in uniform and there are also civilian prosecutors; we understand from one of the High Courts. There were some international observers, family members of the defendants, and French and English-speaking lawyers sitting in the public gallery, although the majority seemed to be English speaking.
27. The defendants arrived separately with their prison guards. First, Nkongho Felix Agbor Balla and Fontem Neba. Second, Mancho Bibixy and the other 25 accused. The reason for this is that they are being held in separate prisons. Felix Agbor Balla and Fontem Neba are held at the *Prison Principale de Yaoundé*, a prison for high profile offenders and those accused of terrorism related offences, while the others are held at the central prison in Yaoundé. We understand that the prison conditions of Felix Agbor Balla and Fontem Neba were not good shortly following their arrest, but after representations made by their legal representatives, their conditions have improved. Both seemed to be in good health. It was not permitted to take pictures inside the courtroom. The picture of the plaque outside the Tribunal (Annex D) was taken with the permission of a military officer guarding the compound.

B. *Applicable Law and Procedure*

28. The Military Tribunal has jurisdiction over the offences that the accused have been charged with based on Section 1(2) of the Terrorism Law, which provides that: "[t]he offences provided for in this law shall fall exclusively under the jurisdiction of military tribunals".
29. Section 3 of Law No. 2008/015 of 29 December 2008 "To Organize Military Justice and Lay Down Rules of Procedure Applicable Before Military Tribunals" (the "Military Justice Code") provides that military tribunals be set up in each region of the country. The same Section provides that the Military Tribunal in Yaoundé may

exercise its powers throughout the national territory in the event of exceptional circumstances, such as those specified in Article 9 of the Constitution, which constitute a serious threat to public order or state security, or terrorism. Article 9 of the Constitution refers to a declaration by the President of Cameroon of a state of emergency or a state of siege.[3] The Military Tribunal in Yaoundé asserts its jurisdiction in the case of Nkongho Felix Agbor Balla and Fontem Neba, based on Section 3 of the Military Justice Code, even though the offences they have been charged with took place in the English-speaking regions and there are also military tribunals in those regions.

30. There are no specific rules governing the proceedings at the Military Tribunal. Rather, with regard to procedure and substantive law, the Military Tribunal applies the Terrorism Law, the Military Justice Code, the Criminal Code, and Law N°2005 of 27 July 2005 on the Criminal Procedure Code (the "Criminal Procedure Code "or" CPC").
31. The Terrorism Law takes precedence as *lex specialis*, to the extent that some of its provisions deviate from the Criminal Procedure Code, the Criminal Code, and the Military Justice Code. Section 1(1) of the Terrorism Law provides that: "[t]he provisions of the penal code, the criminal procedure code and the military justice code that are not repugnant to this law shall remain applicable". The Military Justice Code takes precedence over the Criminal Procedure Code and Criminal Code as *lex specialis*, as provided in Section 16(1) of the Military Justice Code: "[t]he procedure applicable before the military tribunal shall be the ordinary law procedure, subject to special provisions provided for by this law." Similarly, Section 2 of the Criminal Procedure Code establishes that: "[t]his Code shall be of general application except where there is provision to the contrary as provided in the Code of Military Justice or in any special law".
32. The main provisions of the Terrorism Law, which deviate from the Military Justice Code and the Criminal Procedure Code, regard the duration of custody and the preliminary inquiry. With regards to remand in custody, Section 11 of the Military Justice Code provides that: "[...] the duration of remand in custody shall be 48 hours renewable once, but this period may be extended to two further periods of 48 hours each on the written authorization of the state prosecutor". Furthermore, Section 12.4 of the Military Justice Code establishes that the State Prosecutor, before the institution of criminal proceedings, may order remand in custody for 10 days, renewable with another 10 days, with authorization of the Minister of Military Justice if it regards a case of flagrante delicto and there is serious corroborating evidence against the suspect. The Terrorism Law deviates from the Military Justice

3 Constitution of the Republic of Cameroon, article 9(1) The President of the Republic may, where circumstances so warrant, declare by decree a state of emergency which shall confer upon him such special powers as may be provided for by law; (2) In the event of a serious threat to the nation's territorial integrity or to its existence, its independence or institutions, the President of the Republic may declare a state of siege by decree and take any measures as he may deem necessary. He shall inform the Nation of his decision by message.

Code by stipulating in its Section 11 "Remand in custody" that "[f]or the purpose of this law, the duration of remand in custody shall be fifteen days renewable upon the authorisation of the State Prosecutor". No time limit is included in this Law on the length of time that a suspect may be held in custody, nor is there a requirement that the authorisation of the State Prosecutor be motivated (see Part V.A below).

33. With regard to the preliminary inquiry, the Criminal Procedure Code stipulates in Section 142(1) that "[p]reliminary inquiries shall be obligatory in cases of felonies unless otherwise provided by law". Section 12(1) of the Military Justice Code provides that

> "[c]riminal proceedings shall be instituted before the military tribunal by the minister in charge of military justice who shall, to that effect, issue either a direct commitment for trial where he deems that the matter be tried or an order to investigate where he deems that the matter calls for preliminary investigation."

Section 12(2) of the Military Justice Code provides that "[n]otwithstanding the provisions of subsection 1 above, preliminary investigation shall be compulsory in criminal matters".

34. The Terrorism Law deviates from the Criminal Procedure Code and the Military Justice Code in that there is never a preliminary inquiry, but a case is always directly referred to the Military Tribunal by the State Prosecutor (*Commissaire du Gouvernement*). Section 12 "Referral Before the Competent Court" of the Terrorism Law provides that: "[f]or the purposes of this law, matters shall be referred to the military tribunal by a direct order to be placed on trial, issued by State Prosecutor".

35. With regard to the offences over which the Military Tribunal has competency, Section 7 "Competence of the Military Tribunal" of the Military Justice Code establishes that the Military Tribunal "shall be competent to hear:

a). Military offences provided for by the code of military justice
b). Any offence committed by servicemen, with or without civil co-offenders or accomplices, in a military establishment or in the exercise of their duties,
c). Offences against the law on war or defence weapons
d). Armed robbery
e). Any offences involving a serviceman or any person considered as such, committed in times of war or in a region under a state of emergency or emergency measures
f). Any offences committed by civilians in a military establishment causing damage to military equipment or installations, or prejudicial to the physical integrity o[f] a serviceman.
g). All offences related to the purchase, sale, production, distribution, wearing or keeping of military effects or insignia as defined by military regulations
h). All offences related to those specified above."

36. In addition to these offences, the Terrorism Law refers to "Acts of Terrorism" as defined in its Section 2.[4] Most of these offences carry the death penalty, with some exceptions.[5] Furthermore, it refers to offences such as "Financing of acts of terrorism" (Section 3), "Laundering of Proceeds of terrorism" (Section 4), and "Recruitment and Training" (Section 5).
37. With regard to the Judges who hear cases at the Military Tribunal, Section 6 of the Military Justice Code establishes that: "[e]xcepting misdemeanours or minor offences, all cases shall be tried by a collegiate bench, composed of a President and two Assessors, one of who shall be a member of the defence force". Section 4(2) provides that: "[t]he President, Vice-President, Examining Magistrates, the State Prosecutor and Deputy State Prosecutors shall be military legal officers or civilian legal officers", and Section 4(3) provides that: "[a]ssessors and Alternate Assessors shall be military legal officers, civilian officers, or officers of the defence forces".
38. In the case of Nkongho Felix Agbor Balla and Fontem Neba, the Military Tribunal consisted of the President and two Assessors, at least one of whom has no legal training, as far as we understand. This would perhaps be common practice in cases where military officials are being tried by a Military Tribunal for offences committed in the line of duty, i.e. a court martial. However, if civilians are being tried by a Military Tribunal, an Assessor without legal training on the bench could potentially be construed as implying a violation of the right to be tried by an a "competent, independent and impartial tribunal" (Article 14(1) of the International Covenant on Civil and Political Rights – "ICCPR"). We understand that the Military Tribunal in Yaoundé has 6 judges in total, two of whom are civilians and 4 are serving military officers. In the case of Felix Agbor Balla and Fontem Neba, all three judges were military offers.

4 **Section 2: Acts of terrorism**

1. Whoever, acting alone as an accomplice or accessory, commits or threatens to commit an act likely to cause death, endanger physical integrity, cause bodily injury or material damage, destroy natural resources, the environment or cultural heritage with intent to:

a. Intimidate the public, provoke a situation of terror or face the victim, the government and/or a national or international organisation to carry out or refrain From carrying out an act, adopt or renounce a particular position;

b. Disrupt the national functioning of public services, the delivery of essential services to the public to create a crisis situation among the public;

c. Create widespread insurrection in the country;

d. Shall be punished with the death penalty.

2. Whoever

a. Provides and/or uses war weapons and equipment;b. Provides and/or uses microorganisms or any other biological agents, in particular viruses, bacteria, fungi or toxins;c. Provides and/or uses chemical, psychotropic, radioactive or hypnotising substances;d. Perpetuates hostage taking;In order to attain the same objectives as those inferred in sub section 1 above shall be punished with the death penalty,

5 Section 7 "Interruption of the offence or its effects "and Section 8: "Acclamation of acts of terrorism", which carry a sentence of a maximum of twenty years imprisonment; the latter and/or a fine from twenty five million francs (25,000,000) FCFA to fifty million (50,000,000).

C. *Deficiencies in the Terrorism Law*

39. This report focuses on the hearing that took place on 27 April 2017 so that it does not offer an in-depth analysis of the Terrorism Law in its entirety or other domestic laws. Such laws are only referred to in Part V for the purpose of assessing whether the hearing reveals a violation of certain rights established in domestic, regional, and international laws. Nonetheless, there are at least three obvious deficiencies of the Terrorism Law that are in clear violation of international and regional standards.
40. First, the period of time that a suspect can be remanded in custody. The Terrorism Law establishes that this is a period of 15 days, which is renewable, without a time limit and without a motivated and judicial decision to prolong such custody. This effectively means that a person can be held in custody for an excessive amount of time upon the order of the State Prosecutor at the Military Tribunal without charges being brought. This impermissible effect is demonstrated in the case of Paul Ayah Abine, who has been held in custody since 21 January 2017 without any charges having been brought against him. We understand that, because of his position as a Deputy Attorney-General of the Supreme Court, he is subject to "Privileged Proceedings" as regulated by Part X, Section 629(1) of the Criminal Procedure Code,[6] which means that magistrates of a "grade at least equal" to his must be appointed to investigate and, if necessary, hear the case. However, such privileged proceedings nor any other reason justifies this prolonged custody.
41. Remand in custody without being charged constitutes a clear violation of Article 9(2) and (3) ICCPR and the African Commission on Human and Peoples' Rights has established a violation of Article 6 of the African Charter in such cases. For example, in *Article 19 v Eritrea* (2007) AHRLR 73 (ACHPR 2007), para. 94:

> "[t]he Eritrean detainees have not been charged, or brought to trial. This in itself constitutes arbitrariness, as the Commission has previously stated. In communication 102/93, the Commission held that, '[w]here individuals have been detained without charges being brought … this constitutes an arbitrary deprivation of their liberty and thus violates article 6.'"

42. Second, the fact that a case can be submitted to the Military Tribunal directly by the State Prosecutor without a preliminary inquiry, violates several rights established in international and regional laws. For example, Article 14(3)(b) ICCPR and Article 7(1)(c) of the African Charter, since it does not allow the accused or his or her legal representative to adequately prepare for the defence because of a lack of information on evidence against the accused. It may also affect the duration of proceedings, as seen in this case, where hearings were adjourned apparently because the prosecution did not have its list of witnesses finalised. This could constitute

6 Section 629(1) CPC: "[w]here a judicial or legal officer is likely to be charged with committing an offence, the competent Procureur General shall request the President of the Supreme Court to appoint an investigating magistrate as well as three other magistrates of a grade at least equal to that of the magistrate incriminated and they shall, if necessary, hear and determine the matter at first instance".

a violation of Article 14(3)(c) ICCPR and Article 7(1)(d) of the African Charter.

43. Third, the broadness of the definition of what constitutes "acts of terrorism" in the Terrorism Law and the wide array of possible offences that would be covered by this Law could lead to arbitrariness in its application. In limitation clauses that allow for the restriction of certain human rights, one requirement is that a restriction must be "provided for by law". In this sense, the United Nations Human Rights Committee has pointed out that "laws" can only be understood as such if they are sufficiently precise. Such precision not only ensures foreseeability, i.e. a citizen can regulate his or her behaviour accordingly because he or she is sufficiently aware of duties and obligations. It also prevents the abuse of vague provisions by State authorities and arbitrariness in the law's application. See, for example:

United Nations Human Rights Committee, General Comment No. 34: Article 19: Freedoms of opinion and expression, U.N. Doc. CCPR/C/GC/34, 12 September 2011

> "[f]or the purposes of paragraph 3 [Article 19 ICCPR], a norm, to be characterized as a "law", must be formulated with sufficient precision to enable an individual to regulate his or her conduct accordingly and it must be made accessible to the public. A law may not confer unfettered discretion for the restriction of freedom of expression on those charged with its execution [...]"

African Commission on Human and Peoples' Rights, Good v Botswana (2010) AHRLR 43 (ACHPR 2010), para. 178:

> "[w]here a government has reason to believe that a citizen or a non-national legally within its territory poses a threat to national security, it should bring evidence before the courts against the person. Not doing so may lead to the possibility of abuse where individuals can be detained or expelled on mere suspicion of being security threats."

Communication 143/95, 150/96, Constitutional Rights Project and Another v Nigeria [(2000) AHRLR 235 (ACHPR 1999)], para 33:

> while [the African Commission] is sympathetic to genuine attempts to maintain public peace, it must note that all too often extreme measures to curtail rights simply create greater unrest. It is dangerous for the protection of human rights for the executive branch of the government to operate without such checks as the judiciary can usually perform.

D. Description Hearing

44. The hearing was opened by the President of the Military Tribunal at 12.14 pm on

27 April 2017. There was an interpreter to provide interpretation from French into English and vice versa. She began interpreting during the first few minutes in a hesitant manner and then stopped after the President appeared to correct her translation. She did not resume her interpretation, except for the submission on the bail application made by the defence team in English, which was translated into French for the judges.

45. The prosecution announced that they have no special submissions to make during the hearing. The prosecution had its witnesses ready, so that the case could be heard on the merits.
46. The President read out the names of all the defendants and each steps forward when his name is called, into the two boxes facing the judges. Felix Agbor Balla, Fontem Neba and Mancho Bibixy are in one box and the 25 other accused in the other box. Since the boxes only have seating for two persons, all accused are standing. The 25 accused are pressed up against each other for lack of space.
47. A lawyer addressed the tribunal saying he represented a civil party who wished to join the proceedings. The defence team challenged the appearance of this lawyer at the tribunal, referring to Rule 47 of the professional rules of conduct, which apparently states that a lawyer cannot act in a case in which another lawyer is the accused, without having obtained authorisation from the President of the Bar Council. The defence team also referred to Section 39 "Relations Between Counsel and Client", subparagraph 3 of Law No. 90/59 of 19 December 1990 to organize practice at the Bar, which establishes that "[i]n the event of an objection […], the advocate shall be bound to prove that he has been briefed by the client".
48. The President read out a letter from the lawyer of the civil party in which he sought the authorisation from the President of the Bar Council. Apparently, the professional rules of conduct state that, if authorisation is not given within 15 days, it must be regarded as having been granted. The President, therefore, accepted that the civil lawyer appeared in these proceedings.
49. The lawyer of the civil party requested an adjournment so that he could inspect the case file. This request was objected to by the defence team saying: "we don't even have access to the case file!". They went on to say that they had asked the prosecution for the file, but were told that it was "his file". The defence team argued that, if the defence lawyer of the civil party indeed represented that party, then his client would have informed him of the facts and the damages incurred. In addition, the defence argued that an adjournment in this case was not provided for by the Criminal Procedure Code, so that the request for adjournment lacked legal basis.
50. The defence team stated that they did not know who the civil party was and what the alleged damages were that they would have incurred, referring to Section 414 of the Criminal Procedure Code.[7] The civil party referred to alleged threats received

7 Section 414 CPC: (1) The prosecution and the civil party shall inform the accused and the person vicariously liable as well as the insurer of the list of their witnesses at least five (5) days before the hearing begins.
(2) The accused, the person vicariously liable and the insurer shall also inform the prosecution and the civil party of the list of their witnesses within the time-limit prescribed in sub-section (1).

by his clients as the reason why they could not be identified.

51. There were some discussions between the lawyer of the civil party and the prosecution, which suggested to the observer that there was some coordination of arguments. Both were seated in the same benches together. The prosecution said that an adjournment was obligatory, referring to the first line of Article 340 of the Criminal Procedure Code.[8] The defence cited the first line in which it is stated that a civil party can join the proceedings at any time before those proceedings end, with reference to Article 385 CPC,[9] and that an adjournment is only necessary if the civil party is absent. The defence argued that this was not the case here, so that the proceedings had to continue. The defence referred to Article 365 of the Criminal Procedure Code, since the prosecution seemed to have its witnesses ready to be heard.[10]
52. The President did not grant an adjournment, apparently without indicating the reasons for that decision. The defence referred to the bail application made on behalf of the accused and wished to make submissions on that application. The Prosecutor and President of the Tribunal said that they had not received the bail application. The defence team referred to the date on which the application was submitted. Copies of the application were eventually handed over to the Prosecution and the Tribunal by the defence.
53. Submissions on the bail application were made by the defence as follows: On 23 March 2017, a bail application was made for Felix Agbor Balla and Fontem Neba. The two men had been in custody since 17 January 2017. The defence counsel

(3) Where the formalities referred to in sub-sections (1) and (2) have not been complied with, the witnesses shall be barred from being heard. However, the court may, with the consent of the parties and of the Legal Department proceed to hear them mention of such consent shall be made in the judgment.

8 Section 340 CPC: (1) A case shall be adjourned whenever the accused or any other party is not present, if from the case-file it is not evident that was duly served with the summons; (2) The same shall apply when an accused on whom personal service has been effected does not appear but gives an acceptable excuse for his absence.

9 Section 385 CPC: (1) Anyone who alleges that he suffered injury as a result of the commission of an offence may make an oral or written application for damages in court.

(2) The civil party shall indicate the damages which he is claiming

(3) Where the victim of an offence has not made an application for damages, the Presiding Magistrate shall ask him if he intends to do so.

(4) The application for damages by a civil party shall be made before the end of the proceedings otherwise it shall be inadmissible.

(5) When a person has applied for damages as a civil party, mention of this fact shall be made in the judgment.

(6) Where the victim of an offence summoned as a civil party does not appear to indicate his claim for damages, the court shall decide on the criminal action only.

In this case, the victim shall retain his right to bring a civil action.

10 Section 365 CPC: (1) Where the accused pleads not guilty, the court shall hear the witnesses for the prosecution and for the civil party in compliance with provisions of sections328 and 330.

(2) At this stage, notwithstanding the provisions of section 361, the Legal Department shall not make any reference to the criminal record of the accused or to any information concerning his character.

(3) If after hearing the witnesses, the submissions of the Legal Department and, where necessary, the observations of the civil party, the court finds that the evidence adduced does not sustain the offence or that the fact do not constitute any offence, it shall discharge the accused.

referred to them as extraordinary men and proceeded to read their curriculum vitae. Counsel said that Cameroon should be proud of these men and not detain them as terrorists. They argued that neither of the defendants had any previous convictions and that the Military Tribunal was under oath to apply the Constitution, which refers to the fact that Cameroon is "[p]roud of [our] linguistic and cultural diversity" and states: "[we] [a]ffirm our attachment to the fundamental freedoms enshrined in the Universal Declaration of Human Rights, the Charter of the United Nations and The African Charter on Human and Peoples' Rights, and all duly ratified international conventions relating thereto." The defence mentioned that the Constitution also refers to the right of presumption of innocence and the right to a fair hearing.

54. The defence went on to state that Article 45 of the Constitution provides that "[d]uly approved or ratified treaties and international agreements shall, following their publication, override national laws, provided the other party implements the said treaty or agreement." In addition, the Criminal Code, Section 2, Ch. 1 establishes that: "[t]his Code and any provision of criminal law shall be subject to the rules of international law and to all treaties duly promulgated and published."

55. The defence stated that no arguments had been made that the continued detention of these two men was essential. Counsel anticipated the prosecution's potential argument that 224(1) and 224(2)[11] CPC determine that bail cannot be granted if the accused are charged with offences punishable by death. However, Section 246 CPC, which refers to judicial supervision, would allow for their release.[12] In addition, international conventions – contrary to Section 224 CPC – make bail possible. The defence referred to the International Covenant on Civil and Political Rights (ICCPR), specifically the right to the presumption of innocence and the right to

11 Section 224 CPC "Conditional Bail": (1) Any person lawfully remanded in custody may be granted bail on condition that he fulfils one of the conditions referred to in section 246 (g), in particular to ensure his appearance either before the judicial police or any judicial authority.
(2) The provisions of sub-section (1) above shal1 not apply 10 persons charged with felonies punishable with life imprisonment or death.

12 Section 246 CPC "Judicial Supervision": The Examining Magistrate may, by a ruling, subject the defendant to judicial supervision or replace such measure, where the defendant is in detention, with one or more of the obligations provided for in sections 41 and 42 of the Penal Code, with one or more of the following:
(a) limit movement to a .specific area determined by the Examining Magistrate; (b) prohibit visit of certain places specified by the Examining Magistrate; (c) to appear when summoned by the authority in charge of supervision and assistance or by any other person appointed by the Examining Magistrate; (d) to abstain from driving all or specified vehicles and, if need be, hand over his driving licence to be registry which shall issue a receipt in acknowledgement thereof; (e) to refrain from receiving certain persons named by the Examining Magistrate and from communicating with them in any from whatsoever; (f) to submit to medical examination, treatment or care, or to be admitted in hospital, especially in case of intoxication and contagious diseases; (g) in order to ensure his appearance he shall: - either deposit a sum of money, the amount and conditions of payment of which shall be fixed by the Examining Magistrate, taking into consideration the resources of the defendant; - or provide one or more sureties in accordance with the provisions of sections 224 and following;
(h) to refrain from carrying out certain professional activities if the offence was committed within the scope or in the course of his professional duties, and if the Examining Magistrate is of the opinion that the continuation of those activities may cause him to commit another offence.

peaceful assembly. The Constitution establishes that the ICCPR is applicable in Cameroon. In addition, with reference to the jurisprudence of the African Court and Commission on Human and Peoples' Rights, it cannot–in good faith–be said that release cannot be considered for Felix Agbor Balla and Fontem Neba.

56. The defence referred to General Comment No. 35, para. 38 of the United Nations Human Rights Committee, as well as to the Tokyo Rules and stated that Section 224(2) CPC is not compatible with Article 9 ICCPR (right to liberty and security of person). They argued that particular groups should not be given preference over others and that it does not only regard the case of these two men. Rather, this case provides a possibility to give effect to the rule of law in Cameroon. Articles 246 and 224 CPC establish a presumption in favour of liberty. Moreover, judicial supervision had been used in other cases in which the accused were charged with the same offences, such as that of Justice Sokem Ngale Mborh. He was released and kept under supervision; under house arrest.
57. Upon request of the defence counsel, the President agreed that Felix Agbor and Fontem Neba could be seated in the box. The other 25 defendants were led back into the benches in the public gallery by a prison guard and were seated. At this time, three hours had passed, during which the accused stood in the heat, 25 persons pressed into a small box against each other, without food or water.
58. Further submissions on bail were made by other members of the defence team. Reference was made to the possibility to grant bail in Article 301 CPC,[13] that there were no exceptional circumstances that justified prolonged detention, and that the two men were detained from 17 January until 27 April, so that their detention lasted for more than three months. A member of the defence team read out the names of the other 26 accused and stated that all submissions made regarding the bail application for Felix Agbor Balla and Fontem Neba, should also be applied by the Tribunal to the bail application for these accused.
59. The prosecution distributed what appeared to be some bars of chocolate to the members of the Tribunal, the prosecution, and some members of the defence team.
60. A member of the defence team said that the 26 other defendants were laymen, students and journalists, "men of the street" who also had a right to be free and to be presumed innocent. Reference was made to the fact that there was no list of witnesses of the prosecution for these accused and that it was not clear which offences they had been charged with. She also referred to the fact that one accused had a medical condition and that in that condition he should not be in prison. She handed over medical records to the President of the Tribunal. The defence argued that some of these accused had been beaten for days and that it was not clear why they would represent a flight risk, given that many of them were farmers. They had already been in detention for 4 to 5 months. No exceptional circumstances were

13 Section 301 CPC: (1) Where a case is not ready for hearing, the court shall adjourn it to its very next sitting and may order the release of the accused on bail, with or without sureties. The court may also order judicial supervision; (2) Where the case is ready for hearing, the court shall proceed in accordance with the provisions of sections 302 and following.

argued to justify their detention. Although some were from Douala, Bamenda and Buea, they were accused of committing offences in Bamenda. The defence team said that the prosecution did not have a valid case against all of these accused.

61. The prosecution did not make substantive submissions on the bail application, arguing that they had not seen it before. The President of the Tribunal adjourned the case to 24 May 2017, supposedly to hear the prosecution's arguments on the bail application and to decide on that application.
62. The hearing closed at approximately 4.15 pm.

V. Rights that Appear to Have Been Violated

63. The observation of the hearing on 27 April 2017 gave rise to some concerns about rights of the defendants that seem to have been violated. In the following paragraphs, the national, regional, and international standards applicable to those rights are referred to. In Part VII, the facts as observed during the hearing (see Part IV.4) will be assessed with reference to these standards to determine whether any violations of national, regional, and international standards have occurred.

A. *Right to Fair Trial*

64. Prior to setting out the applicable standards on the elements of the right to a fair trial that appear to have been violated in this case, namely: (i) the right to an independent and impartial tribunal, (ii) the right to defence (access to the case file), (iii) the right to an interpreter, and (iv) the right to be tried without undue delay, it is important to highlight two other aspects of the right to a fair trial.
65. First, a violation of the right to a fair trial in a case where the defendant is charged with offences carrying the death penalty, implies a violation of the right to life and may entail–as a remedy – the release of the accused. Second, fair trial rights are non-derogable in a situation of internal political instability or public emergency, under the Principles and Guidelines on the Right to a Fair Trial and Legal Assistance in Africa. The African Commission on Human and Peoples' Rights has established that no right contained in the African Charter is derogable in states of emergency and must, therefore, be adhered to by Sates Parties.
66. Under the International Covenant on Civil and Political Rights, the United Nations Human Rights Committee has established that - although the right to a fair trial is not included as a non-derogable right - any trial leading to the possible imposition of the death penalty in a state of emergency should comply with all the requirements of the right to a fair trial, because the right to life is non-derogable.

National Law

Constitution of the Republic of Cameroon, preamble
"[t]he law shall ensure the right of every person to a fair hearing before the courts".
Constitution of the Republic of Cameroon, Article 65
"[t]he preamble shall be part and parcel of this Constitution".

International and Regional Law

United Nations Human Rights Committee, General Comment No. 32, Article 14: Right to equality before courts and tribunals and to a fair trial, U.N. Doc. CCPR/C/GC/32 (2007), para. 59

> In cases of trials leading to the imposition of the death penalty scrupulous respect of the guarantees of fair trial is particularly important. The imposition of a sentence of death upon conclusion of a trial, in which the provisions of article 14 of the Covenant have not been respected, constitutes a violation of the right to life (article 6 of the Covenant).[14]

United Nations Human Rights Committee Munguwambuto Kabwe Peter Mwamba v. Zambia, CCPR/C/98/D/1520/2006, 30 April 2010, para. 6.7

> [t]he Committee recalls that the imposition of a sentence of death upon conclusion of a trial in which the provisions of the Covenant have not been respected constitutes a violation of article 6 of the Covenant. In the present case, the author's death sentence was imposed, in violation of the right to a fair trial, as guaranteed by article 14 of the Covenant, and therefore also in violation of article 6 of the Covenant.

United Nations Human Rights Committee, Paul Kelly v. Jamaica, Communication No. 253/1987, U.N. Doc. CCPR/C/41/D/253/1987 at 60 (1991), para. 7

> [i]t is the view of the Committee that, in capital punishment cases, States parties have an imperative duty to observe rigorously all the guarantees for a fair trial set out in article 14 of the Covenant. The Committee is of the view that Mr. Paul Kelly, victim of a violation of article 14, paragraph 3 (c) and (d) and 5 of the Covenant, is entitled to a remedy entailing his release.

African Commission on Human and Peoples' Rights, Principles and Guidelines on the Right to a Fair Trial and Legal Assistance in Africa

"R. NON-DEGORABILITY CLAUSE

> No circumstances whatsoever, whether a threat of war, a state of international or internal armed conflict, internal political instability or any other public emergency, may be invoked to justify derogations from the right to a fair trial."

14 E.g. communications No. 1044/2002, *Shakurova v. Tajikistan*, para. 8.5 (violation of art. 14 para. 1 and 3 (b), (d) and (g)); No. 915/2000, *Ruzmetov v. Uzbekistan*, para.7.6 (violation of art. 14, para. 1, 2 and 3 (b), (d), (e) and (g)); No. 913/2000, *Chan v. Guyana*, para. 5.4 (violation of art. 14 para. 3 (b) and (d)); No. 1167/2003, *Rayos v. Philippines*, para. 7.3 (violation of art. 14 para. 3(b)).

African Commission on Human and Peoples' Rights Communication 74/92, Commission Nationale des Droits de l'Homme et des Libertés v Chad [**(2000) AHRLR 66 (ACHPR 1995)**], para 21

> The African Charter, unlike other human rights instruments, does not allow for states parties to derogate from their treaty obligations during emergency situations. Thus, even a civil war in Chad cannot be used as an excuse by the State violating or permitting violations of rights in the African Charter.

United Nations Human Rights Committee, General Comment No. 32, Article 14: Right to equality before courts and tribunals and to a fair trial, U.N. Doc. CCPR/C/GC/32 (2007), para. 6.

> [w]hile article 14 is not included in the list of non-derogable rights of article 4, paragraph 2 of the Covenant, States derogating from normal procedures required under article 14 in circumstances of a public emergency should ensure that such derogations do not exceed those strictly required by the exigencies of the actual situation. The guarantees of fair trial may never be made subject to measures of derogation that would circumvent the protection of non-derogable rights. Thus, for example, as article 6 of the Covenant is non-derogable in its entirety, any trial leading to the imposition of the death penalty during a state of emergency must conform to the provisions of the Covenant, including all the requirements of article 14.[15] Deviating from fundamental principles of fair trial, including the presumption of innocence, is prohibited at all times.[16]

1. *Right to an Independent and Impartial Tribunal*

67. See Annex A for the letter of the Law Society of 13 February 2017 on military jurisdiction over civilians and additional regional and international standards.

National Law

Constitution of the Republic of Cameroon, Article 37(3):

> [t]he President of the Republic shall guarantee the independence of judicial power. He shall appoint members of the bench and for the legal department.

Military Justice Code, Section 5(1):

15 General comment No. 29 (2001) on article 4: Derogations during a state of emergency, para. 15.
16 General comment No. 29 (2001) on article 4: Derogations during a state of emergency, para. 11.

[t]he President, Vice-Presidents, Assessors, Examining Magistrates, the State Prosecutor and Deputy State Prosecutors shall be appointed by decree of the Head of State.

Military Justice Code, Section 12(8):

[t]he state prosecutor shall act under the authority of the minister in charge of military justice whose subordinate he is.

Regional law

African Charter on Human and Peoples' Rights, Article 7(1)(d):

[e]very individual shall have the right to have his cause heard. This comprises: [...] (d) the right to be tried within a reasonable time by an impartial court or tribunal.

African Charter on Human and Peoples' Rights, Article 26:

[s]tates parties to the present Charter shall have the duty to guarantee the independence of the Courts [...]

African Commission on Human and Peoples' Rights, Principles and Guidelines on the Right to a Fair Trial and Legal Assistance in Africa

A.4 a) The independence of judicial bodies and judicial officers shall be guaranteed by the constitution and laws of the country and respected by the government, its agencies and authorities; [...] e) Military or other special tribunals that do not use the duly established procedure of the legal process shall not be created to displace the jurisdiction belonging to the ordinary judicial bodies; [...] g) All judicial bodies shall be independent from the executive branch.

African Commission on Human and Peoples' Rights Mauritania: Malawi African Association and Others v Mauritania (2000) AHRLR 149 (ACHPR 2000)

98. The section responsible for matters relating to state security in the special tribunal is headed by a senior military officer who is not required to have a legal training. He is assisted by two assessors, both military men. The special tribunal is itself presided over by an army officer. In the joint procedure on communications 139/94, 154/96 and 161/97 [International Pen and Others (on behalf of Saro-Wiwa) v Nigeria, paragraph 86], the Commission reached the conclusion that the 'special tribunals violate

> article 7(1)(d) of the African Charter because their composition is at the discretion of the executive branch'. Withdrawing criminal procedure from the competence of the courts established within the judicial order and conferring it to an extension of the executive necessarily compromises the impartiality of the courts, to which the African Charter refers. Independent of the qualities of the persons sitting in such jurisdictions, their very existence constitutes a violation of the principles of impartiality and independence of the judiciary and, thereby, of article 7(1)(d).
>
> 99. Article 26 of the Charter states that: 'States parties to the present Charter shall have the duty to guarantee the independence of the courts...'

100. By establishing a section responsible for matters relating to state security within the special tribunal, the Mauritanian state was reneging on its duty to guarantee the independence of the courts. The Commission therefore concludes that there has been a violation of article 26.

International law

International Covenant on Civil and Political Rights, Article 14(1):

> [a]ll persons shall be equal before the courts and tribunals. In the determination of any criminal charge against him, or of his rights and obligations in a suit at law, everyone shall be entitled to a fair and public hearing by a competent, independent and impartial tribunal established by law [...]

United Nations Human Rights Committee, General Comment No. 32, Article 14: Right to equality before courts and tribunals and to a fair trial, U.N. Doc. CCPR/C/GC/32 (2007):

> 19. "[t]he requirement of competence, independence and impartiality of a tribunal in the sense of article 14, paragraph 1, is an absolute right that is not subject to any exception.[17] The requirement of independence refers, in particular, to the procedure and qualifications for the appointment of judges, and guarantees relating to their security of tenure until a mandatory retirement age or the expiry of their term of office, where such exist, the conditions governing promotion, transfer, suspension and cessation of their functions, and the actual independence of the judiciary from political interference by the executive branch and legislature.
>
> 22. The provisions of article 14 apply to all courts and tribunals within the scope of that article whether ordinary or specialized, civilian or military. The Committee notes the existence, in many countries, of military or

17 Communication No. 263/1987, *Gonzalez del Rio v. Peru*, para. 5.2.

special courts which try civilians. While the Covenant does not prohibit the trial of civilians in military or special courts, it requires that such trials are in full conformity with the requirements of article 14 and that its guarantees cannot be limited or modified because of the military or special character of the court concerned. The Committee also notes that the trial of civilians in military or special courts may raise serious problems as far as the equitable, impartial and independent administration of justice is concerned. Therefore, it is important to take all necessary measures to ensure that such trials take place under conditions which genuinely afford the full guarantees stipulated in article 14. Trials of civilians by military or special courts should be exceptional,18 i.e. limited to cases where the State party can show that resorting to such trials is necessary and justified by objective and serious reasons, and where with regard to the specific class of individuals and offences at issue the regular civilian courts are unable to undertake the trials.[19]

25. The notion of fair trial includes the guarantee of a fair and public hearing. Fairness of proceedings entails the absence of any direct or indirect influence, pressure or intimidation or intrusion from whatever side and for whatever motive.

United Nations Human Rights Committee, Abdelhakim Wanis El Abani v. Libya, CCPR/C/99/D/1640/2007, 14 September 2010, para. 7.8

[t]he Committee also notes that Mr. El Abani was tried by a military court even though he was a civilian, having served as a civil judge at the Benghazi court of first instance. The Committee recalls its general comment No. 32 (2007), in which it states that, while the Covenant does not prohibit the trial of civilians in military courts, nevertheless such trials should be exceptional and take place under conditions which genuinely afford the full guarantees stipulated in article 14. It is incumbent upon a State party that does try civilians before military courts to justify the practice. The Committee considers that the State party must demonstrate, with regard to the specific class of individuals at issue, that the regular civilian courts are unable to undertake the trials, that other alternative forms of special or high-security civilian courts are not up to the task and that recourse to military courts ensures the full protection of the rights of the accused pursuant to article 14. In the present case, the State party has failed to comment on the need to have recourse to a military court. The Committee

18 Also see Convention relative to the Protection of Civilian Persons in Time of War of 12 August 1949, art. 64 and general comment No. 31 (2004) on the *Nature of the General Legal Obligation Imposed on States Parties to the Covenant*, para. 11.
19 See communication No. 1172/2003, *Madani v. Algeria*, para. 8.7.

therefore concludes that the trial and sentencing of the author's father to 13 years' imprisonment by a military court discloses a violation of article 14, paragraphs 1 and 3 (a) to (d), of the Covenant.

United Nations Human Rights Committee Ebenezer Derek Mbongo Akwanga v. Cameroon, CCPR/C/101/D/1813/2008, 19 May 2011, para. 7.5

[t]he Committee notes the State party's argument that the author's trial was conducted according to the legislation in force and that he benefited from an official interpreter during the hearings. It also notes the author's argument that the court was not independent, that he had little opportunity to communicate with his lawyer, who had no access to the indictment and was therefore not able to prepare his defence adequately, and that the written evidence on which the indictment was based was not produced in court.

The Committee recalls its general comment No. 32, in which it considers that the State party must demonstrate, with regard to the specific class of individuals at issue, that the regular civilian courts are unable to undertake the trials, that other alternative forms of special or high-security civilian courts are inadequate for the task and that recourse to military courts is unavoidable. The State party must further demonstrate how military courts ensure the full protection of the rights of the accused pursuant to article 14.

In the present case, the State party has not shown why recourse to a military court was required. In commenting on the gravity of the charges against the author, it has not indicated why the ordinary civilian courts or other alternative forms of civilian court were inadequate for the task of trying him. Nor does the mere invocation of conduct of the military trial in accordance with domestic legal provisions constitute an argument under the Covenant in support of recourse to such courts. The State party's failure to demonstrate the need to rely on a military court in this case means that the Committee need not examine whether the military court, as a matter of fact, afforded the full guarantees of article 14. The Committee concludes that the trial and sentencing of the author by a military court discloses a violation of article 14 of the Covenant.

United Nations Basic Principles on the Independence of the Judiciary

1. The independence of the judiciary shall be guaranteed by the State and enshrined in the Constitution or the law of the country. It is the duty of all governmental and other institutions to respect and observe the independence of the judiciary.

> 2. The judiciary shall decide matters before them impartially, on the basis of facts and in accordance with the law, without any restrictions, improper influences, inducements, pressures, threats or interferences, direct or indirect, from any quarter or for any reason.

United Nations Guidelines on the Role of Prosecutors, Adopted by the Eighth United Nations Congress on the Prevention of Crime and the Treatment of Offenders, Havana, 27 August to 7 September 1990

> 4. States shall ensure that prosecutors are able to perform their professional functions without intimidation, hindrance, harassment, improper interference or unjustified exposure to civil, penal or other liability.
>
> 10. The office of prosecutors shall be strictly separated from judicial functions.

2. *Right to Defence (Access to the Case File)*

National law

Constitution of the Republic of Cameroon, preamble

> every accused person is presumed innocent until found guilty during a hearing conducted in strict compliance with the rights of defence.

Criminal Procedure Code, Section 165(5)(a) "Preliminary Inquiry"

> [t]he Legal Department may request to be given certified true copies of the record of proceedings by the registrar of the inquiry. (b) The other parties may also, at their request and upon payment of the required fees, be given copies of any document of the proceedings.

Criminal Procedure Code, Section 171:

> where counsel for the defendant is present during the first appearance, the Examining Magistrate shall not be bound to give the case file of the inquiry to him in advance.

Criminal Procedure Code, Section 172(3)

> [t]he case file of the inquiry shall be placed at the disposal of the counsel at the chambers of the inquiry twenty-four (24) hours before each interrogation or confrontation.

Regional law

African Charter on Human and Peoples' Rights, Article 7(1)(c):

> [e]very individual shall have the right to have his cause heard. This comprises: [...] (c) the right to defense, including the right to be defended by counsel of his choice.

African Commission on Human and Peoples' Rights, Principles and Guidelines on the Right to a Fair Trial and Legal Assistance in Africa

> N. Provisions applicable to Proceedings Relating to Criminal Charges
> 3) Right to adequate time and facilities for the preparation of a defence:
> E [...] (iii) The accused or the accused's defence counsel has a right to all relevant information held by the prosecution that could help the accused exonerate him or herself [...]
> (iv) It is the duty of the competent authorities to ensure lawyers access to appropriate information, files and documents in their possession or control in sufficient time to enable lawyers to provide effective legal assistance to their clients. Such access should be provided at the earliest appropriate time.
> (v) The accused has a right to consult legal materials reasonably necessary for the preparation of his or her defence.

International Law

International Covenant on Civil and Political Rights

> 14. 3. In the determination of any criminal charge against him, everyone shall be entitled to the following minimum guarantees, in full equality: [...] (b) To have adequate time and facilities for the preparation of his defence and to communicate with counsel of his own choosing.

United Nations Human Rights Committee, General Comment No. 32, Article 14: Right to equality before courts and tribunals and to a fair trial, U.N. Doc. CCPR/C/GC/32, 23 August 2007:

> 32. "[s]ubparagraph 3 (b) provides that accused persons must have adequate time and facilities for the preparation of their defence and to communicate with counsel of their own choosing. This provision is an important element of the guarantee of a fair trial and an application of the principle of equality of arms."

> 33. "'Adequate facilities' must include access to documents and other

> evidence; this access must include all materials[20] that the prosecution plans to offer in court against the accused or that are exculpatory."
> 8. The right to equality before courts and tribunals, in general terms, guarantees, in addition to the principles mentioned in the second sentence of Article 14, paragraph 1, those of equal access and equality of arms, and ensures that the parties to the proceedings in question are treated without any discrimination.
> 13. The right to equality before courts and tribunals also ensures equality of arms. This means that the same procedural rights are to be provided to all the parties unless distinctions are based on law and can be justified on objective and reasonable grounds, not entailing actual disadvantage or other unfairness to the defendant.[21]

United Nations Human Rights Committee, Pierre Désiré Engo v. Cameroon, CCPR/C/96/D/1397/2005, 17 August 2009, para. 7.7

> [t]he Committee notes that the author claims to have waited several months to be informed of the charges against him and to be given access to the case file. The State party failed to reply specifically to this point and merely states that the author had access to all the material in the case, without adducing any evidence. In this respect, the Committee finds a violation of article 14, paragraph 3 (a).

United Nations Human Rights Committee, Abdool Saleem Yasseen and Noel Thomas v. Republic of Guyana, Communication No. 676/1996, U.N. Doc. CCPR/C/62/D/676/1996, 31 March 1998, para. 7.10

> [w]ith regard to the missing diaries and notebooks, the Committee notes that the authors claim that these may have contained exculpatory evidence. The State party has failed to address this allegation. In the absence of any explanation by the State party, the Committee considers that due weight must be given to the authors' allegations, and that the failure to produce at the last trial (1992) police documents which were produced at the first trial (1988) and which may have contained evidence in favour of the authors, constitutes a violation of article 14, paragraph 3, (b) and (e), since it may have impeded the authors in preparation of their defence.

United Nations Human Rights Committee, Ramazan Esergepov v. Kazakhstan, CCPR/C/116/D/2129/2012, 4 May 2016, para. 11.4

20 See concluding observations, Canada, CCPR/C/CAN/CO/5 (2005), para. 13.
21 Communication No. 1347/2005, *Dudko v. Australia*, para. 7.4.

> [t]he Committee also notes the author's claim that owing to the restricted access to the majority of the documents related to his case, the author was deprived of his right to prepare his defence. The Committee observes that the State party in its submission has confirmed that the author was provided only with a redacted version of the indictment. The Committee recalls that "adequate facilities" within the meaning of article 14 (3) (b) must include access to documents and other evidence; this access must include all materials that the prosecution plans to offer in court.[22] [...] even if the lawyer had full access to the prosecution evidence, the author himself lacked information permitting him to instruct his lawyer and to refute the criminal charges against him.23 The Committee considers that the facts before it disclose a violation of the author's rights under article 14 (3) (b) of the Covenant.

United Nations Human Rights Committee, Khoroshenko v. Russian Federation, Communication No. 1304/2004, 29 April 2011, para. 9.7

> [t]he Committee notes the author's claims that he was not given adequate time and facilities to prepare his defence [...] that he did not receive copy of the trial's records immediately after the first instance verdict was issued, that despite numerous requests, he was not given some documents, he considered relevant for his defence, [...] the Committee finds a violation of article 14, paragraph 3 (b), of the Covenant.

3. *Right to an Interpreter*

National law

Criminal Procedure Code, Section 354:

> (1) Where an accused speaks a language other than one of the official language understood by the members of the court, or where it is necessary to translate any document produced in court, the Presiding Magistrate shall of his own motion appoint an interpreter of not less than twenty-one (21) years of age, who shall take oath to interpret faithfully the testimonies of persons speaking in different languages or faithfully translate the document in question.
>
> (2) The parties may recuse the interpreter. In this case, the court shall rule immediately on the recusal and such ruling shall not be subject to appeal.

22 See general comment 32, para. 33.

23 See communication No. 1937/2010, *Leghaei et al. v. Australia*, Views adopted on 26 March 2015, para. 10.4.

Criminal Procedure Code, Section 355:

(1) When an interpreter does not give a true and faithful interpretation, any party to the proceedings may point this out and move the court to have the interpreter replaced.

(2) The court may also of its own motion, point out an interpretation which is not true and faithful and shall proceed to replace the interpreter after having heard the parties.

Criminal Procedure Code, Section 356:

[t]he Registrar in attendance, the parties or the witnesses, shall not, even with the consent of the accused, perform the functions of the interpreter.

Regional law

African Commission on Human and Peoples' Rights, Principles and Guidelines on the Right to a Fair Trial and Legal Assistance in Africa

A.2 Fair Hearing

The essential elements of a fair hearing include: a) equality of arms between the parties to proceedings, whether they be administrative, civil, criminal, or military; b) equality of all persons before any judicial body without any distinction whatsoever as regards race, colour, ethnic origin, sex, gender, age, religion, creed, language, political or other convictions, national or social origin, means, disability, birth, status or other circumstances; [...] e) adequate opportunity to prepare a case, present arguments and evidence and to challenge or respond to opposing arguments or evidence; [...] g) an entitlement to the assistance of an interpreter if he or she cannot understand or speak the language used in or by the judicial body [...].

African Commission on Human and Peoples' Rights, Principles and Guidelines on the Right to a Fair Trial and Legal Assistance in Africa

N 4) The right to an interpreter:

a) The accused has the right to the free assistance of an interpreter if he or she cannot understand or speak the language used before the judicial body. b) The right to an interpreter does not extend to the right to express oneself in the language of one's choice if the accused or the defence witness is sufficiently proficient in the language of the judicial body. c) The right to an interpreter applies at all stages of the proceedings, including pre-trial proceedings. d) The right to an interpreter applies to written as well as oral proceedings. The right extends to translation or interpretation of all documents or statements necessary for the defendant to understand the proceedings or assist in the preparation of a defence. e) The interpretation or translation provided shall be adequate to permit the accused to understand the proceedings and for the judicial body to understand the testimony of the accused or defence witnesses. f) The right to interpretation or translation cannot be qualified by a requirement that the accused pay for the costs of an interpreter or translator. Even if the accused is convicted, he or she cannot be required to pay for the costs of interpretation or translation.

African Commission on Human and Peoples' Rights, Mauritania: Malawi African Association and Others v Mauritania (2000) AHRLR 149 (ACHPR 2000), para. 97.

> [t]he right to defence should also be interpreted as including the right to understand the charges being brought against oneself. In the trial regarding [...], only three of the 21 accused persons spoke Arabic fluently, and this was the language used during the trial. This means that the 18 others did not have the right to defend themselves; this also constitutes a violation of article 7(1)(c).

International Law

International Covenant on Civil and Political Rights, Article 14.3(f):

> In the determination of any criminal charge against him, everyone shall be entitled to the following minimum guarantees, in full equality: .... (f) To have the free assistance of an interpreter if he cannot understand or speak the language used in court.

United Nations Human Rights Committee, General Comment No. 32, Article 14: Right to equality before courts and tribunals and to a fair trial, U.N. Doc. CCPR/C/GC/32 23 August 2007, para. 13

> [t]he right to equality before courts and tribunals also ensures equality of arms. This means that the same procedural rights are to be provided to all the parties unless distinctions are based on law and can be justified on objective and reasonable grounds, not entailing actual disadvantage or other unfairness to the defendant. In exceptional cases, it also might require that the free assistance of an interpreter be provided where otherwise an indigent party could not participate in the proceedings on equal terms or witnesses produced by it be examined.

United Nations Human Rights Committee, General Comment No. 32, Article 14: Right to equality before courts and tribunals and to a fair trial, U.N. Doc. CCPR/C/GC/32, 23 August 2007, para. 31.

> [t]he right of all persons charged with a criminal offence to be informed promptly and in detail in a language which they understand of the nature and cause of criminal charges brought against them, enshrined in paragraph 3(a), is the first of the minimum guarantees in criminal proceedings of article 14.

United Nations Human Rights Committee, General Comment No. 32, Article 14: Right to equality before courts and tribunals and to a fair trial, U.N. Doc. CCPR/C/GC/32, 23 August 2007, para. 40.

> [t]he right to have the free assistance of an interpreter if the accused cannot understand or speak the language used in court as provided for by article 14, paragraph 3(f) enshrines another aspect of the principles of fairness and equality of arms in criminal proceedings.[24] This right arises at all stages of the oral proceedings.

United Nations Body of Principles for the Protection of all persons under any form of detention or imprisonment, Principle 14:

> [a] person who does not adequately understand or speak the language used by the authorities responsible for his arrest, detention or imprisonment is entitled to receive promptly in a language which he understands the information referred to in principle 10, principle 11, paragraph 2, principle 12, paragraph 1, and principle 13 and to have the assistance, free of charge, if necessary, of an interpreter in connection with legal proceedings subsequent to his arrest.

United Nations Human Rights Committee, Charles Gurmurkh Sobhraj v. Nepal, CCPR/C/99/D/1870/2009, 11 August 2010, para. 7.2

> [h]e was not afforded the free assistance of an interpreter during the court's proceedings as well as when the judgement was handed down. As the author can neither read, nor understand, nor write Nepali, he could not understand the issues raised during the hearings of the First Instance Court and was therefore unable to prepare his defence, call his witnesses or confront the prosecution witnesses. Considering that the State party has not commented on that allegation, the Committee must give due

24 Communication No. 219/1986, *Guesdon v. France*, para. 10.2.

consideration to the allegations submitted by the author. It refers to its general comment No 32, where it stated that the right to have the free assistance of an interpreter if the accused cannot understand or speak the language used in court as provided for by article 14, paragraph 3(f) enshrines another aspect of the principles of fairness and equality of arms in criminal proceedings.[25]

The importance of this principle has also been emphasized in the Committee's jurisprudence where it considered that the right to a fair trial implies that the accused be allowed, in criminal proceedings to express himself in the language in which he normally expresses himself, and that the denial of an interpreter constitutes a violation of article 14, paragraph 3(e) and (f).26 In the present case, the Committee considers that the author's lack of access to an interpreter from the time of arrest and during the District Court hearings, as well as the lack of access to a lawyer at the initial phase of the procedure, not only violates the two provisions cited above but also violates the right to a defence, under article 14, paragraph 3(a), (b) and (d), of the Covenant.

United Nations Human Rights Committee, Nallaratnam Singarasa v. Sri Lanka, Communication No. 1033/2001, U.N. Doc. CCPR/C/81/D/1033/2001 (2004), para. 7.2

[a]s to the claim of a violation of article 14, paragraph 3(f), due to the absence of an external interpreter during the author's alleged confession, the Committee notes that this provision provides for the right to an interpreter during the court hearing only, a right which was granted to the author. However, as clearly appears from the court proceedings, the confession took place in the sole presence of the two investigating officers – the Assistant Superintendent of Police and the Police Constable; the latter typed the statement and provided interpretation between Tamil and Sinhalese. The Committee concludes that the author was denied a fair trial in accordance with article 14, paragraph 1, of the Covenant by solely relying on a confession obtained in such circumstances.

United Nations Human Rights Committee, Omar Faruk Bozbey v. Turkmenistan, Communication No. 1530/2006, U.N. Doc. CCPR/C/100/D/1530/2006 (2010), para. 7.2

[t]he Committee takes note of the author's claim, not contested by the

25 Ibid., para. 40.

26 Communication No. 219/1986, *Guesdon v. France*, Views adopted on 25 July 1990, para. 10.2. See a contrario communications No. 221/1987 and 323/1988, *Cadoret v. France* and *Le Bihan v. France*, Views adopted on 11 April 1991, paras. 5.7.

State party, that all court proceedings were conducted and the verdict was delivered in the Turkmen language, which he did not understand. The Committee considers that not providing the author with an interpreter when he could not understand and speak the language used in court, constitutes a violation of article 14, paragraph 1 read in conjunction with article 14, paragraph 3(f) of the Covenant.

4. *Right to be Tried Without Undue Delay*

National law

Criminal Procedure Code, Section 340:

(1) A case shall be adjourned whenever the accused or any other party is not present, if from the case-file it is not evident that was duly served with the summons.

(2) The same shall apply when an accused on whom personal service has been effected does not appear but gives an acceptable excuse for his absence.

Criminal Procedure Code, Section 341:

[a]n adjournment shall be at the discretion of the court when the other person summoned are absent or when any of the parties applies for it.

Criminal Procedure Code, Section 342:

[t]he Presiding Magistrate who order an adjournment shall, in a loud voice, announce the reason thereof and the date for the next hearing.

Criminal Procedure Code, Section 384(1):

[i]n the hearing cannot be finished in one sitting, the Presiding Magistrate shall adjourn it and announce the clay and hour when it shall resume.

Criminal Procedure Code, Section 388(1):

[j]udgment shall either be delivered immediately or in the next fifteen (15) days after the hearing closed. When the matter is adjourned for judgment, the Presiding Magistrate shall inform the parties of the day when it shall be delivered.

Military Justice Code, Section 20:

> [j]udgments of the military tribunal shall:
> Be deliver[ed] immediately or within 15 days of the conclusion of proceedings, where the hearing takes place at the seat of the court, and 30 days in circuit court.
> Be written before they are delivered

Set out the reasons upon which they are based in fact and in law, under pain of being null and void.

Regional law

African Commission on Human and Peoples' Rights, Principles and Guidelines on the Right to a Fair Trial and Legal Assistance in Africa

> A2 Fair Hearing:
> [...] i) an entitlement to a determination of their rights and obligations without undue delay and with adequate notice of and reasons for the decisions.

African Commission on Human and Peoples' Rights, Principles and Guidelines on the Right to a Fair Trial and Legal Assistance in Africa

> N. 5) Right to trial without undue delay:
>
> a) Every person charged with a criminal offence has the right to a trial without undue delay. b) The right to a trial without undue delay means the right to a trial which produces a final judgement and, if appropriate a sentence without undue delay. c) Factors relevant to what constitutes undue delay include the complexity of the case, the conduct of the parties, the conduct of other relevant authorities, whether an accused is detained pending proceedings, and the interest of the person at stake in the proceedings.

African Commission on Human and Peoples' Rights, Communication Article 19 v. Eritrea (2007) AHRLR 73 (ACHPR 2007)

> 98. [...] it must be borne in mind that states parties cannot derogate from the Charter in times of war or any other emergency situation. Even if it is assumed that the restriction placed by the Charter on the ability to derogate goes against international principles, there are certain rights such as the right to life, the right to a fair trial, and the right to freedom from torture and cruel, inhuman and degrading treatment, that cannot be derogated from for any reason, in whatever circumstances.
>
> 99. [...] a backlog of cases awaiting trial cannot excuse unreasonable

delays, as the European Court of Human Rights has held. Further, in the case of Albert Mukong, referred to above, the Human Rights Committee stated that states parties to the ICCPR must observe certain minimum standards as regards the condition of detention, regardless of their state of development. The Commission considers that the same principle applies to the length of detention before trial, and that states parties to the Charter cannot rely on the political situation existing within their territory or a large number of cases pending before the courts to justify excessive delay.

International Law

International Covenant on Civil and Political Rights, Article 14(3)(c)

[i]n the determination of any criminal charge against him, everyone shall be entitled to the following minimum guarantees, in full equality: [...] (c) To be tried without undue delay.

United Nations Human Rights Committee, General Comment No. 32, Article 14: Right to equality before courts and tribunals and to a fair trial, U.N. Doc. CCPR/C/GC/32, 23 August 2007.

27. [a]n important aspect of the fairness of a hearing is its expeditiousness.

35. The right of the accused to be tried without undue delay, provided for by article 14, paragraph 3(c), is not only designed to avoid keeping persons too long in a state of uncertainty about their fate and, if held in detention during the period of the trial, to ensure that such deprivation of liberty does not last longer than necessary in the circumstances of the specific case, but also to serve the interests of justice.

What is reasonable has to be assessed in the circumstances of each case, taking into account mainly the complexity of the case, the conduct of the accused, and the manner in which the matter was dealt with by the administrative and judicial authorities. In cases where the accused are denied bail by the court, they must be tried as expeditiously as possible.[27] This guarantee relates not only to the time between the formal charging of the accused and the time by which a trial should commence, but also the time until the final judgement on appeal.[28] All stages, whether in first instance or on appeal must take place 'without undue delay'."

27 Communication No. 818/1998, *Sextus v. Trinidad and Tobago*, para. 7.2. *Ali Medjnoune v. Algeria*, Communication No. 1297/2004, U.N. Doc. CCPR/C/87/D/1297/2004 (2006), para. 8.9

28 Communications No. 1089/2002, *Rouse v. Philippines*, para.7.4; No. 1085/2002, *Taright, Touadi, Remli and Yousfi v. Algeria*, para. 8.5.

63. The way criminal proceedings are handled may affect the exercise and enjoyment of rights and guarantees of the Covenant unrelated to article 14. Thus, for instance, to keep pending, for several years, indictments for the criminal offence of defamation brought against a journalist for having published certain articles, in violation of article 14, paragraph 3(c), may leave the accused in a situation of uncertainty and intimidation and thus have a chilling effect which unduly restricts the exercise of his right to freedom of expression (article 19 of the Covenant).[29] Similarly, delays of criminal proceedings for several years in contravention of article 14, paragraph 3(c), may violate the right of a person to leave one's own country as guaranteed in article 12, paragraph 2 of the Covenant, if the accused has to remain in that country as long as proceedings are pending."[30]

Charles Gurmurkh Sobhraj v. Nepal, CCPR/C/99/D/1870/2009, 11 August 2010, para. 7.4

[o]n the length of the proceedings, the Committee notes the author's argument that from 26 March 2006 until 23 April 2010, 41 hearings have been scheduled which do not include the hearings which were either postponed or cancelled prior to these dates. The Committee also notes that most court hearings were allegedly cancelled or postponed at the last minute and without reasons being provided. The State party has not provided any information on the reason for such delays. The Committee refers to its jurisprudence, where it stated that the right of the accused to be tried without undue delay relates not only to the time between the formal charging of the accused and the time by which a trial should commence, but also the time until the final judgment on appeal.[31]

All stages, whether in first instance or on appeal must take place without undue delay [...]. The Committee reiterates its position that States parties have an obligation to organize their system of administration of justice in such a manner as to ensure an effective and expeditious disposal of the cases.[32] The length of the proceedings before the Supreme Court and most importantly the high number of postponements and cancellations of court hearings cannot be justified under the present circumstances. Accordingly, the Committee finds that the author's rights under article 14, paragraph 3 (c) of the Covenant, have been violated.

29 Communication No. 909/2000, *Mujuwana Kankanamge v. Sri Lanka*, para. 9.4.

30 Communication No. 263/1987, *Gonzales del Rio v. Peru*, paras. 5.2 and 5.3.

31 Communications No. 1089/2002, *Rouse v. The Philippines*, Views adopted on 25 July 2005, para. 7.4; No. 1085/2002, *Taright et al. v. Algeria*, Views adopted on 15 March 2006, para. 8.5.

32 Communication No. 1466/2006, *Lumanog and Santos v. The Philippines*, Views adopted on 20 March 2008, para. 8.5

5. *Right to Pre-Trial Release*

National law

Criminal Procedure Code, Section 19

(1) A person arrested on a warrant shall be brought immediately before the Examining Magistrate or the president of the trial court who issued the warrant, who may order his immediate release if he fulfils any of the conditions referred to in section 246 (g).[33]
(2) (a) If he fails to fulfil the condition, he shall be taken immediately to the prison indicated on the warrant subject to the provisions of sub-section (3) of this section. (b) Within forty-eight (48) hours of the detention of the person, he shall be interrogated by the Examining Magistrate or, as the case may be, at its next sitting by the trial court which issued the warrant.
(3) The Examining Magistrate or the trial court shall decide on his detention in accordance with sections 221 and 222.

Criminal Procedure Code, Section 21:

(1) Except in cases of offences punishable with death, a warrant of arrest may contain an endorsement that the person to be arrested shall be released if he fulfils the conditions listed in the warrant, in such a case, the endorsement shall specify, apart from the magistrate before whom or the court before which the person to be arrested is to appear: either the number of sureties, if any, and the amount by which they bind themselves to pay in case of nonappearance; or the amount of security to be deposited by the person to be arrested.
(2) When such endorsement is made, the judicial police officer shall release the person if the conditions laid down in the preceding sub-section (1) have been fulfilled.

Criminal Procedure Code, Section 119

(a) The time allowed for remand in custody shall not exceed forty-eight (48) hours, renewable once. (b) This period may, with the written approval of the State Counsel, be exceptionally extended twice. (c) Reasons shall be given for each extension.

33 Section 246 CPC: "[t]he Examining Magistrate may, by a ruling, subject the defendant to judicial supervision or replace such measure, where the defendant is in detention, with one or more of the obligations provided for in sections 41 and 42 of the Penal Code, with one or more of the following: [...] (g) in order to ensure his appearance he shall: either deposit a sum of money, the amount and conditions of payment of which shall be fixed by the Examining Magistrate, taking into consideration the resources of the defendant; or provide one or more sureties in accordance with the provisions of sections 224 and following."

Criminal Procedure Code, Chapter IV "Remand in Custody", Section 218:

> (1) Remand in custody shall be an exceptional measure which shall not be ordered except in the case of a misdemeanour or a felony. It shall be necessary for the preservation of evidence, the maintenance of public order, protection of life and property, or to ensure the appearance of an accused before the Examining Magistrate or the court. Provided that a person with a known place of abode shall not be remanded in custody except in the case of a felony.
>
> (2) The Examining Magistrate may at any time after charging the defendant but before the committal order, issue a remand warrant against him; provided that the offence is punishable with loss of liberty. He shall then make a reasoned ruling committing the defendant in custody; the ruling shall be notified to be the State Counsel and to the defendant.

Criminal Procedure Code, Chapter IV "Remand in Custody", Section 221:

> (1) The Examining Magistrate shall specify the period of remand in custody in the remand warrant. It shall not exceed six (6) months. However, such period may, by reasoned ruling of the Examining Magistrate be extended for at most twelve (12) months in the case of a felony and six (6) months in the case of a misdemeanour.
>
> (2) Upon expiry of the period of validity of the warrant, the Examining Magistrate shall, under pain of disciplinary action against him, order the immediate release on bail of the defendant, unless he is detained for other reasons.

Criminal Procedure Code, Chapter V "Bail", Sub-Chapter I "Self Bail", Section 222

> (1) The Examining Magistrate may, at any time before the close of the preliminary inquiry, and of his own motion, withdraw the remand warrant and grant bail.
> (2) Where bail is not granted as of right, or by the Examining Magistrate of his own motion, it may be granted on the application of the defendant or his counsel and after the submission of the State Counsel, when the defendant enters into a recognizance to appear before the Examining Magistrate wherever convened and undertakes to inform the latter of his movements.

Criminal Procedure Code, Chapter V "Bail", Sub-Chapter II "Conditional Bail", Section 224:

(1) Any person lawfully remanded in custody may be granted bail on condition that he fulfils one of the conditions referred to in section 246(g), in particular to ensure his appearance either before the judicial police or any judicial authority.
(2) The provisions of sub-section (1) above shall not apply to persons charged with felonies punishable with life imprisonment or death.

Military Justice Code, Section 11

[...] the duration of remand in custody shall be 48 hours renewable once, but this period may be extended to two further periods of 48 hours each on the written authorization of the state prosecutor.

Military Justice Code, Section 12.4

[t]he State Prosecutor may before the institution of criminal proceedings by the minister in charge of military justice and where persons presumed to have committed a crime or a flagrante delicto have been referred to him and if there is serious corroborating evidence against such persons, order their remand in custody for a period not exceeding 10 days pending the order to institute action issued by the minister in charge of military justice. The duration of remand in custody may exceptionally be extended for a further 10 days period upon the authorization of the minister in charge of military justice.

Anti-Terrorism Law, Section 11 “Remand in custody”

[f]or the purpose of this law, the duration of remand in custody shall be fifteen days renewable upon the authorisation of the State Prosecutor.

Regional law

For the applicable standards of regional law, see Annex A.

International Law

For the applicable standards of international law, see Annex A.

B. Right to Physical Integrity

National Law

Constitution of the Republic of Cameroon, preamble

every person has a right to life, to physical and moral integrity and to humane treatment in all circumstances. Under no circumstances shall any person be subjected to torture, to cruel, inhumane or degrading treatment.

Regional Law

African Charter on Human and Peoples' Rights, Article 5

"[e]very individual shall have the right to the respect of the dignity inherent in a human being and to the recognition of his legal status. All forms of exploitation and degradation of man particularly slavery, slave trade, torture, cruel, inhuman or degrading punishment and treatment shall be prohibited."

African Commission on Human and Peoples' Rights, Principles and Guidelines on the Right to a Fair Trial and Legal Assistance in Africa

A.2 d) Fair Hearing
The essential elements of a fair hearing include: respect for the inherent dignity of the human person.

International Law

International Covenant on Civil and Political Rights, Article 7

No one shall be subjected to torture or to cruel, inhuman or degrading treatment or punishment [...].

VI. Rights apparently respected

68. Some rights were, at least partly, respected during the hearing that took place on 27 April 2017. It concerns the right to a public hearing, the right of defence (with regard to the time available to present submissions to the Tribunal), and – we understand also prior to the hearing - the right of the defendants of unsupervised access to a legal representative of their own choosing. We cannot assess to what extent these rights have been respected at all times, apart from this particular hearing, nor if they have been respected with regard to each of the defendants.
69. With regard to the right to a public hearing, the hearing on 27 April 2017 was open to the public. International observers required a visitor's badge, but family members of the defendants and other members of the public, such as the lawyers supporting their colleagues, did not seem to require a badge.
70. The right to a public hearing is an important right of due process. The interest served by public proceedings is not only to protect the accused against proceedings behind closed doors, in which the guarantees of due process may be violated, but also for the public and society at large to ensure confidence in the administration

of justice.

1. Right to a Public Hearing

National Law

Code of Criminal Procedure, Chapter II "Public Hearing and Maintenance of Order in Court", Sub-Chapter I "Public Hearing", Section 302:

> "(1) Hearing shall be conducted in public. However, when a public hearing is repugnant to public order or morality, the court may, at any time, of its own motion, or on the application of one of the interested parties and after the submissions of the Legal Department, rule either that the proceedings or any part thereof shall be held in camera or that public hearing shall be restricted. Mention of this fact shall be made in the judgment.
>
> (2) In every case, judgment shall always be delivered in public.

Regional Law

African Commission on Human and Peoples' Rights, Principles and Guidelines on the Right to a Fair Trial and Legal Assistance in Africa

> A.3) Public hearing:
>
> [...] c) Adequate facilities shall be provided for attendance by interested members of the public; d) No limitations shall be placed by the judicial body on the category of people allowed to attend its hearings where the merits of a case are being examined; [...] f) The public and the media may not be excluded from hearings before judicial bodies except if it is determined to be (i) in the interest of justice for the protection of children, witnesses or the identity of victims of sexual violence (ii) for reasons of public order or national security in an open and democratic society that respects human rights and the rule of law. [...] j) Any judgement rendered in legal proceedings, whether civil or criminal, shall be pronounced in public.

International Law

International Covenant on Civil and Political Rights, Article 14(1)

> [...] [i]n the determination of any criminal charge against him, or of his rights and obligations in a suit at law, everyone shall be entitled to a fair and public hearing by a competent, independent and impartial tribunal established by law. The press and the public may be excluded from all or part of a trial for reasons of morals, public order (ordre public) or national

security in a democratic society, or when the interest of the private lives of the parties so requires, or to the extent strictly necessary in the opinion of the court in special circumstances where publicity would prejudice the interests of justice; but any judgement rendered in a criminal case or in a suit at law shall be made public except where the interest of juvenile persons otherwise requires or the proceedings concern matrimonial disputes or the guardianship of children.

2. *Right to Defence (Access to Counsel of Own Choosing)*

71. The defendants have had access to legal representatives of their own choosing. We understand that in earlier stages of their detention such access was not easily obtained. However, currently legal counsel can visit their clients at the prison between working hours. This right is restricted to the legal representatives whose names are displayed on a list at the entrance of the prison. We were told that sometimes a payment has to be made prior to a visit taking place, but do not know whether this is the case with regard to all the defendants or if it is requested all or most of the time. If payment would be required, this would constitute an impermissible restriction of the right to defence.

72. It should also be noted that the defence team was not restricted in the time available to present submissions to the Tribunal. In fact, various members of the defence team presented lengthy arguments on the bail application. Therefore, this element of the right to defence was respected.

National Law

Code of Criminal Procedure, Section 122(3)

> [t]he person on remand may at anytime within the period of detention and during working hours, be visited by his counsel, members of his family, and by any other person following up his treatment while in detention.

Code of Criminal Procedure, Section 240:

> [c] ounsel shall visit his client, in detention only between the hours of six (6) am and six (6) pm.

Code of Criminal Procedure, Section 352

> [t]he accused who appears [at a hearing] may be assisted by counsel.

Regional Law

African Charter on Human and Peoples' Rights, Article 7(1)(c)

> [e]very individual shall have the right to have his cause heard. This comprises: [...] (c) the right to defense, including the right to be defended by counsel of his choice.

African Commission on Human and Peoples' Rights, Principles and Guidelines on the Right to a Fair Trial and Legal Assistance in Africa

> A.2 Fair Hearing
>
> [t]he essential elements of a fair hearing include: [...] (f) an entitlement to consult and be represented by a legal representative or other qualified persons chosen by the party at all stages of the proceedings.

International Law

International Covenant on Civil and Political Rights, Article 14(3)(b)

> 3. In the determination of any criminal charge against him, everyone shall be entitled to the following minimum guarantees, in full equality: [...] (b) To have adequate time and facilities for the preparation of his defence and to communicate with counsel of his own choosing.

VII. Conclusions and recommendations

A. Conclusions

1. *The relation between violations of national, regional and international law*

73. When comparing the facts as observed at the hearing of 27 April 2017 with the relevant standards of national, regional, and international law, some conclusions can be drawn regarding whether or not the circumstances at the hearing reveal violations of those standards.
74. If a conduct or occurrence does not constitute a violation of national law, but does constitute a violation of regional and international law, this is generally indicative of the fact that domestic law does not comply with international standards. If that is the case, such domestic laws should be brought into line with regional and international law. Failure to do so amounts to a breach of international obligations.
75. Moreover, if provisions of domestic law do not correspond with the African Charter on Human and Peoples' Rights, this does not only amount to a violation of a particular substantive right, such as the right to a fair trial. The lack of adequate domestic law also constitutes a violation of Article 1 of the African Charter which

establishes that:

> [t]he Member States of the Organization of African Unity parties to the present Charter shall recognize the rights, duties and freedoms enshrined in this Chapter and shall undertake to adopt legislative or other measures to give effect to them.

76. In this regard, the African Commission on Human and People's Rights has established in several cases that the violation of a right contained in the African Charter gives rise to an autonomous violation of Article 1 thereof. It has also ordered that a country, in order to respect its treaty obligations, must bring its legislation and its practices in line with the African Charter.

African Commission on Human and Peoples' Rights, Good v Botswana (2010) AHRLR 43 (ACHPR 2010)

> 226. Article 1 of the African Charter requires member states to recognise the rights, duties and freedoms enshrined in the Charter and to take legislative or other measures to give effect to them.
>
> 228. The African Charter is a legally binding agreement signed and ratified by 53 African states, and this makes it a treaty as defined under international law, and thus it is regulated by the rules of international law. According to the rules of international law, a state can express its consent to be bound by a treaty by ratification. Consent to be bound here means agreeing (committing oneself) to respect, protect and fulfil the provisions of a treaty.
>
> 239. It is also a well-established principle in international law that a state cannot invoke its domestic laws to avoid its international obligations.
>
> 241. In Jawara v The Gambia [, para. 46] the Commission was categorical when it stated that if a state party fails to recognise the provisions of the African Charter, there is no doubt that it is in violation of article 1 of the same. Article 1 of the African Charter thus imposes a general obligation on all states parties to recognise the rights enshrined therein and requires them to adopt measures to give effect to those rights. As such, any finding of violation of those rights constitutes a violation of article 1.
>
> 244. The Commission recommends: […] (ii) The respondent state should take steps to ensure that sections 7(f), 11(6) and 36 of the Botswana Immigration Act and its practices conform to international human rights standards, in particular, the African Charter.

African Commission on Human and Peoples' Rights, Article 19 v. Eritrea (2007) AHRLR 73 (ACHPR 2007), para. 105

> [...] [t]o allow national law to have precedence over the international law of the Charter would defeat the purpose of the rights and freedoms enshrined in the Charter. International human rights standards must always prevail over contradictory national law. Any limitation on the rights of the Charter must be in conformity with the provisions of the Charter.

77. A violation of Article 1 of the African Charter continues to exist until it is remedied by amendment of the national laws and practices that do not correspond with that treaty. Until such remedy takes place, and in any circumstance, according to the domestic law of Cameroon, international law takes precedence over national law, as provided in Article 45 of the Constitution and Section 2, Ch. 1 of the Criminal Code of Cameroon.

2. *Rights Violated*

a) Right to a Fair Trial
(i) Right to be Tried by an Independent and Impartial Tribunal

78. The domestic law of Cameroon, in Section 7 of the Military Justice Code and Section 2 of the Terrorism Law, establishes a wide range of offences that fall under the jurisdiction of Military Tribunals, irrespective of whether the accused are military officers or civilians. Even if the exercise of jurisdiction by Military Tribunals over civilians is in accordance with domestic law, it constitutes a violation of Article 7(1)(d) of the African Charter. It also constitutes a violation of Article 14(1) ICCPR, insofar as military jurisdiction over civilians should be exceptional. The State authorities of Cameroon have not demonstrated the necessity of such jurisdiction in this case. Moreover, this exercise of jurisdiction goes against the African Commission's case-law, as well as its Principles on a Fair Trial (see Part V.A above). In addition, the domestic law that allows for the exercise of this jurisdiction violates Article 1 of the African Charter, since Section 7 of the Military Justice Code and Section 2 of the Terrorism Law are not in accordance with the treaty obligations established in the African Charter.
79. The exercise of jurisdiction by military courts over civilians also raises concerns regarding the independence of the judiciary. This is especially so in cases where the executive may have a particular interest in a certain outcome of proceedings. The independence of the judiciary should be respected at all times and no undue influence or interference should be exercised by the executive or any other power. Similarly, the Prosecution should be able to act without undue interference and independently of the executive and the judiciary. The fact that the Prosecution forms part of the Ministry of Justice or, in the case of the Prosecution at a Military

Tribunal, forms part of the Ministry of Defence, does not pose a problem with regard to its independence *per se*. In fact, in many countries a similar structure will be in place. However, the Prosecution should not need any authorisation of either the Ministry of Justice or the Ministry of Defence to take any action with regard to a case, as was suggested in our meeting with the *Commissaire du Gourvernement*.

80. Another matter of concern is that at least one of the two Assessors in this case was a military officer who does not seem to have legal training. This would constitute normal practice in a court martial, where a decision needs to be made on offences committed by military officers in the line of duty. However, judges who exercise jurisdiction over civilians – whether in a military court or an ordinary court – should have legal training. A lack of such training could result in a violation of the right to be tried by a "competent, independent and impartial tribunal". This would be the case, irrespective of the particular professional competency of the military officer involved.

81. In addition, the United Nations Human Rights Committee has established that a violation of the right to a fair trial in proceedings regarding offences that carry the death penalty, additionally amounts to a violation of Article 6 ICCPR. The African Charter does not allow for any derogation of the right to a fair trial in a state of emergency or internal disturbance (whether formally declared by decree or not). Under the ICCPR, fair trial rights in proceedings regarding offences that carry the death penalty are non-derogable in a state of emergency, because of the corresponding violation of Article 6 ICCPR.

(ii) Right to Defence (Access to the Case File)

82. During the hearing, the defence team stated that they had not seen the case file. We understand that they may not have seen the case files of all the accused, but perhaps of some of them. We have also heard reports that files were either not made available by the prosecution or that photocopies needed to be made, which carried some costs. A lack of access to the case file or a restriction of such access, for example, through high costs of photocopying, constitutes a violation of the right of defence, established in Article 7(1)(c) of the African Charter and Article 14(3)(b) of the ICCPR. Lack of such access makes it impossible for the accused and his or her legal representative to adequately prepare for the defence. In addition, such lack of access violates the principle of equality of arms, which is a fundamental principle that applies in all proceedings and without which a trial does not comply with guarantees of due process.

(iii) Right to an Interpreter

83. During the hearing, no interpretation was provided from French into English apart from the first remarks made by the President of the Military Tribunal and the parties. There was only interpretation from English into French during the

submission of the defence team on the bail application. This interpretation was for the benefit of the Judges of the Military Tribunal, rather than the defendants. All the defendants are English speakers and we understand that the majority of them do not speak or understand French, in any case not well enough to understand the Presiding Judge or the arguments made by the parties in their own trial. Whenever French was spoken, the defendants were evidently disengaged from the proceedings and did not seem to understand what was being said. By contrast, when English was spoken, they were attentively listening to the submissions made.

84. The order of the State Prosecutor in which Nkongho Felix Agbor Balla, Fontem Neba and Mancho Bibixy were charged with certain offences, their provisional detention was ordered, and they were subjected to the jurisdiction of the Military Tribunal in Yaoundé, was in French. We understand that no English version was available. The other 25 defendants were apparently also charged, and their detention ordered, in French. This means that they can neither understand the documents pertaining to their trial nor the submissions made at the hearings. Therefore, they are not able to instruct their counsel. This is of great concern in any proceeding, especially in a criminal proceedings, and even more so in one that takes place before a Military Tribunal in a case where the defendants face the death penalty.

85. This lack of interpretation constitutes a violation of domestic, regional, and international law. More specifically, Section 354 of the CPC and Article 14(3)(f) ICCPR. It also goes against the African Commission's Principles on a Fair Trial, Principle N.4(d) that establishes the right of "translation or interpretation of all documents or statements necessary for the defendant to understand the proceedings or assist in the preparation of a defence". Although some members of the defence team made their arguments in French and the defence team did not challenge the lack of interpretation, as it had apparently done in previous hearings, it is the Presiding Magistrate who must appoint an interpreter "of his own motion" (CPC, Section 354). Therefore, even if no request is made by the defence, it is a State obligation to provide interpretation for the defendant. Moreover, such interpretation should be adequate, which means that an interpreter should be able to interpret legal arguments to an acceptable standard.

86. To submit a person to trial without an understanding of the charges made against him or her, without being able to follow the arguments of their own defence counsel, the prosecution, or the Judges, is a grave violation of the right to a fair trial and of the principle of equality of arms. In addition, if prior to the hearing statements were taken from the accused without interpretation, and those statements are subsequently relied on in proceedings, this constitutes a violation of Article 14(1) ICCPR (See Part V.A above, *Nallaratnam Singarasa v. Sri Lanka*).

(iv) Right to be Tried Without Undue Delay

87. There have been multiple adjournments in the proceedings against the defendants. At the hearing of 27 April 2017, the case was again adjourned, without any decision

being taken on the bail application. Nkongho Felix Agbor Balla and Fontem Neba have been in detention since 17 January 2017 and many of the other 25 defendants have been in detention allegedly since the beginning of December 2016. Such multiple adjournments, for whatever reason they are granted, prevent a trial from taking place without undue delay. There seems to be no specific provision in domestic law that would prevent such delay. However, this delay constitutes a clear violation of Article 14(3)(c) ICCPR and goes against the African Commission's case-law and Principles on a Fair Trial.

88. The United Nations Human Rights Committee has established that the right to be tried without undue delay is even more important in cases in which the accused are charged with offences carrying the death penalty. This is because the accused are held in a state of continuous uncertainty. The psychological impact of this uncertainty may itself constitute a violation of the right to physical integrity established in Article 5 of the African Charter and Article 7 of the ICCPR. Moreover, a delay in proceedings may violate, apart from Article 14(3)(c) ICCPR, other rights such as the right to freedom of expression and the right to leave one's own country (See Part V.A above, United Nations Human Rights Committee, General Comment No. 32).

89. The adjournment of one month given at the hearing of 27 April 217 violates the aforementioned Articles of the African Charter and the ICCPR. In addition, no adjournment of a month can be given, each time, without further motivation in a case of prolonged pre-trial detention. Moreover, as the African Commission has pointed out, a backlog of cases is no excuse for a delay in proceedings (See Part V.A above, *Communication Article 19 v. Eritrea*), although the wide array of offences over which the Military Tribunal has jurisdiction clearly contributes to such a backlog and delay.

B. Right to Pre-Trial Release

90. Nkongho Felix Agbor Balla and Fontem Neba have been detained for more than four months, since 17 January 2017. The other 25 defendants have been detained for more than five months, most of them allegedly since the beginning of December 2016. Persons can only be held in pre-trial detention in exceptional circumstances (see Part V.B above and Annex A, Law Society letter of 25 April 2017). The decision to hold persons in pre-trial detention should be motivated with reference to such exceptional circumstances. Moreoever, each prolongation of such detention should be also be motivated.

91. A lack of motivation upon remand in custody and prolongation of such custody is allowed under Section 11 of the Terrorism Law, as is a potential long duration of such custody. However, this long duration and lack of motivation constitutes a clear violation of Article 6, as well as Article 1, of the African Charter and Article 9(3) of the ICCPR. Moreover, the case of Paul Ayah Abine, who has been detained since 21 January 2017 and has still not been charged, is another example of the

lack of compliance of Cameroon with its international treaty obligations, for which it can be held internationally responsible. In Justice's Ayah's case, Cameroon has additionally violated the right to promptly be brought before a judge, established in Article 7(1)(d) of the African Charter and Article 9(2) and (3) of the ICCPR. The prolonged custody of Justice Ayah, as well as the prolonged pre-trial detention of Nkongho Felix Agbor Balla, Fontem Neba and the 25 other defendants constitutes a clear violation of regional and international standards.

C. Right to Physical Integrity

92. During the hearing, the defendants had to stand for 3 hours in the heat. Moreover, the other 25 defendants had to stand in a box built for two persons, pressed up against each other. We understand that this is not uncommon in Courts in Cameroon. However, it violates the right to physical integrity established in the preamble of the Constitution, Article 5 of the African Charter, and Article 7 of the ICCPR. In addition, the African Commission's Principles on a Fair Trial state that one of the "essential elements of a fair hearing" is "respect for the inherent dignity of the human person". This means that the accused should be treated humanely and with dignity, not only in detention but also during the hearings in proceedings brought against them.

B. Recommendations

93. The Law Society makes the following recommendations to the authorities in Cameroon, on the basis of observations made at the hearing that took place on 27 April 2017 and in addition to the recommendations made in its letters of 13 February and 25 April 2017. These recommendations are not necessarily in order of importance; each needs to be addressed to ensure compliance with regional and international standards:

- The Military Justice Code and Anti-Terrorism Law must be brought in line with international standards. Primarily with regard to the jurisdiction of military tribunals over civilians, as well as the prolonged and unmotivated remand in custody, and the absence of a preliminary inquiry.
- The defence team must have access to the case file and all other documents relating to proceedings against their clients. No restrictions should be placed on such access of whatever nature, such as high costs for photocopying or otherwise.
- Interpretation must be provided at all stages of the proceedings, as well as translation of all documents relating to such proceedings, where the defendants do not understand the language in which they are being tried. Such interpretation must be made available by the Presiding Magistrate "of his own motion" (CPC, Section 354) and be of an adequate standard.
- The defendants must be tried without undue delay, so that no multiple adjournments should be given that unnecessarily delay proceedings. The overburdening

of the Military Tribunal with cases, mostly due to the wide range of offences over which it has jurisdiction, is not a justification for a delay in proceedings.

- An adjournment cannot be one month, each time, in a case in which the defendants are being held in pre-trial detention, especially in cases in which the defendants are being charged with offences that carry the death penalty.
- The defendants should be seated during the proceedings. If there are more defendants than fit into the box established for that purpose, then other provisions should be made, which may include seating in the public gallery under the supervision of a prison guard or a Court official. Defendants could be asked to stand, for example, when their names are read out, to give statements before the Court, when asked to answer a question, or to receive judgment in their case.
- The State must take measures to improve the conditions in the courtroom at the Military Tribunal in Yaoundé, especially making microphones available so that all those present, including the defendants themselves and those seated in the public gallery, can hear the representations being made. This ensures that the right to a public hearing is not illusory. In this regard, Section 306(2) CPC provides: "[...] the Presiding Magistrate may by a reasoned decision, authorize the installation of a sound system in the court room and the use of recording instruments or loudspeakers to enable a wider audience to follow the proceedings".
- We encourage authorities to welcome international observers and provide substantial information in meetings, to the extent possible. This ensures transparency and allows all views to be taken into account.

94. The Law Society expresses its gratitude to all those who were willing to meet with us, as well as to the authorities in Cameroon who received us. We encourage the authorities to take measures to implement the recommendations made in this report.
95. The Law Society will continue to monitor the situation of lawyers and human rights defenders in Cameroon, especially those who are being tried before the Military Tribunal in the case of Nkongho Felix Agbor Balla, Fontem Neba, and others, as well as cases where lawyers and others are being held in custody under its jurisdiction.

Dr. Marina Brilman
International Human Rights policy adviser
The Law Society

Annexes

TWENTY-EIGHT

The Past That Did Not Pass

The Fallacies of "Living Together" and the English Language Press as Site of Anglophone Collective Memory

LYOMBE EKO

The Evil that Men do, Lives After them (Shakespeare, *Julius Caesar*).

The subtitle of this book, "The Past That Did Not Pass" is a contextualized restatement of the tragic historical drama that we call the Anglophone Question in Cameroon. This phrase is informed by the concept of time held by the Kpe-Mboko (Hwakpe/Bakweri and Womboko), a coastal Bantu people whose ancestral home is the Hvako Mountain in Southern Cameroons. The Kpe-Mboko view time as a continuous, episodic, and elastic phenomenon, not a strictly chronological and sequential thing. While chronological and sequential time has three elements– the past, the present, and the future–Kpe-Mboko continuous time has yesterday (*nmwele*), today (*yawono*) and tomorrow (*nmwele*). The very same word, *nmwele,* is used for yesterday and tomorrow, the past and the future. We can only know the meaning of the word *nmwele* in the context in which it is used. Whether we are speaking of yesterday or tomorrow depends on the contextual couching of the word. In the Kpe-Mboko language, context and tone give birth to meaning. Time is analogous to a continuous stream that flows into the ocean, evaporates, turns into clouds and fog over the Hvako mountain, condenses and falls back as rain that joins rivers and streams that flow back to their home in the sea. Fast forward to the past, rewind to the future. Yesterday is transformed into today and tomorrow. Our yesterdays live in our todays and our tomorrows. If yesterday and tomorrow are part of continuous time, tragic pasts don't really pass. History and past geographic phenomena like the volcanic eruptions of Mount Hvako are things of the past, the present and the future.

In this cultural worldview, the past does not pass because the past is both present and prologue. The ancestors go on an eternal journey; they do not pass away. They travel to *molike*, the place of eternal time, yet they are still with us. We speak to them, pour libations to them, and invoke their presence on important occasions. Our ancestors sometimes visit us as spirits, strangers, or even new-born children. According to this continuous conceptualization of time, the wrongs of the past are staring us in the face today. They demand to be righted, or else they will show up again in our tomorrows–in more virulent and destructive forms. The Anglophone Question is an unfinished business from the past that has not passed; that past is World War I.

People around the world live with pasts that have not passed. Seeds of the Anglophone Problem were sown when English was introduced in West Africa in the 18th century and became the foundation of Pidgin English or Creole, the lingua franca of the region. In Cameroon, the Anglophone Problem was created by the Franco-British partition of German Kamerun in 1916 and the ratification of that partition by the Treaty of Versailles of 1919. That treaty put its imprimatur on the transfer and transformation of territories from German Kamerun to Britain Cameroons and French Cameroun. Britain subsequently partitioned the territories it acquired into Northern and Southern Cameroons and moved them to Nigeria to balance the power dynamics between Northern and Southeastern Nigeria. That colonial past and the consequences of its territorial rearrangements have not passed. The wrongs of European colonialism and World War I are staring us in the face. The Nigerian territory that used to be Northern Cameroons ultimately became the hotbed of the Islamist terrorist group, Boko Haram, while the problematic reunification of English and Pidgin-speaking Southern Cameroons with the independent *République du Cameroun* in 196i accelerated the Anglophone Problem. That problem has taken the form of the problematic situation of the citizens of the English and Pidgin-speaking former Southern Cameroons in the highly centralized, ruthless, authoritarian republican chiefery of the Republic of Cameroun, to which the British colonial power, the United Nations, and the region's own ambitious, naïve, and unsophisticated political leaders–Foncha, Muna, Mukete, and others–had consigned it. The Anglophone Question is actually an assemblage of problems about the reality, existence, cultural specificity, peoplehood, autonomy, self-determination, human rights, and freedom of expression that have emerged out of the lived experience of the Anglophone minority in The French-dominated Republic of Cameroon. The multi-faceted Anglophone Problem is about unequal power dynamics, the clash of political, religious and cultural worldviews of the two former United Nations Trust territories/colonies that reunified in 1961 to form the Federal Republic of Cameroon. The colonial past did not pass because *la République du Cameroun* (East Cameroun) came to the Federal Republic with a legacy of French anti-religious, anti-clerical ideology, a secular republicanism mindset, as well as a centralized, Napoleonic administrative system and civil law, while English- and Pidgin-speaking Southern Cameroons (West Cameroon) brought its nonsecular governmentality, British-style parliamentary democracy, common law, and educational system to the federation. The judiciary of post-colonial French Cameroun drew on the codified Napoleonic civil law system, while that of Southern Cameroons was grounded on a contextualized African version of the British common law, and native law.

The decision of the Francophone-dominated Federal Republic of Cameroon to eliminate religious studies from the curriculum of government schools and from the courses that could be counted in the General Certificate of Education for admission to higher educational institutions, French-style professional schools, and government positions, demonstrated the clashing worldviews of the two Cameroon states, and set the stage for the emergence of the Anglophone Question. The emergence of American, British, Jamaican, and Nigerian popular music and films in the 1960s and 1970s cemented the place of Southern Cameroons in the global Anglosphere. Information and Communication Technologies, especially the Internet and social media platforms that were invented in the United States and diffused first to the Anglosphere and then to the rest of the world, made assimilation of the Anglophone minority into French Cameroon an impossibility. The actions and reactions of both territories reflected these pasts that had not passed.

This book has problematized the official Cameroon government posture on the Anglophone Question–there is no Anglophone problem–and questioned the official Cameroon government and Francophone media framing of the problem as "*la crise socio-politique au NOSO*" (the socio-political crisis in the Northwest and Southwest regions). Interestingly, the same arguments that were advanced to support the assimilation of European Jews in the 19th century were also applied to Anglophones in Cameroon. In his essay on the Jewish Question, Marx (1977) noted that radical, atheistic German theologians and philosophers had demanded that in order to live together, Jews and Christians had to renounce their respective religions, which tended to separate them (Marx, 1977). Proponents of *le vivre ensemble* in Cameroon advanced an identical assimilationist argument. They said that all Cameroonians had problems, not just Anglophones. They called on Anglophones to join other Cameroonians to work together to develop the country as one people rather than insist on a linguistic and cultural specificity inherited from colonialism. Anglophones, they claimed, were being egotistical troublemakers for claiming that they were oppressed when all Cameroonians in all parts of the country had identical problems like Anglophones. That position missed the point that Anglophone Cameroonians had been part of the Anglosphere long before German and British colonialism, certainly long before Cameroon became a country. It also missed the point that the Francophone argument was positional. They were arguing from a position of political, linguistic, and economic power. This was the power the elite of a French post-colony that had replicated the authoritarian Napoleonic governmentality and civil law in Cameroon, complete with its appointed "*prefets*" who were called *chef de terre* (lords of the land). Anglophones could not shed their cultural "Anglophoneness"–and their status as former citizens of a British Commonwealth territory, any more than Francophones could shed their inherited "Francophoneness" or their coveted place in *la Francophonie*.

The bone of contention in the Anglophone problem is the status of Anglophones and their former State, Southern Cameroons or West Cameroon, in the ruthless authoritarian State of Cameroon, whose form and nomenclature retrogressed from the Federal Republic of Cameroon in 1961, to the United Republic of Cameroon in 1972, to the Republic of Cameroon in 1984. The changing nomenclature of the State of Cameron over time represents milestones in the progressive assimilation and erasure of the autonomy of the Anglophone state and the descent of Cameroon towards the highly centralized, intolerant, ruthless, authoritarian republican chiefdom that President Paul Biya has ruled single-handedly for more than 42 years. This political retrogression came with a marked diminishment of Anglophone autonomy, specificity, human rights, and political freedoms. That is the core of the Anglophone Problem, which the Ahidjo/Biya regime has tried to use military rather than political means to solve. In its Buea Declaration of 1993, the All Anglophone Conference decried the de facto, second-class citizenship of Anglophones in Cameroon. This declaration of discontent was highlighted by Anglophone lawyers, teachers, activists, and civil society demonstrators who triggered the Anglophone Revolt in 2016.

This book has demonstrated that the Anglophone problem is a multi-faceted problem that demonstrates a paradox. Machiavellian European democracies and federal states–France, the United Kingdom, Switzerland, as well as Israel, have, over the years, directly and indirectly supported the ruthless, anti-democratic, anti-federalist, autocratic African republican chiefdom of Cameroon despite its horrendous atrocities, and the human rights violations committed against the minority English and Pidgin-speaking population of the former Southern Cameroons, Nevertheless, the proximate cause of the Anglophone Revolt of 2016, was the refusal of the republican chieftain to entertain the very idea of federalism, of restoration of the autonomy of the State of West Cameroon, and of local self-government advanced by the Anglophone minority as a solution to the political crisis that had gripped the country.

As this volume has shown, the harsh repression of the Cameroon government in response to the demands of self-determination emanating from the Anglophone regions was combined with bad faith, deceptive, and misleading half-measures decreed by President Biya. These measures were designed to tinker around the edges of the authoritarian politico-cultural status quo and make some cosmetic touch-ups to it for purposes of maintaining it unchanged while misleading the international community that the regime was taking measures to resolve the Anglophone problem. The crux of the authoritarian deception was that discussing the form of the State was out of the question. That is why the rubber stamp Cameroon National Assembly has never debated the Anglophone Problem since the revolt began in 2016. The National Assembly echoed President Paul Biya's "peace through military subjugation" policy. As we have seen, all attempts to put the Anglophone Problem and the philosophical questions it raised on the agenda of the legislative body were dismissed with haughty condescension. An exemplar of the frivolous, superficial treatment the republican chiefdom reserved for the problem is exemplified by initiatives the government took to "resolve" it. In the government's 2019 budget presented to the National Assembly, Prime Minister, Dion Ngute, set forth the following priorities to resolve the "so-called socio-political tensions" in the English-speaking Northwest and Southwest regions:

> *Intensification des actions d'éducation civique, du bilinguisme, du multiculturalisme et la promotion du vivre ensemble.*
>
> Intensification of civic education activities, bilingualism, and multiculturalism and promotion of living together.

These political priorities ignored the core of the problem, focusing instead on funding superficial programs that enriched their Francophone originators and implementers. The impression was that the Anglophone Problem was due to a lack of civic education, bilingualism, and multiculturalism. It is an open secret that in Cameroon, the most bilingual section of the population is the Anglophone minority, which was the subject of concerted efforts and initiatives on the part of France and French Cameroun to assimilate them into *la Francophonie* and transform them into speakers of Parisian French (Betts, 1961). In this assimilationist context, Anglophones had to learn French to survive in the majority French-speaking Cameroon.

The Fallacies of Le Vivre Ensemble (Living Together)

After the eruption of the Anglophone revolt in 2016, one of the slogans the government of Cameroon and its ministers parroted from dusk to dawn like a talismanic incantation was the concept of *le vivre ensemble* (living together). This nebulous phrase became the ideological and propaganda work horse of the Biya *Chefferie républicaine.* It was mouthed repeatedly as a solution to the Anglophone Question, in place of the good faith, democratic political dialogue, negotiation and compromise that was badly needed to solve the problem. The problem is that the politico-sociological concept of *le vivre ensemble* is a concept advanced by French political thinker Ernest Renan in 1882. In his pamphlet, "*What is a Nation*?" Renan (1823-1892) presented the idea of living together in specific politico-cultural contexts. He wrote that a nation consists of a past and a present. The past is the possession in common of a rich legacy of memories and sites of memory; the present is the current consent of the governed to be governed by the governor. Renan (1882) wrote:

> *Une nation est une âme, un principe spirituel. Deux choses qui, à vrai dire, n'en font qu'une, constituent cette âme, ce principe spirituel. L'une est dans le passé, l'autre dans le présent. L'une est la possession en commun d'un riche legs de souvenirs; l'autre est le consentement actuel, le désir de vivre ensemble, la volonté de continuer à faire valoir l'héritage qu'on a reçu indivis.*
>
> A nation is a soul, a spiritual principle. There are two things that, to speak the truth, are just one, which makes up this soul, this spiritual principle. One is in the past, the other in the present. One is the common possession of a rich heritage of memories; the other is essential current consent, the desire to live together, the willingness to continue to assert the common received indivisible heritage.

Therefore, Renan suggests, nations exist because their citizens desire to live together. *Le vivre ensemble* is the willingness to continue to maintain the value of the heritage the nation received as a common possession at the time of its founding (Renan, 1882, p. 26). Deliberate or willful forgetting (remembering to forget or forgetting to remember) destroys the historic inheritance and current consent to be governed.

Furthermore, Renan (1882) holds that Nations are founded on a "social capital" of heroic pasts, great men, and glories (p. 26). The nation of Cameroon does not have such a historic past; it has no great men or great glories. It was the result of the colonial partition of Africa in the Berlin Conference of 1884-1885. The problem is that before the Partition of Africa and the emergence of German Kamerun in 1884, there were Pidgin and English-speaking territories on the coast of the Cameroons from Douala through Bimbia and westwards towards Nigeria. Pidgin was the language of trade–including the slave trade–and communication–between Europeans and the native Douala and Kpe-Mboko coastal Bantu peoples. The territory was part of the so-called West African slave coast. English was formally introduced in 1833 by English Baptist missionary, Rev. Joseph Merrick. The first formal, self-governing, English territory was founded in Ambas Bay–the bay between Down Beach, Limbe and Ewota (Bota) by Rev. Alfred Saker in 1858. That was 26 years before the Partition of Africa and the creation of German Kamerun in 1884. The ensuing German territory of Kamerun, consisted of territories that are now parts of Nigeria, Cameroon, Central African Republic, and Congo. It existed only from 1884-1916, a mere 32 years. German Kamerun was stripped of its Central African and Congolese components, which went to France, and the rest was partitioned between France and the United Kingdom, with the French getting the bulk of the territory. In the course of forty-four years, both territories evolved into distinct Francophone and Anglophone entities. The colonial trustees of both territories, France and the UK, jettisoned the German name, Kamerun, in favor of Cameroun and Southern Cameroons. German was abolished as the official colonial language and replaced by French, in French Cameroun and English, in British Southern Cameroons. This is the historical, politico-cultural context to which *le vivre ensemble* was introduced.

Ironically, in France, *le vivre ensemble* is the mantra that masks the assimilationist ethos of the monocultural reality of the French post-revolutionary "republican" State (Feldblum, 1996). The talismanic word, the mantra of *le vivre ensemble* in France and Francophone Africa is the word "*republicain*." *Le vivre ensemble* is a republican (as opposed to monarchical) concept. In effect, it emanated from the French Revolution of 1789, which bequeathed the French republican State, and the political world, the "left-right" topographical vocabulary–and the acute political and ideological cleavages that have bedeviled France and many other countries ever since (Winock, 1988). In the monocultural context of France, where there are no hyphenated French citizens, *le vivre ensemble* is a "republican" political ideology designed to mask the subtle but unavoidable realities of forcible "republican" cultural assimilation. In France, where "equality" is more important than liberty, and the law takes precedence over rights, all immigrants are expected to shed their religious and cultural affiliations and specificities at the border and become part of *le vivre ensemble à la française* (French-style living together). In other words, they are expected to become assimilated into the monolithic French republican culture (Eko, 2013).

French Jews are the oldest minority in France. They have faced the harsh realities of *le vivre ensemble* (forcible assimilation) from time immemorial (Marx, 1977). Indeed, the Jewish Question in France was grounded in the millennial problem of the forced assimilation of Jews into the Gallic State Catholicism of the ancien regime and the Catho-secularism of Post-revolutionary France (Kochan, 2004; Eko, 2006; Morin, 1991). Jewish resistance to assimilation led to a virulent French anti-Judaic culture that enabled French collaboration with Nazi Germany and facilitated World War II-era deportations of French and other Jews to Nazi concentration camps (Eko, 2006).

Since people can only be governed to the extent they consent to be governed, deliberate or willful forgetting or ignoring national foundational understandings undermines the possibility of a common history by excluding an entire class of memories (Renan, 1882). Renan could have been writing about Cameroon. The Anglophone Revolt in Cameroon represents a failure of the authoritarian republican chiefdom of Cameroon to manage the politico-cultural differences of the country and maintain the consent of the Anglophones to continue to be part of the country. The problem is that the inflexible, hardline, over-centralized authoritarian regime has no checks and balances and does not know how to handle political and cultural differences. To the republican chieftain, the dispersal of power is a sign of weakness. The response of the Ahidjo/Biya republican chieftaincy to the Anglophone Revolt was, therefore, the classic authoritarian response to political dissent–obfuscation of history and ruthless repression. As Renan (1882, p. 26) put it: *"L'unité se fait toujours brutalement"* (unity is aways achieved brutally). It did not have to be that way. Renan (1882) cautions that forgetting "obliterates the desire of formerly hostile parties to live together, or the possibility of social solidarity, by creating a bubbling, poisonous, pool of resentment among an entire group of people" (Renan, 1882, p. 26). This aptly describes the reality of relations between English and French Cameroon.

The Anglophone Question is, in part, the willful forgetting, nay deliberate erasure of the collective political and cultural memory of an autonomous English-speaking state called Southern Cameroons that willingly reunited with *la République du Cameroun* to form the Federal Republic of Cameroon. Willful ignorance and intentional forgetting born of the abuse of power led to the creation of the over-centralized, corrupt, authoritarian republican chiefery called *la République du Cameroun*. The Anglophone Revolt was triggered by Anglophones, who did not want to forget the genesis of Cameroon as a two-state federation of equal autonomous states. These English and Pidgin-speaking people did not want to continue with the status quo that reduced them to second-class citizens and condemned them to underdevelopment. That is the crux of the Anglophone problem. Since 2016, President Biya's ruthless dictatorial government has tried every trick in the book to suppress the uprising and resistance of the freedom-loving people of Southern Cameroons who voluntarily joined their "brothers and sisters" of the French-speaking *La Republique du Cameroun*. The scorched-earth war against Anglophones villages and atrocities against unarmed civilians that have been perpetrated with the material assistance of Israel, France, the UK, Switzerland, China, Russia, and others has undermined, perhaps fatally, the consent that Anglophones had given to Ahidjo and Biya to lead them in a democratic, fair and tolerant Federal Republic of Cameroon.

As applied in Cameroon, *le vivre ensemble* (the desire to live together) is a political and ideological slogan that was copied from France, hook line and sinker, without regard to its historical and politico-cultural relevance, deformed to the point of caricature, and instrumentalized by the Cameroonian republican chieftaincy out of pure political expediency. The ironic incongruity of the situation was totally lost on the Anglophone elite of the Biya regime–even the most ruthless autocratic regimes have token insiders from the subaltern groups–who picked up the French political mantra, translated it as "living together," and parroted it at every formal, and informal opportunity. The Cameroonian *chefferie republicaine* has also chosen to highlight a dubious "one and indivisible" "republican" ideology copied without attribution from Article I of the French Constitution. The article in question states: "France shall be an indivisible, secular, democratic and social Republic…." The Biya regime chose to ignore the idea of the consent of the governed. *Le vivre ensemble* thus imposes a tyrannical peaceful co-existence between Anglophones and Francophones in the untenable status quo that Anglophones had revolted against. As misapplied in Cameroon, *le vivre ensemble* is an ethno-tribal concept. It preaches unquestioning acceptance by Anglophones of an oppressive peaceful co-existence with French Cameroon after Anglophone subjugation and exploitation. It is not a *vivre ensemble* or peaceful co-existence born of dialogue, negotiation and respect for the Other. In Cameroon, that appropriated slogan is the new-found mask of assimilation because it calls on Anglophones to set aside their claims of linguistic, cultural and identitarian specificity and learn to live together with the majority Francophones–as second-class citizens. Living together, without consent, and without understanding each other, simply means the assimilation and dispersal of Anglophone cultural and identitarian specificity into *la Francophonie* (Betts, 1961). The fundament problem of the top-down, rule-by-decree republican chieftaincy of Cameroon is that it does not know how to deal with change–the localization, decentralization and dispersion of power and authority, as well as of political and cultural communication.

According to the Council of Europe, living together is a two-way street that is concerned with addressing discrimination, prejudice and intolerance by Europeans towards immigrants, on the one hand, and preventing and combating violent extremism and radicalization on the part of non-European immigrants, in a sustainable and proactive way, on the other hand (Council of Europe, 2019). Thus, living together is the code phrase for assimilating and integrating immigrants into European societies without prejudice and ensuring that they, in turn, respect European democratic values. This European conceptualization of living together presupposes respect for freedom of expression and plurality of opinions, respect for human dignity, cultural diversity and the rights of others. It is so as to guarantee tolerance, mutual comprehension, the participation of all citizens in public affairs, and giving all citizens access to the media and information (Council of Europe, 2019).

Living together is a national, politico-cultural affair, a matter of a common history, collective and cultural memory, and a common, mutually determined and mutually acceptable future. In Cameroon, the concept of living together is an empty, imported political slogan that is completely devoid of consensual human rights and democratic values. It is definitely not the *vivre ensemble* of France or the living together of the European liberal, communitarian project. In Cameroon, *le vivre ensemble* is just a vacuous, nebulous buzzword plagiarized from Europe and imposed on the multicultural political context of Cameroon without regard to its appropriateness or applicability. Living together is, thus, at best misapplied in the Cameroonian context. In effect, after the commencement of the Anglophone Revolt in 2016, the Biya government began to use *le vivre ensemble* as a slogan to justify the authoritarian political status quo, and engage in dubious, bad faith initiatives aimed at further assimilating Anglophones and exploiting the natural resources of their territory. In Cameroon, that borrowed code phrase masks the imposed assimilationist "consensus" of the authoritarian *chefferie républicaine*, where being a federalist is a criminal offense. Worse than that, the Cameroon government naively believes that mouthing this European slogan in response to legitimate political grievances in Cameroon would end the Anglophone Revolt. The Anglophone Problem is the result of the imposition of the assimilationist authoritarian governmentality of the republican chiefery of French Cameroun on the territory of the English and Pidgin-speaking former State of Southern Cameroons, which has a different collective, politico-cultural memory that draws on diverse sources. These include African cultures, Pidgin English, a system of governance that was generally consonant with the governmentality, the global media and entertainment of the Anglosphere, remnants of German colonialism and tolerance of religion. It is a historical truism that empires and regimes that bind countries together with the iron bands of totalitarian dictatorship seldom outlive the dictators and potentates who incarnate these systems: The Ottoman Empire, the Federal Republic of Yugoslavia, Nazi Germany, the Soviet Union, Ethiopia and Sudan are cases in point. Cameroon is at an impasse. The Anglophone Revolt of 2016 has become a "frozen conflict" that awaits resolution in the post-Biya era. The problem is that Cameroon is a country that is not built on consensus or held together by a democratic system of checks and balances underpinned by shared history, culture, and tolerance. The Anglophone Revolt has, through the unsophistication, internecine bickering, infighting, and fractiousness of the Anglophone leadership on the one hand, the lack of vision and political obduracy of the Biya regime, on the other hand, descended into a state of political impasse. It has become a "frozen question" much like the frozen "Bamileke Question," the political power or lack thereof, of Francophones and Anglophones who originally hail from the Western region of Francophone Cameroon, and the frozen issue of the burial of Cameroon's exiled first president, Ahmadou Ahidjo, in a cemetery in Senegal. Due to these and other "frozen" conflicts, the future stability of post-Biya Cameroon is uncertain at best.

The Last Word: The English-language Press as Site of Anglophone Politico-Cultural Collective Memory

It is said that newspapers are the rough draft of history, the raw material from which historical accounts are written. These journalistic accounts have different political, economic, social, religious, and cultural meanings in different parts of the world. This is particularly true of visual images. They are "pregnant" with the culture-specific mentalities and worldviews of the specific circumstances in which they were published. The Anglophone Question in Cameroon is a multi-faceted phenomenon, a flowing stream of events and occurrences. Newspapers give us snapshots of the salient happenings of the question from the perspective of their publishers and owners. Journalistic fairness, balance and objectivity are thus contextualized. The Anglophone press ensured that Anglophones would not be a perpetually "muted group," "parenthetical citizens" who do not have a voice in the day-to-day management of society (Ardener, 2015, p. 530), and are muted in relation to the dominant structures (Ardener, 2005; Ardener & Ardener, 1972). Anglophone press coverage of the Anglophone Question and the Anglophone Revolt of 2016 should be seen in this context. History will record that the English-language media in Cameroon (specifically newspapers, radio, and more recently the Internet and social media platforms) have, over time, sustained and boosted Anglophone collective and cultural memory in Cameron (Eko, 2003). Despite the dark curtain of censorship that descended upon the nascent Southern Cameroons press after the reunification with French Cameroun in 1961, despite persecution, intimidation, arrests, imprisonment, and even the murder of journalists, the Anglophone press struggled valiantly and often at great personal cost to journalists and publishers, to maintain a semblance of independence, reporting the truth with great fear and caution, but reporting it nevertheless. This section presents select frontpages of Anglophone Cameroon newspapers–with a couple of Francophone outlets thrown in for context–that, taken together, present narratives of the Anglophone Question from 1993 to 2024.

The Rough Draft of the History of the Anglophone Question as Framed on the Front Pages of English-Language Newspapers

The Anglophone Question is the subaltern status of the English-speaking minority in Cameroon, and muting of their politico-cultural, religious and linguistic specificity by the Ahidjo-Biya republican chiefery. The tightly-controlled state media and the heavily censored private media were essentially mute on the issue. Things took a different turn when the collapse of the Soviet Union and the end of the Cold War triggered a hurricane of uprisings and revolts by oppressed minorities across Africa. Cameroon was no exception. The founding of the Social Democratic Front (SDF) party in opposition to the monolithic CPDM in 1990–six of its members were shot dead by security forces after the rally, strikes, demonstrations and ghost towns led to relative political liberalization. This was marked by the emergence of parties opposed to the ruling CNU/CPDM of the Ahidjo/Biya republican chiefdom. This was the context of the emergence of the Anglophone Question in Cameroon. The much-muzzled English-speaking press quickly became platforms on which Anglophone politico-cultural and linguistic apartness were debated and advanced. The Anglophone newspaper front pages and cartoons below–with a few French language cartoons thrown in for illustrative purposes–constitute a rough chronological timeline of the salient events of the Anglophone Revolt from 1993 to 2024. This is a thirty-year period that changed the history of Cameroon for better or for worse, depending on the perspective of the observer. The front pages below show that development. They take us from the Buea All Anglophone Conference of 1993 (AACI) and its Buea Declaration, through AACII and the Bamenda Proclamation, to the Anglophone Revolt of 2016, the Biya regime's stubborn refusal to even discuss the issue in the National Assembly, the degeneration of the political problem to a military conflict, human rights violations by the Cameroon military, gendarmes and police, as well as by ignorant, unsophisticated and ruthless Anglophone non-state combatants who, having lost sight of their objectives, turned on the very people they claimed to want to liberate.

Anglophone newspapers are sites of Anglophone collective memory as marginalized, "parenthetical citizens" (Ardener, 2005, p. 53).

I. Genesis of the Anglophone Revolt: In the beginning were the All Anglophone Conferences of 1993 and 1994

CAMEROON POST

STOP PRESS
Bundestag and American Congress Demand Fresh Presidential Elections in Cameroon

BUEA APRIL 2 - 3 1993 SPECIAL
ALL ANGLOPHONE CONFERENCE

How Nice To Be Home Again

A PEOPLE'S RICH HERITAGE

WEST CAMEROON YESTERDAY

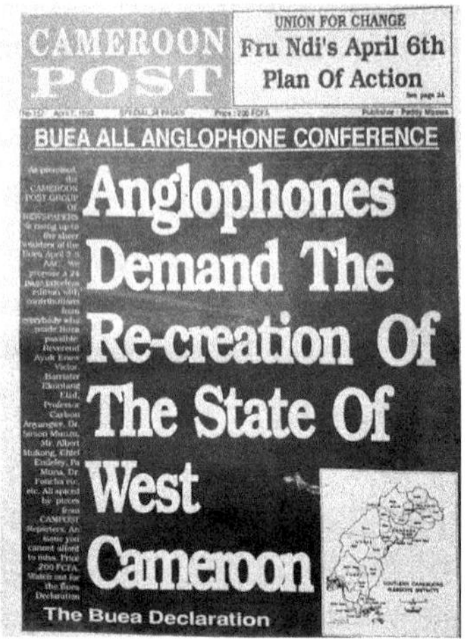

CAMEROON POST

UNION FOR CHANGE
Fru Ndi's April 6th Plan Of Action

BUEA ALL ANGLOPHONE CONFERENCE

Anglophones Demand The Re-creation Of The State Of West Cameroon

The Buea Declaration

Fig. 28.1. Left: "How Nice to be Home Again" Special Report of the All Anglophone Conference of April 2-3, 1993. *Cameroon Post*.

Figure 28.2. Right: Anglophones Demand Recreation of the State of West Cameroon. Report of Buea Declaration of the All Anglophone Conference, *Cameroon Post*, April 7, 1993.

The Guardian Post
DAILY

Vox Pop:
Respondents crucify Minister Atanga Nji Paul on Anglophone marginalisation

Anglophone marginalisation:

Facts & figures that speak!

- Only 76 Anglophones of Biya's 700 Ministers in 34 years
- Only six Anglophones in present 63-member Government
- Only one Anglophone Minister with portfolio out of 38
- Less than 15 Anglophones out of over 130 GMs of State Corporations
- Only 10 Anglophones out of over 130 Board Chairmen of State Corporations
- Only three Anglophone DAGs out of 38 Government Ministries
- No Anglophone SG at the Presidency, Ministers of Finance, Territorial Administration, Defence, GM of SONARA...since independence
- No operational airport, seaport in Anglophone Cameroon
- No Anglophone on the Douala Stock Exchange Board
- Only four Anglophone SGs out of 38 in Ministries
- No Referral Hospital in Anglophone Cameroon
- Only six Anglophones of over 36 Ambassadors
- No English word on FCFA currency
- Only six Anglophones out of 58 SDOs
- Only three Anglophone Army Generals out of 33...

The Guardian Post
DAILY

Corrigendum:

Unending marginalisation:

Anglophones too inferior, incompetent to head these institutions?

Presidency, SG at the Presidency, Finance, Defence, Gendarmerie, Police, Economy, SNH, SONARA, Douala Port Authority, CNPS, CRTV, CAMAIR-Co, SOPECAM, FECAFOOT...

Gov't authorises Mbengwi Ex-students Cooperative Credit Union Limited

CEMAC Summit in Yaounde August 18:
Will Biya cut short holiday to attend gathering?

AFCON:
Deplorable roads, garbage heaps, broken taxis...to welcome guests

Soa District Hospital staff protest unpaid salaries

Figure 28.3. Left: Anglophone Marginalization: Facts and Figures, *The Guardian Post*, May 1993.

Figure 28.4. Right: Anglophone Unending Marginalization. *The Guardian Post*, August 13, 2021

CAMEROON POST

104. April 2 - 9, 1992

Hard Core Opposition Wants Transitional Gov't

Hard core opposition parties which are members of the Alliance For The Reconstruction of Cameroon Through The Sovereign National Conference (ARC-SNC) have called for the formation of a transitional government with the main purpose of convening a sovereign national conference.

In a statement issued in Bamenda March 28, 1992 and signed by the Chairman of the alliance Mr. John Fru Ndi, the ARC-SNC called for the resignation of Mr. Paul Biya and his government.

See Page 3

At Constitution Drafting Technical Committee:

Anglophone Proposal For Federalism Rejected

*Owona Threatens Beti Secession If Anglophones Insist On Federalism

CAMEROON POST

CAM Meeting Holds Against Background Of Threats

* Calls on all educational institutions in Cameroon not to reopen if CEB decree is not signed

See page 11

THE FEDERATION ISSUE

Mitterrand Instructs Biya To Reject Two-State Federation

* Suggests Army Intervention to Crush Anglophone Resistance

Special report on page 3

NEWSLINE

Editorial
Will France Choose For Cameroonians? P.3

Game Plan For August 30/31 National Strike - The FDC to Coordinate Strike in The Centre Province P.3

PTT in Scandal
Peoples' Parcels Wasted In Douala P.6

The Sorry Plight Of Government Sponsored Cameroonian Students In Britain, Germany, Nigeria... P.7

The Agony of the Unibuea Student P.7

Count Down On CANSA Confab
Anglophone Students Converge August 27 P.14

Romancing the Stone
An x-ray of the nefarious French activities in Cameroon P.12

THE NATIONAL EXAMINATION BOARD AFFAIR
"I am not a parent, my children do not study in Cameroon"
Mbella Mbappe
Page 10

THE SO-CALLED COMMUNIQUE FROM SOUTH WEST CHIEFS AND ELITES

Chief Inoni Ephraim Declares Secession

Yaounde SWELA Chapter President, Chief John Agbor Tabi Fires Back

Read our exclusive interview, SWELA communique and other reactions on pages 2, 4 and 5

Figure 28.5. Left: Anglophone Proposal for Federalism Rejected. *Cameroon Post*, April 2, 1992
Figure 28.6. Right: The French Connection: "Mitterrand Instructs Biya to Reject Two-state federation *Cameroon Post*, August 23, 1993."

15 million Fcfa

to be won in BANKO Tuesday, October 18th

The Guardian Post

DAILY

Cherished by many, haunted by some, read by them all

Eto'o, Moukandjo shortlisted for African best player award

Angered by gov't's provocative silence, divide & rule tactic:

Common Law lawyers begin week-long strike today!

Biya expected home today after 32 days abroad

After Bafoussam:

Camair-Co launches flights to Bamenda soon

South West:

Police nab suspected human trafficker with four victims

Trump challenges Clinton to drug test before next Presidential debate

CAMASEJ Buea Sways Students to Embrace Peace as Benchmark for Good Leadership

WAA Cameroon Holds Symposium on Youth Participation in Peace-building Processes in Cameroon

the voice

WEEKENDER

The Audacity of Truth

1993 AAC II Buea Declaration

The Anglophone Voice Biya Refused to Hear

*And Here Comes the Amba Zombi

PM to Buea with Carrot, Defence Minister to Bamenda with Stick

"Tanks' Roll into NW as MINDEF Announces Change in Military Tactics

September 22, No 5

Deifying a Date

The Day Anglophones Poured Out

*Assessing the Trickledown Effect

UK Stunned by Upsurge of Killings, Violence in NW/SW

UNDP Offers Youths Access to Professional Orientation

US President Wants Homosexuality in Cameroon

Yannick Kawa Kawa in Prison

Figure 28.7. Left: Anglophone Common law lawyers kick off the Anglophone Revolt. *Guardian Post,* October 18, 2016.
Fig. 28.8. Right: The Anglophone Voice Biya Refused to Hear. *The Voice*, Friday, September 24, 2021

The Scoop

Association Un Espoir Pour La Vie

A.E.P.

There has been no marriage between British and French Cameroons

- Cardinal Tumi

BBC launches Pidgin English service

CPDM Fako Launches Back To School Campaign

Anglophones Detained in SED bunker moved to Kondengui

PLANET Ananas

THE Sun

Mayor Ekema may have used the backdoor into UB after all

Catholic Bishops maintain Mngr. Bala was murdered

Anglophone crisis:

SDF MPs call for National Dialogue Forum

Headlines

LCC launches three major road projects in Limbe municipality

Insecurity grips Kumba -six bandits nabbed, two drug dealers arrested

Hon. Wirba gets another hero's welcome in Jakiri

-Keeps parliamentary immunity afterall

Two North West Fons perish in ghastly car crash

Figure 28.9. Left: Cardinal Tumi: There was no marriage between British and French Cameroons, *The Scoop*, August 2017.

Figure 28.10. Right: SDF MPS call for National Dialogue Forum, *The Sun*, July 2017

Comment When Sealed Lips Speak

Eden

Teachers' Strike: Detained Principal Released

Prime Minister Yang Admits Anglophone Problem Exists

* Dismisses Atanga Nji's Ranting
* Dissolves The Fame Ndongo Commission
* Strike Continues Indefinitely
* Lawyers Say Laurent Esso's Arrogance Is Killing Dialogue
* A Ten-Point Consensual Agenda Agreed With Teachers

SDF Accuses Govt Of Attempting To Kill Fru Ndi

Maverick Fidel Castro Dies At 90

Wednesday's Clashes Paralyse B'da, Leaves 2 Soldiers Dead

THE INDEPENDENT NEWSPAPER AT THE SERVICE OF THE PEOPLE

The Post

Wache Forever

Biya Designates Social Affairs Minister To Launch Etombi Foundation

No. 02167 FRIDAY, MARCH 12, 2021

WEST CAMEROON:

Sitting On Riches, Walking In Poverty

- Huge Gold Deposits In Donga Mantung, Manyu
- Over 4 Untapped Oil Wells In Ndian, Widikum
- Iron Ore In Mayo-Binka
- Vast Palm Plantations, Timber, Rubber, Banana

VIOLENCE AGAINST MEN:

'My Wife Refused Me Sex, Had A Child With My Friend'

Will President Biya Take COVID-19 Vaccine Like Peers?

President Biya

ALSO INSIDE

Collector's Diary

Turn-ons & Turn-offs For Men, Women

Issues At Stake

When The Belligerents Mortgage Future Of The Nation

Letter From Buea ...

End The War And Many Vices Would End

Morocco's Refusal To Host U17 AFCON: Prejudice Or Fairness?

Fig. 28.11. Left: Prime Minister Yang Admits Anglophone Problem Exists, *Eden*, November 28, 2016."

Figure 28.12. Right: West Cameroon: Sitting on Riches: Walking in Poverty" *The Post*, March 12, 2021.

The Guardian Post
DAILY
Cherished by many, haunted by some, read by them all

Yaounde
Four die of suspected food poisoning

Ceasefire deal:
GOVERNMENT IS ADAMANT.
NO DIALOGUE WITH TERRORISTS
• Ambazonia terrorist leaders themselves sabotage any possibility of "dialogue".

EDITORIAL
Disunited Ambazonians desperate for recognition.

To cushion COVID-19 shocks:
EU disburses 6 billion FCFA to Cameroon

Kamto's lawyer appointed French Justice Minister

The Guardian Post
DAILY
Cherished by many, haunted by some, read by them all

Cholera kills 48 in North region

SDF MPs slam parliament for continuously rejecting debate on Anglophone crisis
• But say only NEC can decide whether party should quit National Assembly, senate in protest

After visit to Cameroon:
US congressman says Anglophone crisis victims need urgent, greater attention

One in 10 children won't complete primary school by 2030 - UNESCO

18 sentenced for competitive entrance exams fraud

13 billion FCFA EU aid to rebuild conflict-ravaged towns in Cameroon

Figure 28.13: Government is Adamant, No Dialogue with Terrorists, *The Guardian Post, 2020.*
Figure 28.14. SDF MPs Slam parliament for continuously rejecting debate on Anglophone crisis, *The Guardian Post,* July 2017

The Guardian Post
DAILY
Cherished by many, haunted by some, read by them all

Biya, Mugabe: Unfair Comparison

Cavaye warns SDF MPs:
"I won't tolerate any debate on Anglophone crisis in parliament"
• The House speaker sounded the warning while receiving SDF MPs after their boycott of the opening session of parliament

After apparent military coup:
Power-drunk Mugabe refuses to resign

THE Sun

THURSDAY, AUGUST 22, 2019

Faculty of Agriculture & Veterinary Medicine
University of Buea
Programmes for Admission in 2019
BSc MSc & PhD

Sisiku Ayuk Tabe & Co trial
The damning verdict
Life imprisonment for all Nera 10 plus heavy fines
Exclusive account of proceedings
Dialogue hopes dampen
Back-to-school in NW,SW in peril
Reactions from across the board

Young Cameroonian creates app to solve school dilemma in NW/SW

Tender result from LCC

Bamenda goes dead as military combats separatists in gun battle

Figure 28.15. Left: Cameroon National Assembly Speaker, Cavaye warns SDF MPS: I won't tolerate any debate on Anglophone crisis in Parliament, *The Guardian Post*, November 2017
Figure 28.16. Right: The Damning Verdict: Ayuk Tabe NERA 10. *The Sun*, August 12, 2019.

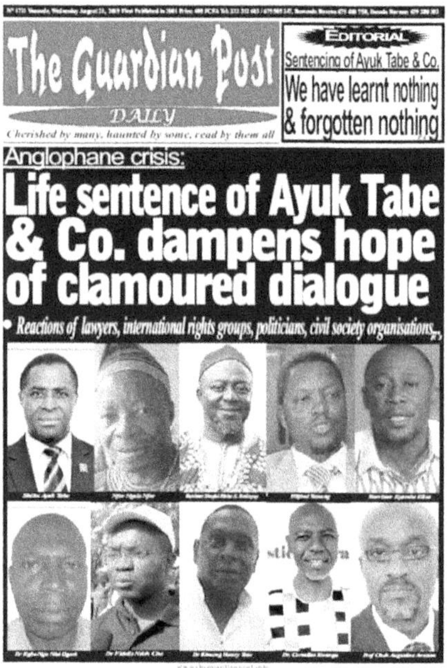

The Guardian Post
DAILY
Cherished by many, haunted by some, read by them all
EDITORIAL
Sentencing of Ayuk Tabe & Co.
We have learnt nothing & forgotten nothing
Anglophane crisis:
Life sentence of Ayuk Tabe & Co. dampens hope of clamoured dialogue
• Reactions of lawyers, international rights groups, politicians, civil society organisations...

«BLEUS» WINNING PRIZE
LA COURSE DES Bleus
325 MILLION / 325 MILLION
THE INDEPENDENT NEWSPAPER AT THE SERVICE OF THE PEOPLE
The WEEKENDER Post
No. 02051 FRIDAY, NOVEMBER 15, 2019 PRICE: FCFA 400
Anti-Riot Police Foil Bikers' Protest Against Governor's Orders
Cameroonians Split Over February 9 Legislative, Municipal Elections
• But ELECAM Gives 15 Days For Parties To Submit Files
PARIS PEACE FORUM:
Biya's Anglophones 'Assimilation Confession' Shocks Cameroonians
P 2&3
MINISTER ATANGA NJI WARNS:
Any Unidentified Biker After December 9, Is A Terrorist
President Paul Biya and Mo Ibrahim in a panel discussion at the Paris Peace Forum
SDF Dumps Decision To Boycott Elections, Strategises To Challenge Adversaries

Figure 28.17 "Life Sentence of Ambazonian Interim President, Ayuk Tabe & Co. dampens hope of clamoured dialogue" *Guardian Post* Wednesday, August 21, 2019

Figure 28.18. Biya's Assimilation Confession Shocks Cameroonians. *The Post*, Friday, November 15, 2019.

Wache Forever
THE INDEPENDENT NEWSPAPER AT THE SERVICE OF THE PEOPLE
The WEEKENDER Post
No. 02137 FRIDAY, OCTOBER 30, 2020 PRICE: FCFA 400
RACE INTO HOUSE OF CHIEFS:
Etina, Ndike Present Consensus List To ELECAM
STOP THE WAR:
Hired Protesters, Commercial Mourners Can't End Cameroon's Bloodbath
Wailing, thousands of protest marches, millions of condemnations, countless hashtags without action will not stop the current killings; only political will and the determination of all citizens will avert this bloodbath
'Evangelist' Atanga Nji's Kumba Sermon Stirs Disapproval
Biya Declares October 31 Day Of National Mourning
False Alarm About Amba Schools Attack Causes Commotion In SW

Figure 28.19. Hired Protesters, Commercial Mourners Can't End Cameroon's Bloodbath, The Post, October 30, 2020.

II. The Biya Regime's Military Subjugation Campaign: The Human Rights and Freedom of Expression Aspects of the Anglophone Problem

THE INDEPENDENT NEWSPAPER AT THE SERVICE OF THE PEOPLE

The Post

ANGLOPHONE CRISIS: Dialogue, President Paul Biya's Credo

NO. 01860 MONDAY, OCTOBER 16, 2017 PRICE: FCFA 400

Buea Midnight 'Mass' Burial Uncovered

Hidden Faces Behind Gruesome Act Unmasked

Was Slain Atanga's Corpse Among Those Buried?

Fako Lawyers Split Ahead Of Court Resumption

SDF Gets First-ever Authorisation To March In Douala

Media House Suspends Worker Over Anglophone Problem

Agbor Balla Rubbishes 'Elites' Visit To Anglophone Regions

Fresh 'mass' grave in Mile 16 Bolifamba New Layout Cemetry

Ntarinkon Cooperative Credit Union Nkwen Branch

Opposite PMI-Nkwen, adjacent Amour Mezam

The Guardian Post DAILY

Cherished by many, haunted by some, read by them all

National Assembly: Gov't tables bill to protect rights of persons with disabilities

Soldiers in search of Amba fighters ransack Shisong Hospital!

Mercilessly torture security guards, molest patients, health officials

Rising violence in NW, SW: US, UK, Switzerland, Canada issue another 'empty' condemnation

China counts achievements, 100 years after creation of Communist Party

Editorial: Cameroon stinking, but grappling to host AFCON!

Limbe City Council: SDO wades in as power tussle goes dirty

Figure 28.20. Right: Buea Midnight 'Mass' Burial Uncovered. *The Post*, October 16, 2017.
Figure 28.21. Left: Soldiers in search of Amba fighters ransack Shisong Hospital. *The Guardian Post*, November 17, 2021.

The Guardian Post DAILY

Cherished by many, haunted by some, read by them all

G20 debt cancellation: IMF says Cameroon can still benefit if...

After Ngarbuh massacre findings: Biya regime under pressure to investigate other alleged military excesses

- Murdering of man who 'released' information to UN on Ngarbuh massacre
- Killing of breastfeeding mother, other civilians in Babanki
- Shooting of civilians to death & burning of corpses in Bali
- Brutal killing of months-old Baby Martha in Muyuka
- Mass killings in Pinyin, Bole-Bakundu, Ndian, Kupe-Muanenguba...
- Slaughtering of physically challenged persons in Belo, Kumba...
- Lootings, rape, burning of villages in NW, SW

African Distribution Company supports fight against COVID-19

'Born again' Biya begins reconciliation process with Anglophones

Analysts say the landmark decisions on Ngarbuh massacre are strong indications that top regime officials whose actions & utterances fueled the armed conflict in NW & SW regions would soon face the music

THE INDEPENDENT NEWSPAPER AT THE SERVICE OF THE PEOPLE

The Weekender Post

Wache Forever

COVID-19 Pandemic Sends Gov't In Search Of Cemetery Space

No. 02089 FRIDAY, APRIL 24, 2020 PRICE: FCFA 400

WICUDA PRESIDENT TELLS GOV'T: We Don't Want Military Base In Ngarbuh

- Will Exhuming Corpses Resurrect The Dead?
- Thank Gov't For inquiry Report
- Appeals Authorities To Investigate Other Atrocities Committed In Mbumland

UN Demands Full Accountability On Ngarbuh Massacre

Michelle Bachelet

Biya Cancels Labour, National Day Celebrations

Shey Henry Nganji, WICUDA National President

Figure 28.22. Right: Biya regime under pressure, *The Guardian Post*, April 24, 2020.
Figure 28.23. Left: Ngarbuh Massacre. We Don't Want Military Base in Ngarbuh, *The Weekender Post*, April 24, 2020.

Partial Cancellation Of Legislative Elections In NW
Don't Sacrifice Us To Appease SDF, NW CPDM Tells Gov't

Violence Must Stop For Dialogue To Continue

THE INDEPENDENT NEWSPAPER AT THE SERVICE OF THE PEOPLE

The Post

Wache Forever

Cameroon Gov't Calls For Vigilance As Nigeria Confirms First Coronavirus Case

No. 02075 MONDAY, MARCH 02, 2020 PRICE: FCFA 400

After Ngarbuh Massacre:
Military Allegedly Kills 15 In Babanki

Administrators Reduce Police, Military Checkpoints After Buea Taxi Drivers' Protest

Children, women mourning victims of Ngarbuh Massacre in church, after the men all escaped and sought refuge in the bushes

Financial Crisis, Unpaid Bills Responsible For Electricity Rationing
- ENEO GM

Biya, Yang, Esso, Motaze, Djoumessi Dragged To Arbitration Tribunal

The Guardian Post
DAILY
Cherished by many, hunted by some, read by them all

Cameroon, Germany seal dev't cooperation deal

I was shot by military
- Pastor injured in Bali church shootings tells congregation

As workers go for months without pay: Lyonga Institute of Science & Technology offers scholarship to children of CDC workers

At least 421 killed in NW, SW within nine months
- Report

Bar Council rubbishes compulsory COVID-19 vaccination

Ntarinkon Credit Union Nkwen Branch
Now operational
Opposite PMI-Nkwen, adjacent Amour Mezam

Figure 28.24. Left: Military kills 15 in Babanki, *The Post*, March 2, 2020.
Figure 28.25. Right: "I was shot by the Military" *The Guardian Post*, October 19 2021.

III. Attacks and Atrocities of Ambazonian Fighters Against Cameroon Military and Against Anglophone Civilians

THE Sun

Fire razes down Sasse

THURSDAY, JANUARY 07, 2021 No. 0632 FCFA 400

International PR firm to lobby for negotiations to resolve Ambazonia war

Deadly attack on Momo SDO's convoy

- Communication Delegate, Becky Liwusi Jeme, five military officers killed
- Convoy was returning to Mbengwi from Ngie and Njikwa after installing D.Os

Buea Diocese:
Enter Bishop Michael Bibi

- After one year as Apostolic Administrator, during which he began a clean sweep of the house and brought order at CUIB and SOBA, Pope Francis Tuesday confirmed the 49-year-old prelate as Bishop of the pioneer diocese in Cameroon
- His immediate challenge shall be to complete the longstanding co-cathedral started by his predecessor, Bishop Immanuel BanlaBushu now on retirement

City SUN
Limbe City Council prioritises stabilisation of finances in 2021
Limbe I mayor tasks staff to step up recovery as council adopts FCFA 980 million budget
Limbe III Council adopts FCFA 650 million to transform municipality in 2021

MINDHU, MINTP, train newly appointed officials

The Guardian Post
DAILY

CRTV in tears as radio Editor-in-Chief drops dead

Bui:
Amba fighters kill NW Penitentiary boss, three warders!

Clergy petition Ngoketunjia SDO over military excesses

Editorial
When parliament speaks truth to Biya, but avoids armed conflict in NW, SW

Secondary education ministry, FECAFOOT to boost youth football

Opposition coalition lobbies Canada to push for electoral reforms

Figure 28.26. Left: Deadly Attack on MOMO SDO's Convoy. *The Sun*, Thursday, January 7, 2021.
Figure 28.27. Right: Amba Fighters kill NW penitentiary boss, three warders, *The Guardian Post*, April 13, 2022.

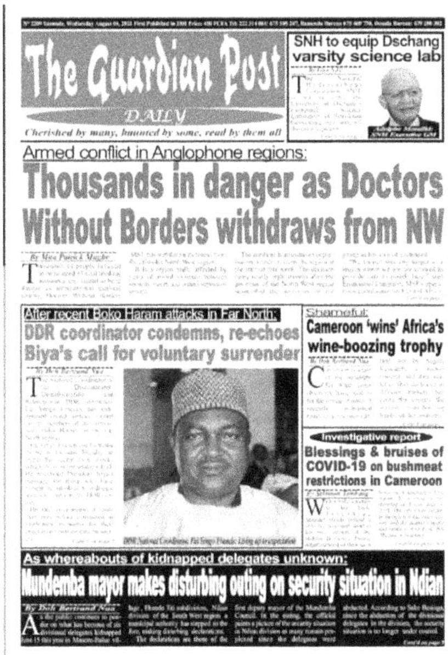

The Guardian Post

DAILY

SNH to equip Dschang varsity science lab

Armed conflict in Anglophone regions:

Thousands in danger as Doctors Without Borders withdraws from NW

After recent Boko Haram attacks in Far North:

DDR coordinator condemns, re-echoes Biya's call for voluntary surrender

Shameful:

Cameroon 'wins' Africa's wine-boozing trophy

Investigative report

Blessings & bruises of COVID-19 on bushmeat restrictions in Cameroon

As whereabouts of kidnapped delegates unknown:

Mundemba mayor makes disturbing outing on security situation in Ndian

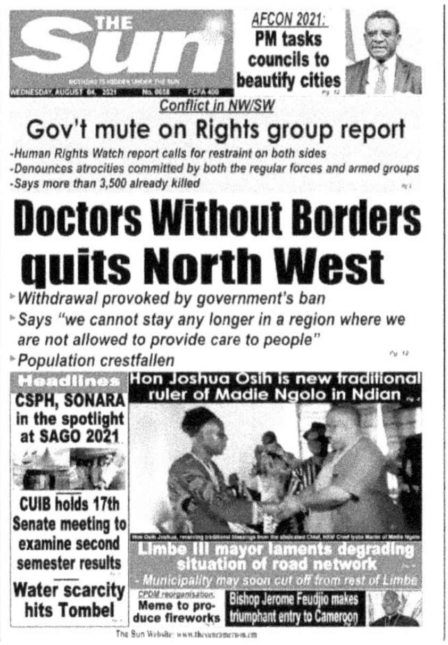

THE Sun

AFCON 2021:

PM tasks councils to beautify cities

WEDNESDAY, AUGUST 04, 2021

Conflict in NW/SW

Gov't mute on Rights group report

-Human Rights Watch report calls for restraint on both sides

-Denounces atrocities committed by both the regular forces and armed groups

-Says more than 3,500 already killed

Doctors Without Borders quits North West

- Withdrawal provoked by government's ban
- Says "we cannot stay any longer in a region where we are not allowed to provide care to people"
- Population crestfallen

Headlines

CSPH, SONARA in the spotlight at SAGO 2021

Hon Joshua Osih is new traditional ruler of Madie Ngolo in Ndian

CUIB holds 17th Senate meeting to examine second semester results

Limbe III mayor laments degrading situation of road network

- Municipality may soon cut off from rest of Limbe

Water scarcity hits Tombel

CPDM reorganisation: Meme to produce fireworks

Bishop Jerome Feudjio makes triumphant entry to Cameroon

Figure 28.28. Left: Thousands in danger as Doctors Without Borders withdraws from NW, *The Guardian Post*, August 4, 2021.

Figure 28.29. Right: Doctors Without Borders Quits Northwest, *The Sun*, August 4, 2021

HE WON 118 MILLION

2 BILLION

THE INDEPENDENT NEWSPAPER AT THE SERVICE OF THE PEOPLE

The Post

WEEKENDER

Wache Forever

Finance Minister Hails Customs Dept For Remarkable 2020 Results

No. 02157 FRIDAY, JANUARY 29, 2021 PRICE: FCFA 400

Panic Grips Limbe After 2 Bomb Blasts

Dschang Road Accident Leaves 53 Dead, 29 Injured

CDC GM Dispels Talk Of Protest, Appeals For Calm

Y'de Inhabitants Decry Surging Robbery In Taxis

Programme Officer Vacancy At UICN

Charred remains of truck and bus

TOGETHER, LET'S TACKLE THE CHALLENGES OF CYBERSECURITY

THE ICT UNIVERSITY

ADMISSIONS ONGOING FOR (FALL) OCTOBER 2023

THE INDEPENDENT NEWSPAPER AT THE SERVICE OF THE PEOPLE

The Post

Wache Forever

Dr. Nkengasong, Cameroonian Authorities Chart Better Ways To Combat HIV/AIDS

No. 02368 MONDAY, SEPTEMBER 11, 2023 FCFA 400

Lockdown Imposes Reign Of Terror

- Separatist Fighters Burn Cars, Kill 3, Injure Others In Buea
- Explosion Kills 1, Injures Over 10 In Limbe
- Fako SDO Bans Night Circulation Of Bikes In Some Areas
- School, Business Activities Halted

ELECAM Launches SW Regional Platform For Permanent Consultation With Stakeholders

CAMTEL GM Promises Expanding Catalog Of Products, Quality Service

Only 46% Of Schools Functioned In NW-SW In 2022-2023 - Barr Agbor Balla

MINPROFF Doles Out FCFA 35M To 200 Buea Flood Victims

SDF's Battle For Peace To Reign In Northwest, Southwest Is Ongoing - Hon. Joshua Osih

Figure 28.30. Left: Panic Grips Limbe After 2 Bomb Blasts, *The Post*, January 29, 2021

Figure 28.31. Right: Lockdown Imposes Reign of Terror. *The Post*, Monday, September 11, 2023.

Everything na double, double
Best Deals #111*0#

THE INDEPENDENT NEWSPAPER AT THE SERVICE OF THE PEOPLE
The Post WEEKENDER
Wache Forever
Kumbo Mayor Launches Holiday Classes, Campaign For Return To Normalcy
No. 02114 FRIDAY, AUGUST 07, 2020 PRICE: FCFA 400

Anglophone Detainee Dies Chained To Sick Bed

Soldiers Implore Population To Identify, Report Amba Explosive Manufacturers

Mgr Kleda's Declaration That Coronavirus Has Been Conquered, Sparks Controversy

Thomas Nganyu Tangem dies, chained to his sick bed

Lawyers At Odds With Motanga's Demolition Campaign

MINCOM Debunks COVID-19 Funds Embezzlement Allegations

The Guardian Post DAILY
Cherished by many, haunted by some, read by them all

Editorial
2025 presidentials
CPDM campaign is on!

Fon Chafah bestows traditional title on US Ambassador

Liberators-turned oppressors:
Amba fighters intensify move to further impoverish Anglophones
- Set taxis on fire for plying streets in Bamenda without being painted in Ambazonia colours

Unite for Health Foundation wins NGO of The Year Award

CENPA crowns Chenwi Peter Most Resilient, Innovative, Dev't-Oriented Mayor

For materialising President Biya's digital transformation vision:
P&T Minister gets Digital, Cybersecurity Champion distinction

Akere Muna, colleague secure release of activist, Junior Ngombe

Figure 28.32. Anglophone Detainee Dies Chained to Sick Bed, *The Post*, August 7, 2020.
Figure 28.33. Amba fighters intensify move to further impoverish Anglophones. *The Guardian Post*, Thursday, August 1, 2024.

The Guardian Post DAILY
Cherished by many, haunted by some, read by them all

Gabon shuts border with Cameroon after failed coup

At New Year wishes ceremony:
Biya ignores Anglophone crisis!
- But diplomats tell him to initiate inclusive dialogue to end conflict in NW, SW
- Pledge to accompany gov't in efforts to restore peace in restive regions

Cameroon ranked among world's authoritarian states

Bishops insist broad-based dialogue only solution to crisis in NW, SW

President Biya at Unity Palace yesterday

Police inspector sacked for receiving 5,000 FCFA bribe

Bolloré Group loses management of Douala Port terminal

ACHAP 9th Biennial Conference

Figure 28.34. Biya Ignores Anglophone Crisis, *The Guardian Post*, January 10, 2019.

IV. Victimization of Independent Anglophone Journalists in Cameroon

The Guardian Post
DAILY
Cherished by many, haunted by some, read by them all

Int'l Call for Tender from the Port of Douala-Bonaberi

When practicing journalism in Cameroon is a crime!

- The case of Buea-based journalist, Samuel Wazizi
- Gov't's silence over his whereabouts ten months after arrest, fuels reports he was tortured to death in detention
- Kamto, Agbor Balla, Michel Ndoki, Kah Walla, PAP, CAMASEJ, SNJC… pressure gov't to produce him dead or alive

The Guardian Post
DAILY
Cherished by many, haunted by some, read by them all

Kribi port, ANOR partner to boost services

Court throws out request to produce Wazizi dead or alive!

Fight against COVID-19:
MINAT boss hands Biya's 170,000 face masks to education ministries

AfDB approves third phase of Ring Road project

June session of parliament begins today

Burundi president dies at 55

Anglophone crisis:
US diplomat urges AU to seek UN Security Council intervention

Figure 28.35. Left: When practicing journalism in Cameroon is a Crime: The Case of the Murder of Samuel Wazizi, *The Guardian Post*, June 3, 2020.

Figure 28.36. Right: Court Throws Out Request to produce Wazizi Dead or Alive, *The Guardian Post*, June 10, 2020.

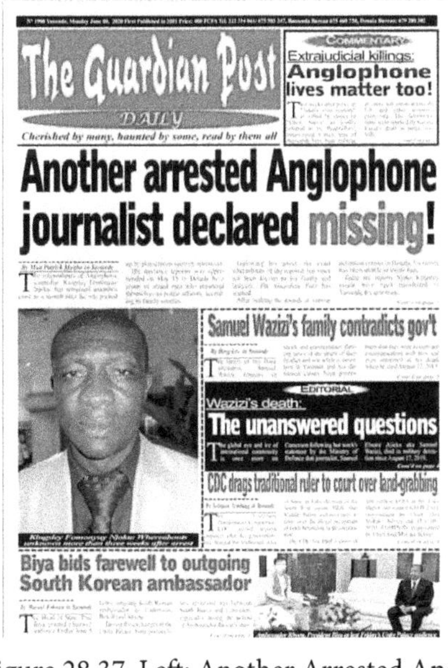

The Guardian Post
DAILY
Cherished by many, haunted by some, read by them all

COMMENTARY
Extrajudicial killings:
Anglophone lives matter too!

Another arrested Anglophone journalist declared missing!

Samuel Wazizi's family contradicts gov't

EDITORIAL
Wazizi's death:
The unanswered questions

CDC drags traditional ruler to court over land-grabbing

Biya bids farewell to outgoing South Korean ambassador

The Guardian Post
DAILY
Cherished by many, haunted by some, read by them all

Vote The Guardian Post 2016 Awards laureates

Consortium President, SG transferred to Yaounde

- Akere, Ben Muna to lead over 30 prominent lawyers to defend arrested Consortium leaders
- Tassang Wilfred escapes arrest, seeks refuge in an embassy in Yaounde
- Uneasy calm reigns in Anglophone Regions

Barrister Ben Muna — Agbor Balla — Tassang Wilfred — Dr. Fontem Neba — Barrister Akere Muna

Gov't shuts down internet in NW, SW
- The move comes a day after gov't warned against propagation of false information on social media

AU offers to mediate between gov't & aggrieved Anglophones

Tchiroma apologises for saying there's no Anglophone problem

Figure 28.37. Left: Another Arrested Anglophone Journalist Declared Missing. *The Guardian Post*, June 4, 2020.

Figure 28.38. Right: Consortium president, SD transferred to Yaoundé, *The Guardian Post*, Jan 10, 2017.

THE INDEPENDENT NEWSPAPER AT THE SERVICE OF THE PEOPLE

The Post

Cameroon Has A Vibrant Economy

Wache Forever

No. 02215 MONDAY, SEPTEMBER 27, 2021 PRICE: FCFA 400

MAJOR NATIONAL DIALOGUE:

After Shadow-chasing Moves, Biya Saddles PM With Preaching Unpopular Special Status

- How Denial Of Federalism Boosted Support For Separatists
- Dion Ngute Expected In B'da To Sing Same Song To Same Wrong Audience

Nso Indigenes Condemn Germany For Continuously Keeping Stolen Statue

5 Ministries Blacklisted For Refusing To Collaborate With CONAC

CPDM Mayor Cries Foul Against Reorganisation Malpractices

Genocide in Ambazonia

We Now Have Two Snakes in Front of Us

IMF completes 4th ECF review for Cameroon, approves FCFA 44M payout

thevoice

The Audacity of Truth

Big Ambazonia Prison Protest Shakes Yaounde

Back to School Without Learning!

Give the Children their Right, Future

Schools Vs Insecurity

EDITORIAL

Genuine Indignation or Image Repair Move?

Figure 28.39. L: After Shadow-chasing Moves, Biya Saddles PM With Preaching Unpopular Special Status. *The Post*, Monday September 27, 2021.

Figure 28.40. R: Big Anglophone Prison Protest Shakes Yaoundé. *The Voice*, July 24, 2019.

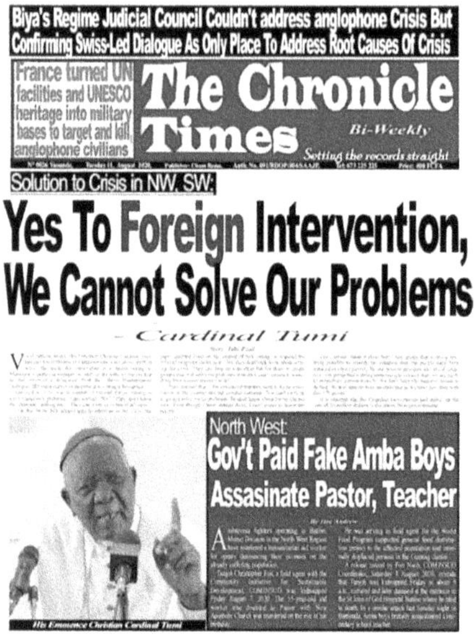
Biya's Regime Judicial Council Couldn't address anglophone Crisis But Confirming Swiss-Led Dialogue As Only Place To Address Root Causes Of Crisis

France turned UN facilities and UNESCO heritage into military bases to target and kill anglophone civilians

The Chronicle Times

Bi-Weekly

Setting the records straight

Solution to Crisis in NW, SW:

Yes To Foreign Intervention, We Cannot Solve Our Problems

– Cardinal Tumi

North West:

Gov't Paid Fake Amba Boys Assasinate Pastor, Teacher

His Eminence Christian Cardinal Tumi

The Guardian Post

DAILY

Cherished by many, haunted by some, read by them all

CAMPOST unveils innovative services on World Post Day

Anglophone crisis:

Tibor Nagy's predictions, inconsistencies spark heated debates

Bamoun gets new Sultan

Presidency recognises Chief Bajon Bihai III as traditional ruler!

ICT University donates 50 MFCFA-worth computers to Chadian varsity

Figure 28.41. L: Yes to Foreign Intervention., We Cannot Solve Our Problems (Cardinal Tumi), *The Chronicle Times*, Tuesday, 11 August 2020.

Figure 28.42. R: Tibor Nagy's predictions, inconsistencies spark heated debates, *Guardian Post*, October 11, 2021.

IV. The International Aspects of the Anglophone Problem as Framed by the English-language Press

The Guardian Post
DAILY
Cherished by many, haunted by some, read by them all
Tiko:
Four die, others hospitalised of alleged food poisoning
Armed conflict in NW, SW:
UN SG accuses military of rape, gross gender-based violence
Kumbo:
Amba fighter allegedly poisons comrade in tussle over lady
Archbishop Nkea inaugurates Una Familia Finance Ltd Yaounde branch office
For selfless service to humanity:
Dr Fuh Calistus wins Philanthropic & Charity Champion Award
Demtou Humanitarian outlines impact of activities in intervention areas

ALL MOBILIZED FOR CYBERSECURITY
The Guardian Post
DAILY
Cherished by many, haunted by some, read by them all
We are recruiting:
Two Desk Editors urgently needed at The Guardian Post
Pressure mounts on France to table Anglophone crisis at UN Security Council
Gov't unveils new Customs measures to sustain economic growth
Mbanga:
Married soldier allegedly kills, buries girlfriend
Human Rights Watch nails gov't, separatists again

Figure 28.43. L: UN SG accuses military of rape, gross, gender-based violence, *The Guardian Post*, Wednesday, April 14, 2021.

Figure 28.44. R: Pressure Mounts on France to table Anglophone Crisis at UN Security Council, *The Guardian Post*, January 14, 2021.

thevoice
The Audacity of Truth
Bi-weekly
Every Monday and Thursday
The Only Revolution in Cameroon is Sharing Money
Ako Kingsley Begins Journey to Celestial Bliss June 18
THE VOICE OFFICE LOCATED AT MELEN OPPOSITE POLYTECHNIC ENTRANCE
thevoice
The Audacity of Truth
ANGLOPHONE CRISIS
UN Security Council Divided 4:1, Russia's Volte-Face
Members Urge Further Mediation to Settle Conflict in Anglophone Cameroon, Prescribe Independent Investigation into Wazizi's Death
Publish Information on Emergency Reserve Use for Covid-19 - HRW
VIEW POINT
Prof. Joseph Owona's 47-Year Crusade against Anglophone Nationalism
OPINION
Cameroun, Where Dictatorship Knows No Bounds!!!
Commonwealth leaders reject automatic second term for Baroness Scotland
Coronavirus Might Become 'Fixture' in Africa for Years
Africa's coronavirus "hotspots" in S. Africa, Algeria, Cameroon: WHO
Islamic militants slaughter 20 soldiers, over 40 civilians in north-east Nigeria

The Guardian Post
DAILY
Cherished by many, haunted by some, read by them all
Proprietor of pioneer private radio in Bamenda dies
Efforts to resolve crisis in NW, SW:
Switzerland offers to facilitate dialogue between gov't, separatists
UN says over 38,000 without shelter due to Anglophone crisis
PM presides over Cameroon football cup final Sunday
Gov't renews 250 billion FCFA contract for road works in Yaounde, Douala
After controversial World Cup match:
FIFA opens investigation against Lionesses
Nexttel affair:
BESTCAM casts doubts on neutrality of inter-ministerial committee
Intensive control of Automobile Stamp Duty for 2019 begins July 1

Figure 28.45. L: UN Security Council Divided. *The Voice*, June 13, 2020.

Figure 28.46. R: Switzerland offers to facilitate dialogue between gov't, separatists, *The Guardian Post* June 30, 2019

The Guardian Post
DAILY
Cherished by many, haunted by some, read by them all

Bamenda, Mbengwi:
Suspected Amba explosives leave two wounded

British MP faults UK gov't over 'shady' trade deal with Biya regime

- Says it's scandalous UK has turned a blind eye on 'slaughtering' of women, children & elderly in NW, SW in preference to clouded trade agreement
- Insists move a slap in the face of a recent US Congress Resolution calling for urgent international action to end Anglophone crisis

West region:
Visiting MINAT boss cautions traditional rulers against petition-writing

Gov't pumps in 10 billion FCFA to resolve water crisis

At least 18 killed in NW, SW within first 20 days of 2021

Tussle over Kumba city top job:
Mewanu in trouble again

- Kumba I councillors to deliberate on city mayor's 'convict' status in stormy session

THE INDEPENDENT NEWSPAPER AT THE SERVICE OF THE PEOPLE
The Post
WEEKENDER
Wache Forever
No. 02198 FRIDAY, JULY 16, 2021 PRICE: FCFA 400

Orange Cameroun Signs Partnership Agreement With University Of Douala

After Biafra-Ambazonia Coalition:
Nigeria Seals Anti-Secessionist Deal With Cameroon

Panic, Uncertainty Grip Nation As Ministerial Bombshell Lurks

Daniel Muna Memorial Clinic:
Ama, George Muna's Court Action Foils 'Board Of Directors Meeting'

Akere Muna Faulted For 'Rough Game'

Biya's envoy, HE Mbayu, and Nigeria's President Buhari exchanging pleasantries

Orange Cameroun Clears Air On Disgruntled Former Workers Defaming Company

MINSEC's Bush-falling Teachers' List:
Witch-hunting Of Perceived Political Opponents Takes Lead

- Staff Who Have Never Left Duty Posts, Country Implicated
- Escapee Inner Circle, Political Friends Shielded By Godfathers

Crucial Role Of Contractors In Mismanaging COVID-19, Other Funds

Figure 28.47. British MP faults UK gov't over "shady" trade deal with Biya regime, *The Guardian Post*, January 21, 2021.

Figure 28.48. Nigeria Signs Anti-Secessionist Deal, *The Post,* July 16, 2021.

The Guardian Post
DAILY
Cherished by many, haunted by some, read by them all

Funeral programme of Joseph Bongkiyung, Dreamland Connect Rock Quarry Manager

Interview:
Canadian High Commissioner on crisis in NW, SW!

- Anglophones have legitimate grievances but secession unrealistic
- Anglophones would be happier if given the autonomy to manage their resources
- Anglophones have lost trust in Biya regime...

Taxation Department
Finance minister upbeat new multipurpose complex would boost productivity

Cameroonian, Diko Mukete, appointed board member of Rwanda Finance

PM launches Vision 2035 Phase II today

THE Sun
MONDAY, OCTOBER 07, 2019

Barrister Ben Muna dies at 79

Major National Dialogue:
Anglophones capture 'Special Status'

- Biya assures recommendations will be considered attentively and diligently
- FCFA 3,500 billion needed to rebuild NW, SW
- Sisiku, others miss out on presidential clemency for anglophone detainees
- SDF tells gov't to copy Canada's example
- 'Diaspora for construction and consolidation of peace' makes major move
- Tibits of MND
- Reactions across the board
- Read excerpts of final report and exclusive Bilingualism and Social Cohesion commission report

Headlines
After release, Kamto says fight continues
People left party leanings behind for interest of Anglophones, country
- Peter Abety

Biz Sun
BICEC fuses with Moroccan bank group BCP
SW Customs chief arrested over rice deal

Figure 28.49. L: Canadian High Commissioner on crisis in NW, SW! *The Guardian Post*, November 16, 2020.

Figure 28.50. R: Anglophones "Capture Special Status," *The Sun*, October 7, 2019..

The Guardian Post
DAILY
Cherished by many, haunted by some, read by them all

SDF justifies low key 30th anniversary celebration

Frontline Southern Cameroons activist, Njoh Litumbe, dies!

After recovering from COVID-19:
Lawyer says inmates stigmatising Mebe Ngo'o's wife

PM Dion Ngute receives Kleda over COVID-19 herbal cure

The late Mola Njoh Litumbe

Priest rubbishes allocation of 4 billion FCFA car loan to MPs
- But lawmakers fire back, say amount insignificant compared to benefits of other state functionaries

Figure 28.51. L: "France will participate in the reconstruction of the Northwest and Southwest (NOSO) but there must first be a peace agreement between the government and armed groups" Christophe Guilhou, French Ambassador, (CRTV, April 19, 2020).
Figure 28.52. R: Frontline Southern Cameroons Activist, Njoh Litumbe Dies. *The Guardian Post*. May 17, 2020.

THE INDEPENDENT NEWSPAPER AT THE SERVICE OF THE PEOPLE
Wache Forever
The Post
How Biya Snubbed Cardinal Tumi, Charlotte Depanda
No. 02168 MONDAY, MARCH 15, 2021 PRICE FCFA 400

Secessionists Are Those Who Govern Cameroon, Not Us - *Sisiku*

CPDM To Count Militants, Not Reorganise Organs

Sisiku Ayuk Tabe, incarcerated President of Republic of Ambazonia

Violation Of Foumban Conference Terms Caused Anglophone Crisis
- *Hon. Tomaino Ndam Njoya*

Hon. Tomaino Ndam Njoya

SDF Braces Up For Grand Come-back

THE INDEPENDENT NEWSPAPER AT THE SERVICE OF THE PEOPLE
Wache Forever
The Post
Maurice Kamto's Meeting With Tibor Nagy Sparks Controversy
NO. 02064 MONDAY, JANUARY 13, 2020 PRICE: FCFA 400

ANGLOPHONE CRISIS:
African Bar Demands UN Organised Referendum To End War

Despite Rising Kidnappings Of Opposition Politicians
ELECAM Board Chair Insists Elections Must Hold

Antonio Guterres, UN Scribe, will he harken to the call of the African Bar Association?

MINFI Circular On Monitoring, Control, Execution Of 2020 State Budget

Figure 28.53. L: Secessionists Are Those Who Govern Cameroon, Not Us, *The Post*, Monday, March 15, 2021.
Figure 28.54. R: African Bar Association Demands UN Organized Referendum to End War, *The Post*, January 13, 2020.

THE INDEPENDENT NEWSPAPER AT THE SERVICE OF THE PEOPLE

The Post

Wache Forever

Chiefs Send Efasamoto, Nyango Namuna After Kumba Massacre Perpetrators

No. 02137 MONDAY, NOVEMBER 02, 2020 PRICE: FCFA 400

AFTER NATIONAL MOURNING, OUTPOURING:

Time To End The War

Kumba

Figure 28.55. Time to End the War, *The Post*, November 2, 2020.

VI. Anglophone and Francophone Cartoon Predictions: Fast Forward to the Past that did Not Pass or Rewind to a Future That May Come to Pass?

Le Popoli

JOURNAL SATIRIQUE

CAMEROUN

AU PAYS DE TOUTES LES INCERTITUDES

BOKO HARAM A T'IL JAMAIS ETE AFFAIBLI?

LE BIDOUNG CHALLENGE A LA FIFA

THE INDEPENDENT NEWSPAPER AT THE SERVICE OF THE PEOPLE

The Post

Wache Forever

With Meagre FCFA 2.3Bn Budget, Can NASLA Fast-track Decentralisation?

No. 02130 MONDAY, OCTOBER 05, 2020 PRICE: FCFA 400

ANGLOPHONE CRISIS:

Bishops Caution: Beware, The Worst May Still Be Ahead

Death Snatches Cameroon Bar Council President

Late Batonnier Charles Tchakoute Patie

Southern Cameroons Has Never Been Independent – Prof Victor Julius Ngoh

Prof. Ngoh

Douala Grand Mall To Go Operational In November

ELECAM Publishes List Of Voters Ahead Of Regional Elections

Noni Fons Denounce Marginalisation By Nso, Petition MINAT

Figure 28.56. L: Francophone Cartoonist, Nyemb Ntoogue (Nyemb Popoli) "In the Country of All Uncertainties," *Popoli* (Douala, Cameroon, 2018).

Figure 28.57. R: Prophetic warning of Anglophone Bishops of the Northwest asnd Southwest regions. *The Post*, October 2, 2020.

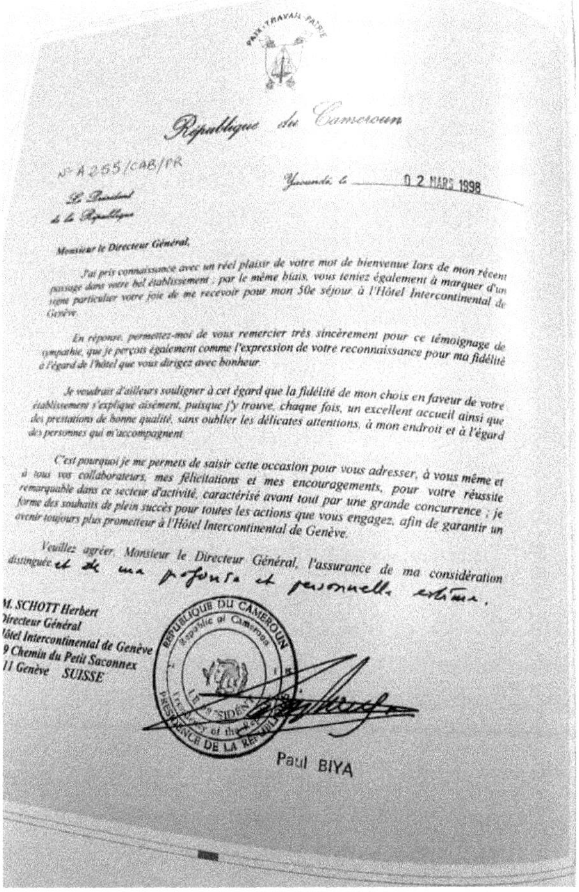

République du Cameroun

N° A255/CAB/PR

Yaoundé, le 0 2 MARS 1998

Le Président de la République

Monsieur le Directeur Général,

J'ai pris connaissance avec un réel plaisir de votre mot de bienvenue lors de mon récent passage dans votre bel établissement ; par le même biais, vous teniez également à marquer d'un signe particulier votre joie de me recevoir pour mon 50e séjour à l'Hôtel Intercontinental de Genève.

En réponse, permettez-moi de vous remercier très sincèrement pour ce témoignage de sympathie, que je perçois également comme l'expression de votre reconnaissance pour ma fidélité à l'égard de l'hôtel que vous dirigez avec bonheur.

Je voudrais d'ailleurs souligner à cet égard que la fidélité de mon choix en faveur de votre établissement s'explique aisément, puisque j'y trouve, chaque fois, un excellent accueil ainsi que des prestations de bonne qualité, sans oublier les délicates attentions, à mon endroit et à l'égard des personnes qui m'accompagnent.

C'est pourquoi je me permets de saisir cette occasion pour vous adresser, à vous même et à tous vos collaborateurs, mes félicitations et mes encouragements, pour votre réussite remarquable dans ce secteur d'activité, caractérisé avant tout par une grande concurrence ; je forme des souhaits de plein succès pour toutes les actions que vous engagez, afin de garantir un avenir toujours plus prometteur à l'Hôtel Intercontinental de Genève.

Veuillez agréer, Monsieur le Directeur Général, l'assurance de ma considération distinguée et de ma profonde et personnelle estime.

M. SCHOTT Herbert
Directeur Général
Hôtel Intercontinental de Genève
9 Chemin du Petit Saconnex
11 Genève SUISSE

RÉPUBLIQUE DU CAMEROUN
Republic of Cameroon
PRÉSIDENCE DE LA RÉPUBLIQUE

Paul BIYA

Figure 28.58. Biya's Letter to the InterContinental Hotel (March 2, 1998). This is a response to a letter from the hotel management thanking the president on the occasion of his 50th stay in the hotel (source: Facebook)

Conclusion

The Anglophone newspaper front pages above are journalistic framings and "couchings" (Eko, 2019) of salient slices of the reality, the lived experience of the English and Pidgin-speaking Cameroonians in the suffocating, assimilative reality of the republican chiefdom of Cameroon. These edited snapshots of slices of reality are positional depictions, stories told from the perspective of Anglophones. These narratives provide "first blush" or surface descriptions and explanations of what has been problematized as the Anglophone Problem. These published slices of lived experience remind us that the Anglophone Problem in Cameroon is a historical relic, an unsolved problem left over from World War I and the Versailles Treaty of 1919. The problems caused by the partition of German Kamerun by colonial powers–the United Kingdom and France–and the transfer of these territories–(and the peoples in them)–from one colonial territory or sphere of influence to another, have not passed. The Anglophone Problem persists because of French, British, Russian, Swiss, Nigerian, and Israeli economic and political self-interest.

Identitarian conflicts are usually intractable conflicts that are not resolved by the argument of force.

This purposive selection of Anglophone newspaper front pages is only a partial record, a "rough draft" of the political, cultural and identitarian history of the Anglophone Problem in Cameroon. The trade union of Anglophone journalists, the Cameroon Association of English-speaking journalists (CAMSEJ), as well as good faith members of the Francophone *Syndicat Nationale des Journalistes du Cameroun* (SNJC) as well as independent newspapers like *Le Messager*, *Le Messager Popoli*, *Expression Nouvelle,* and *Popoli*, will no doubt contribute to this rough draft of history. Professional historians, political scientists, psychologists, sociologists, ethnographers, and anthropologists will shed light on the person and regime of President Paul Biya and his republican chiefery. When the Paul Barthélémy Biya bi Mvondo presidency passes into history, as all presidencies must, it will have, like all ruthless authoritarian regimes that were contemporaneous to it or preceded it on the African continent, a past that would not have passed. History will recall that Cameroon's Chief of State was one of the tiniest paradigmatic exemplars of African authoritarianism leadership, right up there with Ahmed Sekou Touré of Guinea, Sani Abacha of Nigeria, Moammar el Ghaddafi of Libya, Hosni Mubarak of Egypt, Macias Nguema of Equatorial Guinea, Ahmadou Ahidjo of Cameroon, Hastings Kamuzu Banda of Malawi, Emperor Jean-Bédel Bokassa of the Central African Republic, Mohammadu Buhari of Nigeria, Mobutu Sese Seko Kuku Ngbendu wa za Banga of Zaire/Congo (Kinshasa), General Denis Sassou Nguesso of Congo Brazzaville, General Al Bashir of Sudan, Hissène Habre of Chad, Idi Amin Dada of Uganda, Mengistu Haile Mariam of Ethiopia, Robert Mugabe of Zimbabwe, Isaias Afewerki of Eritrea, and Pieter Botha of South Africa. We add two honorary members to that group: Ariel Sharon and Benjamin Netanyahu of Israel, partners in crimes against humanity in Africa. Under their premierships, sections of the Israeli military trained and armed the killing human "machines" of several African despots. These ruthless autocrats all have problematic legacies, pasts that have not passed, pasts that will not pass as long as their wrongs have not been righted.

Despite the relative calm that has returned to the Anglophone Northwest and Southwest regions of Cameroon, anyone who thinks that the Anglophone Problem has been resolved, that the argument of force has triumphed over the force of argument, is living in a political fantasy land. As long as the Cameroon government and Anglophone religious, political and civil society leaders have not organized a sincere, frank, open, and democratic dialogue on the Anglophone problem, a dialogue where the force of argument triumphs over the argument of force, the problem will persist. As long as Anglophones continue to be treated as muted, second-class citizens targeted for assimilation, the Anglophone Problem will continue to exist. As long as the National Assembly continues to bury its head in the sand and refuses to discuss the phenomenon and find solutions to it, the Anglophone Problem will persist. As long as French language–only military tribunals take precedence over civilian justice in adjudicating the political issue of Anglophone identity and culture, the Anglophone Problem will Persist. As long as Anglophone and Francophone federalists are not allowed to hold ideas about federalism without interference, as long as they are not allowed to work towards a return to the Federal Republic of Cameroon, the Anglophone

Problem will continue to exist.

The large number of Anglophone political prisoners in the notorious Kondengui prison, and the rest of the *ngatta* (penitentiary) network proclaim loudly and clearly that the Anglophone crisis is a past crisis that has not passed. As long as torture centers continue to exist, as long as military tribunals continue to try Anglophone civilian prisoners of conscience, as long as Anglophone suspects arrested in the Northwest or Southwest regions are deported to Yaoundé for torture, detention and trial in military tribunals, the Anglophone Problem will persist. As long as Anglophone resistance continues in the form of Monday "ghost town" strikes in the Northwest and Southwest regions, as long as the English language continues to be taught in schools, colleges, and universities, the Anglophone Problem will persist. As long as the Bible continues to be read in English, the Anglophone Problem will continue to exist. As long as a large and growing Cameroon Anglophone Diaspora exists in the United States, the United Kingdom, Canada, and other parts of the Anglosphere, the longevity of the Anglophone problem is assured. The large number of Cameroonian refugees in Nigeria and Ghana, including refugee children born in the bush and refugee camps, the large numbers of internally displaced persons inside Anglophone Cameroon, as well as Francophone Cameroon, ensure that the Anglophone Problem will continue to persist. As long as independent Anglophone newspapers and websites continue to report on the erasure, muting or assimilation of Anglophones, the Anglophone Problem will Persist. Finally, as long as cell phones, photographs, video, computers, databases, Information and Communication Technologies, the Internet, social media platforms, and artificial intelligence continue to exist, the Anglophone Problem will continue to persist. It is a past that will not pass despite the ruthless attempts of the republican chiefery to suppress it.

References

Ardener, S. (2005). Ardener's "Muted Groups": The genesis of an idea and its praxis. Women and Language, Vol. 28, (2), Pp. 50-54,72.

Bauer, B. (1843). The Jewish Question. Braunschweig.

Betts, R. (1961). *Assimilation and Association in French Colonial Theory, 1890-1914*. New York: Columbia University Press.

Council of Europe (2019). Learning to live together - Council of Europe report on the state of citizenship and human rights education in Europe. Retrieved from: https://book.coe.int/en/human-rights-democratic-citizenship-and-interculturalism/7927-learning-to-live-together-council-of-europe-report-on-the-state-of-citizenship-and-human-rights-education-in-europe.html

Eko, L. (2006). New Medium: Old Free Speech Regimes: The Historical and Ideological Foundations of French and American regulation of Bias-Motivated speech and Symbolic Expression on the Internet. *Loyola of Los Angeles, International and Comparative Law Review*, 28 (1) Winter.

Eko, L. (2013). *American Exceptionalism, the French Exception and Digital Media Law*. Lanham, MD. Lexington Books.

Eko, L. (2003). The English-Language Press and the 'Anglophone Problem' In Cameroon: Group Identity, Culture, and the Politics of Nostalgia. *Journal of Third World Studies*

Feldblum, M. (1991). Reconstructing Citizenship: The Politics of Nationality Reform and Immigration in Contemporary France. Albany, N.Y.: SUNY Press.

Hewlett, N. (2005). France and Exceptionalism, in *The French Exception*, Emmanuel Godin and Tony Chafer, (eds.) pp. 3-15. New York: Berghahn Books

Kochan, L. (2004). The Making of Western Jewry. Palgrave Macmillan.

Marx, K. (2012). On the Jewish Question. In *Karl Marx, Early Political Writings*, Joseph J. O'Malley (ed.). Cambridge: Cambridge University Press Retrieved from: https://www.cambridge.org/core/books/abs/marx-early-political-writings/on-the-jewish-question/93471F579F16DAE2891943F33BB4ADFE

Morin, E. (1990). *Le trou noir de la laicité* (The black hole of secularism). *Le Débat* No. 58, p. 38.

Mudimbe, V.Y. (1994). *The idea of Africa.* Bloomington, Indiana: Indiana University Press.

Renan, Ernest (1882). *Qu'est-Ce Qu'une Nation*? (What is a Nation and Other Political Writings. Paris: Calman Levy.

Winock, M. (1988). *Le Veto. La droite et la gauche* (The veto, the right and the left). *Le Monde*, August 19, p. 2).

Epilogue: Summary of the Anglophone Problem in Pidgin Sayings and Proverbs

Anglophone Palava for Cameroon: Jam Pas Die Monkey Chop Pepper

Jam pass die, monkey chop pepper.

Chop Broke Pot, Chop Broke Kontri

God kratch matches!
Satan burn kontri

God kratch matches!
Chop Broke Pot chakara kontri
Tori Long, tam Short

Massa Chop Broke Pot dong kam
Mami Chop Troway Pan don kam
Chop Broke Pot no kno tomorrow
Chop troway Pan no wan kno tomorrow

Monkey di work, baboon di chop
Jam pass die, monkey chop pepper
Jam pass die, dog chop ye vomit
Jam pass die, dog chop grass

Kontri dong chakara
Gun halla, pipo run for bush
Pipo dem suffa pass mark
Soja dem burn pipo dem house
Kraze pipo dem burn school
Gun halla fo kan kan side
Faya! Blood di comot leke wata
Na who well?

BBC Burning Cameroon Screenshot

Ah tok ah die
Ah no tok ah die
You tok you die
You no tok you die
We tok we die
We no tok we die
Dem tok dem die
Dem no tok dem die
Wuna tok, wuna die
Wuna no tok, wuna die.

Chop Broke Pot dong sen soja
Two-side Cutlass dong kam
Two-head snake dong kam
Chop Die dong tanap
Chop no Flop dong kam
Chop no Pay dong kam
Big Belle dong kam
Big Mop dong kam,
Koni man dong kam

Jaga Jaga man, Anji dong kam
Kata kata man, panji dong komot
Wuru Wuru wuman, manji dong shidon
Faya burn old pa fo hause
Faya burn old mami fo haus
Devil faya, faya Devil

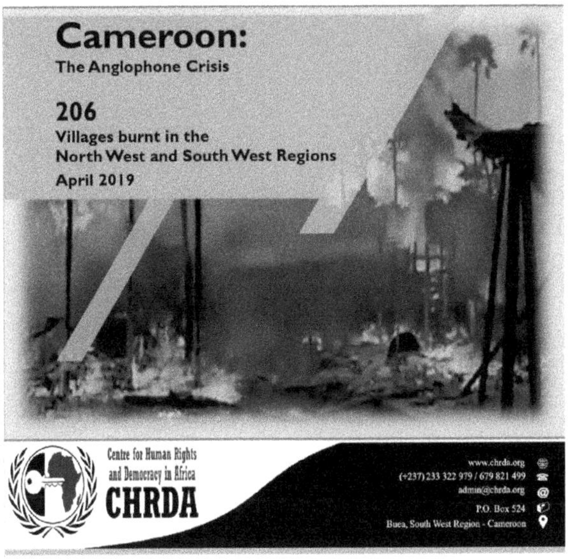

Cameroon Anglophone Crisis, 206 villages burnt, CHRDA (2019)

Opsai dong trong
Jam pass die, monkey chop pepper again!
Monkey tie teet
Man pikin tie heart
Wuman pikin tie sanja

Ah tok, ah die
Ah no tok, ah die
You tok, you die
You no, tok you die
We tok, we die
You tok you die, you no tok you die
Wuna tok, wuna die
Wuna no tok, wuna die.

Mboma sey day nobi one!

Mboma (Green mamba) say day no be one, smo smo katch monkey

Chakara Pipo

Wandaful ting!
Chop Broke Pot
Chop no Flop
Chop no Pay
Chop Die
Two-side cutlass
Two-head snake
Koni man
Tip man
Kata Kata man
Wuru Wuru wuman
Kongossa pipo
Dem dong chakara Kontri

Opsai di kene-kene for dry season
Rain no dey, poto poto plenti

God kratch maches, wata katch faya
Dust and achis faya plenti for rain season
Rain fall, dust cover kontri
Sun di shine, poto poto di plenty
Na lock mop!

Who well?

Pikin go school ih die
Pikin no go school ih die
Ticha go school ih die
Ticha no go school ih die
Docta go hospito soja katcham
Nurse go work soja dem killam
Soja turn ticha
Lawyer turn prisoner man

Mboma say day nobi one.

Mboma sey day nobi one.

Na helele oh!

Helele fo Bamenda
Helele fo Buea
Helele fo Bambalang
Helele fo Wum
Helele fo Ngarbur
Helele fo Kumba
Helele fo Bui
Helele fo Mamfe
Helele fo Momo
Helele fo Bali
Helele fo Ekona
Helele fo Muyuka
Helele for Ndian
Helele fo Akwaya
Helele fo Lebialem

All pipo dem run for bush
Man lep ih lep
Woman lep ih no lep
Wata Go lef Stone

Ah tok ah die
Ah no tok ah die
You tok you die
You no tok you die
We tok we die
We no tok we die
Dem tok dem die
Dem no tok dem die.
Wuna tok, wuna die
Wuna no tok, wuna die.

Trouble dong pass mark.
Ah kongossa, ah die
Ah no kongossa, ah die
You kongossa, you die
You no kongossa, you die
We kongossa, we die
We no kongossa, we die
Wuna kongossa, wuna die
Wuna no kongossa, wuna die

Ah chop ah die
Ah no chop ah die
You chop you die
You no chop, you die
You no chop, you die
We chop we die
We no chop we die
Wuna chop wuna die
Wuna no chop wuna die

Ah run ah die
Ah no run ah die
Ah run for before ah die
Ah run for back ah die

Papa run ih die

Papa no run ih die
Mami Pikin run ih die
Mami Pikin no run ih die
Pikin cry ih die
Pikin no cry ih die

Mboma sey do me, ah do you, God no go vex.

II. Chop Broke Pot dong bring Die on top Die

Die na Die na Die
Dem halla: Man no run oh!
Who well?
Ah run ah die
Ah no run ah die
You run you die
You no run you die
We run we die
We no run we die
Wuna run, wuna die
Wuna no run wuna die

Ah run for before ah die
Ah run for back ah die
We tanap we die
We shidon we die

We lap we die
We no lap we die
We cry we die
We no cry we die

Poor man no di vex.

Ah sick ah no die
You sick you no die
We sick we no die

Mboma sey dey no be one
One day one day
God go cratch matches!
Wata go leave stone
Garri go pas wata

Mboma sey day no be one

Jam pass die
Monkey vomit pepper
One day, one day...
Chop Broke Pot, Chop no Flop, Chop Die go kick bucket
Arata die, na ye mop
Die na die

Tori for Chop Broke Pot long, tam short

Man pass man
Iron pass iron
God pass man
Do me ah do you
God no go vex

Banana Go Ripe
If tam fo banana fo ripe dong ketch
Ih mus ripe
Do how do how

Ih go ripe
Lef am fo bush
Ih go ripe
Bring am fo haus
Ih go ripe
Put am fo under bed
Ih go ripe
Put am up fo banda
Ih go ripe
Do how do how
Ih go ripe
Jam pass die monkey vomit pepper.

Tonda faya Dem

God kratch matches!
Tonda faya Chop Broke Pot
God kratch matches!
Tonda faya Big Belle
God kratch matches
Tonda faya Chop Die
God kratch matches!
Tonda faya Chop no Pay
Man no be God!
Arata die, na ye mop
Chop Broke Pot die, na ye belle
Chop Broke Pot
Chop Broke Mop
Man no run

Wata go leave stone: Palava finish

Wata go leave stone. Mboma kam, mboma go, pipo dem remain

Man pass man
Iron pass iron
We sick, we no die
Man no die, man no rotten.

Case go change
Chop Broke Pot kam, Chop Broke Pot go
Koni man die, koni man bury am
Wata go leave stone
Big Belle kam, Big Belle go
Pipo dem remain
We dey lek we no dey
Man no die, man no rotten!

Ah tok ah die
Ah no tok ah die
You tok you die
You no tok you die
We tok we die
We no tok we die
Dem tok dem die
Dem no tok dem die
Wuna tok, wuna die
Wuna no tok, wuna die.

Palava nova finish

Appendix VIII

Barrister Femi Falana's "Request to President Buhari to Bring Back Naturalized Nigerians, refugees and Asylum seekers who were illegally deported to Cameroon on January 26, 2018 by the National Security Adviser, Major-General Babagana Monguno (Rtd).

FALANA & FALANA'S CHAMBERS

Barristers, Solicitors, Legal Consultants & Notary Public

LEGAL PRACTITIONERS

Femi Falana S.A.N. FCI Arb
Funmi Falana B.Sc. LL.B. LL.M. B.L. ACI Arb., Notary Pub.
Ifeanyi Maduabuchi, LL.B, B.L
Tajudeen Akingbolu LL.B, B.L
Sola Egbeyinka LL.B, LL.M, B.L
Samuel Ogala LL.B, B.L
Modupe Oreo-Ekpadi LL.B, B.L
Adedotun Isola_Osobu LL.B, B.L
Stanley Imhanruor LL.B, B.L
Chukwuma Onwuemene LL.B, B.L
Ayodeji Morakinyo LL.B, B.L
Femi Adedeji LL.B., B.L
Olukitan Olatigbe Agbaje LL.B, B.L
Ahmed Gbadamosi LL.B, B.L
Folarinde Falana LL.B, B.L
Folawemi Falana LL.B, B.L
Fadun Akeem LL.B, LL.M, B.L
Harrison Oseogwina LL.B, B.L
Wisdom Elum LL.B, B.L
Oludolapo Abejide LL.B, B.L
Taiwo E. Olawanle LL.B, B.L
Marshal Abubakar LL.B, B.L
Adebayo Oniyelu LL.B, B.L

LAGOS

25, Adekunle Fajuyi Way,
GRA, Ikeja, Lagos, Nigeria.
Tel.: +234 80 3305 2979
+234 80 2106 3232
E-mail: fflitigation@gmail.com

ABUJA

22, Mediterranean Street,
Imani Estate,
Off Shehu Shagari Way,
Maitama District,
Abuja, Nigeria
Tel: +2348033004903
E-mail: fflitigation@gmail.com

EKITI

106, Ajilosun Street
Ado-Ekiti,
Nigeria.
E-mail: fflitigation@gmail.com

February 2, 2018

President Mohammadu Buhari G.C.F.R.
Presidential Villa,
Three Arms Zone,
Abuja, FCT.

Your Excellency,

REQUEST TO BRING BACK NATURALISED NIGERIANS, REFUGEES AND ASYLUM SEEKERS WHO WERE ILLEGALLY DEPORTED TO CAMEROON ON JANUARY 26, 2018 BY THE NATIONAL SECURITY ADVISER, MAJOR-GENRERAL BABAGANA MONGUNO (RTD)

We are solicitors to the 51 Cameroonian Refugees and Asylum Seekers who were illegally arrested, detained and deported from Nigeria to Cameroon on Friday, January 26, 2018 by the National Security Adviser, Major-General Babagana Monguno (rtd). We write this protest letter on behalf of our clients whose names and status are set out in the List of Deportees attached to this letter.

With respect, the facts and circumstances of the illegal deportation of our clients from Nigeria to Cameroon and the reckless violations of their fundamental rights by the National Security Adviser are hereby stated as follows:

Social Justice For All

1. Our clients are not illegal immigrants in Nigeria. Two of them are naturalized Nigerian citizens while others are recognized refugees and political asylum seekers in Nigeria.

2. Twelve of our clients who are the leaders of the people of Southern Cameroon and who have been living in Nigeria for several years were assembled for a meeting at Nera Hotel, Abuja on Saturday, January 6, 2018 to discuss the challenges faced by the over 10,000 Cameroonians who have sought political asylum in Nigeria due to persecution and repression under the Paul Biya regime in Cameroon.

3. But before the commencement of the meeting a team of armed security personnel invaded the venue, abducted our clients and took them away to an undisclosed place. The said abduction was reported by the Premium Times edition of Sunday, January 7, 2018.

4. In spite of the detailed report of the credible online news medium the Police and the security agencies denied knowledge of the abduction of our clients. Consequently, all efforts made by the lawyers, doctors and family members of our clients to visit them in custody were frustrated without any legal justification. Even Mrs. Nalowa Bih who is pregnant was denied medical attention by the National Security Adviser.

5. However, a representative of the Office of the United Nations Commissioner for Refugees in Nigeria was allowed to visit our clients at the request of the Ministry of Foreign Affairs. During the visit, the United Nations representative found that our clients were held in an underground cell at the headquarters of the Defence Intelligence Agency on the orders of the National Security Adviser.

6. On account of the refusal of the National Security Adviser to allow access to our clients by their lawyers, relatives and doctors we filed an application at the Abuja Judicial Division of the Federal High Court on Thursday, January 25, 2018 for the purpose of securing their fundamental rights to personal liberty and freedom of movement.

7. Notwithstanding the pending suit and the intervention of the Office of the United Nations Commissioner for Refugees, the National Security Adviser expelled our clients from Nigeria and deported them to Cameroon on Friday, January 26, 2018.

8. Although the National Security Adviser was ashamed to disclose the deportation of our clients from Nigeria the Government of Cameroon has celebrated the deportation and threatened to prosecute our clients for unspecified crimes. Thus, with the connivance of the National Security Adviser the Government of Cameroon has since held our clients in an undisclosed military custody in Cameroon.

9. Out of the 51 people who were expelled from Nigeria the Government of Cameroon has maintained that the National Security Adviser handed over to it 47 deportess. Up till now, the National Security Adviser has not accounted for the whereabouts of the remaining 4 detainees!

Your Excellency will therefore agree with us that the arrest, detention and deportation of our clients from Nigeria to Cameroon by the National Security Adviser cannot be justified on the following grounds:

a. Based on the appeal by Nigeria for a peaceful resolution of the political crisis in Cameroon the people of Southern Cameroon filed a suit at the Federal High Court to determine whether the people of Southern Cameroon are not entitled to self-determination within their clearly defined territory separate from La Republique Du Cameroun.
b. By a consent judgment delivered by the Court on March 5, 2002, the Federal Government was directed to file a suit at the International Court of Justice to have a judicial confirmation of the human right of the people of Southern Cameroon to self determination. Attached herewith and marked annexure A is a certified true copy of the judgment.

c. The Federal Government also undertook to take other measures as may be necessary to place the case of the people of Southern

Cameroon for self determination before the United Nations General Assembly and other international organizations.

d. Even though the suit has not been filed at the International Court of Justice the Federal Government has continued to recognize the human rights of our clients and other people of Southern Cameroon to self determination.

e. The National Security Adviser knew that two of our clients are naturalized Nigerians, six are refugees while 37 others are political asylum seekers who are entitled to be protected by the Federal Government of Nigeria. For the avoidance of doubt, the Office of the United Nations Commissioner for Refugees in Nigeria drew the attention of the National Security Adviser to the legal obligations of Nigeria to respect the rights of our clients.

f. Under the National Security Agencies Act (Cap N74) Laws of the Federation of Nigeria, 2004 and the Immigration Act 2015 the National Security Adviser is not competent to arrest, detain and deport any alien or immigrant from Nigeria to any other country.

g. The Minister of Interior in charge of immigration and related matters as well as the Federal Commissioner for Refugees empowered to safeguard the interest and treatment of persons who are seeking to become refugees or persons seeking political asylum in Nigeria and other matters incidental thereto were not consulted by the National Security Adviser before the deportation.

h. The Secretary to the Government of the Federation who is charged with the responsibility for matters relating to refugees or refugee status by Section 2 of the National Commission for Refugees (Establishment Etc) Act and the Attorney-General of the Federation in charge of extradition were also not consulted by the National Security Adviser before the deportation.

i. By virtue of Section 1 of the National Commission for the Refugees etc Act (Cap N21) Laws of the Federation of Nigeria, 2004 the

Government of Nigeria has prohibited the expulsion, extradition or deportation of any person who is a refugee to the frontiers of any territory where -- (a) his life or freedom would be threatened on account of his race, religion, nationality, membership of a particular group or political opinion; or (b) his life, physical integrity or liberty could be threatened on account of external aggression, occupation, foreign domination or events seriously disrupting public order in any part or the whole of that territory."

j. The human right of any person in Africa to enter Nigeria, reside, seek and obtain asylum has been guaranteed by Article 12 (3) of the African Charter on Human and Peoples' Rights (Ratification and Enforcement) Act. (CAP 10) laws of the Federation of Nigeria, 2004 which provides that "every individual shall have the right, when persecuted to seek and obtain asylum in other countries in accordance with the laws of those countries and international conventions."

k. The Federal Republic of Nigeria is a signatory to the 1951 United Nations Convention Relating to the Status of Refugees and the 1969 Organization of African Unity Convention on Refugees and the African Charter on Human and Peoples Rights which have guaranteed the rights of refugees and asylum seekers in Nigeria.

Since the Government of Nigeria has never violated the provisions of the United Nations Convention Relating to Refugees and the OAU Convention on Refugees by deporting refugees and asylum seekers to any country where they might be persecuted we are compelled to urge Your Excellency to grant the following requests:

1. Order the National Security Adviser to produce the missing 5 deportees and bring back to Nigeria our clients who have been deported to Cameroon without any further delay.

2. If the National Security Adviser is unable to bring back our clients to Nigeria he should be removed from office for the brazen impunity

which has exposed Nigeria to ridicule before the comity of law abiding nations.

3. The Federal Government should prevail on the Government of Cameroon not to persecute our clients so as to prevent the United Nations from sanctioning Nigeria for violating the provisions of the 1951 United Nations Convention Relating to Refugees.

Please, Your Excellency, accept, as usual, the assurances of our highest esteem and regards.

Yours sincerely,

FEMI FALANA ESQ, SAN, FCI Arb.

IN THE FEDERAL HIGH COURT
IN THE ABUJA JUDICIAL DIVISION
HOLDEN AT ABUJA.

SUIT NO. FHC/ABJ/CS/30/2002

BETWEEN

CERTIFIED TRUE COPY
FEDERAL HIGH COURT
ABUJA
Signature............
Dat 5-3-2002

1. DR. KEVIN NGWANG GUMNE)
2. AUGUSTINE FEH NDANGAM)
3. CHIEF ETTE OTUN AYAMBA)
4. PROF. VICTOR MUKWELE NGOH)
5. DR. MARTIN NGEKA LUMA)
6. NFOR NGALA NFOR)
7. HILTER HUMPHREY MBINGLO) PLAINTIFF(S)
8. DOBGIMA HENRY K. MUNDAM)
9. SIMON NINPA)
10. SHEY TAFON)
11. PAUL YIWIR)
12. ISAAC SONA)

(For themselves and on behalf of the peoples of Southern Cameroons)

FEDERAL HIGH COURT
ABUJA
Cashier's Office
Date 05/3/2002
PAID ON CR NO
Z002161047

AND

ATTORNEY GENERAL OF THE FEDERAL REPUBLIC OF NIGERIA) DEFENDANT(S)

TERMS AGREED BY THE PARTIES TO BE EMBODIED IN THE ORDER OF THE COURT

TAKE NOTICE that the parties hereto have agreed to the terms contained in the subjoined schedule and pray this court to stay further proceedings in this suit upon the said Terms. [Draft Order attached]

SCHEDULE

1. The Federal Republic of Nigeria shall institute a case before the International Court of Justice concerning the following:

(a) Whether the Union envisaged under the Southern Cameroons Plebiscite 1961 between La Republique Du Cameroun and Southern Cameroons legally took effect as contemplated by the relevant United Nations Resolutions particularly United Nations General Assembly Resolution 1352 (XIV) of 16th October 1959 and United Nations Trusteeship Council Resolution 2013 (XXIV) of 31st May 1960.

(b) Whether the termination by the Government of the United Kingdom of its trusteeship over the Southern Cameroons on 30th September 1961 without ensuring prior implementation of the Constitutional arrangements under which the Southern Cameroons and La Republique Du Cameroun were to unite as one Federal State was not in breach of Articles 3 and 6 of the Trusteeship Agreement for the Territory of the Cameroons under British Administration approved by the General Assembly of the United Nations on 13th December 1946, the United Nations General Assembly Resolutions 1352 of 16th October 1959; 1608 of 21st April 1961, the United Nations Trusteeship Council Resolution 2013 (XXIV) of May 31 1960 and Article 76 (b) of the Charter of the United Nations.

(c) Was the assumption of Sovereign Powers on 1st October 1961 and the continued exercise of same by the Government of La Republique Du Cameroun over Southern Cameroons after the termination by the Government of the United Kingdom of its Trusteeship over (the territory) legal and valid when the Union between the Southern Cameroons and La Republique Du Cameroun contemplated by the Southern Cameroons Plebiscite 1961 had not legally taken effect?

FEDERAL HIGH COURT
ABUJA
Cashier's Office
Date 05/3/2002
PAID ON CR NO
Z002161036

(d) Whether the peoples of Southern Cameroons are not entitled to self-determination within their clearly defined territory separate from La Republique Du Cameroun.

(e) Whether it is the Southern Cameroons and not La Republique Du Cameroun that shares a maritime boundary with the Federal Republic of Nigeria.

2. The Federal Republic of Nigeria shall take any other measures as may be necessary to place the case of the peoples of the geographical territory known as at 1st October 1960 as Southern Cameroons for self determination before the United Nations General Assembly and any other relevant International organizations.

Dated at Abuja this ......5TH...... day of ....MARCH.......... 2002

PLAINTIFFS' COUNSEL

1. **KOLA AWODEIN S.A.N**

....

2. **CHIEF K.K. ASU**

....

3. **TAYO OYETIBO ESQ**

....

4. **IBUKUN AJOMO ESQ**

....

DEFENDANT'S COUNSEL

F. K. BEBU ESQ

....

LIST OF DEPORTEES

S/No	Name	Sex	Age	Nationality
1	Dr. Cornelius Kwanga	M	47	Cameroonian
2	Dr. Nfor Ngala Nfor	M	66	Cameroonian
3	Elias Eyambe Esq	M	49	Cameroonian
4	Shufai Blaise Berinyu	M	51	Cameroonian
5	Mrs. Nalowa Bih Esq	F	53	Cameroonian
6	Mr. Julius Ayuk Tabe	M	53	Cameroonian
7	Professor Augustine Awasom	M	50	Cameroonian
8	Dr. Henry Kimeng	M	50	Cameroonian
10	Dr. Ojong Okongo	M	58	Cameroonian
11	Dr. Fidelis Nde Che	M	47	Cameroonian
12	Mr. Wilfred Tassang	M	48	Cameroonian
13	Mrs. Winifred Augustine	F	52	Nigerian
14	ThankGod Genesis	M	21	Nigerian
15	Nasiru Bah	M	23	Nigerian
16	Tita Tebio	M	32	Cameroonian
17	Bame Emanuel	M	21	Cameroonian
18	Casius Lendzemo	M	30	Cameroonian
19	Nangsiyung Christian	M	22	Cameroonian
20	Nynyki Ernest	M	27	Cameroonian
21	Elvis Fonyun	M	24	Cameroonian
22	Romeon Sevidee	M	25	Cameroonian
23	Wired Zenyuy Leonard	M	27	Cameroonian
24	Amos Bentar	M	28	Cameroonian
25	Lontun Wilfred	M	21	Cameroonian
26	Ahmadu Hassan	M	25	Cameroonian
27	Adones Martin	M	21	Cameroonian
28	Lukong Abdullahi	M	43	Cameroonian
29	Edwin Dubila	M	24	Cameroonian
30	Yiven Emmanuel	M	24	Cameroonian
31	Franklin Emia	M	24	Cameroonian
32	Demian Bongbem	M	22	Cameroonian
33	Salah Edmond	M	22	Cameroonian
34	Nwanyam C. Sumgwa	M	23	Cameroonian
35	Kidze Telson Tanlaka	M	17	Cameroonian
36	Tukon Devine	M	26	Cameroonian
37	John Nkwah	M	19	Cameroonian
38	Anifakah Kiven	M	19	Cameroonian
39	Katat Ezekiel	M	32	Cameroonian
40	Peniel Teri	M	20	Cameroonian
41	Ngoram Emile	M	28	Cameroonian
42	Nyefeh Boris	M	23	Cameroonian
43	Muhammadu Rabiu Audu	M	38	Cameroonian
44	Joseph Bongumnyi	M	23	Cameroonian

45	Pius Ngoran	M	33	Cameroonian
46	Ashime Brown	M	23	Cameroonian
47	Lukong Abdulrahaman	M	34	Cameroonian
48	Fon Stanley	M	23	Cameroonian
49	Sekeh Mulligan	M	26	Cameroonian
50	Nsoye Ignatius	M	22	Cameroonian
51	Voman Romarious	M	25	Cameroonian
52	Zakariyau Nsavolzenyuy	M	30	Cameroonian

Appendix IX

Appendix IX Abduction and Extra-judicial Rendition of the Nera 10: A Legal Analysis by Barrister Charles Taku, International Human Rights Lawyer.

Abduction and Extra-judicial Rendition of the Nera 10: A Legal Analysis

The abduction and extra-ordinary rendition of the Nera 10 from Abuja, as well as the abduction and extra-judicial deportation of other Cameroonian refugees and asylum seekers, including women and children, from Nera Hotel Abuja, Chalsma Hotel, Calabar, and other locations in Nigeria, to torture and detention centers, and ultimately the Yaoundé Military Tribunal, without giving the abductees and deportees due process of law, shocked the Nigerian legal and human rights community. Though there was no extradition treaty between Nigeria and Cameroon, what was shocking, from a rule of law perspective, was that the matters were sub-judice. Nigerian courts had been seized about the matter of the arrests and detention of the Cameroon political refugees by the Nigerian security operatives, but the Nigerian government demonstrated a wanton disregard for Nigerian and international the law. The Anglophone Cameroon Common Law lawyers also found Nigeria's lack of interest in the niceties of international law, as well as its snubbing of the United Nations High Commission for Refugees (UNHCR) quite troubling. A Cameroon Anglophone Common Law luminary, Chief Charles Taku, a traditional Chief from Lebialem, Southwest region, and an international lawyer specializes in International Criminal, Humanitarian, and Human Rights Law and Practice, penned a response to the abductions and deportations. Chief Taku, who represented clients as Lead Counsel at the International Criminal Tribunal for Rwanda (UNICTR), Special Court for Sierra Leone, the International Criminal Court (ICC), the United Nations Human Rights Committee in Geneva, and the African Court on Human and People's Right in Arusha Tanzania, wrote the piece below entitled: "Unmasking Another International Conspiracy: Hail the Rule of Law." Barrister Taku's piece is instructive:

UNMASKING ANOTHER INTERNATIONAL CONSPIRACY: HAIL THE RULE OF LAW

Chief Charles A. Taku

> Chief Charles A. Taku, a traditional Chief from Lebialem, Cameroon, is an International Lawyer with thirty-six years' of trial experience. He specializes in International Criminal, Humanitarian, and Human Rights Law and Practice. Chief Taku has represented clients as Lead Counsel at the International Criminal Tribunal for Rwanda (UNICTR), Special Court for Sierra Leone, the International Criminal Court (ICC), the United Nations Human Rights Committee in Geneva, and the African Court on Human

and People's Right in Arusha Tanzania.

The judgment of the Nigeria Federal High Court in Abuja on March 1, 2019, declaring illegal and unconstitutional, the abduction and deportation to Cameroun of the President of the Interim Government of the Southern Cameroons/Ambazonia Sisiku Ayuk Tabe, members of the Interim Government and several Southern Cameroons refugees carries significant symbolic weight.

The judgment has comprehensively determined the legal status of the abductees which was in controversy since Cameroun characterized them as terrorists on the account of alleged crimes committed against Cameroun from the territory of Nigeria; so, the Isa Tchiroma and the Court-martial alleged. The Federal High Court of Abuja Nigeria on the territory of which the crimes alleged in the court-martial were allegedly committed has decided that they are persons who were legally in the territory of Nigeria as refugees under the protection of international conventional law at the time of their abduction and deportation. They were not therefore terrorists nor did their presence and activities constitute terrorism to warrant their being characterized as terrorists to warrant abduction and deportation to face a court-martial. Even if they were terrorists, international law still outlawed the abduction and deportation without compliance with the municipal and international rule of law.

This judicial determination settles a key issue in the subsequent case brought against the victims by Cameroun, the state to which they were deported. The failure of the court-martial in Cameroun where the abductees are forcefully subjected over their objections, to take judicial notice of the Judgment of the Abuja Federal High Court will have bilateral relations and multilateral treaty obligations consequences on the two countries, in the short and long term. Nigeria and Cameroun are state parties to the 1951 United Nations Convention on Refugees and its Additional Protocol 1967. Both countries are state parties to the OAU 1969 Convention Governing the Specific Aspects of the Refugee Problem in Africa which came into force in 1974.

The refugee problem globally and in Africa is a matter of significant international emergency, if not a humanitarian crisis. Without the existing multilateral treaty regime to manage this humanitarian crisis, millions, of the world's vulnerable refugee population will be pursued across international boundaries and slaughtered by the murderous regimes and criminal squads from whom they fled in the search for protection. International law mandates state parties to the Refugee Convention to open their frontiers to allow refugees fleeing from wars, genocide, crimes against humanity and other life-threatening conditions to their lives to provide them protection. International law outlaws the abduction, deportation, rendition or the refoulement of persons who have sought refugee status to the countries from which they fled. Once the status of refugees is sought or obtained, the person concerned becomes a ward of international law under the Refugee Convention and its Additional Protocol. State Parties to the Refugee Convention are mandated to ensure compliance and indeed are obligated to submit periodic reports on compliance with their treaty obligations under the convention. Nigeria and Cameroun had a multilateral obligation to ensure that the refugee status of the abductees in Nigeria was respected and protected.

Their mandate and responsibility are to the international community, since the 1951 Refugee Convention has near world wide membership. By engaging in criminal conduct to abduct and deport the victims to face a court-martial that applies the death penalty to Cameroun, Nigeria and Cameroun betrayed, violated and endangered the multilateral treaty regime and a protected international human rights value system.

The Federal High Court Judgment provided an opportunity to Nigeria to explain to the world, the rationale and legality of the abductions. It is significant that Nigeria did not convince the court that the abduction and deportation was informed by any compellable reasons justifiable in municipal and /or international law. Nigeria did not convince the court of any legally justified reason to violate with impunity the Nigeria Federal Constitution (1969), its multilateral treaty obligations under the UN Refugee Convention and its Additional Protocol, the African Convention, the International Covenant on Civil and Political Rights and the Rome Statute. There is no compelling reason to explain why Nigeria mortgaged its reputation, its influence in Africa and its claims to lead and represent Africa as a world power at the UN Security Council to fulfil the dictatorial and criminal proclivities of a regime baying for the blood of millions of Southern Cameroonians. Hundreds of thousands of Southern Cameroonians have been deported by Cameroun from their ancestral home which are systematically torched as a deliberate government policy as senior military commanders and civilian government officials have admitted, across the border with Nigeria. The victims who at a great risk of a genocide sought international protections within the territory of Nigeria are living under continuing threat of abduction and assassination, after Nigeria provided support to Cameroun to pursue the commission of international crimes against them in the territory of Nigeria.

The answer as to what endeared President Mohammadu Buhari to place Nigeria at the centre of an unfolding genocide, rather than acting as a facilitator of negotiations and peace may not be answered in this one critical historic judgment. Yet the judgment has the merit of laying an enduring foundation for answers to be provided within the compelling injunction of history. The truth, it is said, will never die with those who thought they could imprison it with sheer political chicanery and stealth transborder corrupt operations. Truth is as stubborn as a rock. Nigeria and Cameroun are aware, and this is important, that the underlying cause of the war declared by Paul Biya as a proxy of France, are the resources within the territory of the Southern Cameroons. These minerals are the umbilical cord to the perennial Nigeria misadventure that has devasted the Niger Delta, its ecosystem, maritime resources, economy and human health. Time will reveal if there are a convergence of economic and hegemonic interests by the known yet, invisible political god fathers enforcing the genocide using Nigeria and Cameroun proxies.

I learnt from my years as a lead counsel at the Special Court for Sierra Lone, in the case of the Revolutionary United from for Sierra Leone (RUF)-Morris Kallon that minerals are the curse of Africa. That is why Central Africa Republic has never been at peace since independence despite its mineral rich capabilities. The Democratic Republic of the Congo is one case in point; so also, Burundi where abundant mineral resources have attracted the interest and wrath of neo-colonial economic and natural resource predators.

The bazaar auctioning of the Southern Cameroons at independence as my late friend

Dr Bate Besong stated, or the Mc McLeod slave deal, as the father of Ambazonia Fon Gorgi Dinka described it, was intended to silence the liberating ambition of Ambazonia patriots. For the record, the slave and bazaar dealers did not know that Ambassbay from which Ambazonia derived its name, stood watch over the liberating spirit of its Ambazonia offspring. Ambassbay is a natural environment for the sharks in the Ambazonia sea as opposed to the neighbouring sea which is inhabited by "crayfish". Those with a good sense of aquatic life know that a shark is not an ordinary fish, surely not a crayfish. And this is where the difference lies.

This judgment of the Abuja Federal High Court conveys an underlying message to the abductors that the abduction of Southern Cameroons leaders and citizens will have consequences that may potentially threaten peace and security in the Gulf of Guinea. That Nigeria has become a key ally of the state actor that declared the war of choice that have the capacity of igniting a conflagration in the Gulf of Guinea affecting its own citizens and interests on both sides of the borders, is a matter of profound concern.

The judgment is a municipal judgment on compliance by Nigeria of its multilateral treaty and constitutional obligations. Finding that Nigeria violated its municipal laws and treaty obligations, is an important contribution to international law. This judgment therefore must be served on the United Nations Secretariat, the United Nations High Commissioner for Refugees in Geneva, all the permanent and non-permanent members of the Security Council through their permanent representations in New York, all ECOWAS state parties through their diplomatic representations in Abuja, the EU state parties present in Brussels, the AU Commission, and give wide publicity.

This judgment negates the charge by Cameroun that the abductees were and are terrorists. Nigeria did not make this charge before and during the hearing. Nigeria should be concerned that persons found to be refugees by its own judiciary are facing a court-martial based on international and municipal violations of its own government. With this judgment, the blood of the abductees and other Southern Cameroonians will lay on the hands of Nigeria should they be further held in violation of this judgment or should they be executed pursuant to the court-martial.

International law mandates that any offence committed on the territory of Nigeria can be investigated and prosecuted by Nigeria failing which Nigeria can send the refugees to a third country willing to accept them but not to the country from which they fled and sought refuge in Nigeria. Will Nigeria submit itself to a court-martial in Cameroun to provide evidence of acts alleged in the charges before the court-martial that were allegedly committed in Nigeria? Does Nigeria recognize a court-martial for civilians which is international human rights jurisprudence has characterised as torture and thus illegal? Does Nigeria by the abductions give legal approval to the crime of abduction which criminalised under the Rome Statute which Nigeria is a state party? Is abduction of civilians not one of the crimes alleged against Boko Haram in which hundreds of thousands of Nigerian civilians have lost their lives? The Abuja High Court trial was an occasion for Nigeria to prove that abduction is legal when conducted by a state actor but illegal when carried out by non-state actors. Nigeria failed to prove this or even convince the court that this crime may be legal under such or other circumstances.

Nigeria under President Mohammadu Buhari tends to disobey court orders and indeed disobeyed the order of the Federal High Court in Abuja made by Justice Gabriel Kolawole dated December 2, 2016 ordering the release of Ibrahim el Zazaky the leader the Shiite Muslim Movement who was abducted by the DSS on December 13, 2015. The DSS alleged that he was detained at his own request for protection. The Judge was unpersuaded on the grounds that protective custody was unknown to law or National Security Agencies Act establishing the DSS. Since December 29, 2015, Colonel Abubakar Malami former National Security Adviser of President Goodluck Jonathan has remained in jail despite court orders for his release.

However, in a suit brought by a constitutional lawyer Johnmary Jideobi praying the court to void the SAN of the Attorney General of the Federation, Abubakar Malami for professional misconduct for advising the Federal Government to disrespect court orders, the Attorney General refused being held accountable for advising the Federal Government to disrespect court orders and that he was not informed about the detentions and so his advice was never sought in the cases. The Attorney General argued in his defence that in cases where his advice was sought, he advised, and the Federal Government complied with court orders. He cited the release on bail of Mazi Nnamdi Kanu the leader of Independent People of Biafra (IPOB) and that of the survivals of an attack on an uncompleted house in Abuja which was stormed and murdered by some operatives of the National Intelligence Services after the Nigeria Human Rights Commission ordered that victims and their dependents be compensated.

This defence by the attorney therefore begs the questions, if he was never informed how then did, he enters appearance to defend the illegal actions of the Nigeria Government?

Africa, and African leaders should hail the Judgment of the Federal High Court of Nigeria in Abuja and pressurise Nigeria and Cameroun to execute it without delay. This judgment protects the municipal and international protections of refugees afforded by multilateral treaties and municipal constitutional provisions. The international multilateral treaty regime has been tested and proved to be critical in checking the excesses and exactions of the world refugee crisis and the humanitarian calamity that is rocking the conscience of humanity. In their imposed inhuman dungeons Sisiku Ayuk Tabe and the Ambazonia abductees represent the face of humanity at risk. This judgment protects that human value represented by Sisiku Ayuk Tabe. African leaders and the international community should applaud this judgment and pressurise Nigeria and Cameroun to obey and execute it.

This judgment should be a shock reminder to everyone, the powerful and the weak, that a refugee is a protected ward of humanity and the legal regimes emplaced to protect him or her attest to this fact. Abducting and deporting refugees to be court-martialled or placing them in harm's way tantamount to driving a sword on the collective conscience of humanity. This should not be allowed to happen without consequences.

I have a message for those responsible for the abduction and court-martial of civilian victims. Respecting this judgment may be the only opportunity for them to avoid placing their own poisoned chalices to their own lips. Babatoura Ahmadou with the use of terror pursued nationalists who sought refuge in foreign lands but died a refugee himself in solitude in distant Senegal. The refugee status he imposed on others and pursued, abducted and killed or assassinated them was the status that protected and sustained him until he died. In 1968, Joseph Desire Mobutu otherwise called Mobutu Sese Seko lured and murdered Pierre Mulele over strong world-wide appeals and condemnation. Mobutu died a miserable refugee in Morocco. The extensive empire he acquired through, murder, looting and plundering the mineral resources of his country are in ruins. The blood of the thousands he slaughtered to keep himself in eternal power still haunts the memory of him. His countrymen and women are even traumatised, turning his extensive empire into the memorial for his innocent victims.

This recorded history may already have extended a hand of invitation to the actors in the theatre of criminality and violations that the Federal High Court High Court in Abuja addressed in this judgment. Whether they will on their own volition abide by this judgment, is not known to me. However, this judgment is addressed to the collective conscience of Humanity represented by the multilateral treaty regime which the court found was violated. The multilateral treaty regime must demonstrate that it has teeth and that it must not condone or encourage the impunity of state violators of their treaty obligations, lest it wrongly encourages non-state actors. Nigeria itself has a refugee problem in far and distant lands, including Cameroun. It will be unfortunate if Nigerians allow their government to determine their fate through the legitimisation of the violations found in this judgment.

I wish to conclude by addressing a few words to Ambazonians who should be strategizing on how to rely on this judgment to highlight their predicament worldwide where ever they find themselves. I am appalled by how much social media activism and sideshows are distracting them from following the rapidly evolving events that may determine their fate yet again while they are asleep or self-destructing in search of power. While internal squabbles must be addressed, that cannot override rallying behind the Interim Government that instructed the lawyers working on this and other cases to raise the profile of the cases to the highest levers of international intervention. While not trivialising the complaints or matters which some components of the struggle may hold dear to their hearts, and I will not and never get involved in such squabbles, I strongly advise all Ambazonians, to henceforth recognize that the Abuja abduction of Sisiku Ayuk Tabe and others and their deportation to Cameroun requires a strong international legal intervention. It is a crime against the Rome Statute which Nigeria is a state party. The unwritten underpinning of the Judgment indeed has this implication. It has violated the UN multilateral treaty regime and that of the AU.

Social media activism alone will not get this judgment executed, enforced. It will not rely on the judgment to pursue all international crimes and violations in which hundreds and thousands of civilians are systematically exterminated and civilian settlements, places of worships and hospitals are torched and reduced to rubbles. It is therefore advisable to support the IG to move quickly to fulfil these tasks while other weighty issues are internally reviewed and quickly redressed without the intension of rocking the boat for the sake of power. Protracted disagreement empowers adversaries. Clearly established areas of agreement should be identified, and prioritised and collective action sought to attain the position outcomes while perennial disagreements struggle for institutional solutions. What cannot wait even for a minute are contributions intended for the collective good, the protection of victims, refugees, vulnerable categories and preventive and protective strategies.

Chief Charles A. Taku

Appendix X

Letter of Eitay Mack to Israeli Defense Export Agency, Israeli Ministry of Defense

איתי מק, עו"ד
Eitay Mack, Advocate
ايتاي مِك، محام

מרכז כלל, משרד 745, רח' יפו 97, ירושלים ■ טל' 02-5877766, פקס 02-5877744
Clal Center, Office 745, 97 Yaffo St., Jerusalem ■ Tel 02-5877766, Fax 02-5877744
eitaymack@gmail.com

February 7, 2018

To:
Racheli Chen
Head of DECA – Israeli Defense Export Controls Agency
Israeli Ministry of Defense

Subject: Urgent request to Apply Article 9 of the Defense Export Control Act in the case of the BIR Unit in Cameroon

1. This letter is sent on behalf of human rights activists Aya Gavriel, Yael Frenkel, Sahar Vardi, Vered Keisar, Shai Eistein, Guy Butavia, Ofer Neiman, Niv Hachlili, Guy Yadin-Evron, Noam Yadin, Elisheva Kravtzov, Uri Agnon, Gal Alfasi, Vered Bitan, Amir Bitan and Yaniv Yurkevich and on my behalf.

2. Since October 2016, a severe political crisis is taking place in the English-speaking provinces of Cameroon, situated in the country's south western and north western provinces, near the border with Nigeria.

3. These regions span 16,364 sq. km, out of Cameroon's 475,442, and 5 out of the 24 million citizens of Cameroon reside there. These areas contain the political base of the main opposition party - the Social Democratic Front (SDF), and they are very significant economically, especially for the oil industry, which amounts to 10% of the country's GDP.

4. The background for the political crisis relates to the establishment of Cameroon: Between 1885-1915 the entire area of Cameroon was a German colony. After WWI, the League of Nations divided the mandate over the area between France and Great Britain. French Cameroon was granted independence from France on 1.1.1960 while British Cameroon was granted independence from Britain, and decided to unite with the former French Cameroon on 1.10.1961.

5. During the French and British mandate in Cameroon, each of the two administered the area under its control differently. In the British mandate areas, the official language was English, the legal system was that of Common Law, and society, the currency and the education systems were based on the British model. Furthermore, Britain allowed a relative freedom of expression and press, and autonomous local institutions. By contrast, the French mandate was highly centralized, the legal system was the Continental one, and the official language was French. The less democratic nature of the French mandate reflected on the centralized development of state institutions in Cameroon after the unification of the French and British parts. Thus, mass political arrests of dissidents and critics of the regime began as early as 1962.

6. The consent to unification given by the residents of the British mandate territory, was based on making Cameroon a federation, including the recognition of English as an official language with French, and stipulating that the President and his deputy, at any time, would represent both states. In spite of that, between 1961 and 1972, the autonomy of the English-speaking regions was denied in a creeping process, and the regime became centralized by the French-speaking majority. Thus, for example, in 1966 Cameroon became a one-party state – "Cameroon National Union"; in May 1972, the Federation was effectively annulled and the united "Republic of Cameroon" was founded; only in 1990 did Cameroon become a multi-party state again, and the aforementioned SDF party was founded; As of 2017, the overwhelming majority of power positions in the executive, judicial and legislative branches is held by representatives of the French-speaking provinces.

7. While some leaders from the English-speaking provinces acted in international forums to promote their independence, separatist groups which called for a violent struggle were established, and Cameroonians from these provinces who immigrated to other countries supported politically and economically their relatives who remained there. But only in 2016 did the situation become volatile, in a manner which risks the entire country's stability.

8. The crisis began on 11.10.2016 when lawyers went on strike. They demanded that State laws be translated into English, criticizes the takeover of the Continental legal system, and the appointment of French-speaking judges to courts in the English-speaking provinces. Their strike and protests gained wide support and public interest in the ongoing discrimination and marginalization in Cameroon against the English-speaking provinces. In addition, calls for a return to a federation or for full independence grew.

9. On 21.11.2016, the teachers also went on strike and began to protest, due to the appointment of teachers who did not speak English and the attempt to marginalize the British educational model in schools and universities in these provinces.

10. Strikes and demonstrations by teachers and lawyers began a "snowball" in the English-speaking provinces, which are being oppressed heavy-handedly. Cameroon's security forces, including the BIR unit, have used live ammunition against protesters, raided universities, businesses and residential buildings, beat civilians, raped students and arrested the political leadership of these regions, which have become de-facto military zones. One of the detainees is a judge of the Supreme Court of Cameroon[1]. The school system was closed for a year, and in January 2017, the State blocked Internet access in the area for several months, which harmed many businesses. Some of those arrested have been tried by military courts, based on draconian anti-terror laws. Tens of thousands have fled to refugees camps in Nigeria[2], and many have left their villages are hiding in the forest.

11. On 15.12.2016[3], the African Commission on Human and Peoples' Rights Published a condemnation of security forces' violence in the English-speaking provinces:

> **The Commission's Country Rapporteur for Cameroon and Special Rapporteur on Human Rights Defenders in Africa, Hon. Commissioner Reine Alapini-Gansou, is deeply concerned by the deteriorating human rights situation in Cameroon, in particular: killings of civilians; the deployment of armed military personnel, special security forces (BIR) and war machines to these two regions; the disproportionate and deathly use of force and violence to dispel peaceful and unarmed Lawyers, Teachers, Students, civilians and protesters in Bamenda, Buea and Kumba; the raping of students in Buea; the arbitrary arrests, detention and merciless beatings orchestrated by the police, gendarmerie, military and the BIR following strikes and protests that have been going on since October 2016.**

---

[1] http://www.africareview.com/news/979180-3783018-q8q6se/index.html

[2] http://www.unhcr.org/news/briefing/2017/12/5a38dc054/unhcr-steps-support-cameroonians-fleeing-nigeria.html ; http://www.unhcr.org/news/briefing/2018/1/5a61b3bc4/concern-grows-women-children-fleeing-cameroon.html ; https://www.reuters.com/article/us-cameroon-separatists-nigeria/at-least-15000-cameroonian-refugees-flee-to-nigeria-amid-crackdown-idUSKBN1F01Q6

[3] http://www.achpr.org/press/2016/12/d340/

3

The Special Rapporteur has received information that the strikes and protests are allegedly provoked by what has been dubbed, "the Anglophone problem," due to discontented Anglophone Lawyers, Teachers and Civil Society in English speaking Cameroon legitimately and peacefully seeking a halt to: the gradual, but systematic destruction and obliteration of the Common Law Legal System and the Anglosaxon System of Education; the marginalisation and neglect by the administration of Cameroon of the two English speaking regions of Cameroon; and the return to Federal system of governance.

The Special Rapporteur is particularly concerned about the alleged deaths of more than nine (9) Cameroonians during the protests in Bamenda, Buea and Kumba, and the allegations that the Government is planning mass arrest, kidnappings and assassination of leaders of Lawyers' associations, Teachers' unions, Civil Society and human rights defenders as a means to thwart the Anglophone cause.

12. During October 2017[4], following intensified protest in the English-speaking provinces marking the day of independence from Britain, the violent repression by the security forces increased, especially by the BIR unit. Any assembly of more than four people was banned. Bus stations, restaurants and stores were closed. Security forces set up checkpoints limiting freedom of movement between various parts of the English-speaking provinces, lookout posts were established on the roofs of buildings and the Minister of Communication announced he would close any media outlet which supported those calling for independence.

13. On 29.1.2018[5], the African Commission on Human and Peoples' Rights, published another statement condemning security forces' violence in the English-speaking provinces:

Since October 2016, the human rights situation in the Republic of Cameroon has continued to worsen following brutal crackdowns on legitimate and peaceful protests by lawyers, teachers and members of civil society of the English-speaking regions of North-West and South-West, who called for the

[4] https://af.reuters.com/article/africaTech/idAFKCN1C61BR-OZATP

[5] http://www.achpr.org/press/2018/01/d384/

4

preservation of the Anglophone legal and educational systems in their regions, an end to marginalisation, and for better management of the regions by the State in terms of development and infrastructure.

The Commission is particularly concerned about the deployment of soldiers in these regions, the disproportionate use of force against unarmed civilians, and the intermittent shutdown of means of communication such as Internet connection.

The Commission is deeply concerned about reports of cases of enforced disappearance, arbitrary detention under deplorable conditions, prohibition of peaceful demonstrations, and constant insecurity leading to the displacement of more than 5,000 Anglophone Cameroonians to Nigeria since the beginning of the crisis without means of subsistence and access to basic necessities.

The Commission strongly condemns the ongoing violence and human rights violations in Cameroon, in particular the militarisation of the English-speaking regions and the disproportionate use of force against the population.

Therefore, along with a condemnation of violence by Cameroon's security forces, the Commission called for the following:

The Commission calls upon the Government of the Republic of Cameroon to fulfil its obligation to protect, and to:

1. **Put an immediate end to the use of force against unarmed civilians;**
2. **Ensure respect for the right to freedom of expression and information, freedom of association and assembly, and the right to liberty and security of the person enshrined in the Charter;**
3. **Ensure the immediate release of all persons arbitrarily detained since October 2016 following the protests;**
4. **Conduct impartial and independent investigations into allegations of extrajudicial killings, enforced disappearances, inhuman and degrading treatment, and**

5

human rights violations reported to have been committed by police, gendarmerie and military officers;

5. **Initiate constructive dialogue without delay, towards putting an end to the suffering of the population.**

14. Human rights groups and activists in Cameroon report that the unit which terrorizes the population of the English-speaking provinces the most is the BIR unit, also named "The Israeli Unit". According to reports, soldiers of this unit raid villages, conduct processions with military gear at the heart of residential neighborhoods, are involved in looting, torture, the beating of men, women and children and also in live firing on protesters and civilians, as well as the demolition of commercial and residential buildings.

15. The unit was established in 2001, officially in order to combat crime organizations. In fact, the unit, along with Cameroon's Presidential Guard, is intended to secure the dictatorial regime of Paul Biya, who has ruled the country since 1982. Biya has established these units due to his mistrust towards the military and his fear of a military coup against him. The BIR unit is directly subordinate to the President and it is accountable only to him, which is exceptional.

16. Although the BIR unit also receives arms and training from the US, it is named "The Israeli unit", since according to reports, and this is exceptional, in addition to Israeli training and advice services, an Israeli ex-IDF officer commanded the unit - Lt. Colonel (reserve) Avi Sivan (former head of the Israeli Duvdevan unit during the first Intifada)[6], who was killed in a helicopter crash in Cameroon in 2010. Prior to providing dictator Biya with security services, Sivan has served as the Israeli military attache in Cameroon. According to reports, after Sivan's death, another Israeli ex-IDF officer replaced him[7].

17. From footage of the BIR unit, published by the media, and delivered to us by human rights activists from Cameroon, one can conclude that its soldiers are using Israeli weapons, including Galil, Galil Ace, Tavor rifles and Negev machine-guns[8]. See for example:

---

[6] https://www.makorrishon.co.il/nrg/online/1/ART2/181/108.html ; https://www.alafnet.com/cameroon-biyas-military-adviser-dies-in-helicopter-crash/ ; http://www.mako.co.il/news-channel2/Channel-2-Newscast/Article-6130775493a7c21004.htm

[7] http://www.jeuneafrique.com/mag/276021/politique/cameroun-paul-biya-sous-protection-israelienne ; http://www.jeuneafrique.com/183587/politique/mort-du-monsieur-s-curit-de-paul-biya-dans-le-crash-d-un-h-licopt-re/ ; https://www.washingtonpost.com/news/global-opinions/wp/2017/07/26/in-the-war-on-boko-haram-is-the-u-s-turning-a-;

[8] https://www.youtube.com/watch?v=SKSWiKzC4P0

7

8

18. Early in 2014, BIR became Cameroon's special military unit to combat the murderous terrorist group Boko Haram. The latter has murdered thousands of civilians in Northern Cameroon, kidnapped women and girls to be used as sex slaves, and has made 200,000 people refugees.

19. Unfortunately, similarly to the case of Nigeria, the justifiable war on the terrorist group Boko Haram has become a war on civilians of communities and ethnic groups from which combatants had been enlisted into the terrorist group, while committing grave violations of human rights and war crimes. Cameroon's security forces have carried out torture, disappearance, extrajudicial executions, rape and illegal deprivation of liberties.

20. The BIR unit, which leads the fight against Boko Haram, is one of the main units accused of crimes. Thus, for example, Amnesty International's 2017 report[9] "Cameroon's Secret Torture Chambers" documents severe torture of civilians - women and men - as well as children and disabled people, in unofficial detention facilities, in bases serving the BIR unit for operational activity, and even in its headquarters in the north of the country. Torture includes: Beating (by electric cables, wood or metal sticks and rods, chains, Machetes and more), repeated beating of the feet to prevent the detainee from walking, tying the detainee's arms and legs behind their back together (called "The Goat"), tying the detainee's arms and legs together behind their back and hanging them in the air (called "The Swing"), asphyxiation by shoving the detainee's head into a water container, causing burns to the detainee's body, pulling out nails, electrocution and more. The detainees had to perform their bodily functions on themselves or in a bucket, and they did not receive medical care.

[9] https://www.amnesty.nl/content/uploads/2017/07/Cameroon-EN-FINAL-lite.pdf?x25872

9

21. Even if the BIR unit was not involved in crimes against civilians in Cameroon, as part of the war on Boko Haram and in general, a special anti-terror military unit, whose task is counter-insurgency, is certainly inappropriate for handling legitimate civil protest by teachers, lawyers, students and others, and the decision to send it to the English-speaking provinces attests to dictator Biya's true intention - elections will be held in Cameroon this year, and the 85 year old Biya fears that the protest will spread to other provinces, where the political and economic conditions are no less grim.

22. Under these circumstances, in view of the crimes in which the BIR unit is involved across Cameroon, especially in the past year in the British-speaking provinces, and fearing that the grave political crisis in Cameroon may spiral out of control into a full civil war, I would ask you to freeze or cancel all security export licenses to the BIR unit, until one can make sure that it is possible to verify that its soldiers are no longer involved in severe violations of human rights, that the crimes which were committed are investigated and those responsible are brought to justice, and that the crisis in Cameroon is over.

23. This case does not involve "normal" Israeli security exports being used for grave violations of human rights, but rather - a real intervention by the Israeli Ministry of Defense in the political life of another country, in a neo-colonial manner. The citizens of Israel, the State of Israel or the Knesset have never declared war on the residents of the English-speaking provinces of Cameroon, and have never voted to support the eternal reign of an aging dictator.

24. In view of the rapid escalation in Cameroon, I would be thankful for your swift reply.

Eitay Mack, Adv.

10

Appendix XI

Submission of the Commonwealth Human Rights Initiative (CHRI, 2018)

Commonwealth Human Rights Initiative

working for the *practical* realisation of human rights in the countries of the Commonwealth

September 2018

Submission to the Commonwealth Ministerial Action Group (CMAG)

The Commonwealth Human Rights Initiative (CHRI) joined by the undersigned Commonwealth, international, and regional civil society groups draw the attention of CMAG to the number of indiscriminate killings, arbitrary arrests, detention without recourse to justice, and torture in Cameroon. Amnesty International have reported that 20 protesters have been killed, and information from UN agencies and Cameroonian civil society indicate that as a result of the ongoing crisis, more than 411,000 have now been displaced, 128 villages burnt, and more than 1,000 individuals are in detention.

It is clear that the Government of Cameroon is now in breach of the Commonwealth Charter, the Latimer House Principles, and the Harare Declaration. In the spirit of that Declaration's call for 'non-governmental Commonwealth organisations to play their full part in promoting these objectives, in a spirit of co-operation and mutual support,' CHRI, joined by the undersigned groups, call on CMAG to now add Cameroon to its formal agenda.

It is imperative that CMAG act; the crisis has moved beyond the stage where considering lessons learnt from other bilingual states is either appropriate or acceptable. Indeed, a crisis which began with protests by lawyers, students, teachers and civil society groups from the Anglophone community against marginalisation and discrimination has deteriorated to a situation where security forces have brutally dispersed demonstrators resulting in deaths and injury. Protestors have been detained unlawfully, freedom of assembly, access to the internet and information constrained, and access to justice severely impaired.

The appendix to this statement goes into more detail, but of major concern are the fact that:

- Security forces have reacted to protests with excessive force resulting in protestors death
- Counter terrorism laws have been used to arrest protestors and journalists

- Prisoners have been denied due process
- Protestors in police custody, including minors, have been tortured to extract confessions
- The independence of the judiciary has been compromised
- Internet connections and access to social media platforms have been blocked

Signed
The Commonwealth Human Rights Initiative (CHRI)
African Centre for Democracy and Governance
Africans Rising
Afrika Youth Movement
All Party Parliamentary Human Rights Group (UK)
Association for the Protection of Natural Resources in Cameroon
CIVICUS: World Alliance for Citizen Participation
Centre for Human Rights and Democracy in Africa
Commonwealth Association for Health and Disability
Commonwealth Lawyers Association
Commonwealth Journalists Association
Crisis Action
Dominicans for Justice and Peace
East African Civil Society Organizations' Forum
Freedom House
Friends of Assam and Seven Sisters
Institute of Commonwealth Studies
International Bar Association's Human Rights Institute
International Federation for Human Rights (FIDH)
Minority Rights Group International
Nouveaux Droits de l'Homme Cameroun
Public Media Alliance
Royal Commonwealth Society, Cameroon
Soroptimist International: a Global Voice for Women
The Commonwealth Equality Network
Un Monde Avenir
United Nations Association - UK
World Dynamics of Young People (WDYP) – Cameroon

British Commonwealth Human Rights Initiative

The Commonwealth Human Rights Initiative (2018) Submission to the Commonwealth Ministerial Action Group (CMAG). Retrieved from: https://www.humanrightsinitiative.org/download/1537957787Cameroon%20CMAG%20submission.pdf

The Commonwealth Human Rights Initiative (CHRI) joined by the undersigned Commonwealth.

Appendix XII

Letter from President Trump informing Congress of his decision to terminate the designation of the Republic of Cameroon as a beneficiary sub-Saharan African country under the African Growth and Opportunity Act (AGO) (2019).

Message to the Congress

— FOREIGN POLICY | Issued on: October 31, 2019

★ ★ ★

TO THE CONGRESS OF THE UNITED STATES:

In accordance with section 506A(a)(3)(B) of the Trade Act of 1974, as amended (19 U.S.C. 2466a(a)(3)(B)), I am providing notice of my intent to terminate the designation of the Republic of Cameroon (Cameroon) as a beneficiary sub-Saharan African country under the African Growth and Opportunity Act (AGOA).

I am taking this step because I have determined that the Government of Cameroon currently engages in gross violations of internationally recognized human rights, contravening the eligibility requirements of section 104 of the AGOA.

Despite intensive engagement between the United States and the Government of Cameroon, Cameroon has failed to address concerns regarding persistent human rights violations being committed by Cameroonian security forces. These violations include extrajudicial killings, arbitrary and unlawful detention, and torture.

Accordingly, I intend to terminate the designation of Cameroon as a beneficiary sub-Saharan African country under the AGOA as of January 1, 2020. I will continue to assess whether the Government of Cameroon engages in gross violations of internationally recognized human rights, in accordance with the AGOA eligibility requirements.

DONALD J. TRUMP

THE WHITE HOUSE,
October 31, 2019.

Appendix XIII

AFRICAN BAR ASSOCIATION

January 10, 2020
The Hon. Boris Johnson
Prime Minister of Great Britain
10 Dowing Street
London, United Kingdom

Dearest Prime Minister,
The Injustice in Southern Cameroun

On behalf of the Governing and Executive councils of the African Bar Association, I bring you greetings and warm solidarity from the entire Lawyers in Africa and use this media to congratulate you and your party for winning the confidence of the people of your country and gaining an emphatic election victory at the last General election in the U.K.

It is my hope Mr. prime Minister and the hope of thousands of African Lawyers and Millions of ordinary Africans particularly those of the commonwealth of Nations that have common heritage with the U.K that your tenure will be especially successful in proffering solutions to a myriad of socio-economic and political problems facing Africa especially the Anglophone Zone.

Sir, the severe civil conflict in Cameroun which has been on for almost four (4) years now and which has festered into full blown carriage of indescribable magnitude has been of serious concern to the African bar Association as early as its roots.

The inability of dictatorships to see a country governed by Law rather than by flat and self will is mostly responsible to the dangerous dimension which the civil war in Cameroun has assumed with the massive and merciless killings of men, women, children, the old and people with disability are not left out.

Trenches have been dug and the Government in Cameroun has been encouraged to kill and imprison more as the United Nations, the Commonwealth of Nations and Great countries like Great Britain which handled Southern Cameroun to Francophone Cameroun have refused to participate; the Cameroon government is still to make its intentions known.

The African bar Association, in the meanwhile, has been doing some background research and has found following which may serve as guidelines for a way forward:

1. Pursuant to UNGA Res. 1352 (XIV) 16 October 1959, a UN-organized plebiscite

was conducted in the British Cameroons on the 11 and 12 February 1961; in the Southern Cameroons on the 11th and Northern Cameroons on the 12th

2. The questions in plebiscite as contained in that Resolution were:
   "(a) Do you wish to achieve independence by joining the independent federation if Nigeria?"
   "(b) Do you wish to achieve independence by joining the independent republic of the Cameroons"?
3. The terms of Res. 1352 (XV), contrary to those of UNGA Res. 1350 (XIII) of 13 March 1959 on Northern Cameroons and the plebiscite in British Togoland, show that the British Southern Cameroons plebiscite was not about the integration of the British Southern Cameroons into the Republic of Cameroon but about independence, although in association with either Nigeria or Cameroon.
4. Cameroon did indeed agree as contained in the plebiscite document called the "Two Alternatives" that should the vote go in favour of British Southern Cameroons achieving independence in association with Cameroon, the union would be a "federation of two states equal in status". This same commitment has been made by the then President of Cameroon Amadou Ahidjo before the 4th committee in 1959 when he said: "We (French Cameroons) are not annexationists. If our brothers of the British zone which to unite with independent Cameroon, we are ready to discuss the matter with them, but we will do so on a footing of equality.
5. The result of the vote in the Southern Cameroons was in favour of achieving independence in association with the Republic of Cameroon.
6. In pursuance of the promise of independence by joining, the UN adopted Res. 1608 (XV) on 21 April 1961 in which it called (para 5) for a tripartite conference of the Government of the Southern Cameroons, the Administering Authority and the Republic of Cameroon to urgently work out the terms of the proposed union.
7. As we write, there is no shred of evidence anywhere that the Administering Authority ever implemented that Resolution or that the tripartite conference ever held.
8. The UN actually followed up the promise of "independence by joining' and did conduct a vote on Southern Cameroons independence on 21 April 1961, which came out overwhelmingly in favour: 64 votes for, 23 against and 10 abstentions
9. The UN General Assembly set the date of Southern Cameroon's independence to be 1 October, 1961, close to two years after the Republic of Cameroon had her own independence on 1 January 1960. Upon achieving independence the Southern Cameroons would join with French Cameroon.
10. Very surprisingly, Cameroon voted against Southern Cameroons independence in Res. 1608 (XV) of 21 April 1961.
11. The determining resolution governing decolonization under the UN system was Res. 1514 (XV) of 14 Dec. 1960, which declared unconditional independence for all trust and non-self-governing territories, whether big or small.
12. Again, we find no evidence that the Administering Authority, the UK, ever compiled with Res. 1514 with regard to the Southern Cameroons.

13. The greatest shortcoming on the part of the UN is that while it adopted Resolution 1608 (XV) calling for a tripartite conference to work out the terms of association between the British Southern Cameroons and the Republic of Cameroon, it never created any mechanism to monitor and report on the implementation of that resolution. Consequently, the idea that the Southern Cameroons actually achieved independence on 1 October and then joined the Republic of Cameroon were all assumptions, which turned out not to be true.
14. Without the implementation of Resolution 1608 (XV) and the landmark Res. 1514, no union was achieved, no terms of the relationship were worked out and the British Southern Cameroons become a prey to Cameroon, even though Cameroon voted against union with the Southern Cameroons.
15. 15. On 30th September 1961, the UK, for an unknown reason, ignored both the elected and functional government of the Southern Cameroons headed by Dr. John Ngu Foncha as well as the British Southern Cameroons House of Assembly and transferred the British Southern Cameroons to the Republic of Cameroon, which took possession and has been in control ever since.
16. Some opinions have suggested that the Republic of Cameroon's seat at the UN also represents that of the Southern Cameroons. We note that the Republic of Cameroon joined the UN on 20th September 1960, at a time when the British Southern Cameroons was still a Trust Territory of the UN. There is no miracle by which Cameroon's seat can represent the two countries given the fact noted above.

Remarks

1. It is to be noted that this matter falls squarely within international law. Both parties were and are subjects of international law; the British Southern Cameroons was a trust territory of the United Nations; it has international boundaries separating it from the Republic of Cameroon; those boundaries have never been adjusted under Article 102 of the UN Charter; it had an elected and functional government at the time it was surrendered by the UK to the Republic of Cameroon. The House of Assembly of the British Southern Cameroons never passed any law to form a federation with the Republic of Cameroon.
2. The result of the fact that the famous Declaration on the Granting of Independence to Colonial Countries and Peoples (Res. 1514), was never implemented is that the Southern Cameroons was never decolonized! It was a fundamental condition of that Resolution that for decolonization to have been considered as effective, power should be transferred by the colonial power to the indigenous population. However, the Administering Authority transferred power to a third party without any terms having been worked out. The transfer deprived the British Southern Cameroons of the opportunity to work out the terms of union by herself. As a trust territory of the UN, decolonisation could not occur without any witness from the UN.
3. The UN and the Administering Authority (the UK) were mere custodians over the territory and people of the British Southern Cameroons. They had no competence to transfer the territory to any third party, nor could any

such purported transfer be valid.

4. The African Bar Association has not found a single article of the UN Charter, UN Resolution of the African Union Constitutive Act nor any instrument of international law which gives the Republic of Cameroon jurisdiction over the Southern Cameroons!
5. We have also found no evidence that any real federation was created between the two countries, since that was called a federation was simply an amendment of the internal law of the Republic of Cameroon, law No. 64/21, declaring the formation of a federation with the British Southern Cameroons.
6. Article 47 of the so-called federation declared that no idea to ever change the federal form of the state could be accepted.
7. A few years down the road, 1972, Cameroon got the population of French Cameroon, which was four times that of the British Southern Cameroons, to participate in a vote to abolish the federation. Of course, it was abolished, meaning in effect that the people of the British Southern Cameroons ceased to have any say in matters concerning their future and destiny.
8. The African Bar Association would like to draw your attention to this very pertinent point: all African countries have agreed on one fundamental principle: that only by respecting boundaries inherited from colonization can there be peace in Africa. This can be emphasized in the Cairo Declaration of July 24 1964; the Algiers Declaration of July 1999 and is entrenched in the African Union Constitutive Act, meaning that her treaty obligations compel her to respect her boundaries acquired at independence, on 1 January 1960.

WAY FORWARD

The African Bar Association calls for Truth, Justice and the Rule of Law as a way forward.

1. The conflict in Cameroon is not a conflict that can be settled by guns. It is not a conflict that can be settled by ignoring the facts, by ignoring justice, truth and the rule of law. Any solution that purports to ignore these factors would simply be preparing for future wars. The mistake that was made in 1961 by ignoring the wishes of the people of the British Southern Cameroons should not be repeated after close to 60 years of additional knowledge on human relations. Rather, the present war should be looked upon as a golden opportunity to correct the injustices that led to this war.
2. A solution imposed by Cameroon or the by the international community will also not be sustainable. Even if Cameroon were to win the war, that would not be a solution. What is certain is that the awareness of the people of the Southern Cameroons; their determination to continue the resistance after successfully resisting Cameroon for the last 58 years; their financial, social and economic power will only grow, leading to new wars. They are acutely aware of the injustice they are suffering. Thus, no amount of persuasion and blackmail will cause them to give up the struggle.

3. The double standards that say that territory is more important to Cameroon than to the people of the British Southern Cameroons; that Cameroon has a right to rule its own territory and cross over and rule that of the British Southern Cameroons; that territorial integrity applies only to Cameroon and not the people of the British Southern Cameroons with a territory of their own: that everything should be done to keep the two people together, knowing fully well that that is only to encourage domination and subordination of one people by another contrary to the Articles 19 and 20 of the African Charter on Human and Peoples Rights, are not solutions at all. They are apartheid being promoted for absolutely spurious reasons. They neither serve Cameroon nor the people of the British Southern Cameroons; they just keep them fighting each other forever. Africans are acutely conscious of the dangers of promoting such double standards and apartheid, which have generated nothing but conflicts in Africa.
4. The African Bar Association has also fully aware that once justice and restitution are done, there will be peace between the two peoples. They will become the best of friends, as we have seen with al colonial masters and their colonies, despite their bitter past. Injustice is the cause of wars and enmity; once justice, is done both sides always become happier.
5. Given all these considerations, the African Bar Association is of the strong opinion that rather than let third parties suggest solutions for a problem which they are not suffering, the best and most transparent and democratic solution would be a UN-organized referendum in the British Southern Cameroons for its people to pronounce themselves on whether they wish to continue to live under Cameroon; to form some kind of association with Cameroon documented by treaty or to govern themselves within their own internationally defined territory. Scotland, Quebec, New Caledonia, Bougainville, the UK itself with the European Union, South Sudan and many other countries have resorted to referenda to settle such supreme matters of interest to their people. There is no reason to deny the people of the Southern Cameroons as similar opportunity for this supreme matter. We firmly believe that the people should be given a chance to speak for themselves. This would automatically lead to a ceasefire. The conditions for such a referendum can be worked out to ensure transparency and fairness.
6. If however any of the major powers is not comfortable with a UN-organized referendum, the next best solution would be to refer the matter to the ICJ for an opinion on whether the territory of the Southern Cameroons belongs to the Republic of Cameroon or to the people of the British Southern Cameroons. Claims over territory in Africa cannot be assumed; they must be proven using Article 4 (b) of the African Union Constitutive Act as a basis for all claims.
7. The African Bar Association notes that it is extremely strange that the Republic of Cameroon seems to be avoiding the Swiss Meditation. The Swiss Mediation or any other third party mediation is a golden opportu-

nity for the Republic of Cameroon to prove to the world its claims and show that the so-called separatists have no case. Instead, however, it is Cameroon that is avoiding the opportunity.

Both of these solutions would settle the matter conclusively and on a lasting basis. However, the referendum solution is by far quicker and less subject to any external distortion than going to the ICJ

The African Bar Association, like the rest of the international community is anxious to see a quick and decisive end to this brutal conflict so that at last the killings may stop, children may go to school, and the people may come out of the bushes. We believe that there will be no stability for Cameroon and the gulf of Guinea as long as the rights of the people of the Southern Cameroons are suppressed. But resolving this conflict on the basis of truth, justice and the rule of law would be the happiest day for the two parties.

Once again, on behalf of the African Bar Association, I thank you for taking prompt action on this letter.

Hannibal Uwaifo
President

Appendix XIV

Open Letter to Her Excellency, Madam Doris Leuthard, President of the Swiss Confederation Federal Chancellery (October 7, 2917)

Open Letter

7th October 2017

Her Excellency, Madam Doris Leuthard
President of the Swiss Confederation
Federal Chancellery
Federal Palace West Wing
3003 Bern
info@bk.admin.ch

His Excellency Walter Thurnherr,
Federal Chancellor
Information Service
Federal Palace West Wing
3003 Bern
Email: info@bk.admin.ch

Email: media@bk.admin.ch

His Excellency Didier Burkhalter Federal Councillor
The Federal Department of Foreign Affairs (FDFA)
Attention: Human Security Division
FDFA Directorate of political affairs
Bundesgasse 32
3003 Bern
Email: pd-ams@eda.admin.ch

Your Excellencies,

Subject: President Paul Biya of Cameroon Masterminds Massacre of Unarmed Civilians from Geneva, Switzerland.

We, a collection of English-speaking citizens from the former UN Trust Territory of Southern Cameroons, which is now part of *la Republique du Cameroon*, and residing in all continent of the world, have the honour to approach your excellencies with a shocking matter of gross human rights violations and death in Cameroon, that is being masterminded from the territory of Switzerland.

In effect, on 1st October 2017, from the comfort and luxury of the InterContinental Hotel, Chemin du Petit-Saconnex 7-9, 1209 Geneva, Switzerland, President Paul Biya ordered the Cameroon armed forces to carry out a bloody massacre that led to the death of more than 100 unarmed civilians, and the wounding of hundreds of others, in the English-speaking region of Cameroon. The most heinous act of this inhumane atrocity was the use of military helicopters to shoot at unarmed civilian demonstrators, and drop fragmentation grenades on them. Please see this report from the Reuters News Agency (https://www.reuters.com/article/us-cameroon-protests/cameroon-army-helicopters-shot-separatist-protesters-witnesses-idUSKBN1CB2BP).

Our relatives in Cameroon witness the attacks and saw the dead and wounded. More than that, leaked Cameroon army logs of the events of 1st October 2017 are chilling in their reckless and wanton disregard for human life:

"[01/10 à 16:33] +237 99104845: À Buea, les insurgés veulent prendre le palais du Gouverneur construit par les Allemands aujourd'hui avant 18h, car disent-ils, c'est leur capitale. Mais les FMO tiennent jusqu'à présent.

[01/10 à 16:33] +237 99104845: Survol à basse altitude et largage des grenades F4 à partir des hélicos"

More than 100 people were killed in this ground and air attack on unarmed civilians, and hundreds were seriously wounded. The mortuaries in the region are full and dead bodies are still being discovered. President Biya masterminded this inhumane attack from the InterContinental Hotel in Geneva, where he has been, and is still living for a few weeks now. Please note that the 237 in the military log is the telecommunications country code of Cameroon. The Cameroon telephone number +237 99104845 from which the messages were sent to President Biya in Geneva, belongs to Cameroon's military intelligence.

Your Excellencies, the government of Switzerland, which has allowed President Paul Biya to make Switzerland his home for long periods of time, needs to know that President Paul Biya is a ruthless authoritarian, republican monarch, who has been president of Cameroon for 35 years and has set the stage for his reelection for another 7-year term in 2018. Under his rule, millions of Cameroon citizens are mired in abject poverty and have no access to the basic necessities of life: clean drinking water, sanitation, healthcare, education or electricity.

Since October 2016, President Biya has ordered a bloody crackdown on the population of the English-speaking regions of Cameroon for daring to request a return to the federal system of government that was abolished by Biya and his predecessor, and replaced with a highly centralized Napoleonic system of rule-by-decree that took away all the rights of the English-speaking minority. Biya has collectively punished this community for daring to demonstrate against their poverty, marginalization and second-class citizenship, while the oil, timber, and other natural resources of their region are exploited by Biya and his family and used to finance their luxurious lifestyle in Switzerland, the United States, France, and other parts of Europe.

Furthermore, in response to calls from the English-speaking minority for change, President Biya cut off Internet connections to that region for more than 100 days. There is an Internet blackout in that region as we speak, in order to prevent the world from knowing the extent of the atrocities perpetrated on civilians. Since November 2016, Cameroon armed forces have opened fire indiscriminately on unarmed, demonstrating students, killing many of them. Female students of the University of Buea have been raped with impunity. The leaders of the unions of English-speaking lawyers, teachers, and students who went on strike calling for a return to federalism were arrested, jailed in inhuman conditions and tortured for 7 months. These civilians were promptly charged with terrorism and other offenses carrying the death penalty, at the Yaoundé Military Tribunal. Hundreds of people from the English-speaking community are still being arrested and lockup up in overcrowded jails in Cameroon as we speak. Their crime is to call for a restoration of their federal state that was abolished in 1972

What should be of concern to Switzerland and Europe is that the military crackdown and massive human rights abuses ordered by President Biya, Supreme Commander of the Cameroon Armed Forces, from the InterContinental Hotel in Geneva, has caused many people to flee Cameroon. They are already joining the flood of refugees headed for Europe...and Switzerland.

We understand that Switzerland is a world leader in the defense of human rights. The Swiss federation's stated policy is that: "The promotion of peace and human rights is a priority of Swiss foreign policy. The centrepiece of this policy is the protection of individuals and their dignity. Every human being should be able to live in peace, free of fear and need."

We know that through his prolonged stays in Switzerland, President Paul Biya provides the InterContinental Hotel Group very lucrative business. However, there is clearly a disconnect between Switzerland's active engagement in human rights promotion and protection, and the fact that it allows President Paul Biya, a massive violator of human rights, who kills and jails people merely for supporting a federal system of government, to live in Switzerland.

Your excellencies, we kindly request you to review the conditions under which President Biya resides in Switzerland and oversees massive violations of human rights from Swiss territory. We request you to ask the Swiss Ambassador in Cameroon and representatives of the International Red Cross Society to visit the English-speaking Northwest and Southwest regions of Cameroon, as well as Biya's notorious jails and dungeons in Yaoundé to see for themselves the massive human rights violations being carried out by Biya's army right now.

Sincerely,

The Collective of English-speaking Southern Cameroonians in the Diaspora.

P/s This letter is unsigned because it is public. If we sign it, the Biya regime will retaliate against our families in Cameroon. We have therefore asked members of our community to send individual copies of the letter to the Swiss government in lieu of their signatures.

Appendix XV

Buea Declaration of the All Anglophone Conference (1993)

ALL ANGLOPHONE CONFERENCE

THE BUEA DECLARATION

Issued by the ALL ANGLOPHONE CONFERENCE

Held At Buea On 2nd and 3rd April, 1993

IN THE NAME OF THE ALMIGHTY GOD FROM WHOM ALL LIFE, WISDOM, POWER, GLORY AND PROTECTION PROCEED:

WE, THE PEOPLE OF ANGLOPHONE CAMEROON, represented by over five thousand Delegates drawn from the thirteen Divisions of our Territory (Boyo, Bui, Donga-Mantung, Fako, Kupe –Mwanenguba, Lebialem, Manyu, Meme, Menchum, Mezam, Momo, Ndian, Ngokitunjia) and from all over the rest of Cameroon, among whom, Elder Statesmen and Senior Citizens, Traditional Rulers, Religious and Spiritual Leaders, Leaders of Political Parties, Members of Parliament and of the Economic and Social Council, Farmers, Workers, Students and Elites of all Professions, meeting at Mount Mary Maternity Centre in the historic town of Buea from the 2nd day to the 3rd day of April 1993 in an All Anglophone Conference for the purpose of adopting a common Anglophone stand for the announced national debate on constitutional reform and of examining several other matters related to the welfare of Ourselves, our Posterity, our Territory and the entire Cameroon Nation,

DO SOLEMNLY MAKE THE DECLARATION herein contained for which we offer the following justification:

TODAY, NO GROUP OF PEOPLE who freely chose to join a political Union would want to be treated as a captive people. In 1961 the people of Southern Cameroons through a United Nations-supervised plebiscite decided to enter into a political Union with the people of La Republique du Cameroun whom they considered as their brothers and fellow countrymen. They did so, by the grace of God, FREELY and without the involvement or participation of the people of La Republique du Cameroun. Their aspiration was to establish a unique Federation on the continent of Africa, and to evolve a bicultural society in which the distinct heritage of each of the partners to the union would flourish. We believed that such a lofty goal could be achieved. During these past thirty-two years, however, our common experience in the Union leaves us in no doubt that far from attaining theses ends; we have become a people with a problem.

Our problem, which the intolerant and hypocritical attitude of our Francophone brothers would rather suppress, springs from a breach of trust on the part of Francophone leadership and from a lack of openness in matters of public interest. Within these thirty-two years, our Union accord has been violated. We have been disenfranchised, marginalized, and treated with suspicion. Our interests have been disregarded.

Our participation in national life has been limited to non-essential functions. Our natural resources have been ruthlessly exploited without any benefit accruing to our territory or to its people. The development of our territory has been negligible and confined to areas that directly or indirectly benefit Francophones. Through manoeuvres and manipulations, we have been reduced from partners of equal status in the Union to the status of a subjugated people.

The common values, vision, and goals which we share as a people and those of our Francophone partners in the Union are different, and clearly cannot blend within the framework of a Unitary state such as was imposed on us in 1972. We are by nature pacifist, patient and tolerant and have demonstrated those qualities since we came into this Union. Our Francophone brothers believe in brutalising, torturing, maiming and assassinating dissenters. They have raped our women and daughters and used hand and rifle grenades against peaceful demonstrators. We find such barbarism alien to us and short of the civilised standards of all democratic societies.

We subscribe fully to the Voltairean dictum that: "I wholly disapprove of what you say, but will defend to death your right to say it". Our idea of freedom of expression and of the press leads us to believe in the open discussion of public issues that affect our lives. Our Francophone brothers suppress freedom of expression and practice censorship of the press. The democratic principle of majority rule the minority rights leads us to believe in the rights and freedoms of the minority. Successive Francophone-led Regimes in this country have pursued a policy of assimilation aimed at wiping out our identity. Thus, our vision of a bicultural society has become an illusive, unattainable goal, and will remain so unless and until we devise a better framework within which this aspiration can find expression.

IN BUEA TODAY, we make an important decision. For the benefit of those who hereafter may doubt the rectitude of our intentions we place on record the following facts:

1. THE PRE-PLEBISCITE ACCORD

The United Nations document entitled, THE TWO ALTERNATIVES which was widely circulated on the eve of the plebiscite to explain to the people the implications of their choice, and the Joint Declaration by Prime Minister J.N Foncha and President Ahmadou Ahidjo contained therein, made it clear to the people of Anglophone Cameroon that, in the event of their opting for the second alternative, they would, at independence, be forming a Federation of two States with equal status.

It was clear that the majority in one state would not be allowed to impose its will or interests on the other state. In 1972, all this was disregarded. Not only did the Francophone majority impose their will, fraudulent, on the Anglophone minority, but they also brought to an end the equality of status between the two founding components of Cameroon.

2. THE CONSTITUTION OF CAMEROON

The Union between the Southern Cameroons and La Republique du Cameroun has proceeded these past thirty-two years without any constitutional basis. Without the process of negotiating the terms of reunification having been completed, without any federal constituent assembly having met, without any draft federal constitution having been established, the National Assembly of la Republique du Cameroun, meeting without any Southern Cameroons participation, adopted proposed amendments to the constitution of La Republique du Cameroun, of 4th May 1960. The latter Constitution, as thus amended, was promulgated by Mr. Ahmadou AHIDJO, president of La Republique du Cameroun, on 1 September 1961, one month before the reunification of the two Cameroons was to take effect, as the Constitution of the Federal Republic of Cameroon. In so far as the Legislature of one component of a future Federation cannot validly act as the Legislature of that Federation, the so- called Federal Constitution of 1 September 1961 was null and void ab initio. No valid constitutional or other legal basis has ever existed for the reunification of the two Cameroons and for the common governance of the two territories.

Without prejudice to the fact that the supposed Federal Constitution of 1 September 1961 was clearly a nullity, it is to be observed that Article 47 of that constitution stated that the latter could only be amended by an Act of Federal Parliament and gave the majority of deputies representing each of the two Federated States power to veto an amendment by voting against any bill for such amendment. The same article made it clear that no bill intended to impair the unity and integrity of the Federation could be introduced.

The supposed Federal Constitution of 1 September 1961 laid down a specific procedure for amendment. In disregard of this special procedure, President Ahidjo chose to organise a referendum, in which Francophones took part, to end the Federation. The so called "Peace Revolution" of 1972 was a ploy by Francophones to use their overwhelming majority to alter the basis of reunification for which Anglophones and Anglophones ONLY, had voted. The 1972 referendum was illegal in so far as it was not in conformity with the procedure which the Constitution itself had laid down for the amendment of its provisions and also in so far as its aim was not only to impair the Federation's unity and integrity, but to abolish the Federation itself. The unconstitutionality of the referendum of 20 May 1972 attaches to, and affects, all enactments following therefrom, notably the constitution of 2 June 1972 and its subsequent amendments.

There is need now to establish, for the first time, the constitutional basis and the legal framework of the Union between La Republique du Cameroun and the Southern Cameroons.

3. EXPLOITATION AND RAPE OF OUR ECONOMY

The unconstitutional and illegal imposition of the Unitary form of government was aimed not only at dismantling the institutions of the Anglophone State (Legislature, Government, House of Chiefs, Judiciary, Police force, etc.), but also at exploiting and raping our economy:

a) Successive Francophone Regimes have since stepped up the exploitation of our natural resources, especially oil and timber.

b) They have destroyed the effective system of financing small-scale industries and enterprises which Anglophone Cameroon had established through the creation of such institutions as the West Cameroon Development Agency and the Cameroon Bank. They killed the Bank.

c) They looted the West Cameroon Marketing Board which Anglophone Cameroon had set up prior to independence and misappropriated with impunity its huge financial reserves of over 78 billion francs.

d) They closed down the West Cameroon Electricity Corporation (POWERCAM) and, with it, our cheap source of hydro-electricity supply at yoke and compelled us to make use of supplies from their source which, enjoying a monopoly of supply and being aimed at excessive profit-making, charges very expensive prices. They completely demolished all out hydro-electric installations instead of maintaining them as stand-by sources and confiscated the assets of the West Cameroon Electricity Corporation.

e) They contrived to squeeze out Anglophone business and to maintain an exclusive grasp and control over finance and business. They fix the terms and conditions of credits and control access to finance institutions both public and private. As a result, familiar Anglophone Businesses starved of credits, such a as Fomenky's Direct Suppliers, Niba Automobile, Nangah Company, Kilo Brothers and the Che Company, are no more.

f) They closed down our Agro-Industrial establishments such as the Santa Coffee Estate and, later, the Wum Area Development Authority and the Obang Farm Settlement.

g) They shut our sea and air-ports. The present Bamenda Airport, abandoned with unfinished structures and insufficient equipment, can in no way compensate for the closure of the Victoria deep sea-port, the Tiko International Airport, the Besongabang Airport, the Bali Airport, the Weh Airstrip, the inland port of Mamfe and the beautiful port of Ndian. They closed down our indigenous airline, the Cameroon Air Transport (CAT). The law-abiding victims of all these acts were powerless because there was no legal framework within which they could seek and obtain redress.

h) They have taken away from us the responsibility to plan our towns and to maintain in them the high standard of sanitation that used to prevail. They have destroyed the system of local government and of community development which we had instituted in Anglophone Cameroon. Today, our main towns which used to boom with commercial activity- Mamfe, Kumba, Tiko, Nkambe, Wum, Victoria, etc. – have been reduced to ghost towns. In the meantime, no Francophone towns and cities have suffered a similar fate. They continue to boom.

4. ROAD INFRASTRUCTURE

The government of Anglophone Cameroon pursued a policy of maintaining all-season roads. To this end, particularly difficult stretches of roads such as the Supe and he Sabga Hills, were tarred. The streets of all divisional chief towns were tarred. The Francophone-led governments have failed to maintain these roads and streets. Worse than that, they have destroyed what we had. Under the pretext of resurfacing our roads which were tarred prior to reunification, they dug up the existing tar, destroyed the roads, and in that state, abandoned them as in the case of Kumba-Mbonge, and the Kumba-Tombel roads. Today, the streets of Kumba, the economic capital of the South West Province, are pool of mud in the rainy season, while Nkambe and Kumbo in the North West wallow in dust up to one foot thick in the dry season. In thirty-two years of independence and reunification, the government has not added a single kilometer of road to the network that existed in Anglophone Cameroon prior to reunification, other than the few kilometers from the Mungo Bridge to Tiko, from Victoria to Idenau and from Santa to Bamenda which were done primarily to serve the economic and commercial interests of Francophones and to provide easy access to oil installations manned and exploited by Francophones for the benefit of Francophones. Ndian, the division off whose shores the nation's oil is produced is without roads. Twice we have witnesses grandiose and pompous ceremonies to mark commencement of construction work on the Kumba –Mamfe road. Till today, that road remains unconstructed. President Ahidjo had never before cut a tape over an untarred road. He did so for the first time at Mamfe. More recently, Mr. Paul Biya publicly announced that he would personally supervise the construction of the Ring Road in the North West Province. There is as yet no sign that the construction of the Ring Road will at last begin.

The neglect of roads in Anglophone Cameroon has had disastrous economic and social consequences for our people and for the development of our territory. We had an all-season Trunk A road running from Victoria through Kumba, Mamfe, and Bamenda to Wum and Nkambe. In their deliberate policy to subjugate us, our Francophone brothers have abandoned the maintenance of this important road. They have, instead, developed the Douala-Bafoussam road so as to compel us in travelling from Bamenda to Buea or Victoria, to pass through their territory.

5. ROAD CHECKPOINTS

The hundreds of police, gendarmes and customs checkpoints on our roads today seem normal and acceptable to Francophones. They really make this country strange to Anglophones. Between Bamenda and Victoria, there are about 35 checkpoints. This unnecessary restriction on the free movement of people, goods and services serves no useful purpose as traffic cases rarely go to the courts. What may originally have been an exercise with a noble objective has been reduced to a system of road tolls instituted by the Forces of Law and Order with the tacit approval of the government.

6. DIVIDE AND RULE

We achieved independence and went into Union with La Republique Du Cameroun as a single entity. The Francophone government divided our Territory into the North-West and South-West provinces without any prior consultation with us. Francophones now plan to go one stage further by fusing the North West Province with the Francophone Western Province and the South West province with the Francophone Littoral Province ostensibly so as to create bilingual Provinces. These moves are, in fact, aimed at the cultural assimilation and annihilation of Anglophone Cameroon. Enforced uniformity, it is hoped, would eventually wipe out Anglophone identity, and secure long term control of our natural resources for the benefit of France. This surreptitious plan is diabolical and unacceptable to us, especially as its implementation can only take place through the fanning of North West/ South West misunderstandings with the complicity of certain self-seeking Anglophones.

7. MARGINALISATION OF ANGLOPHONES

Since the inception of the Federation, Anglophone Cameroonians have only played second-fiddle to their Francophone compatriots, starting with the first Prime Minister of West Cameroon, who, on assuming the role of vice-president of the Federal Republic, set the general pattern of the Anglophone role since then. Anglophones have been appointed mainly into subordinate positions to assist Francophones, even where the latter have been less qualified or less competent.

For 32 years since reunification, Ministries such as those in charge of Territorial Administration, the Armed Forces, Education, Finance, Commercial and Industrial Development, Foreign Affairs, etc have never been headed by Anglophones. When the Prime Minister is Francophone, there is no Secretary General at the Presidency and no vice Prime-Minister. The Prime Minister wields real power and authority. But when that office comes to an Anglophone, he is hedged in between a Francophone Secretary General at the Presidency and another at the prime Minister's office. At the same time he is saddled with not one, but two, Deputy Prime-Ministers on whom real power devolves.

In the Foreign Service, Anglophones rarely get appointed as Cameroon's Ambassador to London, Washington, New York, Lagos or Paris. These key diplomatic posts are reserved exclusively for Francophones.

In Home Affairs there is a rapidly growing tendency to post only Francophone to Anglophone Cameroon in such top administrative positions as Governor, senior Divisional Officer, Legion Commander etc.

8. HUMAN RIGHTS ABUSES

Unlawful detentions, imprisonment, unwarranted searches and seizures, torture by savage agents of the CENER operating La Balancoire, harassment by uncouth gendarmes: these are some aspects of the intolerable Cameroonian reality. Of the hundreds of cases of Human Rights Abuses under a Francophone-led government, we may mention the following among atrocities committed during these past weeks. In November 1992, a young business executive, Che Ngwa Ghandi, was tortured and regularly beaten be CENER agents and gendarme officers until he died. On Thursday 25 March 1993 gendarmes opened automatic machine gun fire on a group of peaceful demonstrators in Bamenda killing three and wounding twenty. On the 18th and 25th of March 1993, in the course of peaceful political demonstrations, 46 Anglophone Cameroonians were arrested, beaten, tortured, and detained in Victoria. Two of these victims, both of them women, were admitted into hospital with severe injuries

9. CIVIL LIBERTIES AND THE DUE PROCESS OF LAW

Before reunification we were certain of the protection and enjoyment of our individual and civil liberties. One could not be arrested and left to languish in prison without being charged. It was unheard of for people's private premises to be searched without a warrant. The police did not carry guns everywhere. We knew nothing of the night raids called KALE-KALE. The opponents of reunification had warned against these forms of repression which even then were already being practiced in La Republique du Cameroun. Today, 32 years later, Anglophones regret that they had not heeded theses warnings.

In a real democracy, everyone is presumed to be equal before the law, and there is certainty that justice would be done if the law is violated. In Cameroon under the Francophone leadership, executive interference with the judicial process and with the enforcement of judicial decisions is commonplace. Judges have been reduced to agents of the Minister of Justice while the courts have become departments and services within the Ministry of Justice. The most glaring and dramatic among the thousands of instances of executive disregarded of the judiciary recently occurred when, on Monday 23 December 1992, the Bamenda High Court ordered in Ruling No HCB (CRM) 92 that 173 persons detained and tortured at the Maximum Security Detention Centre (BMM) be released,. In contempt of the court's decision, government arbitrarily decided that the court order would not be obeyed. The 173 men and women were instead moved, on the 27th of December, under the most inhumane and degrading conditions of transportation imaginable, to Yaoundé to stand trial before a Francophone Court. This teleguiding of justice and the interference with it by government are unknown to us, Anglophones.

10. DISRIMINATION IN EDUCATION AND TRAINING

Anglophones are systematically discriminated against in the admission of students into professional schools and other institutions of higher learning, notably the National School of Administration and Magistracy (ENAM) where the Anglophone sections have been abolished, and the Higher Teacher, s Training College (E.N.S).

Anglophones have virtually been excluded since inception from such institutions as the *Ecole Nationale Superieure Polytechnique*, the *Institute International des Assurances*, the School of surveys, the Business Administration School in Douala, and so on.

There is little or no continuity between the education Anglophone children are given at the primary and secondary levels and the Francophone- dominated, French-oriented education dispensed in our national institutions of higher learning. Many Anglophone youths are forced to travel abroad at great financial costs to themselves and to their families in search of higher education which is of good quality and consistent with their basic education. Anglophones returning to Cameroon with foreign academic and professional qualifications are subjected to the evaluation and equation of their diplomas and degrees before they can be considered for employment. They often have to wait for as long as 5 years for the "equivalence" process to be completed. The files of over 700 Anglophone civil servants are at present lying in the Ministry of the Civil service, some of them for over seven years, awaiting "reclassification" of the persons concerned.

After so many years of neglect, good quality secondary technical education for Anglophone has ceased to exist. What a contrast with the technical and commercial education that, in the days of the Federation, was provided by such renowned institutions as the Government Technical College, Ombe!

11. FRANCOPHONE EXPLOITATION AND DOMINATION

Instances of Francophone exploitation and domination of Anglophones are many. We cite the following examples:

a) The University of Buea is officially designated as being "Anglo-Saxon". It is located in Anglophone Territory and run by Anglophones for the education, primarily, of Anglophones. All this notwithstanding, Francophone government officials in Buea and Yaoundé arrogantly instructed the Management of the Buea University to deny the use of the latter's premises and facilities for the purpose of holding the present All Anglophone Conference. Thus were we reduced to beggars in our own land, confirming once more that we have become a subjugated people.

b) After reunification all Cinemas Theatres in Victoria, Buea, Kumba and Bamenda and other Anglophone towns were compelled to show only French-language films.

c) When there is a football match in France, the entire Cameroon nation is held to ransom by CRTV as the match is shown, sometimes live, on Cameroon Television. The Cameroon Radio and Television Corporation (CRTV) does not react in the same manner when a football or other sporting encounter takes place in England or involves an English team.

d) Television films and programmes originally made in English are shown in Cameroon only after they have been translated into French, and only in their French version.

e) Broadcast time on Radio and Television is very unevenly divided between English and French programmes, even though it does not take longer to inform, educate or entertain in French than it does in English. In the end, Anglophones who share equally in the burden of financing Cameroon Radio and Television, get far less than ¼ of the service provided by this public utility.

f) Whereas all of Cameroon's oil resources at present originate from the Anglophone part of the country only, all oil-related public corporations- SNH, SONARA, SCDP, HYDRAC, etc. – are predominantly staffed by Francophones.

g) Notwithstanding that all of Cameroon's oil exploration, production and transformation takes place in Anglophone Cameroon, oil-derived revenues are paid to the state directly in Yaoundé.

h) It was a Francophone who appeared in Victoria to buy the property of the National Produce Marketing Board when the organisation wound up. It was a Francophone who appeared in Buea proposing to buy all of the Buea Clerk's Quarters. It was a Francophone who appeared in Bamenda wanting to buy all of CAPMAE and its installations. It was a Francophone who appeared in Buea wanting to but the Government Printing Press. It was a Frenchman who was employed to liquidate PAMOL in Ndian. He failed to proceed with the liquidation. For more than four years now, he has been exploiting PAMOL Plantations for the personal benefit of himself and of his Francophone associates and patrons.

i) In spite of the officially bilingual character of Cameroon, and in spite of its wide international spread and high international standing, English is treated as a secondary language in Cameroon. Official texts and documents are issued mainly, and often exclusively in French.

j) The independence which the judiciary enjoyed in Anglophone Cameroon has been eroded under successive Francophone-led governments.

k) In total disregard of the special place occupied in the governance of Anglophone Cameroon by traditional authority, a Francophone-led government arbitrarily abolished the West Cameroon House of Chiefs.

l) We have been made to suffer all the evils of association of Cameroon's economy and public finances with those of France without any corresponding benefits accruing to us. In 32 years since reunification, there are hardly any French-financed development projects, businesses or investments of social or economic consequence in Anglophone Cameroon.

m) Ours must be the only known situation in the world where there exists a system of law without a legislature. Whereas successive constitutions of Cameroon have contained provisions purporting to preserve the body of law in force in Anglophone Cameroon before the advent of the Unitary State, since the abolition of the Federated State of West Cameroon and its law-making institutions, there now exists no institutional framework for amending or reforming that body of law. The Francophones who have dominated the law-making process since 1972 have never cared to take the measures necessary to ensure that this body of law is in tune with modern times and with the present-day aspirations of Anglophone Cameroonians in the domains affected and governed by those laws.

12. INTERNATIONAL ISOLATION OF ANGLOPHONE CAMEROON

By Cameroon's special language of diplomacy, the people of Gabon, Central African Republic, Chad and Congo are our 'brothers". Each of these peoples is a neighbor and "a brother" of All of us. But when it comes to Nigeria and Nigerians, our language of diplomacy changes. Francophones Cameroonians blame Nigeria for practically everything in Cameroon. Consequently, our Mamfe/Ekok road (one of the busiest in the entire country) is the most neglected because it leads to Nigeria.

It was Anglophone Cameroon that left Nigeria in order to form a Cameroon Federation. If therefore, there was reason to feel any animosity towards Nigeria and Nigerians, it logically should come from Anglophone Cameroonians. Francophones forget that just as their "brotherliness" vis a vis Gabonese, Chadians etc, is enhanced by their common Francophone heritage, so do Anglophone Cameroonians feel a "brotherliness" towards Nigerians born of a common Anglophone heritage.

In reality, the observed Francophone attitude towards Nigerians is only one manifestation of a rather generalised phenomenon, namely, the isolation of Anglophone Cameroon in Cameroon's international relations. It is within this same tendency that we must place the reluctance of the Francophone-led government to fulfill the essential conditions for the admission of Cameroon into the Commonwealth, long after Cameroon became a full member of the Francophonie.

WE RECALL THAT before our Territory attained Independence in 1961, we had been practicing parliamentary democracy in a politically pluralistic society which has far more developed than what obtains in Cameroon today, three decades later. We regarded democracy as a way of life, and as an ideal towards which to strive. We were neither saints nor angels; far from it. But we believed then, as we do now, that whenever a government becomes fraudulent, intolerant and repressive, it is the democratic right of the people to change that government and vote in another. We were spared such a task in Southern Cameroons by the relative uprightness of our government then and by the effectiveness of our system of public accountability. As will be recalled, our first government in Southern

Cameroons, led by Dr. E.M.L Endeley, of blessed memory, organised a general election in which it was defeated by the newly-emerging opposition. In keeping with the Anglophone conception and practice of democracy, Dr. Endeley conceded defeat and a peaceful change of government took place.

At this point in the history of our Union with La Republique du Cameroun, exactly thirty-two years, one month and twenty-three days since our people voted to form a Federation with the people of La Republique du Cameroun:

WHEREAS the people of the Southern Cameroons, and they alone, voted freely in the 1961 plebiscite to achieve independence by joining La Republique du Cameroun in a Union erected on a decentralized Federal structure;

WHEREAS by the provision of Article 47 of the Constitution, the Unity of the Federal Republic of Cameroon was secured through the prohibition of any amendments that would impair the unity and the integrity of the Federation;

WHEREAS by the unconstitutional referendum of 20 May 1972 the majority population of La Republique du Cameroun imposed a Unitary State on Anglophone Cameroon, in violation of Article 47 of the Constitution and of the pre-Plebiscite Accord jointly signed by Prime Minister John Ngu Foncha for the Southern Cameroons and president Ahmadou AHIDJO for La Republique du Cameroun and mentioned in the TWO ALTERNATIVES, that neither state shall be allowed to impose its will or its interest on the other;

WHEREAS since May 1972, we have patiently suffered numerous indignities, humiliations and injustices in respect of which we repeatedly cried out for redress;

WHEREAS our several petitions, cries and calls for redress have been repeatedly and callously spurned without serious attention being given to them by successive Francophone-led governments;

WHEREAS our Territory, its natural resources, its environment and our cultural heritage are in imminent danger of destruction;

WHEREAS in our relationship with La Republique du Cameroun the political leadership thereof has time and again demonstrated its bad faith, breach of trust, unwillingness to fulfill promises and undertakings and its propensity for evil, corruption and manipulation;

BUT MINDFUL of the fact that the people, as distinct from the political leadership, of La Republique du Cameroun, may still be desirous of maintaining some of Union with the people of Anglophone Cameroon;

AND WHEREAS it is expedient that such a Union, if it is to last, develop and prosper, should be built on a solid foundation and sustained in a clear atmosphere of openness, trust, mutual respect and a sense of belonging by all;

NOW, THEREFORE, in order to secure these ends by laying a solid foundation of the Union of the two founding entities of present-day Cameroon,

WE SOLEMNLY MAKE THIS DECLARATION:

1) THAT THE IMPOSITION OF THE UNITARY STATE ON ANGLOPHONE CAMEROON IN 1972 WAS UNCONSTITUTIONAL, ILLEGAL AND A BREACH OF FAITH.

2) THAT THE ONLY REDRESS ADEQUATE TO RIGHT THE WRONGS DONE TO ANGLOPHONE CAMEROON AND ITS PEOPLE SINCE THE IMPOSITION OF THE UNITARY STATE IS A RETURN TO THE ORIGINAL FORM OF GOVERNMENT OF

THE REUNIFIED CAMEROON.

3) THAT TO THIS END, ALL CAMEROONIANS OF ANGLOPHONE HERITAGE ARE COMMITTED TO WORKING FOR THE RESTORATION OF A FEDERAL CONSTITUTION AND A FEDERAL FORM OF GOVERNMENT WHICH TAKES COGNIZANCE OF THE BICULTURAL NATURE OF CAMEROON AND UNDER WHICH CITIZENS SHALL BE PROTECTED AGAINST SUCH VIOLATIONS AS HAVE HERE ABOVE BEEN ENUMERATED.

4) THAT THE SURVIVAL OF CAMEROON IN PEACE AND HARMONY DEPENDS UPON THE ATTAINMENT OF THIS OBJECTIVE TOWARDS WHICH ALL PATRIOTIC CAMEROONIANS, FRANCOPHONES AS WELL AS ANGLOPHONES SHOULD RELENTLESSLY WORK.

WE, THE PEOPLE OF ANGLOPHONE CAMEROON, CONVIINCED OF THE JUSTICE OF OUR CAUSE AND RELYING FIRMLY ON THE PROTECTION OF THE ALMIGHTY GOD, DO HEREBY, IN SUPPORT OF THIS DECLARATION AND IN PURSUIT OF THE OBJECTIVES THEREIN SET OUT, MUTUALLY PLEDGE TO EACH OTHER, OUR LIVES, WELL BEING, PROPERTY, CAREERS AND FREEDOM.

GOD BLESS ANGLOPHONE CAMEROON!

GOD BLESS THE FEDERAL REPUBLIC OF CAMEROON!

Done at Buea, this Third Day of April, in the year of our Lord, one Thousand, Nine Hundred and Ninety-three.

Francis K. WACHE Rapporteur,
Sam EKONTANG ELAD Conference Chairman
For Participants at the All Anglophone Conference.
THE BUEA DECLARATION

2nd and 3rd of April, 1993

Revisiting the Genesis of the Anglophone crisis and measures that Anglophones have taken for coexistence to be real in Cameroon.

THE PEOPLE OF ANGLOPHONE CAMEROON held a historic All Anglophone Conference at Buea on 2nd and 3rd April, 1993, for the purpose of adopting a common Anglophone stand on constitutional reform and of examining several others matters related to the welfare of themselves, their posterity, their territory and their country, Cameroon.

We publish in this pamphlet, for the information of the general public, the Resolutions that were adopted, and the Declaration that was issued, by the conference at the end of its deliberations. A comprehensive volume of proceedings of the first-ever All Anglophone Conference is also available.

Each of the historic documents published herein is self-explanatory and calls for no further comment. While the issues which they raise may appear to be of interest specifically to Anglophones, the answers which they propose should serve as a source of inspiration to Cameroonians of other cultures and regions who would want to see some of their specific problems resolved within the framework of a new constitution. We invite them to join hands with us so that, together, we may lay the foundation for a truly united Cameroon in which everyone feels, veritably, a Cameroonian.

THE ANGLOPHONE STANDING COMMITTEE

RESOLUTIONS

WE, THE PEOPLE OF ANGLOPHONE CAMEROON, meeting at the Mount Mary Maternity Centre, Buea, in an All Anglophone Conference from 2nd to 3rd April, 1993, for the purpose of preparing Anglophone participation in the forthcoming National Debate on Constitutional reform and of examining variety of other issues relating to the welfare of ourselves, our posterity, our territory and our country as a whole,

CONSIDERING the invitations issued by the Anglophone Members of the Constitutional Drafting Committee set up in November 1991 at the Yaoundé Tripartite Meeting by which this All Anglophone Conference was convened;

CONSIDERING the general debate in plenary session and in committee during the two days of this conference;

CONSIDERING the numerous position papers that were submitted at this Conference, the substance of which was fully studied in committee;

HEREBY:

1. SALUTE Mr. Sam EKONTANG ELAD, Dr. Simon MUNZU, Dr. Carlson ANYANGWE and Mr. Benjamin ITOE, the Convenors of this unprecedented and historic Conference, and congratulate them for their selfless and patriotic initiative in bringing all Anglophones together;

2. NOTE With satisfaction the massive attendance at the Conference, the effective representation of all Divisions of Anglophone Cameroon and of all socio-professional categories, the eager and enthusiastic participation of all attendants and the orderly and cordial conduct of the proceedings;

3. DECLARE the preparedness of Anglophone to participate in the forthcoming Constitutional Talks with their Francophone brothers and, to this end, resolve;-

a) That there shall be a single and indivisible Anglophone Delegation at the forthcoming Constitutional Talks;

b) That the members of the Anglophone Delegation to the Constitutional Talks shall be those who at the opportune moment and in the spirit of this conference, shall have been mandated as such by the Standing Committee appointed at this conference;

c) That Anglophone Cameroon shall not be bound by any undertakings given at the forthcoming Constitutional Talks by any Anglophone not mandated to attend the conference as a member of the Anglophone Delegation;

d) That the Anglophone Delegation at the Constitutional Talks shall conduct negotiations in close observance of the terms of the Anglophone Draft Constitution tabled at the Talks and that it shall, in any case, be bound by that Draft's proposal regarding the return of Cameroon to the Federal form of Government.

4. CALL on the United Nations and on her Britannic Majesty's Government to attend the forth coming Constitutional Talks pursuant to paragraph 5 and 6 of United Nations Resolution A/C4/L685 abrogating the British trusteeship over Cameroon.

5. CALL on the Cameroon Government to invite delegations of other countries, which wish to do so, to attend the forthcoming Constitutional Talks as observers and moderators.

6. CREATE a committee for the final drafting of the Anglophone Constitutional proposals in accordance with the constitutional guidelines adopted at this Conference.

7. CREATE AN ANGLOPHONE STANDING COMMITTEE of 65 members whose tasks shall be:

a) To determine practical modalities for re-establishing the Institutions of ANGLOPHONE CAMEROON;

b) To follow up the implementation of the decisions of this conference;

c) To work out details of the inter-relationship between the main components of ANGLOPHONE CAMEROON;

d) To propose the ways and means of preserving the historical and cultural unity as well as the territorial integrity of ANGLOPHONE CAMEROON

e) To permanently ensure the non-domination of one section of Anglophone Cameroon by the other;

f) To take all other measures necessary to ensure the effectiveness of the standing Committee, including the modification and/or the expansion of its membership.

8. ON THE EXAMINATION BOARD

a) VEHEMENTLY condemn the breach of faith by the Government of Cameroon in its feet-dragging over this very important question;

b) CALL on Government immediately to sign the necessary instrument for the creation of the Board;

c) SALUTE the industrious and patriotic Anglophone Cameroonians who, at short notice, and braving all hurdles, produced the famous Report on the G.C.E. Examinations;

d) CALL on Anglophones to create a Trust Fund to raise finances for the immediate take-off of the Board.

9. ON THE ANGLO-SAXON UNIVERSITY OF BUEA:

a) CALL on Government to respect the purely Anglo-Saxon nature and the autonomy of the University of Buea:

b) REQUEST Government to provide all the material means necessary for the immediate and effective take-off this University;

c) CALL on Anglophone Cameroonians to create a University of Buea Endowment Fund to ensure that the proper functioning of this baby University of Buea is assured at all times.

10. ON TECHNICAL EDUCATION:

1. CONDEMN 32 years of neglect of this aspect of our education by successive Francophone Governments.

2. CALL a halt to the Frenchification of Technical Education and Examinations in

Anglophone Cameroon.

3. CALL on the Teachers Association of Cameroon and the ANGLOPHONE STANDING COMMITTEE to take all measures necessary to reverse this trend and to correct the situation.

11. ON CAMEROON'S ENTRY INTO THE COMMONWEALTH:

CALL on the Government of Cameroon to end its foot-dragging over this matter by satisfying all conditions necessary for Cameroon's admission into the Commonwealth.

12. CHARGE the Standing Committee with the duty of organising throughout Cameroon, and in Anglophone Cameroon in particular, a campaign of information and explanation concerning the results of this Conference.

13. DEPLORE the total absences from this All Anglophone Conference, without apology, of the Prime Minister and other Anglophone members of government, and wonder whether, in the light of this behavior, they can expect to be regarded as serving the interests of Anglophones at national level.

14. DEPLORE the actions taken under the guidance of Francophone authorities both in Yaoundé and within the South West Province to impede and deny the holding of this All Anglophone Conference on the ideal premises of an Anglo-Saxon University located in Anglophone territory and, ostensibly, managed by Anglophones.

15. EXPRESS Our heartfelt gratitude to the authorities and Management of the Mount Mary Maternity Centre for graciously placing their premises at the disposal of this Conference when all Government Institutions and premises in Buea were denied us for the purpose of holding the Conference.

16. EXPRESS our thanks to the General Organising Committee for their wonderful achievement in the material organisation of the Conference at short notice and under difficult conditions and CONGRATULATE them for this achievement.

17. CONGRATULATE all Anglophones on the success of this Conference which breaks the myth of a NORTH WEST/SOUTH WEST dichotomy and sends to all those who would want to divide Anglophones, so as better to rule them, a clear message that they shall not succeed

18. FINALLY, THANK the Population, Chiefs and Elders of Buea in particular and the South West Province in general, for their hospitality during this Conference.

Done at BUEA, this 3rd Day of April, 1993

Francis K. WACHE Rapporteur Sam EKONTANG ELAD Conference Chairman

For the participants of The ALL Anglophone Conference

THE ALL ANGLOPHONE CONFERENCE
THE BAMENDA PROCLAMATION
K.A
April 29th - May 1st 1994

Appendix XVI

The Bamenda Proclamation of the All Anglophone Conference (1994)

The Second All Anglophone Conference

The Bamenda Proclamation

Issued By The All Anglophone Conference Meeting In Second Session At Bamenda From 29th April To 1st May 1994

The All Anglophone Conference
Second Session Resolutions
Bamenda, April 29 — May 1, 1994

THE PEOPLE OF ANGLOPHONE CAMEROON meeting in the second session of the All Anglophone Conference held in the North West provincial capital of BAMENDA from 29 April to 1 May , 1994 to consider the implication for Anglophone Cameroon of the BIYA Government's arbitrary suspension for nearly one year of the constitutional reform process initiated in November 1992, to evaluate the execution by the Anglophone Standing Committee of the mandate it received from the All Anglophone Conference meeting in its first session at Buea in April 1993, and to examine other issues concerning the People and Territory of Anglophone Cameroon.

CONSIDERING the work accomplished by this Conference both in plenary sessions and in committee;

TAKING COGNIZANCE of proposals, views, opinions and recommendations contained in the various reports, speeches, addresses and statements of officials of the Anglophone Standing Committee and in several position papers submitted by participants at this Conference;

MINDFUL of the reports and recommendations of the various committees, notably the Resolution Committee, the Structures Committee, the Fons and Chiefs Committee and the General Affairs Committee;

HEREBY:

On The Constitutional Reform Process

FORMULATE the position of the Anglophone Cameroon regarding constitutional reform in a solemn statement to be called "The BAMENDA Proclamation" and which shall form an integral part of the Resolutions of this Conference

On The Anglophone Standing Committee's Execution Of Its Mandate And On Organs Of The ACC

2. HEREBY CONGRATULATE the Anglophone Standing Committee for the efficient and courageous execution of the mandate which it received from the first session of the All Anglophone Conference in 1993 despite the very difficult financial, material and human resource conditions in which it had to work and the constant harassment to which it was subjected throughout the year by the authorities of *La République du Cameroun and their*

Anglophone collaborators.

3. FORMALLY AND SOLEMNLY ADOPT the Draft Federal Constitution submitted in 1993 by the Anglophone Standing Committee as the basic Anglophone constitutional proposals to which the Anglophone Delegation to any constitutional talks shall strictly adhere in its negotiations with any other party or parties to such talks.

4. DISSOLVE the Anglophone Standing Committee with effect from the date of the first meeting of the Anglophone Council created at this Conference.

5. CREATE an ANGLOPHONE COUNCIL of fifty-five (55) elected members (of whom 25 shall represent the North West Province, 25 shall represent the South West Province and 5 shall represent Anglophones of the so-called Eleventh Province) with power to co-opt other members as it shall consider necessary in the pursuit of its objectives, and such that at the least ten per cent (10%) of the members shall be women,provided that its total membership shall not at anyone time exceed seventy (70).

6. WITHOUT PREJUDICE to the provisions of paragraph 6–9 inclusive of BAMENDA proclamation, DEVOLVE upon the Anglophone Council all tasks, responsibilities and duties hitherto assigned to, and all power hitherto exercisable by, the defunct Anglophone Standing Committee and all other tasks, responsibilities, duties and power necessary for the effective attainment of the objective of a distinct and autonomous Federated State of Anglophone Cameroon in a bicultural Federal Republic of Cameroon.

7. GRANT the Anglophone Council power to lay down internal rules, regulations and procedures to guide it in the conduct of its business, including those governing disciplinary action against its members.

8. CREATE an Anglophone Advisory Committee of thirty-three (33) member (of whom 15 shall represent the North West Province, 15 shall represent the South West Province and 3 shall represent Anglophones of the so-called Eleventh Province) to be designated by the Anglophone Council from among Anglophone Traditional Rulers, Elder Statesmen, Senior Citizens, Leading Politicians and Religious Authorities sympathetic to the struggle to free the Anglophone People and their Territory from Francophone domination and subjugation whose duty shall be to advise the Anglophone Council on all matters referred to it by the Council.

9. GRANT the Anglophone Advisory Committee power to lay down internal rules, regulations and procedures to guide it in the conduct of its business, including those governing disciplinary action against its members.

10. APPROVE the creation of Anglophone Liaison Committee in every Division, Sub-Division, Town and Village of Anglophone Cameroon or elsewhere in Cameroon or abroad, and Empower the Anglophone Council to define their composition at the various levels, their role, their internal functioning and their links with the Council.

On Other Matters

A. Grassroots Support

11. NOTE WITH SATISFACTION the tremendous progress achieved in the course of the past one year in awakening Anglophone consciousness throughout the country and in all socio-economic classes.

12. CALL UPON the Anglophone Council to take all the measures necessary to maintain

grassroots awareness of the Anglophone problem and of the AAC objectives, methods and procedures for resolving it.

13. WHILE THANKING the entire Anglophone population for the contribution they have so far made to the struggle, Call Upon every Anglophone man, woman and youth to continue to support the cause actively and through all the means available.

B. The Confrontation Of Troops Of The Federal Republic Of Nigeria And Those Of *La République du Cameroun* In the Anglophone Cameroon Territory Of The Bakassi Peninsula

14. APPROVE and Endorse the official statement previously issued by the Anglophone Standing Committee concerning the presence of Nigerian and République du Cameroun troops in the Bakassi Peninsula.

C. The Notion of the Eleventh Province

15. DECLARE that the notion of the Eleventh Province is inconsistent with the restoration of the autonomy of Anglophone Cameroon and the governance of society within a distinct entity of Anglophone Cameroon and Affirm the necessity of all Anglophone to behave, act and be treated as sons and daughters of provinces comprised within the Territory of Anglophone Cameroon.

16. RECOGNISE the social necessity, pending the effective restoration of the autonomy of Anglophone Cameroon, to acknowledge the phenomenon of the "Eleventh Province" in the period of transition to regained Anglophone statehood and to reckon with this phenomenon in the prosecution of the Struggle for the emancipation of Anglophones.

D. The GCE Examinations Board And The University Of Buea Endowment Fund

17. CONGRATULATE the Anglophone People of Cameroon for their victory in the flight to create a separate Board for the GCE and other Anglophone secondary education examinations and Call Upon the newly appointed officials of the Board to administer it in a manner consistent with the aspirations of the Anglophone People in the field of secondary education.

18. RECALLING the call of the All Anglophone Conference in Buea for the creation of a University of Buea Endowment Fund, Note with pleasure and satisfaction that the Fund is now a reality and once more Call on All Anglophone Cameroonians to contribute to the Fund.

E. Voice Of Thanks

19. THANK the Fons and People of Bamenda in particular and the North West Province in general, and especially the Elderly Women of "Takembeng", the Youths of Bamenda and the Leaders of the Churches in Bamenda for their hospitality and for their moral, material and physical support and commitment without which the Conference might not have proceeded to such as successful conclusion.

Done at Bamenda, this 1st day of May,
1994
For and on behalf of Conference
Participants,
Sam EKONTANG ELAD
(Chairman of the Conference)

Appendix XVII

BAMENDA PROVINCIAL EPISCOPAL CONFERENCE [BAPEC] ON THE SOUTHERN CAMEROONIAN ISSUES
THE SECRETARIAT
ARCHBISHOP'S HOUSE
P.O. BOX 82, BAMENDA
NORTH WEST REGION
C A M E R O O N
BAPEC/PRES/2016/30

December 22, 2016,

MEMORANDUM PRESENTED TO THE HEAD OF STATE, HIS EXCELLENCY PRESIDENT PAUL BIYA, BY THE BISHOPS OF THE ECCLESIASTICAL PROVINCE OF BAMENDA ON THE CURRENT SITUATION OF UNREST IN THE NORTHWEST AND SOUTHWEST REGIONS OF CAMEROON

Your Excellency,

For almost one month now there has been a series of unrests and violence in some towns of the Northwest and Southwest Regions(1) of Cameroon occasioned by the strike of the Anglophone Lawyers and of the Teachers' Trade Unions of the English Sub-system of Education. These have led to the loss of human life and to the destruction of property of some of our citizens. There have been flagrant abuses of human rights, as demonstrated by credible eyewitness accounts and by pictures on local television channels and social media. This has led to a premature end to the first term of the school year and paralysed the court system in these regions to the detriment of school children, students, parents and the administration of justice. At the moment, it seems that the government and the striking groups have reached an impasse and it is not likely that the schools are going to open even when the second term begins for the rest of the country. These unrests are symptomatic of a deeper unease among the inhabitants of this geographical circumscription of our nation.

We, the Bishops of the Ecclesiastical Province of Bamenda, which is coterminous with the Northwest and Southwest Regions, where we hold responsibility as Shepherds, cannot remain indifferent to this situation. The Church, in this season, celebrates the birth of Jesus Christ, the Prince of Peace. She has as mandate to proclaim the message of peace (Luke 10:5; Matthew 5:9), and has always stood for justice and peace, and worked for the attainment of the common good of society. Because of her role and competence, the Church is not identified in any way with the political community nor bound to any political system(2). This places her in a uniquely privileged position to provide a balanced perspective on the current problem between the government of Cameroon and the population of significant segments of the Northwest and Southwest Regions of Cameroon. It is for this reason that we have presumed to seize the moment and to make the following submission, with a view to assisting the government to seek a lasting solution to this problem and enable its citizens to live in peace and harmony.

Historical Background of the Problem

Most of the territory known today as the Republic of Cameroon was a German protectorate from 1884. However, German Kamerun also included British Northern Cameroons, which elected to become part of Nigeria in the plebiscite of 1961. This protectorate was divided into British and French Cameroons in 1916 and confirmed, with some slight modifications, by the Milner-Simon Agreement of 10 July 1919. British Cameroons, which was comprised of Northern and Southern Cameroons, was one fifth and French Cameroun was four-fifths of the entire territory. They were Class B Mandated Territories of the League of Nations until 1946 when they became United Nations Trust Territories.

British Cameroons and French Cameroun were separate legal and political entities and historians have postulated that although this partition was said to be temporary Britain and France instituted two different administrative styles and systems which were to impact on any subsequent movement towards eradicating the provisional nature of the partition and facilitating reunification.(3) After the Second World War, the United Nations (Article 76, b) explicitly called on the British and French to administer their respective spheres of Cameroon towards self-government. It called on the Administering Authorities to "promote the political, economic, social and educational advancement of the inhabitants of the Trust Territories, and their progressive development towards self-government or independence as may be appropriate to the particular circumstances of each territory and its peoples..."

Before the London Constitutional Conferences of 1957 and 1958, three political options had emerged in British Southern Cameroons, namely independence as a separate political entity, independence in association with Nigeria, and independence by reuniting with French Cameroun. The Mamfe Conference of August 1959, which was called to hammer out consensus among Southern Cameroonians on one of the options, did not succeed to arrive at a consensus. The three political options persisted, with the most popular being independence as a separate political entity, the next being association with Nigeria and the least popular being reunification with French Cameroun.

Paradoxically, the UN General Assembly Resolution 1352 (xiv) on the British Cameroons' Plebiscite of 1961, clearly ruled out the separate independence of Southern Cameroons(4), the most popular of the three options. This was thanks to the British who tactfully blocked every chance of the Southern Cameroonians voting for independence as a separate entity, convincing the United Nations that Southern Cameroon was not economically viable and could only survive by leaning on Nigeria or the Republic of Cameroon, and recklessly steering the Mamfe All Party Conference of August 1959 to ensure that the parties did not achieve consensus(5). In fact, the British wanted Southern Cameroons to gain independence in association with Nigeria. Consequently, the two questions adopted for the plebiscite were:

1. Do you wish to achieve independence by joining the independent Federation of

Nigeria?

OR

2. Do you wish to achieve independence by joining the independent Republic of Cameroun?

Southern Cameroonians were apprehensive of this move and put pressure on John Ngu Foncha to lead a delegation to London in November 1960 to include the option of independence as a separate political entity. The request was rejected. Nevertheless, according to United Nations Resolution 1541(XV) Principles VII and VIII, Southern Cameroons was qualified to achieve independence either through association or integration which "should be on the basis of complete equality between the peoples of the erstwhile Non-Self-Governing Territory and those of the independent country with which it is integrated. The peoples of both territories should have equal status and rights". It was with this understanding that on the 11th of February 1961 British Southern Cameroons voted to join French Cameroun while British Northern Cameroons voted to join the Federal Republic of Nigeria.

The Foumban Conference of 17th- 21st July 1961 agreed broadly what the "marriage" between the two Cameroons was going to look like. The Yaoundé Tripartite Conference of 2nd-7th August 1961 put this agreement in legal form. Worthy of note here is the fact that the draft 1961 Constitution was never presented to the Southern Cameroons House of Chiefs (SCHC) and the Southern Cameroons House of Assembly (SCHA) for deliberation and approval as should have been the case. Further, it was signed by President Ahidjo on the 1st of September 1961 as President of the Republic of Cameroon when the Federal Republic of Cameroon had not yet come into existence. Be it as it may, the two territories came together in this union as a Federation of East Cameroon and West Cameroon (1961 Constitution, Article 1-1).(6).

In September 1966, all the political parties went into dissolution to form one party in the Federal Republic of Cameroon (the Cameroon National Union), giving birth to one party rule. In 1968, Honourable Solomon Tandeng Muna was appointed to replace Honourable Augustine Ngom Jua without the required Parliamentary endorsement and in contravention of the law which did not permit Muna to handle the posts of Federal Vice President and Prime Minister of the State of West Cameroon concomitantly. Southern Cameroonians saw these moves as dictatorial and undemocratic. They had come from a multi-party democratic society where free debate, alliances, consensus, and respect for the Constitution were the accepted modus operandi.

Referendum of 20th May 1972

While West Cameroonians were still bracing themselves for life in a political dispensation which they regarded as imposed on them by circumstances beyond their control and struggling to cope with the manoeuvres of President Ahmadou Ahidjo, he proposed a Constitution that would make the Federal Republic a unitary state, the United Republic of Cameroon. As we all know, in those days it was politically unwise and even unsafe to hold and express views different from those of the President on any issue, and so there was no public debate on the constitution. This constitution was voted on in a national referendum organized and conducted by the Cameroon National Union (CNU), by now the sole political party in the Republic. The results show that the overwhelming majority of the electors in East and West Cameroon voted in favour of a unitary state. Looking back at what happened, many Anglophone Cameroonians now believe that this was the high-water mark of Ahidjo's deceit and manipulation of West Cameroonians, and some have linked the birth of separatist movements in Anglophone Cameroon to this referendum.

Subsequent Constitutional Amendments

Three years later, the Constitution was amended to include the post of Prime Minister, appointed by the President. Following another amendment in 1979 the Prime Minister would be the constitutional successor of the President of the Republic. In 1984, a constitutional amendment changed the country's name from the United Republic of Cameroon to the Republic of Cameroon. In the eyes of West Cameroonians, Law No 84-1 of 4 February 1984, was incontrovertible evidence that the original intentions of our Francophone brothers and sisters were to absorb Southern Cameroons and not to treat with it as equals. After thirty-three years of union, we had all ended up as citizens of the Republic of Cameroon or East Cameroon.

The Anglophone Problem

It should be clear, from the brief historical sketch presented above, what the crux of the so-called Anglophone Problem is. No matter what some self-appointed elite and spokespersons for Anglophone Cameroonians as well as government Ministers say in public, the participation of various strata of the population and the growing popularity of separatist movements among young and older members of the Anglophone community demonstrates that there is an Anglophone Problem. There is a consciousness among Anglophone Cameroonians that all is not well and something needs to be done about their plight.

What it is

The Anglophone Problem is:

The failure of successive governments of Cameroon, since 1961, to respect and implement the articles of the Constitution that uphold and safeguard what British Southern Cameroons brought along to the Union in 1961.

The flagrant disregard for the Constitution, demonstrated by the dissolution of political parties and the formation of one political party in 1966, the sacking of Jua and the appointment of Muna in 1968 as the Prime Minister of West Cameroon, and other such acts judged by West Cameroonians to be unconstitutional and undemocratic

iii. The cavalier management of the 1972 Referendum which took out the foundational element (Federalism) of the 1961 Constitution.

1. The 1984 Law amending the Constitution, which gave the country the original East Cameroon name (The Republic of Cameroon) and thereby erased the identity of the West Cameroonians from the original union. West Cameroon, which had entered the union as an equal partner, effectively ceased to exist.
2. The deliberate and systematic erosion of the West Cameroon cultural identity

which the 1961 Constitution sought to preserve and protect by providing for a bi-cultural federation.

The Management of the Anglophone Problem

It is our conviction that the Anglophone Problem would have been solved, or at least mitigated, if it had been well managed by those concerned. A lack of proper management seems to be what has aggravated the problem.

The Government and Government Ministers

It is unfortunate to note that the government of Cameroon seems to have made every attempt to downplay or even deny the existence of an Anglophone Problem. Government Ministers (even those of former West Cameroon extraction) have denied the existence of any such problem in the media and in public speeches. Furthermore, it is widely believed in Anglophone Cameroon that government has consciously created divisions among the English-speaking elite, remunerating some allies with prestigious positions in the state apparatus previously reserved for Francophones only, and repressing all actions designed to improve on the status of Anglophone Cameroonians in the union. This seems to have been proven true in the recent unrests by the utterances of government Ministers in the Press Conference on CRTV, in the dispatch of an Anglophone Elite delegation to the Northwest Region, and in the brutal suppression of protests by certain professional groups and sections of the Northwest and Southwest Regions.

Secessionist Groups

In the face of this denial of the existence of an Anglophone Problem by government and the consequent deafening silence from the government to the cries and protests of Anglophone Cameroonians, certain groups have emerged in Anglophone Cameroon that call for the secession of Anglophone from Francophone Cameroon. The Southern Cameroons Youth League, the Southern Cameroons National Council, and the Ambazonia Movement are some of the most strident of these groups and are currently members of the Unrepresented Nations and Peoples Organisation (UNPO) in The Hague.

Federalists

There are different forms of federalism, and federalists in Anglophone Cameroon will differ as to the specific nature of the federal state they would want. However, they are all agreed that they do require a federation which recognises and preserves the region's peculiarity, as did the 1961 Federal Constitution.

Unitarists

Successive amendments to the Constitution up to and including the Amendments of 1996 insist on the fact that Cameroon is one and indivisible (Article 1-2, 1996). Cameroon is described as a decentralised unitary state. Unitarists believe that everything must be done to avoid federalism or secession. However, even the decentralisation announced by the 1996 Constitution has not been implemented, and government and administration have been highly centralised.

Symptoms of Discontent

What some people mistake for the Anglophone Problem are just symptoms pointing to the fact that an overwhelming majority of Anglophone Cameroonians are not happy in the union which they entered with East Cameroon in 1961. They have complained against widespread and systematic marginalisation in various areas of public life which point to the existence of a huge problem. Some of these symptoms include the following:

Marginalisation in Human Resource Development and Deployment <txb>

1. Anglophone Cameroonians have complained about the fact that National Entrance Examinations into Schools that develop the human resources of this country are set per the French Subsystem of Education which makes it very difficult for Anglophones and Francophones to compete on a level playing field. Majority of the membership of these Examination Boards are Francophone so that the interests of Anglophone candidates are hardly, if ever, protected.
2. Out of the five Ministries concerned with Education, which is the means of the transmission of culture, none of the Minsters is Anglophone and none even qualifies to be a deputy or Secretary of State. This gives the impression of a calculated attempt to kill Anglophone culture.

In human resource deployment, there is a gaping inequality in the distribution of posts of responsibility between Anglophones and Francophones. Of the 36 Ministers who defended the budgets for the Ministries last month, only one was Anglophone. In addition, there seem to be key ministries that have been reserved for Francophone Ministers only and Anglophones do not even qualify to be Secretaries of State under them. These include, but are not limited to, Defence, Finance, Territorial Administration, and Economy. <nl>

1. In the 1961 Constitution, the Vice President was the second most important personality in state protocol. Today, the Prime Minister (appointed Anglophone) is the fourth most important person in State Protocol, after the President of the Senate and the President of the National Assembly. Even so, Anglophone Cameroonians believe that he wields no real authority and, like was the case with J.N. Foncha as First National Vice President of the CPDM, finds it "impossible to use [his] exalted position to help in any way shape or influence the policies of the party and nation."(7) There are clearly Francophone ministers who wield more power than he does. This seems to have been proven true in the last Teachers' strike. When the Prime Minister was in Bamenda negotiating with the Teachers' Union Leaders, a group of Francophone Ministers were giving a Press Conference in Yaoundé on the same issue, giving the impression that the negotiations of the PM in Bamenda were of no consequence.

The Treatment of the English Language

There have been widespread protests about the way the English Language has been treated in the public life of the nation.

1. State institutions produce documents and public notices in French, with no English translation, and expect English speaking Cameroonians to read and understand them.
2. National Entrance Examinations into some professional schools are set in French only and Anglophone candidates are expected to answer them. Sometimes this happens even in the English-speaking regions.

Visitors and clients to government offices are expected to express themselves in French, even in the English-speaking regions, since most of the bosses in the offices speak French and make no effort to speak English.

1. Most Senior Administrators and members of the Forces of Law and Order in the Northwest and Southwest Regions are French-speaking and make no effort to understand the cultures and customs of the people they are appointed to govern.
2. Members of Inspection Teams, Missions and Facilitators for Seminars sent from the Ministries in Yaoundé to the English-speaking Regions are generally predominantly French speaking, and expect to be understood by audiences which are predominantly English speaking.
3. The Military Tribunals in the Northwest and Southwest Regions are basically French courts.

Basic Finance documents which businesses and other institutions are expected to work with are all in French. Examples include the COBAC Code, the CIMA Code and the OHADA Code.

The Flooding of Anglophone Cameroon with Francophone Administrators and Workers

Apart from the fact that Ministers, Directors General, Heads of Parastatals, Senior Divisional Officers, Heads of Law Enforcement Institutions, etc. are disproportionately Francophone, there seems to have been a conscious effort made to flood the Northwest and Southwest Regions with Francophone Heads of Service.

1. The Magistrates in these Regions are disproportionately Francophone. So are the Senior Divisional Officers, the Divisional Officers, Commissioners, and Commandants. In the educational sectors, there are increasingly Francophone principals posted to Anglophone schools. Personnel in Hospitals, Banks and Mobile Telephone Companies (even those which originate from Anglophone countries), are predominantly Francophone. And this extends to even non-expert workers in petrol stations.
2. The situation is aggravated by the fact that these Francophone administrators are often overbearing, very arrogant and treat people as if they were second-class citizens, and have no iota of respect for the dignity of the human person. <nl>

Mismanagement of 'West Cameroon' Patrimony

Apart from neglect of infrastructure in the Northwest and Southwest Regions of Cameroon and the mismanagement and ruin of buoyant companies like Cameroon Bank, West Cameroon Marketing Board, WADA in Wum, West Cameroon Cooperative Movement, etc., oil revenues are alleged to be used by those in power to feed 'the bellies' of their allies, and to stimulate the economy in other regions. In addition, there is also great anxiety in Anglophone Cameroon that its major agro-industrial enterprises, especially the Cameroon Development Corporation (CDC) and Plantations Pamol du Cameroun Ltd (Pamol), are sold or their headquarters moved elsewhere.

The 'Francophonisation' of the English Educational Subsystem and the Common-Law System

The flooding of state Anglophone educational and legal institutions with French-trained and French speaking Cameroonians who understand neither our educational subsystem nor the English Common Law undermines Anglophone education and legal heritage and subverts the original intentions of the founders of the nation to build a bi-cultural nation, respecting the specificity of each region. This is the cause of the current strikes by common law lawyers and teachers.

Admissions into State Professional Schools

The exclusion of qualified Anglophones in admissions into state professional schools (especially Schools of Administration, Medicine and Medical Sciences and Higher Teacher Training) even in the Anglophone Regions is a glaring example of marginalisation which the Teachers Unions cited.

These, and many others, have led to the unease and discomfort of the people of the Northwest and Southwest Regions. They perceived this marginalisation as institutionalised as they have been labelled "Biafrans," "enemies in the house" and "traitors" by highly placed government officials and ministers who were never reprimanded for doing so.

Gradual Erosion of Anglophone Identity

There has been a misleading argument from some quarters where some have argued that an Anglophone is anyone who can speak English, as a way of countering Anglophone Cameroonians who protest the issues we have enumerated above. It might be helpful, for the purposes of our presentation and future discourse, to note here that 'Anglophonism' goes beyond the mere ability to speak or understand the English language. It speaks to a core of values, beliefs, customs, and ways of relating to the other inherited from the British who ruled this region from 1916 to 1961. 'Anglophonism' is a culture, a way of being which cannot be transmitted by merely learning a language. In fact, as Dr. Anthony Ndi intimates, Southern Cameroonians had "a distinctive outlook and way of life that went further than the mere fact that the educated ones among them spoke the English Language or a version of it. So, therefore, language could not even be the qualifying factor".(8) This Anglophone identity is the reason most Southern Cameroonians who voted to join the Republic of Cameroon in 1961 did so. It was to preserve their cultural identity as a distinct people.

Anglophone Cameroonians are slowly being asphyxiated as every element of their culture is systematically targeted and absorbed into the Francophone Cameroon culture and way of doing things. These include the language, the educational system, the system of administration and governance (where appointed leaders are sent to lord it over people who cherish elected leaders), the legal system, and a transparent democratic process where elected leaders are answerable to the electorate who put them there in the first place.

Anglophone Cameroonians have seen through this and are raising their voices in protest. The two All Anglophone Conferences (AAC I and II) of the early 1990s, the rise and popularity of the SCNC and other secessionist voices are born of the frustration of Anglophone Cameroonians of being ignored and ridiculed for asking for what they deem to be theirs by right, namely the preservation of their culture. You would remember that, in his resignation letter from the post of first Vice President of the CPDM on the 9th of June 1990, J.N. Foncha cited in point 9 of the letter, as a reason for resigning, the fact that the constitution was "in many respects being ignored and manipulated."

A Natural Reaction

The reaction of Anglophone Cameroonians to preserve their culture can only be described as 'natural'. Is it any surprise that the first Opposition party that forced the door open for multi-partyism in Cameroon, the Social Democratic Front (SDF), came from Anglophone Cameroon? Following the formation of the party, the architect who brought Southern Cameroonians into the union with the Republic of Cameroon, John Ngu Foncha, resigned in disillusionment as the First Vice-President of the CPDM. He explained:

The Anglophone Cameroonians whom I brought into the union have been ridiculed and referred to as 'les Biafrians', 'les ennemies dans la maison', 'les traitres' etc., and the constitutional provisions which protected this Anglophone minority have been suppressed, their voice drowned while the rule of the gun replaced the dialogue which the Anglophones cherish very much.(9)

This is not to say that we do not see the other side of the argument. In any polity formed bytwo or more ethnic, cultural, religious, or linguistic groups, there is bound to be a majority versus minority problem. In any such situation, the wise thing to do would be to make constitutional provisions which would protect and safeguard the existence and rights of the minority, rather than trample on them. The Church teaches that "not even the majority of a social body may violate these rights, by going against the minority, by isolating, oppressing, or exploiting it, or by attempting to annihilate it."(10) Cameroon prides itself as a state of law. In this area, she is at one with the Church which teaches that society should be organised on the principle of the "rule of law". This is the principle "in which the law is sovereign, and not the arbitrary will of individuals"(11) So, apart from the plethora of issues which enhance Anglophone disaffection with the union, there is the additional problem that they are a minority in that union.

Proposed Way Forward

It is not for us to dictate to the Cameroonian people what form the government of this country should take or what solutions should be provided for the problems we have highlighted. The Church respects the legitimate autonomy of the democratic order and is not entitled to express preferences for this or that institutional or constitutional solution. Her contribution to the political order is precisely her vision of the dignity of the person revealed in all its fullness in the mystery of the Incarnate Word(12). That notwithstanding, we feel obliged in conscience as the religious and moral leaders in this part of the country, who exercise care over a people who are hurting, to propose the following lines of action which, hopefully, should lead to peace and harmony among our people.

Honesty in the face of the Anglophone Problem

One of the most disingenuous things any enlightened Cameroonian, talk less of educated Cameroonian of Anglophone upbringing, can do is to deny that there is an Anglophone Problem. If former French President, Jacques Chirac, the Commonwealth, the European Union, and many others have recognised that there is an Anglophone Problem and advised that the government of Cameroon and the discontented Anglophones engage in dialogue, how can Cameroonians deny that there is a problem? To play the ostrich and bury our heads in the sand is to sow disaster for the future of the nation we all love. It is to give way to extremist tendencies in the Anglophone community born of frustration at not being listened to or understood. Is it possible that the government has not heard the cries of distress of the All-Anglophone Conferences which represented a broad base of Anglophone Cameroonians? Is it possible that the government has not heard the Parent-Teacher Associations (PTA), the Common-Law Lawyers, the Teachers' Trade Unions, Students, and others who are not only uncomfortable but are choking under the present dispensation?

Is it possible for us to look this beast in the eye, confront it together and overcome it for the sake of peace and unity in our country? The government's continued denial of any Anglophone Problem, and its determination to defend the unitary state by all available means, including repression, could lead to an escalation of Anglophone demands past a point of no return, and this is not something any responsible citizen would wish for their country.

The All-Anglophone Conferences (AAC) of 1993 and 1994

In May1993, the 65-member Anglophone Standing Committee established by the AAC submitted a draft constitution which would provide for major political, financial, and fiscal autonomy for the two federated states, for the provinces inside both, and for the communities inside each province. They proposed the usual separation of powers between the executive, legislative, and judiciary, and a senate and national assembly for each federated state, as well as a rotating presidency for the Federal Republic, whereby after at most two consecutive mandates of five years an Anglophone would succeed a Francophone (or vice versa). This proposal was even reiterated for each of the federated states to ensure alternation between the provinces. This would be for us a lasting solution to the irksome Anglophone Problem, and would be acceptable to the majority of Anglophone and Francophone Cameroonians.

The Implementation of the 1996 Constitution

We know there is never a perfect constitution and that is the reason why constitutions are amended to make them responsive to changes in time and situation. The 1996 Constitution, even though some have had issues with sections of it, is good enough as an immediate remedy for the 'woes' Anglophones are listing and which make life together in this nation burdensome to them. As the second-best option, we recommend an urgent and immediate implementation of the 1996 Constitution. We recommend that all the institutions created by that constitution be put in place, and that those put in place be empowered with persons charged with rendering them functional. This would include the Regions, the Senate and, by extension, the constitutional council, administrative courts, the minor courts of accounting/auditing. It is important for Cameroonians, especially those who seek protection under the 'rule of law' and of the Constitution, to know that the constitution has really been deployed as a means of regulating the political process in Cameroon. It is our firm belief that if this is done immediately, it would satisfy the majority of Anglophone Cameroonians and silence the calls for secession which have characterized this period of unrest.

Constructive Dialogue and the Establishment of a Roadmap

In the short term and, because the Lawyers and Teachers Strikes have paralysed our legal and school systems, it is imperative for the government to dialogue with the Lawyers and Teachers as soon as possible and agree a possible roadmap regarding their legitimate and genuine demands. We cannot solve a problem if we are unwilling to talk to each other. In the spirit of the African family, we would expect the father of the family to find out from a hurting (even if errant) child what the problem is and what they can do to alleviate their pain and suffering. There are a good number of the problems raised by our lawyers and teachers which can be solved now and there are others which can be solved later, but we need to agree a roadmap and respect it. This will enable the Teachers' Unions to call off the strike and permit our children, who have already lost four weeks of schooling, to return to school. Indeed, openness to dialogue and to cooperation is required of all people of good will, and in particular of individuals and groups with specific responsibilities in the areas of politics, economics and social life, at both the national and international levels(13).

Respect for Human Rights

While it is the duty of administrative and law enforcement officers to maintain peace and order in their areas of jurisdiction, many of them have been unnecessarily overbearing and arrogant. Issuing orders and threats for teachers to return to school, for instance, is not the way to solve their problem. Further, the current unrests have shown up a very ugly and embarrassing side of our administrators and the forces of law and order. Without any provocation from the lawyers or students at the University of Buea (who carried placards saying 'No to Violence' and raised their hands in the air), the forces of law and order brutalized some of them so badly and so inhumanely that seeing the pictures one would have thought they came from the Stone Age. It was shameful to see law enforcement officers drag female students in the mud, spray students' rooms with tear-gas and contaminated water, and then lock some up for days just for exercising a basic human right to make their voices heard in a peaceful manner.

The Church teaches that

> "A just society can become a reality only when it is based on the respect of the transcendent dignity of the human person... Every political, economic, social, scientific, and cultural programme must be inspired by the awareness of the primacy of each human being over society... For this reason, neither his life nor the development of his thought, nor his good, nor those who are part of his personal and social activities can be subjected to unjust restrictions in the exercise of their rights and freedom."(14)

Our administrators and the forces of law and order need to be called to order. In the exercise of their duties for the common good of all citizens, they must never trample on the rights of those citizens and deal out subhuman treatment to them. Such behaviour contravenes the law and provides a seedbed for deep resentment which later manifests itself in very ugly ways.

It is in light of this that we propose that the government should immediately withdraw the forces of law and order from the streets of the Anglophone towns to which they have been deployed, open proper investigations into any abuses of human rights by the forces of law and order, and release or charge those who have been locked up as a result of the recent unrests. In this way, we would have a better climate for the negotiations which have been proposed between the government and the teachers and lawyers.

Justice for All

Every Anglophone group that has raised its voice in protest has chronicled a number of perceived injustices which either the group or the Anglophone community in general suffers. Again, if the government gives them a listening ear, it would become clear to all whether these perceived injustices are founded or just imaginary. As long as these people, rightly or wrongly, continue to feel that they are the victims of injustice, we cannot build 'the Island of Peace' in Central and West Africa we have been proclaiming that we are, and we cannot develop our country without this peace either. We do not believe, in conscience, that locking up people who speak up against injustice (real or imagined) will kill dissent and bring peace. Maybe some examples will help clarify the point we are making.

On the 14th of December 1967, Martin Luther King, Jr. made a statement outside a California prison where Vietnam war protesters were being held. He said: There can be no justice without peace and there can be no peace without justice. On the World Day for Peace, 1st January 1972, Pope Paul VI had as theme for his Message: if you want peace, work for justice. These great crusaders for social justice teach us that without justice, peace will be an elusive goal.

Of course, you would remember the Apostolic Visit of Pope St. John Paul II to Cameroon in August 1985. In his Address to the President, Constituted Bodies, and the Members of the Diplomatic Corps, he said:

> « Devant les conflits qui demeurent ou renaissent, tout le monde doit se poser honnêtement la question de leurs causes. Les injustices commises par certains régimes, concernant les droits de l'homme en général ou les revendications légitimes d'une partie de la population qui se voit refuser la participation aux responsabilités communes, déclenchent des soulèvements d'une violence regrettable, mais qui ne pourront être apaisés qu'avec le rétablissement de la justice. »

These examples show that we need to examine, in a dispassionate manner, the root causes of the unease and unrest in the Anglophone Region of Cameroon and, if these causes are connected to injustice in any form, do all we can to root out those injustices.

Conclusion

Your Excellency,

We stated at the beginning of this Memorandum that it is our bounden duty as Shepherds of the people in the Northwest and Southwest Regions of Cameroon where there are unrests and dissatisfaction, to make a contribution to the solution of the problems that have been posed. We hope that you will find our contribution helpful as you try to navigate this very sensitive and delicate period in our nation's history. We are aware of the gravity of your responsibility before the people of Cameroon and before History, and that is why we tried to do all we could to help. In addition, we commend you and the people of Cameroon to God in prayer, in the belief that He will give you the wisdom you need to carry out this task. We can only add that in this case, time is of the essence as some of our children have already missed school for a month.

A certain religious leader is credited to have said: There really can be no peace without justice. There can be no justice without truth. And there can be no truth, unless someone rises up to tell you the truth. What we have set forth here is what we believe to be the truth, told as part of our prophetic mission, in the hope that it will bring justice, peace, and harmony to this country which we all hold dear to our hearts.

May Mary, Queen of Peace, and Patroness of Cameroon, intercede for us and for our country.

+George Nkuo,
Bishop of Kumbo and President of BAPEC
+Cornelius Fontem Esua,
Archbishop of Bamenda
+Immanuel Bushu,
Bishop of Buea
+Andrew Nkea,
Bishop of Mamfe
+Agapitus Nfon,
Bishop of Kumba

ENDNOTES (Omitted)

Appendix XVIII

HOLY SEE PRESS OFFICE
OFICINA DE PRENSA DE LA SANTA SEDE
BUREAU DE PRESSE DU SAINT-SIÈGE
PRESSEAMT DES HEILIGEN STUHLS

BOLLETTINO
SALA STAMPA DELLA SANTA SEDE

Holy See Press Office Communique: Audience with the President of the Republic of Cameroon, 23.03.2017

The Holy Father Francis today received in Audience, in the Vatican Apostolic Palace, the president of the Republic of Cameroon, His Excellency Mr. Paul Biya, who subsequently met with His Eminence Cardinal Secretary of State Pietro Parolin, accompanied by His Excellency Archbishop Paul Richard Gallagher, secretary for Relations with States.

During the cordial discussions, the existing good relations between the Holy See and Cameroon were evoked, as was the important contribution the Church offers to the development of the country, especially in the fields of education and healthcare. Taking into consideration the peaceful co-existence and mutual respect between the various religious groups, attention was focused on the importance of promoting national cohesion, enhancing the richness of the various historic and cultural traditions of the country, with respect for human and minority rights.

Finally, there was an exchange of views on some themes of international interest, with particular reference to the current challenges affecting the region.

From Vatican City, 23 March 2017

Audiences
Resignations and Appointments
Holy Father's condolences following the attack in London, United Kingdom
Promulgation of Decrees of the Congregation for the Causes of Saints

Appendix XIX

Letter of Cameroon Anglophones in the Diaspora to: Madam Federica Mogherini, High Representative of the Union for Foreign Affairs and Security Policy,

Vice President of the Commission & Mr. Dimitris Avramopoulos

Commissioner for Migration, Home Affairs and citizenship

European Commission (2017)

6th October 2017

Open Letter to:

Madam Federica Mogherini
High Representative of the Union for Foreign Affairs and Security Policy
Vice President of the Commission
Rue de la Loi 200 / Wetstraat 200
1040 Bruxelles / Brussel
Postal address: building BERL - 1049 - Bruxelles / Brussel
Belgique
Tel: +32 229-91111

Email: Federica.mogherini@ec.europa.eu

Mr. Dimitris Avramopoulos
Commissioner for Migration, Home Affairs and citizenship
European Commission
Rue de la Loi/Wetstraat 200
1049 Brussels, Belgium

Email: dimitris.avramopoulos@ec.europa.eu

Dear Honourable Commissioners Mogherini & Avramopoulos

Subject: Cameroon President Paul Biya's Massacre of Unarmed Civilians Creates Future Refugee Problem for Europe

We, a collective of English-speaking citizens from the former UN Trust Territory of Southern Cameroons, which is now part of la République du Cameroun, and residing in all continents of the world, have the honour to write you, about life and death matters that will soon affect immigration in Europe. In effect, on the 1st of October, 2017, from the comfort and luxury of the InterContinental Hotel in Geneva, President Biya of Cameroon ordered the Cameroon armed forces to carry out a bloody massacre that led to the death of more than 100 unarmed, impoverished civilian men, women and children in the English-speaking region of Cameroon, Africa.

The massacre of 1st October 2017, occurred after a popular uprising in the English-Speaking Southern Cameroon region against the brutality, oppression and marginalization perpetrated on the English-speaking community by President Biya. On that fateful day, helicopter gunships of the Cameroon army flew low over unarmed civilian demonstrators, opened fire and dropped grenades on them. Military forces on the ground opened fire at escaping unarmed men, women and children at close range. More than 100 people were killed in cold blood. Biya presided over this massacre from the comfort of his luxurious presidential suite at the InterContinental Hotel in Geneva, Switzerland. Below is an excerpt of leaked Cameroon army war logs communicated to Biya in Geneva. Please note that the telephone country code from which the messages came was 237, the code for Cameroon:

"[01/10 à 16:33] +237 99104845: À Buea, les insurgés veulent prendre le palais du Gouverneur construit par les AIIemands aujourd'hui avant 18h, car disent-ils, c'est leur capitale. Mais les FMO tiennent jusqu'à présent.

[01/10 à 16:33] +237 99104845: Survol à basse altitude et largage des grenades F4 à partir des hélicos"

Bodies of the dead are still being discovered in the town of Buea. The United Nations, Amnesty International, the United States and scores of human rights organizations have condemned these gross violations of human rights. The military occupation and repression continue as we speak. Hundreds of English-speaking Cameroonians have fled into Nigeria and other countries. Many of the victims of President Biya's violence will eventually join the flood of migrants heading to Europe.

Honorable Commissioners, you need to know that President Paul Biya is a ruthless, authoritarian ruler who has been president of Cameroon for 35 years. In Cameroon millions of citizens are mired in abject poverty, and have no access to the barest necessities of life : Clean drinking water, sanitation, healthcare, education, and electricity. Since November 2016, President Biya has ordered a bloody crackdown against the minority English-speaking population of Cameroon, for daring to demonstrate against their poverty, marginalization, and second-class citizenship, while the oil, timber and other resources of their region are exploited by Biya and his family, and used to finance their luxurious lifestyle in Switzerland, the United States, and other parts of Europe.

In response to calls for change, Biya cut off the Internet to the English-speaking region of Cameroon for more than 100 days in order to collectively punish the 8 million people of the region and keep the world from knowing of his atrocities. His forces of law and disorder have opened fire indiscriminately on unarmed, demonstrating students, killing many, and raping others. The civilian leaders of the English-speaking union of lawyers, teachers and students who called for change were arrested, detained for months, tortured, and charged with offenses carrying the death penalty at the Yaoundé Military Tribunal. Tens of people are still being held in jail as we speak. Many others are in exile, seeking to immigrate to Europe and other parts of the world.

We respectfully urge the European Union to urgently review its cooperation with the government of President Biya, who has shown a reckless disregard for human life and human rights, and continues to mastermind the military crackdown on poor, unarmed English-speaking civilians from the safety, comfort, and luxury of the InterContinental Hotel in Geneva, Switzerland, a stone's throw from the United Nations offices.

Sincerely
Signed,
The Collective of English-Speaking Southern Cameroonians in the Diaspora

Appendix XX

Crisis in the Republic of Cameroon Written Statement by Felix Agbor Nkongho Founder and Chairman, Centre for Human Rights and Democracy in Africa Subcommittee on Africa, Global Health, Global Human Rights, and International Organizations U.S. HOUSE OF REPRESENTATIVES COMMITTEE ON FOREIGN AFFAIRS

(June 27, 2018)

Good afternoon, Chairman Christopher Smith, Ranking Member Karen Bass and Esteemed Members of the Subcommittee on Africa, Global Health, Global Human Rights and International Organisations. Thank you for this opportunity to make a statement before you. Thank you as well for highlighting the crisis in Cameroon. The people of Southern Cameroons and all Cameroonians will highly appreciate this hearing on the prolonged crisis.

I am Felix Agbor Nkongho, a human rights lawyer, nonviolent activist and founder of the Centre for Human Rights and Democracy in Africa (CHRDA). The views I express in this testimony are my own and will represent shared sentiments from Southern Cameroonians and Cameroonians.

Over the last 20 months, Cameroon has been the focus of a nation sliding into civil war in Africa, from what started in November 2016 as legitimate grievances by English-speaking lawyers, teachers, students and civil society over the prolonged marginalisation of Southern Cameroonians but peaceful protests turned deadly when the government military shot at peaceful protesters, wounding many and killing several. In my capacity as leader of the lawyers, teachers and civil society organisations who presented the government with grievances, we equally made ourselves available to dialogue for a quick solution. Unfortunately, during the dialogue process, the government rejected talks over a return to federalism which existed from 1961-1972 which guaranteed bilingualism, biculturalism, bijuralism, equal opportunity for all, and provided constitutional provisions for power sharing, economic independence and freedoms. To the dismay of the national, regional and international community, the Cameroon government began arresting activists and leaders including myself. Internet was shut down for 3 months and all forms of dissent were stifled, forcing hundreds into exile. I was charged before the military court with several counts including terrorism, which carried the death penalty. This sparked radicalization of the population and reignited the quest for complete independence of the territory, Southern Cameroons. After several months of protests and calls for the release of all detainees, François Lonseny Fall, Special Representative and Head of the United Nations Regional Office for Central Africa (UNOCA) visited the maximum security prison where we had a meeting, after which he called on the government to release leaders and other detainees.

In August 2017, President Paul Biya ordered the release of several detainees including myself but avoided dialogue prompting mass protest in September 2017 with estimated 500,000 people. The government's response was a brutal crackdown which led to a declaration of independence on October 1, 2017. While approximately 900,000 unarmed protesters were celebrating this declaration, government troops shot at thousands with automatic rifles and helicopters, this marked the start of military attacks upon villages, orders for villages to be evacuated, mass exodus of villagers into Nigeria creating 50,000 refugees and 200,000 internally displaced persons today. All of these prompted an armed campaign by civilians to defend their villages and homes, leading to full-blown armed insurgency.

Cameroon has many features of crisis ridden countries, including its hyper centralized government, weak institutions, endemic corruption, regional tensions, political manipulations, rigged elections and a personalized leadership. While Boko Haram remains a threat to stability and security, the Southern Cameroons crisis represents a more deadly and serious armed conflict which could last longer if not solved. Boko Haram has killed 200 soldiers, gendarmes and policemen including 1900 civilians in 4 years but the Southern Cameroons crisis has killed 90 soldiers, gendarmes and policemen including 3000 civilians in 8 months of armed conflict.

A solution to the Southern Cameroons crisis does not represent a solution to the Cameroon problem, likewise a solution to the Cameroon problem does not address and solve the Southern Cameroons crisis.

Background of the Southern Cameroons crisis

The birth of the Federal Republic of Cameroon on 1st October 1961 marked the reunification of two territories that had undergone different colonial experiences since World War I. The erstwhile German Kamerun was partitioned between the French who practiced assimilation and the British with indirect rule. Cameroon is a country in Central Africa often described as Africa in miniature but has come to the spotlight lately due to crisis of identity and cultural assimilation of the minority English-speaking people. The Southern Cameroons problem popularly known as the Anglophone Crisis is as old as the country Cameroon. It is the expression of a poorly managed decolonisation process, that saw two distinct (British Southern Cameroons and French Cameroon) people come together to form a country void of any real foundations that could guarantee coexistence. A country that has only had two presidents since independence in 1961 with the present Head of State spending close to 4 decades in office.

Cameroon holds a strategic position in the gulf of guinea (rich in crude oil and critical for the stability of West and Central Africa) and is also the main link between these two regions of Africa. Marred with extensive corruption, authoritarian rule, absence of any form of civil rights, poor governance and innate nepotism, the call for greater autonomy by Southern Cameroonians (Anglophones) has never been this resounding as it is today. The Southern Cameroonians otherwise called by the central government as Anglophones, have come to realise that, their place in the failed union with the majority French Cameroon has been nothing less than recolonization characterised with systematic marginalisation, discrimination and subhuman treatment.

History of Southern Cameroons

The Southern Cameroons has a surface area of 43,000 sq. km and a current population of about 8 million people. It is thus demographically bigger than at least 60 UN and 18

AU Member States, and spatially bigger than at least 30 UN and 12 AU Member States. The territory was originally British from 1858-1887. It was ceded to Germany and subsequently incorporated into the contiguous German protectorate of Kamerun, which had been acquired earlier in 1884.

Relation with the British

The Southern Cameroons was thus under British rule from 1858 to 1887, and then from 1915 to 1961, a total period of nearly 80 years. That long British connection left an indelible mark on the territory, bequeathing to it an Anglo-Saxon heritage. The territory's official language is English. Its educational, legal, administrative, political, governance and institutional culture and value systems are all English-derived.

Up to 1960, the Southern Cameroons though under international tutelage was administered by Britain as part of her contiguous colonial territory of Nigeria. But its distinct identity and personality, separate from Nigeria, remained unassailable. UN Resolution 224 (III) of 18 November 1948 protected the Trust Territory from annexation by any colonial-minded neighbour. While acknowledging that the Trusteeship Agreement makes allowance for 'administrative union', the Resolution provides that "Such a union must remain strictly administrative in its nature and scope, and its operation must not have the effect of creating any conditions which will obstruct the separate development of the Trust Territory, in the fields of political, economic, social and educational advancement, as a distinct entity."

Self Rule

In 1954 the Southern Cameroons became a self-governing region within Nigeria and gradually asserted its distinct identity and its aspiration to statehood through increased political and institutional autonomy.

In 1958 the British Government stated at the UN that the Southern Cameroons was expected to achieve in 1960 the objectives set forth in Article 76 b of the UN Charter. Since the Southern Cameroons had already attained self-government status four years earlier in 1954, the objective to be attained in 1960 could only have been full independence. General Assembly Resolution 1282 (XIII) of 5 December 1958 took note of the British statement. The people of the Southern Cameroons therefore legitimately expected to be granted full independence in 1960 given that their country had been self-governing since 1954.

Basic self-government institutions were in place: a Government headed by the Premier as Leader of Government business; a bicameral parliament consisting of a House of Assembly and a House of Chiefs; an Official Opposition in parliament; a Judiciary headed by a Chief Justice; a Civil Service; and police force. The system in place was a democratic and accountable dispensation. In 1959 when the term of office of the incumbent Premier came to an end, peaceful free fair and transparent elections were organised. The opposition won and there was an orderly transfer of power to the in-coming Premier. Consistent with the parliamentary system of government the outgoing Premier became Leader of the Opposition in parliament.

On 1st October 1960 the Southern Cameroons was separated from Nigeria. The

Southern Cameroons Constitution Order in Council came into force. By 1960 the Southern Cameroons had attained a full measure of self-government. Indeed, from 1 October 1960 up to 30 September 1961 it was a full self-governing territory fully responsible for all its internal affairs, except for defense over which matter, along with foreign affairs, Britain continued to exercise jurisdiction.

History of French Cameroon

On 1st January 1960, the attached territory of French Cameroon, also a class B trust territory, achieved independence from France, though with a chronic ongoing anarchy and terrorism there notwithstanding. The French had decided that 1960 was to be the year of independence for its African colonies.

French Cameroun achieved independence under the name and style of La Republique du Cameroun (Present day name of the country) with Mr. Ahmadou Ahidjo as its President. It was admitted to membership of the United Nations on 20 September 1960. The name 'Republique du Cameroun' is variously translated into English as 'Republic of Cameroon' or sometimes simply as 'Cameroon'.

Plebiscite Recommended by United Nations

On 13 March 1959 the General Assembly adopted Resolution 1350 (XIII) recommending a plebiscite in the Southern Cameroons instead of the granting of independence right away. This was followed by another General Assembly resolution, 1352 (XIV) of 16 October 1959, ordering a plebiscite to be held in the Southern Cameroons "not later than March 1961". The people of the Southern Cameroons were to pronounce themselves on 'achieving independence' by the two dead-end alternatives of 'joining' Nigeria or Republic of Cameroon.

Still that same year, some perceptive minds in the Trusteeship Council expressed concerns that after attaining independence on 1 January 1960 Republic of Cameroon could try to annex the Southern Cameroons. The Premier of French Cameroun, Mr. Ahidjo, denied any such intention or the possibility of any such action on the part of independent Republic of Cameroon. At the 849th meeting of the Fourth Committee of the UN, Mr. Ahidjo took the floor and gave the UN the solemn assurance that Republic of Cameroon is not annexationist. He declared: "We are not annexationists. ... If our brothers of the British zone wish to unite with independent Cameroon, we are ready to discuss the matter with them, but we will do so on a footing of equality." Of course this is the reverse on the field.

The United Nations, on April 21, 1961, voted for the independence of the British Southern Cameroons. According to the United Nations Resolution 1608(XV), the Southern Cameroons had a right to sovereignty. The UN General Assembly session voted an overwhelming 64 votes against 23 and 10 abstentions for independence of the Southern Cameroons to take effect on October, 1961. The United States voted for an independent Southern Cameroons. However, France hoodwinked the British and other state to push for the UN coordinated plebiscite.

Plebiscite Process Set in Motion

On 31 March 1960 the Trusteeship Council adopted Resolution 2013 (XXVI) requesting the UK Government "to take appropriate steps, in consultation with the authorities concerned, to ensure that the people of the Territory are fully informed, before the plebiscite, of the constitutional arrangements that would have to be made, at the appropriate time, for the implementation of the decisions taken at the plebiscite."

The Secretary of State put forward the following interpretation as consistent with the plebiscite alternative of 'joining' Republic of Cameroon: "the Southern Cameroons and the Cameroon Republic would unite in a Federal United Cameroon Republic. The arrangements for the union would be worked out after the plebiscite by a conference consisting of representative delegations of equal status from the Republic and the Southern Cameroons. The United Nations and the United Kingdom would also be associated with this conference." Both the Southern Cameroons and Republic du Cameroon agreed to this interpretation

The signed and published Agreement between the Southern Cameroons and Republic of Cameroon provided that in the event of the plebiscite vote going in favour of "achieving independence by joining" Republic of Cameroon, the following would be the broad terms of the 'joining':

1. The Southern Cameroons and Republic of Cameroon would unite to create a Federal State to be called the 'Federal Republic Cameroon', outside the British Commonwealth and the French Community;
2. The component states of the Federation would be the Southern Cameroons and Republic of Cameroon, legally equal in status;
3. Each federated state would continue to conduct its affairs consistently with its colonially-inherited state-culture, with only a limited number of subject matters conceded to the union government;
4. Nationals of the federated states would enjoy Federal Cameroon nationality;
5. The Federation would have a bicameral Parliament consisting of a Federal Senate and a Federal National Assembly; and
6. Federal laws will only be enacted in such a way that no measures contrary to the interests of one state will be imposed upon it by the majority.

The Agreement also stipulated as follows:

1. Constitutional arrangements would be worked out after the plebiscite by a post-plebiscite conference comprising representative delegations of equal status from the Southern Cameroons and Republic of Cameroon, in association with the United Kingdom Government and the United Nations;
2. The post-plebiscite conference would have as its goal the fixing of time limits and conditions for the transfer of sovereignty powers to an organisation representing the future federation;
3. Those entrusted with the affairs of the united Cameroon would put the would-be federal constitution to the people of the Southern Cameroons and Republic of Cameroon to pronounce themselves on it; and

The phrase "to achieve independence by joining Republic of Cameroon" was therefore clearly understood by all concerned (the UN, the UK Government, the Southern Cameroons Government, and the Republic of Cameroon Government) to mean that the Southern Cameroons would attain independence and then form, on the footing of legal equality, a federal union with Republic of Cameroon under an agreed federal constitution as defined in Resolution 1514(XV).

On 11 February 1961 the UN-supervised limited plebiscite took place in the Southern Cameroons. The vote was a plebiscite on political status to enable the people of the Southern Cameroons progress from full measure of self-government to national independence. The vote went in favour of achieving independence 'by joining' Republic of Cameroon rather than Nigeria.

Two months after the plebiscite vote, on 21 April 1961, the UN General Assembly adopted Resolution 1608 (XV) to give effect to the intention expressed by the people of the Southern Cameroons at the plebiscite. Republic of Cameroon, through its Foreign Affairs Minister, Mr. Charles Okala, made a protest against the taking of a vote on the independence of the Southern Cameroons and then voted against Resolution 1608. It speaks volumes that the overwhelming UN vote on the independence of the Southern Cameroons did not go down well with Republic of Cameroon.

In Resolution 1608 (XV) the General Assembly:

1. Endorsed the results of the plebiscite that "the people of the Southern Cameroons decided to achieve independence by joining the independent Republic of Cameroon";
2. Considered that "the decision made by them through a democratic process under the supervision of the United Nations should be immediately implemented";
3. Decided that "the Trusteeship Agreement of 13 December 1946 concerning the Cameroons under United Kingdom administration ... be terminated, in accordance with Article 76 b of the Charter of the United Nations ... with respect to the Southern Cameroons, on 1 October 1961, upon its joining the Republic of Cameroon"; and
4. Invited "the Administering Authority, the Government of the Southern Cameroons and the Republic of Cameroon to initiate urgent discussions with a view to finalizing before 1

October 1961 the arrangements by which the agreed and declared policies of the parties concerned will be implemented."

These said 'agreed and declared policies' were not and have never been finalized.

The Present Crisis and the Federal Constitution

Article 1 of the Federal Constitution of 1961 reads

"1.1. With effect from the 1st October 1961, the Federal Republic of Cameroon shall be constituted from the territory of the Republic of Cameroon, hereafter to be styled East Cameroon, and the territory of the Southern Cameroons, formerly under British trusteeship, hereafter to be styled West Cameroon."

Since 1961 when southern Cameroons decided to join La Republic of Cameroon to form a federation of two equal states, it has been nothing less than a nightmare for Southern Cameroonians. From systematic discrimination, institutional marginalisation, economic exploitations, the identity of the southern Cameroonian in the country has been on a steady and intentional destruction by the majority French Cameroon. The Southern Cameroonian have sought to find out in the most peaceful and civil of ways who he is in Cameroon and the response has always been heavy. Joseph B Ebune (2016) posits in his article on the dilemma of the federal system in West Cameroon "If there was one area where federalism was most negatively exercised in West Cameroon, it was in the economic domain. At independence, the economy of East Cameroon was based on entrepreneurship and industrialisation, and between 1967 and 1971, about 20 billion francs were invested in about 700 industrial firms which included food, chemical, textile, aluminium industries, water and electrical power production (Ekali, 2004). In West Cameroon, only 27 industrial firms mainly plants for agricultural products were operational showing that investment in the industrial sector was low (Ebune, 2016).

Immediately after the reunification process was closed on the 1st of October 1961, the then president of Cameroon Immediately launched his process to annex and recolonise Southern Cameroons.

1. He abolished all political parties in Cameroon by 1965 bringing the country to a one party system. At this time, there was no longer any legitimate organisation to carry on the aspirations of the Southern Cameroons
2. The worst and darkest day in the union, was when in March 1972, president Ahidjo declared that there would be a referendum in Cameroon in May of the same year to change the country from a federation into a unitary state.

    a). This was against the Federal constitution which stated in article 47 that "The amendment may be passed by a simple majority of the membership of the Federal Assembly: Provided that such majority include a majority of the membership elected from each Federated State."

    b). After banning most political parties, no organisation was allowed to carry and defend the aspirations of the people

    c). The vote was against the spirit of the Constitution and the UN led plebiscite in the fact that, it was opened to all Cameroonians. This was intentional and deliberate, given the population disparity in the country at the time. It must be mentioned that, only southern Cameroonians voted for the plebiscite.

    d). More so, the voting was marred by fact that, there were not enough ballot papers to say NO. In fact, in Southern Cameroons that referendum is still considered today as a vote between "Yes and Yes".

3. Fast tracked to 1984, two years after President Paul Biya (Prime Minister from 1975-1982) took office from Ahmadou Ahidjo. He unilaterally changed the name

of the country from United Republic of Cameroon (and also removed one star from the flag which represented Southern Cameroons) and imposed The Republic of Cameroon as the official name of the country.

At that moment, the Southern Cameroons Emancipation struggle was officially born by this decision. First, The Republic of Cameroon, was the name of the French part of Cameroon before the Union. Thus, going back to that name meant two things to Southern Cameroonians.

a). The French part of Cameroon has seceded from the union; and/or
b). They have just annexed or recolonised Southern Cameroons.

- The Southern Cameroons Identity became more glaring. That was when a sitting magistrate who was a southern Cameroonian (Gorji Dinka) took the state of Cameroon to task at the AFRICAN COMMISSION ON HUMAN AND PEOPLES' RIGHTS. He then created the Southern Cameroons National Council (SCNC).
- In 1990, there was a wave of political awareness across sub Saharan Africa which led to the creation of the first opposition political party (SDF) in Cameroon. This Party was created in Bamenda with the principal objective of politics for the identity of Southern Cameroons.
- The first multiparty presidential elections took place in 1992 and it was widely claimed to have been won by the opposition SDF party. But that victory was never to be given and again, it added another block to the frustrations of Southern Cameroonians.
- In 1993 and 1994 a historical All Anglophone Conference was held in Buea and Bamenda Respectively. The resolutions of the conference have never been implemented and one of it was a return to a federal system of governance.
- The French Led central Government decided to dilute the calls for a return to federation by calling for an inconsequential tripartite meeting. The meeting was boycotted by the main opposition party in Cameroon (SDF) and none of the proposals of Southern Cameroonians were considered. The Francophone majority decided to distract Anglophones and opted for a unitary decentralised state. It is worth mentioning that, as we speak, 22 years after the 1996 constitution, nothing has been implemented.

Immediate Causes

Tensions started to gain momentum in May 2015, when Common Law lawyers (after a meeting in Bamenda) sent a memorandum to the head of state asking him to review the Southern Cameroons identity in the union. This was a direct consequence of the systematic and continuous dilution of the common law practice in Southern Cameroons by civil law trained magistrates who couldn't speak or understand the English language. It is worth mentioning that, English language is the natural language of expression in the Anglophone regions. Thus dispensing justice in a language the people do not understand was tantamount to injustice.

The letter of the lawyers saw no response, neither in action or administrative formalities. One year later, the lawyers met in Buea and made a second declaration reaffirming that initial declaration made one year ago. Still, there was total silence, nonchalance and disregard.

In October 2016, the Common Law Lawyers decided to call for an indefinite peaceful strike. They were met with heavy repression from the central government. Lawyers were beaten and professional regalia seized. The people were still on the watch and were totally disappointed with the treatment given lawyers.

By November 21st 2016, after a series of warnings, the teachers of the English Educational subsystem decided to down their tools for an indefinite strike. At this point, it had moved from Common Law Lawyers to teachers and again due to the high handedness of the regime, no solution was given to the request of the teachers. It soon moved into a community problem for all Southern Cameroonians. There were many questions than answers. The police brutality and political denial of the problem further estranged the people.

The crisis reached its peak and collective acceptance from all Southern Cameroonians in December 2016 when an Anglophone Civil Society Consortium was formed to speak on behalf of the Southern Cameroons which I was the president. On the 8th of December 2016, some 4 protesters were killed in Bamenda raising more questions from the people. Government then started dialogue with Consortium leaders in December 2016. But after failing to convince them of any concrete and factual decision taken, the government turned around and arrested these leaders from Buea and Bamenda and were taken to Yaoundé and tried in a military court. It must be mentioned here that, these people were arrested from an Anglophone region and deported to a Francophone region where the language of expression is French, thereby validating the very grievances raised by Anglophones.

These leaders were arrested alongside many other peaceful activist majority of whom have been sentenced to 15 years in jail. Thousands of such activists are still in prison in Yaounde and across the countries, some missing or in mass graves. Some have had their fate decided using the inhumane anti-terrorism law giving them heavy jail terms. Within this period, there were still continuous arrests and killings.

Centre for Human Rights and Democracy has documented more than 1200 detainees in several prisons across the country all linked to peaceful protests or activism.

Two Crucial Moments

On October 1st, 2017 the people of Southern Cameroons in their millions peacefully went out to symbolically declare independence from The Republic of Cameroon. It was a peaceful demonstration that saw the young, the old, women and children come out to create a new country called AMBAZONIA. This day goes down in history as very symbolic for the people and also very bloody. The military responded by shooting unarmed civilians at close range and according to amnesty, over 44 people were shot dead that day, however Centre for Human Rights and Democracy documented almost 1000 killed. This was done under the control and coordination of an interim government.

On January 5th, 2018 some leaders who formed an interim government were arrested in Nigeria and deported to Cameroon. They have since been held incommunicado. Nobody has seen them, no sign of life and no access to lawyers, or family members. The Red Cross has not been able to have contact with them. This further intensified a military campaign by civilians, supported by the diaspora to fight for their rights, protect the innocent people that were been killed, protect families that were burnt in houses by the Cameroonian military.

Human Rights Abuses

Over the last 5 months, the armed conflict between both belligerents have given rise to several human rights abuses. While the government of Cameroon bears a huge responsibility including several crimes considered against humanity, armed groups have also committed several crimes. As confirmed by the US Ambassador to Cameroon, Peter Henry Barlerin, the government has burned down entire about 87 villages, burned down houses with several old people burnt to death, shot civilians, targeted killings, torture and several cases of extrajudicial execution. Meanwhile, armed groups have kidnapped several administrators and traditional rulers, burned administrative buildings and schools, killed several people in revenge killings for allegedly cooperating with the government, collected ransom in exchange for freedom and killed government soldiers.

The Centre for Human Rights and Democracy in Africa has documented thousands of cases including testimonies from victims. We are willing to share these confidential reports with Congress, Foreign Affairs Committee and the subcommittee.

Risk of Imminent Genocide

Some people in the Anglophone regions had long declared that there is a genocide happening in Cameroon and yes, there are signs of a genocide. The fact that people are indiscriminately killed just because they are English speakers points clearly that there is a risk that genocide is imminent. If we go by Amnesty International's report and the declarations of US Ambassador to Cameroon, Peter Henry Barlerin, it is safe to say that the conflict in Southern Cameroons have more ingredients of a genocide.

Looking at the 10 stages of a genocide as defined by Gregory H. STANTON, we can easily notice that these stages are already evident with the crisis:

1. CLASSIFICATIONS: People are divided in the crisis as "us" against "them".
2. SYMBOLISATION: People are forced to identify themselves. We give names as Anglophones, Biafra, Bamenda, separatists, terrorist, extremist, etc;
3. DISCRIMINATION: A dominant group uses law, custom, and political power to deny the rights of other groups. That is what the majority led French central Government is doing on the minority Anglophones using the anti-terrorism law.
4. DEHUMANISATION: One group denies the humanity of the other. This has been seen on several occasions. The governor of the Southwest region referred to Anglophone protesters as Dogs. Even journalists on a local TV station have in a generalised manner called Anglophones as rats;

5. ORGANISATION: Genocide is always organised, usually by the state, often using militias to provide deniability of state responsibility. In Cameroon, the BIR is a specialised ethnic unit for this task. Trained and equipped by the Israelites and US governments respectively. We have seen anti-terrorism equipment given by the US used on armless civilians in the Anglophone regions.
6. POLARISATION: The government broadcast propaganda to turn the population against Anglophones. This is very particular of state television CRTV and Vision 4 television where Francophones are invited to debate about the Anglophone problem. The obvious is that they rain insults and derogatory statements towards Anglophones with impunity.
7. PREPARATION: They often use euphemisms to cloak their intentions, such as referring to their goals as "counter-terrorism." They have built armies, bought weapons and trained their troops and militias to fight "Terrorist". But who are these terrorist?
8. PERSECUTION: Beginning of murders, theft of property, trials and massacres like we have seen in Menka Pinyin and recently in Mbengwi;
9. EXTERMINATION: When it is sponsored by the state, the armed forces often work with militias to do the killing. Sometimes the genocide results in revenge killings by groups against each other, creating the downward whirlpool-like cycle of bilateral genocide (as in Burundi). Already dead bodies are dismembered; rape is used as a tool of war to genetically alter and eradicate the other group. Destruction of cultural and religious property is employed to annihilate the group's existence from history. This is the case of the over 87 villages burnt down with ancestral and sacred places destroyed. We have seen images of the military killing and displaying human remains as a sign of victory as to say, we have killed the animals.
10. DENIAL: Cameroon, several credible international organisations and the international community are still in denial of what is happening. It is worth recalling that the government of Cameroon has refused to provide access to the UNHCR for investigations and Red Cross. It is among the surest indicators of further genocidal massacres. Alleged mass graves have been discovered in many localities in the Anglophone Regions (Tinto, Kwakwa, Mbonge, Lebialem, Munyenge, Batibo, Bali etc). The recent killings of 34 in Santa (Menka-Pinyin) is a crystal example where every person on the scene was killed and the only survivor who was later taken to the hospital due to bullet wounds was pulled out of hospital by the military with his two brothers and executed. Leaving no trace of what happened. If we still think this is not a planned and coordinated genocide, then what else can it be?

Contextualisation and Why United States Must Intervene

The international community and the United States in particular must intervene to stop this conflict before it gets to the broader sphere. The conflict in these regions have the potentials to explode into a sub-regional crisis that will generate more poverty and political problems for the future. The following situational awareness must be considered so as to initiate a timely and efficient intervention:

1. The Anglophone regions (Southern Cameroons) is situated at the Gulf of Guinea which is rich in crude oil;
2. The region is so volatile with armed conflicts in many countries such as Central Africa Republic, Equatorial Guinea, Nigeria, etc;
3. The Anglophone regions (Southern Cameroons) is between West (ECOWAS) and Central (CEMAC) Africa. Thus, a strategical link for commerce, trade and business;

Why must the United States be worried about the Southern Cameroons crisis?

America is looked upon as the ideal place in the world where human rights are respected, where freedoms are guaranteed and human dignity assured. Besides, America voted in favour for UN Resolution 1608 of an independent Southern Cameroons. Moreover, many people had erroneously thought that, with the heavy military artillery of the Central Government in Yaoundé, the Anglophone people will be beaten to submission within days. However, it is seemingly clear that, the fight to self-determination is real and might last a long time if solutions are not achieved early enough.

Several factors indicate that this conflict might last a long period of time.

1. The crisis has moved from guerrilla tactics to direct confrontations;
2. There is a multitude of armed groups all fighting for the Independence of the Southern Cameroons;
3. The objective for Independence is very clear to most of the people and the population supports it;
4. The Anglophone diaspora are in full support of an armed struggle and finance it.
5. Most parts of Southern Cameroons are totally inaccessible by road, telephone and even Radio and TV signals. It is thus easy for pockets of resistances to exist in such places for a longer period;
6. The Government's refusal to initiate dialogue with legitimate Anglophone leaders;

Considerations to Be Made

The longer the crisis persist, there is a likelihood of other bi-products of conflict. Given that, Cameroon has been an example for peace in Africa for decades and the above situational analysis, America must intervene so as to:

1. Reduce the influx of political refugees and asylum seekers as a result of the conflict (21000 Refugees already registered with UNHCR and Nigerian authorities confirming about 50,000 refugees in Nigeria and over 160,000 internally displaced persons);
2. Schools in this territory have been closed, as the lack of education persists, this creates a risk for youths to join armed groups;
3. With the proliferation of arms and armed groups, insecurity in the region is very high and could easily fuel hostage taking, theft and other crimes;
4. Economic stagnation, poverty, and famine in the regions;
5. Many armed groups signal the risk to disarm these groups in the long run;
6. The likelihood of epidemics as a result of lack of social amenities. Today, women

are in the rainforest, beaten by snakes and there are no vaccines. They are having children in bushes, which is unhealthy and dangerous should there be any outbreak of an epidemic;

7. The future of youths not pursuing education has been compromised and it will have a huge social impact.

Recommendations to Congress

The Anglophone Crisis

- Pressure the Cameroon government to allow independent investigations into alleged crimes against humanity and gross abuses of human rights by credible international bodies, regional partners and national civil society organisations.
- Reexamine the current defense and development aid especially in cases of government security using weapons meant for the fight against Boko Haram in the Anglophone regions and on civilians.
- Urge Congress to hold frequent hearings on Cameroon including a full committee hearing, Centre for Human Rights and Democracy is willing to testify before congress with regards to the crisis.
- Insist to the Cameroon government to engage in inclusive dialogue on Federalism and Independence of Southern Cameroons with legitimate leaders of the people without preconditions.
- Help identify possible national mediators and support civil society actors including the Catholic Church.
- Urge for all parties to negotiate for a ceasefire as a confidence building measure towards negotiations for the end of this conflict.
- Engage with the The United States Ambassador to the United Nations to bring this crisis for debate at the UN Security Council.
- Provide humanitarian support to refugees and internally displaced persons.
- Support an international process for a referendum to listen to the voice of the people on the desire regarding the form of the State.
- Call for the release of all prisoners linked to sentences from the anti-terrorism law.
- Call on the government to release 47 Cameroonians deported from Nigeria.
- Engage with US allies such as Israel to review military support and cooperation with Cameroon's elite army BIR in cases of human rights violations by troops trained and supported by them.
- Collaborate with US allies, France, Britain, Israel, European Union to pressure the Cameroon government to seek dialogue and negotiations in order to end conflict.
- United States to place travel restrictions and sanctions on government members fueling the crisis.
- Continue to condemn all forms of violence on both sides.

Upcoming Elections

Continue to urge president Paul Biya to think about his legacy and also put forward a clear succession path to avoid a power vacuum or crisis in case of incapacitation or death.

Increase international support, attention and monitoring as elections in Cameroon are marred by fraud and rigging. The need for more international credible observers on the ground to monitor polling stations and weigh on legitimacy of results.

Pressure the government of Cameroon to engage in negotiations to end the conflict prior to elections, otherwise there is a high risk for no voting in Anglophone regions.

Increase support for civil society organisations due to the lack of a strong opposition and media censorship.

Appendix XXI

Schweizerische Eidgenossenschaft
Confédération suisse
Confederazione Svizzera
Confederaziun svizra

Federal Department of Foreign Affairs FDFA
Directorate of Political Affairs DP
Sub-Saharan Africa and Francophonie Division

CH-3003 Berne, FDFA, DB

Bern, 17 November 2017

Open letter of The Collective of English-speaking Southern Cameroonians in the Diaspora

Dear Sir or Madam,

I refer to your open letter sent on behalf of The Collective of English-speaking Southern Cameroonians in the Diaspora regarding the human rights situation in Cameroon and in particular in its English speaking regions.

As mentioned in your letter, the protection and promotion of human rights is a priority of Switzerland's foreign policy. Switzerland firmly believes that the respect of human rights is an indispensable condition for genuinely sustainable social and economic progress in a manner that benefits every individual. As a country with several linguistic and other national minorities, Switzerland attaches great importance to their needs and rights. Switzerland supports in this regard the relevant UN resolutions as well as the mandates of UN human rights experts, such as the Special Rapporteur on minority issues, and participates at the yearly UN Forum on Minority Issues in Geneva. Further, the rights to freedom of peaceful assembly and to freedom of association are a priority for Switzerland as they are, together with the right to freedom of expression, key prerequisites for any democratic society. Switzerland is in particular strongly committed to protecting and promoting human rights in the context of peaceful protest and it has introduced four resolutions on this issue within the Human Rights Council.

Switzerland is concerned about the human rights situation in Cameroon. Through its Embassy in Yaoundé and in its bilateral contacts with Cameroon's authorities, we address human rights issues on a regular basis, including the complex situation in the English speaking regions. In his last meetings with high level authorities of the government of Cameroon, the Swiss Ambassador in Yaoundé expressed his concern about the situation in the two abovementioned provinces. He also paid a visit to the Southwest region last month.

Federal Palace West Wing, CH-3003 Bern
www.fdfa.admin.ch

President Biya's stays in Switzerland were either of private nature or of official nature in the framework of multilateral conferences in Geneva.

I can assure you that Switzerland will continue to follow closely the human rights situation in Cameroon and promote the protection of human rights, including those of persons belonging to national or ethnic, religious and linguistic minorities, in the framework of its bilateral relations with Cameroon as well as on the multilateral level.

Yours sincerely,

Ambassador Anne Lugon-Moulin
Head of Sub-Saharan Africa and Francophonie Division

Appendix XXII

Appendix XXI.1

H.Res.718 - Condemning the actions taken by the Government of the Republic of Cameroon against Patrice Nganang and others, and for other purposes. 115th Congress 2d Session (2017-2018)

Condemning the actions taken by the Government of the Republic of Cameroon against Patrice Nganang and others, and for other purposes.

IN THE HOUSE OF REPRESENTATIVES
January 29, 2018
Mr. Zeldin submitted the following resolution; which was referred to the Committee on Foreign Affairs

---

RESOLUTION

Condemning the actions taken by the Government of the Republic of Cameroon against Patrice Nganang and others, and for other purposes.

Whereas, on January 17, 2017, the Government of the Republic of Cameroon shut down mobile internet access to English-speaking regions of Cameroon after clashes involving separatists;

Whereas, on October 1, 2017, the Department of State expressed serious concern over the Government of Cameroon's use of force to restrict free expression and violence against protestors in the country's English-speaking regions;

Whereas the Office of the United Nations High Commissioner for Human Rights (OHCHR) publicly urged the Government of Cameroon to halt violence after 17 people had reportedly been killed and dozens wounded and arrested in demonstrations in the country's English-speaking regions since October 1, 2017;

Whereas the Government of Cameroon has retained control of electronic media by refusing to grant licenses to private radio and television stations and has intensified political attacks against the independent press;

Whereas commenting unfavorably on political or human rights issues frequently results in official repercussions for writers and journalists in Cameroon;

Whereas publishing material critical of the Government of Cameroon on political or human rights issues frequently results in official repercussions for writers and journalists;

Whereas Patrice Nganang criticized the Government of Cameroon for its marginalization of English-speaking persons and publicly criticized President Biya on online media outlets;

Whereas Patrice Nganang is highly educated, with a Ph.D. in comparative literature and is currently a professor of cultural studies and comparative literature at the State University of New York at Stony Brook;

Whereas, on December 6, 2017, Patrice Nganang was arrested at Douala International Airport and charged with violating the antiterror law for insulting President Biya;

Whereas Patrice Nganang was taken into custody and detained in the Kondengui Central Prison in Yaoundé, Cameroon, for approximately 20 days;

Whereas the Government of Cameroon delayed a public hearing for Patrice Nganang and neglected to issue a warrant of criminal charges;
Whereas hundreds of English-speaking detainees have been beaten or mistreated in custody;
Whereas these actions of the Government of Cameroon constitute gross and reprehensible violations of international law and basic human rights;
Whereas the police, gendarmerie, and Government authorities reportedly continued to arrest and detain persons arbitrarily, often holding them for prolonged periods without charge or trial and at times incommunicado; and
Whereas there are numerous documented accounts of citizens of Cameroon being imprisoned and beaten for publicly reporting on unrest in Cameroon's English-speaking regions or criticizing President Biya: Now, therefore, be it
Resolved, That the House of Representatives—
(1) strongly condemns the actions taken by the Government of the Republic of Cameroon against Patrice Nganang and the English-speaking minority of Cameroon;
(2) affirms that the United States continues to hold the Government of Cameroon responsible for upholding all the rights of its citizens, regardless of political views or beliefs; and
(3) urges the Government of Cameroon to extend to all of Cameroon's citizens, including political dissidents, the rights guaranteed by the Universal Declaration of Human Rights of the United Nations and other international covenants on human rights, including the freedoms of expression with equal protection under law.

Appendix XXI.2

African Literature Association

Statement on the Detention of Patrice Nganang (December 10, 2017).
The African Literature Association strongly condemns the irregular detention of one of our members, Professor Patrice Nganang, on December 7, 2017, at the Douala airport by the Cameroonian police following the publication in Jeune Afrique's online news journal of an article critical of the Biya government's repression of activism in predominantly Anglophone regions of Cameroon. Nganang, born in Yaoundé, Cameroon, and educated both in Cameroon and in Germany, holds a Ph.D. in Comparative Literature and is currently a professor of Cultural Studies and Comparative Literature at Stony Brook University in New York state. In Spring 2018, he is scheduled to serve as an Old Dominion Professor at Princeton University and to take up a fellowship at Princeton's Humanities Council. Nganang is the author of several prize-winning novels, including *Mount Pleasant* (*Mont Plaisant*) and *Dog Days* (*Temps de Chien*), as well as several books of essays and poetry.
The ALA joins PEN USA and other friends of freedom of expression in calling for the immediate release of Professor Nganang.
As Pen USA reports:
Investigating corruption or commenting unfavorably on political or human rights issues frequently results in official repercussions for writers and journalists in Cameroon. Nganang is only the latest example of a string of writers commenting on sensitive subjects who risk police questioning, lawsuits, detention, or imprisonment.
"Detaining an important independent voice like Patrice Nganang, who has used his writing to investigate the consequences of violence, is indicative of a movement by the government to silence all political criticism and dismantle the right to free expression," said Karin Deutsch Karlekar, PEN America Director of Free Expression at Risk Programs.
In addition to calling upon the Cameroonian government to release Prof. Nganang, unharmed, the ALA encourages members and readers of African literature to join us in taking the following actions:
1) Please call the Cameroon embassy in your home country/country of residence and demand the immediate release of Prof. Nganang
List of embassies here: https://embassy.goabroad.com/embassies-of/cameroon
2) Please also contact a Committee to Protect Journalists representative, either in the US where Nganang lives or your local representative.
Contact info here: https://cpj.org/about/staff.php
3) Please contact Amnesty International: https://www.amnesty.org/en/about-us/contact/
4) Please contact Human Rights Watch: https://www.hrw.org/contact-us
5) Please spread the word using the social media tags #FreeNganang and #Patricenganang

Appendix XXI.3

Patrice Nganang Patrice Nganang Statement to US Congress
June 29, 2018.

Is it impossible to speak of any segment of the unrest that has erupted in the North West and the South West of Cameroon since November 2016, without understanding it as a metaphor of the general Anglophone problem? The answer is simple: No. Why is it so? Answer: Because each aspect of the Anglophone problem brings us to the root of it, which is the wrong done to our people. How can one right that wrong? Answer: By giving our people, and they now call themselves Ambazonians, their statehood back.

To get to this conclusion, it is important to not take the question at its face value, for that question can be transformed into various forms: from 1961, the date of the federation of the two formerly German colonies that were then called Gross kamerun, to 1994, during thirty-three years thus, why was there no university of English tradition in Cameroon? Since 1916, why did it take until 2016, one hundred years then, for Cameroon to awaken to the fact that it had lawyers of British tradition in its populace, and needed to respect their judicial system based on common law? Why is there no noteworthy hospital in the part of Cameroon that speaks English? Why is there no science and technology university in the North West or South West? Why does the biggest city in English-speaking Cameroon, Bamenda, have the worst roads in the country?

The list of what reveals the depth of the injustice done to our people since 1961 is endless, but its systematically criminal nature can only be understood if one also remembers that oil was discovered in that part of the country as early as 1970, and its extraction as well as the amount of the revenue it generates have always been a state secret – run straight from Yaoundé, from the Presidency of the Republic, and managed off-shore by French companies, and on-shore by SONARA, the State oil company, a company always headed by a Francophone, mostly from the tribe of the President, and that means never headed by an Anglophone since its creation, a company whose major shares until 2010 were held by two French companies, Total and Elf.

I was challenged to speak only French around SONARA, writes a former employee, Oliver Zhie, I worked with one sub-company there. All my Francophone colleagues addressed me like this, 'hey Bamenda!'. There is a lot of hate there.

Now, in Cameroon, 'Bamenda', is the slang word by which Francophone people associate Anglophones with servitude, as it means slave, and servant.

Today's upheavals have a long history, and no aspect of Cameroon's political life is immune of it. To give you an example, even Cameroon's awakening to democracy in 1992 – and the opposition party in the country, SDF, Anglophone-based, was born in blood –has been spearheaded by the Anglophone revolt, the Anglophone dissent, the Anglophone discontent.

A quick rundown of the transformation of the Anglophone problem into violent discontent, and this means, of the quite impossible existence of an Anglophone identity inside the Cameroonian public landscape becomes essential when one remembers that the person who effectively transformed what from November 20, 2016 to December 7, 2017 was mostly a corporatist demand of lawyers and teachers into a popular uprising was simply a radio journalist – 'No Fear' Mancho Bibixy, and before his arrest, he used to have one of the most popular talk radio shows in Bamenda.

His arrest triggered a riot in the city, and he was sentenced a few months ago – in French bien sûr - to fifteen years in jail, on charges of 'terrorism', 'secession', 'revolution', 'hostility against the fatherland', 'propagation of false information', 'insurrection and 'contempt of authorities', and of paying an impossible fee, by the military tribunal, during a session headed by a Francophone judge, Abega Mbezoa, of the ethnic group of the President.

And yet as outrageous as it is his sentencing is but a small chapter of a general and systematic marginalization of the English-speaking population that effectively started in 1972, and was sanctioned by the State on April 14, 1984 when a decision by the president named the country after what was French Eastern Cameroon until 1961 – la République du Cameroun.

The narrative of Anglophone marginalization can be read in the requests with which Mancho Bibixy kick started what he called the coffin revolution, and that has now become a civil war – he was asking for better roads, for better hospitals, for better services, joining teachers who were asking for a school system that respects their English-language education, and Lawyers asking for a respect for common law. By doing so, he effectively transformed the journalist that he is, into the mouthpiece of our people's anger at being denied access to the basic necessities, despite the richness of their land. Or into the fact that activists from the Diaspora are routinely delivered a refusal of entry into Cameroon by the state police, a "Notification et motivation de decision de refus d'admission sur le territoire Camerounais" even when as nationals with a foreign passport, they are in possession of a regular visa delivered at the Cameroonian embassy. The thousands of people from the Anglophone Diaspora living in Nigeria, but also in South Africa, England, and here, in the United States can testify to that systematic exclusion of their kind. This is to say that it is effectively impossible to disconnect the situation of any Southern Cameroonian, from the impossible condition of being an Anglophone in "la République du Cameroun."

Why is it that from the Consortium's strike to today Cameroon saw a fast erosion of its most talked about peace, and so rapidly sank into a civil war? The answer to this question lies the long history of an impossible cohabitation between two parts of what was a German colony until 1916 and according to the League of Nation and the UN's trusteeship and mandate had to be marshaled in their own right into independence, and the mismanagement of a federal structure they chose by a francophone State incapable of understanding that the gentlemen's agreement that brought Eastern and Western Cameroon together in 1961, was neither a certificate of annexation by one part nor one of surrender by the other, and most importantly, had no precedent amongst the fifty-three African nations.

Was thus a gem, a historical opportunity? As a matter of comparison: Tanganiya and Zanzibar entered into an agreement to form Tanzania, and the wisdom of their statesmen made them understand that their separate traditions also needed a State structure that respected it – they formed a confederation.
Senegal and Gambia entered into a gentlemen's agreement to form Senegambia, but needed only a couple of years to realize their misjudgment, and did not shed any blood to go apart. Why is it that la République du Cameroun has to kill thousands of Anglophone people, has to sink into a civil war because of a gentlemen's agreement the kind of which other African states and leaders walked away from without a bloodshed? The answer lies in the riches of Anglophone lands – oil.
In the fact that the oil that is tapped on Limbe's coasts has never been invested in the North West and South West. And oil is without doubt what explains the rigidity of Paul Biya, the Cameroonian President, when he says that the form of the Cameroonian state cannot be discussed, and it is also what explains a statement of the French President Emmanuel Macron to him, on the eve of what would become the bloodiest national unity day in the country, May 20, 2018:
« Je souhaite également vous dire la solidarité de la France face aux crimes commis contre, notamment des représentants de l'Etat, dans le contexte de tensions que connaissent les régions Anglophones du Cameroun. Je forme le vœu que ces tensions puissent être résorbées de manière pacifique et concertée, dans le strict respect de l'unité et de l'intégrité de votre pays«
I also wish to express the solidarity of France in the face of the crimes committed against representatives of the State, in the context of the tensions in the Anglophone regions of Cameroon. I wish those tensions to be solved in a pacific manner and through dialogue, and this, in the strict respect of the unity and integrity of your country.
'Strict respect'? No word regarding the thousand civilians dead, those of December 2016, September 2017, October 2017, and of literally every day – the Pa Bertika Edward Penda, 95 who died of lack of medication because he was chased from his village, Depanda Bakundu, burned down by Francophone soldiers. No word regarding the students of the university of Buea raped by mainly Francophone soldiers, some of whom became vipers and like Sidonie were shot and killed in Menka-Pilly while protecting herself in the roof of a home.
No word regarding the targeted killing of more and more civilians by Francophone soldiers. No word regarding the thousands of Anglophones hiding in Nigeria because they are unsafe in their homes, dying of malnutrition and hunger in Nigeria, the 75 villages burnt down by Francophone soldiers, the farms looted by Francophone soldiers. No word on the grandmothers and grandfathers – the Mama Monica Appih Sereh, 95, of Kwakwa, or Mama Pauline Ayele Adia, 86, of Mungo Ndoi – who were burned in their homes. No word on the infants killed. No compassion for a Wiyfenga Eileen Fola, 14, whose face was destroyed by a soldier's bullet.
No word on the torture of civilians by Francophone soldiers, on the war crimes that are being committed in Southern Cameroons as I speak. No word on the Anglophone regions that are cut away from the world. No word on the Anglophones, refugees or the like, who are being denied entry into Cameroon even to bury their dead. The victims of the criminal

deeds of the Francophone State speak louder than any protest of mischaracterization – and the victims are all Anglophones.

A demand for the 'strict respect of the country's unity and integrity' is not only a blank check given to a government that is effectively committing a genocide in front of our very eyes, it is also a brutal disregard of Cameroon's history, and particularly of the history of Western Cameroons, for Southern Cameroon was indeed a State before joining Eastern Cameroons – a State with a functioning government, with its own Constitution, a State that had its own newspapers and only relied on Nigeria for more complex structures like a television network. So much disregard for history, and so much disregard for human life by the head of a State like France can only be interest driven, and the interest here is what manufactures the silence of the media in France over the genocide currently happening in Southern Cameroons.

These are important elements to mention and to remember, as la République du Cameroun's behavior as a colonial conqueror in Southern Cameroons is only possible because Cameroon was always governed as a French-speaking country, as a Francophone country, in fact as a country that has never ceased being a French colony, and as such, the international backing of France was always guaranteed to Paul Biya.

For How Long?

The demand for a restoration of statehood in Southern Cameroons, which is tantamount to the demand for a creation of the Federal Republic of Ambazonia, will always be misunderstood if the social movement that carries it is called 'separatism' or 'secession', for secession and separatism result from a prior unitary position. Yet the people of Southern Cameroons were never given the opportunity all African states were given by their colonizer – to vote upon their independence, upon their statehood.

To understand it better, one has to imagine that instead of choosing between independence and the continuation of colonialism or of apartheid as all African nations did between 1956 and 1994, Burkina Faso for example, had to choose to remain with Côte d'ivoire or join Mali, because the three countries composed what was then called the Federation of Mali. The country's fate would have been doomed by the question itself, and yet it is the choice Southern Cameroonians had to face – to join Nigeria, or Eastern Cameroon – the farcicality of which was repeated in 1972 when they had only one option regarding the form of the state – to vote for a unitary system of government.

They were never given the choice all African nations had! Not in 1916, not in 1961, and definitely not in 1972! In other words, the League of Nations, and the United Nations in particular, both dropped the ball on Southern Cameroons, and allowed our people to be governed as if they had been colonized by a francophone State, and in effect by France.

There lies the Anglophone problem, deep seated in it is the very long disregard of a people's right of self-determination, of sovereignty, the consequence of which can be seen in the absence of basic infrastructures in the two Anglophone regions of the country, in the shutting down of the internet across Anglophone lands, in the jailing of Anglophone journalists, and in the sentencing of an Anglophone activists to fifteen years in jail on charges of 'hostility against the fatherland', and in the hundreds and thousands of refugees and internally displaced persons.

In the government of people, there is no lack of wisdom in recognizing that one has committed a mistake. There is no crime in recognizing that one's parent's generation has entered into an agreement with which one cannot live, for education is there to have us realize the mistakes past and it gives us the means to rectify them. That the 1884 generation had signed treaties sealing the fate of our land, did not deter the generation of 1960 from asking for independence for the same land.

After all, there is no such thing as an eternal agreement between men and women who themselves are not eternal. A government is there to protect the life of the people, to give a shelter to minorities and have everyone have their fair share of the riches of the soil. A government that kills people to protect itself has lost its meaning, and has become a manufacture of injustice.

A government that burns villages has become a murdering machine turned against its own population. A government that has its soldiers shoot at hospitals and mosques has lost its right to exist. As for the Anglophone problem, the solution to the deep-seated systematic injustice that created it is multiple, of course, but its multiplicity shall not have us forget the need to also systematically right the wrong, such as to avoid the transformation of what is now a civil war, into a state that is not soon to disappear from the memory of our people, by creating a returning cycle of violence in their midst. To do so there is one door – that door is to come back to the wrong beginning and start anew by restoring the Southern Cameroons statehood. That door is the independence of Southern Cameroons or the Federal Republic of Ambazonia. Needless to say, the fall of Paul Biya is the key to unlock that almighty goal.

CONTRIBUTORS

Lyombe Eko is the William S. Morris endowed professor in Innovation, Information and Journalism at the College of Media and Communication, Texas Tech University. He was born in the colonial Buea Native Authority, Southern Cameroons as a "native subject" of Her Majesty the Queen of England. He attended the Baptist Bible College in Ndu, Donga Mantung, and the Bilingual Grammar School in Molyko, Buea. He earned his B.A. in Foreign Language Studies & Media Communication at the University of Sioux Falls, South Dakota, his M.A. in Media Communication from Wheaton College Illinois, and his doctorate in Journalism and Mass Communication from Southern Illinois University at Carbondale.

Before he joined Texas Tech in 2015, he was an associate professor and Director of Graduate Studies at the University of Iowa School of Journalism and Mass Communication. He was also Director of the African Studies Program at the University of Iowa. He has also taught at the University of Maine in Orono, Maine. Before his academic career, he was a journalist at Cameroon Radio and Television (CRTV) Yaoundé, and an editor/translator at the African Broadcasting Union (URTNA) in Nairobi, Kenya. His documentary, *Kip Keeps Kids*, which focuses on Kenyan Olympic multi-gold medal winner Kipchoge Keino, won an international prize at the Prix Futura TV Festival in Germany. He has published multiple refereed journal articles, and five books on comparative and international communication law and policy. He is the winner of a Texas Tech University President's Book Award, an Independent Publisher Book Award, and an International Book Award.

Marina Brilman holds a PhD in Law from the London School of Economics (LSE), an LL.M from University College London, and a Master's degree in law from the University of Leiden. She was Leading Articles editor at the Leiden Journal of International Law and LLM adviser at the LSE, where she also taught property law to undergraduates. Marina is a qualified lawyer in The Netherlands where she practised in litigation, international arbitration, and commercial law as a senior associate at De Brauw Blackstone Westbroek (previously Linklaters & Alliance).

She was a board member and Latin America programme director of the Dutch NGO Lawyers for Lawyers, a Visiting Professor at the Universidad de Los Andes in Colombia (teaching public international law and human rights to postgraduates), and worked for three years as a staff attorney of the Inter-American Court of Human Rights. Marina has published on human rights in English and Spanish and is a contributor to the International Law Reports, published by Cambridge University Press, on the Inter-American Court's case-law. She is a Visiting Fellow at the London School of Economics (Latin America and Caribbean Centre). In 2017, she carried out a trial observation of Anglophone federalists at the Yaoundé Military Tribunal on behalf of the Law Society of England and Wales. She was formally a board member of Action on Armed Violence (AOAV), London.

Ndiva Kofele-Kale, University Distinguished Professor and Professor Emeritus of Law in Dedman School of Law, joined the SMU faculty in 1989. He received a B.A. degree from Beloit College and M.A., J.D. and Ph.D. degrees from Northwestern University. Prior to SMU, Professor Kofele-Kale taught at the University of Tennessee College of Law. He also worked in private practice as a corporate and securities lawyer at Lord Bissel & Brook in Chicago. Research for his scholarship and teaching focus on public and private international law led to a concentration in global corruption and the right of people to a corruption-free society. A renowned advocate for human rights, Professor Kofele-Kale's writings have contributed to the codification of international human rights law. He has appeared before several treaty-based human rights tribunals, including the United Nations Human Rights Committee, the U.N. working group on arbitrary detention and the African Commission on Human and Peoples' Rights. His book *Combating Economic Crimes: Balancing Competing Rights and Interests in Prosecuting the Crime of Illicit Enrichment* introduced the concept of "patrimonicide", which is the plundering of resources by corrupt political leaders. He was an associate editor of *The International Lawyer* from 1990-1996. He retires as Professor Emeritus of Law.

Ayah Ayah Abine is President of the Ayah Humanitarian Foundation. Along with his father, Justice Ayah Paul Abine, he has been engaged in humanitarian work among Cameroonian refugees in Nigeria as well as Internally Displaced Persons (IDPs) in Anglophone and Francophone Cameroon. The Ayah Humanitarian Foundation was the first entity to help refugees who had fled Cameroon to the Cross River State of Nigeria after the Anglophone armed resistance started in Manyu, and Akwaya became a war zone. Before the Anglophone Revolt of 2016, the Ayah Foundation operated orphanages in the Northwest and Southwest regions of Cameroon. The first affiliate of the Ayah Foundation, the Saint Valentine's Orphanage, was founded by the Ayahs in 1989. The Orphanage consists of two branches: The boys' Orphanage situated at Governor's street Buea Town; and the girls' dormitory situated in Akwaya town.

Honorable Justice Ayah Paul Abine, father of Ayah Ayah Abine, attended the Bilingual Grammar School in Buea. He was an elected Member of the Cameroon National Assembly for Akwaya. He later became a Justice of the Supreme Court of Cameroon. In 2017, while still a sitting justice of the Supreme Court, he was arrested and imprisoned without trial for eight months at the infamous underground dungeon and interrogation center of the National Gendarmerie Headquarters, SED, in Yaoundé, for allegedly saying that the Anglophone Revolt was a political affair and that the arrested leaders of the Anglophone community should be treated in accordance with the law, not as terrorists. He was never formally charged. He was also removed from the Supreme Court without reason–and without his pension. He is now retired but he continues to fight for justice and human rights.

INDEX

www.ingramcontent.com/pod-product-compliance
Ingram Content Group UK Ltd.
Pitfield, Milton Keynes, MK11 3LW, UK
UKHW050427231025
464242UK00004B/5

9 781957 29651